Windows NT Device Driver Development

Peter G. Viscarola
W. Anthony Mason

MACMILLAN
TECHNICAL
PUBLISHING
U·S·A

201 West 103rd Street, Indianapolis, Indiana 46290

International Standard Book Number: 1-57870-058-2

Library of Congress Catalog Card Number: 97-80986

2001   00   99   4   3   2   1

Interpretation of the printing code: The rightmost double-digit number is the year of the book's printing; the rightmost single-digit, the number of the book's printing. For example, the printing code 98-1 shows that the first printing of the book occurred in 1998.

Composed in Sabon and MCPdigital by Macmillan Computer Publishing

Printed in the United States of America

Warning and Disclaimer

This book is designed to provide information about Windows NT device drivers. Every effort has been made to make this book as complete and as accurate as possible, but no warranty or fitness is implied.

The information is provided on an as is basis. The authors and Macmillan Technical Publishing shall have neither liability nor responsibility to any person or entity with respect to any loss or damages arising from the information contained in this book or from the use of the discs or programs that may accompany it.

Publisher
Jim LeValley

Executive Editor
Linda Ratts Engelman

Managing Editor
Caroline Roop

Acquisitions Editor
Karen Wachs

Development Editor
Christopher Cleveland

Project Editor
Brad Herriman

Copy Editor
Nancy Sixsmith

Indexer
Tim Wright

Acquisitions Coordinator
Amy Lewis

Manufacturing Coordinator
Brook Farling

Book Designer
Gary Adair

Cover Designer
Aren Howell

Proofreader
Maribeth Echard

Production
Tim Osborn
Staci Somers
Mark Walchle

Trademark Acknowledgments

All terms mentioned in this book that are known to be trademarks or service marks have been appropriately capitalized. Macmillan Technical Publishing cannot attest to the accuracy of this information. Use of a term in this book should not be regarded as affecting the validity of any trademark or service mark. Windows NT® is a registered trademark of Microsoft Corporation.

Feedback Information

At Macmillan Technical Publishing, our goal is to create in-depth technical books of the highest quality and value. Each book is crafted with care and precision, undergoing rigorous development that involves the unique expertise of members from the professional technical community.

Readers' feedback is a natural continuation of this process. If you have any comments regarding how we could improve the quality of this book, or otherwise alter it to better suit your needs, you can contact us at networktech@mcp.com. Please make sure to include the book title and ISBN in your message.

We greatly appreciate your assistance.

Acknowledgments

Peter G. Viscarola: I never wanted to write a book. Of course, I always thought it would be nice to *have written* a book—who wouldn't want to be able to put "author of such and such" on their résumé, right? But actually *write* one? No thanks, it always sounded like too much work to me. After all, I've got classes to teach, clients to meet, code to write, and a consulting practice to run. Where would I ever find the time to write a book?

Somehow, Linda Ratts Engelman (the Executive Editor for this book series) convinced Tony and me that we really needed to write this book. She convinced us that we just *had* to write this book. She convinced us that we *wanted* to write this book. How she managed to do this without once ever telling us it would be easy or that we really would have the time to do it, I'll never know. But she did it. I am thus grateful to Linda and her powers of persuasion for talking us into doing this project.

I am also thankful for Linda's cool head and good humor in shepherding us through the actual process. If we delivered software the same way that we delivered this book—months late and 60% larger than planned—OSR would be out of business.

I want to thank all the students over the past five years who have told me "You guys really should write a book!" and who insisted that it was an important thing for us to do. If you-all hadn't insisted so strenuously that we should write this book, we never would have agreed to meet with Linda in the first place. So, thank you.

The actual process of writing this book was made much easier for us, and much more pleasant, by Development Editor Chris Cleveland. Chris did everything humanly possible to let us focus solely on writing the book. This relieved us of having to worry about millions of bits of administrivia like manuscript text formats, procedures, conventions, or other publishing arcana. I am most grateful for his willingness to be flexible and advocate for us. His excellent sense of humor and ability to keep things in perspective (of *The Chicago Manual of Style* he once wrote: "I hate that damn orange book") were sometimes the only thing that motivated me to work on the next chapter.

This book could not have been started, never mind completed, without the assistance of the entire staff of OSR Open Systems Resources, our consulting company. I am extremely grateful for all the support I received during the writing process. I am particularly grateful to the consulting associates who assisted with this book: Mark Cariddi for his work on the sample DMA driver and his reviews, Pete Nishimoto for his work on the sample PIO driver and his chapter reviews, and Mark Roddy for his technical reviews which often caught errors nobody else saw. It is a pleasure to work with each one of you.

Our technical editor could not have been more helpful. Many thanks to Mike Barry who, despite the fact that he was already working a million hours per week, took the time to do thorough reviews and keep us focused on the basic technical details the book needed. His support, especially early in the process ("Another great chapter!") was really, really, important.

Finally, I want to thank my wife and my parents, who never complained about my not being around and without whose support and encouragement I would have quit this project within sixty seconds. My wife Karen, especially, was always supportive and always understanding when I had to work every night and every day every weekend for the more than six months it took to actually do the writing. Thanks, sweetie! I couldn't have done it without you.

Peter Viscarola
September 1998

W. Anthony Mason: The suggestion that we write a book has come up several times over the years here at OSR. Each time we would look at our schedules, we would conclude that there was simply no time to actually complete such a complex task—I had previously written a book and knew that it was always considerably more work than it seemed when it started.

Imagine my surprise when I found that Linda Ratts Engelman had convinced us—especially Peter, who is normally quite level-headed and thoroughly willing to say "no" when something just isn't possible—to write this book. And, of course, we found that writing the book took longer than we'd expected. In addition, we found that the demands of our consulting company constantly distracted from the very important task of finishing the book.

While it will come as no small surprise to the readers, this book is fundamentally Peter's work. While I contributed in a few small ways, it fundamentally represents his vision of how to teach people to construct device drivers for Windows NT. Thus, as you read this book and find things praiseworthy, it is Peter's doing.

Of course, my own personal thanks also go out to the MTP staff—I especially enjoyed the comments back from Chris, as well, since he couldn't tell the parts I wrote apart from the parts Peter wrote! Without Chris, and the other MTP folks, this book would not have been a reality.

Throughout the stress of it all, I relied upon my wife Tammy, who was quite understanding about my constant absences—if it wasn't because I was writing small portions of the book, it was because I was trying to pay enough attention to OSR Open Systems Resources to make up for Peter's focus on the book.

Tony Mason
September 1998

About the Authors

Peter G. Viscarola is a founder of, and Consulting Partner at Open Systems Resources (OSR), the world-renowned consulting firm specializing in Windows NT systems internals. During more than 20 years in the computer industry, including more than 10 years as an independent consultant, Peter has developed device drivers and protocol implementations under a wide array of operating systems. Since the release of Windows NT, Peter has designed or developed more than three dozen Windows NT drivers, including drivers for almost every type of programmed I/O and DMA device imaginable. Recent Windows NT driver projects include development of high-speed drivers for ATM®, ISDN, and Frame Relay devices, as well as design of special Kernel mode drivers for a number of unique situations. Peter's particular areas of expertise include networking and high-speed DMA architectures where hardware-driver interactions are critical. Peter has a long background developing and teaching high-tech courses, and is the developer and chief instructor of Open Systems Resources' Windows NT Kernel Mode Device Driver Seminar. Peter attended Columbia University and the University of Michigan, where he studied applied statistics and computer science, and Lesley College where he studied applied management. Peter is a regular contributor to and columnist for *The NT Insider*, Open Systems Resources' journal of Windows NT systems internals. He is a Senior Member of the IEEE and a voting member of the ACM.

W. Anthony Mason is an Open Systems Resources Consulting Partner with experience in a wide array of system software disciplines during the past 16 years. Tony is also internationally recognized expert in file systems technologies. Among his recent projects have been the design and development of several Windows NT installable file system drivers, including both physical media file systems and networked distributed file systems. In addition to his file systems expertise, Tony is Open Systems Resources' resident expert on NT's Memory Manager and Cache Manager subsystems. Tony also has considerable experience designing and developing Windows NT device drivers, his most recent such project being a DMA driver for a high-speed video encryption board. Tony is the architect and major designer and implementor of Open Systems Resources' File System Filter Driver and File System Driver Development Kits. He is also the developer and chief instructor of Open Systems Resources' Developing File Systems for Windows NT Seminar. Tony received his Bachelor of Science degree from the University of Chicago, where he studied mathematics and computer science. Tony is also a regular contributor to *The NT Insider*, Open Systems Resources' journal of Windows NT systems internals.

About the Technical Reviewer

Michael W. Barry contributed his considerable practical, hands-on expertise to the entire development process for *Windows NT Device Driver Development*. As the book was being written, Mike reviewed all the material for technical content, organization, and flow. His feedback was critical to ensuring that *Windows NT Device Driver Development* fits our reader's need for the highest quality technical information.

Mike Barry has 17 years of programming experience. Upon receiving a BSEE from the University of Texas at Austin, Mike went to work for Datapoint Corporation where he was involved in networking and desktop video conferencing. Mike holds numerous patents ranging from video teleconferencing to color-image processing to cluster printing. He has been involved in NT Kernel and User mode programming since the Windows NT 3.1 beta and is considered an expert on the Windows NT operating system. Currently, Mike is Vice President of Development at T/R systems, Inc. (the inventors of cluster printing), where he and his group are pioneering cluster printing systems based on Windows NT.

Mike lives in Atlanta, Georgia, with his lovely wife and two wonderful children. In his free time, he enjoys scuba diving, tennis, camping, water skiing, and knee boarding.

Contents at a Glance

Table of Contents

Introduction

This book describes the workings, both architectural and pragmatic, of standard kernel mode device drivers for Windows NT. It explains how to design and develop these drivers, as well as how to compile, link, and debug them.

The book focuses on standard Kernel mode device drivers, which are the kind of driver you would write to support a custom add-on device in Windows NT. The types of devices for which a standard Kernel mode driver are typically written range from those as simple as a specialized parallel or serial port to devices as complex as DMA-based realtime video encryption devices. While this book might be generally useful to developers writing other types of drivers on NT, we have shamelessly restricted our discussion of details in most cases to those relevant to the development of standard Kernel mode device drivers.

We have designed this book to be useful to software engineers who have never written a device driver, to those who have written drivers on other operating systems, and even to those engineers who have already written a few drivers on Windows NT. The book does assume a basic knowledge of operating systems internals and a solid knowledge of the C programming language. We also assume that the reader has a general understanding of how devices work: what device registers are and how interrupts work. But, even if you've got a vague grasp of these topics, this book should be within your reach.

If you've written lots of device drivers on Windows NT, you will undoubtedly know much of what we present in this book. In fact, you will probably already know the vast majority of the information. However, we hope that we will be able to add at least one or two items of information to the repertoire of even these old NT driver hands.

Not a Cookbook

This book is not a cookbook with easy answers about how to write device drivers. Over the past five years, we've written several dozen NT drivers. We've also taught something like 3,000 students how to write NT drivers in our three day *Windows NT Kernel Mode Device Drivers* seminar. During that time we've come to the conclusion that the cookbook approach to driver writing only works if you're writing a device driver for a cookbook. In other words, it almost never works at all.

Rather, what we have done in this book is identify, organize, and present as clearly as possible all the information that a typical device driver writer will need to truly understand how Windows NT device drivers "work." We have mixed this with pragmatic hints, tips, and details which we have gained through our experience designing and developing NT drivers for the real world. We have deliberately traded breadth for depth. Thus, instead of covering every possible topic that might be of interest to some device driver writer somewhere, we typically focus on those topics that we have found to be critical for device driver writers to understand. We cover those topics fully and in detail.

Basically, our goal was to give you all the information that we wish *we* had when we started writing NT drivers. Understanding this information will allow you to write not just any driver for your device, but the most optimal driver for your device. It will enable you to make your own intelligent design trade-offs. This approach will also allow you to make better sense of the information presented in the Windows NT Device Driver Kit (DDK).

The order in which the material is presented in this book is loosely based on our seminar. Our seminar, and thus this book, utilizes what we have come to call "The OSR Approach" to teaching people how to write device drivers. This approach emphasizes the fact that a device driver is really an operating system extension. In order to extend Windows NT *effectively,* a developer needs to understand many of the details of how the operating system works. Thus, we approach the task of explaining how to write a device driver in the following steps:

1. Start with general Windows NT operating systems concepts relevant to driver writers

2. Progress to more detailed information about the operating system, such as the virtual memory subsystem, interrupt management, and synchronization issues

3. Next discuss in detail how the I/O Subsystem works, and how drivers interact with the I/O subsystem and with each other

4. Discuss in detail the implementation of standard Kernel mode drivers

5. Discuss, in great detail, the implementation of specific categories of standard Kernel mode drivers

6. Use the knowledge of standard Kernel mode drivers to describe alternative Windows NT driver architectures, such as SCSI, NDIS, and Video Miniport drivers.

Organization of the Book

To reinforce the approach described previously, we have divided the book into three parts. Part One (Chapters 1–7) discusses details of the overall Windows NT architecture relevant to driver writers. If you're new to working with the Windows NT operating system at the internals level, understanding the contents of these chapters is absolutely vital to understanding how to design Windows NT drivers. If you're an old hand at working with NT internals, you should still probably skim these chapters to be sure that you're up on all the terminology we use in the remainder of the book.

Part Two (Chapters 8–20) covers the details of implementing standard kernel mode drivers for Windows NT. In this part, we first discuss the basics of the NT I/O Subsystem, and how I/O requests are described and processed. We then move on to a detailed discussion of how Windows NT device drivers are organized. After that, we delve into the major sections of an NT device driver (first Driver Entry, then dispatch entry points, followed by ISRs and DPCs). Next, we cover in great detail how both programmed I/O and DMA data transfers are performed in NT drivers. In so doing, we present code for two nontrivial sample device drivers. Part Two ends with a discussion of how drivers are built and debugged on NT.

As we discuss each of the topics in Part 2, we try to give you the benefit of our experience of writing NT drivers. We tell you not only how certain things are *supposed* to work, but how they actually *do* work in our experience. Our goal here is to help you shorten your learning curve by avoiding many of the mistakes that we have made.

Part Three (Chapters 21–24) expands on the knowledge gained in the other parts of the book, and provides a basic overview of some of the additional driver types used in Windows NT. This part relates the information already presented about standard Kernel mode drivers to File System drivers, NDIS drivers, SCSI Miniport drivers, and Video drivers. In so doing, our goal isn't to cover in any depth or detail how to write these types of drivers. Rather, it is to provide you with enough information to be able to understand the architecture and structure of these special types of drivers.

This book focuses on NT V4.0. However, we have gathered what information on NT V5 that we can (and that we think is reliable) and placed that in Appendix C. As of this writing, NT V5 is still a pretty distant goal. More information about NT V5 can be found on our Web site.

Web Site Support

We have dedicated a portion of the OSR Web site (http://www.osr.com) to supporting this book. On our Web site you will find complete downloadable source code for the sample drivers presented in Chapters 16 and 17. You will also find updates, technical errata, clever utilities, and other things that may be useful to driver writers.

We also will be placing information on our Web site about NT V5 as it becomes available. By the time NT V5 is fully stable, we expect to have the two sample drivers presented in the book available in both NT V4 and NT V5 versions. Come visit our Web site often!

Conventions Used in This Book

The following conventions are used in this book:

Tip

Tips provide you with helpful ways of completing a task

Note

A note explains terms or concepts that relate to what is discussed in the text, but doesn't warrant full explanation in the text, as it may be distracting.

Warning

A warning is a system critical reminder or guideline that provides cautionary advice to help limit exposure to potential problems, failures, security gaps, and so forth.

Function prototypes appear in boxes without shading and provide explanation of function parameters.

Dispatch entry points appear in shaded boxes and provide explanation of entry point parameters.

Bug Bounty

This book contains thousands of technical details. We have worked very hard to try to ensure every one of these details is correct. I have no doubt that we've missed some. Thus, we ask for your help in ferreting out any remaining technical glitches that might remain in this book.

To this end, the authors and Macmillan Technical Publishing are pleased to offer you a "bug bounty" on this book. If you are the first to report a significant technical error in this book, we will provide you with gifts from both OSR and the publisher as a token of our thanks. And, of course, we will keep an up-to-date technical errata available on our Web site. This is part of the commitment to technical accuracy that we make to you, our readers.

Part I

Windows NT Architecture

Chapter **1**

Windows NT Operating System Overview

This chapter will review:

- **Windows NT Major Characteristics**. This section describes the key architectural features of the Windows NT operating system.

- **User Mode Programs and Environment Subsystems**. Environment Subsystems provide the interface between most User mode programs and the Windows NT operating system. This section describes the role that Environment Subsystems play in the Windows NT operating system.

- **The Windows NT Executive**. The Kernel mode component of the Windows NT operating system that interfaces with applications and makes operating system policy decisions is called the Executive. This section provides an overview of the Executive's subsystems, and the functions those subsystems perform.

- **Windows NT Microkernel**. The Windows NT Executive is built on top of a Microkernel, which provides processor-specific support for the Executive layer. This section describes the Microkernel.

- **Hardware Abstraction Layer**. The Hardware Abstraction Layer (HAL) decouples other parts of the operating system from the specific implementation of underlying hardware. This section provides a brief introduction to the HAL.

This chapter provides an overview of the architecture and characteristics of the Windows NT operating system. If you're new to systems programming on Windows NT, the information in this chapter will provide the background you need to understand how the various pieces of the operating system that are discussed in later chapters fit together. Even if you're experienced at using and programming Windows NT, we recommend that you at least briefly skim this chapter to become familiar with the terminology used throughout the book.

Windows NT Major Characteristics

How do you begin to describe an operating system? One way is to look at its major characteristics or key features. The major characteristics of Windows NT are that it implements:

- Multithreading

- Pre-emptive multitasking

- Demand paged virtual memory, which utilizes a single, global common cache

- Multiprocessing

- A processor-independent architecture

- An internal OS structure based on a modified Microkernel model

- Integrated networking

- Multiple operating system emulation

The following sections consider each of these characteristics in a bit more detail.

> ### Note
>
> *Although different processors have differing numbers of privileged execution levels, Windows NT always uses only two processor-privilege levels. It uses the most privileged processor execution level (Ring 0 on x86 architecture systems), which it calls* Kernel *mode. NT also uses the least privileged mode of execution (Ring 3 on x86 architecture systems), which is referred to as* User *mode.*

Multithreading

The Windows NT model for executing programs is: Each program that executes is represented by a *process*. The process is created when program execution is requested (for example, via the Win32 API function CreateProcess(), or via the native NT system service NtCreateProcess()).

A process is simply a container for the various resources and attributes of the program. For example, the process "owns" the address space used by the program. It also owns any *handles* (more about that later) that the program opens. Resource utilization and quotas are tracked by the process. The process also owns one or more *threads* of program execution.

The unit of execution and scheduling on Windows NT is the *thread*. An initial thread is created when a process is created. That thread may create additional threads (via the Win32 API function `CreateThread()` or the native NT `NtCreateThread()` system service) at any time. Unlike in OS/2, for example, no thread within the process has any special status of any kind.

It is absolutely vital to understand that threads in Windows NT are truly the basic units of execution and scheduling. Unlike some UNIX operating systems, Windows NT threads are not "lightweight threads" (although NT does support a variant of lightweight threads called *fibers*).

In Windows NT, each thread has its own scheduling priority and is autonomous in terms of scheduling. That is, the operating system does not take into account the process to which a thread belongs when it makes scheduling decisions. Thus, all other things being equal, two runnable threads within the same process will compete for CPU time in precisely the same way that two runnable threads from two different processes do.

Multitasking

As in any modern, general-purpose operating system, Windows NT allows multiple units of execution to run simultaneously. It rapidly switches among these units of execution, allowing each to run for a short period of time. This characteristic is termed *multitasking*.

In NT, multiple threads may run at one time. The decision of which thread is selected to run is almost entirely based on priority. NT has 32 possible thread priorities:

- Priorities 0–15 are *dynamic* priorities.
- Priorities 16–31 are *real-time* priorities.

NT implements what is known as *pre-emptive multitasking*. In NT, when a thread is selected to run, it is scheduled to run for a time period called a *quantum*. The quantum indicates the maximum length of time the thread will be allowed to run before another thread is scheduled. If the thread waits or is blocked during its quantum, a new thread is scheduled. While a given thread is running, if a thread with a higher priority becomes runnable, the lower priority thread is stopped from running and the higher priority thread is started. If the thread runs for its entire quantum, the system *pre-empts* the thread from running and selects a new thread to run.

The quantum value varies considerably, according to the platform (Intel or Alpha), the operating system type (Workstation or Server), whether the thread in question is in the foreground or background, and the system tuning settings. Suffice it to say that on an x86 architecture system running Windows NT Workstation, the value used for quantum will typically range from 20 milliseconds to 90 milliseconds. On NT Server, the values typically range from 120 milliseconds to 180 milliseconds.

Scheduling is discussed in more detail in Chapter 5, "Dispatching and Scheduling."

Demand Paged Virtual Memory

Windows NT utilizes a virtual memory architecture in which each process has its own 4GB virtual address space. This virtual address space is subdivided into *pages*, in which each page is 4KB on x86 architecture systems or 8KB on Alpha architecture systems. Typically, user applications have access to 2GB of their processes' virtual address space, with the remaining 2GB of address space to be used by the system. A tuning mechanism in Windows NT Enterprise Server allows this to be extended to 3GB (leaving 1GB of address space for use by the system).

Virtual memory pages are loaded on reference. When the amount of virtual memory exceeds the amount of physical memory, excess read-only image pages may be freed (to be reloaded later from their original location), and read-write pages may be temporarily written to one of the available paging files.

The NT virtual memory model allows the same physical addresses space to appear within the virtual address space of multiple processes. This enables the implementation of various methods of inter-process data sharing.

Multiprocessing

Although Windows NT was originally designed to support both asymmetric and symmetric multiprocessing systems, today only symmetric multiprocessing (SMP) systems are supported. In NT's model of SMP, all systems share the same main memory, and each system has equal access to peripheral devices. The operating system runs on all the processors in the SMP system. In Windows NT, there is no concept of "master" or "slave" CPUs, as there is in some other multiprocessing operating systems. In NT, thread-scheduling and interrupt-handling can be equally distributed among all the processors in the SMP complex.

The basic Windows NT architecture supports SMP systems with up to 32 CPUs. The actual number of CPUs that may be enabled, however, is governed by licensing restrictions. By default, Windows NT Workstation systems support up to only two processors. Windows NT Server systems, by default, support up to four processors, and Windows NT Enterprise Server supports up to eight processors. Hardware vendors, with appropriate license rights from Microsoft, can alter these numbers.

Processor Architecture Independence

Windows NT was designed to work on a wide variety of processors. To facilitate this, most Windows NT operating system code is written in the C programming language. Use of Assembly language has been deliberately kept to a minimum. Throughout its history, Windows NT has been supported on a variety of processors. As of this writing, Windows NT supports the x86 and Alpha processor architectures.

The Windows NT operating system code is divided into three major groups:

- The Executive, including the major operating system subsystems
- The Microkernel
- The Hardware Abstraction Layer (HAL)

The relationship among these major groups can be seen in Figure 1.2 (which appears later in this chapter). The Executive-level components utilize services provided by both the Microkernel and the HAL. The HAL and Microkernel work together to isolate the Executive-level components from processor architecture dependencies. This is one of the keys to Windows NT's processor-independent architecture.

Another aspect of Windows NT processor-independence that is of particular interest to driver writers is that Kernel mode drivers are compatible across various processor architectures at the source level. This means that a driver writer need only write a driver once. That driver can then be compiled by using the Windows NT Device Driver Kit (DDK) to support any of the processor architectures that Windows NT supports.

> Note
>
> *Although there are a few drivers that are compatible between Windows NT and Windows 9x, the standard Kernel mode drivers described in this book are not portable across these two operating systems. Windows NT and Windows 9x have very different internal structures, and do not share any significant operating system code between them.*

Microkernel Model

The Windows NT operating system is based on a much-modified version of the Microkernel architecture that was first pioneered by the Mach operating system. Mach was designed by Carnegie Mellon University in the mid- to late-1980s. In Mach, privileged-mode activities were restricted to a very small subset of functions, which resided in the Microkernel.

In Windows NT, the Microkernel is the module of the operating system that typically deals with the mechanics of doing things on the system. It is the Microkernel that is responsible, for example, for handling and routing interrupts, and for saving and restoring thread context during a task-switching operation. The Microkernel has deliberately been kept small and tight, and is for the most part processor-dependent.

Services provided by the Microkernel are utilized by the Executive-level components of the operating system. The Executive-level components are generally responsible for implementing policy (that is, deciding what the operating system should do next).

It is important to realize that Windows NT is an exceptionally well-designed operating system, which never arbitrarily adheres to a given set of architecture constructs. Thus, although policy code is generally not implemented in the Microkernel, exceptions are made when such a division is not practical. One example of this is scheduling. In Windows NT, thread scheduling (or thread *dispatching*, as it's often called) is the responsibility of the Microkernel. Although moving scheduling to an Executive-level component would have been more architecturally correct, the resulting overhead would be unacceptable.

Integrated Networking

From the time of its initial inception, Windows NT was designed to support networking. This is in dramatic contrast to other PC-based operating systems of the time (late 1989 and early 1990), which had networking added to them as an afterthought.

Windows NT has always supported multiprotocol networks. Out of the box, Windows NT supports the following protocol families:

- AppleTalk
- DLC
- NetBEUI
- IPX/SPX
- TCP/IP

Multiple Operating System Emulation

One of the least-known attributes of Windows NT is that it was designed with the goal of being able to emulate multiple operating systems. Thus, NT supports execution of Win32, POSIX, OS/2, DOS, and Windows 3.1 programs with their native semantics.

This is not to say that any programs written for any of the operating systems listed can be executed without restriction on Windows NT. Rather, the point is that Windows NT was designed at a time when there were many different operating systems contending to be "the one dominant operating system." It was not clear, for example, whether the IEEE 1003 (POSIX) standard was going to be preeminent in the marketplace, whether OS/2 was going to become a major success, or whether Windows was going to catch the public's fancy. Thus, being rather clever folks, the Windows NT development team designed an operating system that was capable of emulating each of the popular operating systems of the day, providing their native APIs and semantics.

As the market developed, the Win32 API has become preeminent. As a result, the multiple operating system support features in Windows NT have become less important. More emphasis is now being placed on getting Windows executables to execute as fast as possible. However, understanding that these facilities exist is vital to understanding the overall architecture of Windows NT.

User Mode Programs and Environment Subsystems

Processes in Windows NT typically run under the control of a specific *Environment Subsystem*. An Environment Subsystem is an independent User mode process that exports a set of APIs for use by applications, exercises control over those applications, and communicates with the Windows NT operating system on behalf of those applications. Figure 1.1 shows the relationships between a typical user application program, an Environment Subsystem being used by that user application, and the Windows NT operating system.

As shown in Figure 1.1, a User mode application utilizes one or more APIs that are provided by an Environment Subsystem. These APIs are typically implemented by a client-side DLL, to which the user application links. When the application calls an API function in the client-side DLL (as shown in Step 1 in Figure 1.1), the DLL checks to see if it can handle the request locally. By this, we mean that that DLL can process the request entirely within the client-side DLL, without reference to any other module. If the request can be handled locally, the client-side DLL processes the request and returns an appropriate reply to the requestor.

Most requests cannot be handled directly within the client-side DLL, however. When a function is called, the client-side DLL typically builds a message that represents that function and sends the message to the Environment Subsystem (Step 2 in Figure 1.1). The message is sent using Windows NT's Local Procedure Call facility, a highly optimized interprocess communication method, designed specifically for this purpose.

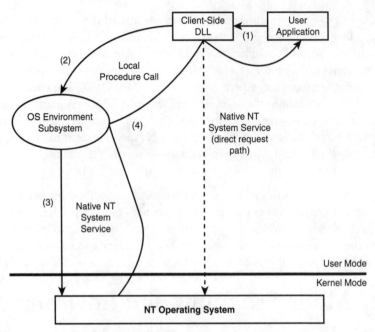

Figure 1.1. *User mode program and Environment Subsystem.*

When a thread running within the Environment Subsystem's process receives the request from the application, it will typically perform any Environment Subsystem-specific processing required, and then translate that request to a native Windows NT system service. The Environment Subsystem then issues the Windows NT system service request on behalf of the user application (Step 3 in Figure 1.1).

The Windows NT operating system processes the system service, and returns its results to the Environment Subsystem, which in turn forwards the relevant portion of the results to the requesting user application. This is shown in Step 4 of Figure 1.1.

Hopefully, an example will make the relationships between the user application, the Environment Subsystem, and the NT operating system clear. Suppose an OS/2 application is running under the control of the OS/2 Environment Subsystem. This application issues a DosExecPgm() function call (which requests the execution of a child process). This function is implemented by code in the OS/2 Environment Subsystem's client-side DLL. When the DosExecPgm() function is called, the code in the DLL assembles all the arguments and a unique code representing the function requested (DosExecPgm(), in this case), and sends all this to the OS/2 Environment Subsystem using NT's LPC facility.

A server thread running as part of the OS/2 Environment Subsystem process receives the message sent by its client-side DLL. It notes that it has received a request to process a DosExecPgm() function. It then does whatever OS/2 sorts of things it needs to do to process this request, implementing OS/2 semantics for the request. For example, the Environment Subsystem determines whether the execution of this new process was requested to be synchronous (in which case, the request is not completed until the requested process exits), asynchronous (and hence parallel with the requesting process), or background (totally independent of the requesting process).

To actually execute the requested process, the OS/2 Environment Subsystem issues the native Windows NT system service NtCreateProcess() to the NT operating system. When the NT process is created in response to the request, the OS/2 Environment Subsystem will keep track of that process as being a child of the requestor. If the new process was requested to be synchronous, the OS/2 Environment Subsystem waits until the process has completed to return status to the requestor. If the request was for an asynchronous OS/2 process, status is returned immediately.

The POSIX Environment Subsystem implements support for fork() and exec() in the same way that the OS/2 Environment Subsystem implements support for DosExecPgm(). The POSIX Environment Subsystem applies POSIX-specific rules and semantics to the function calls it receives. It translates received requests into native Windows NT system service calls on behalf of the requestor, and sends these system service calls to the NT operating system for processing. Results are passed back to the original requesting process.

Originally, the Win32 Environment Subsystem was implemented in precisely the same way as the POSIX and OS/2 Environment Subsystems. However, NT V4.0 introduced a number of optimizations that resulted in much of the Win32 Environment Subsystem. These are discussed later in this chapter, in the section entitled "The Win32 Environment Subsystem."

Bypassing the Environment Subsystem

In some cases, the client-side DLL can directly map a request to a native Windows NT system service. This is the case when the native Windows NT system service is close enough in terms of syntax to the original request, and the Environment Subsystem does not need to perform any "value-added" processing to ensure that its semantics are maintained. This direct path is shown by the dotted line in Figure 1.1.

The most common case when the direct path is used is for file and device I/O operations. In addition to avoiding the overhead inherent in first sending the request to the Environment Subsystem, the direct path allows the I/O operation to initially execute in the context of the requesting thread.

The Native Windows NT API

Windows NT implements a native set of system services that were designed to facilitate operating system emulation. This API was never intended for direct use by applications programmers, however, and is therefore largely undocumented.

A simple example of how the native NT API is specifically aimed at supporting multiple Environment Subsystems is demonstrated by the NtCreateFile() function. This system service may be used to either create a new file or open a file that already exists. In either case, part of the information passed to the NtCreateFile() system service indicates whether the call should treat the supplied filename as case-sensitive or not. This is important because in the Win32 API, filenames are always non–case-sensitive. Thus, the names foo.txt and FOO.TXT (in the same directory) refer to the same file. However, in POSIX, filenames are always considered case-sensitive. Thus, the names foo.txt and FOO.TXT (and Foo.Txt, and FOO.txt, and so on) all refer to different files.

A number of Windows NT native system services are documented in the DDK in their Zw variants. The functions documented include those used for I/O such as ZwCreateFile(), ZwReadFile(), ZwWriteFile(), ZwClose(), ZwSetInformationFile(), and ZwGetInformationFile(). Although either variant of the function may typically be called from Kernel mode, the Zw variant is used in place of the Nt version to cause the previous mode (and hence the mode in which the request was issued) to be set to Kernel mode.

To request a native Windows NT system service, the service parameters are pushed on the stack and the system service is called. On x86 architecture systems, Windows NT native system services are called by using software interrupt 2E. On Alpha systems, system services are called by using the syscall instruction.

The Win32 Environment Subsystem

Starting with Windows NT V4.0, changes were made to the operating system to enable faster support for programs running under the control of the Win32 Environment Subsystem. Prior to NT V4.0, all requests, except for file and device I/O requests, were sent to the Win32 Environment Subsystem in the manner described previously for the POSIX and OS/2 subsystems. Starting with NT V4.0, however, many of the Win32 functions were moved directly into Kernel mode. This allows the Win32 client-side DLLs (the Win32 subsystem uses multiple client-side DLLs) to use the direct path of sending requests directly to the Windows NT operating system more often than was previously possible.

The modules moved from User mode to Kernel mode in NT V4.0 include the Window Manager code, the Graphics Device Interface (GDI), and display drivers. Moving this code into Kernel mode significantly reduces the overhead of making graphics requests. This is because significantly fewer transitions between User mode and Kernel mode are required in NT V4.0 to perform a given function.

The Windows NT Executive

The Windows NT operating system is divided into individual modules, as shown in Figure 1.2.

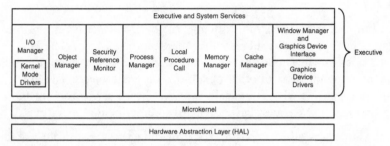

Figure 1.2. *Windows NT operating system structure.*

The Windows NT operating system is comprised of a number of different modules. As Figure 1.2 illustrates, and as previously discussed in this chapter, these modules are grouped together into three groups:

- The Executive, which includes the operating system subsystems
- The Microkernel
- The Hardware Abstraction Layer (HAL)

The Executive is actually a specific module within the NT operating system that is responsible for many miscellaneous functions, including system service dispatching and managing the paged and non-paged system pools. The Executive module utilizes services provided by the other Executive-level components (such as the I/O Manager, Object Manager, and so forth), and thus lends its name to this entire group of operating system modules.

In addition to the Executive module itself, the major components within the Executive level of the operating system are:

- I/O Manager
- Object Manager

- Security Reference Monitor
- Process Manager
- Local Procedure Call facility
- Memory Manager
- Cache Manager
- Win32 support, including Window Manager, and Graphics Device Drivers.

The following sections describe each of these components in more detail.

I/O Manager

As you can probably guess from its name, the I/O Manager is responsible for managing the input/output subsystem of the operating system. The I/O Manager does this by supporting create, read, write, set information, get information, and a whole host of other operations on *File Objects*. The I/O Manager implements what is basically a packet-based asynchronous I/O subsystem that uses I/O Request Packets (IRPs) to describe I/O operations.

The I/O Manager is also responsible for providing a framework for Kernel mode drivers, and provides support for those drivers. Kernel mode drivers are, in fact, dynamically loaded into the operating system and may be thought of as part of the I/O Manager. Because much of this book is about the I/O Manager, and how it supports and provides an environment for device drivers, we will defer any additional discussion of the I/O Manager for later. More general information about the I/O Manager appears in Chapter 9, "The I/O Manager."

Object Manager

The Object Manager is a key part of the Windows NT operating system. Programmers who mostly work in User mode are typically unaware of the Object Manager's existence because it is not directly manipulated from User mode and, by default, its namespace is not visible.

The Object Manager is responsible for maintaining a single namespace for all named objects on the system. It is also responsible for the creation, deletion, and management of named and unnamed NT system objects. The following sections describe some of the major duties performed by the Object Manager that are of particular relevance to driver writers.

Resolving System Names

As mentioned previously, the Object Manager is responsible for maintaining a single namespace for all named system objects. In fact, the Object Manager serves as the root of all namespaces on a Windows NT system. The Object

Manager's namespace can be examined by using the `objdir` utility that is provided with the DDK, or the `winobj` utility that is provided with the SDK. Figure 1.3 shows the Object Manager's top-level namespace, as displayed by `objdir`.

Figure 1.3. *The Object Manager's root namespace.*

To illustrate how the Object Manager's namespace is used in Windows NT, let's examine how the Object Manager works together with the I/O Manager to parse a file specification provided to a file open request.

A user that wants to access a file will typically use the Win32 API to issue a function call that might look something like the following:

```
hFile = CreateFile( "c:\\foo\\bar.txt",          // Dev, path, name
             GENERIC_READ ¦ GENERIC_WRITE,        // Access 0, // Share mode
             NULL, // Security
             OPEN_EXISTING,                        // Disposition
             FILE_ATTRIBUTE_NORMAL,                // Attributes & flags
             NULL);                                // Template file
```

If successful, this function call creates a File Object (that's why the function is called `CreateFile`) that represents an open instance of the named file, on the named path, on the named device. The function returns a handle to this File Object that may be used for subsequent I/O operations on the file.

In assisting the I/O Manager with processing this function, it is the Object Manager that is responsible for initially parsing the supplied name (c:\foo\bar.txt). It passes that part of the name that it cannot parse on to the I/O Manager for interpretation by the appropriate file system.

As previously discussed, when the CreateFile() Win32 API call is issued, the Win32 Environment Subsystem's client-side DLL converts this function call to the native NT system service NtCreateFile(). As part of the process of converting the parameters, Win32 converts the supplied name to a native format name that Windows NT can understand. It does this by pre-pending the supplied name with the string "\??\". Thus, when it issues the native NT system service NtCreateFile(), it does so by using the name \??\c:\foo\bar.txt.

The Executive's system service Dispatcher calls the I/O Manager to process the NtCreateFile() request. The I/O Manager in turn calls the Object Manager to create a File Object to represent the entity named in the function call. Part of the Object Manager's job in creating the File Object is to parse the provided name.

The Object Manager parses the provided name, one piece at a time, with each piece being delimited by a backslash character. Thus, the Object Manager starts by looking to see if it has an entry in its top level namespace that corresponds to "\??". As Figure 1.3 illustrates, in fact it does, and this entry is an Object Manager directory. Figure 1.4 shows a sample of the contents of the Object Manager's \??.

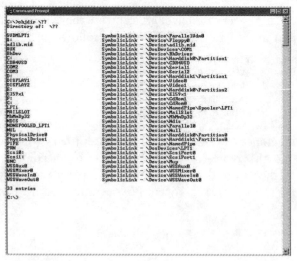

Figure 1.4. *The Object Manager's* \?? *directory.*

With the first piece of the name resolved, the Object Manager next attempts to resolve the next piece of the name within the \?? directory. The next piece of the name is "c:". As shown in Figure 1.4, c: represents a symbolic link to the Object Manager name \Device\Harddisk0\Partition1. Thus, the Object Manager substitutes \Device\Harddisk0\Partition1 for the name c: in the original name.

The Object Manager continues parsing the name. It returns to its base directory and attempts to resolve the first piece of the name, which is now "\Device". As shown in Figure 1.3, this is a directory, which the Object Manager next opens. Figure 1.5 shows the contents of the \Device directory on a sample system.

Figure 1.5. *The Object Manager's* \Device *directory.*

The Object Manager continues parsing pieces of the supplied name. Within the \Device directory, the Object Manager finds an entry that represents Harddisk0. This is also a directory, the contents of which are shown in Figure 1.6.

Now within the \Device\Harddisk0 directory, the Object Manager continues parsing the provided name. The next piece of the name is Partition1, which represents the name of a Device Object within this directory. Because a Device Object was located (and not another Object Manager directory or symbolic link), the Object Manager passes control to the I/O Manager's parse method for Device Objects.

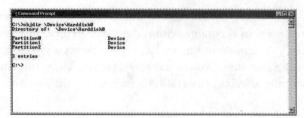

Figure 1.6. *The Object Manager's* \Device\Harddisk0 *directory.*

The Object Manger passes the I/O Manager's parse method the remaining part of the name (\foo\bar.txt) to be resolved. The I/O Manager's parse method resolves this part of the name by finding the File System mounted for the indicated Device Object, building an I/O Request Packet representing the Create File request, and thus passing the renaming part of the name on to the File System for parsing and validation. If the file system decides the supplied name is valid, and if the requested access can be granted to the entity by the file system to the user, then the I/O Manager and Object Manager complete the request successfully, returning a handle to the created File Object.

System Object Management

As mentioned previously, in addition to parsing names, the Object Manager is responsible for the actual creation, deletion, and management of NT system objects. These objects include the File Objects, Device Objects, and Driver Objects used by the I/O Manager; the Process Objects and Thread Objects used by the Process Manager; and Section Objects used by the Memory Manager, among others. The Object Manager is also responsible for maintaining reference counts on system objects, managing object handles, and tracking the access granted to each object via each handle. The Object Manager also supports converting a handle to a given object to a pointer to that object.

To illustrate the I/O Manager's role in the management of system objects, let's expand on the open file example that we started in the previous section.

As discussed in the previous section, to access a file, a user must create a File Object that represents that file. This File Object can be created by using the Win32 API function CreateFile() or directly via the NT native API NtCreateFile(). Both of these functions allow the caller to specify the name of the entity to be accessed (such as the device, directory path, and name of the file to be opened), as well as the access being requested to the entity. NtCreateFile() is processed by the I/O Subsystem, which calls the I/O Manager to create a File Object on its behalf.

If the Object Manager successfully creates the File Object, and if the Object Manager, I/O Manager, and file system successfully parse the supplied file specification, the I/O Manager returns a handle to the newly created File Object to the requestor. This implies that the access requested to the entity underlying the File Object was successfully granted. The Object Manager creates an entry in the handle table for the current process to track this File Object, and records the access that was successfully granted to the object.

On subsequent I/O operations to this File Object, the requestor supplies the File Object handle (typically referred to as a *file handle*, for convenience). Using the current process' handle table, the Object Manager converts the file handle to a pointer to a File Object and increments the reference count on the File Object. At the same time, the Object Manager also checks to see if the access required by the I/O operation that is being requested is allowed by the access that was granted to this File Object when the File Object was created. If the access is not allowed, the I/O Manager immediately aborts the I/O operation with an error status. If the requested access is allowed, the I/O Manager proceeds to build an I/O Request Packet that represents the requested I/O operation on this File Object.

As can be seen from the preceding description, the Object Manager plays a key role in the Windows NT system. It's important to realize that the Object Manager doesn't just work with the I/O Manager, as shown in the preceding example. Rather, the Object Manager works with all the Executive-level subsystems in much the same way as it works with the I/O Manager in the example.

Security Reference Monitor

The Security Reference Monitor is responsible for implementing Windows NT security access policy. As such, it is not of much interest to device driver writers. However, its existence and its responsibilities are worthy of a brief mention.

The Security Reference Monitor implements Access Control Lists (ACLs) and Security Identifiers (SIDs) for use in implementing system security policy. It supports a unique per-thread security profile, and supports security-based validation for access to objects.

It is particularly interesting to note that Windows NT implements a unified security policy. That is, access to all system resources (that are access-controlled) is the responsibility of the Security Reference Monitor. For example, access validation to files on the NTFS file system is implemented not by an internal NTFS security policy, but rather by NTFS utilizing the services provided by the Security Reference Monitor.

Another interesting aspect of the Security Reference Monitor is support for what NT refers to as *impersonation*. This allows one thread to pass along to another thread the right for the second thread to use the first thread's security credentials. This is most often used in client-server operations. In these operations, the client will authorize the server to impersonate the client, thereby allowing the server to use the client's security credentials when performing a particular operation.

Process Manager

The Process Manager is responsible for process and thread creation and deletion. The Process Manager accomplishes this by working with the Object Manager to build Process Objects and Thread Objects, and with the Memory Manager to allocate virtual address space for the process.

Local Procedure Call Facility

The Local Procedure Call (LPC) facility provides a local implementation of the RPC interprocess communication service. LPC supports passing data between clients and servers by using either messages or shared memory. One interesting feature of LPC is that messages may be passed between clients and servers without the overhead of a scheduling operation.

LPC was specifically designed for use between an application and its Environment Subsystem. As a result, the API needed to access LPC is not documented. It is interesting to note that RPC requests between applications on the same Windows NT system will actually use LPC as the transport mechanism.

Memory Manager and Cache Manager

The Memory Manager and Cache Manager together form what we refer to as Windows NT's Virtual Memory Subsystem. The Virtual Memory Subsystem is described in detail in Chapter 3, "Virtual Memory." Here, we will mention some of the main characteristics of NT's implementation of virtual memory as a quick introduction to the topic.

The NT Virtual Memory Subsystem provides a 32-bit demand paged environment. Although 64-bit support is being added to Windows NT, it is not available in NT V4.0 or earlier.

The Virtual Memory Subsystem supports the sharing of physical pages among multiple processes. It supports shared read-only as well as shared read-write memory segments.

The Virtual Memory Subsystem is responsible for implementing Windows NT's data and file caching mechanisms. File data may be accessed on Windows NT via the I/O Manager, using standard read and write operations to files, or via the Memory Manager by mapping the file's data directly into virtual memory. To ensure cache coherency between these two access methods, the Windows

NT Cache Manager implements a single, global, common cache. This single cache is used to cache both process data pages and file data pages.

Win32 Support Components

As discussed previously, the Win32 support components are new to NT V4.0. The Window Manager implements Windowing, Windows messaging, and the like. It comprises much of that code that formerly resided in the User component of the Win32 Environment Subsystem.

The Win32 support components also include the Graphics Device Interface (GDI) and its associated display drivers. These facilities interface between GUI applications and graphics devices, and provide a set of standard text and drawing primitives.

Windows NT Microkernel

The Windows NT Microkernel is responsible for providing processor-specific support for all low-level functions in the operating system. Unlike the HAL, which provides support for processor resources that can change among specific models within a family of processors, the Microkernel provides support for basic architectural constructs, such as handling and dispatching interrupts, saving and restoring thread context, and multiprocessor synchronization.

The Microkernel exports two different types of kernel objects: Dispatcher Objects and Control Objects.

Kernel objects are distinct from Object Manager (or Executive-level) objects. Kernel objects provide the lowest level of support for certain entities. Kernel objects are often the basis for Object Manager objects.

One type of kernel object is the Dispatcher Object. Dispatcher Objects are used for scheduling (or "dispatching," as it's called in Windows NT) and synchronization. Dispatcher Objects are prefixed by a common DISPATCH_HEADER (the definition of which appears in the standard DDK header file, ntddk.h). A picture of the DISPATCHER_HEADER is shown in Figure 1.7.

Dispatcher Objects have an attribute called "signal state." Using the appropriate system service a caller can wait, with an optional timeout, on a Dispatcher Object until the object is signaled. Kernel Dispatcher Objects include events, mutexes, semaphores, and timers.

Many kernel objects may be directly manipulated by device drivers and the Executive. A simple example of such an object is the kernel Event Object. Space for a kernel Event Object may be allocated from any non-paged location, including non-paged system pool. A driver may then initialize this event (using the Microkernel-supplied function KeInitializeEvent()) to either sig-naled or not-signaled state. Any Kernel mode thread with a pointer to this object may then wait for it to become signaled by calling the Microkernel func-tion KeWaitForSingleObject().

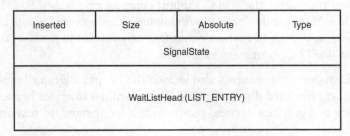

Inserted	Size	Absolute	Type
SignalState			
WaitListHead (LIST_ENTRY)			

Figure 1.7. DISPATCHER_HEADER.

An example of how a Kernel Object can form the basis of an Executive-level object is also provided by the Event Object. Event Objects in the Win32 sub-system (created by the Win32 API function CreateEvent()) are actually Executive-level (Object Manager-created and managed) Event Objects. Each Executive-level Event Object contains a kernel-level Event Object. Waiting for an Executive-level Event Object is accomplished via the Win32 API function WaitForSingleObject() which, once translated to an NT native system service and processed by the Object Manager, results in a call to KeWaitForSingleObject() on the kernel Event Object that forms the basis of the Object Manager's Event Object.

The second type of object exported by the kernel is the Control Object. These objects are used to control specific aspects of system operations. Control Objects include Asynchronous Procedure Call (APC) Objects, Deferred Procedure Call (DPC) Objects, Interrupt Objects, and Profile Objects. Although it is a bit complicated to explain Control Objects at this point, one example is the Interrupt Object. The Interrupt Object is responsible for con-necting a specific interrupt vector to a device driver's Interrupt Service Routine (ISR).

Hardware Abstraction Layer

The Hardware Abstraction Layer (HAL) is responsible for providing a stan-dard interface to processor-specific resources. This standard interface is used by the Microkernel and the Executive-level components. Understanding this stan-dard interface is one of the keys to understanding how Windows NT imple-ments its processor-independent architecture.

The HAL is discussed in detail in the next chapter, Chapter 2, "Achieving Hardware Independence with the HAL."

Chapter 2

Achieving Hardware Independence with the HAL

This chapter will review:

- **The HAL's Role in the Windows NT Operating System.** The HAL provides a standard interface to processor resources for use by the rest of the NT operating system. This section discusses the HAL's specific role in building the portable operating system environment in which NT runs.

- **Device Addressing.** This section describes the abstraction provided by the HAL for identifying a specific device address on a given I/O bus.

- **I/O Architecture.** The HAL provides a set of standard routines that provide access to device registers. This section describes these routines and how they may be used to access device addresses that reside in port I/O space or memory space.

- **Interrupt Management.** This section introduces the HAL's model for interrupt handling.

- **DMA Operations.** The HAL, working with the I/O Manager, provides a unique model for DMA operations on Windows NT. This section introduces the basics of that model.

- **Other HAL Facilities.** This section describes the role the HAL plays in clock and timer management, interfacing to the BIOS, and handling system configuration.

- **Processor Architecture Differences Not Handled by the HAL.** The HAL doesn't even attempt to handle certain basic differences in processor architecture. This section describes a number of those differences.

This chapter discusses how the Hardware Abstraction Layer (HAL) helps provide processor architecture independence on Windows NT systems. You will also learn about some of the fundamental services that the HAL provides. Finally, the chapter ends with a discussion of the types of processor architecture-specific features that the HAL does not include in its abstractions.

The HAL's Role in the Windows NT Operating System

One of the most unique attributes of the Windows NT operating system is that it is not dependent on the design of one particular hardware platform or architecture. This is in strong contrast to earlier systems, such as OS/2, Windows, and DOS, which were very closely tied to their underlying system hardware. The component of Windows NT that provides this hardware independence is the Hardware Abstraction Layer (HAL).

Fundamentally, the HAL is merely a set of operating system services that device drivers utilize to interact with both processor resources and their specific hardware. Although there is no way for NT to enforce the requirement that a device driver utilize the HAL services, the advantages of portability are lost if the HAL isn't used. To use HAL services, device drivers (and other system components) call HAL functions and utilize HAL macros. These functions and macros handle converting the driver's requests into operations appropriate for the particular hardware platform. In many cases, this conversion is straightforward. For some platforms, however, the HAL may have to perform considerable additional processing in order to perform the requested operation.

The HAL implements a standard model (or "abstraction," as it's often called) of available system resources, and a standard view of certain hardware platform capabilities. The HAL also provides a standard interface through which all other Executive-level system components access these resources. This interface does not change, based on the system upon which NT is running. Thus, the HAL maps requests made by other operating system components to its abstract interface to the actual hardware existing on a given platform. Figure 2.1 illustrates this model.

It is very important to understand that the HAL does not provide abstractions for every processor architecture-dependent facility that exists, or that could exist, in a system. Rather, the HAL's abstractions are typically limited to those items that either

- Are regularly used by operating system components other than the Microkernel and the HAL itself

- Could change among specific system implementations within a given processor architecture

Standard HAL Interface: READ_PORT_xxx( ), READ_REGISTER_xxx( ), HalTranslateBusAddress( ), etc.	Standard HAL Interface: READ_PORT_xxx( ), READ_REGISTER_xxx( ), HalTranslateBusAddress( ), etc.
System-specific code to implement standard interface on **single processor x86 systems**	System-specific code to implement standard interface on **specific multiprocessor Alpha system**
Standard x86 HAL	Specific Alpha HAL

Figure 2.1. *The HAL's upper edge stays the same; the actual implementation may change, based on the underlying hardware platform.*

The processor-dependent features that the HAL does *not* implement are discussed in greater detail later in this chapter.

The facilities and resources for which the HAL provides an abstraction include the following:

- Device Addressing
- I/O Architecture
- Interrupt Management
- DMA Operations
- System Clocks and Timers
- Firmware and BIOS Interfacing
- Configuration Management

For device drivers, the HAL's standard interface means that hardware access is platform-independent. Thus, instead of having the particular system platform dictate how a device driver interfaces with its hardware, the driver uses the standard interfaces provided by the HAL. The HAL is responsible for dealing with any platform-specific differences. Because the interface to the HAL does not change from hardware platform to hardware platform, a driver that properly uses the HAL to access its device requires no changes (other than recompilation!) to enable it to run on the various Windows NT hardware platforms.

Note

It's important to understand that the HAL provides an unchanging abstraction of processor architecture-based resources, not an abstraction of specific hardware devices. Therefore, the HAL needs to be changed only when support is required for a different set of processor architecture capabilities. This might include, for example, if support for a new I/O bus needs to be added, or if the mechanics of the way the system clock works changes. The HAL does not provide abstractions of individual devices on the system, such as a serial port, a disk device, or a keyboard.

The HAL provides the following services:

- A common set of services, available on all Windows NT platforms.

- A portable implementation of inherently platform-specific services.

- A uniform mechanism for *ALL* kernel code to access underlying hardware platform resources.

The sections that follow examine some of the resource abstractions provided by the HAL, and describe how the HAL handles them.

Device Addressing

The HAL implements a very flexible model for device addresses. In this model, devices are connected to buses, each of which has its own address space, as illustrated in Figure 2.2.

The HAL views device addresses, as identified by the devices themselves, as strictly bus-relative. These addresses may be located in either port I/O space or memory space. Notice in Figure 2.2 that both PCI buses have the bus-relative address 0xC0000. Similarly, according to the HAL's abstraction, it is possible for two devices on different buses to both have registers located at port I/O space address 0x180.

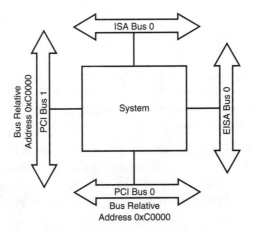

Figure 2.2. *Different bus address spaces.*

Before a device address can be accessed from a driver by using one of the HAL functions described later in this chapter, the address must be converted from a bus-relative address to a HAL-translated address. This translated address is one of the class of addresses called *logical addresses* on Windows NT. A device-logical address is unambiguous and not tied to any particular bus.

It is very important to understand that logical addresses are managed solely by the HAL on Windows NT. This means that logical addresses are best thought of as opaque values, with special meaning only to the HAL. In this way, they are not unlike HANDLEs. Further, how logical addresses are interpreted varies widely among processor architectures and HALs. For example, on one processor architecture, logical addresses might actually be identical to physical addresses in host memory. On another processor, logical addresses might quite literally be encoded values that indicate the bus and port on that bus to which the logical address refers.

I/O Architecture

Perhaps the most significant difference among processor architectures that is relevant specifically to device driver writers is the mechanism by which device control and status registers are accessed. The Intel x86 processor family allows devices to present control and status registers in one of two discrete address spaces: port I/O space or memory space. Because these two address spaces are distinct, x86 architecture processors implement specific instructions that support access to each of these address spaces. Port space addresses are accessed using in and out instructions. That is, addresses that appear on the in or out instruction are interpreted by the processor as addresses in port I/O space. All other instructions (such as mov) interpret any memory references as references to addresses in memory space.

Of course, not all processors support the concept of distinct port I/O and memory spaces. RISC architecture CPUs, such as the Alpha, support only memory address space. Device control and status registers thus appear mapped into memory space, according to a scheme implemented by the system designer.

Complicating this issue is the fact that I/O architecture is not solely a function of the CPU. Rather, it is also a function of the device buses attached to the system. All buses commonly used with x86 architecture systems (including the PCI, ISA, and EISA buses) specifically support the concept of distinct port and memory address spaces.

To enable drivers to support systems with differing I/O architectures without any source code changes, the standard model that the HAL provides to device drivers includes both port I/O and memory spaces. Device drivers access their devices' control and status registers using HAL-provided functions. The HAL in turn implements whatever code is necessary to access the indicated device register on the specific platform on which the driver happens to be running.

Choosing the Correct HAL Function for Device Access

The HAL provides functions that allow drivers to read and write registers in either port I/O space or memory space. These functions are specific to the size of the register being accessed. That is, there are functions to read and to write UCHAR, USHORT, and ULONG registers that reside in either port I/O space or memory space. The complete list of such functions is as follows:

```
READ_PORT_UCHAR()          WRITE_PORT_UCHAR()

READ_PORT_USHORT()         WRITE_PORT_USHORT()

READ_PORT_ULONG()          WRITE_PORT_ULONG()

READ_REGISTER_UCHAR()      WRITE_REGISTER_UCHAR()

READ_REGISTER_USHORT()     WRITE_REGISTER_USHORT()

READ_REGISTER_ULONG()      WRITE_REGISTER_ULONG()
```

The driver selects whether to use the UCHAR, USHORT, or ULONG variant of the function, depending on the size of the device register to be accessed. A UCHAR is defined in NT as an unsigned 8-bit value. A USHORT is defined as an unsigned 16-bit value. A ULONG is defined as an unsigned 32-bit value.

A driver selects whether to use one of the PORT or one of the REGISTER functions, based on the location of the register to be accessed *on the device itself*. Registers located on a device in port I/O space are accessed using the HAL's PORT functions. Registers located on a device in memory space are accessed using the HAL's REGISTER functions.

Thus, if a driver writer wants to access a register on a PCI device, the driver writer must know in advance whether that register is wired to port I/O space or register space on the device. Because the location of a given device register is decided by the device's designer when the device is built, the location of a particular register is never ambiguous, and never varies from system to system. Thus, the driver *never* selects which function type to use, based on the system on which it is running. It is the HAL's job to ensure that the driver's function calls "do the right thing" on the processor architecture on which a driver happens to be running.

Figures 2.3 and 2.4 show the prototypes for the functions READ_PORT_UCHAR() and READ_REGISTER_UCHAR(). The prototypes for the other HAL read functions differ only in the size of the register read and data item returned.

UCHAR
READ_PORT_UCHAR(IN PUCHAR *Port*);

Port: The port I/O address to use for reading this device port.

Figure 2.3. READ_PORT_UCHAR() *function prototype.*

UCHAR
READ_REGISTER_UCHAR(IN PUCHAR *Register*);

Register: The address to use for reading this device register.

Figure 2.4. READ_REGISTER_UCHAR *function prototype.*

Figures 2.5 and 2.6 show the prototypes for WRITE_PORT_UCHAR() and WRITE_REGISTER_UCHAR(). The prototypes for the other HAL write functions differ only in the size of the register and data item written.

VOID
WRITE_PORT_UCHAR(IN PUCHAR *Port*,
                IN UCHAR   *Value*);

Port: The port I/O address to use for writing this device port.

Value: The data value to write to the port.

Figure 2.5. WRITE_PORT_UCHAR() *function prototype.*

VOID
WRITE_REGISTER_UCHAR(IN PUCHAR *Register*,
                IN UCHAR *Value*);

Register: The address to use for writing this device register.

Value: The data value to write to the register.

Figure 2.6. WRITE_REGISTER_UCHAR *function prototype.*

These HAL "functions" are in fact either actual functions or macros, depending upon the precise requirements of the underlying hardware platform. For example, WRITE_PORT_UCHAR() is a function on the x86 platform. The declaration in ntddk.h, specific to the x86 platform is:

```
NTKERNELAPI
VOID
WRITE_PORT_UCHAR(
    PULONG  Port,
    ULONG   Value
    );
```

For the Alpha platform, the declaration is identical. For the Power PC (no longer supported, but still present in ntddk.h), the declaration of WRITE_PORT_UCHAR() is:

```
#define WRITE_PORT_UCHAR(x, y) {           \
    *(volatile UCHAR * const)(x) = y;   \
    KeFlushWriteBuffer();               \
}
```

On the x86 platform, the HAL code that implements the routine for WRITE_PORT_UCHAR() looks something like the following:

```
        mov     edx,[esp+4]
        mov     eax,[esp+8]
        out     dx,eax
```

For the Alpha platform, the code that implements the routine for
WRITE_PORT_UCHAR() looks considerably different from either its x86 or PPC
counterpart. Indeed, the Alpha implementation of this code handles the complex addressing architecture used by the Alpha platform to support port I/O
operations.

Regardless of the precise implementation, the essential point is that the device
driver source code uses the function appropriate for the device register it is
accessing. If the device in question is a PCI device utilizing I/O registers in port
I/O space, the HAL functions for accessing I/O registers in port I/O space are
used. The precise combination of hardware and software used by the platform
to transform the HAL operation into a port I/O access to the device is unimportant to the device driver developer. Thus, device drivers can be developed
in a cross-platform fashion.

> Note
>
> *As noted earlier in the chapter, some functions may have migrated from
> other parts of the operating system into the HAL. In some cases, operations that are described as being part of the HAL are implemented within
> the microkernel. For example, on the x86 platform, the register routines
> (such as READ_REGISTER_UCHAR()) are implemented within the microkernel,
> and not within the HAL itself.*

HAL Buffer Functions

Before completing our discussion of registers and ports, another notable group
of functions provided by the HAL for port and register access are the BUFFER
functions, specifically:

READ_PORT_BUFFER_UCHAR()	WRITE_PORT_BUFFER_UCHAR()
READ_PORT_BUFFER_USHORT()	WRITE_PORT_BUFFER_USHORT()
READ_PORT_BUFFER_ULONG()	WRITE_PORT_BUFFER_ULONG()
READ_REGISTER_BUFFER_UCHAR()	WRITE_REGISTER_BUFFER_UCHAR()
READ_REGISTER_BUFFER_USHORT()	WRITE_REGISTER_BUFFER_USHORT()
READ_REGISTER_BUFFER_ULONG()	WRITE_REGISTER_BUFFER_ULONG()

These functions all read from or write to multiple locations in the data buffer,
accessing a device register that is of the indicated length. Figure 2.7 and Figure
2.8 show the prototypes for READ_PORT_BUFFER_UCHAR() and
WRITE_PORT_BUFFER_UCHAR(), respectively. The other READ_PORT_BUFFER_xxx()
and WRITE_PORT_BUFFER_xxx() functions differ only in the size of the data item
and register referenced.

VOID
READ_PORT_BUFFER_UCHAR(IN PUCHAR *Port*,
    IN PUCHAR *Buffer*,
    IN ULONG *Count*);

Port: The port I/O address to use for reading this device port.

Buffer: A pointer to a buffer to which the read port data is to be copied.

Count: The count of UCHAR values to be read from the port.

Figure 2.7. READ_PORT_BUFFER_UCHAR() *function prototype.*

VOID
WRITE_PORT_BUFFER_UCHAR(IN PUCHAR *Port*,
    IN PUCHAR *Buffer*,
    IN ULONG *Count*);

Port: The port I/O address to which to write the data.

Buffer: A pointer to a buffer from which the port data is to be copied.

Count: The count of UCHAR values to be written to the port.

Figure 2.8. WRITE_PORT_BUFFER_UCHAR() *function prototype.*

For the PORT_BUFFER functions, note that data is always transferred between a single port I/O register location and a range of addresses in the indicated data buffer. That is, WRITE_PORT_BUFFER_UCHAR(PortX, Buffer, NumChars) does the equivalent of:

```
while (NumChars--) {
    WRITE_PORT_UCHAR(PortX, *Buffer++);
}
```

Figure 2.9 and Figure 2.10 illustrate the prototypes for READ_REGISTER_BUFFER_UCHAR() and WRITE_REGISTER_BUFFER_UCHAR(), respectively. The other READ_REGISTER_BUFFER_xxx() and WRITE_REGISTER_BUFFER_xxx() functions differ only in the size of the data item and register referenced.

VOID
READ_REGISTER_BUFFER_UCHAR(IN PUCHAR *Register*,
  IN PUCHAR *Buffer*,
  IN ULONG *Count*);

Register: The starting address of a range of memory-mapped device addresses from which to read.

Buffer: A pointer to a buffer to which the read data is to be copied.

Count: The count of UCHAR values to be read from the register.

Figure 2.9. READ_REGISTER_BUFFER_UCHAR() *function prototype.*

VOID
WRITE_PORT_BUFFER_UCHAR(IN PUCHAR *Register*,
  IN PUCHAR *Buffer*,
  IN ULONG *Count*);

Register: The starting address of a range of memory-mapped device addresses to which the data is to be written.

Buffer: A pointer to a buffer from which the port data is to be copied.

Count: The count of UCHAR values to be written to the register.

Figure 2.10. WRITE_REGISTER_BUFFER_UCHAR() *function prototype.*

It's very important to notice that the REGISTER_BUFFER functions do not work the same way as the PORT_BUFFER functions with respect to the way they handle the device address. The REGISTER_BUFFER functions move data between a range of memory-mapped register locations on the device, and a range of addresses in the indicated data buffer. That is, WRITE_REGISTER_BUFFER_UCHAR(RegisterX, Buffer, NumChars) does the equivalent of:

```
while (NumChars--) {
    WRITE_REGISTER_UCHAR(RegisterX++, *Buffer++);
}
```

Thus, for the PORT_BUFFER functions, a single port device address is used; for the REGISTER_BUFFER functions, a range of memory device addresses is used. This allows the REGISTER_BUFFER functions to be used to move data between host memory and mapped memory areas on a device.

> **Tip**
>
> *Here's a hint that often bites new NT driver writers: In the BUFFER functions, the values provided for Count is the number of data items—which is not necessarily the number of bytes—to be moved. That is, Count is the number of* UCHARs, USHORTs, *or* ULONGs *to be moved, depending on the function chosen.*

Interrupt Management

Because it is the HAL's job to isolate the rest of the system from platform-specific architectural issues, the HAL is responsible for managing and handling interrupts. This includes not only managing the way interrupts are routed, but also assigning relative priorities to the various interrupts. Like device addresses, the HAL's model for interrupt vectors is that such vectors, as identified by the devices themselves, are bus-relative. Thus, before an interrupt vector can be referenced, it must be translated to a logical interrupt priority value.

In Windows NT, device drivers may register to have a function called when a particular device interrupts. The HAL, along with the NT microkernel, is responsible for the specifics of interrupt-controller management and programming. The device driver identifies a HAL-defined interrupt vector to which to connect, and a function to be called when an interrupt occurs at that vector. The HAL (working with the I/O Manager and the microkernel) registers the device driver's Interrupt Service Routine (ISR) function to be called when the indicated interrupt is to be serviced.

Because the number of discrete interrupt priorities—and the ways such priorities are managed—vary widely among processor architectures, the HAL provides an abstraction of hardware logical interrupt priorities. This abstraction is the Interrupt Request Level (IRQL). The HAL provides a set of symbolic values for IRQLs; ranging from the IRQL PASSIVE_LEVEL, which is defined as the lowest possible IRQL on the system, to IRQL HIGH_LEVEL, which is defined as the highest possible IRQL. IRQLs are discussed in much more detail in Chapter 6, "Interrupt Request Levels and DPCs."

> **Note**
>
> *IRQLs have nothing to do with the Windows NT scheduling priority of a thread.*

On some platforms, managing the interrupt controller is a simple task. For example, on a standard x86 platform, the interrupt hardware is a pair of 8259-compatible programmable interrupt controllers (PICs). The second controller is attached to the first controller, with each controller managing eight interrupts, for a total of 15 usable interrupts. The assignment of IRQL values to these individual interrupts is completely a function of the HAL. Thus, there is no absolutely no requirement that the HAL use IRQL 6 for the PIC's IRQ 6!

For more complex systems, programming the interrupt controller is more challenging. Hardware platforms might restrict certain interrupts so they are handled only on specific CPUs. Programmable interrupt controllers must be managed to mask interrupts on some processors while leaving them enabled on other processors. Interrupts may be "cascaded" so that one interrupt represents a set of other interrupts.

Whenever an ISR is to be called in response to a device interrupt, the HAL and microkernel (working together) first raise the system's current interrupt priority to the IRQL that has been assigned to the interrupting device. This has the effect of blocking subsequent interrupts from the interrupting device, and for any device with interrupts of the same or lower IRQL value. Once the device driver's ISR has completed servicing the interrupt, it simply executes a return statement. The IRQL of the system is then altered, as necessary, to service other interrupts that may be pending.

The important thing to realize about interrupt management on NT is that it's almost entirely the HAL's responsibility. Device drivers do not manually "hook" interrupt vectors, program interrupt controllers, or issue IRET or EOI instructions. By using the HAL-supplied functions, drivers are able to work unchanged on the wide array of processor architectures supported by Windows NT.

DMA Operations

The HAL also provides abstractions that support an underlying processor's DMA capabilities. This includes both system DMA and busmaster DMA capabilities. The HAL's model for both system and busmaster DMA are described in detail in Chapter 8, "I/O Architectures," and Chapter 17, "DMA Data Transfers." This section provides merely a brief introduction to these capabilities.

The HAL provides a standard DMA model, in which devices perform DMA operations using logical addresses in host memory. The HAL, working with the I/O Manager, is responsible for providing, translating, and managing these logical addresses.

As discussed previously in this chapter, the address space on each bus connected to the system is considered discrete, as illustrated in Figure 2.2. For the purposes of busmaster DMA, the HAL converts logical addresses used by devices during DMA operations to host memory addresses using map registers as illustrated in Figure 2.11.

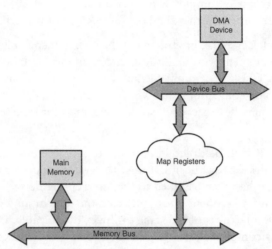

Figure 2.11. *Translating logical addresses to host memory addresses via map registers for DMA operations.*

The HAL also provides an abstraction for use by devices that support System DMA. System DMA utilizes a set of centralized DMA controllers that perform DMA on behalf of suitably configured devices. This frees the devices themselves from having to have a DMA engine on board. The HAL provides a model by which system DMA channels resources may be shared among multiple devices and reserved for use by a specific device for the duration of a transfer. Because System DMA operations may also entail logical to physical host memory address translation, map registers may be used for this process.

Finally, the HAL also provides an abstraction called *system scatter/gather*. This facility provides special support for DMA devices that do not support scatter/gather, that is, devices that are capable of performing DMA operations from only one logical base address per transfer. For such devices, the HAL uses its map registers to create logically contiguous buffers from buffers that are physically discontiguous in host main memory. This facility saves devices that do not themselves support scatter/gather the overhead of having to perform multiple discrete DMA operations for non-contiguous buffers. More details about the HAL's support for scatter/gather and DMA devices appears in Chapter 8, "I/O Architectures," and Chapter 17, "DMA Data Transfers."

Other HAL Facilities

The HAL also provides support for system clocks and timers, firmware and BIOS interfacing, and configuration management.

The HAL provides a standard set of routines used by higher-level entities for programming and handling the system's clocks. This includes both interval-timer management and time-of-day clocks. The abstraction that the HAL presents of these facilities is that the system clock keeps track of time in 100ns-intervals, with time starting on January 1, 1601. Of course, the HAL is responsible for managing the underlying system clocks, and converting between the actual clock frequency and the 100ns-intervals.

When the system is bootstrapped, it is the HAL that is responsible for working with the system BIOS or firmware to determine the system's device configuration. The HAL creates a system-independent description of the hardware present on the system. This configuration information is stored in the Registry, and utilized by the microkernel and I/O Manager.

The HAL is also responsible for retrieving bus-level configuration information (where available) from the underlying architecture. For example, the HAL provides standardized interfaces to retrieve EISA and MCA information from those buses.

Processor Architecture Differences Not Handled by the HAL

As mentioned at the beginning of this chapter, the HAL provides an abstraction of only a subset of features present in a given system. The differences that the HAL handles are primarily those that could be changed relatively easily between implementations of the same processor family. For example, the number of interrupt levels and the way these are managed could conceivably vary among implementations of x86 systems—even among implementations of x86 systems using the same processor. Thus, this is one of the differences handled in the HAL.

There are many differences the HAL does not manage. For example, the HAL does not attempt to handle system architecture differences such as:

- Physical address size
- Virtual memory implementation (LDT/GDT, TLB, etc.)
- Caching/pipelining (separate I&D cache, independently flushed, out-of-order execution, etc.)
- Process/thread context (number, type, and size of registers, etc.)

These attributes are fundamental to a processor's architecture and do not change between different implementations of a particular processor. For example, the number of general-purpose registers on an x86 architecture system is a fundamental architectural feature of the x86 processor that is not going to change from motherboard to motherboard. This is also true of the basic characteristics of virtual memory. It is just not practical to change the hardware implementation of virtual memory without affecting the entire design of the CPU.

These fundamental attributes are mostly managed by the microkernel. To change one of these fundamental attributes requires porting Windows NT to the new architecture. This is a far more involved and complex undertaking than simply changing the HAL.

Chapter 3

Virtual Memory

This chapter will review:

- **Demand Paged Virtual Memory.** Windows NT provides a virtual memory system that loads elements into memory as required. This section describes the rationale and basic mechanism involved in the Windows NT VM system.

- **Address Translation.** A key element of the virtual memory system is translating virtual addresses to physical addresses. This section describes the process Windows NT uses to manage this translation process.

- **Physical-Memory Management.** Because physical memory is a scarce resource, one of the primary goals of the VM system is to ensure proper sharing of this scarce resource between the various programs demanding memory. This section describes the process Windows NT uses to manage this sharing of physical memory in a reasonable and fair manner.

- **Memory-Manager Tuning.** The Memory Manager component of Windows NT allows users to control its behavior using a number of Registry parameters. This section describes those parameters of most interest and describes how they impact the VM system.

- **Drivers and VM.** Windows NT device driver writers must understand how VM works in order to write device drivers that operate correctly. This section describes the key issues confronting device driver developers who must manage virtual addresses in both user and system address spaces.

This chapter discusses general concepts of demand paged virtual memory operating systems, and examines how Windows NT implements its support for virtual memory. A thorough understanding of how Windows NT virtual memory works will clarify the purpose for many of the mechanisms used within a Windows NT device driver for handling memory.

Demand Paged Virtual Memory

Windows NT utilizes a 32-bit pointer value for accessing data within the operating system. Because of this, the address space of any process is 2^{32} bytes, or 4GB. Managing this large address space is a complex and demanding process, requiring that the OS balance the needs of many conflicting demands for physical memory so that the system performs acceptably under a wide variety of loads. This is accomplished by using a virtual memory system.

Windows NT's virtual memory system is a demand paged virtual memory system. Because of this, all references to memory are done by way of an indirect reference—a lookup table. The precise mechanism used for implementing this lookup table is actually quite specific to the processor hardware being used. However, Windows NT implements its common set of functionality uniformly across all the hardware platforms. Figure 3.1 demonstrates an example of this indirection model.

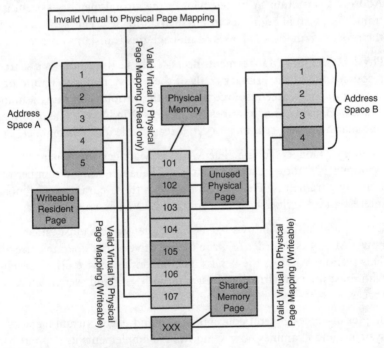

Figure 3.1. *Demand paged virtual memory.*

Figure 3.1 shows two separate address spaces (or "processes," as they are called in Windows NT). Each address space is divided into a set of virtual pages. These virtual pages then in turn may point to physical pages. Because of this virtual-to-physical page mapping, a single physical page can be shared between two separate address spaces—and that shared page can either be read-only or it can be writeable. Further, a shared physical page can have the same virtual address in each address space or it can have different virtual addresses in each address space.

In addition, some physical pages are designated as *free* and are available for use if one of the address spaces needs additional physical memory. For example, Process A in the Figure 3.1 has a virtual page (page 2) with no corresponding physical page. If Process A needs to access data on page 2, the VM system will be required to allocate physical memory (such as free physical page 102) to contain the actual data for virtual page 2.

Note that one advantage of using a lookup table is that more than one such table can exist, although only one table can be in use at any given time. Of course, on a multiprocessor system, each CPU will be using a table. In fact, it is possible for two different CPUs to be using the same table. Thus, Figure 3.1 shows two separate virtual lookup tables. Each table has a set of entries, with each entry potentially referring to a physical page. Given that there are two such lookup tables, each may refer to different pages—or they both may refer to the same common page.

Note

It is important to emphasize that Windows NT implements a hardware platform-independent virtual memory system. Thus, while it is tempting to discuss the characteristics of some particular hardware platform (such as the X86 platform), it does not describe how Windows NT actually works. Instead, this generalized model is mapped onto the support provided by the specific hardware platform. This promotes the flexibility of porting Windows NT to any CPU architecture.

Rationale for Demand Paged Virtual Memory

The demands of the Windows NT virtual memory system are a source of common confusion for new NT kernel driver writers. This is because many of the basic operations performed by device drivers require that the driver writer manipulate memory in order to manipulate and manage these virtual addresses, despite the complexity of the virtual memory system itself.

Given that virtual memory is not required for an operating system, it is useful to explore the reasons why virtual memory turns out to be useful and well worth the complexity involved in supporting it. As well, by better understanding virtual memory, the driver writer is able to exploit that understanding to build Kernel mode device drivers with better performance and a wider range of capabilities.

Many operating systems exist that do not support virtual memory. For example, the venerable MS-DOS does not support virtual memory. Despite this restriction, MS-DOS has proven to be a useful operating system during the past 17 years since it was first introduced.

One universal problem that operating systems have to deal with is scarcity of physical memory. In the case of MS-DOS, a number of techniques evolved to allow physical memory to be shared among multiple programs or even pieces of programs. These techniques enable the system to run programs or utilize data that exceed the size of physical memory.

Even though physical memory is more plentiful today than it was when the Windows NT design team first decided to support virtual memory, physical memory is still a relatively scarce resource that must be shared among all parts of the system. As application programs continue to grow in functionality, and hence in size, virtual memory will continue to play an important role in allowing them to grow yet further.

A number of different techniques have been used by operating systems in the past to allow for memory sharing. For example, one technique was to divide a computer program into a series of discrete pieces. When program code from a particular piece was needed, it was read from disk into memory, overlaying whatever program code was there previously. Although this overlay technique did allow application developers to build feature-rich applications without too much concern over memory limitations, such applications were not necessarily high-performance because of the cost involved in loading the overlay image from disk.

Implementations of simple paging systems were nothing more than a refinement of the overlay technique. Overlay systems had a single overlay region. Code was loaded into that one overlay region, as needed. With these simple paging implementations, memory was divided into a series of discrete pieces (pages), with each of these pages being independently managed. Although this approach minimized some of the disadvantages of overlays, such as the cost of loading the new overlay, actual code was still tied to a particular page. Thus, interactions between the code within each of these pages could cause interactions that in turn made the application run very slowly.

The use of virtual memory solved the "locality" problem because, rather than tying the address being used to a location in physical memory, it refers to a location within a lookup table. By carefully exploiting a virtual-to-physical mapping, the operating system can actually move the contents of individual physical pages to other physical pages. Because each reference to the virtual page is translated via a lookup table, fixing up the lookup table allows this relocation within physical memory without breaking the application.

Virtual memory decouples the various parts of a program from its location in physical memory. By incorporating support for the virtual-to-physical translation within the computer system hardware and ultimately within the CPU itself, the virtual-to-physical translation is done as part of every memory reference.

Of course, using a lookup table that allows an arbitrary location for every byte would be prohibitively expensive. Using the "page" concept, the translation table can instead be used to refer to the location of a range of bytes. Thus, the bytes within a given virtual page correspond one-to-one to the bytes within a specific physical page. Using this scheme, as the size of the page increases; the size of the lookup table decreases. Counterbalancing this, as the size of a page increases; the degree of sharing that can be accommodated decreases. For the systems on which Windows NT currently runs, the page sizes are normally either 4K or 8K bytes.

The next section discusses the duties of the Memory Manager in greater detail.

Note

One optimization that Windows NT utilizes on the Pentium, Pentium Pro, and Pentium II systems is support for large pages. In addition to the normal 4KB-page size supported by these platforms, they also offer support for a 4MB-page size. Although these large pages aren't frequently required, they do turn out to be useful. This is because 4MB of memory is equal to 1024 4KB-pages. Instead of using 1024 virtual-to-physical mapping entries (page table entries), only one is used. This conservation of memory is particularly important in the kernel environment because page table entries are a scarce resource.

For example, on systems with enough memory, Windows NT uses a single 4MB-page for the operating system image, HAL, boot drivers, and initial portion of non-paged pool.

The Memory Manager only uses these large pages in limited circumstances because such large pages are not reclaimed. Thus, any reference to a virtual address within the particular 4MB range will always be valid because the physical memory is locked for use by that virtual page.

Memory Manager Operations

Once all of memory has been divided into a series of physical pages, the Memory Manager within Windows NT controls their use. As individual processes require physical memory, pages are removed from the pool of available pages and assigned to hold information. The actual references to these physical pages are by way of the virtual-to-physical translation table.

Balancing this, the Memory Manager also reclaims pages that are no longer in use or that have not been used in some time. Indeed, one of the most important tasks for the Memory Manager is to ensure that there is always a ready supply of physical pages that are not currently in use. This allows them to be used to satisfy the demand for new physical pages. Indeed, maintaining a ready supply of available physical pages is essential to ensuring that the system continues to operate properly. Once the supply of available physical pages is totally exhausted, it may not be possible for the Memory Manager to recover. In such a case, the system halts with the ominous STOP code NO_PAGES_AVAILABLE.

Because pages can be reclaimed simply because they have not been used recently, it is possible that when the CPU is performing a virtual-to-physical translation, it may find that there is no physical page currently allocated for the given virtual address. This process is known as a *page fault;* when it occurs, the underlying CPU transfers control to the registered page fault handler within the operating system—in this case, the Windows NT Memory Manager. The Memory Manager must then analyze the page fault and determine three things:

1. Was the virtual address actually valid? It is possible that the application has referenced memory that does not exist. If so, the Memory Manager returns an error to the application. Frequently such errors manifest as "Dr. Watson" dialog boxes on Windows NT.

2. Was the page fault caused because the user attempted to access the page in a manner that was "incompatible" with the protection on the page? As we will describe in more detail, each virtual page has protection bits, indicating whether it can be accessed by a user application, or written by the application or the kernel.

3. If the page fault was legitimate, the Memory Manager must then allocate a physical page and retrieve the contents of that page. Typically, they are stored on disk and the Memory Manager must allocate a new physical page and then ask the I/O Manager to read the data from disk into that new physical page. Only then is the page fault resolved.

Thus, the Memory Manager transparently handles page faults. When such page faults occur, the Memory Manager will allocate a new physical page and retrieve its contents (via the I/O Manager, and in turn via the file system), if necessary. This process is referred to as *demand paging* because pages are allocated and their contents are "filled-in" on demand.

Address Space Separation and Control

Windows NT also takes advantage of virtual memory by implementing address spaces. Each address space is represented by its own virtual-to-physical translation table (or, as they are normally called, *page tables)*. Because each set of page tables may define a distinct virtual-to-physical page translation, each set is logically distinct. Furthermore, because the CPU always uses a particular page table when performing operations on memory, it is not possible for a program running in one address space to interfere with a program running in a different address space.

Another mechanism for providing address space separation is provided by the memory-management hardware, and is based upon the protection mode of the memory and the execution mode of the processor. For example, both the Alpha and X86 architecture systems support four such hierarchical protection modes. Regardless of the number of modes available in the processor hardware, Windows NT only uses two: the "least-privileged" mode, referred to as *User mode*; and the "most-privileged" mode, referred to as *Kernel mode*. Note that Windows NT does require the underlying hardware support at least two such protection modes.

Windows NT's virtual memory implementation supports a bit in each virtual-to-physical page table entry that indicates if the page can be accessed from User mode. In NT's model, all valid pages are always accessible from Kernel mode. Thus, if the page protection bit is set so that it indicates that a particular page is accessible from User mode, whenever the processor is running in *any* mode, the software can access the indicated page. If instead the page was set so that it was not accessible in User mode, then that page would be inaccessible when the CPU's execution mode was User mode. The page would be accessible only when the CPU was running at the more privileged Kernel mode. When a page access is attempted from User mode, and such access is not allowed according to the page-protection bit in the virtual-to-physical page table entry, the CPU generates an exception condition, much like it does when the virtual-to-physical translation is not valid.

Windows NT's page-protection mechanism allows the system to partition the memory described by a single page table so that only a portion of it can be accessed from User mode. The remaining portion of the address space described by the page table contains data that is available for use only when the CPU is running in Kernel mode. Thus, because the operating system over-sees all cases in which the CPU transitions from User mode to Kernel mode, Windows NT can protect data that is not accessible from User mode, such as operating system control structures, from damage by errant (User mode) application programs.

User and System Address Spaces

On a single CPU, only one virtual-to-physical mapping can be in use at any time. To provide Kernel mode components (including drivers) with an environment where they know that their memory references are always valid,

Windows NT uses precisely the same virtual-to-physical mappings for a particular range of addresses. Thus, each time a new virtual-to-physical mapping is
loaded into the CPU (a "context switch") some portion of that new mapping
table has exactly the same information as the previous version of the mapping
table. This constant range of addresses is protected from applications because
the individual pages have been marked as *not* being accessible from User mode.
The portion of the address space accessible from User mode is the *user address
space*. The portion of the address space accessible from Kernel mode is the *system address space*. The management, layout, and utilization of these two
address spaces are considerably different and are managed differently by the
Memory Manager. Because of this, you should understand the logistics of the
user address space and how it is handled separately from the system address
space. First, you need to turn your attention to the division of the entire 4GB
address range between these two address spaces.

Figure 3.2 shows the standard division of an address space on Windows NT.
Dividing the address space into two pieces is not the only possible approach.
Some versions of Windows NT support alternative address space divisions.

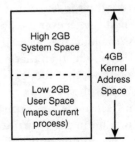

Figure 3.2. *Windows NT Standard Address Space Division. Figure 3.3 shows the "4
Gigabyte Tunable" address space that is supported by Windows NT 4.0 Enterprise
Server.*

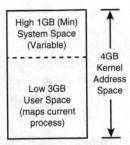

Figure 3.3. *Windows NT 4GB address space division.*

While 4GB may seem like an almost inexhaustible supply of memory, in fact it
can prove to be inadequate for larger server class systems running database

applications. Clearly, the right solution to this is to take advantage of 64-bit pointer support, which yields a 16 exabyte (2^{64}) address space! Unfortunately, such a change will require new hardware and software support and as such is not included in Windows NT V4, nor is it expected to be in Windows NT V5. Instead, Windows NT V5 will provide limited support for a larger address space.

NT V5 supports Very Large Memory (VLM) systems by using 64-bit pointers, but only takes advantage of three additional bits. Three extra bits will extend the size of the virtual address space on Windows NT from 4GB to 32GB. The extra 28GB of address space will be made available to specially written User mode applications and to some parts of the Windows NT operating system itself. Figure 3.4 shows how Windows NT lays out VLM support in NT V5.

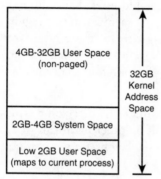

Figure 3.4. *Windows NT VLM address space division.*

Because VLM takes advantage of 64-bit pointers, it will only work on hardware platforms that support such large memory pointers, such as the Alpha or Merced. In addition, VLM has several other unusual properties:

- The VLM virtual-to-physical mapping tables are shared among all processes.

- Physical memory assigned to VLM virtual addresses are not reclaimed until the virtual mapping is deallocated (thus, VLM memory is not "paged").

- Drivers will not need to handle 64-bit virtual addresses, because Windows NT will create 32-bit mappings when communicating with drivers.

Thus, VLM is a limited change to Windows NT to increase the available virtual address space for a range of application programs, such as databases. Note that VLM is a short-term solution within Windows NT that will be addressed in the future 64-bit version.

System Address Space Layout

As noted previously, the Memory Manager handles the system address space differently from the user address space. This is partially due to the unique characteristics of the system address space:

- The system address space is visible, regardless of what user address space is active. This also means that system addresses are valid for all threads in the system.

- The system address space consists of memory regions that are not paged.

- The system address space contains the file system data cache.

Because of these unique characteristics, the system address space is divided into a series of *regions,* each of which is managed differently. For example, the *non-paged pool* is a set of system addresses that point to actual physical memory that is always present. Thus, if memory in this region is referenced and it is not present, the Memory Manager treats it as a fatal error. Similarly, the *paged pool* is a different set of system addresses that act more like memory in an application program. They are paged in as needed, and their physical memory is reclaimed as needed.

Figure 3.5 illustrates the layout of memory on a typical X86-based platform. Note that the specific layout on other platforms or even on other systems may vary, because the details of the layout are not constant across platforms or even releases of Windows NT.

The lowest system space address is the base of the operating system image itself, which is located at `0x80000000`. In addition, for the Pentium class systems, Windows NT may use a large physical page for the operating system, so it will use the remaining memory to load device drivers and the initial portion of non-paged pool.

Beginning at `0xA0000000` is a region for *memory-mapped view* (memory-mapped files are described later in this chapter) within the system address space. Win32k.sys is typically mapped into this region, although this is not required for it to function properly.

The range from `0xA3000000–0xC0000000` is unused so addresses in this range are invalid.

The range of addresses from `0xC0000000–0xC0800000` is used for various Memory Manager data structures that actually describe the virtual page tables and Virtual Address Descriptor (or VAD) tree for the current process. This region is referred to as *hyperspace.* The specifics of the VAD tree are covered later in this chapter.

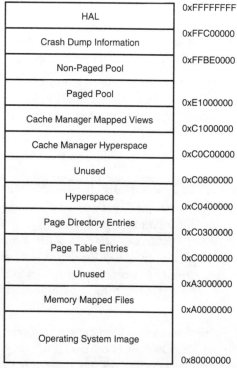

Figure 3.5. *Normal system address space layout (X86).*

The range from 0xC0800000–0xC0C00000 is unused so addresses in this range are invalid.

The range from 0xC0C00000–0xC1000000 is used for managing the working set for the file cache. The *file cache* consists of views into various mapped files and shares physical memory with the rest of the operating system. The file cache's resource consumption requires that it have a *working set* (described later in the section called, "Working Sets"), so that pages can be trimmed—just as if the file cache were a separate process.

The range from 0xC1000000–E1000000 is actually used by the file cache to map views of individual files while they are being read or written via the cache itself. Note that this does not restrict file sizes to 512MB (the size of the range) because a file may be partially mapped. In that case, only a portion of the file itself is mapped at any one time. Thus, by deleting existing maps and creating new maps, it is possible to perform read and write operations on very large cached files.

The range from 0xE1000000–0xFFBE0000 is used for both the paged and non-paged pool within the system, where the paged pool begins at 0xE1000000 and is extended to higher memory addresses. The non-paged pool begins at 0xFFBE0000 and is extended to lower memory addresses.

The range from 0xFFBE0000–0xFFC00000 is used to store information about the location of the paging file located on the boot device, so that in case of a system crash, a copy of physical memory can be copied to that file. It can then be recovered when the system reboots.

The range from 0xFFC00000–0xFFFFFFFF is used to store HAL information.

Note

There is an inherent danger for Kernel mode device driver developers because crash dump information is stored in high memory. This information contains disk block addresses where a crash dump will be written after a system crash. However, it is possible for the Kernel mode device driver to actually overwrite this region in memory. In such a case, writing the crash dump to disk will write it to random locations on the disk itself.

We were working with one client who experienced precisely this problem. After the system would crash, the client would reboot the machine and then receive an ominous warning—No O/S Found. After reinstalling Windows NT several times, we concluded that when the driver did crash, we should reset the system rather than allow it to continue using the debugger. This ensured that crash dump information was not written to disk.

Of course, this simply demonstrates that developing kernel code is inherently riskier than developing application code. Unlike application code, in which the operating system has been designed so it does not trust the parameters passed by application programs, when a Kernel mode device driver passes invalid parameters, they are dutifully used, irrespective of the ultimate repercussions.

With the reorganization of the address space for 4GB, the actual layout of the system virtual address is a bit different on X86 platforms using the 4GT option. Figure 3.6 provides a description of the layout we found on one of our own systems. Of course, this is not the only possible configuration.

Access Control

Earlier, we described how individual virtual pages are access-controlled, indicating whether they can be accessed from User mode. In the Windows NT model, access control has an additional attribute that indicates whether the page can be written. These two access-control bits are used to completely manage access to the given virtual page.

HAL	0xFFFFFFFF
Crash Dump Information	0xFFC00000
Non-Paged Pool	0xFFBE0000
Paged Pool	
Cache Manager Mapped Views	0xE1000000
Operating System Image	0xC2000000
Cache Manager Hyperspace	0xC1000000
Unused	0xC0C00000
Hyperspace	0xC0800000
Page Directory Entries	0xC0400000
Page Table Entries	0xC0300000
Memory Mapped Files	0xC0000000
Operating System Image	0xA1000000
	0xA0000000

Figure 3.6. *System address space layout with 4GT (X86).*

It is important to understand that access control is done on the *virtual* page. There is no inherent protection for a physical page. As it turns out, this is important because the use of page tables effectively means that a single physical page can have multiple virtual references to the physical page. Indeed, one of the common techniques used by drivers to manage buffers is to create a new virtual mapping to a User mode buffer. Instead of relying upon the User mode address to obtain access to the buffer, a system space address is created for the same physical buffer memory.

Windows NT's model of protection is considerably simpler than the models of protection offered by the underlying hardware. This allows NT to support the widest possible variety of processor architectures. For example, on many platforms there are access bits to indicate whether the page may be read, written, or executed; in addition to access controls for each processor mode (except "most-privileged," of course). Thus, with the Windows NT VM protection model, assuming that a page is valid, the following statements are true:

- The page can always be read from Kernel mode.
- It can only be written from Kernel mode if "write access" has been granted.

- It can only be read from User mode if "User mode" access has been granted.

- It can only be written from User mode if both "User mode" access and "write access" have been granted.

- If a page can be read, it can be executed.

By using a simple access model, Windows NT retains a greater degree of platform independence and greater portability. Even with this simple access model, however, Windows NT is fully capable of supporting a wide range of useful virtual memory techniques. Thus, the simplicity does not come at the cost of functionality.

Memory Sharing

The capability for two page tables to reference the same physical memory is a powerful technique. It allows applications to share data between them, without otherwise compromising their independence from one another. It even allows the sharing of code, such as dynamic link libraries (DLLs), between two applications so that only one copy of the DLL is present in memory at any time.

> **Note**
>
> *In our description of DLLs and how they are shared, our interest is in the sharing of the **code** portion of the DLL, including its import table.*

This sharing is possible because the use of a page table allows two (or more) virtual pages to reference the same physical page. As Figure 3.7 shows, using the same physical page for two separate virtual page entries results in shared memory. Any changes made by either application to this shared memory region will be immediately visible to the other application.

As with any virtual page, the attributes stored within that page dictate the allowable access to the memory using that virtual page. There is no requirement that says that, if there are two virtual references to the same physical page, those two virtual page table entries must contain the same attributes. Thus, it is possible for a single page to be readable but not writeable by one process, while the other process can both read and write the image. It would even be possible for the same virtual page table to contain two separate entries pointing to the same physical page, with each entry granting a different type of access.

Copy-On-Write

Support for *copy-on-write* virtual memory is a convenient mechanism for allowing shared memory access when appropriate. When shared memory access is not appropriate, a copy of the memory is made.

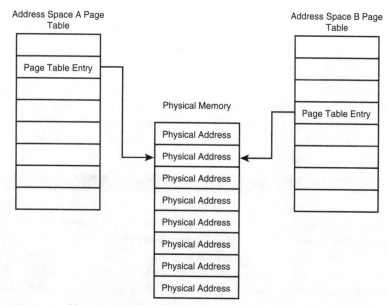

Figure 3.7. *Page tables sharing physical memory.*

Thus, this mechanism preserves physical memory, allows Windows NT to more efficiently utilize this scarce resource, and hence allows Windows NT to efficiently run more applications.

The very name *copy-on-write* tells you exactly what is happening. When the virtual page is first added to the address space, one of its attributes is that the page cannot be written. In addition, a separate attribute indicates that the page is copy-on-write. As long as the page is not being modified, copy-on-write operates very much like any other shared memory page. The only time that its copy-on-write status becomes an issue is when one process attempts to modify the memory. If the memory is merely "shared," the change is visible to each address space that is sharing the page.

> **Note**
>
> *Although the primary use for copy-on-write is for code sharing of DLLs, it can also be used for debugging an application program. In such a case, if the debugger is used to change the contents of a shared code page, such as by setting a breakpoint, that shared page is copied at the point where the first breakpoint is set—ensuring that only the application being debugged is affected.*

When the application program, or the operating system on behalf of the application program, attempts to modify that particular page, a CPU exception of some sort is generated. That exception is caught by Windows NT. Eventually, the exception is handled as a page fault and is dispatched to the Virtual Memory Manager. After analyzing the cause of the page fault, the Memory Manager determines that this particular virtual page is copy-on-write.

The contents of the current physical page are copied to a new physical page. The virtual page table entry is then adjusted to point to the new physical page. Both the copy-on-write and read-only attribute are cleared for that page. From that point forward, subsequent modifications to that page will be made to this private copy of the page. Thus, the page is no longer shared.

Note

We once had a former student report the following problem: Within his driver an application would provide him with a copy-on-write buffer. His driver proceeded to build an MDL and write into the buffer, but, much to his surprise, the original version was actually modified instead of creating a new copy of the data. Indeed, his presentation of the problem at the time was sufficiently confusing and we had to really think about what was going on before we came up with the correct answer.

Within his driver, he created a new virtual mapping to the user's buffer so that he had a system virtual address to the user buffer. This allowed him to use the system virtual address within his driver in an arbitrary context. Because he created a new virtual mapping, the copy-on-write attributes of the original mapping were lost. Thus, when he modified the buffer, the copy operation he expected didn't occur.

Thus, when manipulating user buffers in your Kernel mode device driver, keep in mind that virtual memory attributes, such as read-only, User mode accessible, *and* copy-on-write *are associated with the virtual mapping, not the physical page.*

Although copy-on-write might sound like a rather arcane feature, it is extensively used within Windows NT. Perhaps one of the most common uses of it is for sharing executable code via DLLs. When a DLL is built, the developer specifies what the default load address will be for that DLL. Although most parts of the DLL are written to be position-independent so that they can be loaded almost anywhere in memory, some parts of the DLL are not position-independent.

When Windows NT attempts to load a DLL for an application, it first tries to use virtual memory addresses at the default load address for the DLL. If that address is available and large enough to contain the DLL, it will be loaded into the address space at the default load address location.

However, if the DLL cannot be loaded at its base load address, Windows NT performs relocation on the DLL. This requires that some of the code within the DLL be modified. Rather than make a complete copy of the DLL, Windows NT maps the DLL into the new location. The pages are all set up so they are copy-on-write. Then, as individual pages are written to perform any relocation fix-up that is necessary, the sharing is broken.

This technique ensures that much of the DLL is still shared between applications and that only those small pieces that must be updated are actually copied.

> **Note**
>
> *Although using copy-on-write within DLLs does ensure that they are always mapped into the application address space correctly, this process can slow the loading time of applications. In order to minimize the amount of fix-up that must be performed, individual DLLs should be built so they use a default load address that does not conflict with any other DLL used by the application.*
>
> *Indeed, most of the standard Windows NT DLLs are built so they each use a separate load address. This simple mechanism maximizes the speed at which applications load and thus enhances the performance of the Windows NT systems.*

Copy-on-write is also useful when debugging programs. It is important to ensure that any changes to the program, such as setting a breakpoint within the program, only occurs on the copy being debugged. Otherwise, other running copies of the same code would also execute the same breakpoint! Additionally, it is important that the breakpoint not be written back to the original file. Thus, if the Memory Manager needs to reclaim the page containing the breakpoint, it must store it in a temporary location—not back in the original executable file. The copy-on-write mechanism accomplishes exactly this task.

Because of this, **all** executable user applications are memory-mapped on Windows NT by using this copy-on-write mechanism. The goal is to ensure that executable code sharing is always correct, even if the executable code is modified in one address space.

> **Note**
>
> *The copy-on-write technique is **not** generally useful for sharing data, precisely because it makes a copy of the original page when it is modified. Data-sharing is typically done using standard shared memory because the goal is to ensure that there is only one copy of the data shared between*

continues

Continued

> *multiple address spaces. For example, Win32 maintains a list of all current valid drive letters. This information is maintained in a single physical page that is shared between all processes. Because this information can be updated by any process (via the* DefineDosDevice *API call in Win32, for example), using copy-on-write memory to maintain this global system state would potentially result in every process having its own view of the available drives!*

Memory-Mapped Files

As previously stated, DLLs are loaded into an address space. Although conceptually correct, the reality is a bit more complex. Windows NT uses a mechanism known as *file-mapping* to accomplish this. Normally, applications access files using read and write operations. When a file is memory-mapped, its content is represented as a range of virtual addresses in memory. This is functionally equivalent to an application program allocating memory, reading the contents in from the disk into a buffer in memory, and later writing the contents of that memory buffer back to the file when it is finished. The reading and writing are entirely handled by the Memory Manager rather than by the application. Further, only pages of the file that are actually changed in memory will be written back to the file.

It's important to note that merely mapping a file into the address space of a program does not by itself include reading the file's contents. When a file is mapped, the Memory Manager reserves virtual memory addresses for the file. At that time the Memory Manager also sets up information so that when an address in the memory range is first referenced, the Memory Manager will be called (as a result of a page fault) to read the contents of the referenced page from the file on disk. For example, this technique is used when application programs are executed. Rather than "loading" the image into memory, it is mapped into memory, and then individual page references fault and cause the page to be fetched from the file containing the executable program code.

Because memory-mapped files can actually be shared between address spaces, the Memory Manager not only tracks where a particular file is mapped into an address space, but it also tracks what physical memory is currently being used to store individual pieces of the memory-mapped file. As described later in the chapter, the Memory Manager ensures that only a single copy of the memory-mapped file appears in physical memory so that it can be properly shared between all the address spaces that refer to it. This is done by using an internal Memory Manager structure known as the *Section Object*.

One of the common uses of memory-mapped files on Windows NT is for the instantiation of processes. All executable images on Windows NT are mapped into memory, and loaded as memory-mapped files—with the special copy-on-write attribute discussed in the previous section. If the image is modified within a particular address range (perhaps by setting a debugger breakpoint), the modified pages are no longer shared with the other processes. Instead, those pages are private to that particular address space. Indeed, when the address space is destroyed, such changes are normally discarded because they are no longer needed.

Another common time to use memory-mapped files is when a file is copied. The Win32 API called CopyFile() typically memory-maps the input file. Because the file now appears as a "buffer" in the application address space, it is trivial for it to pass a pointer into the source file (which looks like a memory buffer) to the WriteFile() call, which then writes the data to the destination file.

Of course, there are other uses for memory-mapped files on Windows NT—these are only representative of the types of use found on Windows NT.

Paging

Much of the mechanism discussed thus far has been how virtual addresses are translated into physical addresses. Sometimes, virtual addresses do not in fact have an associated physical address. One reason this occurs is because the Memory Manager vigilantly scans the various address spaces within the system, reclaiming pages from them.

Reclaiming pages refers to the Memory Manager changing individual entries in the virtual page table so that, instead of pointing to the actual physical page, it is marked as invalid. If the virtual page table entry indicates that the page is dirty, the Memory Manager will write the contents of the physical page to its backing store. Typically, this is somewhere on the disk drive.

The driving need here is that the number of physical pages within the system is strictly limited. Thus, it is essential to ensure that this scarce resource is shared fairly. Otherwise, some applications would perform poorly or not function at all because they did not have enough memory. On the other hand, reclaiming pages from one application to give to another application can lead to a condition in which the system spends most of its time performing I/O to disk and reclaiming pages. This condition is known as *memory thrashing*; normally the only way to resolve it is to either use less memory by running fewer applications or to add additional memory to the system.

The remainder of this section discusses the details of how the various demands on physical memory are balanced against one another. These topics include:

- **Working Sets.** The working set is used by the Memory Manager to ensure that no process is deprived of all physical memory, and that no process can use all physical memory.

- **Balance Set Manager.** The Balance Set Manager is used by the Microkernel to periodically call into the Memory Manager to reclaim physical memory from processes that might no longer be using it.

- **Modified Page Writer.** The Modified Page Writer scans all physical pages, looking for dirty pages that should be written.

- **Mapped Page Writer.** The Mapped Page Writer accepts pages from the Modified Page Writer that are part of memory-mapped files and writes them to disk.

- **Lazy Writer.** The Lazy Writer scans data cached by the file systems and writes out any dirty pages to disk. This is how Windows NT implements *write-behind* caching for the file systems.

Working Sets

The Memory Manager on Windows NT maintains a *working set* for each user process. For the system process, a working set is used to track the usage of memory for the file system cache maintained by the Cache Manager. The working set information is used by Windows NT to balance the use of memory between competing processes and the file cache.

Thus, a working set consists of information about the process, including the following:

- **Number of Page Faults.** This information indicates the level of paging activity experienced by this working set.

- **Size.** This information indicates the current size of the working set.

- **Peak Size.** This information indicates the "high-watermark" of the working set.

- **Maximum Size.** This information indicates the largest working set allowed by the system.

- **Minimum Size.** This information indicates the size at which trimming is performed by the system.

For example, a process is not subject to memory trimming until it has reached the Minimum Size of its working set quota, while Maximum Size indicates the threshold beyond which new pages are added at the expense of older pages being removed.

Note that these values are not static. Instead, Windows NT modifies them as necessary to improve the performance of the program. For example, the Maximum Size is increased whenever a process needs additional memory, as detected by the Number of Page Faults and available memory.

This flexible strategy is essential to allowing Windows NT to adjust the basic working set for each process as necessary and as resources are available within the system itself.

Balance Set Manager

The Balance Set Manager, which is part of the Microkernel, is actually a dedicated thread that runs in the system process. As such, it is a Kernel mode-only thread, responsible for performing a variety of background processing operations to optimize memory usage on the Windows NT system.

This background thread awakens periodically and looks for work to perform. On an idle system, the Balance Set Manager typically awakens only to find there is no work to perform and quickly returns back to a blocking (sleep) state.

When the system is active or when it has been recently active, the Balance Set Manager invokes the Memory Manager to actually look through the list of processes and attempt to remove pages from the working set. The Memory Manager's algorithm for this attempts to ensure that it does not trim pages that have recently been loaded (to prevent "memory thrashing") or from processes that are experiencing many page faults. As the demand for memory increases between processes, the Memory Manager trims pages from the working set more aggressively.

Once the Memory Manager has determined that a particular process working set should be trimmed, it then scans the process working set, looking for its oldest pages. As it scans from the oldest to newest pages, the Memory Manager attempts to locate pages that have not been recently used, based on the "accessed" bit that is maintained by the hardware and stored within the virtual page table entry. If the page has not been accessed since the last time the Memory Manager scanned, it removes the page from the working set. Otherwise, the Memory Manager simply clears the "accessed" bit. By using the "accessed" bit, the Memory Manager ensures that it does not trim pages that have been used since the last time trimming was performed. Of course, if the system is experiencing a memory shortage, the period between scanning decreases and hence the number of pages available for trimming increases.

Once a page has been found that should be trimmed, the Memory Manager updates the process virtual page tables to indicate that this page is no longer valid. Thus, the next time that virtual page is accessed, a page fault will result. Separately, the Memory Manager maintains a reference count on the physical page and this reference count is decremented. This is necessary because physical pages might be shared between processes, as described earlier. In the case where the physical page is shared, two separate virtual page tables reference that one page. Clearly, we cannot recycle that page until all such references have been released.

When the reference count for the physical page drops to zero, the page can be recycled. Before the page is reused, it enters an intermediate state known as the *transition state*. In this stage, the physical page has not been reused, so its contents have not changed. If a process references its virtual page table, the entry will be marked as "invalid" and a page fault will occur. While processing this page fault, the Memory Manager will note that this virtual page is "in transition" and, based upon information within the working set, that transitional page is reclaimed. We describe this in more detail later in this chapter in the discussion on "Virtual-to-Physical Address Translation."

Another important task performed by the Balance Set Manager is to swap out kernel stacks. Normally, kernel stacks are "pinned" into memory so they cannot be paged out. Under certain circumstances, however, they can be removed from memory. This can only happen when the process is inactive and the thread in question is in a "User mode" wait state.

Note

The DDK function `KeWaitForSingleObject()` *includes a* `WaitMode` *parameter that indicates the type of wait being performed. The two possible values are* `KernelMode` *and* `UserMode`. *When the thread is blocked in a* `UserMode` *wait state, the Balance Set Manager is allowed to unpin its stack so that the physical memory used for the stack can be reused by the operating system. However, the actual process of removing the kernel stack is done by the Memory Manager. Note that if a thread is blocked in a* `KernelMode` *wait state, its kernel stack cannot be safely unpinned, so the Balance Set Manager leaves it alone in memory. Given that each user thread normally consumes 12KB (X86) or 16KB (alpha) of memory, the capability to share this physical memory is important when many threads are present in the system.*

Of course, for a Kernel mode device driver writer, the fact that the stack can be paged out is not a big concern. This is because most Kernel mode device drivers call `KeWaitForSingleObject()` in a `KernelMode` wait state, and hence the stack cannot be paged out. Further, when the thread is scheduled to run again, its stack is read back in from the paging file and pinned in memory. Thus, when writing a Kernel mode device driver, it is inherently safe to assume that the kernel stack is non-paged memory. Of course, you must then use only the `KernelMode()` wait state because otherwise the kernel stack might be paged!

Modified Page Writer

The Memory Manager actually maintains two separate dedicated high-priority threads for the sole purpose of writing out a steady stream of dirty pages back to the *backing store,* which is typically a disk drive, although it might be a disk drive on a remote system. This background write process is imperative because it ensures that the number of dirty pages never exceeds some threshold.

In essence, the Memory Manager implements a "leaky-bucket" algorithm (akin to filling a bucket with a fire hose and draining it with a pinhole leak). The fire hose is the rate at which application programs can create new dirty pages. The pinhole leak is the rate at which the Memory Manager can write pages back to disk. Given that the speed of modifying memory is nearly five orders of magnitude faster than writing to disk, this is a serious problem.

The real reason this is a problem is that if the number of pages available for recycling falls too low, the Memory Manager will find itself in an untenable situation—one where it requires more physical pages to continue running so that it can write pages out to disk. Such situations ultimately lead to a deadlock of some sort, causing the system to halt.

The Modified Page Writer is responsible for writing pages that have been modified ("dirty pages") back to the paging file. If the modified page is from a memory-mapped file (which is described later in this chapter, in the section entitled "Memory-Mapped Files"), the page is queued and the Mapped Page Writer handles writing them back to the correct file. Once the page has been written, it is no longer dirty; if necessary, it can be reclaimed for use in some other virtual address space. Thus, an available pool of clean pages can always be guaranteed.

Note

The algorithm used by the Modified Page Writer does not write all dirty pages. Instead, it tries to write enough dirty pages to ensure that the supply of clean pages is large enough that the system does not run into a memory exhaustion state—because such a state is fatal.

Thus, the Memory Manager is not concerned about writing out dirty pages to disk to preserve their data contents. Indeed, if an application modifies a very small set of pages on a continual basis, those pages may not ever be written out to disk. This can be a problem with the pages that contain data from a mapped file. In such a case, the data may sit in memory without ever being written out. Application programs that wish to ensure that the data is written to disk must perform this operation

continues

Continued

explicitly. Of course, applications cannot assume that data from a memory-mapped file is only written to disk when they ask. This is because the Memory Manager will write data when it chooses, independent of the needs or requirements of the application.

Mapped Page Writer

The Mapped Page Writer is responsible for writing dirty pages back to memory-mapped files. For those new to Windows NT, this might seem to be a rare condition. In fact, it turns out to be extremely common because essentially all files on Windows NT are memory-mapped into the file cache.

This integrated file cache ensures that the file can be accessed both via the file cache (via the file systems using read and write) as well as via memory-mapped file access. In this case, the data for the mapped files are shared between all the memory-mapped images. Thus, there is only a single copy of the data in memory, which ensures that changes made using read/write are coherent with changes made using memory-mapped access.

As noted previously, other files are also memory-mapped. For example, executable images and DLLs are routinely memory-mapped. Unlike data files, however, such executable images and DLLs are memory-mapped for read-only access. Data files are memory-mapped for read-write access.

The Mapped Page Writer processes individual pages as they are passed to it from the Modified Page Writer. Thus, as memory conditions become low, the Modified Page Writer is writing pages to the paging file and queuing pages for memory-mapped files to the Mapped Page Writer. This is essential because it ensures that writing pages back to disk does not cause page faults (because the file systems themselves use paged memory, this is possible, though rare).

Note

There are a few interesting cases to consider when looking at memory-mapped files. For example, although an executable image is mapped read-only and a data file is mapped read-write, this is problematic when someone copies a file foo.exe *to a different file* bar.exe, *and then executes* bar.exe. *When the file is copied, it is actually modified as if it were a data file. However, when the file is executed, it is mapped into memory in a read-only fashion. Whenever the usage of a file is changing in this fashion (from a data file to an executable or vice versa), the file system is actually responsible for ensuring the consistency of the data of the two separate mappings. Normally, it does this by ensuring that any dirty data (such as for the new file* bar.exe *in our example) has been written to disk, and then deleting the data cached in system memory. Similarly, when the file has recently been executed and then is overwritten, it must delete the data cached in memory and then create a new set of pages to represent the new copy.*

This is one reason that it isn't possible to copy a new executable image over an existing executable image when it is running—the very process of doing this requires that the current in-memory copy be discarded (or "purged") so that the new copy can be stored in memory. Because the current copy is in use, an attempt to purge its pages fails.

Lazy Writer

The Lazy Writer is part of the Cache Manager. As such, it is responsible for writing dirty file cache data back to disk. Unlike the Mapped Page Writer, the Lazy Writer does not attempt to write all dirty data in memory back to disk. Instead, the Lazy Writer attempts to ensure that any dirty cached-file data is written back to disk. It only does this for files that are modified via the read/write path. In this case, the file is memory-mapped into the file cache. The file systems then call the Cache Manager as needed to perform the actual read and write I/O operations.

When an application requests that data be written back to the file, the Lazy Writer copies the data contents of the user buffer to the file cache. The Cache Manager copies the data into these memory-mapped files. As noted with memory-mapped files, the Memory Manager does not attempt to ensure that data in a memory-mapped file is written back to disk—the Memory Manager writes what data it needs to ensure that there are clean pages and no more.

Thus, like any application that uses memory-mapped files, the Lazy Writer must actively write the contents of dirty pages back to disk to ensure that file system data is eventually written. However, by performing the writes in the background, it appears to users that application writes (such as when saving a file from a word processor) complete quickly. Data is then written to disk in the background, while applications can continue ordinary processing.

There is an inherent risk in delaying write operations because the system might fail between the time the application data is copied into the file cache and the time the data is written to disk. To minimize this window of vulnerability, Windows NT uses an aggressive time schedule, so the Lazy Writer begins writing data back to disk in the seconds immediately following the application write. Thus, user data is written back to disk quickly.

Address Translation

Of course, this mechanism in the Windows NT virtual memory system is there to facilitate one fundamental process—address translation. Whenever the CPU is presented with an address—perhaps using the instruction pointer or stack pointer, or using a load or store memory operation—that address is interpreted as a virtual address and is translated to a corresponding physical address.

As we discussed in Chapter 2, "Achieving Hardware Independence with the HAL," and as you'll see in Chapter 8, "I/O Architectures," Windows NT has three different types of addresses:

- **Virtual Addresses.** These addresses are translated into physical addresses prior to actual use.

- **Physical Addresses.** These addresses actually refer to physical memory. Note that such memory always appears on the memory bus, although the actual memory might be normal RAM or it might be memory presented to the system by a device.

- **Logical Addresses.** This "catch-all" case is used for special addresses that are used by the HAL when communicating with a device driver. Thus, the HAL is responsible for managing these addresses.

Understanding the type of address the Kernel mode device driver is using is essential to ensuring that the driver functions properly. For example, using a logical address when the system believes it is a virtual address will cause the address to be translated and the translated address will be used. This typically results in either a system crash (the blue screen of death) or changes to data that you did not want to change, causing instability and improper behavior.

The following sections describe the detailed mechanisms used to map virtual addresses to physical addresses in more detail. In summary, these techniques include:

- **Page Tables.** A page table is the precise mechanism the Virtual Memory system (and sometimes the underlying hardware) uses to translate between a particular virtual address and the specific physical address.

- **Virtual-to-Physical Translation.** The underlying hardware utilizes its own hardware-dependent mechanism to map a virtual address to a physical address. Only when the hardware is unable to accomplish this does it invoke the operating system.

- **Virtual Address Descriptors (VADs).** The Memory Manager uses the VAD to describe the complete virtual memory layout for a given address space. This allows the Memory Manager to resolve page faults quickly and correctly.

- **Context.** Given that there are many address spaces within the system, the context is defined by the address space that is currently in use. This concept is particularly important to kernel mode device driver developers,

because understanding context is essential to writing a correctly functioning device driver.

Page Tables

Typically, the system CPU will translate all virtual addresses to physical
addresses. It does this by using page tables. Figure 3.8 shows how a single virtual address is translated to point to a particular byte on a particular physical
page.

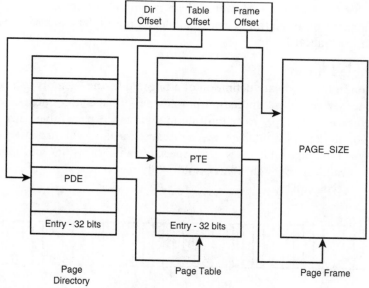

Figure 3.8. *Page tables.*

For the Intel platform, the 10 most significant bits of the virtual address are
used as a reference into the *page directory*. This page directory consists of
nothing more than a series of (virtual) pointers to individual page tables. The
next 10 bits of the virtual address are used as a reference into the page table.
Like the page directory, the page table consists of an array of pointers to individual pages. Unlike the page directory, however, these pointers are physical
references rather than virtual references. This physical reference is to the physical page that contains the data in question.

The last 12 bits of the virtual address are used as an offset to a particular byte
within the physical page. Thus, on the Intel platform we note:

- Each page consists of 4096 bytes of data (2^{12})

- A single page table can contain 1024 page references because the page
  table is 4KB and each reference is 32 bits.

- One page table describes 4MB of physical memory: 1024 entries × 4KB per page.

- A single page directory can contain 1024 page table references because the directory page is 4KB and each reference is 32 bits.

- One page directory page describes 4GB of physical memory: 1024 entries × 4MB per page table.

Of course, the Windows NT virtual memory system is not tied to a particular page size. Although the page size is a manifest constant on any given platform (you can use the PAGE_SIZE constant in the Kernel mode device driver), it can vary from platform to platform. For example, on the Alpha platform, one page is 8KB rather than 4KB.

Page Table Entries

In addition to the hardware definition of a page table, the Memory Manager also defines several other "special-purpose" types of page table entries. These special-purpose entry types store information within the page table when the entry is not marked as valid. This works because the CPU will not interpret the contents of a page table entry if the special "valid" bit is not set to indicate the entry is valid. A page table entry is normally referred to as a PTE. Figure 3.9 shows a typical PTE.

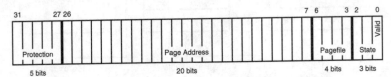

Figure 3.9. *Sample page table entry.*

Note that the PTE is 32 bits wide. Thus, Figure 3.9 labels each of these bits in the sample PTE, as well as the fields within it, to provide a general sense of size and usage for the various fields within a typical PTE. There are, in fact, several different PTE layouts defined by the Memory Manager, with the layout of the bits depending upon the precise type of the PTE. They are:

- **Hardware.** The precise layout of the hardware PTE is specific to the hardware platform.

- **Prototype.** This PTE is used for shared memory pages (more on this later).

- **Demand Zero.** This PTE indicates that the page must be zeroed before it can be used.

- **Paging File.** This PTE indicates that the data contents of this page are stored in the paging file.

- **Unused.** This PTE indicates that the particular entry is available for use.

Hardware PTE

The Hardware PTE type is used whenever the page itself is valid. Typically, this will include information such as:

- One bit to indicate if the page has been accessed. As previously noted, the Memory Manager uses this bit when performing page trimming.

- A few bits to indicate the access rights on the page. For Windows NT, this must support at least User mode and write mode. Frequently, other bits will indicate other access rights, such as execute, or access for other CPU modes.

- The physical address of the page. The Intel platform requires 20 bits, while the Alpha platform requires 19 bits.

- Typically, a few bits are reserved for the OS to use. NT uses these to indicate special page attributes such as copy-on-write.

Prototype PTE

Perhaps the most interesting type is actually the Prototype PTE. The fundamental problem for the Memory Manager is how to handle shared memory pages. Figure 3.10 illustrates the problem that occurs when a shared memory page is currently located in the paging file.

In this case two different page tables (presumably in two different processes) reference the same page. The page contents are currently stored in the paging file. When one process references that shared memory page, the Memory Manager will allocate a new physical page and read the data from the paging file. The second process, with its own page table, still refers to the data in the paging file. Thus, to avoid losing the advantages of data sharing, the Memory Manager needs to update all references to the physical page.

The Memory Manager does this by using a Prototype PTE. These "extra" entries are maintained by the Memory Manager for any shared memory structure. When valid, the particular PTE refers to the physical page containing the data. However, when the particular PTE is not valid, it refers to the Prototype PTE. The Prototype PTE in turn refers to the physical page, if there is one, or to the actual location of the data—such as in a paging file. Figure 3.11 depicts the situation in which the Prototype PTE points to the paging file.

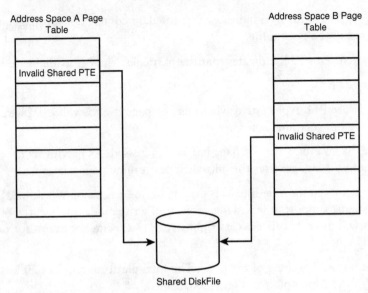

Figure 3.10. *Shared memory.*

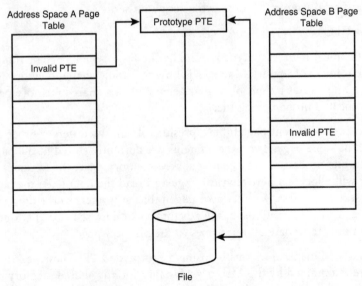

Figure 3.11. *Prototype PTE with data in paging file.*

If the Prototype PTE points to the paging file, and an application references the page using its own page table; the Memory Manager allocates a new page, fixes the prototype PTE so it points to the newly allocated physical page, and fixes the PTE for the application's address space to point to the correct physical page. Figure 3.12 illustrates the references to the correct physical page once the PTE has been fixed up. Note that one address space has a valid reference to the physical page and the other address space still maintains a reference to the Prototype PTE.

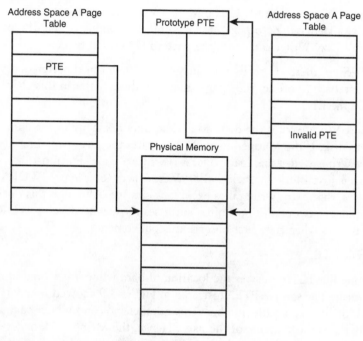

Figure 3.12. *Prototype PTE with data in memory.*

This ensures that if an application in a different address space with a reference to the Prototype PTE references that page, the Memory Manager will adjust its page tables to point to the correct physical page. This situation was illustrated earlier in Figure 3.7.

Demand Zero PTE

A variation on the Prototype PTE is the Demand Zero PTE. This page is established so that it points to a special reserved page that is zero-filled. Attempts to read these pages will return nothing more than zeros. However, when the page is written, a "clean" page (one filled with nothing other than zeros) is substituted. Ensuring that pages filled with zeros are always allocated to new pages ensures that user applications cannot read the previous contents of memory using malloc(). Otherwise, it would be possible for User mode applications to compromise the security of the system by reading the data created by other applications—or even the operating system.

Demand Zero pages actually have an interesting attribute that causes a problem for certain types of storage devices when used with Windows NT. Specifically, Demand Zero pages are automatically marked as "dirty" by the Memory Manager in its private database. When the application modifies the page, the PTE is also marked as dirty. Normally, this doesn't make any difference. However, when the file Cache Manager is the "application" that receives a new, clean Demand Zero page, it is possible that timing of the Mapped Page Writer and Lazy Writer can cause the page to be written twice.

This is because there are really two dirty bits—one bit in the Memory Manager private database (more on the "page frame database" later in this chapter) and one bit in the PTE.

If the Lazy Writer writes the dirty page first, only one copy of the data is written out to disk. If the Mapped Page Writer writes the dirty page first and then the Lazy Writer writes the dirty page, it is written again. For most disk subsystems, this is just a little inefficient. For Write Once Read Many (WORM) storage devices, that extra write takes extra disk storage. Although this doesn't cause an incorrect operation, it often surprises those who develop WORM storage drivers when they first observe this phenomenon.

Paging File PTE

The Paging File PTE describes the location of data while it is stored in the paging file itself. The sample PTE illustrated in Figure 3.9 showed four bits reserved for the paging file number. This number indicates which paging file currently holds the contents of the page. Hence, the Memory Manager can utilize up to 16 paging files, which should be sufficient for even the most extreme environments.

Of course, the same 20 bits that were used to describe the physical page address can be used to describe the location of the data within the paging file.

Unused PTE

The Unused PTE indicates that the PTE entry itself is not presently being used. Thus, any attempts to reference this page will not be resolved by the Memory Manager. Instead, an error will be generated and sent to the application thread that caused the invalid memory reference.

Virtual-to-Physical Address Translation

The precise mechanism that the various hardware platforms use to perform virtual-to-physical address translation is dependent upon the specifics of the underlying hardware platform. Although we have described the page directory, page tables, and physical pages, only some hardware platforms actually support this translation mechanism.

For example, the MIPS family of CPUs does not traverse the page tables when performing virtual-to-physical address translation. Instead, they rely solely upon a Translation Lookaside Buffer (TLB), which is implemented in hardware, and stores the virtual-to-physical mapping in a hardware associative cache. In this case, the CPU uses the virtual address to look up the corresponding physical address in the TLB. If the entry is not present in the TLB, it causes a page fault.

Indeed, all of the hardware platforms rely upon some form of translation buffer mechanism to improve the performance of virtual-to-physical address translation. The size of this translation table is small—it could be as small as a single entry or large enough to contain over a hundred entries.

The translation buffer differs from the page table in that the translation buffer is merely a cache of recently used virtual-to-physical address translations, while the page table describes all possible virtual-to-physical translations. Thus, we rely upon the translation buffer to increase the performance of address translation and fall back to the page tables only when the necessary information is not cached.

For most other platforms, the hardware actually walks through the page tables to translate a virtual address to a physical address. Even some of these platforms utilize a TLB to optimize this process. Utilizing a TLB provides a fast way to cache virtual-to-physical address translation.

Note

For additional information on how the underlying hardware platforms support virtual memory, you should read the Pentium II Family Developer's Manual, Volume 3: Operating System Writer's Guide, *or the* Alpha Architecture Reference Manual. *Each of these manuals describes the details involved in page-fault handling with respect to the particular hardware platform. For the X86 family of processors, Windows NT typically utilizes a "flat model" segmentation scheme with paging, although there is some use of segments for supporting DOS programs.*

There are always addresses that the CPU cannot translate, either because the access to the page is incompatible with the PTE or because the virtual address does not have a corresponding physical address. In either case, these complex problems must be deferred to the Memory Manager itself. This process is a page fault and must be handled by the Memory Manager.

When a page fault occurs, it is actually trapped by the Microkernel. The Microkernel builds a canonical description of the fault and then passes this into the Memory Manager. By building a canonical representation of the page fault, the kernel furthers the platform independence described in Chapter 1,

"The Windows NT Operating System Overview." The information it receives is as follows:

- Whether the fault is a load or store operation
- What virtual address is being accessed
- What the CPU processor mode is when the fault occurs

Note that when the Memory Manager is invoked, the CPU processor mode is KernelMode because processing page faults is a privileged operation requiring OS intervention.

In analyzing a particular page fault, the Memory Manager must first analyze the PTE. In doing so, it must handle some very complex cases. For example, a page fault might occur on multiple processors on a multiprocessor system. Thus, when the Memory Manager is called, it might find that the page causing the fault is actually valid because it has since been updated by a different processor (or even a different thread on the same processor).

A fault might occur in User mode. In this case, the Memory Manager must traverse the page directory, find the page table, and find the specific page table entry. It is even possible while doing this that the Memory Manager will find that the page directory and page table are paged out!

Once the Memory Manager finds the appropriate PTE, it must then determine if the PTE itself is valid. If the PTE is valid, the Memory Manager's work is done—it can just return to the kernel, and the kernel in turn will restart the faulting instruction.

If, as is more often the case, the PTE is invalid, the Memory Manager must check for each of the various conditions that might have occurred. These are based upon the particular type of PTE that is stored in the page table (recall that the Memory Manager defines the contents of a PTE when it is invalid).

For example, if the PTE indicates that the given page is a Demand Zero page, the Memory Manager must actually allocate a new zero-filled page, and update the PTE to point to the newly allocated zero-filled page. Then, when the kernel restarts the faulting instruction, the CPU will be able to access the page.

When a virtual address is in system space, the Memory Manager handles those differently from addresses in Kernel mode. As noted in the section, "System Address Space Layout," the layout of addresses in the system address space is regimented so that the Memory Manager knows how to handle these page faults. This is necessary because the Memory Manager does not manage the system address space the same way it does the kernel address space.

Virtual Address Descriptor

Although the page tables are essential to managing the translation of virtual-to-physical translation, we have thus far ignored the issue of what the Memory Manager does when a virtual page is being "demand-paged." In such a case, the PTE is marked as "invalid" and thus when that page is actually referenced, it causes a page fault.

The Memory Manager must allocate a physical page. In addition, it must also be able to obtain the contents of that page from its current storage location, typically a disk drive. To do this, the Memory Manager must ask the I/O Manager to retrieve the contents of the page. In turn, the I/O Manager calls the actual storage device, typically via a file system, to retrieve the actual data contents of the page.

Thus, given a virtual address, the Memory Manager must be able to locate the data, indicating where the actual data contents of the page are stored. This is done by using the Virtual Address Descriptor (VAD) tree. Each VAD entry describes one range of pages within the address space and indicates where data within that region is actually located. All the VAD entries are stored together in a binary tree and describe how the entire address space for this particular process is constructed. Hence, there is one VAD tree for each address space.

A single VAD entry describes a range of virtual pages. It includes information about the attributes of pages in that range and where the backing store for the virtual pages is located. For example, a VAD entry associated with a memory-mapped file would describe the range of pages in use by that memory-mapped file, and indicate that the address range is "backed" by the mapped file.

An additional example is an application program that allocates storage within its address space, such as by using the standard malloc() call. To accommodate the new range of virtual pages required to describe the additional physical memory that has been allocated, a VAD descriptor would be created (or an existing one extended). Memory that is not associated with a particular file, such as that allocated by a malloc() operation, is backed by the paging file. The paging file is thus nothing more than a special file on disk that is used to store temporary data that should be discarded by Windows NT when the address space is deleted.

The process of adding a new range of addresses into a process is thus divided into two steps:

1. A range of virtual addresses are "reserved," and that information is then stored in the VAD.

2. The VAD is modified to indicate the backing store for the range of addresses.

Thus, Windows NT "commits" the address range to some actual location.

For an example, return to the now familiar case of a DLL. When a DLL needs to be mapped into memory, the first step is to reserve an address range for the DLL. Once that is done, the VAD is updated to point to the DLL file itself, so that the VAD is committed to the DLL file.

The VAD entries are combined together to form a tree structure. Using a tree has several advantages:

- The VAD tree can be searched quickly to find the correct VAD for a given virtual address.

- The VAD tree can represent a sparse address range. Thus, if nothing exists in a given virtual address range, there will not be any information about the VAD tree.

- The VAD tree allows a single VAD to be split into multiple pieces, as necessary.

Context

Perhaps the most important issues with respect to virtual addresses require that the driver writer always consider the context for a given operation. With respect to virtual memory, the context identifies which virtual memory mappings the system is using to translate virtual addresses to physical addresses.

Thus, in a driver, when attempting to access a user address (that is, an address below the 2GB—or 3GB for an Enterprise Server—boundary), the CPU will actually use the current set of page tables to translate that address. Given this, the concept of an *arbitrary thread context* is one in which your driver cannot be certain what set of mappings is in use. Using an arbitrary memory address is likely to lead to one of three possible problems:

- The address will not be valid. In this case, the Memory Manager will raise an exception that must either be handled or the system will crash.

- The address will be valid. In this case, your driver will read (or write) using this essentially arbitrary memory address, with unpredictable results.

- The address will be valid and will point to the correct memory.

It often surprises device driver writers that the third scenario in the preceding list will often occur in their test scenarios. This is because frequently the "arbitrary thread" chosen to perform their work will be the only active program on the system—namely, their test program. In such circumstances, a driver might even appear to work correctly. Instead, the problem shows up during later testing or even after it has been shipped to customers.

An invalid pointer is the most common reason the Windows NT operating system halts. For example, the most frequently observed STOP codes when Windows NT provides the Blue Screen of Death (BSOD) all relate to invalid memory references. The reason that there are several is that the invalid memory reference can occur in several different ranges of memory. The BSOD is described in more detail in Chapter 18, "Building and Debugging."

For example, IRQL_NOT_LESS_OR_EQUAL often indicates that a segment of memory was not valid. Because the page was invalid, a page fault occurred, and control was transferred to the Microkernel. In turn, the Microkernel then determined that the IRQL of the system is at a level where page faults are prohibited (DISPATCH_LEVEL or above). In this case, a bug check is generated immediately. (Chapter 6, "Interrupt Request Levels and DPCs," discusses IRQLs in more detail.)

Another example of an invalid memory reference causing the system to halt is PAGE_FAULT_IN_NONPAGED_AREA. As described previously in the chapter, the Memory Manager organizes the system space portion of the address space into several different ranges, with each range having a particular purpose. One such region is the *non-paged pool*. This region is referred to as *non-paged* because all virtual references within this region of memory are either valid and point to physical memory, or they are invalid. Thus, when a page fault occurs for addresses within this range, the Memory Manager expects to find a physical memory reference. Thus, after the Memory Manager has been invoked to handle the page fault, if it finds that the virtual address is within this range, it halts the system because there is a serious bug—some kernel component, such as a device driver, is referring to non-existent kernel memory addresses.

The third example of an invalid memory reference causing the system to halt is KMODE_EXCEPTION_NOT_HANDLED. This typically occurs when a Kernel mode component, such as a device driver, references an address in user space and it is not valid. In this case, the Memory Manager generates an exception. The Microkernel then scans the kernel stack to determine if there is a registered exception handler. If there is no such exception handler, the Microkernel halts the operating system.

Thus, in order to avoid catastrophic results, it is imperative that a device driver developer understand the context in which it is going to operate. The simplest model for device driver developers is the one in which they can always assume they will not be called in the correct thread context. For example, intermediate- and lowest-level storage drivers typically do not need to worry about context because they are always called with kernel addresses and kernel data structures. Drivers that can be called in thread context, such as all highest-level drivers, or some intermediate drivers, need to always be aware of any context assumptions they are making when developing their driver.

Physical Memory Management

Independent of the translation of virtual-to-physical memory, the Memory Manager must also track the usage of physical memory. When the system first initializes, it determines the available physical memory and builds data structures that are, in turn, used to manage all physical memory in the system (these structures are actually stored in virtual memory—in the non-paged pool to be precise.)

The following sections describe in more detail the three mechanisms used by the Memory Manager to manage the allocation and usage of physical memory:

- **Page Frame Database.** The page frame database is a table describing the state of each physical memory page in the system. By tracking the state of each page (active, free, and so forth) the Memory Manager can reclaim and allocate memory as needed.

- **Page Recovery Algorithm.** The Memory Manager actually handles the transition of pages through several states as part of page recovery. This mechanism ensures that page recovery is both efficient and inexpensive.

- **Section Object.** The Section Object is used by the Memory Manager to track resources that are available to be memory-mapped into the various address spaces.

Page Frame Database

The Memory Manager maintains the *page frame database* to track the state and usage information about each physical page of memory that is present on the system at the time the OS started. The page frame database does not describe device physical memory, a point that is important to understand when building MDLs for device memory.

Individual entries within the page frame database are typically referred to by their page numbers. Hence, this database is normally referred to as the *page frame number (PFN) database*. An individual entry within the page frame database describes how a given physical page is currently being used. On Windows NT, a page is always in one of eight states:

- **Active.** The physical page is in active use. The PFN database includes reference-counting information to indicate the number of active references.

- **Transition**. The physical page is part of one or more working sets, but all PTE entries to it are marked invalid. This state is used as part of recycling the page.

- **ModifiedNoWrite**. The physical page is part of one or more working sets, contains dirty data, but is not presently scheduled to be written to disk.

- **Modified**. The physical page may be part of one or more working sets, contains dirty data, and is presently scheduled to be written to disk.

- **Standby**. The physical page is not part of any working sets, although the page may still contain useful data. This state is the "last resort" for pages before they are recycled for other uses.

- **Zeroed**. The physical page has been completely filled with zeros. The Memory Manager maintains a set of such pages so that when a Demand Zero page fault occurs, it can immediately satisfy it using one of these pages.

- **Free**. The physical page is unused and contains no useful data. Unlike zeroed pages, pages in the Free state may have data remaining in them from their prior use.

- **Bad**. The physical page has been marked as Bad. This can be used with hardware that supports identification and removal of pages that are not performing correctly (perhaps they've failed an ECC check.)

In Figure 3.13, we provide a simple graphic description of these lists. Note that the "pages" are actually tracked via their PFN database entries, with every physical page present on exactly one list. Note that these lists map one-to-one with the various states listed. Thus, a physical page is in the "free" state when it is on the "free" list.

Note that not all physical memory is described within the PFN database. For example, device drivers can indicate the memory that is resident on their device using `MmMapIoSpace()` (the prototype for which is shown in Figure 13.15 in Chapter 13, "DriverEntry"). While the Memory Manager builds a virtual-to-physical translation for this memory, it uses non-paged pool for this purpose. Such memory does not have an entry in the PFN database.

The Page Recovery Algorithm

Note that the Windows NT page recovery algorithm might appear a bit unusual when first described. From the pure operating system perspective, the page reuse mechanism should implement a least-recently-used (LRU) algorithm. Then, each time a page was accessed, it would be moved to the front of the list. As pages were needed for other processes, the Memory Manager would remove them from the tail of the list—in essence, removing those pages that had not been used recently.

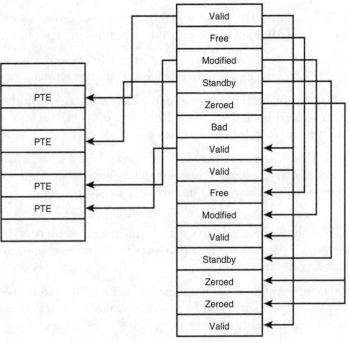

Figure 3.13. *Memory Manager page lists.*

While theoretically optimal, the cost of a strict LRU mechanism requires constantly moving the PFN entries from the middle of the list to the head of the list. For CPUs that didn't support this, the OS would have to ensure that a page fault occurred for every page except the current one. Instead of LRU, Windows NT utilizes a much more efficient three-step, FIFO algorithm for recycling the physical pages. First, as we described earlier, there is an "accessed" bit that is set by the MMU. This allows Windows NT to chose to trim only pages from a particular process working set when the page has not been recently accessed, specifically since the last time the working set was scanned by the Memory Manager. Then, a page is moved to the Transition list. If it is referenced at this point, the data is in memory and the page can be cheaply recovered. Once a page has become the oldest page on the Transition list it is moved to the Standby list. It can still be recovered at this point, but once it becomes the oldest page on the standby list it is reclaimed—either to be zeroed and added to the zero list, or to become part of a processes address space because the physical page has been recycled.

Thus, this algorithm approximates the strict LRU algorithm without the costly overhead of LRU.

Section Object

The Memory Manager in Windows NT exports a single control data structure: the Section Object. Like other objects within Windows NT, the Section Object can be named. Figure 3.14 shows the Devices directory within the Object Manager. This shows one Section Object of particular interest to device driver writers—the PhysicalMemory Section Object. This Section Object can be used from a device driver to map device memory into an application space. This allows device memory to be accessed directly from a custom application, although this should be set up from the device driver.

Figure 3.14. *Physical Memory Section Object.*

Section Objects are used within the Memory Manager to describe anything that can be "mapped" into memory. Perhaps the best example of this is for memory-mapped files, each of which has exactly one Section Object (although there are potentially many open references to that one file, with one file object for each open reference). This mechanism is essential to ensuring that no matter how many mapped instances of a file exist in the system, there is only one copy of the data.

Memory-Manager Tuning

There are a number of instances when it may be necessary to tune the performance of the Windows NT Memory Manager in order to increase the available pool of resources for a particular device driver. Figure 3.15 shows a view of the Registry keys that control the behavior of the Memory Manager.

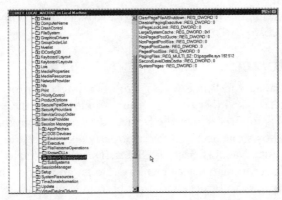

Figure 3.15. *Memory Manager Registry control keys.*

From Figure 3.15, the Registry key values of interest are as follows:

- **DisablePagingExecutive.** This value disables the paging of the operating system and device drivers. A value of zero indicates that paging is enabled, while any non-zero value disables paging. When paging is disabled, the code portion of all drivers in the system are locked into memory.

- **IoPageLockLimit.** This REG_DWORD value ranges from a minimum of 512KB to a value approximately 7MB less than the total physical memory on the system. It is used to restrict the amount of memory that can be locked by a Kernel mode driver on behalf of a User mode process. Drivers that transfer large blocks of data in multi-threaded programs find it useful to increase this value; otherwise, certain operations will fail due to the quota being exceeded.

- **NonPagedPoolSize.** This value establishes the total available non-paged memory size. A value of zero indicates that the "default" value, which is computed based upon the available physical memory, should be used. A larger value indicates the size that should be used. Note that the maximum acceptable value is a function of the available physical memory and the version of Windows NT. For NT V4. SP3 on an X86 platform, the version dependent limit is 128MB.

- **SystemPages.** This value establishes the number of PTEs reserved by the operating system for describing system memory. The default value is a function of the version and platform, but for a typical system it is 10,000. The maximum value also varies as a function of the version and the platform, but it is less than 50,000. Each PTE allows Windows NT to describe one PAGE_SIZE unit of memory (4KB on X86, 8KB on Alpha). Increasing this value is typically necessary when a device has a large amount of memory and the driver must access that memory.

These are only the Memory Manager-related values that are typically of interest to Kernel mode device driver developers. Chapter 4, "The Registry," describes the Registry in more detail.

Drivers and VM

While an understanding of Virtual Memory is useful to gain an appreciation of the operating system, it is also important when developing Kernel mode device drivers because device driver writers routinely must manipulate virtual, physical, and logical addresses.

For example, as you will see in more detail in Chapter 14, "Dispatch Entry Points," the I/O Manager can pass one of three types of addresses containing input from a User mode application:

- The virtual address of the User mode application's buffer

- The virtual address of a system buffer

- The physical description of the user's buffer as a Memory Descriptor List (MDL)

The issue of context will come up again in Chapter 12, "Driver Structure," but for the purposes of discussing virtual memory, knowing the context of a particular operation is critical to being able to handle virtual addresses correctly. This is because for the VM system, context defines which page tables to use when translating the address.

Thus, the virtual address of the User mode application's buffer must be translated by using the same set of page tables that were used by the application when building that buffer. Otherwise, the virtual-to-physical address translation might point to the right physical memory, but often will not.

> ### Note
>
> *It comes as some surprise to new Kernel mode driver developers that when they are in an "arbitrary" context, using a user virtual address may resolve to the correct physical memory. Indeed, frequently this problem may go undetected in the developer's testing environment because the only use of the system is to debug the driver. Hence, often the "arbitrary" context is the last application that ran—the test program! In such a case, the bug often shows up the first time it is tested by a third party that is using the system for other tasks as well as for testing the driver.*

The advantage of using a virtual address for a system buffer is that addresses in the system address space are identical, regardless of the actual context. This is because all contexts share the system space mappings, as described earlier in this chapter. Unfortunately, the I/O Manager accomplishes this by allocating a buffer from the non-paged pool and copying data into it. Although this is acceptable for small blocks of data, it can become unbearably slow for larger blocks of data.

The third alternative is for the I/O Manager to pass a description of the physical pages that make up the user's buffer. Of course, as discussed earlier, a virtual address is not required to point to a valid physical address. Thus, in the process of building the description of the physical pages, the Memory Manager (at the request of the I/O Manager) must ensure that the virtual-to-physical address mapping is valid and remains valid. The process of ensuring that the virtual-to-physical address mapping is valid is known as *probing*. The process of ensuring that a valid virtual-to-physical mapping remains valid is known as *locking*. Hence, the Memory Manager routine that performs this task is `MmProbeAndLockPages()`. The prototype for this function is shown in Figure 16.3 (in Chapter 16, "Programmed I/O Data Transfers.")

Memory Descriptor Lists

The Memory Manager uses the Memory Descriptor List (MDL) structure for describing a set of physical pages that make up the user application's virtual buffer. Once a device driver has an MDL describing a user buffer, that MDL can be used to create a mapping in the system virtual address space or it can be used to obtain logical addresses that can be given to the device for performing Direct Memory Access (DMA.) DMA is described in more detail in Chapter 17, "DMA Data Transfers."

Building a system virtual address mapping is straightforward for the Memory Manager once it has a set of physical page addresses because it can simply find a range of unused PTEs in the system virtual address space, and then fix those PTEs to point to the appropriate physical pages. This is important because if a Kernel mode device driver tries to use the physical address directly, the CPU will perform a virtual-to-physical translation on that physical address. Of course, it is extremely unlikely that this translation will result in a correct operation.

Frequently, Kernel mode device drivers allow the I/O Manager to interact with the Memory Manager when creating the MDLs for a user buffer. Those same drivers then use the MDL as a parameter to pass into the Memory Manager, either to obtain a system virtual address using `MmGetSystemAddressForMdl()`, or by translating the physical addresses within the MDL into logical addresses for use in programming the device using `IoMapTransfer()`. The prototype for `MmGetSystemAddressForMdl()` is shown in Figure 16.1 (in Chapter 16.) The prototype for `IoMapTransfer()` is shown in Figure 17.7 (in Chapter 17.)

It is also possible for Kernel mode device drivers to build MDLs directly from user virtual addresses. Although this is unusual for Kernel mode device drivers, it can prove to be useful under certain limited circumstances. Chapter 16 discusses handling user buffers directly in more detail. Drivers that do manipulate user virtual addresses directly must be certain to handle invalid memory references. For example, the Memory Manager routine `MmProbeAndLockPages()` raises an exception when a user memory reference is invalid.

Structured Exception Handling

One very important technique for handling certain types of memory access problems is *Structured Exception Handling* (SEH). This technique is a feature of the operating system that is supported by the standard Microsoft C/C++ compiler. Although it can be used for general error handling, the interest here is to ensure that user addresses are valid.

Using Microsoft C, SEH is accomplished by using the keywords __try and __except. Microsoft's build environment for Kernel mode drivers (discussed in greater detail in Chapter 18) defines the keywords try and except in terms of the actual compiler primitives. This is done using the arguments -Dtry=__try and -Dexcept=__except when compiling standard C programs.

C++ code compiled using Microsoft's build environment **must** use the native __try and __except versions of these keywords because C++ defines its own exception-handling mechanism using the try and except keywords. This C++ exception-handling mechanism is incompatible with the exception-handling mechanism supported by the Microkernel for Kernel mode device drivers.

> **Note**
>
> *The Structured Exception Handling model described here should not be confused with the termination handling that is also available. A termination handler is a segment of code that will always be executed once a particular region has been entered, regardless of the way control is transferred out of the code region. For example, this is often used to ensure proper cleanup of resources such as locks or allocated memory. A termination handler also uses the __try clause to introduce it, but uses a __finally to represent the termination code. The __try/__except mechanism is independent of the __try/__finally mechanism. The two may be both be used within your code.*

Example 3.1, which follows shortly, demonstrates how to use SEH when accessing an address in the user portion of the address space. A few important notes about SEH on NT:

- The __except clause is executed only if the expression evaluates to TRUE.

- The routine GetExceptionInformation can only be called within the __except expression. This can be used to retrieve extended information about what caused the exception.

- The routine GetExceptionCode can be used within the __except expression or within the __except clause in order to retrieve the basic information about what caused the exception.

- Not all exceptions can be handled. For example, an illegal instruction exception cannot be trapped with an exception handler.

- If an exception does not occur, the code within the exception-handling clause is not called.

Your own driver can generate exceptions using the Executive subsystem routine ExRaiseStatus().

Example 3.1. Using Structured Exception Handling

```
//
// We'll be reading data from the user mode address.  We should make certain it
// is valid.
//
BOOLEAN OsrProbeForRead(Buffer, Length)
{
    ULONG index;
    UCHAR dummyArg;
    PUCHAR effectiveAddress;

    //
    // Probe the input buffer by reading a byte from each page in the range -
    // that's enough.

    try {

        for (index = ADDRESS_AND_SIZE_TO_SPAN_PAGES(Buffer, Length);
             index;
             index--) {

            effectiveAddress = (PUCHAR) Buffer;

            effectiveAddress += ((index-1) * PAGE_SIZE);

            dummyArg = *effectiveAddress;

        }
```

```
} except (EXCEPTION_EXECUTE_HANDLER) {

    DbgPrint("Exception is 0x%x\n", GetExceptionCode());

    return FALSE;

}

//
// If we make it to here, the input buffer is valid.
//

return TRUE;
```

When an exception occurs, the Microkernel analyzes the registered exception handlers until it either finds an exception handler willing to handle the exception or it runs out of exception handlers. An unhandled exception in Kernel mode causes the system to halt.

Example 3.1 demonstrates an unconditional exception handler, because the macro EXCEPTION_EXECUTE_HANDLER is a shorthand expression for TRUE. Thus, the exception handler will always be invoked if there is an exception. If any exception occurs while referencing the memory, in this case it will unconditionally trap into the exception handler. Sometimes, you might only want to handle exceptions that occur because of memory errors, in which case you should provide a function that can be used to examine the cause of the exception and determine whether it should be handled or not (see Example 3.2).

Example 3.2. A Selective Exception Handling Expression

```
ULONG BackgroundExceptionFilter( ULONG Code, PEXCEPTION_POINTERS pointers)
{
    PEXCEPTION_RECORD ExceptionRecord;
    PCONTEXT Context;

    ExceptionRecord = pointers->ExceptionRecord;
    Context = pointers->ContextRecord;

    return EXCEPTION_EXECUTE_HANDLER;
}
```

Example 3.3 demonstrates a code fragment, showing how to use this expression. If an exception occurs while calling the function within the __try block, the Microkernel will call the routine BackgroundExceptionFilter to determine if the exception handler should be invoked. In Example 3.3, it is invoked. An error is printed and processing continues because the exception has been handled.

Example 3.3. Using the Exception Handling Expression

```
runAgain = FALSE;

__try {

    runAgain = (*backgroundTask->BackgroundTaskProc)
               (backgroundTask->Context);

} __except ( BackgroundExceptionFilter(GetExceptionCode(),
                        GetExceptionInformation()) ) {

    DbgPrint(("Unexpected exception when calling routine\n"));

}
```

Note

Perhaps the most challenging part about using SEH is debugging the system when something goes wrong. In such a case, it can be useful to use an exception filter routine, similar to the one in Example 3.2, and utilize a hard-coded breakpoint. By doing this, the debugger is invoked before the stack has been unwound, making it easier to debug what has actually happened.

Chapter 4

The Registry

This chapter will review:

- **Viewing and Modifying the Registry.** This section examines the tools used to navigate and edit Registry entries. Coverage includes the following utilities: `regedt32.exe`, `regedit.exe`, `regdmp.exe`, and `regini.exe`.

- **Registry Organization.** This section explains the hierarchy, values, and data types typically found within the Registry. Coverage of the `UNICODE_STRING` string structure and wide-character null-terminated strings is also included.

- **Registry Keys of Interest to Device Driver Developers.** This section covers the `HARDWARE`, `SOFTWARE`, and `SYSTEM` Registry subkeys that are more relevant to the working environment of device driver writers. Coverage of control sets is also included for further clarification.

This chapter discusses the Windows NT Registry, emphasizing those parts of the Registry that are of interest to Kernel mode device driver developers. Note that this chapter merely introduces the Registry and points out some of the particular keys of interest. The actual Registry entries needed to install and start a driver in Windows NT are described in Chapter 20, "Installing and Starting Drivers."

The Registry is nothing more than a database of configuration and administrative information about the operating system and related utilities. However, because it has evolved to accumulate all the configuration information on Windows NT, the organization of the information within the Registry has become complex.

Although the Registry is described as if it were a single component, it is in fact constructed by combining several independent components called *hives* into a single, coherent namespace. For example, information about the hardware configuration of the current system is recomputed as part of system initialization, and is modified as individual drivers and services load. Other parts of the Registry, such as those used to maintain user-specific and system-specific configuration data, are stored on disk and maintained in memory so they can be quickly accessed as necessary.

Viewing and Modifying the Registry

Although Windows NT provides two separate utilities to examine and modify the Registry, neither of these tools is presented to users via the standard Start menus. Instead, these utilities must either be manually invoked or added to the menus. regedt32.exe is the original utility built by Microsoft for examining and modifying the Registry. This utility is tied tightly to the Windows NT platform and understands certain data types that are unique to Windows NT. regedit.exe is a separate utility that works with any system supporting the Win 32 Registry API—notably Windows 95, Windows 98, and Windows NT 4.0. Figure 4.1 and Figure 4.2 illustrate the basic appearance of the regedit32 and regedit utilities, respectively.

What is available within the Registry is restricted using the standard Windows NT security mechanisms. Thus, each key within the Registry can be protected much like files are protected within the file system. Kernel mode device drivers typically need not worry about this security because Kernel mode access is normally granted as a matter of course.

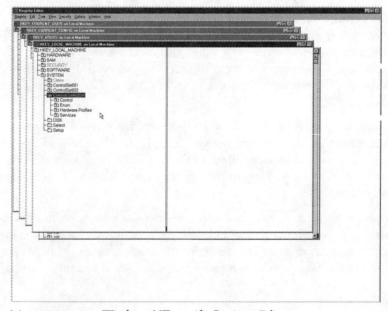

Figure 4.1. regedt32.exe: *Windows NT-specific Registry Editor.*

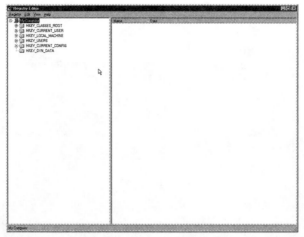

Figure 4.2. regedit.exe: *Win32 Registry Editor for Windows 95/98 and Windows NT.*

Although both the regedit.exe and regedt32.exe utilities perform similar functions, their appearances are distinctive and each provides slightly different features. For example, the two utilities frequently display Registry information in slightly different forms. Figure 4.3 shows the information displayed by the regedt32.exe utility for the HAL resources on a multiprocessor system.

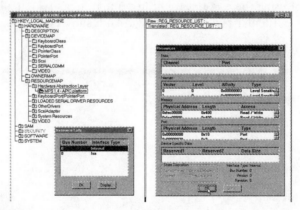

Figure 4.3. regedt32.exe's *presentation of HAL resources.*

Note that by selecting one of the two entries at this level of the Registry (either .raw or .translated), the Registry Editor can display detailed information about this information.

Compare the display in Figure 4.3 to the presentation of the same information by the regedit.exe utility in Figure 4.4.

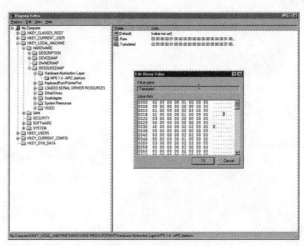

Figure 4.4. `regedit.exe`'s *presentation of HAL resources.*

Instead of providing a detailed display of the meaning of this Registry information, `regedit.exe` presents this information as binary data without any interpretation. Thus, it is useful to know that the `regedt32.exe` utility was constructed with explicit knowledge of the detailed data structures that Windows NT maintains about hardware resources, while the `regedit.exe` utility does not.

One benefit of using the `regedit.exe` utility is that it can search all parts of the Registry for a particular textual value. Figure 4.5 shows the Find option within `regedit.exe`.

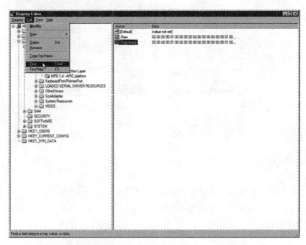

Figure 4.5. `regedit.exe`'s *Find capability.*

Although `regedt32.exe` has a search facility, it is restricted to searching for a textual match, with respect to the name of keys within the Registry. A key in the Registry corresponds to a particular level, much like a directory within Explorer. A key acts as a container of additional keys or values, where values actually contain the data elements within the Registry. The actual organization of the Registry is described in more detail later in this chapter in the section "Registry Organization."

Figure 4.6 shows the Find option used with `regedt32.exe`.

Figure 4.6. `regedt32.exe`'s *Find capability.*

Again, note that the `regedt32.exe` utility's Find option is restricted to searching on the names of individual keys, rather than for textual strings anywhere within the Registry—notably within the data portion of values. Thus, when searching for a particular string anywhere in the Registry, the `regedit.exe` utility may be better suited to the task.

For example, if you wish to find all values that contain data with the word "Microsoft," you cannot do this by using `regedt32.exe`, although you can do so by using `regedit.exe`. You **could** find all the keys that have the word "Microsoft" in their names, but this is often less useful.

In addition to these standard Windows NT utilities, the Windows NT DDK also includes two additional command-line utilities: `regdmp.exe` and `regini.exe`.

The `regdmp.exe` utility can be used to dump all or a portion of the Registry. For example, to dump the HAL portion of the Registry displayed earlier in Figures 4.3 and 4.4, use the command (all one line):

```
regdmp "HKEY_LOCAL_MACHINE\Hardware\ResourceMap\Hardware Abstraction Layer\MPS
1.4 - APIC Platform"
```

This command displays quite a considerable amount of text information that describes this Registry key, but this represents the same information observed earlier using `regedt32.exe` and `regedit.exe`—again, using a different format for the information.

The `regini.exe` utility can be useful when developing drivers because it allows the developer to build a simple textual description of the Registry key and its values rather than building a complete installation program. The Registry keys necessary for driver installation are described in detail in Chapter 20. The `regini.exe` utility takes a text file and builds Registry information based upon the information within the Registry itself. The input of the `regini.exe` utility is compatible with the output of the `regdmp.exe` utility.

Registry Organization

The Registry is organized into a series of different top-level keys. Each key represents a distinct type of information. In Windows NT, the standard top-level keys are as follows:

- **HKEY_CLASSES_ROOT**. This key indicates special handling for various file extensions.

- **HKEY_CURRENT_USER**. This key indicates configuration information for the current logged-on user.

- **HKEY_CURRENT_CONFIG**. This key indicates miscellaneous configuration state.

- **HKEY_LOCAL_MACHINE**. Of interest to device driver writers, this key indicates system state.

- **HKEY_USERS**. This key provides local information on this machine about users.

Note that individual Registry keys may in fact be links to other keys. While reading the contents of the Registry, these links point to other parts of the Registry. For example, the HKEY_CURRENT_USER key points to the correct entry in the HKEY_USERS portion of the Registry. Thus, this linkage is normally transparent to programs and utilities reading the Registry, and it allows Windows NT to construct a logical name space for the Registry, where the "correct" contents are determined by the system as necessary.

Indeed, we will discuss one of these links—the *current control set*—that is important to the configuration state for device drivers later in the section "The SYSTEM Subkey and Control Sets."

Subkeys, Values, and Data Types

Within the Registry, each key may contain additional keys that may also contain values. A *value* has a name that is unique within the current key and has associated data, as well as type information for interpreting the data itself. Figure 4.7 shows a simple example of this hierarchical decomposition.

Figure 4.7. Microsoft *key within* HKEY_LOCAL_MACHINE\SOFTWARE.

Figure 4.7 shows the Microsoft key. Selecting the key displays additional information, as shown in Figure 4.8.

For our purposes, the Windows NT key was selected because it also shows where the current configuration data is maintained within the Registry. For this example, the system used to capture these images was running CurrentBuildNumber 1381 (which indicates that this was an NT V4 system) and the CSDVersion Service Pack 3.

In addition, each of these entries identifies the type of data. For both CurrentBuildNumber and CSDVersion, the REG_SZ indicates that this is a null-terminated string (the "Z" indicates a null-terminated string because the wide character value zero is the null character). The Registry supports a variety of

different data types, but those of primary interest to device driver developers
are as follows:

- **REG_NONE.** No type

- **REG_SZ.** Null-terminated wide character string

- **REG_EXPAND_SZ.** Null-terminated wide character string, with environment
  variable expansion

- **REG_BINARY.** Binary format data

- **REG_DWORD.** 32-bit value

- **REG_DWORD_LITTLE_ENDIAN.** Same as REG_DWORD

- **REG_DWORD_BIG_ENDIAN.** 32-bit value in big endian format

- **REG_LINK.** Link within the Registry

- **REG_MULTI_SZ.** Multiple null-terminated wide character strings; list ends
  with an empty string

- **REG_RESOURCE_LIST.** Resource list

- **REG_RESOURCE_REQUIREMENTS_LIST.** Resource requirements list

- **REG_FULL_RESOURCE_DESCRIPTOR.** Description of device assigned resources

Figure 4.8. Windows NT *key within* HKEY_LOCAL_MACHINE\SOFTWARE\Microsoft.

Managing Wide Character Strings

Describing strings on Windows NT can be confusing because Windows NT
provides two different ways to represent strings. One is using the
UNICODE_STRING structure, which is declared for the DDK in ntdef.h as:

```
typedef struct _UNICODE_STRING {
    USHORT Length;
    USHORT MaximumLength;
    PWSTR  Buffer;
} UNICODE_STRING;
```

The other mechanism used to describe a string is to follow the convention that
it is terminated by a null character. The rich programming environment of the
Windows NT DDK utilizes both forms of strings, with some functions taking
wide character strings and others taking pointers to the UNICODE_STRING data
structure. Furthermore, the DDK documentation uses these terms interchangeably. We have found that new device driver developers often first experience
these two different mechanisms when they begin interacting with the Registry
itself.

One technique you can use when managing these strings is to maintain them
by using the UNICODE_STRING structure, but ensure that there is an additional
wide character at the end of the Buffer pointed to by the structure. In this case,
the Length field in the structure indicates the size in bytes of the string stored
within the Buffer, while the MaximumLength field will indicate a size of at least
two bytes more than the Length (because it requires two bytes to store a single
null wide character terminator).

Registry Keys of Interest to Device Driver Developers

For device driver developers, there are only a few keys of general interest within the Registry. These keys are located within the HKEY_LOCAL_MACHINE top-level
key (refer to Figure 4.1).

HARDWARE

The HARDWARE subkey describes the current hardware configuration, including
resources that have been reserved for use by a particular device by its device
driver. This key is entirely dynamic and is reconstructed each time the system
boots. Thus, if a device driver does not load, its device resources will not be
present in this portion of the Registry because they have not been reserved with
the operating system. The HARDWARE key is the first key available as the operating system initializes.

Individual values stored within the HARDWARE subkey can describe complete sets of configuration or resource information. For example, Figure 4.9 shows the information displayed for an Ethernet card on a particular system. These resources have been reserved by the device driver to ensure that other devices on the system do not use the same resources.

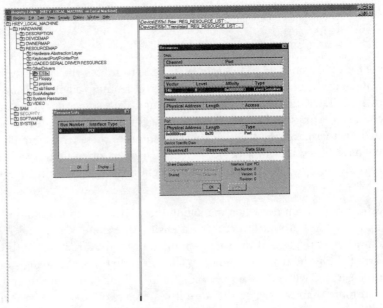

Figure 4.9. *Resources in use by an Ethernet device.*

An example of a utility that reads this information and displays it is the standard diagnostic program winmsd.exe. This program reads the Registry information and displays the resource utilization list, as shown in Figure 4.10.

Figure 4.10. winmsd.exe *reporting I/O port usage.*

Although these values are certainly of interest to device driver writers, they are never directly created by the device driver. Instead, device driver writers rely upon I/O Manager functions, such as `IoAssignResources()` or `IoReportResourceUsage()` (described in Chapter 13, "Driver Entry"). These routines in turn create and record the necessary Registry information.

SOFTWARE

The `SOFTWARE` subkey describes the configuration state and information for the various software packages installed on the system. Figure 4.8 showed one piece of information that can be useful to a device driver—the current version and CSD (patch) applied to the system. Typically, device drivers do not store information in this portion of the Registry because it is typically used by the various services and applications installed on the system.

Comparing the `Classes` subkey of `SOFTWARE` side-by-side with the top-level `HKEY_CLASSES_ROOT` reveals that they are identical (see Figure 4.11).

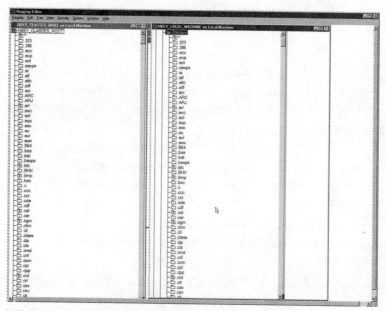

Figure 4.11. `HKEY_CLASSES_ROOT` *and* `HKEY_LOCAL_MACHINE\SOFTWARE\Classes`.

Rather than being two identical copies of the same information, one is a link to the other. For any application program or device driver that reads this information, either path will point to exactly the same information.

The SYSTEM Subkey and Control Sets

The SYSTEM subkey contains all static configuration information, and is of particular interest to device drivers because it includes the static configuration information about which drivers can be loaded on this system. Figure 4.12 shows the layout of the SYSTEM subkey.

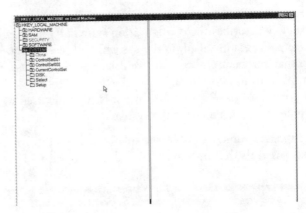

Figure 4.12. SYSTEM *subkey.*

The actual system startup information is maintained as a *control set.* Each control set describes the parameters to use when initializing the system, the drivers and services to load, and other information essential to proper configuration of the system as it is booted.

The Registry actually maintains as many as four such control sets. Figure 4.12 illustrated two control sets: ControlSet001 and ControlSet002. The key CurrentControlSet is actually a link within the Registry to the control set used when the system started.

The Select key within the Registry indicates the interpretation of the four possible control set values and their mapping to the actual control sets. These values are as follows:

- **Default.** This value is the "default" control set that should be booted when the system is started.

- **Current.** This value is the "current" or actual control set that was booted when the system was started.

- **Failed.** This value is a control set that was overridden manually (during boot loading).

- **LastKnownGood.** This value is the last control set that was in use when someone successfully logged onto the system.

These values are set and modified as changes to the control set are made to add or remove services, as well as when a boot fails because the control set is invalid and has been replaced by the system. For example, when Windows NT boots, it provides a mechanism for reverting to the "last known good" configuration. This means that the control set indicated by the LastKnownGood value in the Registry will be used to determine the control set to use.

A control set—such as CurrentControlSet—is made up of four subkeys: Control, Enum, Hardware Profiles, and Services. Of these, Control and Services are of interest to device driver developers.

Figure 4.13 illustrates the Control subkey, which describes system startup and tuning parameters that are used to control the precise manner in which Windows NT will operate.

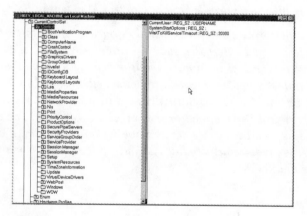

Figure 4.13. *Control set.*

For example, the CrashControl subkey describes what the system should do if a system crash occurs—including creating a crash dump, rebooting, and so forth. Some of the information, such as the DumpFile value, is used when the system reboots to indicate where the crash dump should be copied because it is stored in the paging file when the system crashes.

The GroupOrderList and ServiceGroupOrder subkeys control the order in which device drivers load during system initialization. These keys are described in greater detail in Chapter 20.

The Session Manager subkey (this is not the same as the SessionManager subkey, which is a different subkey but is in the same location and has a deceptively similar name) contains configuration information used by the executive subsystems during their own initialization. For example, as described in Chapter 3, "Virtual Memory," the Memory Manager uses the values in the Memory Management subkey. This was shown in Figure 3.15.

The Services subkey describes the services, including device drivers, which can be loaded by the system. This key is scanned three times during system initialization just to determine the correct set of drivers and services to load as part of starting up the Windows NT system. Chapter 20 describes this process in greater detail.

The Services subkey contains listings for device drivers; for other types of Kernel mode drivers, such as file system drivers or file system recognizer drivers; and for User mode services.

Note

*The Service Control Manager (*services.exe*) actually scans the* Services *subkey when it first initializes. It builds an in-memory database of the information it finds in the* Services *subkey. Chapter 20 describes the programmatic interface into the Service Control Manager in more detail.*

Because it performs a scan of this subkey once when it starts, if the Registry is changed externally, such as with regedt32.exe, *the Service Control Manager does not know about the changes to the Registry until the next time it scans it—the next time the system starts up. Because the Service Control Manager is normally used to start new services (such as with the Control Panel applet or the* net start *command-line command), if it scans its own list of services and doesn't find the entry, it cannot load it. Hence, the requirement that a system be rebooted after manually changing the Registry.*

Chapter *5*

Dispatching and Scheduling

This chapter will review:

- **Dispatching.** Dispatching is the process of switching from one thread of execution to another thread of execution. This section describes the basic dispatching model on Windows NT.

- **Scheduling.** Scheduling is the process of determining which thread is to execute next on a given processor. This section describes the basic scheduling model on Windows NT.

This chapter discusses the basics of scheduling on Windows NT. Note that this chapter is not intended to be an exhaustive treatise on Windows NT scheduling; it is designed to emphasize those portions of scheduling that are of interest to device driver writers.

Scheduling is, in fact, often one of the most complex parts of any operating system. In this regard, Windows NT is no exception. For example, the Windows NT scheduling algorithm for multiprocessor systems has changed throughout the lifetime of Windows NT to further tune its performance. Sometimes achieving this optimal performance means that the default scheduling rules are set aside. This chapter does not describe these details because they are beyond the scope of interest for device driver writers and are subject to change between versions of Windows NT.

Dispatching

Dispatching is the way the operating system switches between threads—the units of execution on Windows NT. As such, dispatching is distinct from the act of *scheduling*, which is the determination of the next thread to run on a given CPU. Thus, we start by describing the process of dispatching (switching between threads) in this section, and we discuss scheduling (choosing which thread to run next) in the next section.

Windows NT is organized around the concepts of *processes* and *threads*. All threads are associated with a particular process, and each process encapsulates shared resources, such as the VM page tables discussed in Chapter 3, "Virtual Memory." Thus, two threads within the same process have access to the same resources, while two threads within different processes normally do not share resources.

> ### Note
>
> *Threads between processes can share resources, but it requires explicit programming so that each of the threads can locate the resource. For example, two threads might open the same file and share the data contents of that file. Normally, this is done by using a "well-known name" for the shared resources, and this is allowed by several Win32 APIs that are used for opening or creating resources.*
>
> *An example of this is the event that can be shared between two or more applications, or even between an application and a Kernel mode driver. Such an event is normally created by using the* CreateEvent() *API available in Win32. By providing the optional name for the event, the event is visible to all applications within the system. Indeed, a Kernel mode driver can even access this event by using the standard DDK API call* IoCreateNotificationEvent(). *There is one trick. Win32 API operations create their events in a special directory within the Object Manager namespace—the* BaseNamedObjects *directory. Thus, this name must be explicitly used for the Kernel mode API, while it is not used for the Win32 level API.*

Threads are the units of execution within Windows NT. What this means is that each "thread" consists of sufficient information for the OS to be aware of the state of a particular thread at any point in time. In addition, the OS must also have enough information to be able to safely change that thread's state. Typical states for threads are as follows:

- **Wait.** A thread in the wait state is blocked from running until some event (or set of events) occurs.

- **Ready.** A thread in the ready state is eligible to run but must wait until NT decides to schedule it.

- **Running.** A thread in the running state is presently active on some CPU in the system.

For example, when a device driver calls the function KeWaitForSingleObject() to wait for an event to be signaled, the Microkernel places the current thread into a wait state. This is accomplished by using a KWAIT_BLOCK member that is present in the thread control block—the ETHREAD or KTHREAD structure, which are normally used interchangeably. This is because the KTHREAD structure represents the Microkernel state for the given thread, and is just the first part of the ETHREAD structure, which represents the executive state for the given thread.

The ETHREAD structure keeps track of all threads, regardless of their state. If the thread is waiting to run because it is ready, it will be tracked via the ready queue, which is a kernel data structure used to track threads while they await being scheduled.

When the thread is running, the kernel's processor control block, the KPRCB (which is referenced from the PCR) identifies which thread is active at the time, as well as two other threads—the next thread to run and the idle thread. The idle thread runs whenever no other threads are ready to run in the system. In such a case, the idle thread performs some CPU-specific operations waiting for something to happen—frequently the idle thread will continue to run until a device interrupts because some I/O operation has completed. This will eventually cause a thread to become ready to run.

When the kernel switches from one thread to another thread (a process referred to as *dispatching*), it stores the current thread's context, such as the contents of various CPU registers. The kernel then loads the new context, such as those CPU registers, of the next thread to run. This is done by the routine KiSwapThread(). This is why KiSwapThread() is frequently seen on the stack of threads not currently running. Figure 5.1 shows, with the aid of the kernel debugger, a thread's stack ending with KiSwapThread().

Another routine that is called to perform dispatching is KiSwitchToThread(). This function dispatches to a particular thread. This technique is important for optimizing client/server communications via the LPC subsystem. Specifically, KiSwitchToThread() allows a thread to send a message and then switch control to the recipient of that message (see Figure 5.2).

Because all threads call KiSwapThread() and KiSwitchToThread(), the return of the threads implies that they have been rescheduled. The thread continues running at the point where the dispatch—the call to KiSwapThread() or KiSwitchToThread()—occurred. Because the register state was restored, the OS creates the illusion that multiple threads were running in parallel by using this technique.

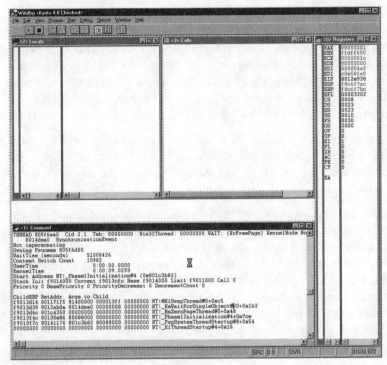

Figure 5.1. *Kernel debugger display of blocked thread.*

Of course, because Windows NT supports symmetric multiprocessing as described in Chapter 1, "Windows NT Operating System Overview," it is actually possible for multiple threads to be running in parallel—one on each CPU. However, the basic mechanism used in a multiprocessor (MP) system for dispatching is quite similar to the mechanism used in a uniprocessor (UP) system.

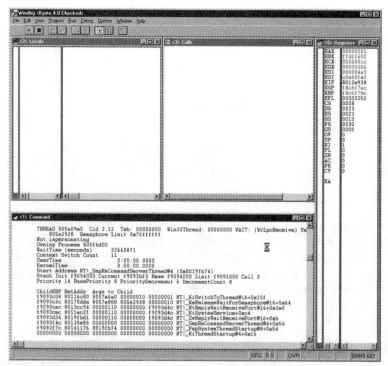

Figure 5.2. *Kernel debugger display of* KiSwitchToThread() *call.*

Scheduling

Although *dispatching* is the process by which the OS switches from one thread to another, *scheduling* is the process by which the OS picks the next thread to run. For example, if you look at the kernel processor control block (KPRCB) for the Alpha platform as it appears in ntddk.h, you'll note that it includes the field NextThread which indicates the next thread to run:

```
typedef struct _KPRCB {

//
// Major and minor version numbers of the PCR.
//

    USHORT MinorVersion;
    USHORT MajorVersion;

//
// Start of the architecturally defined section of the PRCB. This section
// may be directly addressed by vendor/platform specific HAL code and will
// not change from version to version of NT.
//
```

```
    struct _KTHREAD *CurrentThread;
    struct _KTHREAD *NextThread;
    struct _KTHREAD *IdleThread;
    CCHAR Number;
    CCHAR Reserved;
    USHORT BuildType;
    KAFFINITY SetMember;
    struct _RESTART_BLOCK *RestartBlock;

//
// End of the architecturally defined section of the PRCB. This section
// may be directly addressed by vendor/platform specific HAL code and will
// not change from version to version of NT.
//
} KPRCB, *PKPRCB, *RESTRICTED_POINTER PRKPRCB;
```

This architecture allows the kernel to be disconnected from the actual scheduling algorithm, in keeping with the original design goal that the microkernel avoid implementing operating system *policy* whenever possible. Thus, the executive subsystems can implement scheduling policy without requiring any changes in the underlying dispatching scheme as implemented in the microkernel.

The code within the kernel that is responsible for dispatching control to a new thread always runs at or above IRQL DISPATCH_LEVEL. This is necessary because there are a number of intermediate states, such as when the registers for the threads are being restored, where it is not safe to allow for arbitrary preemption. Thus, we typically describe the dispatcher as running at IRQL DISPATCH_LEVEL.

Other code within the system also runs at IRQL DISPATCH_LEVEL, and any such code is similarly protected against pre-emption. *All* such code is restricted from dispatching—and the results of performing a dispatching operation at IRQL DISPATCH_LEVEL are unpredictable. Under some circumstances, the system will crash; in other circumstances, performing a dispatching operation at IRQL DISPATCH_LEVEL may interfere with the correct operation of arbitrary user threads.

Note

The effect of disabling dispatching when running at IRQL DISPATCH_LEVEL can be seen in the following example. We recently heard from one unfortunate driver writer who wanted to understand why his call to KeWaitForSingleObject() *returned* STATUS_SUCCESS, *even though the event was never signaled. After some discussion, we learned that this call was being made from a* Deferred Procedure Call *(DPC) in the context of the system idle thread (DPCs are discussed in detail in Chapter 15, "Interrupt Service Routines and DPCs"). The call to*

KeWaitForSingleObject() called the dispatch code. The dispatch code determined that there were no threads to run, so it would explicitly choose to run the system idle thread. The dispatcher thus returned STATUS_SUCCESS, *so ultimately* KeWaitForSingleObject() *also returned* STATUS_SUCCESS, *even though the event was not signaled. All we could say was "Yikes!"*

The balance of this section covers the following topics:

- **Thread Priorities**. Although individual components within the executive are allowed to augment the basic scheduling policy, the kernel provides a default scheduling mechanism based on priorities.

- **Pre-emption**. To ensure that system resources are shared between all threads on the system, the kernel restricts them to running for no longer than some small period of time. When that time expires, another thread is scheduled—a process referred to as *pre-emption*.

- **The Impact of Scheduling on Drivers**. Scheduling requires that Kernel mode device drivers be constructed so that their shared data structures are properly protected.

Thread Priorities

A *priority* is a numeric value that indicates the relative importance of a particular thread with respect to scheduling. As Figures 5.1 and 5.2 demonstrated, there are actually *two* priority fields:

- Priority. The value for this field is the current numeric value that will actually be used for scheduling.

- BasePriority. The value for this field indicates the minimum value for Priority. In other words, the OS can adjust the Priority of a given thread arbitrarily, as long as it is equal to or greater than the BasePriority value for that thread.

On Windows NT, numeric priority values range between 0 and 31, although the value 0 is reserved by the operating system. Thus, no threads, except specially designated OS threads, may use this priority. This range is divided into two categories: *dynamic* priorities and *real-time* priorities.

Dynamic priorities are values between 1 and 15. They are referred to as "dynamic" because the operating system varies the priority of threads in this range. Thus, for example, it is not possible for a thread in this range to "steal" the CPU and cause starvation of other threads that are waiting to run.

Real-time priorities are values between 16 and 31. They are referred to as "real-time" because the operating system does not vary the priority of threads in this range. Real-time range threads can continue to control the CPU, as long as no other threads of equal or higher priority are scheduled. Thus, it is possible for a real-time thread to "steal" the CPU and cause starvation of other threads that are waiting to run. Because of this, the right to use real-time priorities is restricted to those users or processes having the necessary privilege.

> **Note**
>
> The Priority *value determines whether the thread is "real-time" or "dynamic," not the* BasePriority *value. Indeed, it is quite possible for a thread to have a* BasePriority *value in the "dynamic" range and a* Priority *value in the "real-time" range. This is indicative that the* Priority *value has been modified by code outside the microkernel.*

Establishing Thread BasePriority Values

For either dynamic or real-time priorities, the BasePriority is established when the thread is first created and may be programmatically adjusted via such calls as KeSetBasePriorityThread() (see Figure 5.3). Typically, the BasePriority value is established by the subsystem to which the thread is bound. For example, Win32 combines two values: The priority of the process (the value of which is not used as part of scheduling) and the relative priority of the thread, as specified to the Win32 API call CreateThread(). Other subsystems presumably make similar decisions about their respective threads.

LONG
KeSetBasePriorityThread (IN PKTHREAD *Thread*
　　IN LONG *Increment*);

Thread: A pointer to a thread object for which the base priority is to be set.

Increment: A priority increment to apply to this thread's base priority.

Figure 5.3. KeSetBasePriorityThread() *function prototype.*

Adjusting Priority Values for Dynamic Threads

For dynamic threads, the Priority starts out equal to the BasePriority, but may be adjusted by the operating system. This is based upon the particular scheduling requirements of the various executive components—again, relieving the microkernel of the burden of implementing anything other than the basic scheduling algorithm. Examples of events that impact the current priority are as follows:

- **I/O completion.** When a device driver completes an I/O request, it indicates an optional priority boost given to the thread's current priority. (See Figure 13.2, `IoCompleteRequest()`.)

- **`KeSetEvent()`.** When a device driver sets an event, it indicates (as shown in Figure 5.4) an optional priority boost given to the thread's current priority.

- **Quantum exhaustion.** When a thread has run for its complete time slice, or *quantum*. In this case, the OS decreases the current priority back toward the base priority. Quantum exhaustion is discussed later in this chapter.

- **Not running.** When a thread has not run for a period of time, the OS provides it with a priority boost to ensure it has a chance to run. This prevents CPU starvation.

There are other reasons the OS also adjusts the `Priority` value of a given thread, but the first two are those most directly applicable to Kernel mode device driver writers, and allow Kernel mode drivers to participate in the scheduling algorithm for threads.

LONG
KeSetEvent (IN PRKEVENT *Event*,
　　IN KPRIORITY *Increment*,
　　IN BOOLEAN *Wait*);

Event: A pointer to an event object to be changed to signaled state.

Increment: A priority increment to apply to any waiting threads.

Wait: TRUE if the call to **KeSetEvent** is to be followed immediately by a call to **KeWaitXxx**.

Figure 5.4. `KeSetEvent()` *function prototype.*

Adjusting `Priority` Values for Real-Time Threads
For real-time threads, the OS never adjusts the `Priority` value, although it can be changed programmatically, such as with the call `KeSetPriorityThread()` (see Figure 5.5). Because of this, and because the OS will not boost threads into the real-time range, real-time threads must be used with caution because a thread with a real-time `Priority` value runs, as long as it does not wait, until some other thread of equal or greater `Priority` becomes ready to run.

> KPRIORITY
> **KeSetPriorityThread** (IN PKTHREAD *Thread*,
>   IN KPRIORITY *Priority*);
>
> *Thread*: A pointer to a thread object for which the current priority is to be set.
>
> *Priority:* A priority to set for this thread's current priority.

Figure 5.5. KeSetPriorityThread() *function prototype.*

Viewing Threads by Priority Level and State

The OS maintains a sorted list of threads, based upon their priority level. One thread is identified by using the KPRCB, and this is the thread that will run next. In addition, other threads are maintained in the *ready queue*. Figure 5.6 shows a listing of the currently ready threads, plus the currently running thread information by using the kernel debugger.

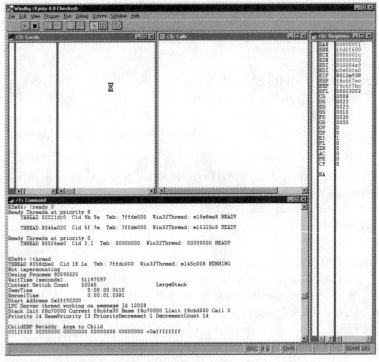

Figure 5.6. *Kernel debugger display of running and ready threads.*

Figure 5.7 shows the PCR describing the current state of this processor. From the PCR, you can see the value of CurrentThread (0x8058DBE0), NextThread (0x0), and IdleThread (0x80145A80)—these values were extracted from the KPRCB via the PCR.

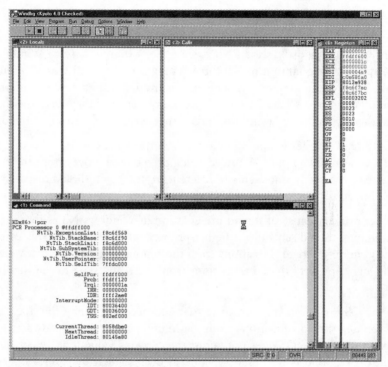

Figure 5.7. *Kernel debugger display of* PCR *Information.*

A NextThread value of zero indicates that no thread has yet been selected to run, even though there are threads currently in the ready queue. The OS will select a new thread to run once the currently running thread exhausts its quantum (due to *pre-emption*—described in the next section) or blocks, waiting for some event.

Pre-emption

As was mentioned in Chapter 1, Windows NT is a pre-emptive, multithreaded, and multitasking operating system. It employs a traditional operating system technique to provide this multitasking capability by associating a *quantum* with each thread when it starts running. This quantum is the period of time that this particular thread will execute.

Periodically, a hardware clock generates an interrupt. Each time that interrupt occurs, the OS updates its current time and determines what actions, if any, it should take. One such action is to decrease the remaining quantum for the currently running thread. Once the current thread has been running for a time period equal to or greater than its quantum, the microkernel invokes the scheduling algorithm to choose a new thread to run.

The precise value of the quantum for a given thread depends upon the particular version and type of Windows NT system. For example, on one Windows NT v4 system, the quantum for all threads on a server system was 120 milliseconds. Threads running on the same hardware that used the Workstation version of Windows NT had a 60-millisecond quantum if they were the foreground thread, and only 20 milliseconds if they were a background thread.

When a thread finishes its quantum and a new thread is scheduled to run, the thread has been *pre-empted*. A thread being pre-empted moves from the running state to the ready state. This is different from when a thread dispatches—when a thread dispatches, it moves from the running state to the waiting state.

The other primary cause of thread pre-emption in Windows NT is that the currently running thread schedules a higher-priority thread to run. In this case, the currently running thread transitions from the running state to the ready state, and the higher-priority thread transitions from the ready state to the running state.

When the OS pre-empts one thread so that another thread may run, the currently running thread transitions from the running state to the ready state. For real-time threads, the OS does not adjust the Priority value. For dynamic threads, the OS adjusts the Priority value by decreasing it by PriorityDecrement +1. Thus, even when PriorityDecrement is zero, the Priority field is decreased by one—but never less than the thread's BasePriority. Note that the value for the PriorityDecrement field was listed in Figures 5.1 and 5.2 as part of the standard thread information. The DecrementCount field is used by the LPC subsystem when using the KiSwitchToThread() call.

Once the new Priority value has been computed for the thread, it is placed in the ready queue. Figure 5.8 shows this process for a thread "A" that has run to the end of its quantum.

The Priority value for thread "A" is decreased by at least one (assuming Priority > BasePriority), and it is then inserted at the tail of the priority queue associated with its new priority. As depicted in Figure 5.8, thread "B" will be the next thread to run.

Figure 5.9 shows the case for quantum exhaustion with real-time threads.

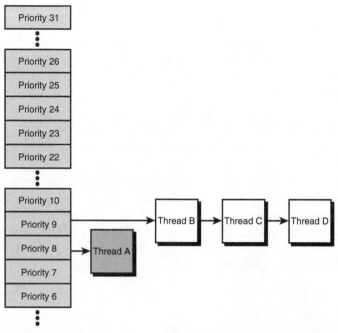

Figure 5.8. *Ready queue after dynamic priority thread "A" exhausts its time quantum.*

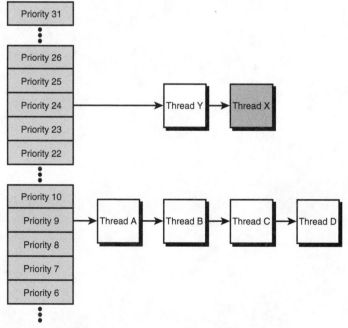

Figure 5.9. *Ready queue after real-time priority thread "X" exhausts its time quantum.*

In this case, the Priority value of the thread does not change. In the example, the next thread to run will be thread "Y." Because the Priority value of real-time threads does not decay, and because the Microkernel will not boost the Priority value of dynamic threads into the real-time range, such threads must be used with care because they can steal the CPU so that it is not available for lower-priority threads.

The Impact of Scheduling on Drivers

With respect to the impact of scheduling, writing a Kernel mode device driver is akin to writing a multithreaded Win32 application program. As noted in Chapter 3, the system address space is shared between all threads in the system. Because of this, Kernel mode device drivers must assume that their code will be utilized by many different system threads. Even in a uniprocessor environment, it may be possible for a thread running through the driver's code to be pre-empted. Thus, it is the responsibility of the driver writer to ensure correct serialization of threads with respect to one another.

Chapter 6

Interrupt Request Levels and DPCs

This chapter will review:

- **Understanding Interrupt Request Levels (IRQLs).** Understanding IRQLs is key to understanding how Windows NT works. This section defines IRQLs and explains the basics of how they are used.

- **How IRQLs Are Used.** This section delves into more detail on how Windows NT uses each of the individual IRQL levels, from IRQL PASSIVE_LEVEL through IRQL HIGH_LEVEL.

- **Deferred Procedure Calls (DPCs).** This section describes DPCs in detail, including how DPCs are invoked by the Windows NT operating system, key DPC characteristics, and the details of how DPCs work on multiprocessor systems.

- **The DpcForIsr.** This section describes the specific instance of the DPC implemented by the I/O Manager for interrupt completion.

Windows NT synchronizes Kernel mode activity by using a set of Interrupt Request Levels (IRQLs). This chapter describes in detail how IRQLs are used by Windows NT to achieve synchronization within the operating system. Once you thoroughly understand IRQLs, you will become familiar with the processing that occurs at each IRQL. This includes processing Deferred Procedure Calls (DPCs), which are used to perform callback processing of non-time-critical operations within the operating system.

Understanding Interrupt Request Levels (IRQLs)

In Windows NT, higher-priority activities or events interrupt those activities or events running at lower priorities. Consider, for example, how the device Interrupt Service Routines (ISRs) are managed. If the serial port device's ISR (typically a relatively low-priority device in the system) is running, and a clock interrupt occurs on the same processor, the serial port device's ISR will stop executing and the clock's ISR will be started. When the clock's ISR is completed, control is transferred back to the serial port device's ISR at the point where it was previously interrupted.

The relative priority of an activity within the Windows NT operating system is defined by its Interrupt Request Level (IRQL). The current processor's IRQL indicates the relative priority of the activity currently taking place on that CPU. IRQL values are assigned to both software and hardware activities, with software IRQLs being lower than hardware IRQLs. If an event occurs on a given processor that has a higher IRQL than the processor's current IRQL, the higher-priority event will interrupt the lower-priority event. If an event with an IRQL lower than the processor's current IRQL occurs on that CPU, processing of that event waits until all other events at higher IRQLs have been processed. Thus, the processor's current IRQL functions as an interrupt mask, deferring (masking) those activities requested at the same or lower IRQLs than the processor's current IRQL.

Because Windows NT executes on a broad range of system architectures, some of which differ widely in terms of their hardware priority support, NT uses a set of mnemonics to define IRQL values. Table 6.1 shows the standard Windows NT IRQL names, how they are used, and the numeric value assigned on x86 systems.

Table 6.1. Windows NT IRQL names.

IRQL Mnemonic	Numeric value on x86 Architecture Systems (for reference)	Example of Usage
HIGH_LEVEL	31	NMI, machine check
POWER_LEVEL	30	Power failure handling
SYNCH_LEVEL	30	Synchronization level
IPI_LEVEL	29	Inter-processor interrupt
CLOCK2_LEVEL	28	Clock handling

IRQL Mnemonic	Numeric value on x86 Architecture Systems (for reference)	Example of Usage
PROFILE_LEVEL	27	Profile timer
	12–27	Device IRQs on some x86 systems
DISPATCH_LEVEL	2	Dispatcher and DPCs
APC_LEVEL	1	Kernel APC handling; Paging
PASSIVE_LEVEL	0	Ordinary thread execution in both Kernel and User modes

The lower-level IRQLs (IRQLs PASSIVE_LEVEL through DISPATCH_LEVEL) are used internally for synchronization of the operating system software. These IRQLs are modeled as software interrupts. IRQLs above DISPATCH_LEVEL, whether they have a specific mnemonic or not, reflect hardware-interrupt priorities. Thus, these hardware IRQLs are often referred to as Device IRQLs (or DIRQLs).

The specific values assigned to the IRQL mnemonics vary from system to system. The relationship between the software IRQLs, and the fact that the software IRQLs are lower priorities than the hardware IRQLs, remains constant, however. Thus, IRQL PASSIVE_LEVEL is always the lowest IRQL in the system, APC_LEVEL is always higher than PASSIVE_LEVEL, and DISPATCH_LEVEL is always higher than APC_LEVEL. All these IRQLs are always lower than the lowest DIRQL.

Unlike the software IRQLs, the values assigned to and the relationship among the hardware IRQLs can change, depending on the system's hardware implementation. For example, as Table 6.1 illustrates, on x86 architecture systems, IRQL PROFILE_LEVEL is lower than IRQL IPI_LEVEL, which is in turn lower than IRQL POWER_LEVEL. On MIPS systems, however, IRQL POWER_LEVEL and IRQL IPI_LEVEL are the same value, and both are lower than IRQL PROFILE_LEVEL.

IRQLs Are Not Scheduling Priorities

A very important point to understand is that IRQLs are not the same as Windows NT process-scheduling priorities. In fact, all User mode thread execution takes place at IRQL PASSIVE_LEVEL. Scheduling priorities are artifacts of the Windows NT Dispatcher, which uses them to determine which thread to next make active.

IRQLs, on the other hand, are best thought of as interrupt priorities used by the operating system. An interrupt at any IRQL above PASSIVE_LEVEL will interrupt even the highest-priority User mode thread in the system. This is because, as stated previously, all user threads run at IRQL PASSIVE_LEVEL when they are running in User mode.

Determining the IRQL

The current IRQL is tracked on a per-CPU basis. A Kernel mode routine can determine the IRQL at which it is running by calling the function KeGetCurrentIrql(), the prototype for which is shown in Figure 6.1.

```
KIRQL
KeGetCurrentIrql();
```

Figure 6.1. KeGetCurrentIrql() *function prototype.*

KeGetCurrentIrql() returns the IRQL of the current CPU.

Most device driver routines are called by the I/O Manager at an architecturally defined IRQL. That is, the driver writer knows the IRQL(s) at which a given function will be called. Kernel mode routines may change the IRQL at which they are executing by calling the functions KeRaiseIrql() and KeLowerIrql(), the prototypes for which are shown in Figure 6.2 and Figure 6.3, respectively.

```
VOID
KeRaiseIrql(IN KIRQL NewIrql,
        OUT PKIRQL OldIrql);
```

NewIrql: The value to which the current processor's IRQL is to be raised.

OldIrql: A pointer to a location into which is returned the IRQL at which the current processor was running, before the IRQL was raised to *NewIrql*.

Figure 6.2. KeRaiseIrql() *function prototype.*

```
VOID
KeLowerIrql(IN KIRQL NewIrql);
```

NewIrql:The value to which the current processor's IRQL is to be lowered.

Figure 6.3. KeLowerIrql() *function prototype.*

Because IRQLs are a method of synchronization, most Kernel mode routines (specifically, device drivers) must **never** lower their IRQL beyond that at which they were called. Thus, drivers may call `KeRaiseIrql()` to raise to a higher IRQL, and then call `KeLowerIrql()` to return back to the original IRQL at which they were entered (from the I/O Manager, for example). However, a driver must **never** call `KeLowerIrql()` to lower its IRQL to a level less than that at which it was entered. Doing so can cause highly unpredictable system operation, which will likely end with a system crash.

How IRQLs Are Used

IRQLs are the chief method used for prioritizing operating system activities within Windows NT. Raising the IRQL allows an operating system routine to both control its re-entrancy and to ensure that it can continue its work without pre-emption by certain other activities. The following sections describe how the most common IRQLs are used within Windows NT.

IRQL PASSIVE_LEVEL

IRQL PASSIVE_LEVEL is the ordinary IRQL of execution in the operating system, both in User mode and Kernel mode. A routine running at IRQL PASSIVE_LEVEL is subject to interruption and pre-emption by almost anything else happening in the system. Thus, threads running at IRQL PASSIVE_LEVEL are subject to pre-emption by the Dispatcher at the end of their quantum. Pre-emption was discussed in Chapter 5, "Dispatching and Scheduling."

Most executive-level routines in Windows NT (that is, Kernel mode routines other than the Microkernel and the HAL) strive to keep the IRQL as low as possible. In most cases, this results in most routines running at IRQL PASSIVE_LEVEL. This policy maximizes the opportunity for higher IRQL activities to take place.

IRQL APC_LEVEL

IRQL APC_LEVEL is used by Kernel mode routines to control re-entrancy when processing Asynchronous Procedure Calls (APCs) in Kernel mode. APCs are operating system function callbacks that are required to take place within a particular process and thread context.

To fully understand how IRQL APC_LEVEL is used, take a look at an example of how APCs are used within the kernel. When the I/O Manager ultimately completes an I/O request for an application, it returns to the thread two longwords that make up the I/O status. The I/O status is returned in a location indicated by the application as part of its call to an I/O system service. In order for the I/O Manager to return the I/O status to the application, it must execute in the context of the application's process. That is, the application's address space must be mapped in the lower portion of kernel virtual address space (as discussed in Chapter 3, "Virtual Memory").

Of course, I/O operations are typically asynchronous in Windows NT, and thus may complete in an arbitrary thread context. The problem is, therefore, how the I/O Manager will return to the context of the requesting thread, so that it can complete the I/O request and return its I/O status information. The I/O Manager does this by requesting a special kernel APC. Specifically, the APC that is requested is the Special Kernel APC for I/O Completion, which is discussed in more detail in Chapter 10, "How I/O Requests Are Described," and in Chapter 14, "Dispatch Entry Points." The I/O Manager requests this APC and indicates the thread to which the APC is to be queued and a function to be called when the APC is granted.

The APC is requested by generating a software interrupt at IRQL APC_LEVEL. If the thread that is the target of the APC is currently executing on the current processor, and the current IRQL is less than APC_LEVEL, the Special Kernel APC for I/O Completion will be serviced immediately. The IRQL is raised to IRQL APC_LEVEL and the Special Kernel APC for I/O Completion routine is called.

If the target thread is currently executing on the current processor, but the processor's IRQL is IRQL APC_LEVEL or higher, the request for an APC_LEVEL interrupt is recorded and the APC is queued to the thread. The requested APC_LEVEL interrupt will be recognized when the IRQL drops to below APC_LEVEL. If at that time the currently executing thread is the target thread, the APC will be dequeued from the thread and the Special Kernel APC for I/O Completion will be processed.

If the target thread is not executing on the current processor, the Microkernel queues the APC to the thread, clears the APC_LEVEL interrupt on the current processor, and returns. The Special Kernel APC for I/O Completion will be processed when the target thread is next scheduled and the system is running at, or about to return to, an IRQL less than IRQL APC_LEVEL.

The point of this example is that when an APC is to be queued, it is queued to a particular thread. If that thread is running on the current processor, and the current processor's IRQL is below APC_LEVEL, the Special Kernel APC for I/O Completion is processed immediately. Thus, by manipulating the IRQL, the currently executing kernel routine can block the delivery of APCs. Further, because Kernel mode APC processing occurs at IRQL APC_LEVEL, the processing of Kernel mode APCs is serialized.

Although the entire foregoing discussion is correct, there are a number of subtleties that affect the delivery of Kernel mode APCs that we have glossed over. This is intentional. The point here is not to document in detail all of the undocumented behavior of Kernel mode APCs. Rather, it is our intention to provide a real example of how IRQL APC_LEVEL is used within the kernel.

IRQL DISPATCH_LEVEL

IRQL DISPATCH_LEVEL is used within Windows NT for two different activities:

- Processing Deferred Procedure Calls (DPCs)
- Running the Dispatcher (NT's scheduler)

DPC processing is discussed later in this chapter, in a section of its own. Therefore, we limit our present discussion to the Dispatcher. The Dispatcher, as described in Chapter 5, is Windows NT's thread scheduler. It is responsible for implementing the NT scheduling algorithm, which chooses what thread is executed and implements pre-emption at quantum end.

The Windows NT Dispatcher receives requests to perform a reschedule operation at IRQL DISPATCH_LEVEL. When the operating system decides to change the thread that is running on the current processor, it can sometimes call the Dispatcher directly. However, when the system is running at an IRQL higher than DISPATCH_LEVEL, it requests a DISPATCH_LEVEL software interrupt. This results in the Dispatcher running on the current processor the next time IRQL DISPATCH_LEVEL is the highest-priority interrupt to be serviced by the system.

Consider, for example, the case of a thread running in User mode. Because it is running in User mode, this thread is, of course, running at IRQL PASSIVE_LEVEL. While the thread is running, the clock is periodically interrupting to indicate the passage of time to the operating system. With each clock tick that passes, the clock interrupt service routine decrements the remaining quantum of the currently running thread. When the thread's remaining quantum is decremented to zero, the clock interrupt service routine generates a DISPATCH_LEVEL interrupt to request the Dispatcher to run and choose the next thread to run. Because the clock's interrupt service routine runs at an IRQL that is higher than DISPATCH_LEVEL (it runs at IRQL CLOCK2_LEVEL on x86 processors), processing of the request for the Dispatcher is deferred.

After generating the DISPATCH_LEVEL interrupt, the clock interrupt service routine finishes whatever other work it has to do and returns to the Microkernel.

The Microkernel then recognizes the next highest-priority interrupt that is pending. Each interrupt is serviced in turn. When there are no interrupts to service above DISPATCH_LEVEL, the DISPATCH_LEVEL interrupt service routine is executed. This interrupt service routine processes the DPC list (discussed later), and invokes the Dispatcher to choose a new thread to run.

When the Dispatcher is invoked, it notices that the current thread's quantum has been decremented to zero. The Dispatcher then implements Windows NT's scheduling algorithm to determine the next thread to be scheduled. If a new thread is chosen (the previously executing thread could be rescheduled), a context switch occurs. If there are no APCs pending for the newly selected thread, the thread's code will be executed when the system returns back to IRQL PASSIVE_LEVEL.

Other Kernel Routines Running at IRQL DISPATCH_LEVEL

IRQL DISPATCH_LEVEL is an important priority in Windows NT. Because the Dispatcher runs at IRQL DISPATCH_LEVEL, any routine that runs at IRQL DISPATCH_LEVEL or above is not subject to pre-emption. Thus, when a thread's quantum expires, if that thread is currently running at IRQL DISPATCH_LEVEL or above, it will continue to run until it attempts to drop the current processor's IRQL below DISPATCH_LEVEL. This should be obvious, because running at a given IRQL blocks the recognition of other events requested at that IRQL or at any lower IRQLs.

What may be less obvious is that when code is executing at IRQL DISPATCH_LEVEL or above, it cannot wait for any Dispatcher Objects that are not already signaled. Thus, for example, code running at IRQL DISPATCH_LEVEL or above cannot wait for an event or mutex to be set. This is because the act of yielding the processor requires (at least conceptually) the Dispatcher to run. However, if a routine is running at or above DISPATCH_LEVEL, the DISPATCH_LEVEL interrupt will be masked off and therefore not immediately recognized. The result? A return directly back to the code that issued the wait operation!

Even less obvious may be the fact that code running at IRQL DISPATCH_LEVEL or above may not take any page faults. This means that any such code must itself be non-paged, and must touch only data structures that are non-paged. This is essentially because code running at or above IRQL DISPATCH_LEVEL can't wait for a Dispatch Object to be signaled. Thus, even if a paging request was processed, the thread with the page fault couldn't be descheduled while the needed page was read in from disk!

DIRQLs

As mentioned previously, the IRQLs higher in priority than IRQL DISPATCH_LEVEL are called Device IRQLs (DIRQLs). These IRQLs are used for processing hardware interrupts from devices. When a device of a given IRQL interrupts, the interrupt service routine for that device executes at the synchronize IRQL that was specified when the device driver for that device connected to the interrupt. Connecting to interrupts and specifying a synchronize IRQL is described in detail in Chapter 13, "Driver Entry."

A vitally important point about DIRQLs is that these IRQLs do not necessarily preserve the relative priorities that may be implied by a given bus's external interrupt signaling method. For example, the HAL has complete discretion in terms of how it maps IRQs (bus Interrupt ReQuest lines) to IRQLs. In some HALs, such as the standard x86 architecture multiprocessor HAL, the IRQ assigned to a device may have no relationship to the IRQL assigned to that device (beyond ensuring that the device is mapped to an IRQL within the range of Device IRQLs).

Note

Because this can be such an important point for device driver writers in certain systems, we'll say it again: The relationship between two IRQs assigned to two particular devices is not necessarily preserved when IRQLs are assigned to those devices. Whether a device with a more important IRQ is assigned a higher (that is, more important) IRQL is totally up to the HAL. Indeed, in most standard x86 multiprocessor HALs for systems that use APIC architectures, the relationship of IRQ to IRQL is not preserved.

Suppose a system has two devices configured: Device A and Device B. Because the driver writer considers Device A more important than Device B, he assigned Device A to a more important (numerically lower) IRQ than device B. On some systems, such as DOS or Win9x, this implies that Device A can interrupt Device B. On Windows NT, the relationship between the interrupt priorities of these two devices is up to the HAL. Assigning them to particular IRQs indicates nothing beyond which line each device asserts when it wants to request an interrupt.

IRQL HIGH_LEVEL

IRQL HIGH_LEVEL is always defined as the highest IRQL on a Windows NT system. This IRQL is used for NMI (Non-Maskable Interrupt) and other interrupts of very high priority. In the exceedingly rare case in which a device driver needs to disable interrupts on a particular processor for a short period, the driver may raise its IRQL to HIGH_LEVEL. However, a device driver raising to IRQL HIGH_LEVEL is considered a very drastic step, and it is almost never required in Windows NT.

> **Note**
>
> *Raising the IRQL to* HIGH_LEVEL *should be something that most drivers in Windows NT never do. Disabling interrupts is a commonly used method for achieving synchronization on other operating systems (such as DOS or Win9x). However, on Windows NT, simply raising to IRQL* HIGH_LEVEL *for synchronization purposes will not work on multiprocessor systems. Kernel mode code performs serialization by using spin locks, which are described in detail in Chapter 7, "Multiprocessor Issues."*

Deferred Procedure Calls (DPCs)

In addition to its use for running the NT Dispatcher, IRQL DISPATCH_LEVEL is also used for processing Deferred Procedure Calls (DPCs). DPCs are callbacks to routines to be run at IRQL DISPATCH_LEVEL. DPCs are typically requested from higher IRQLs to allow more extended, non-time-critical, processing to take place.

Let's look at a couple of examples of when DPCs are used. Windows NT device drivers perform very little processing within their interrupt service routines. Instead, when a device interrupts (at DIRQL) and its driver determines that a significant amount of processing is required, the driver requests a DPC. The DPC request results in a specified driver function being called back at IRQL DISPATCH_LEVEL to perform the remainder of the required processing. By performing this processing at IRQL DISPATCH_LEVEL, the driver takes less time at DIRQL, and therefore decreases interrupt latency for all the other devices on the system.

Another common use for DPCs is in timer routines. A driver may request to have a particular function be called to notify it that a certain period of time has elapsed (this is done using the KeSetTimer() function, which is described in Chapter 16, "Programmed I/O Data Transfers"). The clock interrupt service routine keeps track of passing time, and when the specified time period has elapsed, requests a DPC for the routine that the driver specified. Using DPCs for timer notification allows the clock interrupt service routine to return quickly, but still results in the specified timer routines being called without undue delay.

DPC Objects

A DPC is described by a DPC Object. The definition of a DPC Object (KDPC) appears in ntddk.h and is shown in Figure 6.4.

DPC Object (KDPC)

Importance	Number	Type
	DpcListEntry	
	DeferredRoutine	
	DeferredContext	
	SystemArgument1	
	SystemArgument2	
	Lock	

Figure 6.4. *DPC Object.*

A DPC Object may be allocated by a driver from any nonpageable space (such as nonpaged pool). DPC objects are initialized by using the function KeInitializeDpc(), the prototype for which appears in Figure 6.5.

VOID
KeInitializeDpc(IN PKDPC *Dpc,*
        IN PKDEFERRED_ROUTINE *DeferredRoutine,*
        IN PVOID *DeferredContext*);

Dpc: Points to the DPC object to be initialized.

DeferredRoutine: A pointer to the function to which the deferred call is to be made at IRQL DISPATCH_LEVEL.

DeferredContext: A value to be passed to the *DeferredRoutine* as a parameter, along with a pointer to the DPC object and two additional parameters.

Figure 6.5. KeInitializeDpc() *function prototype.*

A request to execute a particular DPC routine is made by placing the DPC Object that describes that DPC routine into the DPC Queue of a given CPU, and then (typically) requesting an IRQL DISPATCH_LEVEL software interrupt. There is one DPC Queue per processor. The CPU to which the DPC Object is queued is typically the current processor on which the request is issued. How the processor for a particular DPC is chosen is discussed later in this chapter, in the section "DPC Object Characteristics." A DPC object is queued by using the KeInsertQueueDpc() function, as shown in Figure 6.6.

VOID
KeInsertQueueDpc(IN PKDPC *Dpc*,
     IN PVOID *SystemArgument1*,
     IN PVOID *SystemArgument2*);

Dpc: Points to the DPC object to be queued.

SystemArgument1: A value to be passed to the *DeferredRoutine* as a parameter, along with a *SystemArgument2*, a pointer to the DPC object, and the *DeferredContext* argument specified when the DPC Object was initialized.

SystemArgument2: A value to be passed to the *DeferredRoutine* as a parameter, along with *SystemArgument1*, a pointer to the DPC object, and the *DeferredContext* argument specified when the DPC Object was initialized.

Figure 6.6. KeInsertQueueDpc() *function prototype.*

Invoking and Servicing DPCs

Issuing a DISPATCH_LEVEL software interrupt results in the processor recognizing the interrupt when it becomes the highest IRQL event pending on that processor. Thus, after calling KeInsertQueueDpc(), typically the next time the processor is ready to return to an IRQL below DISPATCH_LEVEL, it will return instead to IRQL DISPATCH_LEVEL and attempt to process the contents of the DPC Queue.

> **Note**
>
> *As noted earlier in the chapter, IRQL DISPATCH_LEVEL is used both for dispatching and for processing the DPC Queue. In NT V4, when a DISPATCH_LEVEL interrupt is processed, the entire DPC Queue is serviced first, and then the Dispatcher is called to schedule the next thread to run. This is reasonable because the processing done within a DPC routine could change to alter the state of the thread scheduling database, for example, by making a previously waiting thread runnable.*

The DPC Queue is serviced by the Microkernel. Each time the DPC Queue is serviced, all entries on the DPC Queue for the current processor are processed. One at a time, the Microkernel removes a DPC Object from the head of the DPC Queue, and calls the *DeferredRoutine* indicated within the DPC Object. The Microkernel passes as parameters to the *DeferredRoutine* a pointer to the DPC Object, plus the contents of the *DeferredContext, SystemArgument1*, and *SystemArgument2* field of the DPC Object.

Because the DPC Queue is serviced at IRQL DISPATCH_LEVEL, DPC routines are called at IRQL DISPATCH_LEVEL. Because the DPC Queue is serviced whenever IRQL DISPATCH_LEVEL is the highest priority IRQL to be serviced (such as immediately after an interrupt service routine has run and before returning to the interrupted user thread), DPCs run in an *arbitrary thread context.* By arbitrary thread context, we mean that the DPC executes in a process and thread that may be entirely unrelated to the request that the DPC is processing. Execution context is described in more detail in Chapter 11, "The Layered Driver Model."

The DPC routine completes its processing and returns by executing a return statement. On return from a DPC routine, the Microkernel attempts to remove another DPC Object from the DPC Queue and process it. When the DPC Queue is empty, DPC processing is complete. The Microkernel proceeds to call the Dispatcher.

Multiple DPC Invocations

A given DPC is described by a specific DPC Object. As a result, whenever KeInsertQueueDpc() is called and detects that the DPC Object passed to it is already on a DPC Queue, KeInsertQueueDpc() simply returns (taking no action). Thus, whenever a DPC Object is already on a DPC Queue, any subsequent requests to queue that same DPC Object that occur prior to the DPC Object being removed from the DPC Queue are ignored. This makes sense because the DPC Object can physically be linked into only one DPC Queue list at one time.

The next obvious question might be: What happens when a request is made to queue a DPC Object, but the system is already executing the DPC routine indicated by that DPC Object (on the current or a different processor)? The answer to this question can be found by a careful reading of the previous section of this chapter. When the Microkernel services the DPC Queue, it removes the DPC Object at the head of the queue, and *then* calls the DPC routine indicated by the DPC Object. Thus, when the DPC routine is called, the DPC Object has been removed from the processor's DPC Queue. Therefore, when a request is made to queue a DPC Object and the system is executing within the DPC routine specified in that DPC Object, the DPC is queued as normal.

DPCs on Multiprocessor Systems

Contrary to what has been stated in other publications, and as should be evident from the preceding discussions, a single DPC routine may be actively executing on multiple processors are the same time. There is absolutely no interlocking performed by the Microkernel to prevent this.

Consider the case of a device driver that has multiple requests outstanding on its device at a time. The driver's device interrupts on Processor 0, the driver's interrupt service routine executes, and subsequently requests a DPC to complete interrupt processing. This is the standard way that drivers work in Windows NT. When the interrupt service routine completes and the system is ready to return to the user thread that was interrupted, Processor 0's IRQL is lowered from the DIRQL at which the ISR ran to IRQL DISPATCH_LEVEL. As a result, the Microkernel services the DPC Queue, removing the driver's DPC Object and calling the indicated DPC routine. The driver's DPC routine is now executing on Processor 0.

Just after the driver's DPC routine has been called, the device once again interrupts. This time, however, for reasons known only to the hardware, the interrupt is serviced on Processor 1. Again, the driver's interrupt service routine requests a DPC. And, again, when the interrupt service routine is complete, the system (Processor 1) is ready to return to the interrupted user thread. During this process, Processor 1's IRQL is lowered to IRQL DISPATCH_LEVEL, and the Microkernel services the DPC Queue. In so doing (and still running on Processor 1), it removes the driver's DPC Object and calls the driver's DPC routine. The driver's DPC routine is now executing on Processor 1. Assuming that the driver's DPC routine has not yet completed running on Processor 0, note that the same DPC routine is now running in parallel on both processors.

> ### Note
>
> *This example highlights the importance of utilizing the proper set of multiprocessor synchronization mechanisms in drivers. Specifically, spin locks must be used to serialize access to any data structures that must be accessed atomically within the driver's DPC if the driver's design is such that multiple DPCs can be in progress simultaneously. Spin locks are described in detail in Chapter 7, "Multiprocessor Issues."*

DPC Object Characteristics

DPC Objects have two characteristics that influence the way they are processed. These characteristics are the Importance and Number fields, which can be seen in Figure 6.4 and are discussed in greater detail in the sections that follow.

DPC Importance

Each DPC Object has an importance, which is stored in the DPC Object's
Importance field. The values for importance are enumerated in ntddk.h as being
HighImportance, MediumImportance, and LowImportance. The importance of a DPC
Object affects where in the DPC Queue the DPC Object is placed when it is
queued, and whether or not an IRQL DISPATCH_LEVEL interrupt is issued when
the DPC Object is queued. KeInitializeDpc() initializes DPC Objects with
MediumImportance. The Importance of a DPC Object can be set by using the
function KeSetImportanceDpc(), the prototype for which appears in Figure 6.7.

VOID
KeSetImportanceDpc(IN PKDPC *Dpc,*
        IN KDPC_IMPORTANCE *Importance*);

Dpc: Points to the DPC object in which the Importance field is to be set.
Importance: The importance value to set into the DPC Object.

Figure 6.7. KeInsertQueueDpc() *function prototype.*

DPC Objects with either MediumImportance or LowImportance are placed on the
end of the DPC Queue when they are queued. DPC Objects with
HighImportance are queued at the beginning of the DPC Queue.

The importance of a DPC Object also affects whether or not a DISPATCH_LEVEL
software interrupt is generated when the DPC Object is placed on the DPC
Queue. When a HighImportance or MediumImportance DPC Object is queued to
the current processor, a DISPATCH_LEVEL interrupt is always generated. The
DISPATCH_LEVEL interrupt is generated for LowImportance DPCs or for DPCs that
are specifically targeted to a processor other than the current processor, according to a complex (and undocumented) scheduling algorithm.

> ### Note
>
> *Most device drivers should never need to set the importance of their DPC
> Objects. In the rare case that the latency between requesting a DPC and
> that DPC running is excessive, and the driver writer is not able to solve
> this latency through other means, you can try setting the DPC Object to
> HighImportance. Typically, however, device drivers on Windows NT do
> not alter their DPC importance from the default of MediumImportance.*

DPC Target Processor

In addition to an importance, each DPC Object has a *target processor.* This
target processor is stored in the Number field of the DPC Object. The target

processor indicates whether or not a DPC is restricted to execute on a given processor on the system, and, if so, on which processor. By default, KeInitializeDpc() does not specify a target processor. Consequently, by default, DPCs will run on the processor on which they were requested (that is, the DPC will be invoked on the processor on which KeInsertQueueDpc() was called).

A DPC may be restricted to executing on a specific processing using the KeSetTargetProcessorDpc() function, the prototype for which is shown in Figure 6.8.

VOID
KeSetTargetProcessorDpc(IN PKDPC *Dpc*,
      IN CCHAR *Number*);

Dpc: Points to the DPC object for which the target processor is to be set.

Number: The zero-based processor number on which the DPC is to be executed.

Figure 6.8. KeSetTargetProcessorDpc() *function prototype.*

Note

Like DPC importance, a DPC's target processor is almost never set by a device driver. The default behavior, which is for the DPC to execute on the current processor, is the behavior that is almost always desired.

When a specific target processor is set for a DPC Object, that DPC Object will always be queued on the indicated processor's DPC Queue. Thus, for example, even though KeInsertQueueDpc() is called on Processor 0, a DPC Object with its target processor set to Processor 1 will be inserted on the DPC Queue for Processor 1.

The DpcForIsr

As discussed previously in this chapter, the most common use of DPCs is for Interrupt Service Routine (ISR) completion. To make it easy for device drivers to request DPCs for ISR completion from their ISRs, the I/O Manager defines a specific DPC that may be used for this purpose. This DPC is called the *DpcForIsr*.

The I/O Manager embeds a DPC Object in each Device Object that it creates. This embedded DPC Object is initialized by a device driver, typically when the driver is first loaded, by calling the function IoInitializeDpcRequest() (see Figure 13.18 and the related description in Chapter 13). IoInitializeDpcRequest() takes as input a pointer to the Device Object in which the DPC Object is embedded, a pointer to a driver function to call, and a context value to pass to that function. IoInitializeDpcRequest(), in turn, calls KeInitializeDpc() to initialize the embedded DPC Object, passing the pointer to the driver's function as the *DeferredRoutine* parameter and the context value as the *DeferredContext* parameter.

To request the DPC from its ISR, a driver simply calls IoRequestDpc() (see Figure 13.2 and surrounding text), passing a pointer to a Device Object. IoRequestDpc() in turn calls KeInsertQueueDpc() for the DPC Object embedded in the Device Object.

Because all device drivers have Device Objects, and all drivers that utilize interrupts also utilize DPCs, using the I/O Manager's DpcForIsr mechanism is very convenient. In fact, most device drivers in Windows NT never directly call KeInitializeDpc() or KeInsertQueueDpc(), but call IoInitializeDpcRequest() and IoRequestDpc() instead.

Chapter 7

Multiprocessor Issues

This chapter will review:

- **The Problem with Shared Data.** This section describes the problem with sharing data between two simultaneously executing entities.

- **Using Locks to Serialize Access to Shared Data.** This section describes how locks are used to serialize, and thus protect, access to shared data.

- **Spin Locks.** Spin locks are the tools provided by the NT operating system to allow Kernel mode programmers to protect shared data. This section describes the two types of spin locks available to driver writers on Windows NT. It also describes how these locks are implemented on both multiprocessor and uniprocessor systems.

- **Spin Lock Issues.** This section discusses a few implementation issues with using spin locks efficiently.

Because Windows NT supports multiprocessing, all Kernel mode code must be multiprocessor-safe. Multiprocessor safety involves maintaining cache coherency among processors, virtual memory issues, and even interrupt handling. Fortunately, the Microkernel and the HAL handle most of these issues transparently to the driver writer.

However, as discussed briefly in several prior chapters, driver writers must be careful to properly synchronize access to shared data structures. Of course, care in synchronizing access to shared data is required anytime a routine can be re-entered. This is the case, even on a uniprocessor implementation of Windows NT. However, adding multiproessor support makes such synchronization even more vital. This chapter describes the problems inherent in sharing data structures in a multiprocessor environment. You will also become familiar with the tools that Windows NT makes available to driver writers to help solve those problems. The chapter concludes the discussion of multi-processor issues with a description of enforcing atomic operation on uniprocessor systems.

The Problem with Shared Data

Anytime a data structure is shared among two threads of processing, there is the potential for sharing problems if each thread does not have exclusive access to the data being shared for the time period during which the data is being modified. Consider, for example, two threads, each of which attempts to increment a reference count on a data structure (see Figure 7.1).

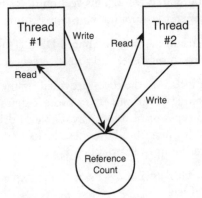

Figure 7.1. *The need for synchronizing access to shared data structures.*

Thread #1 reads the reference count, increments it, and writes it back to its storage location in memory. Thread #2 does the same thing—it reads the reference count, increments it, and writes it back to memory. A problem occurs either if Thread #1 is pre-empted between the time it reads the value and the time it writes it back, or if Thread #1 and Thread #2 execute in parallel on two different processors. The problem scenario is:

1. Thread #1, executing on Processor 0, reads the reference count from the data structure into a register. The value read for the reference count is zero.

2. Thread #2, simultaneously executing on Processor 1, reads the reference count from the data structure into a register. The value read for the reference count is also zero.

3. Thread #1 increments the value. The reference count value that Thread #1 has in its internal register is now one.

4. Thread #2 increments the value. The reference count value that Thread #2 has internally is now one.

5. Thread #1 writes the value back to storage. The reference count is one.

6. Thread #2 writes the value back to storage. The reference count is one.

This sequence of processing results in a reference count that is incorrect because, with two threads actively referencing a data structure, the reference count should obviously be two.

Using Locks to Serialize Access to Shared Data

The solution to the problem of simultaneous access to shared data is to use a lock to guard the reference count. Before the reference count can be modified, the lock must be acquired. After the reference count has been modified, the lock is released. Thus, using locks to properly implement the reference count example described in the last section, the sequence of operations is as follows:

1. Thread #1, executing on Processor 0, attempts to acquire the lock that guards the reference count. The lock is successfully acquired.

2. Thread #2, simultaneously executing on Processor 1, attempts to acquire the lock that guards the reference count. The lock cannot be acquired because it is already owned by Thread #1. Thread #2 therefore waits.

3. Thread #1 reads the reference count from the data structure into a register. The value read for the reference count is zero.

4. Thread #1 increments the value. The reference count value that Thread #1 has in its internal register is now one.

5. Thread #1 writes the value back to storage. The reference count is one.

6. Thread #1 releases the lock guarding the reference count.

7. Thread #2 resumes executing.

8. Thread #2 reads the reference count from the data structure into a register. The value read for the reference count is one.

9. Thread #2 increments the value. The reference count value that Thread #2 has internally is now two.

10. Thread #2 writes the value back to storage. The reference count is two.

11. Thread #2 releases the lock guarding the reference count.

This sequence of processing results in a reference count that is correct.

An appropriate Dispatcher Object, such as a mutex, can be used for synchronization to guard the shared data structure. This works fine, as long as all the threads that modify the data being shared execute only at IRQL PASSIVE_LEVEL or IRQL APC_LEVEL. Thus, using a mutex would be a perfect solution for synchronizing access to data that is shared between two user threads because User-mode threads always execute at IRQL PASSIVE_LEVEL.

However, using a Dispatcher Object such as a mutex would not be possible if any thread that modifies the shared data is running at IRQL DISPATCH_LEVEL or above. This is due to the fact that running at IRQL DISPATCH_LEVEL or higher blocks recognition of the DISPTACH_LEVEL interrupt that is used to trigger the Dispatcher. Thus, it is impossible for a thread running at IRQL DISPATCH_LEVEL or above to yield control of the processor to wait, in case the Dispatcher Object is not available. This was discussed in detail in Chapter 6, "Interrupt Request Levels and DPCs."

Spin Locks

Fortunately, there is a simple solution to sharing data when one or more of the modifying threads may be running at IRQL DISPATCH_LEVEL or above. The solution is to use a spin lock.

Spin locks are standard Windows NT data structures, located in nonpageable memory. Every spin lock has an IRQL implicitly associated with it. That IRQL is at least IRQL DISPATCH_LEVEL, and it is the highest IRQL from which the lock may ever be acquired. Spin locks may be used only by routines running in Kernel mode because they imply a transition to an IRQL above PASSIVE_LEVEL. Figure 7.2 illustrates the process of acquiring a spin lock on a multiprocessor system.

As Figure 7.2 illustrates, the reason spin locks have their name is that if the lock is not available, the thread that attempts to acquire the lock simply spins (or "busy waits" as it is often called), repeatedly trying to acquire the lock until the lock is free. Of course, because this spinning occurs at IRQL DISPATCH_LEVEL or above, the processor on which the lock is being acquired is not dispatchable. Thus, even when the currently executing thread's quantum expires, the thread will continue running.

When an attempt is made to acquire a spin lock, the routine called to acquire the lock does not return to the caller until the lock has been acquired. In addition, there is no interface available to driver writers to enable the specification of a timeout value. Finally, there is no interface available to check the state of a spin lock before attempting to acquire it.

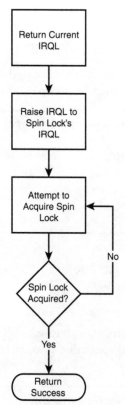

Figure 7.2. *Acquiring a spin lock on a multiprocessor system.*

There are two kinds of spin locks: Executive Spin Locks and Interrupt Spin Locks. Each of these spin locks is acquired in a different way, and is used for a slightly different purpose. The following sections describe each of these spin locks in detail.

Executive Spin Locks

Executive Spin Locks are the type of spin lock most frequently used in an NT device driver. They are defined in ntddk.h as data structure type KSPIN_LOCK. Executive Spin Locks operate at IRQL DISPATCH_LEVEL. Storage for an Executive Spin Lock is allocated by the lock's creator from nonpageable storage. For device drivers, this means that spin locks are typically allocated from non-paged pools. After space for the lock has been allocated, the lock is initialized by using the function KeInitializeSpinLock(), the prototype for which is shown in Figure 7.3.

VOID
KeInitializeSpinLock(IN PKSPIN_LOCK *SpinLock*);

SpinLock: A pointer to previously allocated storage for spin lock to be initialized. This storage must be non-pageable.

Figure 7.3. KeInitializeSpinLock() *function prototype.*

Once a spin lock has been initialized, it may be acquired. Executive Spin Locks may be acquired by callers running at less than or equal to IRQL DISPATCH_LEVEL by calling KeAcquireSpinLock(), the prototype for which is shown in Figure 7.4.

VOID
KeAcquireSpinLock(IN PKSPIN_LOCK *SpinLock*,
        OUT PKIRQL *OldIrql*);

SpinLock: A pointer to previously initialized spin lock to be acquired.

OldIrql: A pointer to a location into which to return the IRQL at which the processor was executing prior to the spin lock being acquired.

Figure 7.4. KeAcquireSpinLock() *function prototype.*

When KeAcquireSpinLock() is called on a multiprocessor system, the steps shown earlier in Figure 7.2 are taken. The current IRQL at which the processor is running is first saved. Next, KeAcquireSpinLock() raises the IRQL on the current processor to IRQL DISPATCH_LEVEL. The function next tries to acquire the indicated spin lock, repeatedly if necessary, until the attempt succeeds. When the indicated spin lock has been acquired, KeAcquireSpinLock() returns to its caller.

Spin locks are mutual exclusion locks. This means that they may be acquired by only one requestor at a time. Spin locks are not recursively acquirable. An attempt to acquire a spin lock that is already held by the calling thread is a fatal error and will result in the (Free Build of the) system hanging.

Note

> *Remember: After an Executive Spin Lock has been successfully acquired, the caller is running at IRQL* DISPATCH_LEVEL. *Thus, for the entire time that the spin lock is held, only actions that are legal at IRQL* DISPATCH_LEVEL *(as discussed in the previous chapter) may be taken by the driver.*

Of course, if the caller knows that it is already running at IRQL DISPATCH_LEVEL, returning the current IRQL and then attempting to raise it to IRQL DISPATCH_LEVEL is a waste of time. This would be the case, for example, when a driver is running within a DPC routine. Therefore, NT provides an optimized version of KeAcquireSpinLock() for use when the caller is already running at DISPATCH_LEVEL. This function is called KeAcquireSpinLockAtDpcLevel(). The prototype for this function is shown in Figure 7.5.

VOID
KeAcquireSpinLockAtDpcLevel(IN PKSPIN_LOCK *SpinLock*);

SpinLock: A pointer to previously initialized spin lock to be acquired.

Figure 7.5. KeAcquireSpinLockAtDpcLevel() *function prototype.*

KeAcquireSpinLockAtDpcLevel() works exactly the same way as KeAcquireSpinLock() except, as previously mentioned, it assumed the caller is running at IRQL DISPATCH_LEVEL. It therefore does not bother to raise the IRQL of the current processor to IRQL DISPATCH_LEVEL and, because the pre-call IRQL is assumed to be DISPATCH_LEVEL, it does not return the previous IRQL to the caller.

It is very important to note that it is a very serious logic error to acquire an Executive Spin Lock when running at an IRQL greater than IRQL DISPATCH_LEVEL. This is because the IRQL of an Executive Spin Lock is IRQL DISPATCH_LEVEL, which is the highest IRQL at which an Executive Spin Lock can be acquired. Because Executive Spin Locks cannot be acquired from IRQLs above DISPATCH_LEVEL, Executive Spin Locks can never be acquired from within an interrupt service routine. Attempting to acquire an Executive Spin Lock from an IRQL greater than DISPATCH_LEVEL results in a crash with the error code IRQL_NOT_GREATER_OR_EQUAL.

Executive Spin Locks that were acquired with KeAcquireSpinLock() must be released using the function KeReleaseSpinLock(). Executive Spin Locks that were acquired with the function KeAcquireSpinLockAtDpcLevel() must be released using the function KeReleaseSpinLockFromDpcLevel(). The prototypes for these two functions are shown in Figure 7.6 and Figure 7.7, respectively.

VOID
KeReleaseSpinLock(IN PKSPIN_LOCK *SpinLock*,
    IN KIRQL *NewIrql*);

SpinLock: A pointer to a spin lock to release.

NewIrql: IRQL to which to return after the spin lock has been released.

Figure 7.6. KeReleaseSpinLock() *function prototype.*

VOID
KeReleaseSpinLockFromDpcLevel(IN PKSPIN_LOCK *SpinLock*);

SpinLock: A pointer to a spin lock to release.

Figure 7.7. KeReleaseSpinLockFromDpcLevel() *function prototype.*

Both of these functions release the indicated spin lock, and thus make it available for acquisition by another requestor. The only difference between the two is that after releasing the spin lock, KeReleaseSpinLockFromDpcLevel() stays at IRQL DISPATCH_LEVEL, whereas after releasing the spin lock, KeReleaseSpinLock() returns to the IRQL indicated by *NewIrql* on the function call.

> *Tip*
>
> *Notice that the names of the routines used to acquire a spin lock from* DISPATCH_LEVEL *and to release it are not symmetrical. The function to acquire the spin lock is* KeAcquireSpinLock**At**DpcLevel()*; the function to release a spin lock thereby acquired is* KeReleaseSpinLock**From**DpcLevel()*. Also, notice that these calls refer to IRQL* DISPATCH_LEVEL *as "DPC level." This name is slang for the IRQL level at which DPCs run—* DISPATCH_LEVEL*. Officially, however, there is not now, and never has been since NT V3.1, an IRQL* DPC_LEVEL *defined in* ntddk.h.

Using Multiple Executive Spin Locks Simultaneously

In complex drivers, it is often necessary to acquire a second Executive Spin Lock while already holding another Executive Spin Lock. Although the DDK clearly states that driver writers should "avoid using nested spin locks" (section 16.2.5 of the Kernel-Mode Guide), this is not typically possible. The problem the DDK is trying to help avoid is the problem of deadlocks. The process illustrated in Table 7.1 shows one example of a deadlock.

Table 7.1. A "deadly embrace" deadlock.

Code Path on Processor #1		Code Path on Processor #2
Attempt to acquire spin lock FOO (successful)		Attempt to acquire spin lock BAR (successful)
Do some work		Do some work
Acquire spin lock BAR	←Deadlock→	Acquire spin lock FOO

In Table 7.1, the thread executing on Processor #1 calls KeAcquireSpinLock() and successfully acquires the spin lock at location FOO. It does this presumably because it needs to modify the data located in a shared data area protected by FOO. More or less simultaneously, the thread running on Processor #2 calls KeAcquireSpinLock() to acquire the spin lock at location BAR. Again, this is assumed because this thread needs to modify the data protected by the BAR spin lock. Next, the thread running on Processor #1 decides that it (also) needs to modify the data protected by the BAR spin lock. Thus, it calls KeAcquireSpinLock(), specifying spin lock BAR. Because spin lock BAR is currently held by the thread running on Processor #2, the thread on Processor #1 spins, waiting for the lock to become available. Finally, the thread running on Processor #2 that is holding the BAR spin lock decides that it needs to modify some data protected by the FOO spin lock. The Processor #2 thread then calls KeAcquireSpinLock() in an attempt to acquire spin lock FOO. Of course, because the thread running on Processor #1 is holding the FOO spin lock, the thread running on Processor #2 spins, waiting for the FOO spin lock to become free.

The result? The system is hopelessly deadlocked. This type of deadlock is called a "deadly embrace." When will this situation be resolved? Whenever the user presses the reset button on the system!

This situation is all too common in the real world of developing device drivers. Consider the device driver that needs to remove a request from one queue while placing it on another. If each queue is guarded by a different spin lock and the locks are not managed correctly, the deadlock problem cited earlier is a real possibility.

Fortunately, such problems are very easy to avoid. Whenever multiple locks are used, a locking hierarchy must be defined. The locking hierarchy simply lists all the locks in the system that could possibly be held simultaneously, and prescribes the order in which these locks must be acquired whenever multiple locks are required. A locking hierarchy is typically created by listing the locks used in a system, from left to right, in order of frequency of their acquisition. This list becomes the hierarchy. Whenever multiple locks must be held simultaneously, the locks are acquired in the order in which they appear in the list. This process works with any number of locks.

For our FOO and BAR spin lock example, cited earlier, we could create a simple locking hierarchy that lists: FOO, BAR. This hierarchy means that "any time we need to hold both Executive Spin Locks FOO and BAR, acquire FOO first and then acquire BAR." Note that if we need to acquire *only* BAR to modify the data that it protects, we do not necessarily need to also acquire FOO. We need to acquire both spin locks only when we need to simultaneously modify the data that both spin locks protect. And, when we need to hold both spin locks, we must acquire them in the order specified in the hierarchy.

> **Note**
>
> *The order in which the locks are released is not important (as long as the correct IRQL is preserved). You can't cause a deadlock by releasing spin locks in the wrong order.*

The example illustrated in Table 7.2 shows the FOO and BAR example from Table 7.1 corrected to properly implement the locking hierarchy previously mentioned.

Table 7.2. Using two Executive Spin Locks—deadlock-free.

Code Path on Processor #1	Code Path on Processor #2
Attempt to acquire spin lock FOO (successful)	Attempt to acquire spin lock BAR (successful)
Do some work	Do some work
Acquire spin lock BAR	Release spin lock BAR
Do more work	Attempt to acquire spin lock FOO (spin, waiting)
Release spin lock BAR	
Release spin lock FOO	Succesfully acquire spin lock FOO
	Attempt to acquire spin lock BAR
	Do some other work
	Release spin lock BAR
	Release spin lock FOO

In Table 7.2, the thread on Processor #1 acquires spin lock FOO, and the thread on Processor #2 acquires spin lock BAR, just as it was before the locking hierarchy was introduced. When the thread on Processor #1 needs to acquire BAR, it may simply acquire it because it has already acquired FOO, and the locking hierarchy states that if both FOO and BAR are required, BAR may not be acquired unless FOO is already held. Thus, when the thread on Processor #2 decides that it needs to hold both FOO and BAR simultaneously, it first releases BAR. This is because, according to our locking hierarchy, if both FOO and BAR are needed, FOO must be acquired before BAR can be acquired. With BAR released, the thread on Processor #2 is free to attempt to acquire FOO (which eventually succeeds after a short wait), and then acquire BAR.

The result? Processing is deadlock-free.

> **Note**
>
> *The only trick to using locking hierarchies is that the code that acquires multiple spin locks must be aware of which spin locks it requires, and which spin locks have already been acquired. This isn't impossible, or even extraordinarily difficult. It just requires some advance planning and design on the part of the driver writer.*

Debugging Executive Spin Locks

It is a little-known fact that the Checked Build of Windows NT (described in Chapter 18, "Building and Debugging") provides a few helpful assists for debugging problems with Executive Spin Locks—at least on x86 architecture systems. As with many internal features of Windows NT, these are not documented, so their behavior is subject to change without notice.

One helpful feature in the Checked Build checks to see whether a thread attempts to acquire a spin lock that it already owns. If this occurs, the Checked Build crashes with a STOP error. Kii386SpinOnSpinLock will be found a few locations down the kernel stack. The kernel virtual address of the spin lock is the STOP code. If a debugger is hooked up when the crash occurs, a message similar to the following is displayed:

```
*** Fatal System Error: 0xF962F6A0 (0x00000000,0x00000000,0x00000000,0x00000000)
```

The error code (0xF962F6A0 from the preceding message) is the kernel virtual address of the spin lock that has been attempted to be recursively acquired. The current thread is the thread that attempted to recursively acquire the lock.

Similarly, the Checked Build includes a spin lock timeout. This timeout appears to be rather short (less than a second). Therefore, it is possible to encounter this timeout on the rare occasion when you have a hotly contested spin lock on a system with many processors, when one processor has to wait a long time for the lock. If a debugger is not hooked up to the checked system when the time-out occurs, the system crashes with a KMODE_EXCEPTION_NOT_HANDLED error. If a debugger is attached when the timeout occurs, the message "Hard coded breakpoint hit" is displayed. At the top of the kernel stack will be the function SpinLockSpinningForTooLong. Simply resuming from the breakpoint (typing "G" in WinDbg) will result in additional attempts to acquire the spin lock, with corresponding time out.

Interrupt Spin Locks

Interrupt Spin Locks, which are sometimes referred to as *ISR spin locks*, are the rarer of the two types of spin locks on Windows NT. Interrupt Spin Locks operate at a DIRQL, specifically the *SynchronizeIrql* that is specified when a driver calls IoConnectInterrupt() (which is described in Chapter 13, "Driver Entry"—refer to Figure 13.7 and the surrounding text). Interrupt Spin Locks are always associated with a particular Interrupt Object, and are thus associated with a particular interrupt service routine for a particular device. Interrupt Spin Locks are typically stored within an Interrupt Object, although they may be stored externally to the Interrupt Object and be pointed to by a field in the Interrupt Object (again, see Chapter 13 for a complete explanation). Interrupt Spin Locks are initialized by the I/O Manager when IoConnectInterrupt() is called.

The Interrupt Spin Lock for a particular interrupt service routine is always acquired by the Microkernel prior to its calling the interrupt service routine. The Microkernel releases the Interrupt Spin Lock after the interrupt service routine returns.

> **Note**
>
> *Note that if the appropriate Interrupt Spin Lock is acquired and released by the Microkernel around a driver's interrupt service routine, that interrupt service routine will always be running holding the spin lock. This means that the ISR connected to a given vector by a given Interrupt Object will never be running on two processors simultaneously! This is described in much greater detail in Chapters 13 and 15.*

Driver routines other than the interrupt service routine may acquire a particular Interrupt Spin Lock by calling KeSynchronizeExecution(). This is the only way that an Interrupt Spin Lock can be acquired by a driver (aside from having the Microkernel automatically acquire the Interrupt Spin Lock prior to calling the driver's interrupt service routine). KeSynchronizeExecution() in particular, and Interrupt Spin Locks in general, are described in more detail in Chapter 15, "Interrupt Service Routines and DPCs."

Spin Lock Implementations on Uniprocessor Systems

The Windows NT operating system code is different on uniprocessor systems than it is on multiprocessor systems. For example, because there is only one processor on a uniprocessor system, spinning waiting for a spin lock to become free is not useful (because there is no other processor on which a thread could release the lock!).

Using spin locks, however, results in execution of the "locked" code sequence at IRQL DISPATCH_LEVEL. This masks DISPATCH_LEVE interrupts on the processor, and thus disabled preemption on that processor. Consider, for example, the case of inserting an entry into a doubly linked list. On a multiprocessor system, you might worry about a DPC routine executing on this processor or another processor attempting to simultaneously update the same list. On a uniprocessor system, you would still need to be assured that the thread inserting the entry was not interrupted at IRQL DISPATCH_LEVEL or pre-empted (that is, descheduled) midway through its insertion. If another thread were to come along and attempt to insert an entry into the same list, the list would obviously be corrupted.

Thus, even on uniprocessor systems, drivers must protect atomic operations by using locks. Where code may be running at IRQLs greater than or equal to IRQL DISPATCH_LEVEL, such atomic operations must be protected with spin locks.

Figure 7.8 illustrates NT's implementation of spin locks on uniprocessor systems.

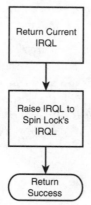

Figure 7.8. *Acquiring a spin lock on a uniprocessor system.*

KeAcquireSpinLock() is implemented on uniprocessor systems as, basically, a call to KeRaiseIrql(). Because raising the IRQL to IRQL DISPATCH_LEVEL or above results in dispatching being disabled, a thread that runs at one of these

IRQLs will continue to run until it lowers its IRQL below IRQL
DISPATCH_LEVEL. Similarly, KeReleaseSpinLock() on uniprocessor systems simply
results in the IRQL being lowered, as in a call to KeLowerIrql(). The atomic
execution of the code between the calls to KeAcquireSpinLock() and
KeReleaseSpinLock() is maintained.

Maybe make a note that it is not a good idea to take a shortcut and simply
raise the IRQL to dispatch level using KeRaiseIrql instead of a spin lock.

Spin Lock Issues

There are a number of issues that must be considered when using spin locks.
For example, the length of time a spin lock is held should be kept to the shortest amount of time reasonably necessary. After all, other processors could be
spinning, waiting for the lock to become free.

On the other hand, it is likely to be a worse error to repeatedly acquire and
release the same spin lock. Acquiring and releasing a spin lock is almost sure to
be expensive on any system because an interlocked memory operation is
required.

> ### Note
>
> *The DDK provides a recommended guideline of 25 microseconds as the
> maximum amount of time a spin lock should be held. This guideline is
> just plain silly. The 25-microsecond value is actually a holdover from the
> earliest days of NT. Consider the fact that the work that can be done in
> 25 microseconds on a 700MHz Alpha processor is certainly much differ-
> ent from the work that can be done in 25 microseconds on a slow 486
> processor! Why would elapsed time matter?*
>
> *The only real guideline is to "be careful" to hold spin locks only as long
> as they are actually needed. True, this doesn't provide a handy numerical
> guideline to follow. But it is the only true guideline. Similarly, balance the
> cost of holding a spin lock with the cost of releasing and reacquiring the
> same lock. In most cases, it is our experience that it is better to hold a
> lock for a little longer than it is to drop and reacquire the lock repeatedly.*

Part II

The I/O Manager and Device Driver Details

Chapter 8

I/O Architectures

This chapter will review:

- **Programmed I/O Devices**. This section discusses Programmed I/O devices that move data under program control between the device and host memory.

- **Busmaster DMA Devices**. This section discusses Busmaster DMA devices that autonomously transfer data between themselves and host memory, using intelligence built into the device.

- **System DMA Devices**. This section discusses System DMA devices that utilize a systemwide DMA controller, provided as part of the basic system logic set, to transfer data between themselves and host memory.

Devices utilize different mechanisms to move data between the device and host memory. Windows NT places devices, and hence their drivers, into one of three major categories depending on their capabilities:

This chapter describes each of these three types of devices and how drivers deal with them on a Windows NT system.

Programmed I/O Devices

Programmed I/O (PIO) devices are usually the simplest of the three main categories of devices. The driver for a PIO device is responsible for moving the data between host memory and the device under program control. This characteristic is, in fact, what gives this category its name. A driver may access a PIO device via shared memory, memory space registers, or port I/O space registers. How the device is accessed depends on the device's design. Figure 8.1 illustrates the relationships between a device driver, a PIO device, and a user application's data buffer in host memory.

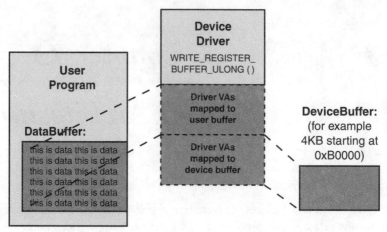

Figure 8.1. *Accessing a shared memory buffer on a PIO device.*

The device shown in Figure 8.1 has a 4KB-memory buffer. This buffer is part of the hardware device itself, not something created by the driver. During initialization, the driver maps the device's memory buffer into kernel virtual address space via calls to the Memory Manager.

To transfer data to the device, the driver moves the data under program control to a location within the device's memory buffer. The move would most likely be performed by using the HAL function WRITE_REGISTER_BUFFER_ULONG ().

The destination address that the driver uses for the move would be the kernel virtual address that the driver previously mapped to the device. The code the driver might use to implement the write operation might be something like the following:

```
WRITE_REGISTER_BUFFER_ULONG(deviceBuffer, userBufferVa, longwordsToCopy);
```

In the preceding code, the variable deviceBuffer contains the kernel virtual address of the destination location in the device's memory buffer. The variable userBufferVa contains the kernel virtual address of the user buffer to copy. The variable longwordsToCopy contains the number of longwords to be copied to the device.

This one statement copies the indicated number of longwords from the requestor's buffer to the device buffer.

Figure 8.2 shows a similar arrangement to that shown in Figure 8.1, but in this example, the interface to the device is via a longword register located in memory space.

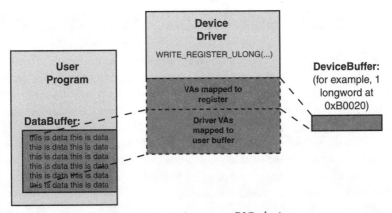

Figure 8.2. *Accessing a memory space register on a PIO device.*

During initialization, the driver will map the physical addresses that the device's memory space registers occupy into kernel virtual address space. The driver then accesses the device using the HAL routines READ_REGISTER_ULONG() and WRITE_REGISTER_ULONG().

One example of the configuration shown in Figure 8.2 would be when the register shown is the data input register for the device. When the driver for this device has a buffer of requestor data to provide to the device, it copies the contents of the requestor's buffer to the device's data input register, one longword at a time. Thus, given that:

- deviceAddress contains the kernel virtual address of the device's register

- longwordsToCopy contains the number of longwords to be moved to the device

- userBufferVa is a PULONG containing the kernel virtual address of the user buffer to copy

The driver might use the following code to move the data from the requestor's buffer to the device:

```
While(longwordsToCopy--) {
    WRITE_REGISTER_ULONG(deviceAddress, *userBufferVa++);
}
```

The driver simply steps through the requestor's data buffer, one longword at a time, moving each longword of data to the device's data input register. The move is accomplished by using the appropriate HAL function.

A point that should not be missed in the preceding two examples is that the device is always accessed by using the HAL functions. Although sometimes it works, it would not be correct to access the device by using RtlCopyMemory(), memcpy(), *or even by simply dereferencing a pointer. Using the HAL routines ensures cross-platform compatibility. As discussed in Chapter 2, "Achieving Hardware Independence with the HAL," you should not be too concerned that the HAL routines will introduce unnecessary overhead in these operations. The HAL strives to perform operations with as little overhead as possible, consistent with cross-platform compatibility and data integrity.*

Figure 8.3 shows a final example of a PIO device.

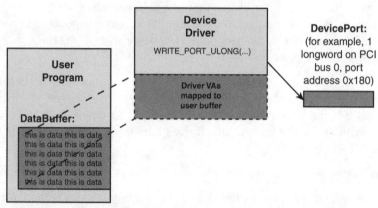

Figure 8.3. *Accessing a port I/O space register on a PIO device.*

Figure 8.3 shows that the interface to the device in question is via a longword register in port I/O space. Because this register is not in memory space, the driver does not need to (and, in fact, cannot) map the register into kernel virtual address space. Instead, to access the port I/O space register, the driver uses the HAL READ_PORT_ULONG() and WRITE_PORT_ULONG() functions.

Given that:

- deviceAddress contains the (translated) port I/O space address of the device's data input register

- longwordsToCopy contains the number of longwords to be moved to the device

- userBufferVa is a PULONG containing the kernel virtual address of the user buffer to copy

The code a driver might use to write to this device is the following:

```
While(longwordsToCopy--) {
    WRITE_PORT_ULONG(deviceAddress, *userBufferVa++);
}
```

In this example, the data is moved by using the HAL function from the user's buffer to the device's port I/O space data input register.

Although each of the three aforementioned devices is accessed in a slightly different way, they all share one common attribute. To get data to the device or retrieve data from the device, the driver is required to "manually" move the data under program control. This data movement consumes CPU cycles. So, while the driver is moving data between a requestor's buffer and a peripheral, the CPU is not being used to do other useful work, like processing a user's spreadsheet. This is the primary disadvantage of a PIO device.

Busmaster DMA Devices

Busmaster DMA devices vary enormously in both architecture and complexity. The single characteristic that these devices have in common is that a Busmaster DMA device autonomously transfers data between itself and host memory. The device driver for a Busmaster DMA device gives the device the starting *logical address* of the data to be transferred, plus the length and direction of the transfer; and the device moves the data itself without help from the host CPU. Because the host CPU is not required to perform the transfer, Busmaster DMA devices leave the host CPU free to perform other useful work.

> *Note*
>
> *It is vital to understand that DMA transfers on NT are always performed by using logical addresses. Logical addresses were explained in Chapter 2, "Achieving Hardware Independence with the HAL," and are discussed further in the section "Logical Addresses," which appears later in this chapter.*

Two Categories of Busmaster DMA Devices

Windows NT categorizes Busmaster DMA devices as being one of two types. The specific functioning of a device's hardware determines into which category a given device falls. The two categories are Packet-Based DMA devices and Common-Buffer DMA devices.

Packet-Based DMA devices are the most common type of Busmaster DMA device. Packet-Based DMA devices typically transfer data to/from different logical addresses for each transfer. Typically, these devices transfer data directly from the data buffer within the requestor's process. Thus, for each transfer, the driver provides the device with the logical base address and length of the requestor's data buffer, as well as the direction of the transfer. The device interrupts when the transfer is completed.

Common-Buffer DMA devices typically utilize the same buffer for all transfer operations. Many network interface cards are Common-Buffer DMA devices. In these devices, the driver and the device have a buffer in host memory in common. The buffer typically contains control structures, the format of which is defined by the device and understood by the driver. These control structures typically describe pending transfers to or from the device. The driver maps the common buffer into kernel virtual addresses space, and thus accesses it by using kernel virtual addresses.

During initialization, the driver typically provides the device with the logical address of the base of the common buffer. When the driver has a transfer request for the device, it fills information about that request into the shared data structures in the common buffer. The device accesses these control structures (via Busmaster DMA) as required to identify and process requests, and ultimately to return status to the driver.

The two types of DMA devices, and the specifics of their support in Windows NT, are described in detail in Chapter 17, "DMA Data Transfers."

Logical Addresses

DMA operations from devices on a Windows NT system are performed to logical addresses. These logical addresses are managed by the HAL, and correlate to physical host memory addresses in a hardware-specific and HAL-specific manner.

In the standard NT DMA model supported by the HAL, logical addresses are translated to host memory physical addresses by the HAL through the use of map registers. Figure 8.4 shows the HAL's standard view of how devices and host memory are connected.

A device bus has a logical address space, managed by the HAL, which is different from the physical address space used for host memory. When processing a DMA transfer request, a device driver calls the I/O Manager and HAL (using the function IoMapTransfer (), described in detail in Chapter 17) to allocate a set of map registers, and program them appropriately to perform the DMA data transfer. Each map register can relocate up to one physical page of addresses (which is 4KB on current x86 systems, 8KB on current Alpha systems).

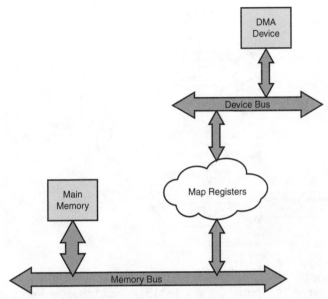

Figure 8.4. *Logical DMA addresses mapped to physical addresses via the HAL's use of map registers.*

It is important to understand that map registers are part of the HAL's standard abstraction of system facilities. How the logical addresses used in DMA operations are implemented, including how these logical addresses are translated to physical addresses and thus even how map registers themselves are implemented, is entirely a function of how a particular HAL is implemented on a given platform.

Some HALs, such as those for certain Alpha platforms, implement logical-to-physical address translation using Translation Lookaside Buffers (TLBs), located in bus bridge logic provided by the platform hardware. In this case, the translation of logical addresses to physical addresses is performed by a combination of hardware (the TLB) and software (the HAL). Thus, in this case, the HAL's conceptual map registers are implemented by using actual hardware (window) registers.

Other HALs perform logical address to physical address translation entirely in software. For example, consider the problems inherent in ISA bus devices addressing the full extent of memory on x86 architecture systems. The ISA bus has only 24 address bits, which only allows devices on the bus to address memory locations up to 16MB. Consequently, memory above 16MB is not directly reachable via DMA from the ISA bus. To support DMA operations on the ISA bus, most common x86 HALs implement a software-only map register scheme, such as that shown in Figure 8.5.

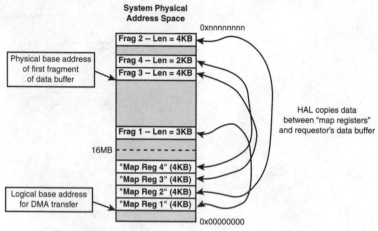

Figure 8.5. *Map registers implemented in software.*

In Figure 8.5, the HAL implements map registers by allocating a physically contiguous set of 4KB buffers below 16MB. Each of these buffers serves as a map register. The HAL allocates these buffers once, at system startup time. When supporting a DMA transfer request for an ISA bus device driver, the HAL reserves a set of these buffers. The HAL provides the device driver with the physical address of a mapping register (that is, actually the physical address of one of the buffers in low memory) as the logical address to be used by the device for the DMA operation. The HAL is responsible for copying the data between the actual requestor's data buffer and the low memory map register.

Note that, irrespective of how the HAL actually implements map registers, the conceptual abstraction of map registers exported by the HAL is always the same. In this model, DMA operations are always performed to logical addresses, never physical addresses. Further, in this model, the HAL is responsible for translating logical addresses to physical addresses through the use of map registers.

Scatter/Gather

Because Windows NT uses virtual memory, the physical memory pages that comprise a requestor's data buffer need not be contiguous in host memory, as illustrated in Figure 8.6.

Simple DMA devices are capable of transferring data by using only a single logical base address and length pair. Therefore, drivers for such devices must reprogram the device for each logical buffer fragment in the requestor's buffer. This can require both extra overhead and latency.

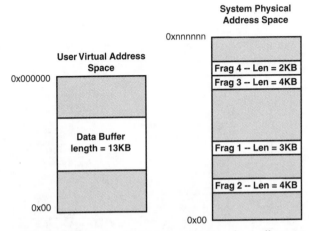

Figure 8.6. *Virtually contiguous data buffers need not be physically contiguous.*

More-sophisticated DMA devices support an optional feature called *scatter/gather*. This feature, also known as "DMA chaining," allows the device to be programmed with multiple pairs of base addresses and lengths simultaneously. Thus, even a logically fragmented requestor's buffer can be described to the DMA device by its driver in one operation.

To help reduce the overhead required to support devices that do not implement scatter/gather, the HAL implements a facility known as *system scatter/gather*. To implement this feature, the HAL utilizes its map registers to create a single, contiguous, logical address range that maps to the requestor's noncontiguous buffer in physical memory. This contiguous logical address range can then be addressed by a device that does not support scatter/gather with a single logical base address and length.

As with other logical-to-physical address translation operations, how the HAL implements system scatter/gather is totally platform- and HAL-specific. On systems utilizing actual hardware-translation schemes, HALs may implement system scatter/gather by using these translation registers, as shown in Figure 8.7.

On systems in which map registers are implemented by the HAL in software, such as most x86 architecture systems, the HAL implements system scatter/gather exactly the same way it implements DMA on the ISA bus. Refer again to Figure 8.5. To support DMA devices that do not implement their own scatter/gather, the HAL allocates a block of physically contiguous "map registers" from low memory, and provides the base address of this buffer to the device driver as the logical address of the requestor's buffer. For a read operation (from the device) the HAL provides the logical base address to the device, the device performs the DMA transfer, and then the HAL copies the data from the "map registers" to the actual requestor's data buffer. For a write operation (to the device), the HAL copies the contents of the requestor's data buffer to the physically contiguous "map registers" prior to the DMA transfer.

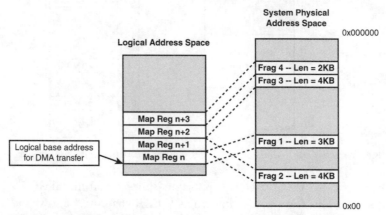

Figure 8.7. *Using hardware map registers to support system scatter/gather.*

The HAL's system scatter/gather support mostly frees drivers for DMA devices from having to program their devices multiple times to perform a single DMA request. The cost of this support obviously varies. On systems where map registers are implemented in hardware, little or no extra overhead results from the HAL's support of this feature. In fact, system scatter/gather on these systems is clearly "a win" in terms of saving CPU time and increasing transfer speed.

On systems that do not have hardware map registers, the advantage is less clear. The overhead of recopying all the data for each user DMA transfer must be balanced against the overhead of the device driver having to reprogram the device multiple times to perform each requested DMA transfer. Whether this is a savings or not is likely to be rather system dependent.

> ### Tip
>
> *In most HALs, a device driver can bypass the HAL's system scatter/gather support by setting the* ScatterGather *field of the* DEVICE_DESCRIPTION *data structure to* TRUE *prior to calling* HalGetAdapter *(). This eliminates the intermediate buffering performed by most x86 architecture HALs.*
>
> *This can be especially useful for taking performance measurements of your driver, both with and without the system scatter/gather facility enabled. However, be aware that this also eliminates the very helpful hardware-based scatter/gather support that may be provided in other HALs.*

System DMA Devices

System DMA (also called slave DMA) is a vestige of the original IBM PC design. In the original IBM PC, the 8080 CPU didn't have enough horsepower to do everything that needed to be done. Therefore, an Intel 8237-5 chip was configured on the motherboard as a systemwide DMA controller. This controller was originally used to offload memory-refresh operations and floppy disk transfers from the CPU.

Later systems (such as the PC AT and PS/2) modified the original design slightly, moving memory refresh logic to dedicated hardware, and adding a second 8237-compatible DMA controller (for a total of eight DMA channels). However, the concept of a systemwide DMA controller being available has stuck. And, even though nobody has even seen an Intel 8237-5 chip in years, the presence of eight general-purpose DMA controller channels is now a fundamental part of "industry standard" PC-compatible design. To this day, most floppy disk controllers still utilize System DMA for their device support.

System DMA provides the capability for a device on the system to use a common DMA controller to perform transfers between itself and host memory. This capability results in a device that is inexpensive (like a PIO device), but that can move data without using host CPU cycles (like Busmaster DMA).

System DMA, as it is supported in Windows NT, is very much like Busmaster DMA, with the following exceptions:

- System DMA devices share a DMA controller that is provided as part of the system, whereas Busmaster DMA devices have a dedicated DMA controller built into their devices.

- System DMA devices do not support scatter/gather.

- The HAL programs the System DMA controller; the device then utilizes the functionality of the System DMA controller to transfer data between itself and host memory.

> Note
>
> *Though it's rare, System DMA can be supported on buses other than the ISA, EISA, and MCA bus. Some HALs could actually have the capability to support System DMA on the PCI bus! This feature could be used, for example, by a floppy disk controller that happens to be attached to the system's internal bus. We don't actually know whether any existing hardware actually uses such facilities in any real-world NT systems, however.*

The System DMA controller provides eight channels for DMA support. NT allows devices to share these channels; however, only one device may use a given channel at a time. Like Busmaster DMA devices, System DMA devices may support Packet-Based System DMA or Common-Buffer System DMA. Common-Buffer System DMA is also referred to as "auto-init" System DMA.

The HAL is responsible for supporting system DMA on Windows NT platforms. Drivers never interface directly to the system DMA components on Windows NT. Rather, the system DMA controllers are programmed via the HAL. As with Busmaster DMA, the HAL uses map registers to translate between logical DMA addresses and host memory addresses.

Few new devices are developed today that utilize System DMA. Use of this facility is typically restricted to legacy floppy disk drives and some sound cards.

Chapter 9

The I/O Manager

This chapter will review:

- **I/O Subsystem Design Characteristics: An Overview.** This section introduces the I/O Subsystem and the attributes discussed in the remaining sections of the chapter.

- **Key Design Characteristics Explained.** The remaining sections in the chapter describe in more detail the major design characteristics of the NT I/O Subsystem of interest to driver writers.

The Windows NT I/O Manager defines the structure of and provides interfaces to Windows NT Kernel mode drivers. This chapter describes the design characteristics of the I/O Manager, and hence the characteristics of the entire Windows NT I/O Subsystem. This chapter also describes the major data structures used and managed by the I/O Manager. The chapter concludes with a preview of the Windows NT layered driver model and its use of Packet-Based I/O.

I/O Subsystem Design Characteristics: An Overview

In this chapter, the Windows NT I/O Subsystem refers to all those components that together provide the capability to perform I/O to peripherals on the system. This includes the I/O Manager and all the Kernel mode device drivers in the system.

Unlike the I/O subsystems in other operating systems, such as DOS or Win9x, the Windows NT I/O Subsystem was designed from the ground up to have a well-defined, yet extensible interface that accommodates modern intelligent peripherals. The Windows NT I/O Subsystem has more in common with the

VMS and UNIX operating systems than with Windows or DOS. In fact, driver writers familiar with VMS or many of the common UNIX variants will find much about the NT I/O Subsystem that is familiar.

The following list provides the major design characteristics of the Windows NT I/O Subsystem. The Windows NT I/O Subsystem is:

- Consistent and highly structured
- Portable across processor architectures
- Configurable
- As frequently pre-emptible and interruptible as possible
- Multiprocessor safe on MP systems
- Object-based
- Asynchronous
- Packet-driven
- Layered

The remaining sections of the chapter briefly discuss each of these NT I/O Subsytem characteristics.

The NT I/O Subsystem Is Consistent and Highly Structured

The NT I/O Manager provides the interface between device drivers and the remainder of the Windows NT operating system. This interface is provided by the I/O system services, which provide basic I/O support to the operating system through the implementation of its functions: NtCreateFile(), NtReadFile(), NtWriteFile(), NtDeviceIoControlFile(), and a few other less well-known native APIs. Figure 9.1 illustrates the relationship between the I/O Manager, the I/O system services, device drivers, and user applications.

The I/O system services provide a device-independent interface between applications that issue requests and the rest of the I/O subsystem. This interface does not change, regardless of the mode (Kernel or User) from which the request is being initiated, the environment subsystem (such as Win32, POSIX, or none) under which the requestor is running, or the device to which the requestor is communicating.

Viewed from another perspective, the I/O system services and I/O Manager always provide Kernel mode drivers with a standard description of I/O requests. This standardization frees Kernel mode drivers from having to deal with differences among requestors.

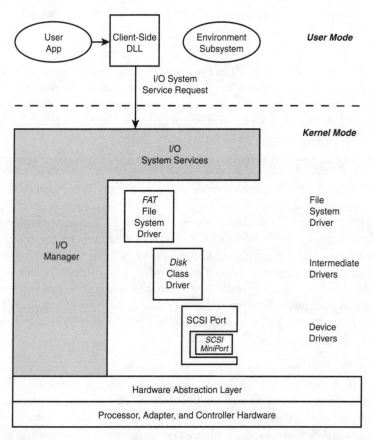

Figure 9.1. *The relationship of the I/O Subsystem to user applications.*

A final aspect of the I/O Subsystem being consistent and highly structured is that the I/O Manager clearly defines the basic ways in which drivers interact, both with the I/O Manager and with other drivers. The I/O Manager defines a detailed and specific set of interfaces to be implemented by device drivers. These interfaces are well-documented. Further, the I/O subsystem itself provides a broad set of support routines which may be called by device drivers to facilitate certain operations.

The NT I/O Subsystem Is Portable Across Platforms

Like the rest of the Windows NT operating system, the I/O subsystem is independent from the CPU architecture upon which it is running. This platform independence is provided through use of functions provided by the Microkernel and the HAL.

Device drivers are written in C, like the I/O Manager itself, and may be moved among processor architectures simply by being recompiled. Because the HAL provides Kernel mode drivers with a standard abstraction of the underlying processor facilities, drivers need not be concerned with the architectural specifics of the processor on which they are running.

> **Note**
>
> *While it is true that Kernel mode drivers are typically written in C, it is also possible to write Kernel mode drivers in C++ using one of the commercially available packages of class libraries. However, the native interfaces between the I/O Manager and Kernel mode drivers are C Language interfaces. Additionally complicating the picture for C++ developers is that the operating system does not supply a C++ runtime library, and Microsoft does not officially support development of Kernel mode drivers in C++. So, while developing Kernel mode drivers for Windows NT in C++ is certainly possible, it is presently a bit more complicated than simply using C.*

The Windows NT operating system uses a set of NT-specific data types that are specifically designed to be independent of processor architecture. These data types are defined in the include file `ntdef.h`. This include file is automatically referenced when `ntddk.h`, the master include file used for writing drivers, is included. To help ensure cross-platform compatibility, driver writers should use the NT-specific data types instead of the more traditional C language data types. Table 9.1 provides some examples of common C language data types and their NT equivalents:

Table 9.1. Standard C language/NT data type equivalents.

Standard C Data Type	NT Data Type
char	CHAR
short	SHORT
long	LONG
int64 (64-bit signed integer)	LONGLONG

Standard C Data Type	NT Data Type
unsigned __int64 (64-bit unsigned integer)	ULONGLONG
unsigned char	UCHAR
unsigned short	USHORT
unsigned long	ULONG
unsigned char *	PUCHAR
unsigned short *	PUSHORT
unsigned long *	PULONG
unsigned char (used for logical value)	LOGICAL or BOOLEAN

Note

It can be useful, and almost interesting, to read ntdef.h. *In addition to the typedefs previously referred to, it includes definitions for several utility macros that might be useful to driver writers. Check it out!*

You might find it hard to believe that efficient device drivers can be written for Windows NT with absolutely no CPU architecture dependencies. However, the HAL and Microkernel do such a good job of isolating drivers from processor differences that platform-independent drivers are indeed the rule. One of the authors has written a number of drivers that were initially designed, tested, and released on x86 architecture platforms, which were later ported to Alpha architecture platforms without any more trouble than recompilation. The key to such success is assiduously following the standard NT driver model, and carefully using the HAL's abstractions.

The NT I/O Subsystem Is Configurable

All Kernel mode drivers in Windows NT are dynamically loaded. Typically, drivers are started at system startup time. However, drivers may also be loaded after the system has started either programmatically or manually on command.

When a driver is loaded, it determines information about the configuration of the devices it intends to support, and of the system when necessary, dynamically. The driver does this by calling functions provided by the I/O Manager, by querying the Registry, by interacting with the HAL, or through a combination of these means. In any case, drivers use the NT-prescribed methods for determining device configuration to dynamically determine the configuration of their devices. Properly written device drivers in Windows NT do not contain machine- or processor architecture-dependent values.

The NT I/O Subsystem Is Pre-emptible and Interruptible

As mentioned in Chapter 6, "Interrupt Request Levels and DPCs," executive level components such as the I/O Subsystem strive to keep their IRQLs as low as possible during as much of their processing as possible. Keeping the IRQL low allows more important, more time-critical, processing to take place rapidly in the system.

This I/O Manager helps keep drivers pre-emptible and interruptible as much as possible by calling most driver entry points at the lowest possible IRQL. Most of the time, this results in driver entry points being called at IRQL PASSIVE_LEVEL.

The NT I/O Subsystem Is Multiprocessor Safe

Like the rest of the Windows NT operating system, the I/O Manager is designed to run on multiprocessor systems. Given the wide availability of multiprocessor systems, most Kernel mode drivers should be designed, implemented, and tested with multiprocessor support.

Proper support for multiprocessor systems entails appropriately guarding shared data that can be simultaneously accessed on multiple CPUs. When this data is accessed only at IRQL PASSIVE_LEVEL, a variety of techniques may be used to appropriately serialize access. When shared data may be accessed at IRQL DISPATCH_LEVEL or above, spin locks must be used. Spin locks were discussed in detail in Chapter 7, "Multiprocessor Issues."

Even if a driver does not support execution on multiprocessor systems, it should be multiprocessor safe. This means that if a driver is restricted to running on only uniprocessor systems, at startup it should check the number of CPUs on the system and refuse to load if there is more than one CPU. This number of processors in the system may be determined by querying the location KeNumberProcessors, as shown in the following example:

Example 9.1. Checking the number of CPUs in a system.

```
//
// Ensure that we've been loaded on a system with only
// one active CPU
//
if (*KeNumberProcessors > 1) {

    //
```

```
// Refuse to load by returning any error code.
// STATUS_DEVICE_CONFIGURATION_ERROR is as good as
// any other.
//
return(STATUS_DEVICE_CONFIGURATION_ERROR);
}
```

The NT I/O Subsystem Is Object-Based

The Windows NT I/O Subsystem is based on a collection of "objects." These objects are defined by the Microkernel, HAL, and the I/O Manager and exported to other Kernel mode modules, including device drivers. The I/O Manager and device drivers use these objects, as well as other data structures, in performing their functions.

As mentioned in Chapter 1, the NT operating system in general, and the I/O Subsystem in particular, is *object-based*, but not necessarily *object-oriented*. The majority of the operating system is written in C, with a few processor specific portions of the Microkernel and HAL written in Assembly. Thus, the definitions for the objects that the operating system uses are simply typedefs for structures defined in C. These definitions are typically exported for use by drivers in the file ntddk.h.

Objects are created by drivers by calling defined operating system functions. When an object is created by calling a Kernel mode function, a pointer to that object is usually returned. Most objects used within the I/O Subsystem are considered *partially opaque*. This means that a subset of fields within the object can be directly manipulated by kernel modules, including drivers. Examples of partially opaque objects include Device Objects and Driver Objects, both of which are discussed in more detail later. A few objects used within the I/O Subsystem (such as DPC Objects or Interrupt Objects) are considered *fully opaque*. This means that Kernel mode modules (other than the creating module) must call functions that understand and manipulate the fields within the object.

How does a driver know which objects are partially opaque and which are fully opaque? And how does a driver know which fields in a partially opaque object can be modified? The answers are simple: Where there are routines provided to manipulate the fields within an object, those routines should **always** be used. Also, the *Kernel Mode Drivers Reference Manual* in the DDK documents the accessible fields in a variety of objects. If the field isn't documented, Microsoft would like you to consider the field opaque.

The remainder of this section describes some of the objects that are most commonly used within the I/O subsystem. For each, we give the object's name, describe its purpose, and briefly describe its structure. Figure 9.2 shows the relationship among several of these objects.

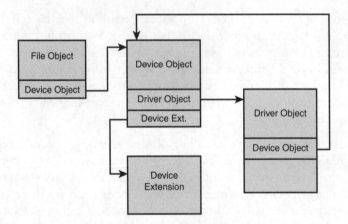

Figure 9.2. *Structures commonly used within the I/O subsystem.*

File Objects

The File Object is defined by the NT structure FILE_OBJECT, which is illustrated in Figure 9.3.

A File Object represents a single open instance of a file, device, directory, socket, named pipe, mail slot, or other similar entity. A single shared file that is opened multiple times will have one File Object for each time the file is opened. File Objects are created by the NtCreateFile() system service, or its Win32 equivalent, CreateFile(). When a File Object is created, a handle to that File Object is returned to the creator. This handle identifies the file for subsequent operations, such as read, write, or device control operations.

CSHORT Size		CSHORT Type	
PDEVICE_OBJECT Device Object			
PVPB Vpb			
PVOID FsContext			
PVOID FsContext2			
PSECTION_OBJECT_POINTERS SectionObjectPointer			
PVOID PrivateCacheMap			
NTSTATUS FinalStatus			
PFILE_OBJECT RelatedFileObject			
BOOLEAN WriteAccess	BOOLEAN ReadAccess	BOOLEAN DeletePending	BOOLEAN LockOperation
BOOLEAN SharedDelete	BOOLEAN SharedWrite	BOOLEAN SharedRead	BOOLEAN DeleteAccess
ULONG Flags			
UNICODE_STRING FileName			
LARGE_INTEGER CurrentByteOffset			
ULONG Waiters			
ULONG Busy			
PVOID LastLock			
KEVENT Lock			
KEVENT Event			
PIO_COMPLETION_CONTEXT CompletionContext			

Figure 9.3. *The File Object.*

While the I/O Manager creates a File Object for each open instance of a file or device, manipulation of File Objects is typically restricted to the I/O Manager and file systems. Device drivers rarely refer to the File Objects created for open instances of their devices.

Driver Objects

The Driver Object describes where a driver is loaded in physical memory, the driver's size, and its main entry points. The format of a Driver Object is defined by the NT structure DRIVER_OBJECT. Figure 9.4 illustrates the fields in a Driver Object.

CSHORT Size	CSHORT Type
PDEVICE_OBJECT Device Object	
ULONG Flags	
PVOID DriverStart	
ULONG DriverSize	
PVOID DriverSection	
PDRIVER_EXTENSION DriverExtension	
UNICODE_STRING DriverName	
PUNICODE_STRING Hardware Database	
PFAST_IO_DISPATCH FastIoDispatch	
PDRIVER_INITIALIZE DriverInit	
PDRIVER_STARTIO DriverStartIo	
PDRIVERA_UNLOAD Driver Unload PDRIVER_DISPATCH	
MajorFunction[IRP_MJ_MAXIMUM_ FUNCTION +1]	

Figure 9.4. *The Driver Object.*

The Driver Object is created by the I/O Manager. The I/O Manager provides a pointer to a driver's Driver Object when a driver is first loaded. As part of standard initialization processing, during its Driver Entry routine, a driver fills into its Driver Object pointers to the remainder of its entry points. For example, a driver fills into its Driver Object a pointer to a routine for each I/O major function code that the driver supports. This is described in detail in Chapter 13, "Driver Entry."

Device Objects

The Device Object represents a physical or logical device that can be the target of an I/O operation. The format of the Device Object is defined by the NT structure DEVICE_OBJECT (see Figure 9.5).

Unlike many operating systems, in Windows NT, Device Objects are created directly by drivers themselves. While a Device Object may be created at any time by a driver by calling IoCreateDevice(), Device Objects are normally created when a driver is first loaded. When a driver creates a Device Object, it also specifies the size of the Device Extension to be created. The Device Extension is a per-device area that is private to the device driver. The driver can use this area to store anything it wants, including device statistics, queues of requests, or other such data. The Device Extension is typically the main global data storage area. Both the Device Object and Device Extension are created in non-paged pool.

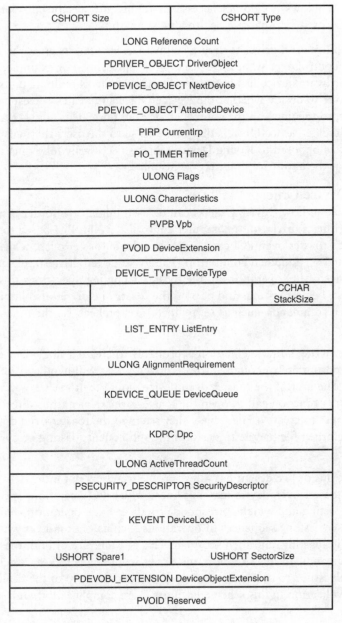

CSHORT Size			CSHORT Type	
LONG Reference Count				
PDRIVER_OBJECT DriverObject				
PDEVICE_OBJECT NextDevice				
PDEVICE_OBJECT AttachedDevice				
PIRP CurrentIrp				
PIO_TIMER Timer				
ULONG Flags				
ULONG Characteristics				
PVPB Vpb				
PVOID DeviceExtension				
DEVICE_TYPE DeviceType				
				CCHAR StackSize
LIST_ENTRY ListEntry				
ULONG AlignmentRequirement				
KDEVICE_QUEUE DeviceQueue				
KDPC Dpc				
ULONG ActiveThreadCount				
PSECURITY_DESCRIPTOR SecurityDescriptor				
KEVENT DeviceLock				
USHORT Spare1			USHORT SectorSize	
PDEVOBJ_EXTENSION DeviceObjectExtension				
PVOID Reserved				

Figure 9.5. *The Device Object.*

When a Device Object is created, it is optionally assigned a name by the driver. This name will be the native Windows NT name for the device. Device Objects that are not named are typically used for internal operating by a device driver, and are not directly accessible outside the driver that created them. Named Device Objects are accessible via the NtCreateFile() system service. Device names in Windows NT do not necessarily follow any specific convention. Thus, it is possible to name a device almost anything.

The capability for a driver to create its own Device Objects gives the driver complete control over what a Device Object represents. For example, if a particular hardware device has one controller that controls multiple units, it is up to the driver to decide whether the Device Objects it creates corresponds to the controller, to the units on the controller, or even both. This allows the driver writer to create Device Objects that make sense to the users that will be accessing them, as opposed to having Device Objects necessarily following the specifics of the hardware that may be installed.

Using Device Objects

An example of how Device Objects can be used might be in order. Assume you're writing a driver for a computer controlled 32-bit PCI-based toaster oven. Each toaster oven PCI card controls a single toaster oven, which is probably located on a kitchen countertop. The toaster oven driver implements a whole range of I/O operations to the toaster, including operations to set toast brownness, begin toasting, and pop up the toast. The driver also implements a set of oven commands, such as set temperature, preheat, set the timer, and the like.

The driver writer's first inclination is probably to create a single Device Object named, appropriately enough, "Toaster Oven," that will handle all these requests. The user of the toaster oven device would then issue a Win32 CreateFile() function call to open the toaster oven device (thus directing the I/O Manager to create a File Object that refers to the toaster oven device), and use the returned file handle to perform the subsequent toasting or oven operations.

However, this device design has a few problems. Users not intimately familiar with the toaster oven device may not know which I/O operations specifically refer to toasting and which correspond strictly to oven operation. This could lead to users issuing sequences of operations such as: set toast brownness, preheat, begin toasting, and then set timer. This is a mixture of both toaster and oven commands. In this situation, the driver would have to keep track of the commands issued to determine the mode (toaster or oven) of the device. Request validation in this scheme becomes more complicated than it should be.

An alternative approach would be for the driver to create two Device Objects instead of one. One Device Object would be the "Toaster" device; the other would be the "Oven" device. When a user wants to perform toasting operations they (naturally) open the Toaster device. When they want to perform oven operations, they would open the Oven device. Thus, the user's intent—to toast or to use the oven—is clear from the start.

Each I/O operation that can be issued by a user is associated with either the toaster or the oven device. This makes the user's interface to the device easier to understand. In addition, using two separate Device Objects makes the driver's job of request validation much simpler. Once the user has opened the Toaster device, any oven requests (such as preheat or set timer) sent by the user to that device will be rejected by the driver. Similarly, toaster requests sent to the oven device would be rejected. Of course, the driver would need to keep some global state to ensure that when the toaster device was opened, the oven device on the same toaster oven could not be opened simultaneously.

Deciding precisely what a Device Object represents when designing a new device driver is a major architectural decision. Choosing correctly can result in a driver that is both easier to use and easier to develop.

> ### Note
>
> *While a toaster oven might seem a silly example, there are many real devices that follow the toaster oven model. We designed a driver for a bus-based industrial controller that precisely fits this model. The device could be accessed in either of two modes. By making each of these access modes a separate Device Object, documentation and use of the device were significantly simplified. Even more importantly, the job of designing, writing, and testing the driver was made much easier.*

Interrupt Objects

The Interrupt Object is created by the I/O Manager, and is used to connect a driver's interrupt service routine to a given interrupt vector. The structure, KINTERRUPT, is one of the few fully opaque structures used in the I/O Subsystem. Its internal format does not appear in ntddk.h.

Adapter Objects

The Adapter Object is used by all DMA drivers. It contains a description of the DMA device, and represents a set of shared resources. These resources may be a DMA channel or a set of DMA map registers. Use of this object facilitates resource sharing in DMA operations.

The format of the Adapter Object is defined by the HAL. A pointer to an
Adapter Object is returned to a driver as a result of calling HalGetAdapter().
The Adapter Object is fully opaque. Its structure is defined as ADAPTER_OBJECT.
Its internal format does not appear in ntddk.h.

The NT I/O Subsystem Is Asynchronous

One of the main design characteristics of the Windows NT I/O Subsystem is
that it uses an asynchronous I/O model. Figure 9.6 illustrates the comparison
between synchronous and asynchronous I/O approaches.

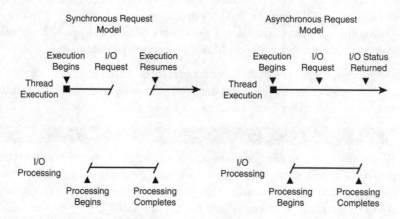

Figure 9.6. *Synchronous versus asynchronous I/O.*

In an inherently synchronous I/O model, a thread that initiates an I/O operation is blocked while the I/O operation is processed. Thus, the request to perform a read or write operation, for example, does not return until that read
or write operation has completed. This is the model used, for example, in
MS-DOS.

In contrast, the Windows NT I/O Subsystem supports asynchronous I/O. In
Windows NT, I/O requests are described by an I/O Request Packet, a pointer
to which is passed to a driver for processing. At any point during processing, a
driver may indicate that the I/O operation is pending. This allows the requesting thread to (optionally) continue execution, thus overlapping its I/O operation with performing useful work.

Of course, threads in Windows NT may optionally request to wait until a
requested I/O operation completes before resuming processing. This is, in fact,

the default for I/O operations initiated via the Win32 environment subsystem. In this case, the thread waits on a Dispatcher Object until the request completes. The Dispatcher then finds another ready thread to run.

Having an inherently asynchronous I/O subsystem results in some interesting attributes. For one, a single thread may have multiple I/O operations in progress simultaneously. These requests may be to different devices, or to the same device. Another interesting attribute is that when multiple I/O operations are outstanding simultaneously, the requests will not necessarily complete in the order in which they were initiated.

To make these concepts clear, take a look at a simple example. Consider a thread that issues four simultaneous I/O requests to the same file, with the following parameters:

- Read 1000 bytes starting at byte offset 80000 in the file
- Read 1000 bytes starting at byte offset 81000 in the file
- Read 1000 bytes starting at byte offset 0 in the file
- Read 1000 bytes starting at byte offset 15000 in the file

The Windows NT I/O Subsystem does not make any guarantees about the order in which these I/O requests will complete. Such ordering is totally file system dependent, and will likely be the result of the prior activity that has taken place on the file.

The NT I/O Subsystem Is Packet-Driven

As previously mentioned, the Windows NT I/O Subsystem is a packet-driven system. In this system, each I/O operation can be described by a single I/O Request Packet (IRP). The I/O Manager builds the IRP as a result of a request to one of the I/O system services. Once the IRP has been built and initialized, a pointer to the IRP, and a pointer the Device Object to which the IRP was directed, is passed to the appropriate driver. IRPs are discussed in greater detail in Chapter 10, "How I/O Requests Are Described."

The NT I/O Subsystem Is Layered

The Windows NT I/O Subsystem uses a layered driver model. In this model, layers or "stacks" of drivers work together to process I/O requests. This layering is shown in Figure 9.1, which appears earlier in the chapter.

At the highest level of the stack are File Systems Drivers. These drivers are typically responsible for name space management and mapping file-relative I/O requests to volume-relative requests. Below File System Drivers sit Intermediate Drivers. These drivers perform value-added or class-based processing for devices. At the bottom of the stack are device drivers. These drivers actually interact with and manage hardware.

It is important to understand that not every I/O request on Windows NT goes through every layer in the stack. If a requestor issues an I/O operation to the toaster device that was previously discussed, this request would be serviced directly by the toaster device driver.

The concept of layering in the Windows NT I/O Subsystem is described in detail in Chapter 11, "The Layered Driver Model."

Chapter 10

How I/O Requests Are Described

This chapter will review:

- **IRP Structure.** This section describes the format of an I/O Request Packet (IRP) and its I/O Stack locations.

- **Data Buffers.** Driver writers have a choice of how the I/O Manager describes a requestor's data buffers. This section describes the three choices.

- **I/O Function Codes.** I/O functions in Windows NT are described by using major and minor function codes. These codes are reviewed in this section.

- **Predefined and Custom I/O Control Functions.** When an I/O operation requests a particular device's specific function, an I/O Control (or IOCTL) function is used. This section describes both the IOCTL functions that are predefined by NT for standard devices and how a driver writer defines custom I/O Control functions for a device.

- **I/O Request Parameters.** This section describes how function-specific parameters are retrieved from the current I/O Stack location in the I/O Request Packet.

Windows NT describes I/O requests by using a packet-based architecture. In this approach, each I/O request to be performed can be described by using a single I/O Request Packet (IRP).

When an I/O system service is issued (such as a request to create or read from a file), the I/O Manager services that request by building an IRP describing the request, and then passes a pointer to that IRP to a device driver to begin processing the request.

IRP Structure

An IRP contains all the information necessary to fully describe an I/O request to the I/O Manager and device drivers. The IRP is a standard NT structure of type "IRP." Figure 10.1 shows the structure of an IRP.

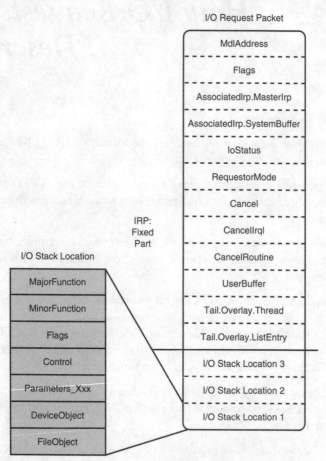

Figure 10.1. *Format of the IRP and I/O Stack locations.*

As you can see in Figure 10.1, each I/O Request Packet may be thought of as having two parts: A "fixed" part and an I/O Stack. The fixed part of the IRP contains information about the request that either does not vary from driver to driver, or it does not need to be preserved when the IRP is passed from one driver to another. The I/O Stack contains a set of I/O Stack locations, each of which holds information specific to each driver that may handle the request.

Although the size of a particular IRP is fixed when it is created by the I/O Manager, every IRP that the I/O Manager creates is not the same size. When the I/O Manager allocates an IRP, it allocates space for the fixed portion of the IRP plus enough space to contain at least as many I/O Stack locations as there are drivers in the driver stack that will process this request. Thus, if an I/O request were issued to write to a file on a floppy disk, the stack of two drivers that would process this request would probably be similar to the stack shown in Figure 10.2.

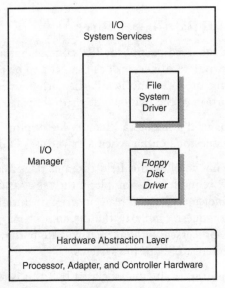

Figure 10.2. *Example of a stack of two drivers.*

The I/O Manager creates an IRP to describe this request that has at least two I/O Stack locations: one location for the File System Driver and a second location for the Floppy Disk device Driver.

We said the IRP in the example has *at least* two I/O Stack locations. To avoid allocating every IRP from NT's nonpaged pool, the I/O Manager maintains a pair of *lookaside lists* that hold preallocated IRPs.

> **Note**
>
> *In NT V4, one of these lookaside lists holds IRPs that have a single I/O Stack location. The other lookaside list holds IRPs that have three I/O stack locations.*

The I/O Manager always attempts to use an IRP from these lists, if possible. Thus, for an I/O request directed to a stack of two drivers, the I/O Manager attempts to use one of the IRPs from the lookaside list of IRPs that has three

I/O Stack locations. If there are no IRPs available on the appropriate lookaside list, or if an IRP with more than three I/O Stack locations is needed, the I/O Manager simply allocates the IRP from the nonpaged pool.

> **Note**
>
> *Because IRPs are always allocated from nonpaged system space, they are never paged out. As a result, drivers may reference IRPs at any IRQL (without being concerned about causing a potentially fatal page fault at elevated IRQL).*

Fields in the IRP's Fixed Part

As stated previously, the fixed part of the IRP contains information that either does not vary from driver to driver or does not need to be preserved when the IRP is passed from one driver to another. Particularly interesting or useful fields in the fixed portion of the IRP include the following:

- **MdlAddress**. This field points to a Memory Descriptor List (MDL) that describes the requestor's buffer when a driver uses Direct I/O.

- **Flags**. As the name implies, this field contains flags that (typically) describe the I/O request. For example, if the IRP_PAGING_IO flag is set in this field, this indicates that the read or write operation described by the IRP is a paging request. Similarly, the IRP_NOCACHE bit indicates that the request is to be processed without intermediate buffering. The Flags field is typically of interest only to file systems.

- **AssociatedIrp.MasterIrp**. In an associated IRP, this is a pointer to the master IRP with which this request is associated. This field is likely to be of interest only to the highest-layer drivers, such as file systems drivers.

- **AssociatedIrp.SystemBuffer**. This location points to an intermediate buffer in nonpaged pool space for the requestor's data, when a driver uses buffered I/O.

- **IoStatus**. This is the I/O Status Block that contains the ultimate completion status of the IRP. When an IRP is completed, the IoStatus.Status field is set by the completing driver to the completion status of the I/O operation, and the IoStatus.Information field is set by the driver to any additional information to be passed back to the requestor in the second longword of the I/O Status Block. Typically, the IoStatus.Information field contains the number of bytes actually read or written by a transfer request.

- **RequestorMode**. This field indicates the mode (Kernel mode or User mode) from which the request was initiated.

- **Cancel**, **CancelIrql**, and **CancelRoutine**. These fields are used if the IRP needs to be cancelled while in progress. **Cancel** is a BOOLEAN which, when set to TRUE by the I/O Manager, indicates that the cancellation of the I/O operation described by this IRP has been requested. **CancelRoutine** is a pointer to a function set by a driver using the appropriate NT-supplied routine, to a function for the I/O Manager to call to have the driver cancel the IRP. Because the **CancelRoutine** field is called at IRQL DISPATCH_LEVEL, **CancelIrql** is the IRQL to which the driver should return. Chapter 14 contains more details on cancel processing.

- **UserBuffer**. This field contains the requestor's virtual address of the data buffer associated with the I/O request, if any.

- **Tail.Overlay.DeviceQueueEntry**. This field is used by the I/O Manager for queuing IRPs for drivers that use System Queuing. System Queuing is described in detail in Chapter 14.

- **Tail.Overlay.Thread**. This field is a pointer to the requestor's thread control block (ETHREAD).

- **TailOverlay.ListEntry**. While a driver owns an IRP, it can use this field for linking one IRP to the next.

Fields in the IRP I/O Stack Location

Each I/O Stack location in an IRP contains information for a specific driver about the I/O request. The I/O Stack location is defined by the structure IO_STACK_LOCATION. To locate the current I/O Stack location within a given IRP, a driver calls the function IoGetCurrentIrpStackLocation(). A pointer to the IRP is the sole parameter on the call. The return value is a pointer to the current I/O Stack location.

When the I/O Manager initially allocates the IRP and initializes its fixed portion, it also initializes the first I/O Stack location in the IRP. The information in this location corresponds with information to be passed to the first driver in the stack of drivers that will process this request. Fields in the I/O Stack location include the following:

- **MajorFunction**. This field indicates the major I/O function code associated with this request. This indicates the type of I/O operation to be performed.

- **MinorFunction**. This field indicates the minor I/O function code associated with the request. When used, this modifies the major function code. Minor functions are used almost exclusively by network transport drivers and file systems, and are ignored by most device drivers.

- **Flags.** This field indicates the processing flags specific to the I/O function being performed. This field is of interest mainly to file systems drivers.

- **Control.** This field represents a set of flags that are set and read by the I/O Manager, indicating how it needs to handle a particular IRP. For example, the SL_PENDING bit is set in this field (by a driver's call to the function IoMarkIrpPending()) to indicate to the I/O Manager how completion is to be handled. Similarly, the flags SL_INVOKE_ON_CANCEL, SL_INVOKE_ON_ERROR, and SL_INVOKE_ON_SUCCESS indicate when the driver's I/O Completion Routine should be invoked for this IRP.

- **Parameters.** This field comprises several submembers, each of which is specific to the particular I/O major function being performed.

- **DeviceObject.** This field contains a pointer to the device object that is the target of an I/O request.

- **FileObject.** This field is a pointer to the file object associated with an I/O request.

After the fixed portion of the IRP and the first I/O Stack location in the IRP are appropriately initialized, the I/O Manager calls the top driver in the driver stack at its dispatch entry point that corresponds to the major function code for the request. Thus, if the I/O Manager has just built an IRP to describe a read request, he will call the first driver in the driver stack at its read dispatch entry point. The I/O Manager passes the following as parameters: a pointer to the IRP that was just built and a pointer to the device object that corresponds to the device on which the driver is to process the request.

Describing Data Buffers

The descriptor for the requestor's data buffer appears in the fixed portion of the IRP. Windows NT provides driver writers with the following three different options for describing the requestor's data buffer associated with an I/O operation:

- **Direct I/O.** The buffer may be described in its original location in the requestor's physical address space by a structure called a Memory Descriptor List (MDL), which describes the physical addresses of the requestor's user mode virtual addresses.

- **Buffered I/O.** The data from the requestor's buffer may be copied from the requestor's address space into an intermediate location in system address space (by the I/O Manager before the driver gets the IRP), and the driver is provided a pointer to this copy of the data.

- **Neither I/O.** The driver is provided with the requestor's virtual address of the buffer.

Drivers must choose a single method for the I/O Manager to use to describe all the read and write requests that are sent to a particular device. The choice is made when the Device Object is created (typically at initialization time) by setting bits in the Flags field of the Device Object. A different method from the one chosen for read and write requests, however, may be used for each Device I/O Control (IOCTL) code supported by the driver. I/O function codes and IOCTLs are covered in detail later in the chapter.

Describing Data Buffers with Direct I/O

Direct I/O is most often used by "packet-based" Direct Memory Access (DMA) device drivers. However, it may be used by any type of driver that wants to transfer data directly between a user buffer and a peripheral without having the overhead of rebuffering the data (as with Buffer I/O, described later in the chapter), and without having to perform the transfer in the context of the calling process (as with Neither I/O, also described later in the chapter).

If a driver chooses Direct I/O, any data buffer associated with read or write I/O requests will be described by the I/O Manager by using an opaque structure called a Memory Descriptor List (MDL). This MDL describes the data buffer in its original location within the requestor's physical address space. The address of the MDL is passed to the driver in the IRP in the MdlAddress field.

Before the IRP is passed to the driver, the I/O Manager checks to ensure that the caller has appropriate access to the entire data buffer. If the access check fails, the request is completed by the I/O Manager with an error status, and the request is never passed on to the driver.

After the access check is completed, but still before the IRP is passed to the driver, the I/O Manager locks the physical pages that comprise the data buffer in memory (thus making all the requestor's data buffer nonpageable). If this operation fails (for example, if the data buffer is too large to fit into memory at one time), the request is completed by the I/O Manager with an error status. If the locking operation succeeds, the pages remain locked for the duration of the I/O operation (until the IRP is ultimately completed).

When an IRP is ultimately completed (by calling IoCompleteRequest()) and the MdlAddress field is non-zero, the I/O Manager unmaps and unlocks any pages that were mapped and locked. The I/O Manager then frees the MDL associated with the IRP.

Understanding MDLs

A Memory Descriptor List (MDL) is capable of describing a single data buffer that is contiguous in virtual memory, but is not necessarily physically contiguous. As shown in Figure 10.3, a single virtually contiguous requestor's buffer may span several noncontiguous physical pages. An MDL is designed to make it particularly fast and easy to get the physical base addresses and lengths of the fragments that comprise the data buffer. The definition for the MDL structure appears in NTDDK.H.

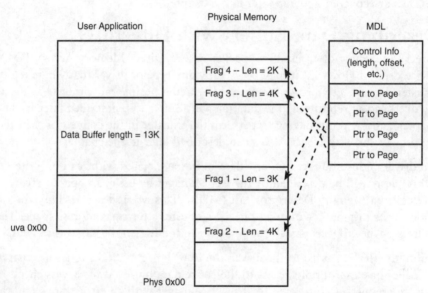

Figure 10.3. *A requestor's data buffer (shown both in virtual and physical address space) and an MDL that describes it.*

Figure 10.4 shows the contents of an MDL. Even though the structure of an MDL is well known, it is one of the few truly opaque data structures in Windows NT. By *opaque*, we mean that the structure of the MDL can never be assumed by a driver. Thus, the fields of the MDL should never be directly referenced by a driver.

The I/O and Memory Managers provide functions for getting information about a data buffer using an MDL. These functions include the following:

- **MmGetSystemAddressForMdl()**. This function returns a kernel virtual address that may be used in an arbitrary thread context to refer to the buffer that the MDL describes. As can be seen in Figure 10.4, one of the fields in the MDL contains the mapped system virtual address associated with the MDL, *if one exists*. This function is in fact a macro in NTDDK.H.

The first time this function is called, it calls `MmMapLockedPages()` to map the buffer described by the MDL into kernel virtual address space. The returned kernel virtual address is then stored in the `MappedSystemVa` field of the MDL. On subsequent calls to `MmGetSystemAddressForMdl()`, the value that was previously stored in `MappedSystemVa` is simply returned to the caller. Any mapping that is present is deleted when the MDL is freed (that is, when the I/O request is ultimately completed).

- `IoMapTransfer()`. This function is used primarily by DMA device drivers to get the logical base address and the length of each of the fragments of the data buffer for use in a DMA operation.

- `MmGetMdlVirtualAddress()`. This function (which is actually a macro) returns the requestor's virtual address of the buffer described by the MDL. Although this virtual address is of direct use only in the context of the calling process, this function is frequently used by DMA device drivers because the requestor's virtual address is one of the input parameters to `IoMapTransfer()`.

- `MmGetMdlByteCount()`. This function, which is another macro from NTDDK.H, returns the length, in bytes, of the buffer described by the MDL.

- `MmGetMdlByteOffset()`. This function, which is yet another macro, returns the offset to the start of the data buffer from the first page of the MDL.

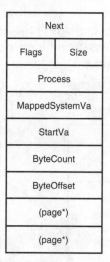

Figure 10.4. *Memory Descriptor List (MDL).*

Thus, given an MDL, a driver writer may use the appropriate function to conveniently accomplish either of the following tasks:

Map the requestor's buffer into kernel virtual address space (by calling `MmGetSystemAddressForMdl()`).

Get the logical base address of the physical fragments that comprise the requestor's buffer for use in a DMA transfer (by calling `IoMapTransfer()`).

Whichever function the driver writer chooses, the requestor's data is available to the driver directly from within the requestor's buffer. No intermediate buffering or recopying of the requestor's data is performed by the I/O Manager.

> **Note**
>
> *One particularly interesting field in the MDL is called* Next. *This field is used to build "chains" of MDLs that together describe a single buffer that is not virtually contiguous. Each MDL in the chain describes a single virtually contiguous buffer. MDL chains are designed for use by network drivers only, and are not supported by most of the I/O Manager's standard functions. Therefore, MDL chains may not be used by standard device drivers in Windows NT.*

Describing Data Buffers with Buffered I/O

An alternative to Direct I/O is Buffered I/O. In this scheme, an intermediate buffer in system space is used as the data buffer. The I/O Manager is responsible for moving the data between the intermediate buffer and the requestor's original data buffer. The system buffer is deallocated by the I/O Manager when the IRP that describes the I/O request is ultimately completed. Figure 10.5 illustrates how Buffered I/O works.

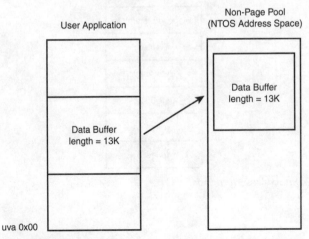

Figure 10.5. *How Buffered I/O works.*

To prepare a Buffered I/O request, the I/O Manager checks to ensure that the caller has appropriate access to the entire length of the data buffer, just as it did for Direct I/O. If the caller does not have appropriate access, the request is completed and is not passed along to the driver. As an optimization, this check is not performed if the request originated in Kernel Mode.

The I/O Manager next allocates a system buffer from the nonpaged pool with a size that is (at least) equal to that of the data buffer. If this is a write operation, the I/O Manager then copies the data from the requestor's buffer to the intermediate buffer. Whether the request is for a read or a write operation, the Kernel virtual address of the intermediate buffer is passed to the driver in the AssociatedIrp.SystemAddress field of the IRP. The length of the requestor's buffer is passed in the Parameters union in the IRP's current I/O Stack location. For a read operation, the length of the requestor's buffer is located in Parameters.Read.Length; for a write operation, the length of the requestor's buffer is located in Parameters.Write.Length.

> **Note**
>
> *Even though the* AssociatedIrp.SystemAddress *field is part of the AssociatedIrp structure in the IRP, this use of the field has nothing to do with associated IRPs!*

Because the address of the intermediate buffer corresponds to a location in the system's nonpaged pool, the address is usable by the driver in an arbitrary thread context. The system buffer is virtually contiguous. There is no guarantee, however, that the system buffer will be physically contiguous. When using Buffered I/O, the memory pages comprising the original data buffer are not locked during the I/O operation. Thus, their pageability is not affected by the I/O operation.

Before an IRP for a write operation described with Buffered I/O is sent to a driver, the I/O Manager copies the data from the requestor's buffer to the system space buffer. When a read operation using Buffered I/O is ultimately completed, the I/O Manager is responsible for copying the data from the intermediate buffer back to the requestor's data buffer. As an optimization, the I/O Manager delays this copy operation until the thread issuing the I/O request is next scheduled (using a "special Kernel APC for I/O completion"). When the requestor's thread is next ready to run, the I/O Manager copies the data from the intermediate system buffer back to the requestor's buffer and frees the system buffer. This optimization not only avoids possible page thrashing, it also serves a "cache-warming" function—preloading the processor cache with data from the buffer so that it is ready for rapid access by the requestor on return from the I/O request.

Buffered I/O is most often used by drivers controlling programmed I/O devices that use small data transfers. In this case, it is usually very convenient to have a requestor's data described by using a system virtual address.

Describing Data Buffers with Neither I/O

The final option for having a requestor's data buffer described by the I/O Manager is called Neither I/O. This option is called Neither I/O because the driver does not request either Buffered I/O or Direct I/O. In this scheme, the I/O Manager provides the driver with the requestor's virtual address of the data buffer. The buffer is not locked into memory—no intermediate buffering of the data takes place. The address is passed in the IRP's UserBuffer field.

Obviously, the requestor's virtual address is only useful in the context of the calling process. As a result, the only drivers that can make use of Neither I/O are drivers that are entered directly from the I/O Manager, with no drivers above them, and can process (and, typically, complete) the I/O operation in the context of the calling process. Therefore, drivers for conventional storage devices cannot use Neither I/O, because their Dispatch routines are called in an arbitrary thread context. Most typical device drivers cannot use Neither I/O because the I/O requests in these drivers are often started from their DpcForIsr routine, and are thus called in an arbitrary thread context.

If used appropriately and carefully, Neither I/O can be the most optimal method for some device drivers. For example, if a driver performs all of its work synchronously and in the context of the calling thread, Neither I/O saves the overhead of creating an MDL or recopying the data that would be required by Direct and Buffered I/O. These savings can be significant. How about a driver that can't complete *every* request it receives synchronously in the context of the calling thread, you might ask? If such a driver only *occasionally* needs to intermediately buffer the data or create a descriptor that allows the data buffer to be referenced from an arbitrary thread context, the overhead saved by using Neither I/O may be worthwhile.

Evaluating Available Data Buffer Descriptor Options

How do you decide whether to use Direct I/O, Buffered I/O, or Neither I/O in your driver? There's one case where the choice is made for you: If you are writing an Intermediate driver that will be layered above another driver, you must use the same buffering method that the device below you uses.

For device drivers, the choice is clearly an architectural decision that will affect both the complexity and performance of the driver. If you have a compelling reason to use Neither I/O and you can meet the requirements for its use, you should choose Neither I/O.

Most device drivers, however, do not use Neither I/O because of the constraints involved. Drivers that transfer at least a page of data or more at a time usually perform best when they use Direct I/O. Although the I/O Manager locks the pages in memory for the duration of the transfer, Direct I/O avoids the overhead of recopying the data to an intermediate buffer. Using Direct I/O for large transfers also prevents tying up large amounts of system pool. Also, most DMA drivers want to use Direct I/O. Drivers for packet-based DMA devices want to use it because this allows them to easily get the physical base address and length of the fragments that comprise the data buffer. Drivers for "common buffer" DMA devices want to use it to avoid the overhead of an additional copy operation.

Drivers that move data relatively slowly using Programmed I/O, have operations that pend for long periods of time, or transfer data in small blocks, will most profitably make use of Buffered I/O. These drivers include those that are used for traditional serial and parallel port devices, as well as most simple machine control drivers.

Buffered I/O is the simplest method to implement because a pointer to a virtually contiguous buffer in system space containing the data is provided in the IRP.

Although the choice of Buffered I/O versus Direct I/O is an important one, it is far from critical in most cases. It has been our experience that first-time NT driver writers often spend inordinate amounts of time worrying about which method to use. If it is not clear which method you should use in your driver, and if you're writing a driver for a programmed I/O-type device, start by using Buffered I/O. After writing your driver, you can experiment to see whether switching to Direct I/O will improve performance. After all, the only differences between the two from a programming standpoint are where you look in the IRP for your information (Irp->AssociatedIrp.SystemBuffer, versus Irp->DmaAddress) and one function call (to MmGetSystemAddressForMdl() to get a system virtual address mapping a buffer described by an MDL). Hardly a problem at all!

For convenience, the differences between Direct I/O, Buffered I/O, and Neither I/O for read and write operations are summarized in Table 10.1 that follows.

Table 10.1. Characteristics of Direct I/O, Buffered I/O, and Neither I/O.

	Direct I/O	Buffered I/O	Neither I/O
Requestor's Data	Described by MDL	Intermediately buffered in nonpaged system pool	Described by requestor's virtual address

continues

Table 10.1. Continued

	Direct I/O	Buffered I/O	Neither I/O
Status of Requestor's Original Buffer While I/O Operation Is in Progress	Locked in memory by I/O Manager	Remains unlocked	Remains unlocked
Buffer Description in IRP	Irp->MdlAddress contains pointer to MDL	Irp->Associated Irp.SystemBuffer contains kernel virtual address of intermediate buffer in non paged pool	Irp->User Buffer contains (unvalidated) requestor's virtual address of buffer
Context	MDL usable in Kernel Mode in arbitrary thread context	Kernel virtual address usable in Kernel Mode in arbitrary thread context	Usable only in context of calling thread

I/O Function Codes

Windows NT uses I/O function codes to identify the specific I/O operation that will take place on a particular file object. Like most operating systems, Windows NT I/O function codes are divided into major and minor I/O functions. Both appear in the IRP in the driver's I/O Stack location. Major function codes are defined with symbols starting IRP_MJ. Some of the more common major I/O function codes include the following:

- **IRP_MJ_CREATE.** This major function code creates a new file object by accessing an existing device or file, or by creating a new file. This function code represents requests issued via the CreateFile() Win32 function or the NtCreateFile() native NT system service.

- **IRP_MJ_CLOSE.** This major function code closes a previously opened file object. This function code represents requests issued via the CloseHandle() Win32 function or the NtClose() native NT system service.

- **IRP_MJ_READ.** This major function code performs a read operation on an existing file object. This function code represents requests issued via the ReadFile() Win32 function or the NtReadFile() native NT system service.

- **IRP_MJ_WRITE.** This major function code performs a write operation on an existing file object. This function code represents requests issued using the WriteFile() Win32 function or the NtWriteFile() system service.

- **IRP_MJ_DEVICE_CONTROL.** This major function code performs a driver-defined function on an existing file object. This function code represents requests issued using the Win32 function DeviceIoControl() or the NtDeviceIoControlFile() native NT system service.

- **IRP_MJ_INTERNAL_DEVICE_CONTROL.** This major function code performs a driver-defined function on an existing file object. There are no user-level APIs that correspond with this function. This function is typically used for inter-driver communication purposes.

> **Note**
>
> *The complete list of I/O function codes appears in NTDDK.H. Functions other than those listed in the preceding section are typically of interest only to file systems, network drivers, or other very specialized drivers, however, and will never be encountered by ordinary device drivers.*

Minor I/O function codes in Windows NT are defined with symbols that start with IRP_MN_. Windows NT mostly avoids using minor function codes to overload major functions for device drivers, favoring instead the use of I/O Control codes. Therefore, almost all IRPs received by device drivers have a minor function code of IRP_MN_NORMAL (which, not surprisingly, has the value 0x00). In general, minor I/O function codes are used exclusively by file systems and network transports. For example, one file system-specific minor I/O function code is IRP_MN_COMPRESSED, indicating that the data should be written to the volume in compressed format.

The major and minor I/O function codes associated with a particular IRP are stored in the MajorFunction and MinorFunction fields of the current I/O Stack location in the IRP. These fields may therefore be referenced, as shown Example 10.1.

Example 10.1. Checking an IRP's major and minor function codes.

```
IoStack = IoGetCurrentIrpStackLocation(Irp);
If (IoStack->MajorFunction == IRP_MJ_READ) {
    If (IoStack->MinorFunction != IRP_MN_NORMAL {
        // do something

}
```

Understanding Device I/O Control Functions (IOCTLs)

Most of the Windows NT major I/O function codes should be fairly self-explanatory. IRP_MJ_DEVICE_CONTROL and IRP_MJ_INTERNAL_DEVICE_CONTROL, however, probably require a bit of explanation. IRP_MJ_DEVICE_CONTROL is the major function code used for IRPs resulting from calls to the Win32 function DeviceIoControl() or the native NT function NtDeviceIoControlFile(). Figure 10.6 shows the prototype of the the Win32 DeviceIoControl() function.

```
BOOL DeviceIoControl(
        HANDLE  hDevice,              // handle to device of interest
        DWORD   dwIoControlCode,      // control code of operation to
                                      // perform
        LPVOID  lpInBuffer,           // pointer to buffer to supply
                                      // input data
        DWORD   nInBufferSize,        // size of input buffer
        LPVOID  lpOutBuffer,          // pointer to buffer to receive
                                      // output data
        DWORD   nOutBufferSize,       // size of output buffer
        LPDWORD lpBytesReturned,      // pointer to variable to rcv byte
                                      // count
        LPOVERLAPPED lpOverlapped     // pointer to overlapped
                                      // structure
);
```

Figure 10.6. DeviceIoControl() *function prototype.*

The only difference between IRP_MJ_DEVICE_CONTROL and IRP_MJ_INTERNAL_DEVICE_CONTROL is that there is no API to request that the I/O Manager build IRPs with a major function of IRP_MJ_INTERNAL_DEVICE_CONTROL from user mode. Therefore, the IRP_MJ_INTERNAL_DEVICE_CONTROL major function code can be used only by device drivers that create IRPs manually. IRPs with this function code could be used, for example, to provide a private communications mechanism between two drivers. In fact, this is the way the SCSI Class Drivers send requests to the SCSI Port Driver. Because IRPs of this type could never be built by a user-mode program, the communication mechanism is somewhat more secure than it would be if it used regular IRP_MJ_DEVICE_CONTROL functions.

So how is IRP_MJ_DEVICE_CONTROL typically used? When a driver supports a particular type of device, that device is likely to have a set of specialized functions that can be controlled via the driver. These are functions other than those that can be described using the standard IRP_MJ_CREATE, IRP_MJ_CLOSE, IRP_MJ_READ, and IRP_MJ_WRITE function codes. For example, the device driver for a SCSI tape unit might want to provide a mechanism that enables users to send a request to erase a tape. Such device-specific requests are described using the IRP_MJ_DEVICE_CONTROL major function code. This major function code simply means "other" (that is, a request other than Create, Close, Read, or Write is being made). Specifically, the device control function to be performed (such as "erase the tape") is indicated by an I/O control code (or IOCTL) that is passed as part of the request.

Standard devices that appear in Windows NT systems have predefined sets of I/O control codes that they implement. The I/O control codes for these functions are described in the Windows NT Kernel-Mode Driver Reference manual, and are defined in NTDDK.H. For example, the I/O control code used to request the SCSI Tape driver to erase a tape is IOCTL_TAPE_ERASE. Similarly, the I/O control code that sets the output volume for the audio channel of a CD-ROM drive is IOCTL_CDROM_SET_VOLUME. If you write a driver for a device that corresponds to one of the standard devices in the system, your driver is expected to implement the standard I/O control codes for that device type.

Defining Custom IOCTLs

Drivers for nonstandard devices may also want to provide I/O control codes that correspond to the specific functions that they perform. For example, if we were writing a device driver for a toaster, we would need to implement an I/O control code that enabled a user to send a request to the driver to set the toast brownness level on the device. We accomplish this by defining a custom I/O control code for each function that we want to implement.

Some operating systems allow the driver writer to choose values for custom I/O control codes at random (values of "1" and "2" are particularly popular). Windows NT, however, actually attaches meaning to the values of I/O control codes, as shown in Figure 10.7.

Fortunately, Windows NT provides a macro that defines custom control codes, saving us from having to manually pack bits into the I/O Control Code longword. This macro is named, appropriately, CTL_CODE. The CTL_CODE macro is defined in both NTDDK.H (for use by drivers) and in WINIOCTL.H (for use by applications programs). This allows a single header file, defining the custom IOCTLs that a driver implements, to be shared by the driver and any application programs that may issue IOCTL requests to the driver. The CTL_CODE macro takes the following arguments:

```
CTL_CODE(DeviceType, Function, Method, Access)
```

The purpose of each argument is described in the sections that follow.

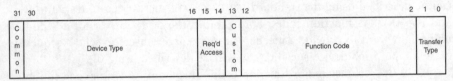

Figure 10.7. *Format for I/O control codes.*

CTL_CODE *DeviceType* **Argument**

The *DeviceType* argument for the CTL_CODE macro is a value (of type DEVICE_TYPE) that indicates the category of device to which a given I/O control code belongs. Standard NT devices have standard NT device types (FILE_DEVICE_DISK for disk drives, FILE_DEVICE_TAPE for tapes, and so on) that are defined in the same .H files as the CTL_CODE macro. Custom device types, for devices such as our toaster that don't correspond to any standard NT device, may be chosen from the range of 32768-65535. These values are reserved for use by Microsoft customers. If you're defining a custom device type, it doesn't matter what value you choose within this range. Even if you choose the same value as another custom device on your system, everything will still work fine.

> **Note**
>
> *In addition to its use in the CTRL_CODE macro, there is another place the DEVICE_TYPE of a device is specified. The DEVICE_TYPE is also provided when a Device Object is created using the function IoCreateDevice(). The creation of Device Objects is described in Chapter 13, "Driver Entry." Typically, the DEVICE_TYPE that is specified when a Device Object is created by a driver is that same DEVICE_TYPE that is specified when any custom IOCTLs are defined for that device by the driver. However, NT does not require that a Device Object with a particular DEVICE_TYPE receive or process IOCTLs only of that same DEVICE_TYPE.*

CTL_CODE *Function* **Argument**

The *Function* argument to the CTL_CODE macro is a value, unique within your driver, which is associated with a particular function to be performed. For example, we would need to choose a particular function code that represents the "set toast brownness level" function implemented by our toaster driver. Custom function codes may be chosen from the range of values between 2048–4095. Again, the specific value you choose doesn't really matter, even if you choose the same function value that another driver already uses, as long as the value is unique within your driver.

CTL_CODE *Method* **Argument**

The *Method* argument indicates to the I/O Manager how the data buffers supplied with this request are to be described. To understand what this parameter relates to, take another look at the Win32 DeviceIoControl() function prototype (refer to Figure 10.6).

First, notice that there are *two* data buffers available on the function call. DeviceIoControl() is a very rare type of I/O system service because it provides the capability to supply multiple data buffers on a single request. Next, notice the unusual naming of these two buffers, relative to the direction of data movement of their contents. According to the comments in the prototype, the InBuffer contains data to be provided by the requestor to the driver. That is, the direction of movement of the data in the InBuffer is *in to the driver*. This buffer is typically used to transfer parameters or short chunks of data from the requestor to the driver. The comments in the function prototype indicate that the OutBuffer contains data coming *from the driver*. In fact, this buffer is typically used to move larger chunks of data between the requestor and driver *in either direction*. It might have been easier for all of us if they had just named these buffers BufferA and BufferB!

How the I/O Manager decribes these two buffers to a driver is indicated by the *Method* argument of the CTL_CODE macro. Possible values supplied for this argument are as follows:

- **METHOD_BUFFERED.** Both the InBuffer and the OutBuffer are handled as Buffered I/O.

- **METHOD_IN_DIRECT** and **METHOD_OUT_DIRECT.** The InBuffer is handled as Buffered I/O and the OutBuffer is handled as Direct I/O. The only difference between METHOD_IN_DIRECT and METHOD_OUT_DIRECT is the access check that is performed when validating the OutBuffer (METHOD_OUT_DIRECT checks the OutBuffer for read access; METHOD_IN_DIRECT checks the OutBuffer for write access).

- **METHOD_NEITHER.** Both the InBuffer and OutBuffer are handled as Neither I/O. The requestor's virtual address of each buffer is provided in the IRP.

For METHOD_BUFFERED, the system buffer allocated by the I/O Manager is large enough to hold the contents of the requestor's InBuffer or OutBuffer, whichever is larger. If an InBuffer was specified on the request, and its length is not zero, the contents of the InBuffer are copied to the intermediate system buffer. These operations are illustrated in Figure 10.8. As for any Buffered I/O request, the address of the system buffer is placed in the IRP in the AssociatedIrp.SystemBuffer field.

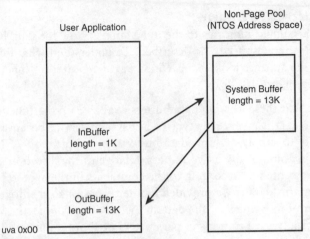

Figure 10.8. *An illustration of* METHOD_BUFFERED.

The IRP containing the request is then passed to the driver. The intermediately buffered input data may be read and acted on (even recopied, if necessary) by the driver. The driver then places any results to be returned in the OutBuffer in the intermediate system buffer, starting at the beginning of the buffer, directly over any input data that may have been present. When the request is ultimately completed, if an OutBuffer was specified on the request and its length is not zero, the number of bytes indicated in the IRP's IoStatus.Information field is copied from the intermediate buffer to the requestor's OutBuffer (limited, of course, to the size of the OutBuffer). As with any Buffered I/O request, the system buffer is deallocated when the IRP is ultimately completed.

In METHOD_IN_DIRECT and METHOD_OUT_DIRECT, the InBuffer (if one is specified and if its length is not zero) is handled exactly as for Buffered I/O. That is, an intermediate system buffer is allocated, and the data is copied from the requestor's InBuffer to the intermediate system buffer. A pointer to the system buffer is provided in the IRP in the AssociatedIrp.SystemBuffer field. The OutBuffer (if one is specified and if its length is not zero) is handled exactly as for Direct I/O. That is, the OutBuffer is checked for appropriate access, its physical pages are locked in memory, and an MDL is built describing it (see Figure 10.9). As with Direct I/O, a pointer to the MDL is provided in the IRP's MdlAddress field.

The only difference between METHOD_IN_DIRECT and METHOD_OUT_DIRECT is the access check performed by the I/O Manager on the OutBuffer. For METHOD_IN_DIRECT, the I/O Manager checks to ensure that the requestor has read access to the entire extent of the OutBuffer. In this case, the OutBuffer would be used for input to the driver. If METHOD_OUT_DIRECT is used, the I/O Manager checks to ensure that the requestor has write access to the entire extent of the OutBuffer.

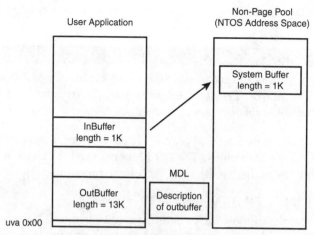

Figure 10.9. *An illustration of* METHOD_IN_DIRECT *and* METHOD_OUT_DIRECT.

In METHOD_NEITHER, both buffers are treated as in the Neither I/O method. That is, no access checking or intermediate buffering is performed, and no MDLs are built. The requestor's virtual addresses are provided in the IRP. The requestor's virtual address of the OutBuffer is supplied in the IRP in the UserBuffer field in the fixed portion of the IRP. The requestor's virtual address of the InBuffer is provided in the IRP in the I/O Stack location at Parameters.DeviceControl.Type3InputBuffer.

> ### Note
>
> *A couple of words on IOCTL buffering methods seem to be in order. Although the* DeviceIoControl() *function enables the specification of two buffers, most IOCTLs use only a single buffer and some require no buffer at all. Also, the same constraints apply to using* METHOD_NETIHER *that apply to using Neither I/O for read and write operations. That is, for* METHOD_NEITHER *to be used, the request must be processed in the context of the calling process.*

CTL_CODE Access **Argument**

The Access argument to the CTL_CODE macro indicates the type of access that must have been requested (and granted) when the file object was opened for a given I/O control code to be passed on to the driver by the I/O Manager. The possible values for this argument are as follows:

- **FILE_ANY_ACCESS.** This value indicates that any access may have been specified on the CreateFile() call.

- **FILE_READ_ACCESS.** This value indicates that read access must have been requested.

- **FILE_WRITE_ACCESS.** This value indicates that write access must have been requested.

The *Access* argument is required because I/O control operations are not intrinsically read or write operations. The I/O Manager needs to know what type of access to check for in the handle table before the function is allowed.

Using the CTL_CODE Macro

By way of example, suppose we're defining some custom I/O control codes for our toaster device. The definitions might be something like the following:

Example 10.2. Defining custom I/O control codes for a device.

```
#define FILE_DEVICE_TOASTER 53334
#define IOCTL_TOASTER_START_TOASTING        \
            CTL_CODE(FILE_DEVICE_TOASTER, 2048,
                            METHOD_BUFFERED, FILE_ANY_ACCESS)
#define IOCTL_TOASTER_EJECT_TOAST                \
            CTL_CODE(FILE_DEVICE_TOASTER, 2049, \
                            METHOD_ BUFFERED, FILE_ANY_ACCESS)
#define IOCTL_TOASTER_SET_BROWNESS            \
            CTL_CODE(FILE_DEVICE_TOASTER, 2050,    \
                            METHOD_ BUFFERED, FILE_WRITE_ACCESS)
```

Here, we chose a random value that represents the device type for our toaster device. We also defined three custom I/O control codes for this device using the CTL_CODE macro: IOCTL_TOASTER_START_TOASTING, IOCTL_TOASTER_EJECT_TOAST, and IOCTL_TOASTER_SET_BROWNESS. For each of these custom I/O control codes, we chose a function value from the range that is reserved for Microsoft customers that makes the I/O control code unique within our driver. For all three of these I/O control codes, we specified the buffers to be handled as Buffered I/O by specifying METHOD_BUFFERED. In order to be able to issue the SET_BROWNESS I/O control code, the issuing user must previously have successfully opened the toaster device for write. For the START_TOASTING and EJECT_TOAST I/O control codes to be issued, however, no specific access needs to be requested when the toaster device was opened.

The issues involved in choosing the most appropriate buffering method to use for a custom IOCTL are pretty much the same as those involved in choosing the best method to use for read and write functions. Driver writers should keep in mind that InBuffer and OutBuffer need not be used in every IOCTL that is implemented. If small amounts of data or control information are to be transferred, the InBuffer is typically used and the OutBuffer is not referenced. Unless METHOD_NEITHER is specified, the data from the InBuffer is always intermediately buffered, if present. Thus, if only the InBuffer is to be used, the driver may define the IOCTL with METHOD_BUFFERED, METHOD_IN_DIRECT, or METHOD_OUT_DIRECT.

When large amounts of data are to be transferred in either direction between a driver and a requestor's buffer, the OutBuffer is typically used. On these requests, the InBuffer is most often not referenced. For these IOCTLs, the driver writer needs to choose whether the data being transferred between the driver and the requestor's InBuffer should be intermediately buffered. To intermediately buffer this data, the driver writer chooses METHOD_BUFFERED. To have the pages comprising the requestor's buffer locked into memory and described by an MDL, the driver writer will specify METHOD_IN_DIRECT (for data being transferred from the requestor's buffer to the driver) or METHOD_OUT_DIRECT (for data being transferred from the driver out to the requestor's buffer).

Single requests that use both buffers tend to pass parameters or control information in the InBuffer, and to pass the data for the driver to operate on in the OutBuffer. Because the InBuffer is always described by using Buffered I/O, the choice of how the data for the OutBuffer is to be described to the driver (and the direction of data movement) dictates the choice of which buffering method to use, as previously described.

Finally, regardless of whether one or both buffers are used in a request, METHOD_NEITHER may be appropriate when a driver can process the request in the context of the calling thread.

As a convenience, Table 10.2 summarizes the differences between the various buffering methods for IOCTLs, and where the information about each request can be found in the IRP.

I/O Request Parameters

Parameters, as specified by the requestor, which are specific to a particular major I/O function code, are located in the parameters field of the current I/O Stack location in the IRP. The definitions for the parameters fields available to device drivers appear in NTDDK.H. The locations of parameters in the current I/O Stack location for the most common I/O functions of interest to device drivers are described in the following list:

- **IRP_MJ_READ.** Parameters for this function code are as follows:

    - **Parameters.Read.Length.** A ULONG, which contains the size in bytes of the requestor's buffer.

- **Parameters.Read.Key.** A ULONG, which ontains the key value to be used with this read. This is typically used for supporting byte-range locking of files.

- **Parameters.Read.ByteOffset.** A LARGE_INTEGER, which contains the offset (typically in a file) at which this read operation should begin.

- **IRP_MJ_WRITE.** Parameters for this function code are as follows:

  - **Parameters.Write.Length.** A ULONG, which contains the size, in bytes, of the requestor's buffer.

  - **Parameters.Write.Key.** A ULONG, which contains the key value to be used with this write. This is typically used for supporting byte-range locking of files, which is only of interest to file system drivers.

  - **Parameters.Write.ByteOffset.** A LARGE_INTEGER, which contains the offset (typically in a file) at which this write operation should begin.

- **IRP_MJ_DEVICE_CONTROL.** Parameters for this function code are as follows:

  - **Parameters.DeviceIoControl.OutputBufferLength.** A ULONG, which contains the length, in bytes, of the OutBuffer.

  - **Parameters.DeviceIoControl.InputBufferLength.** A ULONG, which contains the length, in bytes, of the InBuffer.

  - **Parameters.DeviceIoControl.ControlCode.** A ULONG, which contains the I/O control code that identifies the particular device control function being requested. This control code usually is previously defined by the driver using the CTL_CODE macro.

  - **Parameters.DeviceIoControl.Type3InputBuffer.** A PVOID, which contains the requestor's virtual address of the InBuffer. It is typically used only when an IOCTL uses METHOD_NEITHER.

Note that IRP_MJ_CREATE has a set of parameters in the current I/O Stack location, but these parameters are usually of interest only to file system drivers.

As an example of the way this information is used for an IRP_MJ_READ operation, the offset from which to start reading and the number of bytes to read are located in the current I/O Stack location, as shown in Example 10.3:

Example 10.3. Locating parameters for a read request.

```
IoStack = IoGetCurrentIrpStackLocation(Irp);
Offset = IoStack->Parameters.Read.ByteOffset;
BytesToRead = IoStack->Parameters.Read.Length;
```

Table 10.2. IOCTL buffering methods.

	METHOD_BUFFERED	METHOD_IN_DIRECT	METHOD_OUT_DIRECT	METHOD_NEITHER
InBuffer Uses	Buffered I/O	Buffered I/O	Buffered I/O	Requestor's virtual address
InBuffer (if present on call) located via	Kernel virtual address in Irp->AssociatedIrp.SystemBuffer			Requestor's virtual address in **Parameters. DeviceIoControl. Type3InputBuffer** of current I/O Stack
InBuffer length	Length in bytes in **Parameters.DeviceIoControl.InputBufferLength** of current I/O Stack Location			
OutBuffer Uses	Buffered I/O	Direct I/O	Direct I/O	Requestor's virtual address
OutBuffer (if present on call) located via	Kernel virtual address in Irp->AssociatedIrp.SystemBuffer	MDL pointed to by Irp->MdlAddress	MDL pointed to by Irp->MdlAddress	Requestor's virtual address in Irp->UserBuffer
OutBuffer length	Length in bytes in **Parameters.DeviceIoControl.OutputBufferLength** of current I/O Stack Location			

As a further example, our toaster driver might use the code in Example 10.4 to identify the particular operation being requested and the length of the buffers being supplied:

Example 10.4. Identifying requested IOCTL operation and supplied buffer lengths.

```
IoStack = IoGetCurrentIrpStackLocation(Irp);

Code = IoStack->Parameters.DeviceIoControl.IoControlCode;

Switch(Code) {
    case IOCTL_TOASTER_SET_BROWNESS:

        //
        // InBuffer contains longword indicating browness
        // level requested
        //
        InLength =
            IoStack->Parameters.DeviceIoControl.InputBufferLength;

        if (InLength != sizeof(ULONG)) {
            status = STATUS_BAD_PARAMETER
        }
```

continues

Continued

```
        //
        // The OutBuffer will receive the browness level actually set
        //
        OutLength =
            IoStack->Parameters.DeviceIoControl.OutputBufferLength;

        if (OutLength != sizeof(ULONG)) {
            status = STATUS_BAD_PARAMETER
        }

        // Handle this function...
        break;

    case IOCTL_EJECT_TOAST:

        // Handle this function...
        break;

    case IOCTL_SET_BROWNESS:

        // Handle this function...
        break;
}
```

In Example 10.4, the driver retrieves the particular I/O control code from the current IRP Stack location in the location `Parameters.DeviceIoControl.IoControlCode`. The driver then switches, based on this code. In processing the `IOCTL_TOASTER_SET_BROWNESS` function, the driver retrieves and validates the lengths of the requestor's `InBuffer` and `OutBuffer`. The size of the `InBuffer`, as indicated by the requestor, is retrieved from `Parameters.DeviceIoControl.InputBufferLength` in the current I/O Stack location. The size of the OutBuffer (as indicated by the requestor) is retrieved from `Parameters.DeviceIoControl.OutputBufferLength`.

Handling and Processing IRPs

On receiving an I/O request via an I/O system service, the I/O Manager allocates and builds an IRP that completely describes that request. The IRP is allocated from nonpaged space, using either a preallocated IRP in one of the I/O Manager's lookaside lists, or by allocating the IRP directly from nonpaged pool. The I/O Manager initializes the fixed portion of the IRP (in the format indicated by the driver) with the description of the requestor's buffer. The I/O Manager then initializes the first I/O Stack location in the IRP with the function codes and parameters for this request. The I/O Manager then calls the first driver in the driver "stack" to begin processing the request.

Chapter 11, "The Layered Driver Model," covers in detail exactly how the request is processed.

Case Study: When Neither I/O Was the Only Alternative

We have a colleague, a very talented Windows NT driver writer, who works for an imaging company. This company makes high-resolution hardcopy imaging devices (printers, really) that are capable of rendering color images. The images printed are typically many megabytes in length. The imaging hardware itself is a programmed I/O-type device with many megabytes of shared RAM.

After the device is set up appropriately, image rendering is performed with standard IRP_MJ_WRITE functions from a user-mode program. Each write request describes a multimegabyte buffer that contains a single image to be rendered. Operation of the device is synchronous and single-threaded. Only one rendering operation can be in progress at a time, and until that rendering operation is completed, another one cannot be started.

The driver for this device would typically utilize Direct I/O, due to the size of the user buffer. In testing his initial Direct I/O design, however, our colleague ran into a problem: On a system with limited amounts of physical memory, it was sometimes impossible to lock down the entire data buffer containing an image. When it was possible, locking down such a large amount of physical memory often caused the system to slow down unacceptably. What did he do to fix this?

The answer was to use Neither I/O to describe the write operations. Because no drivers can be layered over this device and requests are sent directly to this device driver from user mode applications, this driver will be called in the context of the requesting process. In addition, because the device itself is inherently synchronous, there was no problem with "blocking" the user mode application while moving data from the requestor's data buffer and the device's shared memory.

By using Neither I/O, the user virtual address of the requestor's data buffer was retrieved from the IRP and used as the source address for the copy operation to the device. During the copy operation, if portions of the requestor's data buffer were not resident, they were simply automatically page-faulted into memory. Because all processing was performed in the driver's Dispatch entry point, processing was performed at IRQL PASSIVE_LEVEL, and page faults presented no problem.

Chapter **11**

The Layered Driver Model

This chapter will review:

- **User Mode versus Kernel Mode Drivers.** Windows NT supports many different driver architectures. In this section, we describe the difference between User mode drivers and Kernel mode drivers.

- **Intermediate and Device Driver Layering.** Windows NT utilizes a layered driver architecture. This section describes how Intermediate drivers locate and layer themselves over lower-layer device drivers.

- **File System Driver Layering.** This section covers how File System drivers are dynamically located at the top of the storage driver stack.

- **Processing I/O Requests in Layers.** With the details of how driver stacks are built already discussed, this section describes how I/O requests are processed by being passed from driver to driver until they are completed.

- **Completion Notification.** This section describes how higher layer drivers may optionally be notified of the ultimate completion of an I/O request they have passed on to one or more underlying drivers in the driver stack.

- **Special Understandings Between Drivers.** The standard method of passing IRPs from driver to driver is not used by all drivers. This section discusses some alternative methods that drivers use to communicate.

- **Filter Drivers.** This section describes how one driver may dynamically attach and layer itself above another driver. This process allows the attaching driver to intercept or "filter" the I/O requests originally destined for the driver that was attached.

- **Fast I/O.** This section describes optimization of the normal "packet-based" I/O model used by most drivers, which NT supports.

It's not uncommon for people to get confused when they first start to learn about writing Windows NT drivers. Part of the reason for this confusion is the fact that Windows NT does not have a single driver model. Rather, there are many different things called "drivers" in Windows NT. At the highest level, the types of drivers may be divided into two categories: User mode drivers and Kernel mode drivers.

Although this book focuses on Kernel mode drivers, a brief mention of User mode drivers might be useful. User mode drivers aren't what most people typically think of when they think of "drivers." User mode drivers are specific to a particular environment subsystem and provide support to applications that run under the control of that subsystem. User mode drivers often provide a subsystem-specific interface to a standard Kernel mode driver.

In the Win32 Environment Subsystem, User mode drivers are implemented as Dynamic Linked Libraries (DLLs). One of the types of User mode drivers used by Win32 in NT 4 is Multimedia drivers. Win32 Multimedia drivers are called by the Windows Multimedia DLL (WINMM.DLL) to perform various functions. These User mode drivers may keep local state and information, and even pop-up dialog boxes to request user input. The drivers may be "software-only" or may utilize hardware by forwarding requests using standard APIs (such as CreateFile(), ReadFile(), WriteFile(), and DeviceIoControl()) to an underlying Windows NT Kernel mode driver. As an example, most Audio Compression Manager (ACM) drivers, which implement audio compression algorithms, are User mode, software-only drivers. On the other hand, Multimedia Control Interface (MCI) drivers are User mode drivers that typically interact with underlying hardware through the use of a collaborating Kernel mode driver. Figure 11.1 illustrates the interaction between a user application, the Win32 Environment Subsystem, a User mode driver, and its related Kernel mode driver.

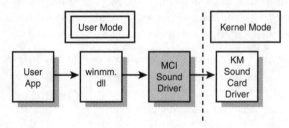

Figure 11.1. *How User mode drivers fit in.*

Kernel Mode Drivers

As distinct from User mode drivers, Kernel mode drivers form part of the Windows NT Executive layer and run in Kernel mode, as their name implies. Kernel mode drivers are accessed and supported by the I/O Manager. Requests are sent to the I/O Manager as a result of executing an I/O system service, such as a Win32 `CreateFile()` or `ReadFile()` function, or a Windows NT native function such as `NtCreateFile()` or `NtReadFile()`.

The four types of Kernel mode drivers are as follows:

- File System drivers

- Intermediate drivers

- Device drivers

- Mini-drivers

These drivers can be grouped together in "stacks" that work together to completely process a request targeted at a particular Device Object, as shown in Figure 11.2.

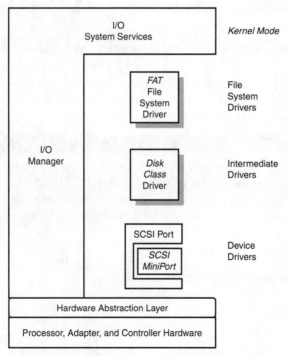

Figure 11.2. *A typical NT driver stack.*

File System Drivers

File System drivers exist at the top of the NT Kernel mode driver stack. File System drivers play a special role in Windows NT because they are tightly coupled with the NT Memory and Cache Manager subsystems. File System drivers may implement a physical file system, such as NTFS or FAT; however, they may also implement a distributed or networked facility such as NT's LanMan Redirector, or NT's named pipe communication mechanism. File System drivers may also implement a "pseudo-file" system. Development of NT File System drivers is currently unsupported by Microsoft, is almost entirely undocumented, and requires a special Installable File Systems development kit from Microsoft. Further discussion of File System drivers appears in Chapter 21, "File System Drivers."

Intermediate Drivers

Intermediate drivers form the middle layer of the NT driver hierarchy, sitting below File System drivers and above Device drivers. In fact, there may be multiple Intermediate drivers in a stack of NT drivers. Intermediate drivers provide either a "value-added" feature (such as mirroring or disk-level encryption) or class processing for devices. In either case, Intermediate drivers rely upon the Device drivers below them in the NT driver hierarchy for access to a physical device.

The most common type of Intermediate driver is the Class driver. A Class driver typically performs processing for a category of device, having common attributes, which is physically accessed via a separately addressable shared bus. For example, the Disk Class driver performs processing for disk-type devices that are located on a SCSI bus.

> **Note**
>
> *In NT 4, for the sake of uniformity and simplicity, the Disk Class driver also handles requests that go to the ATAPI (ATDISK) driver. This is because the ATAPI driver was implemented as a "SCSI Miniport" driver, even though it does not sit on a SCSI bus! Mini-drivers are covered later in the chapter.*

Another example of a Class driver is the Tape Class driver, which handles tape-oriented requests for SCSI tape drives.

Device Drivers

Device drivers are what most people think of first when they hear the term "drivers." These are the third type of Kernel mode driver in Windows NT. Device drivers interface to hardware via the Hardware Abstraction Layer

(HAL). In general, device drivers control one or more peripheral devices, in response to a user request. Device drivers may receive and process interrupts from their hardware. device drivers may exist alone or may be located under an Intermediate driver in a driver stack. If a device driver exists in a driver stack, it is always at the bottom of the stack. An example of a device driver in a driver stack is the NT serial port driver. Our Toaster example driver, mentioned in previous chapters, would also be a device driver. The Toaster driver would probably exist on its own, without an Intermediate or File System driver above it.

Mini-Drivers

The final type of Kernel mode driver in Windows NT is the Mini-Driver. Although Mini-Drivers are typically device drivers in NT 4, there are also Mini-Drivers that are Intermediate drivers. What distinguishes a Mini-Driver from other Device drivers is that the Mini-Driver exists within a "wrapper." The Mini-Driver's interfaces are typically restricted to those provided by the wrapper, which dictates the structure of the Mini-Driver. This structure is usually very specific to the type of peripheral being supported. For example, the interface for network Mini-Drivers is highly specific to sending and receiving communications messages.

Because the wrapper provides a special environment for the Mini-Driver, most properly written Mini-Drivers restrict themselves to calling only interfaces that are provided by their wrapper. Thus, the Mini-Driver does not call any of the functions supplied by the I/O Manager. Instead, it calls functions provided by the wrapper, which in turn may call the I/O Manager's functions, as required. Figure 11.3 shows a diagram of a Mini-Driver within its wrapper.

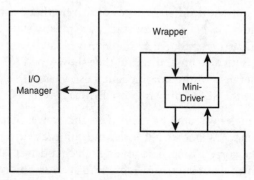

Figure 11.3. *Mini-Driver/wrapper structure.*

The purpose of the Mini-Driver approach is to make it relatively easy to write drivers for common peripherals, such as video cards, net cards, and SCSI adapters. All common processing is done in the wrapper; the only work done by the Mini-Driver is the actual interfacing with the hardware. A bonus of this approach is that its use makes it quite easy to implement an operating system-independent driver scheme. Because all interfaces between the Mini-Driver and the "outside world" are typically via its wrapper, if the wrapper exists on multiple operating systems, the Mini-Driver will automatically be supported.

Perhaps the best-known example of a Mini-Driver is the SCSI Miniport driver. The Miniport driver exists inside the wrapper provided by the SCSI Port driver. The SCSI Miniport driver's structure is dictated by the SCSI Port driver. The SCSI Port driver handles all the work common to queuing and processing SCSI requests, including building an appropriate SCSI Command Data Block. The Miniport driver's job is restricted to placing the request on the hardware in a manner that is specific to its particular SCSI adapter. In addition to Windows NT, Microsoft has provided a SCSI Port driver wrapper for Windows 95. Thus, SCSI Miniport drivers are compatible across these two operating systems. Although we don't specifically discuss Mini-Drivers in detail in this book, Chapters 22–24 in Part 3 offer a brief overview of SCSI, Video, and NDIS Miniport drivers.

Even though different types of Kernel mode drivers can be very different, they all still exist within the larger framework supplied by the I/O Manager. Thus, the underlying concepts for the various types of Kernel mode drivers are all the same. The differences come in the details of the way each type of driver is implemented.

Intermediate and Device Driver Layering

So, now that you know the different types of drivers that exist, how are they organized into stacks? In NT 4, driver stacks are mostly static, being created when the system is first started. An example driver stack was shown earlier in Figure 11.2. This is a conceptual diagram that shows the FAT File System driver that uses the services of the Intermediate Disk Class driver, which in turn uses the services of the SCSI Port/MiniPort Device driver.

Driver stacks are mostly created by the drivers themselves. The correct creation of a driver stack under Windows NT 4 depends on each driver in the stack being started at the correct time. The time at which a driver is started is determined by its Registry parameters (for more information on driver startup time, see Chapter 4, "The Registry," and Chapter 20, "Installing and Starting Drivers").

The first driver to start in the example stack shown in Figure 11.2 is the SCSI Miniport driver. When the Miniport driver is started, it causes its wrapper, the

SCSI port driver, to start. The SCSI Port/Miniport driver searches the bus and finds SCSI adapters that it will control. For each adapter found, the SCSI Port driver creates a Device Object named \Device\ScsiPortX, where X is an ordinal number representing a particular SCSI adapter.

After all the SCSI Miniport drivers configured in the system have started, the Class drivers are started, one at a time. These are the Intermediate drivers in the driver stack, and include (for example) the Disk Class driver, the CD-ROM Class Driver, and the Tape Class driver. When a Class driver starts, it looks for Device Objects that represent SCSI Port devices, since these are the devices over which it will layer. The Class driver does this by calling the IoGetDeviceObjectPointer() function shown in Figure 11.4.

NTSTATUS
IoGetDeviceObjectPointer(
    IN PUNICODE_STRING *ObjectName*,
    IN ACCESS_MASK *DesiredAccess*,
    OUT PFILE_OBJECT **FileObject*,
    OUT PDEVICE_OBJECT **DeviceObject*);

ObjectName: Name of Device Object being sought.

DesiredAccess: Represents the access required to the indicated Device Object.

FileObject: Pointer to the File Object used to access the device.

DeviceObject: Pointer to the Device Object with the name ObjectName.

Figure 11.4. IoGetDeviceObjectPointer() *function prototype.*

Note that the IoGetDeviceObjectPointer() function takes the name of the Device Object to find, and returns a pointer to the Device Object ultimately associated with that name. The function works by sending a Create request to the named device. If this request fails, either no device named ObjectName exists or the caller cannot be granted the access indicated by DesiredAccess. If the Create request succeeds, a File Object is created, which increments the reference count of the Device Object to which the File Object belongs. The I/O Manager then artificially increments the reference count on the File Object by one, and sends a Close request to the device. As a result of this entire process, the Device Object (whose pointer is returned in DeviceObject) cannot be deleted until its reference count is decremented. Thus, the lower-layer Device Object cannot "go away" while the Class driver has a pointer to it.

The Device Object's reference count is decremented when the Class driver calls ObDereferenceObject() on the File Object, which results in the File Object's reference count going to zero. When a File Object's reference count becomes zero, the reference count in the Device Object associated with that File Object is decremented.

Notice that when a Class driver calls IoGetDeviceObjectPointer() to search for SCSI Port devices, it does so by name. The Class driver sequentially searches for devices named \Device\ScsiPort0, \Device\ScsiPort1, \Device\ScsiPort2, and so on until IoGetDeviceObjectPointer() returns an error.

Next, having found one or more SCSI Ports, the Class driver enumerates the individual device units on each of these SCSI Ports. The Class driver does this by sending requests to the SCSI Port/Miniport driver. For each device the Class driver finds that it can control, it creates one or more Device Objects. The Class driver also "claims" the device by sending a request to the SCSI Port driver, thus preventing a different Class driver from later trying to control the same device.

The specific process that the Disk Class driver follows is an example of the general process. The Disk Class driver enumerates the device units on each SCSI Port. For each disk found, the Disk Class driver creates a Device Object named \Device\HardDiskX\Partition0 (where X is the ordinal number of the disk). This Device Object represents the (entire raw) disk volume itself. In addition, the Disk Class driver creates one Device Object for each logical partition on the disk with a format that it can identify as supportable under Windows NT. These Device Objects are named \Device\HardDiskX\PartitionY, where X is the ordinal disk number and Y is the ordinal partition number starting at one on that hard disk. The system later assigns actual drive letters (such as C:, D:, and so on) to these devices in the form of symbolic links.

For each Device Object created, the Class driver stores away the Device Object pointer for the underlying device to which its device is linked. That is, for each Disk Device Object it creates, the Disk Class driver stores (in the disk Device Object's Device Extension) the pointer to the SCSI Port Device Object on which that disk unit resides.

Whenever a Device Object is created for a device that is to be layered above another device, the high-level Device Object must be initialized carefully to reflect the attributes of the lower-layer device. The information about the lower-layer device comes from its Device Object, or even from interrogating the lower-layer physical device itself.

In initializing their Device Objects, the Class drivers use information from both the SCSI Port's Device Object and from the physical device units that they support. For example, a Disk Class driver checks the information returned from interrogating the physical device to determine whether the device is removable. If the device is removable, the Disk Class driver sets the FILE_REMOVABLE_MEDIA flag in the Characteristics field of the Device Object, as appropriate.

Another field that must be carefully initialized is the StackSize field in the Device Object. The StackSize field indicates the number of I/O Stack locations required for requests going to that device and any devices below it. Intermediate drivers set the StackSize field of their Device Objects to one greater than the contents of the StackSize field in the Device Object of the device over which they are layered. Because the device driver is usually the last (that is, lowest) driver in the stack, the value in the StackSize field in the Device driver's Device Object is normally 1.

Finally, the Buffering method and alignment requirement must also be preserved from lower- to higher-layer Device Objects. The Buffering method indicates how the driver wishes to have read and write type requests described to it, as described in Chapter 10, "How I/O Requests Are Described." This is indicated by the flags DO_BUFFERED_IO or DO_DIRECT_IO in the Device Object. Either of these flags, if set in the lower-layer Device Object, must also be set in the higher-layer Device Object. Therefore, when the Class driver creates its Device Objects, it initializes the Flags field of its Device Objects to reflect the Buffering method indicated in the SCSI Port device.

The AlignmentRequirement field in the Device Object indicates the required base alignment of data buffers sent to the device. The alignment requirement of the lower-layer device must also be reflected in any higher-layer Device Objects. Therefore, when the Class driver creates its Device Objects, it initializes the AlignmentRequirement field of the Device Objects it creates by using information from the SCSI Port Device Object.

With all the Class Device Objects created, the first two members of the driver "stack" are complete—Class devices over SCSI Port devices. If one SCSI adapter existed in a system, with one SCSI disk having two recognizable partitions on that SCSI adapter, the created Device Objects look like those shown in Figure 11.5. Note that this creates a many-to-one relationship between Intermediate-layer Device Objects and Device Objects created at the lowest layer, which is typical in NT.

We used the SCSI Port driver and Class drivers as examples to illustrate how a driver stack is built; however, the process is identical for all stacks involving Intermediate and Device drivers. The Device driver starts, then one or more Intermediate drivers layer above the Device driver, identifying by name the Device Objects of the Device driver that are to be supported. The Device Objects created for the Intermediate driver must carefully reflect the information in the device's Device Objects.

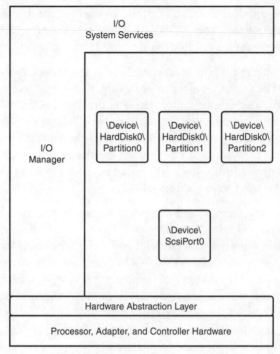

Figure 11.5. *Disk Class Device Objects layered over the SCSI Port Device Object.*

Note that the driver stack created by this process is static. Only at initialization time do the Class drivers search for SCSI Port devices on which the supported devices may exist. Therefore, if a SCSI device is added after the Class driver starts (as a result, for example, of plugging in a PC Card SCSI Adapter), the SCSI Class drivers never see this new port device and never attempt to enumerate its bus to find potentially supportable Class devices. Also note that the Class drivers are dependent on the actual name of the SCSI Port device. For example, if somebody creates a unique Device driver—not utilizing the SCSI Miniport architecture—that names its SCSI Port Device objects something other than \Device\ScsiPortX, these Device Objects are never found. Continuing this example, even if this Driver creates Device Objects named \Device\ScsiPortX, the values for x must monotonically increase, starting with zero, due to the specific algorithm used by the Class drivers.

File System Driver Layering

File System drivers (FSDs) are at the top of the Windows NT driver stack. FSDs are added dynamically to the driver stack, as opposed to the way Intermediate drivers are added.

The first time an I/O operation is directed to a file-structured device, the I/O Manager initiates a Mount operation for the device. The file-system recognition process then takes place. During file-system recognition, each FSD of an appropriate type for the device encountered is called to see whether it recognizes the file structure on the media being accessed. If the FSD recognizes the file structure present on the media, it creates a Device Object that represents a mounted instance of that file system on the particular device.

The I/O Manager recognizes file-structured devices through the existence of a Volume Parameter Block (VPB) for the device. The VPB links the Device Object that represents the partition (created by the Class driver) with a Device Object that represents a mounted instance of a file system on that partition (created by an FSD). On first access, if a VPB exists for the device and if the DeviceObject pointer in the VPB is NULL, the I/O Manager initiates the Mount operation. Figure 11.6 shows the format of the VPB and its relationship to the Class driver's Device Object.

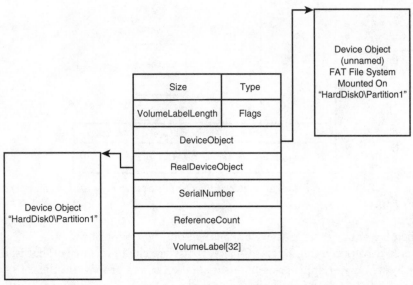

Figure 11.6. *How File System Device Objects and Disk Class Device Objects are linked by a VPB.*

Using the previous example driver stack, the first time an I/O operation is directed to device \Device\HardDisk0\Partition1, the I/O Manager notices that this is a file-structured device and that it does not presently have a file system associated with it. As a result, it will pass a Mount request to registered disk type file systems, one at a time, asking them if they recognize the file structure on the partition as a type that they support. Disk file systems ordinarily encountered on Windows NT 4 include NTFS and FAT. The first file system that recognizes the format of the data on the partition will mount the device successfully. As part of the mount process, the FSD creates an (unnamed) Device Object that represents the instance of the mounted file system on that partition. This results in the driver stack shown in Figure 11.7.

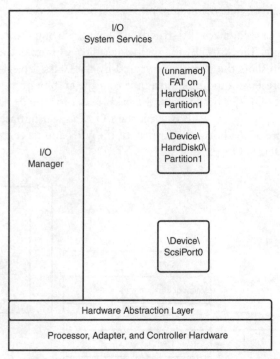

Figure 11.7. *A complete stack of Device Objects: File System over Disk Class over SCSI Port.*

When the FSD creates its Device Object, it observes most of the same rules for layered drivers creating Device Objects that were cited previously. That is, the File System driver appropriately sets its StackSize and propagates the AlignmentRequirement field from the lower-layer Device Object. Note, however, that the Buffer method is specifically not preserved by File System drivers (because FSDs use method Neither for their read and write operations).

With the creation of the File System Device Object, the driver stack is complete. In our example illustrated in Figure 11.2, we have a File System driver over an Intermediate (Class) driver, which is layered over a Port/Mini-Port Device driver.

Finding the Driver at the Top of the Stack

Of course, not every I/O request starts at a File System driver. Although we frequently discuss layering in Windows NT in terms that might imply there are always multiple layers in every driver stack, this isn't necessarily true! Requests are ordinarily directed to the driver that owns the Device Object named in the Create operation. Thus, if the Create operation specifies a device named "Toaster," the request goes directly to the Device driver for the Toaster device. This is the normal case for devices that are used for special purposes, such as industrial or process control. These devices are not typically file-structured and do not typically have Class drivers associated with them. Instead, these drivers create Device Objects that are directly accessed by applications (via the Win32 CreateFile() function or the NT native system service NtCreateFile()).

The one interesting exception to this rule is File Systems. When a user wants to open a file on a disk, the name C:\top\fred.txt might be specified. Although the device in this example, C:, corresponds to a Class driver's Device Object (probably the Device Object named \Device\HardDisk0\Partition1), the request does not first go to the Class driver; it goes to the File System driver. This is because when the Create operation is processed, the I/O Manager looks to see if a VPB is associated with the device being accessed. If a VPB exists, the I/O Manager checks to see if a file system has been mounted on the device. If a file system has not been mounted on the device, the Volume Recognition process (also called the Mount process) is initiated, as previously described. If a file system has been mounted on the device, the I/O Manager substitutes the File System's Device Object for the originally requested Device Object. Thus, the request is passed to the File System driver at the top of the driver stack, instead of directly to the Class driver.

Understanding Driver Structure

At this point, it is useful to briefly discuss the structure of NT Kernel mode drivers. All of the concepts in this section will be discussed completely, and in much greater detail, in ensuing chapters of the book. This section just presents the briefest possible summary of these concepts to facilitate our continuing description of driver layering.

All standard NT Kernel mode drivers (that is, all drivers other than Mini-Drivers) share a common basic structure. In Windows NT, drivers have specific entry points that are called by the I/O Manager to perform particular functions.

When a driver is first loaded, it is called at its DriverEntry entry point. Within this entry point, a driver is responsible for determining its configuration, and for performing all necessary driver- and device-initialization processing.

In addition to DriverEntry, a Kernel mode driver may have up to one Dispatch routine for each major I/O function code that it supports. When the I/O Manager has a request of a particular type that it wants a driver to process, it calls the driver at the Dispatch routine that corresponds to the request's major function code. A pointer to the IRP describing the request and a pointer to the Device Object representing the device are passed as arguments by the I/O Manager to the Dispatch routine. Upon being called at one of its Dispatch routines, the driver must validate the request and process it as far as possible. When an IRP is ultimately completed, the driver completing the request calls the IoCompleteRequest() function, passing a pointer to the IRP being completed as one of the arguments.

Processing I/O Requests in Layers

Windows NT uses a layered driver model to process I/O requests. In this model, drivers are organized into stacks. Each driver in a stack is responsible for processing the part of the request that it can handle, if any. If the driver's processing of the request results in its completion, the driver calls IoCompleteRequest()to complete the request. If the request cannot be completed, information for the next lower-level driver in the stack is set up and the request is then passed along to that driver.

As discussed in Chapter 10, "How I/O Requests Are Described," I/O requests in Windows NT are described by using I/O Request Packets (IRPs). When the I/O Manager receives an I/O system services call, it allocates an IRP with at least as many I/O Stack locations as there are drivers in the driver stack. The I/O Manager determines this quantity by examining the StackSize field of the top Device Object in the stack. The I/O Manager then initializes both the fixed part of the IRP and the IRP's first I/O Stack location. The I/O Manager then calls the first driver in the stack at its appropriate Dispatch routine to start processing the request.

When a driver is called with an IRP to process, it examines both the information in the fixed portion of the IRP and the information in its I/O Stack location. On receiving the IRP, a driver calls IoGetCurrentIrpStackLocation() to get a pointer to the current I/O Stack location within the IRP and examine the IRP's parameters. The driver may do the following:

- Process the IRP itself.

- Pass the IRP on to a lower-layer driver to process and complete, sometimes after the higher-layer driver has performed some preliminary processing.

- Hold on to the IRP, and create one or more additional IRPs that are passed to lower-level drivers to allow the higher-level driver to ultimately satisfy the request.

Processing the IRP Itself

If the driver can complete the IRP itself, either immediately or by queuing the IRP for later processing, it will do so.

One example of a driver completing an IRP immediately is when it finds an invalid parameter passed in the IRP. This might be an invalid buffer base alignment or byte offset, for example. Other examples include a request to a Device driver to read the temperature from a thermocouple device or a range of blocks from a disk.

Passing IRPs to Lower-Layer Drivers

If a driver decides that it cannot completely handle a particular request itself, it can decide to pass that request on to the next lower-level driver in its driver stack. The driver may do this either immediately upon receiving the request, or after partially processing a request. In order to pass an IRP to another driver, the driver must set up the next I/O Stack location in the IRP for the underlying driver to which the request will be passed. The driver calls the IoGetNextIrpStackLocation() function to get a pointer to the next I/O Stack location. Using this pointer, the driver fills in the parameters of the request that need to be passed to the next-lowest-level driver. The request is then passed to a specific lower-level driver by calling the IoCallDriver() function. This function takes two arguments, as shown in Figure 11.8.

NTSTATUS
IoCallDriver(IN PDEVICE_OBJECT *DeviceObject*,
    INOUT PIRP *Irp*);

DeviceObject: A pointer to the Device Object, owned by the nextlowest-level driver in the stack, to which the request is to be sent.

IRP: A pointer to the IRP to be sent to the next lowest-level driver.

Figure 11.8. IoCallDriver() *function prototype.*

When might a driver pass on a request for further processing? Consider the case of a File System driver (FSD) that processes a noncached write operation to a disk. When the FSD receives and validates the parameters of the request, the *ByteOffset* parameter in the IRP's I/O Stack location reflects an offset from the start of a file. Using the file's metadata information (which the FSD itself maintains), the FSD sets up the *ByteOffset* parameter in the next I/O Stack location to be relative to the start of the disk. The FSD then sets up the remainder of the next I/O Stack location (such as the length of the write and the disk driver's Device Object pointer) and passes the request to the disk driver for processing.

Another example of a driver that passes a request on to a lower-level driver is an Intermediate driver that performs disk-level encryption. When called with an IRP for a write operation, the encryption driver first encrypts the contents of the data buffer. The encryption driver then passes the IRP to the lower-level disk Device driver so that buffer is written to disk.

There's a final, and very specific, case in which a driver might pass along a request to a lower-level driver. Whenever a higher-level driver receives an IRP_MJ_DEVICE_CONTROL function with an I/O Control Code that it does not recognize as its own, it is required to pass that request down to the driver directly below it. This scheme enables users to send control type requests to underlying devices by using a handle to a File Object that corresponds, for example, to a specific file on that volume.

An example of this scheme is the previously cited I/O Control Code IOCTL_CDROM_SET_VOLUME. If a user has an audio file open on a CD-ROM drive, the user can issue a Win32 DeviceIoControl() function call, specifying this I/O control code to set the volume of the CD-ROM's audio channel. This IOCTL is handled by a combination of the CD-ROM Class driver and the SCSI Port/Miniport drivers, on which the CD-ROM device resides. When the CDFS (CD File System) driver receives this IOCTL, it doesn't recognize it as a request that it supports. As a result, the CDFS simply passes the request on to the next-lowest driver in the stack.

The call to the IoCallDriver() function causes the I/O Manager to "push" the I/O Stack, resulting in the I/O Stack location that had been "next" becoming "current." The IoCallDriver() function call also causes the I/O Manager to find the driver associated with the target Device Object and to call that driver's Dispatch routine that corresponds to the Major Function code in the now-current I/O Stack location. It is important to understand that the call to IoCallDriver() causes the I/O Manager to directly call the target driver's Dispatch routine after performing a minimal amount of processing; the I/O Manager does not delay, queue, or schedule this call in any way. Thus, a higher-level driver's call to IoCallDriver() does not return until the Dispatch routine of the called driver performs a return operation.

When the target driver receives the request passed from the higher-layer driver, it simply repeats the process already described: it gets the request's current I/O Stack location (by calling IoGetCurrentIoStackLocation()), examines the parameters passed in the IRP, and determines whether it can process the I/O request itself. If the target driver cannot process the I/O request, it sets up the next IRP Stack location in the IRP and calls the next-lowest-level driver in the stack. This process is repeated until the request is finally completed. Figure 11.9 shows the layered driver process.

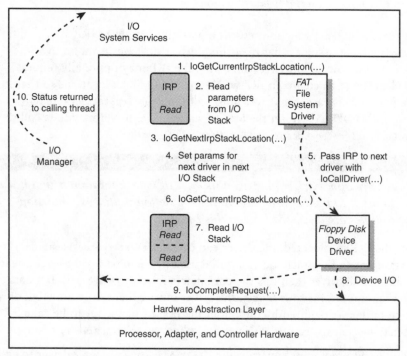

Figure 11.9. *The layered driver process.*

Creating Additional IRPs to Be Passed to Lower-Level Drivers

A variation on passing an IRP to a lower-level driver is when a driver chooses to process an IRP by creating one or more additional (new) IRPs and passes these IRPs to a lower-level driver. IRPs may be created by a driver using a variety of methods, the most common of which is to call the IoAllocateIrp() function. Figure 11.10 shows the prototype for the IoAllocateIrp() function.

> PIRP
> **IoAllocateIrp**(IN CCHAR *StackSize*,
>   IN BOOLEAN *ChargeQuota*);
>
> *StackSize:* Number of I/O Stack locations required in the IRP
> *ChargeQuota:* Indicates whether the current process' quota is to be charged

Figure 11.10. `IoAllocateIrp()` *function prototype.*

The `IoAllocateIrp()` function returns a partially initialized IRP. By default, `IoAllocateIrp()` assumes that the calling driver does not want an I/O Stack location of its own. The driver allocating the IRP may optionally request `IoAllocateIrp()` to create an IRP with enough I/O Stack locations so that it can have one. In this case, the driver must call `IoSetNextIrpStackLocation()` (a macro in NTDDK.H) to set the Stack location. The driver may then call the `IoGetCurrentIrpStackLocation()` function.

Note

One reason a driver may want its own I/O Stack location is that it wants to use it to pass information to its completion routine. Completion routines are discussed later in this chapter.

Once the IRP is allocated, the driver can call `IoGetNextIrpStackLocation()` to get a pointer to the Stack location to be used by the next lowest-level driver in the stack. The driver then fills the parameters in to the I/O Stack. If a data buffer is required for the request, the driver must either set up an MDL or a system buffer, as required by the Buffer method of the driver to be called. The IRP may be sent to the target driver by calling the `IoCallDriver()` function.

A slightly different approach to calling `IoAllocateIrp()` is for a driver to call the `IoMakeAssociatedIrp()` function. Figure 11.11 shows the prototype for the `IoMakeAssociatedIrp()` function.

> PIRP
> **IoMakeAssociatedIrp**(IN PIRP *MasterIrp*,
>   IN CCHAR *StackSize*);
>
> *StackSize:* Number of I/O Stack locations required in the IRP
> *MasterIrp:* Pointer to an IRP with which the newly created IRP is to be "associated"

Figure 11.11. `IoMakeAssociatedIrp()` *function prototype.*

`IoMakeAssociatedIrp()` allows the creation of IRPs that are "associated" with a "master" IRP. The driver that calls `IoMakeAssociatedIrp()` must manually initialize the `AssociatedIrp.IrpCount` field of the master IRP to the count of associated IRPs that are created prior to calling `IoMakeAssociatedIrp`. Associated IRPs are the same as any other IRP in NT, except that when an associated IRP is completed, the `IrpCount` field in its master IRP is decremented. When the `IrpCount` field in the master IRP reaches zero, the I/O Manager automatically completes the master IRP.

There are some restrictions that must be observed when using associated IRPs, however. Associated IRPs may only be used by the topmost driver in a stack. Ordinarily, this is a File System driver. An example of one way that a File System driver can use an associated IRP is when the FSD receives a request to perform a nonbuffered read from file, in which the corresponding disk blocks are not contiguous. In this case, the FSD can create a set of associated IRPs, with the original file-oriented read as the master IRP. The FSD sends each of the associated IRPs down to the next lower-layer driver for processing. When all the associated IRPs that were created for the master IRP are complete, the I/O Manager automatically completes the master IRP, which represents the originally requested read operation.

Advantages of the Layered Driver Model

The layered driver model that NT uses has a number of advantages, as highlighted in the following list.

- The layered driver model allows each driver to specialize in a particular type of function. For example, it decouples file systems from having to know about disk drives.

- The layered driver model allows, in most cases, functionality to be dynamically added to a driver stack. Take the case of the disk-level encryption driver again, for example. Disk-level encryption can be added, without any changes to the FSD or device driver, by simply inserting the encryption driver into the stack.

- The layering scheme utilized by NT is flexible enough to allow an I/O request to be completed at any layer. Requests do not always travel down the entire stack to be processed. For example, when an FSD receives a read operation and the data to satisfy that read is in the FSD's cache, the FSD completes the read request directly.

Completion Notification

A driver may wish to be informed when a request that it has passed to a lower-level driver is completed. It can do this by calling the `IoSetCompletionRoutine()`

function prior to passing the IRP to an underlying driver. Figure 11.12 shows the `IoSetCompletionRoutine()` function prototype. Figure 11.13 shows the prototype for the driver function that is called as a result of calling `IoCompleteRequest()` on an IRP that has a completion routine set.

```
VOID
IoSetCompletionRoutine(IN PIRP Irp,
        IN PIO_COMPLETION_ROUTINE  CompletionRoutine,
        IN PVOID  Context,
        IN BOOLEAN  InvokeOnSuccess,
        IN BOOLEAN  InvokeOnError,
        IN BOOLEAN  InvokeOnCancel);
```

Irp: Pointer to the IRP which, when completed, results in the CompletionRoutine being called

CompletionRoutine: Pointer to the function to call when the IRP is completed

Context: Driver-defined value to be passed as an argument to the *CompletionRoutine*

InvokeOnSuccess, InvokeOnError, InvokeOnCancel: Parameters which, when set to TRUE, indicate that the CompletionRoutine is to be called when the IRP is completed with the indicated status

---

Figure 11.12. `IoSetCompletionRoutine()` *function prototype.*

```
NTSTATUS
CompletionRoutine(IN PDEVICE_OBJECT DeviceObject,
        IN PIRP Irp,
        IN PVOID Context);
```

DeviceObject: Pointer to Device Object on which original IRP was received by this driver

IRP: Pointer to IRP being completed

Context: Driver-defined context value passed when IoSetCompletionRoutine() was called

---

Figure 11.13. *Driver's CompletionRoutine() function prototype.*

The IoSetCompletionRoutine() function is actually a macro defined in NTDDK.H. Invoking this function causes a pointer to a completion routine and the supplied completion routine's context argument to be stored in the *next* I/O Stack location in the IRP. The appropriate flags are also set in that I/O Stack location's Flags field, to indicate the conditions (success, error, or cancel) under which the completion routine is to be invoked.

When IoCompleteRequest() is called, the I/O Manager starts at the current I/O Stack location and walks backward up the stack, calling completion routines as it goes. Completion routines are called serially, one after another. Figure 11.14 illustrates this process. Again, these calls are made directly by the I/O Manager from within the IoCompleteRequest() function: there is no queuing or scheduling involved. Additionally, note that the Completion routine is called at the same IRQL at which IoCompleteRequest() was called. This may be any IRQL, up to and including IRQL DISPATCH_LEVEL.

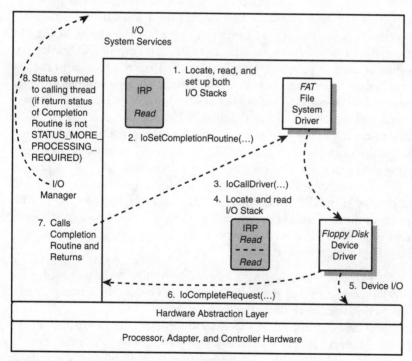

Figure 11.14. *The Completion routine process.*

Storing the Completion routine information in the IRP's next I/O Stack location, instead of in the current I/O Stack location, has some interesting implications. One is that if a driver sets a Completion routine in an IRP and later calls IoCompleteRequest(), that Completion routine is never invoked. This is because when IoCompleteRequest() is called, the I/O Manager processes Completion routine call-backs, starting with the current I/O Stack location. Because the current driver's Completion routine is stored in the next I/O Stack location, the Completion routine of any driver calling IoCompleteRequest() never gets called.

Another implication of storing the Completion routine information in the next I/O Stack location is that a driver that is the lowest driver in the stack, typically the device driver, must *never* attempt to set a Completion routine to be called. Because this will be the driver calling IoCompleteRequest, this would be an error in any case; however, this procedure error may have additional consequences because there is no valid I/O Stack location following the I/O Stack location used by the lowest driver in the stack!

Driver Capabilities in a Completion Routine

What can a driver do in its Completion routine? As you'll see from its prototype, a driver is called at its Completion routine with a pointer to the IRP being completed. The contents of the IRP are still valid when the Completion routine is called. Thus, a driver may (once again) get a pointer to its I/O Stack location by calling IoGetCurrentIrpStackLocation(). The current IRP Stack location may thus be used to pass information from the Dispatch routine to the Completion routine. Likewise, because the IRP is not yet fully complete, the AssociatedIrp.SystemBuffer and the MdlAddress fields are as valid as they were when the IRP was initially passed to the driver's Dispatch routine. Using the appropriate fields, the driver may examine or even change the user data being returned. The driver can also change the I/O Status being returned to the user (by changing the contents of IoStatus.Status or the contents of IoStatus.Information in the IRP). The only information that the driver will find is *not* still present in the IRP is the content of the *next* I/O Stack location. With the exception of the MajorFunction, DeviceObject, and Completion-related fields, the contents of all lower I/O Stack Locations are cleared by the I/O Manager before the Completion routine is called.

One particularly useful technique in a Completion routine is the capability of a driver to reclaim ownership of the IRP passed to it. This can be accomplished by the Completion routine returning with the status STATUS_MORE_PROCESSING_REQUIRED. If a Completion routine exits with any other status, the I/O Manager simply continues its "walk" backward through the I/O Stack locations in the IRP, looking for Completion routines to call. When the I/O Manager reaches the I/O Stack location for the first driver in the stack, ultimate completion processing for the IRP takes place.

When a driver returns STATUS_MORE_PROCESSING_REQUIRED from its Completion routine, the I/O Manager immediately stops Completion processing of the IRP.

The ownership of the IRP is left with the driver. The driver may choose to perform additional processing of the IRP itself or it may choose to pass the IRP on to another driver for additional processing. When processing for that IRP is eventually complete, the driver completing that IRP once again fills in the Status and Information fields of the IoStatus block in the IRP, and calls IoCompleteRequest() for that IRP. At this point, the I/O Manager performs Completion processing for the IRP, looking for Completion routines to call starting at the current I/O Stack location and walking backward up the I/O Stack.

As may be evident from the preceding discussion, drivers can use Completion routines for a wide variety of purposes. For example, a Class or File System driver may want to know the Completion status of a disk read, so that if the read fails, it can reissue the request. Alternatively, an Intermediate disk block encryption driver may need to know when read operations are completed on a disk volume, so that it can decrypt the read data.

Troubleshooting Tip

A common mistake is made in implementing Completion routines that wish to resubmit an IRP to a lower-layer driver. The mistake is that the driver calls IoCallDriver() from its Completion routine to pass the IRP to the underlying driver. Although this might initially sound like a good idea, recall that Completion routines may be called at any IRQL <= DISPATCH_LEVEL. Because IoCallDriver() results in a target driver's Dispatch routine being called directly, this also results in the target driver's Dispatch routine being called at IRQL DISPATCH_LEVEL. This is likely to be a fatal error, resulting in a system crash, because most drivers expect their dispatch routines to be called at IRQL PASSIVE_LEVEL or 'IRQL APC_LEVEL. To avoid this, Completion routines that are called at IRQLs IRQL DISPATCH_LEVEL should send the IRP to a worker thread running at IRQL PASSIVE_LEVEL. The worker thread can then call IoCallDriver() to resubmit the IRP to the underlying driver.

Special Understandings Between Drivers

Of course, there are plenty of exceptions to the standard way that NT drivers layer themselves upon one another. It is not that uncommon, in fact, for two drivers to have what we call a "special understanding" that enables them to pass requests between one another using something other than the standard mechanism.

The simplest way that two drivers can communicate is to simply call each other's routines directly. Because all drivers reside within the system process' address space, this is fairly easy. One way of implementing this particular special understanding is for two drivers to link against the same Kernel mode DLL. On loading, each driver creates and initializes a structure into which it places pointers to the entry points it wishes to export to the other driver, and calls a function in a DLL to store this information. When one driver wishes to call the other, it simply does so through a set of functions provided by the DLL, which calls the appropriate function through one of the previously provided pointers.

This is precisely how TDI (Intermediate layer) drivers interface with NDIS drivers. The NDIS wrapper is the common library DLL. When the TDI has a message that it wants the NDIS driver to send, it calls a function in the NDIS wrapper, which in turn directly calls the NDIS driver. The status returned by the NDIS driver is returned by the NDIS wrapper as the status of the TDI's call. Likewise, when the NDIS driver receives a message, it passes that message to the TDI by calling the TDI's Receive function through a function provided by the NDIS wrapper.

Other drivers may implement a similar scheme to allow them to call each other's functions directly, without the use of an intermediate DLL, as shown in Figure 11.15.

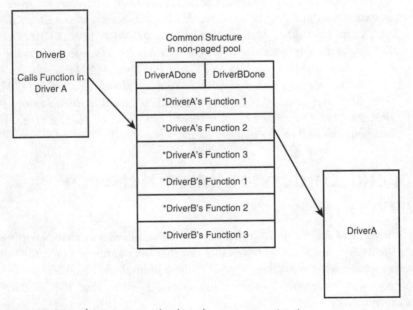

Figure 11.15. *Inter-driver communication via a common structure.*

In this scheme, one of the drivers—we'll call it Driver A—creates a common structure in a nonpaged pool. Driver A fills into the structure pointers to the functions it wants Driver B to be able to call. Driver A then sends a pre-arranged IRP to Driver B (using IoCallDriver()), passing a pointer to the structure in a prearranged field in Driver B's I/O Stack location. Driver B then fills its function addresses into the structure, and completes the IRP (by calling IoCompleteRequest()). This I/O completion signals to Driver A that Driver B has completed its initialization processing of the structure. Each driver now has all the information it needs to call the functions that were exported by the other driver. We have used this scheme a number of times in drivers we have written, with excellent results.

The Class drivers and SCSI Port drivers use yet another "special understanding" to facilitate their communication. When it receives an IRP, the Class driver builds an auxiliary data structure called a SCSI Request Block (SRB) in a nonpaged pool. A pointer to this structure is stored in a prearranged field in the SCSI Port driver's I/O Stack location. When the SCSI Port driver receives the IRP, it primarily looks to the SRB for information to describe the request.

Why do NT drivers go to the trouble of creating such "special understandings" between each other? One obvious reason is that two drivers want to be able to pass more information than is conveniently possible using the IRP structure. This is the reason that the Class and SCSI Port drivers use the SRB. Another common reason is that if two drivers communicate very frequently, they may just not want the bother or overhead of creating IRPs every time they want to communicate. For example, if Driver A frequently wants to pass the value of a single parameter to Driver B, it may not make sense to create an IRP and call IoCallDriver() to pass this parameter.

The disadvantages of creating a "special understanding" between two drivers really need to be examined before embarking on such a scheme. How extensible is the scheme that's being created? Will it work in future versions of Windows NT? Is it maintainable? Given that IoCallDriver() has very little overhead, is a sufficient amount of time or overhead really being saved to justify "rolling your own" scheme?

Filter Drivers

No discussion of driver layering in NT would be complete without a discussion of Filter drivers. The Windows NT I/O Manager includes the capability for one Kernel mode driver to "attach" one of its Device Objects to a Device Object created by a different driver. The result of this is that IRPs destined for the driver associated with the original Device Object will be sent to the driver associated with the "attached" Device Object. This attached driver is a Filter driver.

The Filter driver can then examine, modify, complete, or pass along the IRPs it receives to the original driver. Filter drivers may be inserted at any layer in the Windows NT driver stack.

There are a couple of different mechanisms that allow a Filter driver to attach its Device Object to that of another driver. One way is for the Filter driver to first find the Device Object for the device it wants to attach using `IoGetDeviceObjectPointer()`, which was discussed previously. The Filter driver then attaches its Device Object to the found Device Object using the `IoAttachDeviceToDeviceStack()` function. Figure 11.16 shows the prototype for the `IoAttachDeviceToDeviceStack()` function.

PDEVICE_OBJECT
IoAttachDeviceToDeviceStack(
       IN PDEVICE_OBJECT *SourceDevice*,
       IN PDEVICE_OBJECT *TargetDevice*);

SourceDevice: Pointer to original Device Object to be attached

TargetDevice: Pointer to Filter driver's Device Object

Figure 11.16. `IoAttachDeviceToDeviceStack()` *function prototype.*

Every Device Object has a field named `AttachedDevice`, which points to the Device Object of the first Filter driver that has attached this Device Object. If the `AttachedDevice` field of the Device Object is `NULL`, there are no attached devices. If the `AttachedDevice` field is not -zero, it points to a Filter driver's Device Object. `IoAttachDeviceToDeviceStack()` finds the end of the `AttachedDevice` list for the Device Object pointed to by *TargetDevice*, and points the `AttachedDevice` field of this final Device Object to the Filter driver's Device Object. Figure 11.17 illustrates a series of Device Objects attached to each other.

The return value of `IoAttachDeviceToDeviceStack()` is a pointer to the Device Object to which the Filter driver's Device Object has been attached. The Filter driver can use this pointer to pass requests on to the original device. Although this pointer is usually the same as the *TargetDevice* pointer, it may be that of another Filter driver that has attached the same device (refer to Figure 11.17).

Another way for a Filter driver to attach its Device Object to that of another device is to call the `IoAttachDevice()` function. This function, the prototype for which is shown in Figure 11.18, simply combines the functionality provided by `IoGetDeviceObjectPointer()` and `IoAttachDeviceToDeviceStack()`.

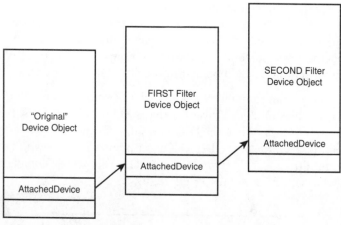

Figure 11.17. *A set of attached Device Objects.*

NTSTATUS
IoAttachDevice(IN PDEVICE_OBJECT *SourceDevice*,
    IN PUNICODE_STRING *TargetDevice*,
    OUT PDEVICE_OBJECT **AttachedDevice*);

SourceDevice: Pointer to Filter driver's Device Object

TargetDevice: Unicode string that contains the name of the device to be attached

AttachedDevice: Pointer to Device Object that has been attached

Figure 11.18. `IoAttachDevice()` *function prototype.*

What effect does attaching a device have? The main one is that any Create I/O request that is issued to an attached device is redirected to the last Device Object in the list of attached devices. This action results in the request being sent to the (Filter) driver associated with that Device Object. Thus, if a user issues a `CreateFile()` Win32 function for the "original" Device Object in Figure 11.17, the request is redirected to the Filter driver that created the SECOND Filter Device Object.

This operation (Create requests being redirected to the last attached device in the list) is also illustrated by the Device Object pointer returned by the `IoGetDeviceObjectPointer()` function. Recall that Intermediate drivers use this function to retrieve a pointer to a Device Object of a lower-layered device, by specifying the name of that lower-layered device's Device Object. When an Intermediate driver attempts to locate a lower-level device by calling

`IoGetDeviceObjectPointer()`, the pointer returned will be that of the last attached device in the list of attached devices, if that Device Object is attached. Thus, again using Figure 11.17 as an example, if an Intermediate driver were to issue `IoGetDeviceObjectPointer()` for the "Original" device, the Device Object pointer returned would be that of the SECOND Filter device.

Let's look briefly at an example. Suppose the SCSI Mini-port and Port drivers start as normal. Next, a Filter driver for the SCSI Port driver starts. Next, the Disk Class driver starts. When the Disk Class driver calls `IoGetDeviceObjectPointer()`, the Device Object pointer returned will be a pointer to the Filter driver's Device Object. Figure 11.19 shows the completed stack of Device Objects, with Filter driver inserted.

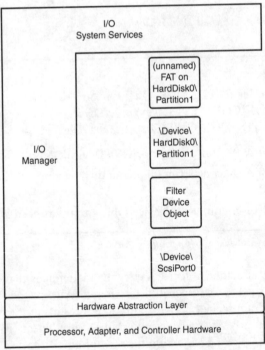

Figure 11.19. *A stack of Device Objects, including one that filters the ScsiPort device.*

It is very important to remember that the I/O Manager only runs the `AttachedDevice` list to find the last attached Device Object as a result of processing a Create request. *No redirection occurs when* `IoCallDriver()` *is called.* Therefore, for a Filter driver to be successful, it must attach any device in which it is interested before a higher-layered device calls `IoGetDeviceObjectPointer()` (which, as previously discussed, issues a Create) to find its Device Object.

Filter Driver Usage Guidelines

In our practical experiences with Filter drivers, we have developed a set of rules that well-behaved Filter drivers must follow. These rules are as follows:

- If inserting a Filter driver into the device stack causes anything to break, it's automatically the Filter driver's fault. The onus is thus on the Filter driver to adapt itself and to make sure that everything is working correctly after it is introduced. This is true, even if the Filter driver needs to compensate for an error in a lower-layered driver!

- It is up to the Filter driver to understand how the device to which it attaches works. If the Filter driver can't "understand" the requests that it receives, it is not the fault of the device to which it attaches.

- Filter drivers must appear to any drivers that layer above them as close to the original device as possible.

- Filter drivers must plan to work well with other Filter drivers. These include Filter drivers that attach a device before them and Filter drivers that attach the device after they have attached it.

The importance of these rules can be demonstrated with a couple of simple examples. Take the case of a Filter driver that attaches the SCSI Port driver, as in our previous example. In this case, the IRPs that the Filter driver receives have SRBs associated with them. As we said earlier, most of the information about the request being sent from a Class driver to the SCSI Port driver appears in the SRB. If the Filter driver isn't aware of the "special understanding" between the Class and SCSI Port drivers, it is surely missing a lot of information!

Another example involves Filter drivers that attach themselves above File System drivers. Not only must these Filter drivers understand the requests that File System drivers expect to receive (no mean feat, considering that this information is not documented by Microsoft), but they also must be sure that they don't do anything to cause the File System driver to malfunction. What makes this particularly tricky is that File System drivers typically use method Neither to describe their I/O requests. Thus, I/O requests for FSDs *must* be passed to the FSD in the context of the thread originally initiating the request. If a Filter driver changes the context of the request, by sending a request off to be processed by a worker thread, for example, the File System driver stops working. According to our Filter driver rules, this is the Filter driver's fault.

Fast I/O

As we mentioned at the start of this chapter, File System drivers are very close-ly coupled with the NT Memory and Cache Manager subsystems. Thus, requests to read or write to a File Object often result in nothing more than a cached operation in the File System. None of the other driver layers are involved. Because these cached operations can be very fast, the I/O Manager implements an optimized method for dealing with these requests. This method is called "Fast" or "Turbo" I/O.

A driver that supports fast I/O creates what is called a Fast I/O Dispatch Table. The structure (FAST_IO_DISPATCH) is documented in NTDDK.H. A driver that supports Fast I/O points the FastIoDispatch field of its Driver Object to this table. When the I/O Manager receives an I/O request, *for certain drivers and functions,* it checks to see if the driver supports Fast I/O for this function before it builds an IRP. If the driver supports Fast I/O for this function, the I/O Manager calls the driver at its Fast I/O entry point, in the context of the requesting thread, with the parameters supplied with the request. If the driver can completely handle the request in its Fast I/O routine, it does so, and returns TRUE as the result of the call to its Fast I/O entry point. If the driver cannot handle the request in its Fast I/O routine, it returns FALSE.

When a driver returns FALSE as a result of a call to one of its Fast I/O entry points, the I/O Manager proceeds as if no Fast I/O entry point had been sup-plied. That is, the I/O Manager builds an IRP in the normal way and calls the driver with that IRP.

Fast I/O is usable by only a small number of Windows NT drivers. First of all, except for its use in TDI devices, it comes into use only for drivers that are the top driver in a stack. In addition, the I/O Manager restricts most operations, including read and write operations, to File System drivers only. That is, unless a driver is a File System driver, the I/O Manager never even looks for a Fast I/O entry point for most operations.

However, one operation for which the I/O Manager does support Fast I/O for non-File System drivers is IRP_MJ_DEVICE_CONTROL. That is, when processing a Device Control system service (as a result of calling the Win32 function DeviceIoControl() or issuing the NtDeviceIoControlFile() native NT system ser-vice), the I/O Manager always checks to see whether the top driver in the stack supports Fast I/O. If it does, it calls its Fast I/O entry point for Device Control functions. Figure 11.20 shows the prototype for the FastIoDeviceControl() entry point.

```
BOOLEAN
FastIoDeviceControl(PFILE_OBJECT  *FileObject,
        IN BOOLEAN  Wait,
        IN PVOID  InputBuffer,
        IN ULONG  InputBufferLength,
        IN OUT PVOID  OutputBuffer,
        IN ULONG  OutputBufferLength,
        IN ULONG  IoControlCode,
        OUT PIO_STATUS_BLOCK  IoStatus,
        IN PDEVICE_OBJECT Device);
```

FileObject: Pointer to the File Object on which this operation is taking place

Wait: TRUE if the driver can wait while processing this request

InputBuffer: Requestor's virtual address of InBuffer, supplied on the request

InputBufferLength: Length, in bytes, of the InputBuffer

OutputBuffer: Requestor's virtual address of OutBuffer, supplied on the request

OutputBufferLength: Length, in bytes, of the OutputBuffer

IoControlCode: I/O Control Code specified in the request

IoStatus: Pointer to I/O Status Block to be filled in by driver if return value is TRUE

Device: Pointer to Device Object on which request is being issued

Figure 11.20. `FastIoDeviceControl()` *entry point prototype.*

Although Fast I/O can indeed be a valuable optimization, most device drivers will not or cannot make use of even the Device I/O Control functionality that it provides. The major restriction imposed by Fast I/O is that the driver must be at the top of the stack. For drivers that meet this requirement, the same restrictions imposed by METHOD_NEITHER for Device Control operations exist. That is, the driver must be able to completely process the request in the context of the calling thread. Although some drivers can profitably make use of this functionality, they are the exceptions.

Case Study: The Importance of Load Order

We had a student a few years back who became all excited when he heard about Filter drivers. "This is exactly what I need," he said, "to implement a read-only filter for SCSI devices." Apparently this is a project with which he had been tasked, and until coming to class he could think of no way to address his problem.

So, he went off and wrote his Filter driver. As he described it to us in a number of email messages, this Filter driver layered itself over the SCSI Port driver. Whenever it received an IRP with a write request for a restricted device, it simply completed the IRP with STATUS_ACCESS_DENIED. Although we pointed out to him that this would solve only part of his problem (for example, this solution addressed neither delete nor rename operations!), he insisted that his manager would be happy just to have the functionality that he had planned.

A short time later, we received an emergency phone call from the student. Filter drivers didn't work for him! Although he had written his driver according to the instructions we provided in our class and his Filter driver loaded without any errors, it never received any IRPs! Was NT broken? Did we lead him astray about Filter drivers?

When we asked him to explain how he was doing his testing, the problem soon became apparent: He was doing his testing on a spare disk drive on the same SCSI controller as his system disk. By his own description, he started his system, logged in, and then used the Devices Control Panel applet to start his Filter driver. He could see his driver print debug messages on loading, and he knew that it loaded successfully because he never received any IRPs.

The problem occurred, of course, when his Filter driver was loading. When the system started, the SCSI Port driver loaded, and then the Disk Class driver loaded. Sometime after both of these drivers started, our student logged into the system. It was then that he started his Filter driver. Recall that the only time the list of attached Device Objects is traversed is during Create processing. Therefore, because the Disk Class driver had already started, it already issued its call to IoGetDeviceObjectPointer to get a pointer to the Device Object of the SCSI Port driver. The Disk Class driver then used this pointer whenever it sent requests to the SCSI Port driver using IoCallDriver.

Sometime after this initialization took place, our student's Filter driver loaded and successfully attached the SCSI Port driver. However, because the Disk Class driver already got its pointer to the SCSI Port driver's Device Object, no requests ever went to the Filter driver.

The fix? Simply change the time at which the Filter driver loaded. By having the Filter driver automatically start during system startup and specifying an appropriate value for the "Group" startup parameter, the driver started after the SCSI Port driver but before the Disk Class driver.

Another mystery solved!

Chapter **12**

Driver Structure

This chapter will review:

- **DriverEntry Points.** In this section, we provide a description of the most common entry points in Windows NT device drivers. We also indicate where in the book information about these entry points can be found.

- **Understanding Driver Organization.** Before we can discuss the details of each driver entry point in the following chapters, it's important to understand the general concepts of the way Windows NT device drivers are organized. In this section, we look at a device driver as a whole and describe when the various entry points in a driver are called. We also examine the typical path that a driver implements to process a request.

Before discussing the details of the processing that takes place at the major entry points in a driver, which we do in the next chapter, it is helpful to discuss the basics of driver structure. This structure includes the various entry points in a Device driver, the context in which a driver's entry points may be called, and the flow of processing for typical requests.

DriverEntry Points

The Windows NT driver architecture uses an entry point model, in which the I/O Manager calls a particular routine in a driver when it wants the driver to perform a particular function. Of course, at each entry point the I/O Manager passes a specific set of parameters to the driver to enable it to perform the requested function.

The basic driver entry points, used by most NT Kernel mode device drivers, are as follows:

- **DriverEntry.** The I/O Manager calls this function in a driver when a driver is first loaded. Drivers perform initialization for both themselves and any devices they control within this function. This entry point is required for all NT drivers. The DriverEntry entry point is described in detail in Chapter 13, "DriverEntry."

- **Dispatch entry points.** A driver's Dispatch entry points are called by the I/O Manager to request the driver to initiate a particular I/O operation. A driver can have up to one Dispatch entry point for each major I/O function that it supports. Dispatch entry points are described in detail in Chapter 14, "Dispatch Entry Points."

- **Interrupt Service Routine (ISR).** This entry point is present only if a driver supports interrupt handling. Once a driver has connected to interrupts from its devices, its ISR will be called whenever one of its devices requests a hardware interrupt. ISRs are described in detail in Chapter 15, "Interrupt Service Routines and DPCs."

- **DpcForIsr and/or CustomDpc.** A driver uses these entry points to complete the work that needs to be done as a result of an interrupt occurring or another special condition. DpcForIsr and CustomDpc entry points are discussed in detail in Chapter 15.

Other entry points are applicable to the processing of a specific IRP or set of IRPs. These entry points include the following:

- **Cancel.** A driver can define a Cancel entry point for each IRP that it holds in an internal queue. If the I/O Manager needs to cancel a specific IRP, it calls the Cancel routine associated with that IRP. Cancel operations and the Cancel entry point are discussed in detail in Chapter 14.

- **Completion routine.** As discussed in Chapter 11, "The Layered Driver Model," a higher-layer driver can establish a Completion routine in an IRP. The I/O Manager calls this routine after all lower-layer drivers have completed the IRP.

Finally, several entry points are applicable only if specific functionality is used or supported by a driver. Most of these entry points apply only to specific types of drivers. The entry points include the following:

- **Reinitialize.** The I/O Manager calls this entry point, if one has been registered, to allow a driver to perform secondary initialization. The Reinitialize entry point is discussed in detail in Chapter 13.

- **StartIo.** The I/O Manager utilizes this entry point only in drivers that use System Queuing (described in Chapter 14). For such drivers, the I/O Manager calls this entry point to start a new I/O request. The StartIo entry point is discussed in detail in Chapter 14.

- **Unload.** The I/O Manager calls this entry point to request the driver to ready itself to be immediately removed from the system. Only drivers that support unloading should implement this entry point. The Unload entry point is discussed in Chapter 13.

- **IoTimer.** The I/O Manager calls this entry point approximately every second in drivers that have initialized and started IoTimer support. This entry point is discussed in Chapter 13.

- **Fast I/O.** Instead of one entry point, this is actually a set of entry points. The I/O Manager or Cache Manager calls a particular Fast I/O routine to initiate a specific "Fast I/O" function. These routines are almost exclusively supported by file system drivers. Fast I/O entry points were discussed in Chapters 10 and 11, and are further discussed in Chapters 13 and 15.

- **AdapterControl.** The I/O Manager calls this entry point to indicate that the driver's shared DMA resources are available for use in a transfer. Only certain DMA device drivers implement this entry point. This entry point is discussed in detail in Chapter 17, "DMA Data Transfers."

- **Timer DPC.** This entry point is called when a driver-requested timer expires. Timer entry points are discussed in Chapter 15 and Chapter 16, "Programmed I/O Data Transfers."

- **Synchronize Function.** The I/O Manager calls this entry point in response to a driver's request to acquire one of its ISR Spin Locks. This entry point is described in detail in Chapter 15.

Understanding Driver Organization

Of course, a driver is more than a random collection of entry points. Throughout this section, we'll discuss, in general terms, when and how the I/O Manager calls the major driver entry points. We also discuss the processing that takes place at these entry points. Finally, we discuss how a typical I/O request moves through a driver during its processing.

The goal of the sections that follow is to introduce you to the general operation of a Windows NT driver. Bear in mind that the details of the processing that takes place at each entry point, and all the exceptions to the general rules that are presented, are described in later chapters.

Loading and Initialization

As discussed in previous chapters, NT drivers are dynamically loaded. In NT 4, drivers are almost always loaded during system startup. When a driver is loaded, the I/O Manager calls its DriverEntry entry point. A pointer to the driver's Driver Object and a pointer to a Unicode string containing the driver's registry path are passed as parameters to the driver at its DriverEntry entry point. It is during DriverEntry processing that a driver performs internal initialization, and locates and initializes hardware that it will control.

If a driver returns an error status to the I/O Manager's call to DriverEntry, the driver is unloaded from the system (unless the driver was started at boot time; see Chapter 20, "Installing and Starting Drivers") and the I/O Manager makes no further references to the driver. On return from DriverEntry with success, the I/O Manager begins passing I/O requests to the driver, in the form of IRPs, in response to user requests.

Some drivers or devices might take a long time to perform initialization or require their devices to be initialized in stages. After initial processing in DriverEntry, a driver can call the I/O Manager to register a Reinitialization entry point after such a driver has determined that it will load successfully. The Reinitialization entry point is called after all the other drivers in the system that are waiting to be loaded have completed loading.

Request Processing for Device Drivers

Figure 12.1 is a flow chart that illustrates the typical sequence of request processing for device drivers. Use this flow chart to follow the steps described in the remainder of this section. Although every device is not constrained to follow this precise processing sequence, this is the basic sequence utilized by many NT drivers for typical devices.

Dispatch Routine Processing

When the I/O Manager has a request for a driver to process, it calls the driver at the Dispatch entry point associated with the request's major function code. For example, when the I/O Manager has an IRP with an IRP_MJ_READ function code for a particular driver to process, it calls that driver's Dispatch Read entry point. As parameters to the driver's Dispatch entry point, the I/O Manager passes a pointer to the Device Object to which the request is directed and a pointer to the IRP that describes the request. Drivers may have up to one Dispatch entry point per function code that they support.

When called at its Dispatch entry point with an IRP, it is the driver's job to process the IRP as far as possible before returning to the I/O Manager. The status that the driver returns from its Dispatch routine is the status of the I/O request for which the driver was called. Thus, if the driver can complete the request in its Dispatch routine, it does so and returns the status of the request to the I/O Manager. The reason for completing the request may be that one or more of the request's parameters were in error (such as the buffer length being inappropriate for the device), or that the driver could complete the request on the device successfully.

If immediate completion of the request is not possible, the device driver queues the IRP for later processing. This is the typical case for most device drivers. A typical driver, upon receiving a request to perform a data transfer function, such as an IRP with a major function code of IRP_MJ_READ, cannot immediately complete the request because one of the following is true:

- The driver needs to wait for the device to become available before the operation can be initiated. In this case, the driver marks the IRP as pending and places the IRP on a queue of pending requests.

- The driver can initiate the operation, but it needs to wait for the requested data to become available on the device or the transfer to complete. In this case, the driver marks the IRP as pending and stores a pointer to the in-progress IRP.

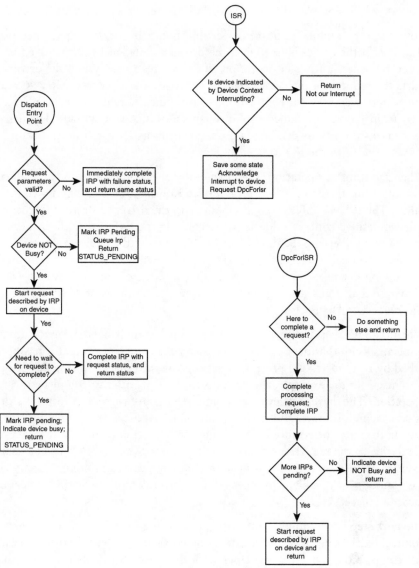

Figure 12.1. *Typical sequence of request processing for device drivers.*

In either case, the driver returns STATUS_PENDING to the I/O Manager. To indicate that the I/O request is presently in progress on the device driver, the I/O Manager returns STATUS_PENDING at this point to the thread that requested the I/O operation.

ISR and DpcForIsr Processing

When a device driver returns from a call to its Dispatch entry point with a request pending, when does that request ultimately get completed? Although this depends on the specific architecture of the device, it is safe to say that the request will be completed as a result of a Deferred Procedure Call (DPC).

Consider, for example, a simple device that is capable of one single operation at a time. If the device is free when the driver is called at its Dispatch entry point to process a transfer operation (such as a read or a write), the driver starts the request on the device. The driver saves a pointer to the IRP so that it can be retrieved later for completion, and it indicates that the device is now busy (using some internal control mechanism of its own devising). The driver next marks the IRP as pending and returns from its Dispatch routine with STATUS_PENDING to the I/O Manager.

When the transfer operation is complete, the device interrupts. As a result of this interrupt, the driver's Interrupt Service Routine (ISR) for the device is called. The driver's ISR is passed a pointer to the driver's Interrupt Object and a driver-defined context value as parameters. In the ISR, the driver determines (typically by querying the device hardware) whether the device indicated by the context argument is currently requesting an interrupt. If the device indicated by the context argument is requesting an interrupt, the driver acknowledges to its hardware that it has seen the interrupt, saves any required state for later use, and requests a DpcForIsr.

When the DPC is processed, the driver is called at the DpcForIsr entry point associated with that device. The driver determines the reason that it has been called by referring to the previously saved state information or the device hardware itself. In the example, the driver is in the DpcForIsr to complete a transfer operation. The driver retrieves the pointer to the in-progress IRP that it stored in its Dispatch routine, and performs any hardware-specific completion processing that may be required. This might include actually moving the data from the device to the requester's data buffer (for a programmed I/O type device), re-enabling interrupts on the device, or (for some devices) nothing at all. With the request now completely processed, the driver completes the IRP by calling IoCompleteRequest().

The next step is very important: Prior to returning from its DpcForIsr entry point, the driver needs to propagate its own execution. Because the driver has just completed a request in the DpcForIsr, the device is usually now available to start a new request. Therefore, before returning from the DpcForIsr, the driver checks to see whether there are any requests queued, waiting for the device to become available.

If there are requests queued, the driver starts one of these requests (it chooses which one to start by using an internal algorithm). If there are no pending requests, the driver clears its own internal indication that the device is busy. In either case, the driver returns from its DpcForIsr entry point.

The example discussed also illustrates how a request is processed if the device driver's Dispatch routine was called and it determined that the device was busy and the request could not be immediately started. In this case, the driver marks the IRP pending, and queues the request. The driver starts this request in the DpcForIsr entry point as a result of a previous request being completed.

Although the previous example was for a transfer request, the same sequence of operations would take place for any interrupt driven request. Even polled drivers follow a similar sequence. Such drivers typically utilize a private worker thread to periodically query a device's registers. When an in-progress request is complete, a polling driver typically requests a CustomDpc entry point, in place of the DpcForIsr entry point, to complete the request.

Request Processing for Intermediate Drivers

The sequence of processing requests for Intermediate layer drivers is typically simpler than that for device drivers. So, as for device drivers, when the I/O Manager has a request to be processed, it calls an Intermediate driver at the Dispatch entry point that corresponds to the request's major function code. When it's called at its Dispatch entry point, an Intermediate driver processes its request as far as possible, returning the status of the request to the I/O Manager as the status of its Dispatch entry point.

For an Intermediate layer driver, processing a request entails validating it and, if it is found to be valid, typically using IoCallDriver() to pass the IRP to a lower-layer driver for further processing and ultimate completion. Typically, the status returned by the next lowest layer driver to the IoCallDriver() function call is returned by the Intermediate driver as the status from its Dispatch entry point.

Optionally, the Intermediate driver can set a Completion routine in the IRP, prior to passing the IRP along to a lower-layer driver. This is done by using the function IoSetCompletionRoutine(). When a Completion routine is set by an Intermediate driver for a given IRP, the driver is called at its Completion routine when all the lower-layer drivers have completed the IRP. The process by which Intermediate drivers pass requests on for processing and are called back at their completion is described in detail in Chapter 11, "The Layered Driver Model."

As an example, consider how the Disk Class driver processes a read request. The Disk Class driver is called at its read Dispatch entry point, with an IRP having a major function code of IRP_MJ_READ. The driver validates the parameters in the IRP. If any of the IRP's parameters is not valid, the IRP is immediately completed with an error status, and the Disk Class driver returns that same error status from its read Dispatch entry point to the I/O Manager.

If the IRP's parameters are valid, the Disk Class driver will process the request by sending it along to the appropriate Disk Device driver, which is usually the next lower-layer driver below the Disk Class driver. The Disk Class driver sends the request to the disk Device driver by calling IoCallDriver(). The Disk Class driver then returns from its read Dispatch routine, returning the status returned by IoCallDriver() to the I/O Manager.

Dynamic Unloading

Windows NT supports not only the dynamic loading, but also the dynamic unloading of a driver from the running system. Support for dynamic unloading is optional in a driver. A driver indicates to the I/O Manager that it can be dynamically unloaded by supplying a pointer to an Unload entry point in its Driver Object.

After a driver has been requested to dynamically unload, when there are no further I/O requests in progress for any of the driver's Device Objects, the I/O Manager calls the driver at its Unload entry point. A pointer to the driver's Driver Object is passed as a parameter. When called at its Unload entry point, the driver basically undoes the work it did within its DriverEntry routine. The driver resets any devices under its control and disables the interrupts from those devices. The driver disconnects from interrupts, deletes its Device Objects, pending timers are stopped, and all other driver-allocated structures are returned to the pool.

> **Note**
>
> *If a driver chooses to support dynamic unloading, it must properly unload when the I/O Manager calls its Unload entry point. It cannot "choose" not to unload after it has been called. Indeed, the driver is unconditionally unloaded once this entry point has returned.*

Request Processing Context

When a driver is called to process a request, what context is it called in? Stated simply, this question means: What is the current thread, as established by the (NT Microkernel) dispatcher? Because every thread belongs to only one process, the current thread implies a specific current process. Together, the current thread and current process imply all those things (handles, virtual memory, scheduler state, and registers) that make the thread and process unique.

Process Context

Recall that in Windows NT, a process is really just a container for a set of threads. The process contains most of the resources and attributes used by each of its threads.

A simple example of process context is handles, such as those returned from the Win32 function CreateFile() (or the NT native function NtCreateFile()). Because handles are specific to a particular process, a handle created within the context of one process is of no use in another process's context.Because handles are "owned" by a process, they can be shared by all the threads in that process.

Virtual memory context is perhaps the aspect of process context that is most important to driver writers. Recall that NT maps user processes into the low 2GB of virtual address space, and processes the operating system code itself into the high 2GB of virtual address space. When a thread from a user process is executing, its virtual addresses range from 0 to 2GB, and all addresses above 2GB are set to "no access," which prevents direct user access to operating system code and structures. When the operating system code is executing, the virtual addresses for the operating system code range from 2–4GB, and the current user process (if there is one) is mapped into the addresses between 0 and 2GB.

> **Note**
>
> *In Windows NT Enterprise Server, user processes may have up to 3GB of virtual address space. Thus, in this version of the system, user processes are mapped into the low 3GB of virtual address space, with the operating system mapped into the high 1GB.*

In NT, the code mapped into the high 2GB of address is the operating system code, which includes all drivers, and paged and nonpaged pool. This mapping never fundamentally changes (well, to be precise, *most* of the mapping never changes. The data mapped in the "hyperspace" area, for example, does change). However, the user code mapped into the lower 2GB of address space changes, based on which process is current.

In NT's specific arrangement of virtual memory, a given valid user virtual address *x* within process P (where *x* is less than or equal to 2GB) corresponds to the same physical memory location as kernel virtual address *x*. This is true, of course, only when process P is the current process and (therefore) process P's physical pages are mapped into the operating system's low 2GB of virtual addresses. Another way of expressing this last sentence is "This is true only when P is the current process" or "This is true only in the context of process P." So, for all user processes, user virtual addresses and kernel virtual addresses up to 2GB refer to the same physical locations, given the same process context.

Thread Scheduling Context

Another aspect of context that's important to drivers is thread scheduling context. When a thread waits (such as by issuing the Win32 function WaitForSingleObject() for an object that is not signaled), that thread's scheduling context stores information that defines what the thread is waiting for. When issuing an unsatisfied wait, the thread is removed from the ready queue, to return only when the wait has been satisfied. This occurs when the Dispatcher object for which the thread was waiting becomes signaled.

Classes of Context

In NT, Kernel mode drivers run in three different classes of context:

- System process context
- Specific thread (and process) context
- Arbitrary thread (and process) context

During its execution, certain parts of every Kernel mode driver eventually run in each of the three context classes listed previously. For example, a driver's DriverEntry() function always runs in the context of the system process, which is the process that is first created when the system starts. It has an arbitrary user process mapped into the lower 2GB of the kernel's virtual address space.

On the other hand, a driver's DpcForIsr entry point always runs in what's referred to as an "arbitrary thread context." This means that the thread that is the current thread, in terms of the dispatcher, is unrelated to the request(s) being processed in the DpcForIsr while the DpcForIsr is executing. Because any thread might be the current thread, any user process (or no user process) might be mapped into the lower 2GB of kernel virtual addresses. This "works" because the code for the DpcForIsr is running in the high 2GB of system virtual addresses, and the code mapped at these addresses (as already mentioned) does not change from process to process.

Dispatch Routines and Context

The context in which a driver's Dispatch routine runs is a particularly interesting issue. In some cases, a driver's dispatch routines run in the context of the calling user thread. Figure 12.2 shows why this is so.

When a user thread issues an I/O function call to a device, for example by calling the Win32 ReadFile() function, this results in a system service request. On Intel architecture processors, such requests are implemented by using software interrupts that pass through an interrupt gate. The interrupt gate changes the processor's current privilege level to Kernel mode, causes a switch to the kernel stack, and then calls the system service dispatcher. The system service dispatcher in turn copies the system service arguments from the user stack to the kernel stack, and calls the I/O Manager to build an IRP and call the Read Dispatch routine of the top driver in the driver stack. All this happens at IRQL PASSIVE_LEVEL.

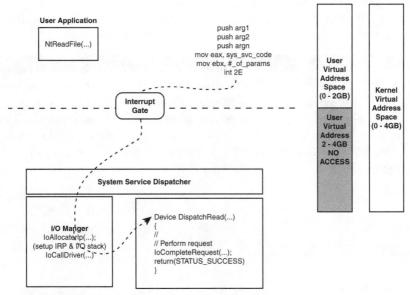

Figure 12.2. *Calling a stack of drivers in requestor's context.*

Throughout this entire process, no queuing of the I/O request takes place. Therefore, no change in thread and process context could have taken place. In this example, then, the Dispatch routine for the driver at the top of the stack is called in the context of the thread that issued the ReadFile() request. This means that when the driver's Read Dispatch routine is running, it *is* the calling thread executing the Kernel mode driver code.

Thus, any driver that is called directly by the I/O Manager, with no other intervening drivers, is called in the context of the calling thread. This includes File System drivers, for example, because they sit at the top of their driver stacks. It also includes device drivers that provide functions directly to User mode applications with no intervening intermediate or file system drivers, such as the Toaster driver mentioned in earlier chapters.

A driver's Dispatch routine does not always run in the context of the requesting thread, however. If a driver is layered below another driver, its Dispatch routine almost always assumes that it is running in an arbitrary thread context. This is because, as described in Chapter 11, a higher-layer driver may queue any request it receives for later processing. When the driver later decides to pass that request to a lower-layer driver, it can be running in a different thread context from which the request was received. Of course, the higher-layer driver may queue some requests and not others. The context in which the lower-layer driver is called may, therefore, sometimes be that of the requesting thread, and at other times not. Because the lower-layer driver has no way of knowing when it is being called in the context of the calling thread and when it is not, the lower-layer driver must always assume its context to be arbitrary.

> ### Note
>
> *A filter driver, attaching over a device driver that would otherwise be called in the context of the requesting thread, cannot cause the device driver to be called in a different thread context and then malfunction. This is because, according to the rules for filter drivers in Chapter 11, if inserting a filter driver above another driver causes the driver being filtered to break, this is a problem in the filter driver.*

Chapter 13

DriverEntry

This chapter discusses the details of processing at the DriverEntry entry point. It also discusses how drivers may support dynamic unloading by supplying an Unload routine. Specifically, this chapter will review:

- **Determining Device Configuration.** Because drivers in Windows NT are loaded dynamically, they must dynamically locate the device(s) that they will support. In this section, we describe how a driver finds the devices it will support.

- **Creating Device Objects.** In Windows NT, Device Objects are created dynamically by the device driver. In this section, we discuss in detail how Device Objects are created, and how devices are made accessible to users.

- **Claiming Hardware Resources.** In this section, we describe how a driver reserves specific hardware resources—such as I/O Ports, shared memory regions, IRQs, and DMA channels—for its own use.

- **Translating Bus Addresses.** Hardware resources used by devices are bus-specific. Before these resources can be used by a driver via the HAL, they must be translated to systemwide logical values. This section describes how this is done.

- **Exporting Entry Points.** In this section, we describe how a driver makes its many entry points known to the I/O Manager.

- **Connecting to Interrupts and the Registering DpcForIsr.** Most drivers are interrupt-driven. In this section, we describe how a driver connects its Interrupt Service Routine to a particular device's interrupts, and how the driver registers its DPC routine for ISR completion.

- **Getting an Adapter Object.** DMA device drivers need an Adapter Object in support of almost all their transfer operations. This section describes how a driver gets a pointer to its Adapter Object.

- **Performing Device Initialization.** This section briefly discusses device-specific initialization that a driver may need to perform.

- **Other DriverEntry Operations.** Some drivers have special needs. In this section, we discuss some optional operations that some drivers may need to perform during DriverEntry.

- **Dynamic Driver Unloading.** Just as drivers are dynamically loaded in Windows NT, they can also optionally be dynamically unloaded. In this section, we describe how a driver can declare its support for dynamic unloading.

The I/O Manager calls a driver's DriverEntry function when the driver is loaded. In NT, only one instance of a driver is loaded, regardless of the number of physical devices that the driver will control. Thus, a driver's DriverEntry entry point is called by the I/O Manager only once, regardless of the number of devices the driver will control. DriverEntry is called at IRQL PASSIVE_LEVEL in the context of the system process. Figure 13.1 shows the prototype for the DriverEntry entry point.

NTSTATUS
DriverEntry(IN PDRIVER_OBJECT *DriverObject*,
    IN PUNICODE_STRING *RegistryPath*);

DriverObject: A pointer to the Driver Object for the driver being loaded.

RegistryPath: A pointer to a Unicode string containing the driver's Registry path name, which is usually something like \HKEY_LOCAL_MACHINE\SYSTEM\Current Control Set\Services\DriverName

When Called: When driver is loaded

Context: System Process

IRQL: PASSIVE_LEVEL

Figure 13.1. *DriverEntry entry point.*

The return value from DriverEntry is NTSTATUS. If the driver returns a status indicating success, the I/O Manager immediately allows processing of requests for the Device Objects created by the driver. If a status other than success is returned, the driver is unloaded.

The specific work performed by a driver in DriverEntry does, of course, depend on the type of device being supported. The main job of a driver when called at DriverEntry is to do whatever is necessary to ready itself and its devices to process I/O requests. The typical steps that a driver performs at the DriverEntry include the following:

1. Locate physical hardware devices that the driver will control.

2. Create one or more Device Objects.

3. Claim hardware resources to be used by the driver and, where necessary, translate those resources for use by the driver with the HAL.

4. Export other driver entry points (such as Dispatch entry points).

5. Connect to interrupts and register a DpcForIsr.

6. For DMA devices, describe the device's characteristics and get an Adapter Object.

7. Do whatever initialization and setup is necessary to make the devices under the driver's control ready for processing.

People new to writing NT drivers are often surprised at the length and complexity of the processing that takes place during DriverEntry. Because all drivers determine their configuration and reserve resources in NT when they load, however, all the work needed to prepare the driver and its devices for operation takes place during DriverEntry.

Determining Device Configuration

Unlike other operating systems, drivers in NT locate the hardware resources for the device(s) they support dynamically when they are loaded. Hardware resources, in this case, refer to the I/O ports, shared memory segments, device registers (in both memory and port space), interrupt vectors, and system DMA channels that a device utilizes. The three ways to locate this information in NT are as follows:

- **Query the system's device-configuration data.** During startup, the system locates and identifies a subset of devices that are present on the system. Information about these devices may be retrieved using the `IoQueryDeviceDescription()` function.

- **Query bus configuration data.** Drivers for PCI, EISA, and MCA devices may retrieve information about device identification and configuration for any given slot on these buses. This retrieval operation is accomplished using the `HalGetBusData()` function.

- **Query the driver's "Parameters" subkey in the Registry.** During the driver's installation procedure, information about a device's configuration can be requested from the user and stored in the Registry. Drivers may retrieve this information by using the `RtlQueryRegistryValues()` function. More information about driver installation procedures can be found in Chapter 20, "Installing and Starting Drivers."

The method that a driver uses is a function of the type of device it supports. Many drivers use a combination of methods. For example, a driver for a serial port device typically queries the system's configuration data to determine its hardware resources. This method is used because serial port devices are one of the standard devices discovered and identified during system startup. For a more complex device, such as an exotic PCI-based serial port, the process can be more involved. For example, the driver might attempt to augment the system configuration data by also retrieving the device-specific PCI slot configuration data.

On the other hand, a driver for a PCI-based Toaster device typically relies solely on querying each slot on each PCI bus that's present on the system to locate its hardware resources. Because Toasters aren't standard devices, the system can't locate them during startup. Thus, it's completely up to the driver to locate such devices.

Regardless of any other method used to identify hardware resources, most drivers also retrieve device or driver-specific information from the driver's "Parameters" subkey in the Registry. This information, which was usually stored by the driver's installation procedure when the driver was installed, can include any information relevant to the driver, such as information to override default configuration values or even license information.

Resource Lists, Descriptors, and Partial Descriptors

Before discussing the methods used to retrieve configuration information, it might be helpful to discuss the major structures that the NT Configuration Manager uses to describe hardware resources. All the structures described in this section are defined in NTDDK.H.

The Configuration Manager describes individual hardware resources by using a `CM_PARTIAL_RESOURCE_DESCRIPTOR` structure. This structure would contain, for example, the base address and length of an I/O port; or the level, vector, and affinity of an interrupt. These `CM_PARTIAL_RESOURCE_DESCRIPTOR` structures may be grouped together in a `CM_PARTIAL_RESOURCE_LIST` that contains a count of the `CM_PARTIAL_RESOURCE_DESCRIPTOR` structures it contains. All the resources used by a particular device, for example, would be grouped together in a single `CM_PARTIAL_RESOURCE_LIST`.

The values contained in a CM_PARTIAL_RESOURCE_LIST are the untranslated, bus-relative values, however. These values are only meaningful when the bus type and bus number on which they appear are also supplied. Thus, the CM_PARTIAL_RESOURCE_LIST is part of a CM_FULL_RESOURCE_DESCRIPTOR that also includes the InterfaceType (which indicates the bus type) and the bus number with which the CM_PARTIAL_RESOURCE list is associated. To enable the description of multiple sets of resources across multiple buses, the CM_FULL_RESOURCE _DESCRIPTOR may be contained in a CM_RESOURCE_LIST. The CM_RESOURCE_LIST contains a count of the number of CM_FULL_RESOURCE_DESCRIPTORs that it contains. Figure 13.2 shows the relationship of these structures.

```
CM_RESOURCE_LIST
     ULONG Count
     CM_FULL_RESOURCE_DESCRIPTOR List[1]
          INTERFACE_TYPE InterfaceType
          ULONG BusNumber
          CM_PARTIAL_RESOURCE_LIST PartialResourceList
               USHORT Version
               USHORT Revision
               ULONG Count
               CM_PARTIAL_RESOURCE_DESCRIPTOR  PartialDescriptors[1]
                    UCHAR Type
                    UCHAR ShareDisposition
                    USHORT Flags
                    union  u
                         Port        // Type == CmResourceTypePort
                         PHYSICAL_ADDRESS Start
                         ULONG Length

                         Interrupt        //Type == CmResourceTypeInterrupt
                         ULONG Level
                         ULONG Vector
                         ULONG Affinity

                         Memory        // Type == CmResourceTypeMemory
                         PHYSICAL_ADDRESS Start
                         ULONG Length

                         Dma         //  Type ==CmResourceTypeDma
                         ULONG Channel
                         ULONG Port
                         ULONG Reserved1

                         DeviceSpecificData // CmResourceTypeDeviceSpecific
                         ULONG DataSize
                         ULONG Reserved1
                         ULONG Reserved2
```

Figure 13.2 *Relationship of Resource Lists, descriptors, and partial descriptors.*

Querying System Configuration Data

As discussed earlier in this chapter, NT is able to locate and identify some subset of devices that is connected to the system during system startup. These subsets include devices that comprise the system itself, such as the CPU, floating-point unit, and certain buses. Of more interest to driver writers, however, is that many "standard" devices, such as disk, keyboard, serial, and parallel devices, are also detected.

The way system devices are detected is dependent on the system architecture. For X86 architecture systems, the NTDETECT program queries the BIOS to locate and identify such devices. For RISC architecture systems, such as the Alpha, the Advanced RISC Consortium (ARC) console firmware performs the task of locating and identifying standard devices. Whichever way the detection is performed, the data is first stored in memory in a standardized format and then later written to the Registry under the
\HKEY_LOCAL_MACHINE\HARDWARE\DESCRIPTION key. You can examine this key yourself (using the regedit or rededt32 utilities) to get an idea of the sorts of devices that the system finds during startup on your system.

Because the configuration information is stored in the Registry in a well-known location, drivers may use any method they like to retrieve this information. Methods include using RtlQueryRegistryValues() or directly using the native Zw functions. However, due to its ease of use, most drivers choose to use the I/O Manager-provided function IoQueryDeviceDescription() for this purpose. Figure 13.3 shows the prototype for the IoQueryDeviceDescription() function.

```
NTSTATUS
IoQueryDeviceDescription(IN PINTERFACE_TYPE  BusType,
        IN PULONG  BusNumber,
        IN PCONFIGURATION_TYPE  ControllerType,
        IN PULONG  ControllerNumber,
        IN PCONFIGURATION_TYPE  PeripheralType,
        IN PULONG  PeripheralNumber,
        IN PIO_QUERY_DEVICE_ROUTINE  CalloutRoutine,
        IN PVOID  Context);
```

BusType: A pointer to the interface type being sought (such as Isa, PCIBus, and similar).

BusNumber: A pointer to a ULONG containing the zero-based bus number for which information is being sought.

ControllerType: A pointer to the controller type (such as DiskController, SerialController, etc.).

ControllerNumber: A pointer to a ULONG containing the zero-based controller number.

PeripheralType: A pointer to a value indicating the type of peripheral for which information is being sought. Drivers looking for controller information set this and *PeripheralNumber*, following, to NULL.

PeripheralNumber: A pointer to a ULONG containing the zero-based peripheral number.

CalloutRoutine: A pointer to a routine in the driver to call with information about each item found. The prototype for this function is shown in Figure 13.4.

Context: A driver-defined value to be passed as a parameter to the *CalloutRoutine*.

Figure 13.3. *IoQueryDeviceDescription function prototype.*

IoQueryDeviceDescription() enables a driver to retrieve information about the buses on a system and the controllers that appear on those buses. A driver might call this function to determine which serial port controllers appear on the ISA bus in the system, for example. The IoQueryDeviceDescription() function also enables drivers to directly determine to which controller certain specific peripheral devices are attached. A driver can call IoQueryDeviceDescription() to find to which serial port in the system a mouse that it controls is attached, for example.

For the IoQueryDeviceDescription() function, interfaces (which are really buses) are defined as being one of the enumerated values of INTERFACE_TYPE. Examples of enumerated values include Isa, Eisa, and PCIBus. Similarly, controllers and peripherals are specified as values of CONFIGURATION_TYPE. Example values for controllers are DiskController, KeyboardController, ParallelController, and SerialController. Examples of peripheral values are DiskPeripheral, FloppyDiskPeripheral, and PointerPeripheral (for the mouse).

> ### Note
> The complete definitions of these enums appear in NTDDK.H.

When calling IoQueryDeviceDescription() the *BusType* parameter is required. If a driver wants to locate information about its devices on a particular bus, it supplies the value indicating that bus for *BusType*. Most drivers of standard system devices don't limit the devices they support to residing on a particular bus, however. In this case, IoQueryDeviceDescription() is called in a loop that supplies values for *BusType* from 0 to MaximumInterfaceType. Calling IoQueryDeviceDescription() does not, however, require the provision of either a *ControllerType* or *PeripheralType*. However, the values for these parameters must be set with care and with regard to each other. If a driver is searching for controllers of a specific type to support, but does not care about peripherals, it sets *PeripheralType* to NULL. On the other hand, if a driver is searching for a specific *PeripheralType*, it *must* specify the *ControllerType* on which the particular peripheral device resides. Failing to provide a *ControllerType*, even if a specific *PeripheralType* is specified, results in IoQueryDeviceDescription() returning only information about the various buses in the system. For example, suppose that a driver is capable of supporting a particular type of mouse, regardless of whether it is on a serial controller or on its own interface card. This driver would call IoQueryDeviceDescription() twice, each time specifying *PeripheralType* PointerPeripheral: once specifying *ControllerType* SerialController and a second time specifying *ControllerType* MouseController.

When IoQueryDeviceDescription() is called to retrieve information about a particular controller or peripheral, it calls the driver at the driver's *CalloutRoutine* for each matching item found. Figure 13.4 shows the prototype for this

CalloutRoutine. The *CalloutRoutine* is called at IRQL PASSIVE_LEVEL in the same context as that in which the driver called IoQueryDeviceDescription(). Within the *CalloutRoutine,* the driver can perform whatever functions it requires to validate or further identify the device it will support.

```
NTSTATUS
QueryDeviceCalloutRoutine(IN PVOID Context,
        IN PUNICODE_STRING PathName,
        IN INTERFACE_TYPE BusType,
        IN ULONG BusNumber,
        IN PKEY_VALUE_FULL_INFORMATION *BusInformation,
        IN CONFIGURATION_TYPE ControllerType,
        IN ULONG ControllerNumber,
        IN PKEY_VALUE_FULL_INFORMATION
                            *ControllerInformation,
        IN CONFIGURATION_TYPE PeripheralType,
        IN ULONG PeripheralNumber,
        IN PKEY_VALUE_FULL_INFORMATION
                            *PeripheralInformation);
```
Context: The driver-supplied context value specified on the call to IoQueryDeviceDescription.

BusType: The interface type of the bus described in BusInformation.

BusNumber: The zero-based bus number of the bus described by BusInformation.

BusInformation: A pointer to a vector of KEY_VALUE_FULL_INFORMATION structures describing the bus.

ControllerType: The type of the controller described by ControllerInformation.

ControllerNumber: The zero-based number of the controller described by ControllerInformation.

ControllerInformation: A pointer to a vector of KEY_VALUE_FULL_ INFORMATION structures describing the controller.

PeripheralType: The type of peripheral described by PeripheralInformation.

PeripheralNumber: The zero-based number of the peripheral described by PeripheralInformation.

PeripheralInformation: A pointer to a vector of KEY_VALUE_FULL_ INFORMATION structures describing the peripheral found.

Figure 13.4. *CalloutRoutine from IoQueryDeviceDescription function prototype.*

Probably the trickiest part of using IoQueryDeviceDescription is figuring out how to interpret the bus, controller, and peripheral information passed to the *CalloutRoutine*. The prototype shown in Figure 13.3 shows that this information is passed to the driver in a pointer to a pointer to a KEY_FULL_VALUE_INFORMATION structure. This really means that the driver is passed a pointer to an array of KEY_FULL_VALUE_INFORMATION structures.

The first entry in the array, which has the symbolic index IoQueryDeviceIdentifier, contains the information from the Identifier value in the Registry. This comprises the name, if any, of the component.

The second entry in the array, IoQueryDeviceConfigurationData, contains the data from the ConfigurationData value in the Registry.

The third array element, IoQueryDeviceComponentInformation, comprises the data from the ComponentInformation value in the Registry.

The KEY_FULL_VALUE_INFORMATION structure contains the name and data for the Registry value that's being returned. The data field for the IoQueryDeviceConfigurationData entry is a CM_FULL_RESOURCE_DESCRIPTOR, which contains all the information known about the DMA, interrupt, shared memory, port, and device-specific resources used by the device.

> ### Note
>
> *Certain devices, such as those for floppy disks, serial ports, and keyboards, retrieve device-specific data using* IoQueryDeviceDescription(). *This data specifies configuration information, such as media density, port speed, and which LEDs to light by default on the keyboard. The format for device-specific data is defined by structures named* CM_XXX_DEVICE_DATA, *where* XXX *is the name of the device. Refer to NTDDK.H for the definitions of these structures. Also, see the appropriate example drivers in the DDK (such as the sermouse driver) for ways to use this data.*

The DDK contains several example drivers that use IoQueryDeviceDescription. The example that we find easiest to follow is the intpar driver (\ddk\src\comm\intpar). In the file initulo.c, the function ParGetConfigInfo demonstrates how to call IoQueryDeviceDescription to look for a particular controller (ParallelController, in the example) across all the buses defined in the system. The intpar driver's *CalloutRoutine* is ParConfigCallback. This function demonstrates how to get the CM_FULL_RESOURCE_DESCRIPTOR from the PKEY_FULL_VALUE_INFORMATION structure passed with the controller information.

Querying Bus-Configuration Data

Drivers for PCI, EISA, and MCA bus devices, other than those that the system locates and identifies during startup, need to get their device information from the relevant bus. As mentioned earlier, some drivers for "standard" system devices that reside on the PCI, EISA, or MCA bus may also want to supplement the information they can retrieve from the Registry by querying the bus-supplied configuration information.

Drivers can query bus-supplied information for their devices by searching each applicable bus in the system for their device. This is done using the HalGetBusData function shown in Figure 13.5.

ULONG
HalGetBusData(IN BUS_DATA_TYPE *BusDataType*,
        IN ULONG *BusNumber*,
        IN ULONG *SlotNumber*,
        IN PVOID *Buffer*,
        IN ULONG *Length*);

BusDataType: The type of data to be returned, such as PCIConfiguration, EisaConfiguration, or POS.

BusNumber: The zero-based bus number for which data is being sought.

SlotNumber: The bus-defined slot number for which data is being sought. For PCIConfiguration, this is the AsULONG member of the PCI_SLOT_NUMBER structure.

Buffer: A pointer to a buffer into which the requested data is to be returned. This buffer may be from local storage or paged or non-paged pool.

Length: The length, in bytes, of the supplied buffer. For PCIConfiguration data, this buffer should be at least 256 bytes long.

Figure 13.5. *HalGetBusData function prototype.*

Drivers call HalGetBusData for each slot on each bus on which their device is supported. From each call, HalGetBusData returns the bus-configuration data for the device in the indicated slot. The format of the data varies, according to the type of bus being searched.

Calling `HalGetBusData()` and `HalAssignSlotResources()` for PCI Bus Devices

For PCI buses, `HalGetBusData()` is called with a *BusDataType* of `PCIConfiguration`. In this case, the *SlotNumber* parameter is not an integer; it is a `PCI_SLOT_NUMBER` structure. This structure contains a union, one member of which is a ULONG. This part of the union is used when passing the slot number information as the *SlotNumber* parameter on `HalGetBusData()`. The other member of the union is a sequence of bit fields that indicate the device and function number for which PCI configuration information is being sought. Figure 13.6 shows the `PCI_SLOT_NUMBER` structure.

AsULONG		
Reserved	Function	DeviceNumber

Figure 13.6. `PCI_SLOT_NUMBER` *structure.*

On return from `HalGetBusData()`, the contents of *Buffer* contain contents of PCI configuration space for the device and function indicated by *SlotNumber*, which NT describes by using the `PCI_COMMON_CONFIG` structure. The return value of the function indicates the length of the data returned in *Buffer*, which for all valid devices and functions is 256. If `HalGetBusData()` returns a value of two, no device exists at the indicated *SlotNumber* (that is, no device exists corresponding to the device number and slot number supplied on the call). In this case, the `VendorId` field of the returned `PCI_COMMON_CONFIG` structure contains the reserved value `PCI_INVALID_VENDOR_ID`. If the return value from `HalGetBusData()` is zero, the PCI bus indicated in *BusNumber* does not exist. Because PCI buses are assigned contiguous numbers starting with zero, discovering that a particular PCI bus does not exist means that no other PCI buses exist with greater numbers.

> **Note**
>
> *Drivers must never attempt to subvert the Hardware Abstraction Layer (HAL) and manipulate PCI configuration registers directly. Doing this is, at best, platform-specific; and, worse, it can cause the HAL problems. To get or set information in PCI configuration space, always use the provided HAL functions.*

A driver attempts to find its devices on all the PCI buses connected to a system. The driver does this by enumerating all the devices and functions on all the PCI devices in the system. This may be done by calling HalGetBusData() for PCI_MAX_FUNCTION for each device and for PCI_MAX_DEVICES for each bus, until HalGetBusData() returns a value of zero, which indicates that there is no such PCI bus in the system. For each call that returns a valid PCI_COMMON_CONFIG structure in Buffer, the driver checks the VendorId and DeviceId fields of the structure looking for a match for the Vendor ID (VID) and Device ID (DID) of its device. If the VID and DID match the VendorID and DeviceID fields in the PCI_COMMON_CONFIG structure, the driver saves away the *BusNumber* and *SlotNumber* on which the device was found.

The code to do this is probably easier to understand than the preceding explanation, so refer to Example 13.1.

Example 13.1. Finding devices on PCI buses connected to the system.

```
//
// Keep looking at buses until there are no more
//
moreBuses = TRUE;
for (busNumber = 0; moreBuses; busNumber++) {
    //
    // Ennumerate all the devices on this bus
    //
    for (deviceNumber = 0;
         moreBuses && deviceNumber < PCI_MAX_DEVICES;
         deviceNumber++)  {

        //
        // Ennumerate all the functions on each device
        //
        for (functionNumber = 0;
             moreBuses && functionNumber < PCI_MAX_FUNCTION;
             functionNumber++)  {

            slotNumber.u.bits.Reserved = 0;
            slotNumber.u.bits.DeviceNumber = deviceNumber;
            slotNumber.u.bits.FunctionNumber = functionNumber;

            //
            // Get the configuration space for the adapter in this slot
            //
            length = HalGetBusData(PCIConfiguration,
                        busNumber,
                        slotNumber.u.AsULONG,
                        configInfo,
                        sizeof(PCI_COMMON_CONFIG) );
```

continues

Continued

```
        //
        // A return value of zero indicates no more PCI buses on the system
        //
        if (length == 0) {
            moreBuses = FALSE;

            break;
        }

        //
        // If there's nothing in this slot, PCI_INVALID_VENDORID is
        // returned as the vendor ID. If this is the case, just
        // continue running the bus.
        //
        if (configInfo->VendorID == PCI_INVALID_VENDORID)  {

            continue;
        }
        //
        // Is this the PCI device for which we've been searching?  It is
        // if both the vendor and device ID match
        //
        if ( (configInfo->VendorID == OSR_PCI_VID) &&
             (configInfo->DeviceID == OSR_PCI_DID) )  {

            ULONG index;

            //
            // FOUND IT!
            //
            //   ***Driver does something useful here, including (at least)
            //      storing away the slot and bus numbers.
            }
        }
    }
}
```

> **Note**
>
> *Although PCI bus numbers are continuous, starting with zero, this is not true for device numbers. Thus, to find all their devices, drivers have to query devices zero through* PCI_MAX_DEVICES *on every valid bus.*

A driver might be able to take some shortcuts in Example 13.1, depending on the device the driver supports. Although most device drivers in NT are capable of supporting multiple devices, those that support only a single unit can stop their search as soon as they find their device. In addition, drivers of single-function devices (which are by far the majority of devices) can just query function zero of each device, instead of enumerating every function on every device.

> **Note**
>
> *"What about devices that exist behind PCI-PCI bridges?" you ask. NT conveniently handles the bridge for you. Therefore, no special handling is required for devices that are located behind bridges.*

Once the driver finds its devices, and the bus number and slot number for each device has been saved, the device's hardware resources can be determined. Drivers should almost never read and interpret a device's hardware resources directly by using the information returned by HalGetBusData(). Instead, PCI drivers call the HalAssignSlotResources() function, shown in Figure 13.6, which returns the actual device hardware resources in a CM_RESOURCE_LIST.

```
NTSTATUS
HalAssignSlotResources(IN PUNICODE_STRING  RegistryPath,
        IN PUNICODE_STRING  DriverClassName,
        IN PDRIVER_OBJECT  DriverObject,
        IN PDEVICE_OBJECT  DeviceObject,
        IN INTERFACE_TYPE  BusType,
        IN ULONG  BusNumber,
        IN ULONG  SlotNumber,
        IN OUT PCM_RESOURCE_LIST  *AllocatedResources);
```

RegistryPath: A pointer to a Unicode string containing a Registry key, under which information about requested resources will be stored. If *DeviceObject* is NULL, this may be the same as the *RegistryKey* passed in to DriverEntry. If *DeviceObject* is not NULL, this value must point to a key under the driver's Registry key.

DriverClassName: An optional Unicode string that provides a name for the subkey under HKEY_LOCAL_MACHINE\HARDWARE\RESOURCEMAP, under which the driver's configuration information will be stored.

DriverObject: A pointer to the driver's Driver Object, as passed in at DriverEntry.

DeviceObject: A pointer to the Device Object for which these resources are being claimed. If this value is NULL, resources are being claimed for driver-wide use.

BusType: The interface type on which the device resides.

SlotNumber: The slot number in which the device resides. For PCIBus interfaces, this is the AsULONG field of the PCI_SLOT_NUMBER structure.

AllocatedResources: A pointer into which the function returns a pointer to a CM_RESOURCE_LIST, describing the resources which have been claimed for the device in slot SlotNumber on Bus BusType.

Figure 13.7. `HalAssignSlotResources()` *function prototype.*

The driver passes `HalAssignSlotResources()` the location of the device via the *BusType, BusNumber,* and *SlotNumber* parameters. `HalAssignSlotResources` returns a `CM_RESOURCE_LIST`, describing the device's hardware resources. A pointer to this structure is returned in *AllocatedResources.* The storage for the `CM_RESOURCE_LIST` is allocated within the function from nonpaged pool. After extracting the information from this structure, the driver must return the storage for the `CM_RESOURCE_LIST` to pool (by calling `ExFreePool()`).

In addition to returning the resource information to the driver, `HalAssignSlotResources()` automatically reserves the resources in the list for use by the driver by calling `IoAssignResources()` (described later in this chapter). The primary resources requested in the call to `IoAssignResources()` are the resource values specified in the PCI Configuration space. When possible, `HalAssignSlotResources()` may also provide alternative acceptable values to `IoAssignResources()`. The *RegistryPath*, *DriverClassName*, *DriverObject*, and *DeviceObject* parameters on the call to `HalAssignSlotResources()` are identical to those same parameters in `IoAssignResources()`. See the discussion of `IoAssignResources()` following Figure 13.12 for more information on these parameters.

Because of its integration with the HAL and I/O Manager, `HalAssignSlotResources()` should be used by PCI drivers to determine and reserve hardware resources for the devices they support, whenever possible. Calling `HalAssignSlotResources()` for a particular device fails in some rare cases, however. This is typically due to an error in the PCI configuration information in the device itself. In other cases, a device may have unusual requirements that need to be communicated to the driver in a nonstandard way. Finally, perhaps a device has data in the device-specific portion of its PCI configuration space that needs to be retrieved by the driver. In these cases, drivers may fetch device-configuration information directly from the device's PCI configuration space. If device configuration for a PCI device is determined by a method other than calling `HalAssignSlotResources()`, the driver should register the device's resources by calling `IoAssignResources()`. Note also that drivers may write to PCI configuration space, when necessary, by using `HalSetBusData()` and `HalSetBusDataByOffset()`.

Calling `HalGetBusData()` for EISA or MCA Bus Devices

Drivers for EISA and MCA bus devices search these buses for their devices using `HalGetBusData()`, in a manner similar to that of the PCI buses described in the preceding section. For the EISA and MCA buses, the *SlotNumber* parameter is a ULONG integer, not a structure. For EISA buses, the *BusDataType* parameter is `EisaConfiguration`; for MCA buses it is `POS`.

EISA configuration information is returned in much the same format as it is returned from the EISA BIOS routines. The buffer passed on the `HalGetBusData()` call is filled with a `CM_EISA_SLOT_INFORMATION` structure, which will immediately be followed by zero or more `CM_EISA_FUNCTION_INFORMATION` structures.

`POS` information is returned for MCA buses in a `CM_MCA_POS_DATA` structure.

For both EISA and MCA bus devices, drivers determine a device's hardware resources by directly reading the information returned by HalGetBusData(). Drivers for devices on these buses do not call HalAssignSlotResources().

Querying the Registry

Some drivers may have no way to determine their device configuration, other than querying the Registry. These drivers include almost all non-PNP ISA devices. Other drivers that determine some of their device-configuration information by using other means, such as calling HalGetBusData(), can store additional information in the Registry, which needs to retrieved during DriverEntry processing. This data can include any device-specific parameters, including tuning, configuration, or even license information.

By convention, drivers store device specifics in the Registry under the key \HKEY_LOCAL_MACHINE\SYSTEM\CurrentControlSet\Services*DriverName*\Parameters, where *DriverName* is the name of the driver. Drivers that support multiple device units typically create subkeys under the   *DriverName* key. Thus, a driver with two devices can have the following three keys:

```
\HKEY_LOCAL_MACHINE\SYSTEM\CurrentControlSet\Services\DriverName\Parameters
\HKEY_LOCAL_MACHINE\SYSTEM\CurrentControlSet\Services\DriverName\Device0\
                                                               Parameters
\HKEY_LOCAL_MACHINE\SYSTEM\CurrentControlSet\Services\DriverName\Device1\
                                                               Parameters
```

In this scheme, configuration information that applies to the entire driver appears under the ...*DriverName*\Parameters key, whereas configuration information that applies to a particular device appears under the appropriate device-specific key.

> *Note*
>
> *Where and how a driver stores its device-specific configuration information in the Registry is up to the driver, and its installation and configuration programs. No specific structure is required by Windows NT.*

Although there are several ways that a driver can query the Registry for device-specific configuration parameters, calling RtlQueryRegistryValues() is clearly the easiest. You may doubt this the first time you read the description for RtlQueryRegistryValues() in the DDK, however, because this function can be used in many different ways. Here, we describe a way to use the function that's truly quick and easy. When you look through the sample drivers in the DDK, you'll see that they most frequently call RtlQueryRegistryValues() this same way. Our description of RtlQueryRegistryValues() is restricted to this one method of using the function. For more information, see the complete description in the DDK. The prototype for this function is shown in Figure 13.8.

NTSTATUS
RtlQueryRegistryValues(IN ULONG *RelativeTo,*
    IN PWSTR *Path,*
    IN PRTL_QUERY_REGISTRY_TABLE *QueryTable,*
    IN PVOID *Context,*
    IN PVOID *Environment);*

RelativeTo: The symbolic value that indicates the base of the Path parameter. Where Path specifies a complete Registry key, this is RTL_REGISTRY_ABSOLUTE.

Path: A pointer to a wide string that contains the Registry path of the information to be read.

QueryTable: A pointer to a vector of structures describing the information to be retrieved from the Registry. The table ends with an all-zero element.

Context: A driver-defined context argument to be passed when each query routine, if any, is called.

Environment: A pointer to the environment with which to interpret REG_EXPAND_SZ values. Drivers typically pass this parameter as NULL.

Figure 13.8. `RtlQueryRegistryValues` *function prototype.*

`RtlQueryRegistryValues()` takes a *Path,* indicating where it should start reading in the Registry. This function also takes as input *QueryTable,* which is a pointer to a vector of `RTL_QUERY_REGISTRY_TABLE` entries, each entry of which describes a value to be read from the Registry. Each *QueryTable* entry specifies the name of the value to be read, and it can also supply a default value to be used if the entry is not present. Setting *RelativeTo* to `RTL_REGISTRY_ABSOLUTE` causes *Path* to be interpreted as an absolute Registry path.

What's particularly useful about the `RtlQueryRegistryValues()` function is that it can be used to query multiple values from the Registry and supply appropriate defaults for each, all in one call.

Given the following definitions and the *RegistryPath* parameter passed in at DriverEntry:

```
PWCHAR pathToRead;
RTL_QUERY_REGISTRY_TABLE queryTable[2];
```

```
        ULONG zero = 0;
        ULONG bufferCount = 10;
    #define MAX_PATH_LENGTH 256
```

Example 13.2 demonstrates calling RtlQueryRegistryValues().

Example 13.2. Calling RtlQueryRegistryValues()*.*

```
        //
        // Create a wide character string that starts with our Registry
        // Path (passed in to DriverEntry) and adds "\Parameters" to it.
        //
        pathToRead = ExAllocatePool(PagedPool, MAX_PATH_LENGTH);

        RtlZeroMemory(pathToRead, MAX_PATH_LENGTH);
        RtlMoveMemory(pathToRead, RegistryPath->Buffer, RegistryPath->Length);
        wcscat(pathToRead,L"\\Parameters");

        //
        // Zero the parameter table
        // Note: A fully zeroed entry marks the end of the table
        //
        RtlZeroMemory(&queryTable[0], sizeof(queryTable));


        //
        // Set up the parameters to read and their default values
        //
        queryTable[0].Flags = RTL_QUERY_REGISTRY_DIRECT;
        queryTable[0].Name = L"BufferCount";
        queryTable[0].EntryContext = &bufferCount;
        queryTable[0].DefaultType = REG_DWORD;
        queryTable[0].DefaultData = &zero;
        queryTable[0].DefaultLength = sizeof(ULONG);
        //
        // Get the values from the Registry
        //
        code = RtlQueryRegistryValues(
                    RTL_REGISTRY_ABSOLUTE | RTL_REGISTRY_OPTIONAL,
                    pathToRead,
                    &queryTable[0],
                    NULL,
                    NULL);

        if(!NT_SUCCESS(code))  {

            DbgPrint("RtlQueryRegistry FAILED! Code = 0x%0x\n", code);
        }

        DbgPrint("Value for BufferCount = %d.\n", bufferCount);
```

Drivers that determine their device configurations from the Registry should read the user-supplied configuration information, and then attempt to reserve the indicated resources before trying to access them. For example, a driver might read the port address for its master control registry from the Registry where the port address was stored, based on user input during the driver's installation or configuration process.

Prior to actually using the value it reads, the driver should call `IoAssignResources()` (or `IoReportResourceUsage()`, both of which are described later in this chapter in the section "Claiming Hardware Resources") to attempt to reserve the indicated port address. If the driver is successful in reserving the address, it may then go on to verify that the address is valid by accessing the device. If the request to reserve the hardware resource fails, another driver has already claimed the indicated resource. This conflict will have to be corrected before the driver can successfully control this particular device.

> **Note**
>
> *Drivers in NT generally avoid searching for device ports by walking through port space and attempting to find ports associated with particular devices. This is due to the "danger" to system stability inherent in doing this. Remember, multiple users can be using a particular machine simultaneously.*

Creating Device Objects

After a device driver has determined the devices it will support, it creates one or more Device Objects to represent those devices. The general concepts relating to Device Objects were discussed in detail in Chapter 9, "The I/O Subsystem." This section covers ways to create Device Objects and make them accessible to user mode programs.

A Device Object represents the entity that can be the target of a `CreateFile()` request to the I/O Manager or referenced from another driver for communications using `IoGetDeviceObjectPointer()`. As discussed in Chapter 9, the decision of what a Device Object corresponds to for a particular driver is probably the most important architectural decision that the driver writer makes. Drivers create Device Objects using the `IoCreateDevice()` function, the prototype for which is shown in Figure 13.9. Device Objects are always created in non-paged pools.

```
NTSTATUS
IoCreateDevice(IN PDRIVER_OBJECT  DriverObject,
        IN ULONG  DeviceExtensionSize,
        IN PUNICODE_STRING  DeviceName,
        IN DEVICE_TYPE  DeviceType,
        IN ULONG  DeviceCharacteristics,
        IN BOOLEAN  Exclusive,
        OUT PDEVICE_OBJECT  *DeviceObject);
```

DriverObject: A pointer to the Driver Object passed in to DriverEntry.

DeviceExtensionSize: The size, in bytes, of a per-device storage area to be allocated along with the Device Object. The format and contents of this storage area are defined by the driver.

DeviceName: If a named Device Object is being created, this is a pointer to a Unicode string containing the name of the device. This name should typically be in the Object Manager's "\Device" directory.

DeviceType: One of the predefined DEVICE_TYPEs if a Device Object for a standard device is being created; otherwise, a random value from the range "reserved to Microsoft customers."

DeviceCharacteristics: A set of flags that indicate the overall characteristics of this device. Examples include FILE_READ_ONLY_DEVICE and FILE_REMOVABLE_MEDIA.

Exclusive: A boolean value, set to TRUE, to indicate that only one file handle may be open on this device at a time.

DeviceObject: A pointer to receive the pointer to the created Device Object.

Figure 13.9. `IoCreateDevice()` *function prototype.*

The *DriverObject* parameter on the `IoCreateDevice` call is a pointer to the Driver Object passed in to the driver by the I/O Manager at the `DriverEntry` entry point.

Device Extensions

A driver may also choose to create a Device Extension when it creates a Device Object. The Device Extension is also located in nonpaged pool. The Device Extension is a structure associated with a device that is reserved for use solely by the driver. The driver determines its format and controls its use, and its size is passed by the driver as the *DeviceExtensionSize* parameter to `IoCreateDevice()`. Drivers typically use the Device Extension to store device-specific data, including device statistics, listheads for queues of requests, synchronization objects like mutexes, and spin locks to protect these fields.

Device Names

The Device Object name supplies the native Windows NT name for a device. These names are Unicode strings, and should be created in the Object Manager's Device directory. A pointer to the UNICODE_STRING structure that contains the name of the device is passed as the *DeviceName* parameter on IoCreateDevice(). Device names may be any legal Object Manager name, which means that they can contain any character other than a path separator. Although there appears to be no absolute limit on the length of Device Object names, for practical purposes, names are limited in length to MAX_FILENAME_LENGTH (256 bytes).

How are Device Objects for standard Windows NT devices named? They are typically named with the name of the device, and immediately followed by the unit number, starting at zero. For example, the first CD-ROM device on the system is named CdRom0 and the first floppy disk drive is named Floppy0. In order to allow other drivers to locate their devices, drivers that implement standard Windows NT devices (such as disks, floppys, CDs, and serial and parallel ports), call IoGetConfigurationInformation() to determine the next available unit number for their devices. The prototype for this function appears in Figure 13.10.

IoGetConfigurationInformation() returns a pointer to the I/O Manager's memory-resident CONFIGURATION_INFORMATION data structure. This structure contains a count of the number of devices of each type found. Drivers supporting any of the device types tracked by this structure should use the value from this structure to set the unit numbers for their devices. As it creates each device, the driver should increment the value in the CONFIGURATION_INFORMATION structure.

PCONFIGURATION_INFORMATION
IoGetConfigurationInformation( );

This function takes no parameters.

Figure 13.10. IoGetConfigurationInformation *function prototype.*

Device Types and Characteristics

The *DeviceType* and *DeviceCharacteristics* parameters to IoCreateDevice() may require some explanation. *DeviceType* is the value that indicates the type of device. The value for the *DeviceType* parameter is the same as the *DeviceType* parameter on the CTRL_CODE macro that is used for defining Device I/O Control codes.

For drivers of standard devices, such as disks, tapes, or serial ports, NT defines standard device numbers in NTDDK.H. These definitions start with FILE_DEVICE, for example; FILE_DEVICE_DISK for a standard disk type device. Custom devices assign their own device types from the range reserved for custom devices, which is 32768–65535. If you're implementing a standard device, you should use the standard type value when you create your device. If you're implementing a custom device, the value you choose really doesn't matter, as long as it's in the range reserved for custom devices. The value you use here should, of course, be the same as that used to define any Device I/O Control codes (but, in fact, it doesn't strictly have to be!).

> *Note*
>
> *Custom device types are not registered with Microsoft. Frequently, this can cause some concern for device driver writers, who fear that they might choose a custom device type that is the same as some other device's custom device type. Although this can occur, for an application to actually use this device type in passing I/O Control operations to your driver, it must also know the* name *of the driver. Because it isn't possible for two devices using the same name to coexist on a particular host, there really is no reason to worry about "collisions" of custom device types.*

The *DeviceCharacteristics* parameter is a set of flags that indicate a standard set of attributes. The values for these flags include FILE_REMOVABLE_MEDIA, FILE_READ_ONLY_DEVICE, and FILE_REMOTE_DEVICE. These values are also of interest only to drivers of standard devices.

Device Exclusivity

A final parameter of interest on the IoCreateDevice() function is the *Exclusive* parameter. When this parameter is set to TRUE, only one single open File Object at a time is allowed by the I/O Manager on the device. All subsequent IRP_MJ_CREATE requests, after the first successful one, will be rejected by the I/O Manager before they reach the driver, until the first File Object is closed. Setting this parameter to FALSE causes all IRP_MJ_CREATE requests to be sent to the driver, where it may decide which requests, or how many simultaneous open requests, to grant.

> **Note**
>
> *Of all the parameters on all the functions in* DriverEntry, *it's our experience that the* Exclusive *parameter is the one set incorrectly most often. Almost all devices will want to set* Exclusive *to* FALSE, *which results in the driver getting every valid IRP_MJ_CREATE issued for the device. Contrary to the DDK documentation, this flag has nothing to do with how many threads can send I/O requests to the device (except that if only one open is possible, only those threads in that process can successfully send requests to the device).*

Example 13.3 demonstrates calling IoCreateDevice(). Of course, the DDK has many similar examples.

Example 13.3. Creating a Device Object.

```
//
// Initialize the UNICODE device name. This will be the "native NT" name
// for our device.
//
RtlInitUnicodeString(&devName, L"\\Device\\OSRDevice");

//
// Ask the I/O Manager to create the device object and
// device extension
//
code = IoCreateDevice(DriverObj,
                      sizeof(OSR_DEVICE_EXT),
                      &devName,
                      FILE_DEVICE_OSR,
                      0,
                      FALSE,
                      &devObj);
```

Device-Naming Considerations

It is interesting to note that naming the Device Object is, in fact, optional. An unnamed Device Object can obviously not be the target of a call to CreateFile(), IoGetDeviceObjectPointer(), or IoAttachDevice() because these functions require the name of the device being targeted. Therefore, unnamed Device Objects are created relatively rarely. When they are created, they are typically restricted to being used for internal control purposes within a driver. File System drivers also create unnamed Device Objects to represent the instance of the file system mounted on a particular device partition.

When a Device Object is created, it is initialized by the I/O Manager. A pointer to the device's Device Extension is returned as the DeviceExtension field of the Device Object. Device drivers for storage devices will want to initialize the AlignmentRequirement field of newly created Device Objects to one of the FILE_xxxx_ALIGNMENT values defined in NTDDK.H, as well as setting the SectorSize field to an appropriate value. Drivers with particular requirements may also wish to set the StackSize field, which indicates the number of I/O Stack locations required by this device, and any other devices, layered beneath it. The I/O Manager initializes this value to one when the Device Object is created.

After the Device Object is created, the driver needs to set the Device Object's Flags field to indicate the way the driver wants IRP_MJ_READ and IRP_MJ_WRITE requests to be described. The options available to a driver were described in detail in Chapter 10, "Describing I/O Requests." If the driver elects to have Read and Write requests described by using Buffered I/O, the DO_BUFFERED_IO bit must be set in the Flags field. If the driver wants to use Direct I/O, the DO_DIRECT_IO bit must be set. To use Neither I/O, neither bit is set (hence, its name). What do you get if you set *both* bits? This is an invalid combination, but it seems to always result in getting Buffered I/O (well, at least today). Finally, remember that Device Control (IOCTL) functions can use a different buffering method from that chosen for IRP_MJ_READ and IRP_MJ_WRITE requests.

> *Note*
>
> *Although we discuss their creation in the chapter on DriverEntry, Device Objects may, in fact, be created any time a driver is running at IRQL* PASSIVE_LEVEL. *If a driver creates a Device Object outside of its DriverEntry routine, the driver must manually clear the* DO_DEVICE_ INITIALIZING *bit in the Device Object's Flags field. On return from DriverEntry, the I/O Manager clears this bit for all Device Objects created within DriverEntry.*

Device Symbolic Links

Recall that applications are under the control of their subsystems. Typical Windows NT subsystems, notably the Win32 and NTVDM subsystems, restrict their applications so that they can access only certain devices. Thus, simply creating and naming a Device Object is not sufficient to allow that device to be easily accessed by such a user mode application. Furthermore, most of the familiar device names (such as C: or COM1) are not native NT names. These names are symbolic links within the Object Manager namespace to the native NT names of the devices.

Typically, whenever a Win32 application calls CreateFile(), the Win32 subsystem prefixes the name supplied on the call with the string "\??\". This causes the Object Manager to look for the name supplied, starting in its "??" directory. This directory (which, prior to NT 4.0, was named DosDevices) contains logical links from the familiar names to the native NT Device Objects in the Object Manager's "Device" directory. Thus, "\??\LPT1" is a symbolic link, probably to the device named "\Device\Parallel0".

To enable users to access devices you create, you need to create a symbolic link from the Object Manager's "??" directory to the native NT name for your Device Object. Note that because this link is created on a name basis, you will not be able to create a symbolic link to it if your device object is unnamed. The function that is used to create symbolic link is named, appropriately enough, IoCreateSymbolicLink(), the prototype for which appears in Figure 13.11.

NTSTATUS
IoCreateSymbolicLink(IN PUNICODE_STRING *SymbolicLinkName*,
    IN PUNICODE_STRING *DeviceName*);

SymbolicLinkName: A pointer to a Unicode string that contains the name of the symbolic link to be created. To make devices accessible to Win32 subsystem applications, this link should be created in the Object Manager's "\??" directory.

DeviceName: A pointer to the native NT device name for which the symbolic link is being created.

Figure 13.11. IoCreateSymbolicLink() *function prototype.*

The two parameters to this function are self-explanatory. An example of the IoCreateSymbolicLink() function appears in Example 13.4.

Example 13.4. Creating a symbolic link for a Device Object.

```
RtlInitUnicodeString(&linkName, L"\\??\\MyDevice");

code = IoCreateSymbolicLink(&linkName, &devName);
```

Example 13.4 creates the symbolic link "\??\MyDevice" to the native NT device with a name equal to the Unicode string contained in &devName. Thus, User mode applications in the Win32 subsystem would attempt to open this device using the CreateFile() function in a manner something like the following:

```
Handle = CreateFile("\\\\.\\MyDevice",
                GENERIC_READ|GENERIC_WRITE,
                0,
                0,
```

```
OPEN_EXISTING,
0,
0);
```

Note that the name of the symbolic link and the native NT name of the device need not be related in any way. Furthermore, multiple symbolic links may be created to point to a single native NT device.

> **Note**
>
> *Symbolic link names must be valid in the environment in which they will be used. For example, although the I/O Manager allows you to create a symbolic link named "\??*.*", it is unlikely a Win32 user that tries to open your device using this symbolic link name will get what he expects!*

One final note on symbolic links: it is a mistake to assume that *not* creating a symbolic link for your device means that User mode applications can never open the device. Creating or omitting a symbolic link to a native NT device name does not provide any measure of security to a created device. User mode applications that use the native NT API can, of course, access devices by their native NT names. And, although applications that run under the control of the Win32 subsystem cannot directly open devices by using their native NT names, the applications can programmatically create symbolic links that can open the devices. This is done by using the Win32 DefineDosDevice() function.

> **Note**
>
> *Some symbolic links, such as the drive letters, are created by the I/O Manager, based upon which devices are present during boot loading. Because of this, some devices that load later must create their own symbolic links. Devices should always do this by using a Win32 program or helper service that uses the DefineDosDevice() function. This ensures that other Win32 applications, such as Explorer, are notified when their drive letters are created and deleted. Otherwise, Win32 programs may not be notified of the change.*

Claiming Hardware Resources

Once a driver's hardware resources are identified, the next step is for the driver to attempt to claim the identified resources with the I/O Manager. Claiming the resources has three purposes:

1. It allows the I/O Manager and HAL to ensure that the resources a driver expects to use are valid.

2. It allows the I/O Manager to determine that resources that are exclusively required by a driver are not already in use by another driver.

3. It allows configuration-display programs (such as winmsd) to display helpful information about which resources are being used, and by which drivers and devices.

When resources are claimed by a driver, the I/O Manager makes an entry in the Registry under the \HKEY_LOCAL_MACHINE\HARDWARE\RESOURCEMAP key, indicating the hardware resources the driver uses.

Most drivers written since the release of NT V3.51 claim resources by using the IoAssignResources() function. The prototype for this function appears in Figure 13.12. IoAssignResources() (almost) completely replaces the original function that was used for this purpose: IoReportResourceUsage(). IoReportResourceUsage() can still be called, and it has a couple of unusual features that IoAssignResources() does not have. However, most people writing new drivers should call IoAssignResources() because of its much greater functionality.

NTSTATUS
IoAssignResources(IN PUNICODE_STRING *RegistryPath*,
     IN PUNICODE_STRING *DriverClassName*,
     IN PDRIVER_OBJECT *DriverObject*,
     IN PDEVICE_OBJECT *DeviceObject*,
     IN PIO_RESOURCE_REQUIREMENTS_LIST
                                RequestedResources,
     IN OUT PCM_RESOURCE_LIST **AllocatedResources*);

RegistryPath: A pointer to a Unicode string that contains a Registry key, under which information about requested resources will be stored. If the value for *DeviceObject* is NULL, this may be the same as the *RegistryKey* passed in to DriverEntry. If *DeviceObject* is not NULL, this value must point to a key under the driver's Registry key.

DriverClassName: An optional Unicode string that provides a name for the subkey under HKEY_LOCAL_MACHINE\HARDWARE\RESOURCEMAP, under which the driver's configuration information will be stored.

DriverObject: A pointer to the driver's Driver Object, as passed in to DriverEntry.

DeviceObject: A pointer to the Device Object for which these resources are being claimed. If this value is NULL, resources are being claimed for driver-wide use.

RequestedResources: A pointer to a Resource Requirements List that describes the resources needed for this device, as well as optionally describing alternative resources.

AllocatedResources: A pointer into which the function returns a pointer to a CM_RESOURCE_LIST that describes the resources that have been claimed for the device.

Figure 13.12. `IoAssignResources()` *function prototype.*

Drivers that claim resources by using `IoAssignResources()` are typically limited to those for ISA, EISA, and MCA bus devices. Drivers for PCI bus devices call `HalAssignSlotResources()`, which internally calls `IoAssignResources()` on behalf of the driver. Therefore, the only time drivers for PCI bus devices directly call `IoAssignResources()` is when they add resources to those that were reserved by `HalAssignSlotResources()`. How IoAssignResources are used to add resources to those previously allocated is discussed later in this section.

Resources to be claimed in a call to IoAssignResources() are described to the
I/O Manager using an IO_RESOURCE_REQUIREMENTS_LIST. This Resource
Requirements List contains one or more Resource Lists
(IO_RESOURCE_LIST), each of which contains one or more Resource
Descriptors (IO_RESOURCE_DESCRIPTOR). Each Resource Descriptor describes a single hardware resource (a port, interrupt, memory range, or DMA channel) that
the driver wishes to claim. Attributes of the resources include whether the port
address is in memory or Port I/O space, whether a shared memory segment is
read-only or read-write, and whether interrupt resources are edge- or level-
triggered. Each resource is also indicated as either being required for exclusive
use or being sharable. See the complete description of the IoAssignResource()
function's parameters in the DDK.

IoAssignResources() is very powerful in that it allows drivers to indicate both
preferred resources and possible alternatives as part of its Resource
Requirements List. The I/O Manager assigns preferred resources when they are
available, but if another driver has already claimed a preferred resource, the
I/O Manager will attempt to fulfill the driver's request by using one of its alternatives. Drivers may also indicate certain hardware resources as having no
alternatives. On successful return from IoAssignResources(), the driver receives
a CM_RESOURCE_LIST that describes all the resources that have been claimed by
the driver.

Thus, for example, a driver for an ISA bus device might indicate that it has an
I/O Port resource (its main control and status register) located at port I/O
address 0x300, that this resource is 8 bytes long, and that there are no alternatives acceptable to the driver for this resource. This ISA card I/O port address
would presumably be set on the card using jumpers, and therefore could not be
changed programmatically by the driver. The driver might also indicate that it
requires the use of IRQ 9 and that no other IRQ is acceptable (again, probably
due to a hardware constraint on the device). The driver might further indicate
that its device has a 1KB shared memory segment and that the preferred location for this segment is 0xC0000. The driver can also indicate that alternative
acceptable base addresses for this segment are 0xD0000 and 0xE0000. This is
done by setting up a single Resource List that contains multiple Resource
Descriptors. One Descriptor would describe the required port I/O address, one
Descriptor would describe the required IRQ, one Descriptor would describe
the preferred memory segment base address, and one Resource Descriptor
would describe each of the two alternative acceptable memory base addresses.
An example of how these lists might be set up appears in Example 13.5.

Given the following declarations:

```
PIO_RESOURCE_REQUIREMENTS_LIST resReqList;
PIO_RESOURCE_LIST resList;
```

```
                PIO_RESOURCE_DESCRIPTOR resDescriptor;
                ULONG sizeToAllocate;
                PCM_RESOURCE_LIST cmResList;
```

The code is as follows:

Example 13.5. Calling IoAssignResources().

```
        sizeToAllocate = sizeof(IO_RESOURCE_REQUIREMENTS_LIST) +
                            sizeof(IO_RESOURCE_LIST) +
                            sizeof(IO_RESOURCE_DESCRIPTOR) * 5;


        resReqList = ExAllocatePool(PagedPool, sizeToAllocate);

        RtlZeroMemory(resReqList, sizeToAllocate);

        resReqList->ListSize = sizeToAllocate;
        resReqList->InterfaceType = Isa;
        resReqList->BusNumber = 0;
        resReqList->SlotNumber = 0;

        //
        // There is one Resource List
        //
        resReqList->AlternativeLists = 1;


        resList = &resReqList->List[0];

        resList->Version = 1;
        resList->Revision = 1;

        //
        // This Resource List contains 5 Resource Descriptors
        //
        resList->Count = 5;

        resDescriptor = &resList->Descriptors[0];

        //
        // Set the required port resource
        //
        resDescriptor[0].Option = 0;                    // Required - No alternative
        resDescriptor[0].Type = CmResourceTypePort;
        resDescriptor[0].ShareDisposition = CmResourceShareDeviceExclusive;
        resDescriptor[0].Flags = CM_RESOURCE_PORT_IO;


        resDescriptor[0].u.Port.Length = 8;
        resDescriptor[0].u.Port.Alignment = 0x01;

        resDescriptor[0].u.Port.MinimumAddress.LowPart = 0x300;
        resDescriptor[0].u.Port.MinimumAddress.HighPart = 0;
```

```
resDescriptor[0].u.Port.MaximumAddress.LowPart = 0x307;
resDescriptor[0].u.Port.MaximumAddress.HighPart = 0;


//
// Next, the interrupt resource
//
resDescriptor[1].Option = 0;              // Required - No alternative
resDescriptor[1].Type = CmResourceTypeInterrupt;
resDescriptor[1].ShareDisposition = CmResourceShareDeviceExclusive;
resDescriptor[1].Flags = CM_RESOURCE_INTERRUPT_LATCHED;

resDescriptor[1].u.Interrupt.MinimumVector = 9;
resDescriptor[1].u.Interrupt.MaximumVector = 9;


//
// Next, the shared memory segment.
//

//
// Start with the descriptor for the preferred base address
//
resDescriptor[2].Option = IO_RESOURCE_PREFERRED;
resDescriptor[2].Type = CmResourceTypeMemory;
resDescriptor[2].ShareDisposition = CmResourceShareDeviceExclusive;
resDescriptor[2].Flags = CM_RESOURCE_MEMORY_READ_WRITE;


resDescriptor[2].u.Port.Length = 0x400;
resDescriptor[2].u.Port.Alignment = 0x1;

resDescriptor[2].u.Port.MinimumAddress.LowPart = 0xC0000;
resDescriptor[2].u.Port.MinimumAddress.HighPart = 0;

resDescriptor[2].u.Port.MaximumAddress.LowPart = 0xC0400;
resDescriptor[2].u.Port.MaximumAddress.HighPart = 0;

//
// Next, specify the first alternative
//
resDescriptor[3].Option = IO_RESOURCE_ALTERNATIVE;
resDescriptor[3].Type = CmResourceTypeMemory;
resDescriptor[3].ShareDisposition = CmResourceShareDeviceExclusive;
resDescriptor[3].Flags = CM_RESOURCE_MEMORY_READ_WRITE;


resDescriptor[3].u.Port.Length = 0x400;
resDescriptor[3].u.Port.Alignment = 0x1;

resDescriptor[3].u.Port.MinimumAddress.LowPart = 0xD0000;
resDescriptor[3].u.Port.MinimumAddress.HighPart = 0;
```

continues

Continued

```
resDescriptor[3].u.Port.MaximumAddress.LowPart = 0xD0400;
resDescriptor[3].u.Port.MaximumAddress.HighPart = 0;

//
// Next, specify the second alternative
//
resDescriptor[4].Option = IO_RESOURCE_ALTERNATIVE;
resDescriptor[4].Type = CmResourceTypeMemory;
resDescriptor[4].ShareDisposition = CmResourceShareDeviceExclusive;
resDescriptor[4].Flags = CM_RESOURCE_MEMORY_READ_WRITE;


resDescriptor[4].u.Port.Length = 0x400;
resDescriptor[4].u.Port.Alignment = 0x1;

resDescriptor[4].u.Port.MinimumAddress.LowPart = 0xE0000;
resDescriptor[4].u.Port.MinimumAddress.HighPart = 0;

resDescriptor[4].u.Port.MaximumAddress.LowPart = 0xE0400;
resDescriptor[4].u.Port.MaximumAddress.HighPart = 0;

code = IoAssignResources(RegistryPath,
                &className,
                DriverObj,
                NULL,
                resReqList,
                &cmResList);

    if(!NT_SUCCESS(code) )   {

        DbgPrint("*** IoAssignResources Failed.  Code = 0x%0x\n", code);

    } else {

        // Decode the CM_RESOURCE_LIST here to determine the resources
        //  the I/O Manager has claimed for the driver

    }
```

Note in Example 13.5 that the type of bus (INTERFACE_TYPE), bus number, and slot number are specified in the IO_RESOURCE_REQUIREMENTS_LIST. For ISA bus devices, the slot number is not used.

On return from IoAssignResources() (after checking to ensure a successful status return), the driver examines the returned CM_RESOURCE_LIST to determine which of its alternative resources the I/O Manager claimed for it. The returned information must be stored, and the memory that the I/O Manager reserved for the CM_RESOURCE_LIST must be freed by the driver (by calling ExFreePool()).

So, in one call, a driver may indicate the required, preferred, and alternative resources that it needs. However, IoAssignResources() has yet another interesting feature—it enables drivers to specify complete alternative resource schemes. Although most devices are not able to take advantage of this capability, this feature enables a driver writer to establish alternative Resource Lists, with the I/O Manager being required to choose one of the Resource Lists from among the set of alternatives. The Resource Descriptors within the Resource List indicate the hardware resources required by the indicated alternative. This enables a driver, for example, to indicate that it requires the I/O Manager to allocate resources from one of the following alternatives:

Base address 300, IRQ 5, and shared memory address 0xC0000

or

Base address 0x300, IRQ 11, and base address 0xD0000

The Resource Lists may even contain preferred and alternative resources. Again, we don't see many driver writers being able to make use of this functionality, but it's nice to know it's there.

We strongly encourage people who write drivers for non-plug-and-play devices to take advantage of the flexibility provided by IoAssignResources(). If your device can be programmatically set to work with a variety of hardware resources, you should always build your Resource List with one preferred resource and as many individual alternative resources as your hardware and driver can accommodate. Letting the I/O Manager choose individual resources, based on the resources already in use by the system, helps avoid hardware conflicts that are otherwise not resolvable.

> ### Note
>
> *The alternative to* IoAssignResources() *is the* IoReportResourceUsage() *function. The example drivers in the DDK all call* IoReportResourceUsage() *because they were written prior to the availability of* IoAssignResources(). *However,* IoReportResourceUsage() *has two features that* IoAssignResources() *does not. First, it allows a driver to override any conflicts detected by the I/O Manager and HAL, thus forcing resources to be reserved for a driver's exclusive use, even if those resources are already claimed by another driver. Second, it allows drivers to claim device-specific resources (* CmResourceTypeDeviceSpecific() *). The capability to override conflicts is of dubious value (two devices can't be using the same I/O port, for example). However, the capability to claim device-specific data resources may be useful to some drivers of standard system devices identified with* IoQueryDeviceDescription().

IoAssignResources() enables a driver to claim its resources on a per-device basis or on a driver-wide basis. Resources that are claimed on a per-device basis are reserved by the driver for use with a specific Device Object, and can be released separately from resources claimed for driver-wide use or for other devices. Resources that are claimed on a driver-wide basis are generally those hardware resources that are used by the driver in general, not for just one particular device. Whether resources are being claimed on a per-device or driver-wide basis is determined by the *DeviceObject* and *RegistryPath* parameters on the call to IoAssignResources().

If resources are being claimed on a driver-wide basis, *DeviceObject* is set to NULL, and *RegistryPath* is set to the value that was passed into DriverEntry by the I/O Manager. On the other hand, if resources are being claimed on a per-device basis, *DeviceObject* points to the Device Object with which the resources are associated and *RegistryPath* must point to a unique key under the driver's HKEY_LOCAL_MACHINE\SYSTEM\CurrentControlSet\Services*DriverName* Registry key. Although there's no established convention about how to name this key, we usually just specify a key under *DriverName* equal to the unit number. Thus, the *RegistryPath* used for claiming resources for the first Toaster device would be HKEY_LOCAL_MACHINE\SYSTEM\CurrentControlSet\Services\Toaster\0.

Although it might seem that the distinction between per-device and driver-wide resources is more architectural than practical, there's actually a very pragmatic consequence of this choice. IoAssignResources() can be called to claim an initial set of resources, to release a previously set of claimed resources, or to add to or delete from a pre-existing list of resources. Suppose that your driver needs to claim resources for each of its three devices. In all likelihood, the code in your driver will probably call IoAssignResources() three times, once for each device. If you call IoAssignResources() three times, each time indicating that the resources are being claimed on a driver-wide basis, the resources that you indicate on each subsequent call after the first will *replace* the previously claimed set of resources. On the other hand, if you call IoAssignResources() with *DeviceObject* pointing to a different Device Object each time and have a separate *RegistryPath* specified on each call, the result claims the sum of all the resources on each of the three calls. This is probably what you had in mind.

As already mentioned, previously claimed resources may be released using IoAssignResources(). All resources that are allocated for a device on per-device basis or for a driver on a per-driver basis may be returned by calling IoAssignResources() with a *RequestedResources* set to NULL. Specific resources may be released by calling IoAssignResources() with an IO_RESOURCE_ REQUIREMENTS_LIST, including IO_RESOURCE_DESCRIPTORs for all the resources that your driver wants to retain and omitting those it wants to release. In all instances, the *DeviceObject*, *RegistryPath*, and *DriverClassName* parameters must be specified exactly as they were when the resources were claimed.

Drivers for PCI bus devices almost never call IoAssignResources() directly because HalAssignSlotResources() (used by almost all drivers of PCI bus devices) internally does this automatically. However, PCI device drivers do call IoAssignResources() on the rare occasions when they need to add an additional hardware resource to those already claimed, or to release resources previously obtained by calling HalAssignSlotResources().

We should probably mention something at this point about the *DriverClassName* parameter to IoAssignResources(). *DriverClassName* is a strictly optional parameter that enables the driver to specify a name for the subkey under \HKEY_LOCAL_MACHINE\HARDWARE\RESOURCEMAP, under which the driver's resources will be recorded. If a *DriverClassName* is not specified, the driver's resources will be recorded under the OtherDrivers subkey.

Translating Bus Addresses

Regardless of how the hardware resources for a device are determined, until their addresses are translated they are bus-specific. That is, the addresses returned for ports, registers, and other shared memory spaces as read from the Registry, read from the bus configuration data using HalGetBusData(), returned from HalAssignSlotResources(), or returned from IoQueryDeviceDescription() are only valid if the bus type and bus number are also specified. This is due to the following two facts about the HAL's abstraction of a system's architecture:

1. Multiple buses, of the same or different types, may be connected to the system simultaneously. These buses may each have their own bus-specific address spaces.

2. A bus's address space does not need to be the same as the system's physical address space.

Figure 13.13 shows a system configured with two separate (not bridged) PCI buses on the same system, plus one EISA bus and one ISA bus.

> *Note*
>
> *Don't worry about whether or not this is a good bus configuration or a reasonable system to build, or whether it's allowed by the various hardware specifications. The point here is that the HAL allows this configuration.*

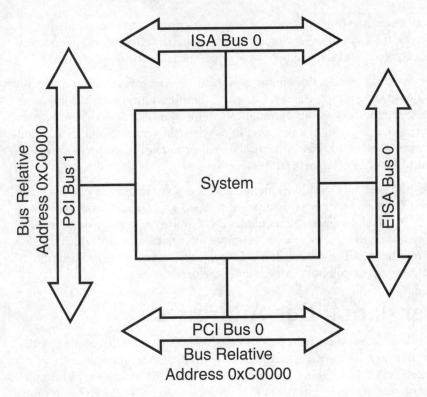

Figure 13.13. *Different bus address spaces.*

According to the HAL's system abstraction, these buses may have overlapping bus-specific address spaces. That is, each bus may have an address 0xC0000 that translates to a different logical address that is used to uniquely access the bus address via the system.

The designer of the overall system hardware (that is, the processor, bus support, and memory subsystem) is responsible for determining how buses are attached to the system and for creating a discrete mapping between bus-specific addresses and unambiguous logical addresses. The HAL for supporting that system is responsible for knowing how to perform these translations.

Thus, before a port or memory address for a device on a specific bus can be accessed by a driver, it must be translated to a logical address. This translation is performed by using the HalTranslateBusAddress() function, the prototype for which is shown in Figure 13.14.

BOOLEAN
HalTranslateBusAddress(IN INTERFACE_TYPE *InterfaceType,*
　　IN ULONG *BusNumber,*
　　IN PHYSICAL_ADDRESS *BusAddress,*
　　IN OUT PULONG *AddressSpace,*
　　OUT PPHYSICAL_ADDRESS *TranslatedAddress);*

InterfaceType: The interface type for which the address passed in BusAddress is to be translated.

BusNumber: The zero-based number of the bus for which the address passed in BusAddress is to be translated.

BusAddress: The bus-relative device address to be translated.

AddressSpace: A pointer to a ULONG. As input to the function, it contains a code that indicates the address space in which the device's hardware address resides. On successful return from the function, it contains a code that indicates the address space in which the *TranslatedAddress* resides on the current processor. Values defined for x86 architecture systems include 0x00 indicating memory space and 0x01 indicating Port I/O space. RISC processors may define additional values.

TranslatedAddress: A pointer into which is returned a logical address that can be used with the HAL access function (READ/WRITE_PORT_xxxx or READ/WRITE_REGISTER_xxxx) to access *DeviceAddress* on InterfaceType bus number *BusNumber.*

Figure 13.14. `HalTranslateBusAddress()` *function prototype.*

`HalTranslateBusAddress()` takes input parameters that specify a bus relative address, plus the address space in which the address resides, the bus type, and the bus number. Although the address, bus type, and bus number may be determined dynamically from device-configuration information, the space in which the device address resides (that is, Port I/O space or memory space) is a function of the device itself. `HalTranslateBusAddress()` returns an unambiguous logical address that the driver may subsequently use to refer to that device. The function also returns the address space in which that returned address resides on the current system. Note that the returned logical address can be a physical address (in either Port I/O space or memory space—as it is on most x86 architecture systems) or a logical address, which is useful only for the purposes of calling the HAL access function (as it is on some Alpha systems).

Mapping Logical Addresses to Kernel Virtual Address Space

Because the HAL's system abstraction includes Port I/O space, logical addresses in Port I/O space are assumed to be directly accessible by the driver using the appropriate READ_PORT_XXXX and WRITE_PORT_XXXX HAL access function. Logical addresses in memory space, however, can only be referenced from a driver using kernel virtual addresses. So, if HalTranslateBusAddress() returns a logical address in memory space (as opposed to port space), the driver must ask the Memory Manager to map that logical address into kernel virtual address space so the driver can access it. This is done by using the MmMapIoSpace() function, the prototype for which is shown in Figure 13.15.

PVOID
MmMapIoSpace(IN PHYSICAL_ADDRESS *PhysicalAddress,*
    IN ULONG *NumberOfBytes,*
    IN BOOLEAN *CacheEnable);*

PhysicalAddress: The physical address to be mapped into kernel virtual address space.

NumberOfBytes: The size, in bytes, of the address space to map.

CacheEnable: A boolean value, indicating whether the address range should be cachable by the processor's cache. TRUE means that the address range may be cachable.

Figure 13.15. *MmMapIoSpace function prototype.*

MmMapIoSpace() maps a physical or logical address into kernel virtual address space. The driver passes the logical address returned from HalTranslateBusAddress() as the *PhysicalAddress* parameter. The length of the device's memory located at this address is specified in the *NumberOfBytes* parameter. The driver also specifies whether the addresses being mapped will be eligible for caching by the CPU in the *CacheEnable* parameter.

> **Note**
>
> *CacheEnable controls internal CPU caching of the address range,* and is not related to the disk or virtual memory caching performed by the Cache Manager. *For simplicity and to ensure consistency between memory contents and what is on the device, most drivers should set CacheEnable to* FALSE.

Examples: Translating Bus Addresses

Let's look at a couple of examples to see how HalTranslateBusAddress() and MmMapIoSpace() work, and how they are used by a driver. For the purposes of these examples, assume that Port I/O address 0x300 is a valid address on the indicated PCI bus. Examples 13.6–13.8 all use the following definitions:

```
INTERFACE_TYPE  interfaceType;
ULONG  busNumber;
PHYSICAL_ADDRESS busAddress;
ULONG addressSpace;
PHYSICAL_ADDRESS translatedAddress;
BOOLEAN result;
PVOID deviceAddressToUse;
ULONG value;
```

Translating Bus Addresses on a Standard x86 Architecture System

The parameters for this example are as follows:

- **System configuration.** Standard X86 architecture processor, 1 PCI bus, and one ISA bus

- **HAL.** Standard x86 single processor HAL

- **Device.** PCI device with 4-byte base port address at 0x300, in Port I/O space

Example 13.6. Translating Bus Addresses on a Standard x86 Architecture System.

```
interfaceType = PCIBus;
busNumber = 0;
busAddress = 0x300;
addressSpace = 0x01;      // 0x01 == Port I/O space; 0x00 == Memory space

result = HalTranslateBusAddress(PCIBus,          // Interface type
                                0,               // Bus Number
                                0x300,           // Bus Address
                                &addressSpace,   // Ptr to address space
                                &translatedAddress); // Ptr to logical
                                                 //     address to return
```

In Example 13.6, the value returned in the addressSpace variable is 0x01, denoting that the returned address is in Port I/O space; and the value returned in the variable translatedAddress is 0x300. How do we know this? We know this because standard x86 processors implement Port I/O space, and that space is shared across all busses. Therefore, there's not much for HalTranslateBusAddress to do!

The I/O port on the device can then be read using the low 32-bits from the
translatedAddress variable and the HAL function READ_PORT_ULONG, as follows:

```
deviceAddressToUse = translatedAddress.LowPart;

value = READ_PORT_ULONG(deviceAddressToUse);
```

The READ_PORT_ULONG function on x86 system results in an IN instruction being
issued to perform the indicated read from Port I/O space.

Translating Bus Addresses for a MIPS System

In this example, the device is the same as in Example 13.6, but the system configuration is different. The parameters for this example on translating bus
addresses are as follows:

- **System configuration.** MIPS R4000 processor, 1 PCI bus and one ISA bus

- **HAL.** Standard MIPS single processor HAL

- **Device.** PCI device with 4-byte base port address at 0x300 in Port I/O
  space

Example 13.7. Translating Bus Addresses for a MIPS System.

```
interfaceType = PCIBus;
busNumber = 0;
busAddress = 0x300;
addressSpace = 0x01;      // 0x01 == Port I/O space; 0x00 == Memory space

result = HalTranslateBusAddress(PCIBus,               // Interface type
                                0,                    // Bus Number
                                0x300,                // Bus Address
                                &addressSpace,        // Ptr to address space
                                &translatedAddress);  // Ptr to logical
                                                      //     address to return
```

In Example 13.7, the value returned in the addressSpace variable will most likely be 0x00, denoting that the returned address is in memory space; and the
value returned in the variable translatedAddress will likely be some very large
value ending in 0x300. We know this because standard MIPS platforms do not
have a separate Port I/O space. Thus, the system hardware designer maps
"port I/O space" addresses into some set of reserved physical addresses on the
system.

Because the value returned in the addressSpace variable indicates that the
returned logical address is in memory, the next thing that needs to be done is
to call MmMapIoSpace(), as follows:

```
deviceAddressToUse = MmMapIoSpace(translatedAddress,  // logical address to map
                                  0x08,               // length of space
                                  FALSE);             // indicate not cacheable
```

This call to MmMapIoSpace() maps the returned logical address into kernel virtual
address space, making it accessible by the driver. The driver may then read
from the device's register by using the returned variable deviceAddressToUse and
the HAL's READ_PORT_ULONG function, as follows:

```
value = READ_PORT_ULONG(deviceAddressToUse);
```

This function results in a read from the indicated memory location. Despite the
fact that the translatedAddress variable returned from HalTranslateBusAddress()
indicated that the address resides in memory space on this processor, we still
use READ_PORT_ULONG to read it. This is because the actual device address (the
one on the hardware device) is in port space. The actual device address, not the
AddressSpace value returned by HalTranslateBusAddress, is what determines
which HAL access function to use.

Translating Bus Addresses on an Alpha System

In this example, the device is the same as in the previous two examples (13.6
and 13.7), but the system is an Alpha processor. The parameters for this
example on translating bus addresses are as follows:

- **System configuration.** Alpha processor, 1 PCI bus

- **HAL.** Standard Alpha HAL

- **Device.** PCI device with 4-byte base port address at 0x300 in Port I/O
  space

Example 13.8 Translating Bus Addresses on an Alpha System.

```
interfaceType = PCIBus;
busNumber = 0;
busAddress = 0x300;
addressSpace = 0x01;     // 0x01 == Port I/O space; 0x00 == Memory space

result = HalTranslateBusAddress(PCIBus,         // Interface type
                    0,                          // Bus Number
                    0x300,                      // Bus Address
                    &addressSpace,              // Ptr to address space
                    &translatedAddress);        // Ptr to logical address to
                                                   return
```

In this example, the value returned in the addressSpace variable will most likely
be 0x01, denoting that the returned value is in Port I/O space. Surprise! Even
though the Alpha doesn't have Port I/O space, it returns this indicator to indicate to the driver that calling MmMapIoSpace() is not necessary. The value
returned in translatedAddress is Quasi-Virtual Address (QVA) that encodes the

bus number and bus relative address. This QVA has meaning only to the HAL functions that are called to reference it, as in the following:

```
value = READ_PORT_ULONG(deviceAddressToUse);
```

This call results in the HAL performing the translation of the QVA to a device address when called and then returning the contents of that memory-mapped address.

Highlights of Bus Address Translation

To sum up, every Port I/O address and every memory address for a device needs to be translated from a bus relative value to a logical address before it can be used by the driver. This translation is performed by using HalTranslateBusAddress(). If HalTranslateBusAddress() returns that the returned address is in memory space on the current system, the driver next calls MmMapIoSpace() to map the returned logical address into kernel virtual address space. The returned logical address will be referenced by using the HAL function indicated by the original address space on the device, not the address space returned from HalTranslateBusAddress(). Thus, if an address physically resides in Port I/O space (as defined by the way the hardware device is wired), it is always accessed using the HAL READ/WRITE_PORT_XXXX functions, irrespective of the address space returned by HalTranslateBusAddress(). The HAL and the underlying hardware are responsible for properly resolving the differences. Thus, the driver writer can write a single, portable driver that works on different Windows NT platforms.

Troubleshooting Tip

A common problem that drivers encounter when they attempt to map multiple, large shared-memory segments from their devices into kernel virtual address space is that the call to MmMapIoSpace() *fails. This failure sometimes appears to be random—it happens sometimes but not other times. Because* MmMapIoSpace() *returns a kernel virtual address and not* NTSTATUS, *this failure is indicated by a return value of* NULL. *The likely cause of this problem is that the system has run out of system Page Table Entries (PTEs), with which to describe segments of kernel virtual address space. This problem can be rectified by setting the Registry value* HKEY_LOCAL_MACHINE\CurrentControlSet\Control\SessionManager\Memory Management\SystemPages *to a value between 20000 and 50000.*

Exporting Entry Points

With all of its hardware resources identified and device addresses translated, the driver next exports its entry points to the I/O Manager. This is performed by placing pointers to the driver's various entry points into the Driver Object, which was passed in to the driver at its DriverEntry entry point.

The driver fills entries into the Driver Object MajorFunction vector, with a pointer to a Dispatch routine for each I/O major function code it supports. If the driver uses System Queuing (discussed in Chapter 14, "Dispatch Entry Points"), it places a pointer to its StartIo routine in the StartIo field of the Driver Object. If the driver supports dynamic unloading, it places a pointer to its Unload routine in the Driver Object's DriverUnload field. Drivers that support Fast I/O also fill in a pointer to their Fast I/O Dispatch table in the Driver Object's FastIoDispatch field.

Example 13.9 demonstrates how to fill the various fields into the Driver Object.

Example 13.9. Filling Fields of the Driver Object.

```
//
// Establish dispatch entry points for the functions we support
//

DriverObj->MajorFunction[IRP_MJ_CREATE]          = OsrCreateClose;
DriverObj->MajorFunction[IRP_MJ_CLOSE]           = OsrCreateClose;

DriverObj->MajorFunction[IRP_MJ_READ]            = OsrRead;
DriverObj->MajorFunction[IRP_MJ_WRITE]           = OsrWrite;
DriverObj->MajorFunction[IRP_MJ_DEVICE_CONTROL] = OsrDeviceControl;

//
// Unload function
//
DriverObj->DriverUnload = OsrUnload;
```

As you saw in Example 13.7, drivers only fill in the MajorFunction vector for the I/O Function codes they want to support. Any entries that are not initialized by the driver will be connected to a function in the I/O Manager that returns STATUS_INVALID_DEVICE_REQUEST to any requests. Also, note that some major functions may be connected to the same Dispatch routine, as is the case with IRP_MJ_CREATE and IRP_MJ_CLOSE in the example.

Although these entry points have been filled into the Driver Object, the driver will not start to receive requests via these entry points until it has returned from DriverEntry.

Connecting to Interrupts and the Registering DpcForIsr

The next step in the DriverEntry entry point, at least for any interrupt-driven device, is to connect to interrupts from the device. In this step, the I/O Manager is given a pointer to the driver's Interrupt Service Routine (ISR), to be called each time that an interrupt is received from a particular device. The I/O Manager and the Microkernel create an Interrupt Object that connects (indirectly) the processor's interrupt vector to the driver's ISR. Unlike calls to your Dispatch entry points, which cannot be called until DriverEntry returns, a driver must be ready for its ISR to be called as soon as it connects to interrupts.

Translating Interrupt Levels and Vectors

Like device addresses, interrupts are also bus-specific. Therefore, before a driver can use an interrupt level and vector that it has read from the Registry or identified by using `HalGetBusData()`, `HalAssignSlotResources()`, or `IoQueryDeviceDescription()`, the driver must first translate them to systemwide logical values. This translation is performed by using the `HalGetInterruptVector()` function, the prototype for which is shown in Figure 13.16.

`HalGetInterruptVector()` takes the device's *InterfaceType* and *BusNumber* as parameters, as well as the bus-specific *BusInterruptLevel* and *BusInterruptVector*. For ISA bus devices, *BusInterruptVector* is ignored. The `HalGetInterruptVector()` function returns as its return value the translated interrupt vector, and returns the device interrupt level translated to an IRQL (DIRQL) in the *Irql* parameter.

```
ULONG
HalGetInterruptVector(IN INTERFACE_TYPE InterfaceType,
        IN ULONG BusNumber,
        IN ULONG BusInterruptLevel,
        IN ULONG BusInterruptVector,
        OUT PKIRQL Irql,
        OUT PKAFFINITY Affinity);
```

InterfaceType: The interface type on which the device resides.

BusNumber: The zero-based number of the bus on which the device resides.

BusInterruptLevel: The bus-relative interrupt level used by the device.

BusInterruptVector: The bus-relative interrupt vector used by the device. For ISA bus devices, this parameter is ignored.

Irql: The system IRQL corresponding to *BusInterruptLevel*.

Affinity: The mask of maximal processor affinity. A bit is set for each processor on which the devices interrupt may be service.

Figure 13.16. `HalGetInterruptVector()` *function prototype.*

The maximal mask of processor affinities is returned in the *Affinity* parameter. This value is a KAFFINITY structure, in which each bit corresponds to a potential CPU on the system. Bit zero corresponds to processor zero and bit 31 corresponds to processor 31. A bit is set for each processor on which the interrupt may be received. For NT 4, this is always the mask of active processors on the system. Thus, on a dual-processor system with two processors running, *Affinity* is always returned with the low two bits set; on a quad-processor system, bits 0 through 3 are always set.

Connecting Driver ISR to Interrupts

With the interrupt vector and level translated, the driver may now connect its ISR to the interrupt by using `IoConnectInterrupt()`, the prototype for which is shown in Figure 13.17. Note, a driver must be ready to receive interrupts as soon as it calls `IoConnectInterrupt()`.

```
NTSTATUS
IoConnectInterrupt(OUT PKINTERRUPT  *InterruptObject,
        IN PKSERVICE_ROUTINE  ServiceRoutine,
        IN PVOID  ServiceContext,
        IN PKSPIN_LOCK  SpinLock,
        IN ULONG  Vector,
        IN KIRQL  Irql,
        IN KIRQL  SynchronizeIrql,
        IN KINTERRUPT_MODE  InterruptMode,
        IN BOOLEAN  ShareVector,
        IN KAFFINITY  ProcessorEnableMask,
        IN BOOLEAN  FloatingSave);
```

InterruptObject: A pointer to a location into which is returned, on successful completion, a pointer to the Interrupt Object describing this interrupt and ISR.

ServiceRoutine: A pointer to the driver's interrupt service routine (ISR).

ServiceContext: A driver-defined value to be passed into the ISR when an interrupt occurs. Typically, this is a pointer to the Device Object responsible for the interrupt.

SpinLock: An optional pointer to an externally allocated and initialized spin lock, which is used when supporting multiple ISRs that need to be serialized. Almost always passed as NULL.

Vector: The interrupt vector to connect to, as returned from HalGetInterrupt().

Irql: The IRQL associated with the device, and at which the ISR will execute, as returned from HalGetInterrupt().

SynchronizeIrql: The IRQL at which the ISR will execute. This is almost always set to the same value as *Irql*; however, if *SpinLock* is not zero, this value may be set to a value higher than *Irql* to ensure serialization among multiple devices.

InterruptMode: A value indicating whether the interrupts from this device are LevelSensitive or Latched. Note that interrupts for PCI devices are LevelSensitive.

ShareVector: A boolean value, indicating whether the driver is willing to share this interrupt vector with other devices. Note that PCI devices must share interrupts.

ProcessorEnableMask: A KAFFINITY mask that indicates the processor on which interrupts from this device will be serviced. This value is usually the same as the value returned in Affinity from HalGetInterruptVector().

FloatingSave: A boolean value, indicating whether the floating-point registers should be saved before the ISR is called, and returned when the ISR exits. On x86 architecture processors, this must be set to FALSE.

Figure 13.17. IoConnectInterrupt() *function prototype.*

IoConnectInterrupt() takes as input the *InterruptVector, Irql,* and *Affinity* values returned by HalGetInterruptVector().

If the driver wants to restrict the processors on which interrupts will be processed, it may set *Process EnableMask* to a subset of the values returned in the *Affinity* parameter from HalGetInterruptVector().

> **Tip**
>
> *Although it might initially sound like a good idea to restrict the processors on which interrupts occur for a device, our experience is that it is better not to do so, except in very special circumstances. Setting* ProcessorEnableMask *on* IoConnectInterrupt() *to indicate that the interrupt can be processed on all processors enables the hardware and the HAL to work together to level interrupts and reduce interrupt latency. Restricting interrupts to a subset of the available processors can be a useful tool for well-defined, closed systems with set configurations. These include process control and similar systems.*

The driver specifies the *InterruptMode* (either Latched or LevelSensitive), based on the characteristics of the hardware device. Similarly, the driver sets *ShareVector* to TRUE, if it is willing to share this interrupt vector with other devices; and sets it to FALSE otherwise. Note that PCI devices are required by the PCI specification to share interrupt vectors.

The remainder of the parameters to IoConnectInterrupt() are a bit more arcane. The *FloatingSave* parameter, for example, specifies whether the floating-point registers should be saved before and restored after the ISR is executed. Almost all device drivers set *FloatingSave* to FALSE, which is the only supported value on x86 architecture systems.

This leaves the *SpinLock* and *SynchronizeIrql* parameters. The *SpinLock* parameter is almost always set to NULL by device drivers. This results in the Microkernel using a spin lock internal to the Interrupt Object, to ensure that the ISR is only active on one processor at a time. *SynchronizeIrql* is almost always set to the same value as *Irql* by device drivers. This setting results in the ISR executing at the DIRQL specified by the return from *Irql* by HalGetInterruptVector(). This is the normally desired behavior.

A driver should set *SpinLock* and *SynchronizeIrql* to something other than the recommended values only if the driver supports multiple interrupt sources *and* it needs to serialize executions of the ISRs associated with those interrupts. This is the case, for example, for a device that has two interrupt vectors but a single set of registers. When in the ISR because of one interrupt, the driver needs to be sure that it isn't interrupted by the other interrupt while accessing the registers.

To achieve serialization across two ISRs shared by a common device, IoConnectInterrupt() enables you to specify an external spin lock and the IRQL at which the ISR will be executed. To make use of this feature, a driver allocates space in a non-paged pool for a KSPIN_LOCK structure, and initializes it using KeInitializeSpinLock(). The *SpinLock* parameter on both calls to IoConnectInterrupt() is set to point to this spin lock. The *SynchronizeIrql* parameter is set to the higher of the two device's IRQLs, as returned from HalGetInterruptVector(). Because this results in both ISRs using the same spin lock and executing at the same DIRQL, the two ISRs now cannot ever interrupt each other.

Troubleshooting Tip

It is a serious error, yet a relatively common one, to acquire the spin lock that is optionally pointed to by the SpinLock *parameter within a driver using* KeAcquireSpinLock(). *This action results in the spin lock being acquired at* IRQL DISPATCH_LEVEL. *Although this effectively blocks the ISR using the spin lock from executing on other processors, it can lead to the driver deadlocking the current processor. ISR spin locks may only be acquired by using* KeSynchronizeExecution().

IoConnectInterrupt() returns a pointer to a kernel Interrupt Object, which the driver must store away (typically in the Device Object's device extension) for later use in disconnecting the interrupt or calling KeSynchronizeExecution().

Initializing the DPC Object for the DpcForIsr

After connecting to interrupts, a driver typically calls the
IoInitializeDpcRequest() function. This function takes as input a pointer
to a Device Object and a pointer to the DpcForIsr for that Device Object. The
function, which is actually implemented as a macro in NTDDK.H, initializes
the DPC Object embedded in the Device Object with a pointer to the
DpcForIsr. Consequently, when the driver calls IoRequestDpc(), a DPC is
queued for the driver's DpcForIsr. The prototype for IoInitializeDpcRequest()
appears in Figure 13.18.

VOID
IoInitializeDpcRequest(IN PDEVICE_OBJECT *DeviceObject,*
    IN PIO_DPC_ROUTINE *DpcRoutine);*

DeviceObject: A pointer to the Device Object with which the DPC is
associated.

DpcRoutine: A pointer to the driver's DpcForIsr that will be queued as
a result of the driver calling IoRequestDpc() and specifying
DeviceObject.

Figure 13.18. IoInitializeDpcRequest() *function prototype.*

Of course, drivers are not required to utilize NT's built-in DpcForIsr mechanism. As an alternative, drivers may wish to allocate a block of storage from
non-paged pool, sizeof(KDPC) bytes in length, and initialize it by calling
KeInitializeDpc(). Then, to request a DPC using this DPC object from its ISR,
the driver calls KeInsertQueueDpc(), specifying this DPC structure instead of
IoRequestDpc. Some drivers use this design to separate processing for different
interrupt causes on the same device, queuing a specific DPC to handle each
type of processing.

Getting an Adapter Object

Prior to completing initialization, DMA drivers need to describe the characteristics of each of their devices and indicate the maximum number of map registers that each device will need. The drivers do this by using HalGetAdapter(),
the prototype for which is shown in Figure 13.19.

VOID
HalGetAdapter(IN PDEVICE_DESCRIPTION *DeviceDescription,*
    IN OUT PULONG *NumberOfMapRegisters);*

DeviceDescription: A pointer to the DEVICE_DESCRIPTION structure that details the DMA characteristics of this device.

NumberOfMapRegisters: A pointer to a ULONG, in which the HAL
returns the maximum number of map registers that may be used at one
time by this device.

Figure 13.19. `HalGetAdapter()` *function prototype.*

To indicate a device's characteristics, drivers fill in a DEVICE_DESCRIPTION structure for each of their devices. Drivers typically allocate space for the structure
from the stack or from paged pool. The DEVICE_DESCRIPTION structure contains
information about a device's DMA characteristics. This information includes
whether the device is a busmaster device, whether it supports scatter/gather,
and whether it is capable of understanding 32-bit addresses. This structure also
indicates the maximum transfer length supported by the device.

The DEVICE_DESCRIPTION structure must be completely zeroed before any information is filled into it. Drivers only fill in those fields that are relevant to their
type of device. Therefore, busmaster devices do not put anything in the
`DmaChannel`, `DmaPort`, or `DmaSpeed` fields. The fields themselves are fairly self-
explanatory. The DDK supplies definitions for each field, in case there is any
doubt as to a particular field's meaning.

`HalGetAdapter()` returns a pointer to an ADAPTER_OBJECT as its return value. This
function also returns, as the contents of the *NumberOfMapRegisters* parameter, the maximum number of map registers that the driver may ever use at one
time with the returned Adapter Object. The driver must save each of these values for later use during DMA operations. On return from `HalGetAdapter()`, the
driver-allocated memory for the DEVICE_DESCRIPTION data structure can be
returned to pool.

Note

The NumberOfMapRegisters *parameter is often misunderstood. The
common belief is that this parameter must be set on input to the maximum number of map registers a device requires. This isn't so! The HALs
that we are aware of ignore any values passed in via this parameter.*

*Typical HALs determine the maximum number of map registers that a
device requires by dividing the maximum transfer size (as specified in the*

MaximumLength *field of the* DEVICE_DESCRIPTION *data structure) by the system's page size, and then adding one. This value is compared to any limit that the HAL may impose to determine the maximum number of map registers that a driver may request for a particular adapter. That maximum number of map registers is returned by the HAL as the contents of the* NumberOfMapRegister *parameter.*

Example 13.10 demonstrates how to call HalGetAdapter() for a busmaster DMA device.

Example 13.10. Calling the HalGetAdapter() *function for a busmaster DMA device.*

```
    //
        // Allocate space for the DEVICE_DESCRIPTION data structure
        //
        deviceDescription = ExAllocatePoolWithTag(PagedPool,
                            sizeof(DEVICE_DESCRIPTION), 'pRSO');

        //
        // Important: Zero out the entire structure first!
        //
        RtlZeroMemory(deviceDescription, sizeof(DEVICE_DESCRIPTION));

        //
        // Our device is a 32-bit busmaster PCI device. It does not support
        // scatter/gather.
        //
        deviceDescription->Version = DEVICE_DESCRIPTION_VERSION;
        deviceDescription->Master = TRUE;
        deviceDescription->ScatterGather = FALSE;
        deviceDescription->Dma32BitAddresses = TRUE;
        deviceDescription->BusNumber = devExt->BusNumber;
        deviceDescription->InterfaceType = PCIBus;
        deviceDescription->MaximumLength = OSR_PCI_MAX_TXFER;


        devExt->Adapter = HalGetAdapter(deviceDescription, &devExt->MapRegsGot);

        if(!devExt->Adapter)  {

            DbgPrint("HalGetAdapter FAILED!!\n");

            return(STATUS_UNSUCCESSFUL);

        }

        //
        // Return the memory allocated from pool
        //
        ExFreePool(deviceDescription);
```

Performing Device Initialization

To this point, all the work within DriverEntry has been concerned with finding devices, and initializing the interface between the driver and the operating system. The only thing that remains is to perform any processing required to initialize the devices under the driver's control. On successful return from DriverEntry, all the devices supported by a driver should typically be ready to process I/O requests.

The work required to initialize a device varies greatly, depending on the device type. In general, devices need to be reset and placed in a known state. Some drivers need to download microcode or configuration information to their devices, or set up structures in shared memory.

> **Tip**
>
> *NT drivers can perform I/O directly from Kernel mode. Consequently, downloading information into devices is relatively easy—not nearly the chore it is in some other operating systems. One particularly easy method of doing this is to use* ZwCreateSection() *and* ZwMapViewOfSection() *to memory map the file. The data from the file can then easily be referenced with a pointer to a structure referring to the base of the mapped area, or even simply copied to the device using* RtlMoveMemory()*.*

Some devices take a long time to initialize or must be initialized in stages. In general, if a driver is going to take longer than a few seconds to initialize, it should register for reinitialization by calling IoRegisterDriverReinitialization() during DriverEntry. Figure 13.20 shows the prototype for the IoRegisterDriverReinitialization() function.

VOID
IoRegisterDriverReinitialization(
        IN PDRIVER_OBJECT *DriverObject,*
        IN PDRIVER_REINITIALIZE *DriverReinitializationRoutine,*
        IN PVOID *Context);*

DriverObject: The driver object for which the reinitialization routine is being registered.

DriverReinitializationRoutine: A pointer to a driver reinitialization function.

Context: A driver-defined context value to be passed to the reinitializaton routine.

Figure 13.20. IoRegisterDriverReinitialization() *function prototype.*

When a driver registers for reinitialization, the I/O Manager makes an entry for the driver on its internal reinitialization list. After all drivers with boot and system start times have been called at their DriverEntry entry points, the I/O Manager calls each driver that has registered for reinitialization at its Reinitialization routine. This entry point is shown in Figure 13.21. As shown in the figure, the driver is passed a pointer to its Driver Object, a context value, and a count (starting with 1) of the number of times that the driver's reinitialization routine has been called.

NTSTATUS
DriverReinitialization(IN PDRIVER_OBJECT *DriverObject,*
    IN PVOID *Context,*
    IN ULONG *Count);*

DriverObject: A pointer to the Driver's Driver Object. This is the same Driver Object a pointer to which was passed to the driver at DriverEntry.

Context: A driver-defined context value supplied in the call to IoRegisterDriverReinitialization.

Count: The number of times that this driver has been called at its reinitialization entry point. The first time the driver is called, the count is one.

When Called: For boot-start or system-start drivers: after all drivers in the boot and system start groups have been loaded. For auto-start and demand-start drivers: after DriverEntry is complete.

Context: System Process

IRQL: PASSIVE_LEVEL

Figure 13.21. *Entry point: driver reinitialization.*

During reinitialization processing, a driver may once again register for reinitialization. This results in the I/O Manager replacing the entry for the driver on the end of its internal reinitializaton list. The driver's Reinitialization routine will be called again when all other driver Reinitialization routines have been called.

Drivers that either start at auto-start time or are demand-started may register Reinitialization routines. Doing this, however, results in the driver's Reinitialization routine being called immediately after the driver's DriverEntry routine completes. Practical use of driver reinitialization is, therefore, limited to drivers that start during the boot-start or system-start phases of startup.

Other DriverEntry Operations

Certain drivers may have additional work to perform in DriverEntry. In this section, we describe some of the additional functions that drivers may optionally want or need to perform in their DriverEntry routine.

Intermediate Buffers

Drivers that require static buffers for intermediate storage of data or control structures will typically want to allocate space for those buffers during DriverEntry. The system's paged and nonpaged pools tend to become fragmented over time while the system runs. Therefore, drivers should allocate any static buffers they require, especially large static buffers, during DriverEntry processing.

Drivers that need storage space for control structures or intermediate storage can allocate space directly from the system's paged or nonpaged pools by using ExAllocatePool(). Drivers that require buffer space for DMA operations allocate such buffers in a specific manner, described later in the section titled "Common Buffers for DMA Devices."

Drivers that desire memory that is not subject to internal processor caching can allocate buffers by using the MmAllocateNonCachedMemory() function, the prototype for which is shown in Figure 13.22. This function allocates memory in PAGE_SIZE increments. The buffer returned from this function is non-cached, logically contiguous, and non-paged. It is not necessarily physically contiguous, however. On some systems, it may be easier to allocate large chunks of non-paged memory using MmAllocateNonCachedMemory() than by using ExAllocatePool() for nonpaged pool.

PVOID
MmAllocateNonCachedMemory(IN ULONG *NumberOfBytes*);

NumberOfBytes: The size, in bytes, of the non-cached buffer to be allocated.

Figure 13.22. MmAllocateNonCachedMemory() *function prototype.*

Drivers that require physically contiguous memory for buffers may call MmAllocateContiguousMemory(), the prototype for which is shown in Figure 13.23. Because almost all drivers for DMA devices allocate buffer space using HalAllocateCommonBuffer(), shown in Figure 13.24, other requirements for contiguous memory are rare.

PVOID

MmAllocateContiguousMemory(IN ULONG *NumberOfBytes*
    IN PHYSICAL_ADDRESS *HighestAcceptableAddress*);

NumberOfBytes: The size, in bytes, of the non-cached buffer to be allocated.

HighestAcceptableAddress: The highest physical address at which the top of the buffer may be located.

Figure 13.23. MmAllocateContiguousMemory() *function prototype.*

Common Buffers for DMA Devices

There are several reasons that DMA drivers may need to allocate buffer space during initialization. This is the case when, for example, the driver requires an intermediate buffer from which DMA operations are repeatedly performed. Another reason is that the device utilizes shared host-based memory structures for communications between itself and the driver. In either case, after the driver has gotten a pointer to its Adapter Object, it allocates space for a memory-based "common" buffer. This buffer is termed "common" because it is shared in common between the DMA device that will access the buffer using logical addresses, and the driver that will access the buffer using kernel virtual addresses.

The function used to allocate common buffer space is HalAllocateCommonBuffer(), the prototype for which appears in Figure 13.24.

PVOID
HalAllocateCommonBuffer(IN PADAPTER_OBJECT *AdapterObject*,
    IN ULONG *Length*,
    OUT PHYSICAL_ADDRESS *LogicalAddress*,
    IN BOOLEAN *CacheEnabled*);

AdapterObject: A pointer to the driver's Adapter Object, previously acquired by using HalGetAdapter.

Length: The length, in bytes, of the required common buffer.

LogicalAddress: A pointer to a PHYSICAL_ADDRESS structure into which, on successful return, the function returns the logical address of the allocated common buffer. This address may be used for DMA operations.

CacheEnabled: A boolean value, indicating whether the allocated memory should be eligible for caching in the processor.

Figure 13.24. `HalAllocateCommonBuffer()` *function prototype.*

`HalAllocateCommonBuffer()` takes as input the length of the buffer required and a pointer to the device's Adapter Object. If required for DMA operation on the system, the function also maps the allocated space by using the Adapter Object's map registers. Note that any map registers used by this function are reserved until `HalFreeCommonBuffer()` is called. If cached memory is not required, drivers should set *CacheEnabled* to FALSE. On some platforms, this may make memory allocation easier and less likely to impact the system's nonpaged pool.

> **Tip**
>
> To reduce demands for contiguous memory that is required on some platforms, drivers that need multiple common buffers should call `HalAllocateCommonBuffer()` multiple times instead of calling it once to request a single large buffer.

`HalAllocateCommonBuffer()` examines the device characteristics contained in the Adapter Object, and allocates the memory appropriate for use by the device. For example, the common buffer allocated for system DMA devices that do not support 32-bit addresses will automatically be located in the lower 16MB of physical space within the system.

HalAllocateCommonBuffer() returns a kernel virtual address that the driver may use to access the buffer, and a logical address to be used by the device to perform DMA operations to or from the extent of the buffer.

> ### Note
>
> *Drivers that require buffers for DMA operations* must *allocate them by using* HalAllocateCommonBuffer() *(or a manual alternative to this function). It may seem reasonable to allocate such buffers by calling* HalAllocateContiguousMemory(), *and then get the address of the buffer for DMA by calling* MmGetPhysicalAddress(). *Although this works on current x86 architecture systems, it* does not work *on all platforms. Remember, logical addresses used for DMA operations are not necessarily the same as physical addresses. Some platforms really do use map registers for DMA operations!*

The only proper alternative to using HalAllocateCommonBuffer() that is available to a driver is to manually perform all the activities that HalAllocateCommonBuffer() would do. That is, you can allocate the buffer (contiguously, if necessary), lock it into memory, map the buffer with an MDL, call IoAllocateAdapterChannel() to allocate the necessary map registers, and then call IoMapTransfer() to get the logical address (or addresses) of the buffer.

I/O Timers

Some drivers need to periodically check their devices to ensure that they are operating properly. Additionally, drivers often require a clock with a resolution on the order of seconds, which allows them to time-out operations. Both of these functions can be conveniently implemented by using I/O Timers.

A driver can initialize an I/O Timer on a per-Device Object basis. The timer fires approximately once per second. When the timer is enabled for a device, each time that the timer fires, the I/O Manager calls the driver's I/O Timer routine that is associated with that device at IRQL DISPATCH_LEVEL in an arbitrary thread context. Drivers initialize an I/O Timer by using the function IoInitializeTimer(), the prototype for which is shown in Figure 13.25.

PVOID
IoInitializeTimer(IN PDEVICE_OBJECT *DeviceObject,*
   IN PIO_TIMER_ROUTINE *TimerRoutine,*
   OUT PVOID *Context);*

DeviceObject: A pointer to the driver's Device Object with which the timer is associated.

TimerRoutine: A pointer to the driver's I/O Timer routine, to be called by the I/O Manager once per second when the I/O Timer is running.

Context: A driver-defined context value for the I/O Manager to pass into the driver's I/O Timer Routine when it is called.

Figure 13.25. IoInitializeTimer() *function prototype.*

I/O Timers are typically initialized during a driver's DriverEntry routine.

I/O Timers may be started or stopped on a per-Device Object basis, as required by the driver. I/O Timers are started by using the function IoStartTimer(), the prototype for which is shown in Figure 13.26.

PVOID
IoStartTimer(IN PDEVICE_OBJECT *DeviceObject);*

DeviceObject: A pointer to the driver's Device Object with which this timer is associated.

Figure 13.26. IoStartTimer() *function prototype.*

Figure 13.27 shows the prototype for the driver's I/O Timer routine.

PVOID
IoTimerRoutine(IN PDEVICE_OBJECT *DeviceObject,*
   IN PVOID *Context);*

DeviceObject: A pointer to the driver's Device Object with which this timer is associated.

Context: The context value provided by the driver when it called
`IoInitializeTimer()`.

When Called: Approximately once per second

Context: Arbitrary

IRQL: DISPATCH_LEVEL

Figure 13.27. `IoTimerRoutine()` *entry point.*

Likewise, an I/O Timer may be stopped by using the function `IoStopTimer()`, the prototype for which is shown in Figure 13.28. While a timer is stopped, calls to the driver's I/O Timer routine do not take place.

PVOID
IoStopTimer(IN PDEVICE_OBJECT *DeviceObject);*

DeviceObject: A pointer to the driver's Device Object with which this timer is associated.

Figure 13.28. `IoStopTimer()` *function prototype.*

Note that I/O Timers are provided for low-resolution timing purposes only. The I/O Manager uses a single timer queue entry to process all I/O Timers. When this entry comes due, the I/O Manager calls each I/O Timer routine that has a timer enabled, one at a time. Therefore, although calls to a driver's timer routine are always at least one second apart, they can, in fact, be considerably more than one second apart. Drivers that need higher precision timing may initialize and use kernel timers (using the functions `KeInitializeTimer()`, `KeInitializeTimerEx()`,`KeSetTimer()`, and `KeSetTimerEx()`. These routines are discussed in Chapter 16, "Programmed I/O Data Transfers."

Intermediate and Filter Drivers

Up to this point in the chapter, we've restricted our discussion to initialization operations for device drivers. This is perhaps to be expected, given that the focus of this book is device drivers. However, a few words about the initialization tasks typically performed by intermediate and filter drivers is in order.

Because they do not, by definition, control any hardware, initialization for intermediate drivers is typically much simpler than it is for device drivers. During DriverEntry, intermediate drivers typically get and store away the Device Object address of the underlying drivers that will support them. Precisely how this is done is device-specific. As described in Chapter 11, "The Layered Driver Model," the Disk Class driver, for example, retrieves the Device Object address of any devices named "ScsiPortx" by using the IoGetDeviceObjectPointer() function.

Filter drivers share the characteristics of the devices to which they attach, as well as having characteristics specific to the job they perform. During DriverEntry, filter drivers typically create a new Device Object, and then attach it to the Device Object of the device to be filtered by calling IoAttachDevice() or IoAttachDeviceToDeviceStack(), as described in Chapter 11, "The Layered Driver Model." Any other initialization performed by a filter driver is driver- and device-specific.

Dynamic Driver Unloading

As mentioned previously, just as drivers may be dynamically loaded, drivers in NT may also be dynamically unloaded. Support for dynamic unloading is optional. If a driver supports dynamic unloading, it fills a pointer to its Unload routine into the Driver Object during DriverEntry processing. This was described earlier in this chapter, in the section entitled "Exporting Entry Points."

Drivers may be unloaded, either programmatically or interactively, by users with administrator privilege. A driver's Unload routine is not called by the I/O Manager if there are active references to any of the driver's Device Objects. Note that if a driver elects to supply an Unload routine, and the driver's Unload routine is called, the driver will be unconditionally unloaded on return from its Unload routine. Other than delaying in its Unload routine, there is no way that a driver can decide that it is not ready to be unloaded.

A driver's Unload routine is called at IRQL PASSIVE_LEVEL in the context of the system process. The prototype for this routine is shown in Figure 13.29.

PVOID
UnloadRoutine(IN PDRIVER_OBJECT *DriverObject*);

DriverObject: A pointer to the driver's Driver Object. Context:

When Called: When a driver is to be unloaded

Context: System process

IRQL: PASSIVE_LEVEL

Figure 13.29. UnloadRoutine() *entry point.*

The goal of processing in a driver's Unload routine is, in essence, to reverse the work done at its Dispatch entry point. This includes (for example) stopping any running timers, disconnecting from previously connected interrupts, unmapping any memory that has been mapped by using MmMapIoSpace(), returning any reserved hardware resources, unregistering for shutdown notification if it was so registered, and deleting any created Device Objects.

To facilitate its work, a driver may get a pointer to the first Device Object it created from the DeviceObject field of the Driver Object, a pointer to which is passed to the driver at its Unload routine entry point. Further Device Objects may be found by following the NextDevice pointer in each Device Object.

Before exiting, drivers must be careful to return all the memory they allocate during operation (such as memory that was allocated from the system's paged or nonpaged pools).

> **Tip**
>
> *Making your driver unload properly can be rather time-consuming, due to the effort required to ensure that you can undo all that was done in the driver. However, this can be time well spent. Making your driver dynamically unloadable can greatly speed the debugging process because you will not need to reboot the system every time you want to make a change to your driver code.*

Chapter **14**

Dispatch Entry Points

This chapter will review:

- **Validating requests.** Before a request can be processed, its parameters must first be validated. This section describes that process.

- **Completing requests.** A driver must notify the I/O Manager of each IRP it processes to completion by calling the IoCompleteRequest() function. This section describes how and when IoCompleteRequest() is called.

- **Pending and queuing requests.** Anytime a request cannot be immediately processed and completed within a dispatch routine, a driver has to mark the request "pending" and place it on a queue for later processing. This section describes how a driver can use either System Queuing or Driver Queuing to manage in-process requests.

- **Request processing.** Some requests a driver receives can be processed and completed directly in the Dispatch routine. Other requests are completed asynchronously. This section reviews the various alternatives.

- **Shutdown notification.** One unusual Dispatch entry point is used for driver shutdown notification. This section describes that Dispatch routine.

- **Cancel processing.** What happens when a request that is currently pending in a driver is cancelled? This section describes driver cancellation processing strategies.

This chapter discusses the basics of how a driver receives, pends, queues, and completes I/O requests. It also describes request cancellation. Because so much of how a request is processed depends on the architecture of both the driver and the device, the details of request processing have been separated from the basics that appear in this chapter. The details of request processing specific to programmed I/O devices appear in Chapter 16, "Programmed I/O Data Transfers." The details of request processing specific to DMA devices appear in Chapter 17, "DMA Data Transfers."

When the I/O Manager has an I/O request for a driver to process, the I/O Manager calls the driver at one of its Dispatch entry points. The specific Dispatch entry point called depends on the I/O major function code of the request. During its initialization processing in DriverEntry, the driver provides a pointer to a Dispatch entry point for each I/O major function code it supports by filling in the MajorFunction vector of its Driver Object. The I/O Manager calls the driver's Dispatch entry point, passing a pointer to one of the driver's Device Objects and a pointer to an I/O Request Packet (IRP), as shown in Figure 14.1.

NTSTATUS
DispatchXxxxx(IN PDEVICE_OBJECT *DeviceObject*,
    IN PIRP *Irp*);

DeviceObject: Pointer to a driver-created Device Object on which the I/O request is to be performed.

Irp : Pointer to an I/O Request Packet describing the I/O operation to be performed.

When Called: To process an I/O request.

Context: Typically arbitrary, but top layer driver in driver stack is called in the context of the requesting thread.

IRQL: Typically PASSIVE_LEVEL, but IRP_MJ_READ and IRP_MJ_WRITE entry points for drivers in the storage stack may be called at IRQL APC_LEVEL for paging.

Figure 14.1. *Dispatch entry points.*

When the I/O Manager calls a driver at one of its Dispatch entry points, the I/O Manager is asking the driver to perform the I/O request described by the IRP on the device described by the driver's Device Object.

Dispatch entry points are typically called at IRQL PASSIVE_LEVEL within an arbitrary thread context. There are, however, exceptions to this practice. The IRP_MJ_READ and IRP_MJ_WRITE Dispatch entry points of drivers in the storage stack may be called at IRQL APC_LEVEL to process paging requests. Furthermore, the Dispatch entry point of a driver at the top of its driver stack (that is, the first driver called by the I/O Manager to process a request) runs in the context of the requesting thread.

Warning

Driver writers new to Windows NT often think that Dispatch entry points are called at IRQL DISPATCH_LEVEL. *Not so! The unfortunate use of the term "dispatch" in both places has completely different meanings.*

Note

Although it is neither well documented nor common, Windows NT does allow higher-layer drivers to call the Dispatch routines of lower-layer drivers (using IoCallDriver() *) at IRQL* DISPATCH_LEVEL. *Windows NT's convention for indicating that an IRP is being passed to a driver's Dispatch routine at IRQL* DISPATCH_LEVEL *is set to the IRP's* MinorFunction *field to* IRP_MN_DPC. *Special drivers for audio or video capture, as well as for file systems, deal with such requests. Note that typical device drivers (including those supplied with NT) neither check for nor handle this option. Any device drivers you develop may assume that they will be called according to the IRQL rules mentioned previously.*

The goals of processing at a device driver's Dispatch entry point are as follows:

1. **Validate the I/O request.** If the request is invalid, the driver immediately completes it with an error status. Although the I/O Manager typically has already checked the overall I/O request for validity, the driver checks the IRP for validity in terms of the operation being requested for the specific device. Depending on the device, this check might include validating the length and byte offset of the request or checking to ensure that the supplied I/O control code is valid. The information being validated can come from the fixed portion of the IRP or from the IRP's current I/O Stack location.

2. **Process the IRP as far as possible.** The extent of possible processing varies based on the architecture of the driver, the device, and the I/O function being requested. Most drivers can complete a subset of I/O requests directly within their Dispatch routines. Additionally, a driver can typically initiate the processing of certain requests (such as Transfer functions) within its Dispatch routines, but must await completion of the request before the IRP can be completed. Some drivers may have a subset of requests that cannot even be started on the device from within the Dispatch routine. Some simple requests can be completed entirely within the Dispatch function and require no additional processing by the actual device.

3. **Queue the IRP for further processing if immediate completion is not possible.** If a request cannot be fully processed within the driver's Dispatch

routine, the driver queues the request for completion later. This is the case, for example, when a disk driver initiates a read request for its device. The driver queues the IRP representing that request until the read has been completed. Drivers also queue requests received for a device that is already busy processing another request. Such requests are queued and initiated when the currently in-process request is completed.

The amount and type of "processing" a request entails varies significantly depending on the layer at which the driver resides in the Windows NT driver stack. For device drivers, processing a request usually entails performing the I/O operation described by the request on the device and calling IoCompleteRequest() when the I/O operation is complete. Bear in mind, however, that for Intermediate drivers and FSDs, "processing" a request typically involves only passing the request on to an underlying driver by calling IoCallDriver().

Unless otherwise specifically noted in this chapter, all references to drivers refer specifically to device drivers and not File System Drivers (FSDs) or Intermediate layer drivers.

The value returned by a driver to the I/O Manager from its Dispatch routine reflects the outcome of the I/O operation it was called to dispatch. If the I/O operation described by the IRP was completed by the driver within the Dispatch routine, the driver returns the completion status of the I/O operation. On the other hand, if the I/O operation is queued by the driver for later processing and completion, the driver returns STATUS_PENDING. You will find more about STATUS_PENDING later in this chapter.

Validating Requests

When one of its Dispatch entry points is called, the first step any driver takes is to validate the newly received I/O request. The type of validation that must be performed varies depending on the design of the driver and the particular device being supported. Even the I/O method (direct, buffered, or neither) impacts the type of validation to be performed.

Drivers can assume a few things about the validity of every I/O request they receive. For example, drivers can assume that the I/O request contains a valid IRP_MJ function code in the MajorFunction field of the IRP. Drivers can assume that any requests they receive (other than IRP_MJ_CREATE) have been preceded by an IRP_MJ_CREATE operation. Hence, drivers can assume that the requesting thread has the appropriate security access to the device object to enable it to perform the requested function. Drivers can also assume that received requests are valid based on the requested access specified in the corresponding

IRP_MJ_CREATE request. Thus, if a device is opened only for read data access, the driver should not receive any write data requests; all requests that do not match the originally requested access are completed with an error status by the I/O Manager.

The type of validation that most drivers have to perform is to check the appropriateness of each received request relative to the driver's and device's constraints. For example, drivers usually check to ensure that the length of transfer requests is within the supported limits of both the driver and the device.

> *Tip*
>
> *The I/O Manager considers zero bytes to be a valid buffer length for an I/O operation. When the requestor's buffer length is zero, the I/O Manager does not allocate a Memory Descriptor List (for devices supporting direct I/O) or an intermediate buffer (for devices supporting buffered I/O). Thus, a driver should* always *check for zero length transfers before checking any other parameters.*

If the requested transfer length is not zero bytes, a driver can assume that the requestor's buffer has been described in the method requested according to the Flags bits in the Device Object (for IRP_MJ_READ and IRP_MJ_WRITE operations) or the Method parameter specified on the DEV_CTL macro (for IRP_MJ_DEVICE_CONTROL operations).

Drivers that support Neither I/O for either read/write or device control operations must perform additional checks. Because the requestor's buffer address stored in the UserBuffer field of the IRP is a direct copy of what the requestor specified in its I/O request, this parameter must be validated. At a minimum, drivers validating user mode buffer addresses should check to ensure that the entire buffer resides at an address less than or equal to MM_USER_PROBE_ADDRESS, and that the provided length does not cause the address to "wrap." Drivers that have to check for write access to such a buffer should, at a minimum, also attempt to write to each page in the buffer within a try...except exception handler. Example 14.1 demonstrates this validation operation.

Example 14.1. Buffer validation for Neither I/O.

```
PVOID   address;
PIO_STACK_LOCATION ioStack;
ULONG   length;
BOOLEAN userBufferIsValid;

ioStack = IoGetCurrentIrpStackLocation(Irp);

length = ioStack->Parameters.Write.Length;
```

continues

Continued

```
address = Irp->UserBuffer;

userBufferIsValid = TRUE;

//
// Validate the buffer.  Note: This driver does not consider
// zero to be a valid buffer length!
//
if( (length == 0) ||
    ((ULONG)address+length < (ULONG)address) ||
    ((ULONG)address+length > (ULONG)MM_USER_PROBE_ADDRESS) )  {

    userBufferIsValid = FALSE;

} else  {

    //
    // Probe the input buffer by writing a byte to each page
    // in the range
    //
    try {
        ULONG index;
        PUCHAR addressToTest;

        for (index = ADDRESS_AND_SIZE_TO_SPAN_PAGES(address, length);
             index;
             index--) {

            addressToTest = (PUCHAR)address;
            addressToTest += ((index-1) * PAGE_SIZE);
            *addressToTest = 0x00;
        }

    } except (EXCEPTION_EXECUTE_HANDLER) {

        userBufferIsValid = FALSE;


    }
}

//
// If the buffer failed any of our checks, complete the request
// right now with an error status
//
if (userBufferIsValid == FALSE)  {

    Irp->IoStatus.Status = STATUS_INVALID_PARAMETER;
    Irp->IoStatus.Information = 0;
    IoCompleteRequest(Irp, IO_NO_INCREMENT);

    return(STATUS_INVALID_PARAMETER);

}
```

The code in Example 14.1 first checks to ensure that the supplied address and length are valid. Next, it writes a byte to each page within the buffer, using an exception handler to catch any invalid accesses. If either of these tests fails, the IRP is completed with STATUS_INVALID_PARAMETER (see the next section in this chapter for further information on completing I/O requests).

Drivers should perform any other validity checking that is possible for a request within their Dispatch routines. For example, some requests may be valid only if they have been preceded by other requests or if the device is currently in a particular state. This checking is typically performed within the Dispatch routine.

A final word about validating IRP_MJ_DEVICE_CONTROL and IRP_MJ_INTERNAL_DEVICE_CONTROL requests. Drivers must check the received I/O control code, passed in the current IRP Stack location in the Parameters.DeviceIoControl.IoControlCode field, for validity. Device drivers should reject unrecognized I/O control codes with an appropriate status, typically STATUS_INVALID_PARAMETER. Intermediate and file system drivers, however, must pass any requests containing unrecognized I/O control codes to the driver directly below them in the driver stack. This requirement is discussed in detail in Chapter 11, "The Layered Driver Model."

Completing Requests

To inform the I/O Manager that a request it has processed is complete, a driver fills in the IO_STATUS_BLOCK structure in the IRP with status information about the completed request and calls IoCompleteRequest(). Figure 14.2 shows the prototype for the IoCompleteRequest() function, which may be called at IRQL <= IRQL DISPATCH_LEVEL.

NTSTATUS
IoCompleteRequest(IN PIRP *Irp*,
    IN CCHAR *PriorityBoost*);

Irp: Pointer to an I/O Request Packet describing the I/O operation to be completed.

PriorityBoost: A positive value to be added to the requesting thread's current scheduling priority.

Figure 14.2. IoCompleteRequest() *function prototype.*

The IO_STATUS_BLOCK structure is located in the IoStatus field of the IRP. The IO_STATUS_BLOCK structure comprises two fields, as shown in Figure 14.3.

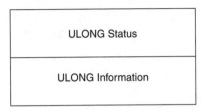

Figure 14.3. *The* IO_STATUS_BLOCK *structure.*

The Status field of the I/O status block is set with an NTSTATUS value indicating the completion status of the I/O request. Successful completion is typically indicated by the value STATUS_SUCCESS. Requests that are invalid or that complete their device operations unsuccessfully should be completed with an appropriate error status. The complete list of status values defined by Windows NT appears in the file NTSTATUS.H in the DDK's \inc directory. Driver writers normally select an error code from this set of NT-defined values.

Although it is not commonly done, driver writers can invent their own error codes. These codes must follow the format shown in NTSTATUS.H and must have the "customer code flag" bit (bit 29) set.

> **Tip**
>
> *One common area of confusion with respect to the use of status codes is their handling by the Win32 subsystem. Win32 translates the standard Windows NT status codes returned by a driver to Win32 error values. The Win32 subsystem uses a predefined mapping to accomplish this translation. The full set of Windows NT error status codes and their Win32 equivalents are given in Appendix A, "Windows NT Status Codes/Win32 Error Codes"; however, note that there are not Win32 status codes that correspond to every Windows NT status code. Any Windows NT status code that has no Win32 equivalent is translated to* ERROR_MR_MID_NOT_FOUND *or another similar, very general, error code by the Win32 subsystem. Windows NT status values with the "customer code flag" set are returned without translation by Win32. Thus, even though your driver returns a particular error code, Win32 may translate that code to an entirely different error code. Other Windows NT subsystems may use an entirely different set of mappings as well.*

Driver writers should always try to use unique error codes to denote each of the error returns associated with processing a particular I/O function in their drivers. Doing so greatly increases the usability of the driver by enabling the requestor to determine precisely what went wrong with the request by examining the returned I/O status. Note that driver writers are generally free to use any of the standard NT error status values, and supply their own interpretation of them. Thus, STATUS_INVALID_DISPOSITION returned from a lathe driver could mean that it is impossible for the driver to complete an operation because of the current state of the lathe, even though the standard NT meaning of this error relates to exception handling.

The Information field of the I/O status block contains additional information about the completion of the request. This field is typically set by the driver to the number of bytes actually transferred as a result of the I/O operation. Thus, for example, an application can perform a read operation, specifying a 2000-byte-long input buffer. The driver completing this request indicates the number of data bytes actually returned in the requestor's buffer by setting the contents of the Information field of the I/O status block in the IRP.

> ### Note
>
> Setting the contents of the IoStatus.Information *field in the IRP to the number of bytes actually read or written for a transfer function is* required, *not optional, whenever the transfer request is completed with a success status. The I/O Manager relies on the contents of this field when, for example, it copies data read with* METHOD_BUFFERED.

One particularly effective use of the Information field is to return additional information when a request is completed with an error status. In this case, the I/O Manager makes no assumption about the contents of the Information field.

Boosting I/O Request Thread Priority

The IoCompleteRequest() function takes as parameters a pointer to the IRP being completed and a *PriorityBoost*. The *PriorityBoost* parameter enables a driver to temporarily increase the priority of a thread in the dynamic priority range, consequently allowing the thread to be optimally responsive to the completion of its I/O request. The value given for *PriorityBoost* is added to the current scheduling priority of the requesting thread (if the thread is in the dynamic priority range).

> ### Note
>
> Because of the way this parameter is processed, no matter what value is provided for PriorityBoost, *the thread's resulting priority is never less than its priority when* IoCompleteRequest() *was called. Therefore,* PriorityBoost *cannot be a negative value. Furthermore, no matter how large the value is for* PriorityBoost, *the requestor's thread can never be*

continues

Continued

> *boosted out of the dynamic range and into the real-time range. A thread*
> *receiving a* PriorityBoost *that would result in its being boosted out of the*
> *dynamic range has its priority set to the highest priority within the*
> *dynamic priority range (15). Finally, let us restate that* PriorityBoost
> *applies only to threads running in the dynamic scheduling range—it has*
> *no effect on threads running in the real-time scheduling range.*

Drivers that do not want to boost the priority of the requesting thread should
specify the value IO_NO_INCREMENT for *PriorityBoost*, which is defined in NTDDK.H
as zero. Drivers should use *PriorityBoost* with care. Recall from the discussion
of scheduling in Chapter 5, "Dispatching and Scheduling," that boosts to a
thread's current priority are cumulative. That is, when multiple I/O requests
are completed for a thread, the *PriorityBoost* specified on each call to
IoCompleteRequest() is added to the thread's current scheduling priority. Thus,
even moderate values for *PriorityBoost* for threads running within the typical
range of priorities can result in a thread reaching priority 15 (the highest
dynamic priority) rapidly.

Although it is not usually a concern for device driver writers, it is important to
note that only the driver actually completing the processing of an I/O request
calls IoCompleteRequest(). Therefore, only one driver in a stack of drivers typically calls IoCompleteRequest() for a given IRP. For example, if DriverA passes
an IRP it received at one of its Dispatch entry points to DriverB for processing
(as an Intermediate layer driver would), only DriverB calls IoCompleteRequest()
for that IRP.

Once a driver calls IoCompleteRequest(), it ceases to "own" the IRP it is completing. No further references to the IRP by the driver can occur after
IoCompleteRequest() is called.

> ### Tip
>
> *Because the Dispatch routine must return the same status as the comple-*
> *tion status of the IRP, many beginning NT driver writers make the error*
> *of completing the IRP within their Dispatch routine and then ending*
> *their dispatch routine with return* Irp->IoStatus.Status. **This is a poten-**
> **tially fatal error** *because the IRP no longer belongs to the driver as soon*
> *as* IoCompleteRequest()*is called.*

How the I/O Manager Completes Requests

It is important to understand the process the I/O Manager typically follows
when IoCompleteRequest() is called. The sequential process is as follows:

1. When IoCompleteRequest() is called, the I/O Manager begins its processing by calling any completion routines that have been registered for this IRP by higher-layer drivers. This process is described in detail in Chapter 11, "The Layered Driver Model."

2. After all registered completion routines (if any) have been called, the I/O Manager checks whether this IRP is an Associated IRP. If an Associated IRP is being completed, the I/O Manager checks whether it is the last IRP associated with its Master IRP; if it is, the I/O Manager calls IoCompleteRequest()for the Master IRP (and waits for completion processing for the Master IRP to finish).

3. If the IRP has an associated MDL (in Irp->MdlAddress), the I/O Manager unlocks the pages in the buffer described by the MDL.

4. Assuming that the request is being completed asynchronously, the I/O Manager queues a Special Kernel APC for I/O Completion function to the thread that initiated the I/O. This results in the *PriorityBoost* being added to the requesting thread's priority. At this point (typically before the APC is actually processed), IoCompleteRequest() returns to the caller.

The Special Kernel APC for I/O Completion function runs the next time the requesting thread is scheduled and is running at IRQL PASSIVE_LEVEL. When the APC runs, the I/O Manager copies the I/O Status Block from the IRP to the requesting process's address space. The I/O Manager also copies any data that has been intermediately buffered to the requestor at this time.

As you can see from this discussion, the overhead involved in a call to IoCompleteRequest() greatly depends on the details of the I/O request being completed. For example, if several higher-layer drivers have registered completion routines (as may be the case for a storage device driver), the time required to call these routines can be considerable. Moreover, if the request being completed happens to be an Associated IRP, the time is further multiplied. On the other hand, if a device driver is not layered below other drivers, the overhead inherent in a call to IoCompleteRequest() is minimal.

The code segment in Example 14.2 shows how a request is completed.

Example 14.2. Completing a request.

```
// Complete the request with success status
//
Irp->IoStatus.Status = STATUS_SUCCESS;
Irp->IoStatus.Information = bytesTransfered;

IoCompleteRequest(Irp, IO_NO_INCREMENT);
```

Example 14.2 shows how IoCompleteRequest() is called for a function that involves transferring data. The Status field of the IRP's I/O Status Block is set to indicate that the request completed successfully; the Information field of the IRP's I/O Status Block is filled in with the number of bytes actually transferred (in this example, this value is taken from a local variable). The IRP is completed by calling IoCompleteRequest(). No increase in the requesting thread's priority is provided as a result of completing this request because IO_NO_INCREMENT is specified as the *PriorityBoost* argument.

Pending and Queuing Requests

Anytime immediate completion of a request is not possible within a Dispatch routine, a driver must indicate to the I/O Manager that the request remains in progress. The device driver does this by returning STATUS_PENDING from its Dispatch routine. STATUS_PENDING indicates that the requested I/O operation is still in progress and that "ownership" of the IRP remains with the driver. Early in the Dispatch routine, before it initiates any processing of the IRP and before the IRP is queued, the driver must also mark the IRP itself pending by calling IoMarkIrpPending(). Failure of the driver to do both of these things causes improper system behavior. Figure 14.4 shows the prototype for the IoMarkIrpPending() function. This function is actually a macro that sets the SL_PENDING_RETURNED bit in the current IRP stack location.

VOID
IoMarkIrpPending(IN PIRP *Irp*)

IRP: A pointer to the IRP which is to be marked as pending.

Figure 14.4. IoMarkIrpPending() *function prototype.*

When SL_PENDING_RETURNED is set in an IRP, it indicates to the I/O Manager that the IRP will be completed by the driver calling IoCompleteRequest()at a later time. Example 14.3 shows a Dispatch routine that returns with the received IRP pending.

Example 14.3. Marking an IRP pending in a Dispatch routine (System Queuing).

```
NTSTATUS OsrSimpleWrite(PDEVICE_OBJECT DeviceObject, PIRP Irp)
{
    PIO_STACK_LOCATION ioStack;
    NTSTATUS code;
```

```
ioStack = IoGetCurrentIrpStackLocation(Irp);

//
// If the Write is too big, fail the request
//
if ( (ioStack->Parameters.Write.Length == 0) ||
        (ioStack->Parameters.Write.Length > OSR_MAX_WRITE) ) {

    Irp->IoStatus.Status = STATUS_INVALID_PARAMETER;
    Irp->IoStatus.Information = 0;

    IoCompleteRequest(Irp, IO_NO_INCREMENT);

    code = STATUS_INVALID_PARAMETER;

} else {

    //
    // We will return with this request pending
    //
    IoMarkIrpPending(Irp);

    //
    // Queue the request and/or start it on the device if necessary
    //
    IoStartPacket(DeviceObject, Irp, NULL, NULL);

    code = STATUS_PENDING;

}

return(code);
}
```

In Example 14.3, the Dispatch routine OsrSimpleWrite() is called to process a
write IRP. The function validates the received IRP by checking to ensure that
the length of the write is not zero and is not longer than the maximum supported by the device. If the length is too large, the driver completes the request,
setting the I/O Status Block Status field in the IRP to STATUS_INVALID_PARAMETER
and the I/O Status Block Information field to zero. The request is then completed by calling IoCompleteRequest(). The function completes by returning
STATUS_INVALID_PARAMETER. If the length of the write is valid, the driver marks
the IRP pending by calling the IoMarkIrpPending() function. Note that the driver does this as soon as the IRP is validated and before any further processing
is performed on the IRP. The driver next uses System Queuing (described later
in this chapter) to either start the request or queue it for later processing. In
this example, the function completes by returning STATUS_PENDING to the I/O
Manager.

> **Warning**
>
> *If a driver is going to queue an IRP it receives in its Dispatch routine, it is vital that a driver mark the IRP pending by calling* `IoMarkIrpPending()` *before it queues the IRP for processing. This is true regardless of the queuing method chosen by the driver (as described later). If the driver queues the IRP first and then marks it pending, incorrect driver or system operation may result.*

A driver can return from its Dispatch routine with an I/O request in progress for two reasons:

- The request has been started on the device, and the driver is awaiting the request's completion.

- The request cannot be started at the current time on the device, and the driver is waiting for the device to become available before it can be started.

A request started on a device may have to pend for many reasons. The obvious case is when the request itself has been passed to the device and the driver is merely awaiting the request's completion to be indicated by the device (through an interrupt, for example). There are, however, other reasons drivers may pend an "in-progress" request. For example, a device may have to reach a specific internal state before a request can be initiated (an old-fashioned disk drive that has to perform a seek before executing a read, or a data communications device that has to have a virtual circuit established before a message can be sent, for example). In all these cases, the driver marks the IRP pending, stores the address of the in-progress IRP in a convenient location (such as the device extension), and returns STATUS_PENDING to the I/O Manager.

It may not always be possible to immediately initiate every request received by a driver. Most devices limit the number of requests they can process simultaneously. For many devices, only one operation can be in progress at a time. When an IRP cannot be immediately initiated, the driver has to maintain a queue of outstanding IRPs. In such cases, the driver marks the IRP pending, places the IRP in a queue, and returns STATUS_PENDING to the I/O Manager from its Dispatch routine.

Windows NT provides two methods drivers can use to queue requests for their devices:

- Drivers can use the NT I/O Manager to queue requests. This is called *System Queuing*.

- Drivers can manage the queuing operation themselves. This is called *Driver Queuing*.

These methods are discussed in the following sections.

System Queuing

The simplest method a driver can use for queuing IRPs is called System Queuing. This method provides a combined capability for managing in-progress and queued requests. In System Queuing, the driver supplies a StartIo entry point. If a request received at a Dispatch entry point is valid and cannot be immediately completed within the Dispatch routine, the driver marks the IRP pending, calls IoStartPacket(), and returns STATUS_PENDING to the I/O Manager. Figure 14.5 shows the prototype for the IoStartPacket() function. The example in the "Pending Requests" section provides an example of how IoStartPacket() is called.

VOID
IoStartPacket(IN PDEVICE_OBJECT *DeviceObject*,
    IN PIRP *Irp*,
    IN PULONG *Key*,
    IN PDRIVER_CANCEL *CancelFunction*);

DeviceObject: A pointer to the Device Object to which the request is directed.

IRP: A pointer to the IRP describing the I/O operation being requested.

Key: An optional pointer to a value used to determine the IRP's position in the queue of pending requests. If the pointer is NULL, the IRP is placed at the end of the queue.

CancelFunction: An optional entry point in the driver that can be called if this request is cancelled by the I/O Manager while it is in the queue.

Figure 14.5. IoStartPacket() *function prototype.*

IoStartPacket() is called with four parameters. The *DeviceObject* and *Irp* parameters are a pointer to an IRP describing an I/O request and a pointer to the Device Object on which to perform the I/O operation described by the IRP. These are typically the same pointers passed into the driver's Dispatch routine by the I/O Manager. The *Key* parameter, if non-zero, points to a value that determines the position of this IRP relative to other IRPs placed on the queue for the same device. The *CancelFunction* parameter, if non-zero, points to a driver-supplied cancel routine that the I/O Manager will call if it has to cancel this request while it resides in the system queue. The process of handling IRP cancellation is discussed later in this chapter in the section "System Queuing and IRP Cancellation."

Calling IoStartPacket() results in the I/O Manager calling the driver at the driver's StartIo entry point if there is a request to process and the device to which the request is directed is free. The I/O Manager maintains a pointer to the in-progress IRP in the CurrentIrp field of the Device Object. Within its StartIo routine, the driver makes the request active on the device. Figure 14.6 shows the prototype for the StartIo entry point.

NTSTATUS
StartIo(IN PDEVICE_OBJECT *DeviceObject*,
    IN PIRP *Irp*);

DeviceObject: Pointer to a driver-created Device Object on which the I/O request is to be performed.

Irp: Pointer to an I/O Request Packet describing the I/O operation to be performed.

When Called: To initiate an I/O request in drivers using System Queuing.

Context: Arbitrary

IRQL: DISPATCH_LEVEL

Figure 14.6. StartIo *entry point.*

The device later indicates to the driver that the in-progress operation is complete, typically by issuing an interrupt. From within the device's Interrupt Service Routine (ISR), the driver requests a DpcForIsr. In the DpcForIsr, the driver completes the in-progress request and calls the IoStartNextPacket() function to propagate its execution. Figure 14.7 shows the prototype for the IoStartNextPacket() function.

VOID
IoStartNextPacket(IN PDEVICE_OBJECT *DeviceObject*,
    IN BOOLEAN *Cancelable*);

DeviceObject: A pointer to the Device Object for which the driver wants to dequeue another packet.

Cancelable: A boolean value indicating whether this request could potentially be cancelled while it is queued.

Figure 14.7. IoStartNextPacket() *function prototype.*

IoStartNextPacket() takes two parameters: *DeviceObject*, which is a pointer to a Device Object on which the driver is requesting that a new request be started; and *Cancelable*, which, when set to TRUE, indicates that the IRPs in this queue are cancelable. If the *CancelRoutine* was set to a non-zero value when IoStartPacket() was called, the *Cancelable* parameter must be set to TRUE when calling IoStartNextPacket().

Calling IoStartNextPacket() results in the I/O Manager calling the driver at the driver's StartIo entry point if there is a request to process for the indicated device.

When System Queuing is used, the I/O Manager keeps track of when a given device (represented by a Device Object) is free or busy, and which IRPs are pending for each device. This tracking is accomplished using a Device Queue Object embedded in the Device Object. The I/O Manager uses this Device Queue Object to manage the system queue of IRPs pending for a given device. The Busy field of the Device Queue Object indicates whether a request is in progress from that Device Queue. The Busy field is set to TRUE immediately before the driver's StartIo routine is called. The Busy field is cleared any time IoStartNextPacket() is called and there are no IRPs pending in the Device Queue.

Although System Queuing is the easiest method a driver can use to manage arriving IRPs, it also has a significant limitation. Drivers that use System Queuing can have only one operation per device in progress at a time.

Note

Using System Queuing (as it is typically implemented) implies that only one IRP can be in progress per device at a time. That means one read **OR** *one write* **OR** *one device controls operation. Not one IRP of each type— just one IRP.*

This IRP in-progress limitation is acceptable to drivers for some devices (such as serial or parallel port devices) which, by their very nature, can have only one request in progress at a time. Drivers that find this limitation unacceptable must use Driver Queuing, described in the following section.

The advantage of System Queuing is that it provides a very clear and easy-to-implement model for managing both in-progress and queued requests. In addition to storing a pointer to the active IRP in the Device Object, the driver is provided with a pointer to the active IRP in both its Interrupt Service Routine (ISR) and DpcForIsr. This is certainly very convenient.

Example 14.3, earlier in this chapter, demonstrates how an IRP is marked pending and provides an example of System Queuing. As you saw in that example, if the IRP's parameters are valid, the IRP is marked pending and IoStartPacket() is called.

Driver Queuing

A driver does not have to rely on the I/O Manager to manage either its in-progress IRPs or queue of pending IRPs. By using Driver Queuing, a driver can decide for itself which and how many operations may be in progress simultaneously on each of its devices. Although more complex to implement than System Queuing, Driver Queuing provides a driver with total control over parallel device operations. This is vital for drivers of modern intelligent, high-speed, I/O peripherals. Using Driver Queuing, a driver can decide, for example, that it can have three writes and two reads in progress at a time, but only when there isn't a device I/O control operation already in progress (or any similar combination of requests).

With Driver Queuing, a driver creates and manages its request queues in any manner it likes. If a received request is valid and cannot be immediately completed within the Dispatch routine, the driver determines whether the request can be started on the device. If it can, the driver marks the IRP pending, starts the request on the device, and returns STATUS_PENDING from its Dispatch entry point to the I/O Manager. The driver stores a pointer to the in-progress IRP in any convenient location (typically, the device extension of the Device Object). If multiple requests are in progress simultaneously, the driver maintains a structure with pointers to each of the in-progress IRPs.

Later, when the device indicates that an in-progress request has completed (typically with an interrupt), the driver locates the IRP that corresponds to that request in a driver-and-device-specific manner (typically in a combination of the driver's ISR and DpcForIsr). The driver completes any processing it may have to perform on the IRP. Within the DpcForIsr, the driver completes the IRP and checks to see whether there are any pending requests in its queue(s) that can be started on completion of the in-progress request. If there are any such requests, the driver starts them on the device, thus propagating its own execution.

If the request cannot be started on the device when it is received in a Dispatch routine (for whatever hardware-specific reason), the driver marks the IRP pending, inserts the IRP into one of its internal queues, and returns STATUS_PENDING to the I/O Manager.

In Driver Queuing, queues of IRPs are usually managed using NT's standard list-manipulation functions. The IRP structure has a LIST_ENTRY the driver can use for this purpose while it owns the IRP. This structure is at Irp->Tail.Overlay.ListEntry. The list head for the queue of IRPs is typically stored in the driver's device extension. Because it is likely that IRPs placed on the queue in a driver's Dispatch routine will be removed within the driver's DpcForIsr, each IRP queue must be protected by a spin lock. This spin lock must be separately allocated and initialized by the driver from a nonpaged pool. The driver can then acquire and release the spin lock in the conventional way, calling KeAcquireSpinLock(AtDpcLevel)() and KeReleaseSpinLock(FromDpcLevel)(). Alternatively, the driver can manipulate the IRP queues by using the executive interlocked ExInterlocked...List() functions. Spin locks are discussed in Chapter 7, "Multiprocessor Issues."

> ### Note
>
> *Drivers must be careful whenever they intermix list access by using the* KeAcquireSpinLock(AtDpcLevel)() *and* ExInterlocked...List(). *The* ExInterlocked...List() *functions allow access to lists at IRQLs > IRQL* DISPATCH_LEVEL. *If a particular list is accessed at IRQL > DISPATCH_LEVEL using the* ExInterlocked...List() *functions, that particular list cannot be accessed elsewhere using* KeAcquireSpinLock(AtDpcLevel)() *functions. Failing to heed this warning can result in deadlocks. Note that* KeAcquireSpinLock(AtDpcLevel)() *and* ExInterlocked...List() *functions **can** be used to access the same list if* ExInterlocked...List() *is never called at IRQLs > DISPATCH_LEVEL.*

Example 14.4 demonstrates Driver Queuing of a write request.

Example 14.4. Driver Queuing of a write request.

```
NTSTATUS OsrWrite(PDEVICE_OBJECT DeviceObject, PIRP Irp)
{
    POSR_DEVICE_EXT devExt = DeviceObject->DeviceExtension;
    KIRQL oldIrql;
    NTSTATUS code = STATUS_SUCCESS;
    BOOLEAN listWasEmpty;
    ULONG temp;

    //
    // (validate any parameters... code omitted)
    //
```

continues

Continued

```
//
// We always return with this request pending
//
IoMarkIrpPending(Irp);

//
// Take out the Write list lock because we'll insert this IRP
// onto the write queue
//
KeAcquireSpinLock(&devExt->WriteQueueLock, &oldIrql);

//
// Is there anything on the list before we insert the arriving IRP?
//
listWasEmpty = IsListEmpty(&devExt->WriteQueue);

//
// Put this request on the end of the write queue
//
InsertTailList(&devExt->WriteQueue, &Irp->Tail.Overlay.ListEntry);

//
// Because we've queued this request, set a routine to be called
// by the I/O Manager in case it needs to cancel this IRP
//
IoSetCancelRoutine(Irp, OsrCancelFromWriteQueue);

//
// Do we need to start this request on the device?
//
// If a request is in progress already, the IRP we just queued will
// start in the DPC when the currently in-progress IRP is completed.
//
if (listWasEmpty)  {

    //
    // No write presently active.  Start this request...
    //
    OsrStartWriteIrp(DeviceObject,Irp);
}

//
// We're done playing with the write queue now
//
KeReleaseSpinLock(&devExt->WriteQueueLock, oldIrql);

return(STATUS_PENDING);
}
```

Although Example 14.4 is, like any well-written source code, self-explanatory, a few specific points are worth noting. The device supported by the example driver function is limited to having one write operation in progress at a time. Instead of maintaining a separate location with a pointer to the in-progress write IRP, or a flag indicating that a write request is presently in-progress on the device, the example uses a single queue of write requests. The request at the head of this queue is always the request currently in progress on the device. Thus, on entry to the routine and after acquiring the spin lock that protects the queue, the driver checks to see whether the write queue is empty (by calling IsListEmpty()). The arriving IRP is then placed at the end of the queue. If the queue was empty on entry, the arriving IRP is at the head of the queue and must be made active on the device. This is done by calling OsrStartWriteIrp(). Before returning with STATUS_PENDING, the spin lock protecting the write queue is released.

Supplementary Device Queues

For the sake of completeness, we should mention that there is a rarely used cross between System Queuing and Driver Queuing that enables drivers to process multiple simultaneous requests. Using this method, drivers create supplementary Device Queues by allocating space for the extra Device Queue Object from a nonpaged pool and initializing it by using KeInitializeDeviceQueue(). IRPs are placed on these supplementary Device Queues by using KeInsertDeviceQueue() or KeInsertByKeyDeviceQueue(), and are removed by calling KeRemoveDeviceQueue() or KeRemoveByKeyDeviceQueue(). Some requests are then processed by calling IoStartPacket()/IoStartNextPacket(); others are processed by using KeInsert(ByKey)DeviceQueue()/KeRemove(ByKey)DeviceQueue(). We are aware of only a single driver (NT's SCSI port driver) that uses this architecture. Although we're sure that supplementary Device Queues can be useful for special circumstances, we can't think of any that justify what we view as the inherent confusion implied in this approach. Thus, we recommend against using supplementary Device Queues unless you take great care to clearly document their use.

Request Processing

As discussed so far, when a device driver is called at one of its Dispatch entry points, it performs the following sequence of events:

1. Validates the received request and completes the request if it is not valid.

2. Processes the request as far as possible. This includes completing the request if all processing can be completed within the Dispatch routine.

3. If the request can be started within the Dispatch routine, marks the request pending and queues it for later completion.

4. If the device required by the request is busy, marks the request pending and queues it for later initiation.

The following sections discuss synchronous processing, asynchronous processing, and a combination of synchronous and asynchronous processing.

Synchronous Processing and Completion

Requests that can be processed and completed immediately within the Dispatch routine should always be handled this way. This method of request completion is called *synchronous completion* because the request completes within the context of the calling thread, which is forced to wait while the request is in progress. For example, most device drivers have no device processing that is required to support the IRP_MJ_CREATE and IRP_MJ_CLOSE functions. Example 14.5 is a very common implementation of a single Dispatch routine that handles both of these functions.

Example 14.5. A typical device driver Create/Close Dispatch routine.

```
NTSTATUS OsrCreateClose(PDEVICE_OBJECT DeviceObject, PIRP Irp)
{
    //
    // Nothing much to do...
    //
    Irp->IoStatus.Status = STATUS_SUCCESS;
    Irp->IoStatus.Information = 0;

    IoCompleteRequest(Irp, IO_NO_INCREMENT);

    return(STATUS_SUCCESS);
}
```

In Example 14.5. the driver simply completes the received request without any additional required processing. Likewise, operations that set or retrieve device state settings or parameters can often be completed synchronously. This is true of many device control requests, such as those shown in Listing 14.6.

Example 14.6. Dispatch device control routine, using synchronous request processing and completion.

```
NTSTATUS ToasterDeviceControl(PDEVICE_OBJECT DeviceObject, PIRP Irp)
{
    POSR_DEVICE_EXT devExt;
    ULONG controlCode;
    PIO_STACK_LOCATION ioStack;
    NTSTATUS code;
    ULONG temp;
    ULONG newBrowness;
```

```
devExt = (POSR_DEVICE_EXT)DeviceObject->DeviceExtension;

//
// Get pointer to our current I/O stack location
//
ioStack = IoGetCurrentIrpStackLocation(Irp);

//
// Retrive specified control code.  This indicates which specific
// device control function to perform
//
controlCode = ioStack->Parameters.DeviceIoControl.IoControlCode;

//
// Default to no information returned
//
Irp->IoStatus.Information = 0;

switch (controlCode) {

    case IOCTL_TOASTER_START_TOASTING:

        //
        // If a browness level for the toast has been set, attempt
        // to start toasting.
        //
        if(devExt->BrownessLevel != 0)  {

            code = ToasterStartToasting(DeviceObject, FALSE);

        } else  {

            code = STATUS_DEVICE_NOT_READY;
        }

        break;

    case IOCTL_TOASTER_EJECT_TOAST:

        //
        // Immediately eject the toast, no matter what's in progress.
        //
        WRITE_PORT_ULONG(devExt->ToasterBaseRegisterAddress+MCSR_OFF,
                         TOASTER_MCSR_EJECT)

        code = STATUS_SUCCESS;

        break;

    case IOCTL_TOASTER_SET_BROWNESS:

        //
```

continues

Continued

```
// Save the previous browness setting
//
temp = devExt->BrownessLevel;

//
// NOTE: This request uses METHOD_BUFFERED.
//
// Is the supplied input buffer a valid length?
//
if ( ioStack->Parameters.DeviceIoControl.InputBufferLength
                    < sizeof(ULONG) ) {

    code = STATUS_INVALID_BUFFER_SIZE;

} else {

    //
    // The length is valid.  Get the new requested browness level
    //
    newBrowness = *(ULONG *)(Irp->AssociatedIrp.SystemBuffer);

    //
    // If the supplied browness level is not valid, don't
    // set it.
    //
    if (newBrowness > TOASTER_MAX_BROWNESS)   {

        code = STATUS_INVALID_PARAMETER;

    } else {

        //
        // Save the browness setting for the next toasting
        // operation. Note that a newBrowness setting of zero just
        // retrieves the current browness level for the device
        //
        if (newBrowness != 0) {

            devExt->BrownessLevel = newBrowness;

        }

        //
        // The request succeeds -- we set the browness level --
        // whether or not we return the previous setting below.
        //
        code = STATUS_SUCCESS;

        //
        // Return the previous browness setting to the user's
        // OutBuffer if the buffer is large enough.
        //
```

```
        if ( ioStack->Parameters.DeviceIoControl.OutputBufferLength
                        >= sizeof(ULONG) ) {

            *(ULONG *)(Irp->AssociatedIrp.SystemBuffer) = temp;

            //
            // Indicate number of bytes being returned
            //
            Irp->IoStatus.Information = sizeof(ULONG);

        }

    }

}

break;

    default:

        //
        // Other IOCTLs are invalid
        //
        code = STATUS_INVALID_DEVICE_REQUEST;

        break;
}

//
// Complete the I/O request
//
Irp->IoStatus.Status = code;

IoCompleteRequest(Irp, IO_NO_INCREMENT);

return(code);
}
```

Example 14.6 processes three device control operations for the Toaster device.
The specific device control operation to be performed is indicated by the I/O
control code. For this example, the codes are as follows:

- IOCTL_TOASTER_START_TOASTING

- IOCTL_TOASTER_SET_BROWNESS

- IOCTL_TOASTER_EJECT_TOAST

You may want to study Example 14.6 closely because it illustrates many of the
concepts discussed throughout this chapter. For example, notice that all the
error cases in this Dispatch routine return unique values. This allows the
caller to easily distinguish between an invalid device control request (which is

completed with STATUS_INVALID_DEVICE_REQUEST) and a valid request that was
sent with an invalid buffer size (completed with STATUS_INVALID_BUFFER_SIZE) or
which was not valid because of the current state of the device
(STATUS_DEVICE_NOT_READY).

The first operation supported in the sample ToasterDeviceControl() function is
IOCTL_TOASTER_START_TOASTING. The driver validates this request by checking to
see whether a toast brownness level has been set (using
IOCTL_TOASTER_SET_BROWNESS) before receiving this request. If the brownness level
has been set, the driver calls ToasterStartToasting() to start the toasting operation and sets the Status field of the IRP's I/O status block to the returned value.
If a brownness level has not yet been set, the driver immediately completes the
request with STATUS_DEVICE_NOT_READY.

The next device control code supported is IOCTL_TOASTER_EJECT_TOAST. To
process this request, the driver sets the TOASTER_MCSR_EJECT bit in the Toaster
device's master control and status register using the HAL function
WRITE_PORT_ULONG. This request cannot fail, and is completed immediately with
STATUS_SUCCESS.

The last operation the ToasterDeviceControl() function supports is
IOCTL_TOASTER_SET_BROWNESS. This is probably the most interesting I/O control
code. Note that IOCTL_TOASTER_SET_BROWNESS uses METHOD_BUFFERED, and the
requestor specifies a ULONG value in the InBuffer containing the new desired setting for the brownness level. If desired, the user can also supply an OutBuffer
with a length at least sizeof(ULONG), which receives the previous brownness
level set in the Toaster. If a brownness level of zero is supplied by the user in
the InBuffer, the brownness level is not altered—only the current brownness
level is returned.

The driver first saves the current brownness setting, which is stored in the
device extension of the Device Object. The driver then validates the size of
input data by checking Parameters.DeviceIoControl.InputBufferLength in the
current I/O Stack location. If the supplied buffer is at least big enough to hold
a ULONG value, the new brownness level is retrieved from the device extension. If
the new requested brownness level is greater than TOASTER_MAX_BROWNESS, the
request is completed with STATUS_INVALID_PARAMETER. If the supplied valid is not
zero, it is saved in the Device Object's device extension. The size of the supplied OutBuffer is then checked. If the OutBuffer is at least big enough to hold a
ULONG value, the previous brownness level is placed in the system buffer, overwriting the input data. The Information field of the I/O Status Block in the IRP
is set to sizeof(ULONG), and the request is completed with STATUS_SUCCESS. This
status results in the I/O Manager copying the ULONG value in the system buffer
to the requestor's OutBuffer.

Note that the processing of IOCTL_TOASTER_SET_BROWNESS raises some issues regarding simultaneous device access. The careful reader will notice that it is possible for two different requestors to be attempting to set the brownness level at the same time. This can occur, for example, on a multiple process system if two threads, each running on a separate CPU, simultaneously issue IOCTL_TOASTER_SET_BROWNESS device control requests. Because Dispatch entry points are typically called at IRQL PASSIVE_LEVEL, simultaneous device access could occur even on a single processor system. One requesting thread could be pre-empted while processing one request, consequently allowing another thread to take control of the CPU and issue a second request.

Two threads simultaneously setting the toaster brownness can result in the current brownness setting being retrieved by both threads, and a new brownness setting being established by each. Depending on the exact timing involved, the previous brownness setting, returned by the Dispatch routine in the OutBuffer, could therefore be incorrect for one of the threads.

Note that the problem of simultaneous access is at least partially mitigated by allowing only one opening of the Toaster device at a time. This can be accomplished either by making the Toaster device an exclusive device (by setting the Exclusive parameter on IoCreateDevice to TRUE when the device is created), or designing the Toaster driver's IRP_MJ_CREATE Dispatch entry point so that any simultaneous open requests after the first are rejected. Even in these cases, two threads in the same process can issue simultaneous requests attempting to IOCTL_TOASTER_SET_BROWNESS.

Is simultaneous access a problem? That depends on the specific device being supported. For a Toaster device, the capability to set the brownness level and receive back the correct previous brownness setting without interruption is probably not critical. Furthermore, based on how toasters are generally used, it's not very likely that multiple threads—in the same or different processes for that matter—will issue requests simultaneously to one toaster.

For a different type of device, however, simultaneous access during a set-parameters operation could be a big problem. To prevent such simultaneous access, the driver need only protect the operation with an appropriate lock. In the case of the Toaster device, the driver would acquire the lock immediately on entering case IOCTL_TOASTER_SET_BROWNESS. The driver would drop the lock just before the break in the case, resulting in an atomic set operation.

> **Note**
>
> *Of course, protecting the set operation with a lock doesn't stop another thread from issuing a simultaneous* IOCTL_TOASTER_SET_BROWNESS *request. The lock just delays the processing of the second request until the initial*

continues

continued

> *request finishes. If you use a lock and allow only one* IRP_MJ_CREATE *to the Toaster device, however, the problem can be caused by only two threads within the same process (or one thread issuing two simultaneous requests). In reality, both of these issues are nonsense; it is simply a usage error and can't be avoided.*

Although not shown in any of the previous examples in the chapter, it is certainly possible to complete IRP_MJ_READ and/or IRP_MJ_WRITE requests synchronously on devices that support such operations. For example, a driver that supports a device in which write operations are processed by copying them to a shared memory segment might support synchronous completion of such requests. In processing these requests, locking must be carefully implemented to avoid jumbling the transfer data.

If you cannot assume that the device is always available to perform an operation, attempting to process requests synchronously can get rather complicated. In this case, synchronous completion requires the driver to block in the Dispatch routine until the device becomes available, perhaps waiting on a Dispatcher Object signaled from a DPC. Although this approach is indeed a valid driver architecture, it is not typical of NT drivers and should generally be avoided. One problem with this design is that it blocks the current thread. If a device driver is not layered under any other drivers (and is hence called in the context of the requestor's thread), the requestor's thread is blocked, keeping it from potentially being able to perform any useful work while waiting for the device to become free. Worse, if a device driver is layered under another driver, the thread being blocked is potentially unrelated to the request being processed! Thus, one user can issue a read request for a disk supported by such an ill-conceived driver on a server, and a totally different user's thread could be blocked while the driver waits for the device to become available. Clearly, this is not a good idea. Another problem created by this approach is that proper cancel operations (discussed later in this chapter in the section, "Cancel Processing") are much trickier to implement in this architecture. Chapter 16 discusses the pros and cons of this topic in more detail.

A better architecture is to process the request asynchronously: Start the request if the device is free, queue it if the device is busy, and in either case, return STATUS_PENDING from the Dispatch routine. This is the typical way NT drivers handle such requests (and we have been discussing this asynchronous approach throughout this chapter).

Asynchronous Processing and Completion

When a driver has to wait for a request to be completed or a device to become available, the best supporting architecture is one that processes requests asynchronously. As described earlier in this chapter, drivers can implement an asynchronous request architecture using either System Queuing or Driver Queuing. In both of these approaches, the driver queues the request and returns STATUS_PENDING to the requestor. This provides the requestor with the option to continue to do useful work while the I/O operation is in progress.

Several examples of asynchronous processing have already been presented. See the functions OsrWrite() and OsrSimpleWrite(), in Examples 14.3 and 14.4, earlier in this chapter.

Combining Synchronous and Asynchronous Approaches

Most well-implemented drivers use a mixture of both synchronous and asynchronous approaches. As mentioned previously, when a driver receives a request, it should validate the request and complete it immediately if the request is not valid. The driver should then process the request as far as possible within the Dispatch routine. When rapid or immediate completion of a request is possible within a Dispatch routine, the driver should complete the request in the Dispatch routine. When processing the request involves waiting a significant period of time for its completion or for the device to become available, the driver should queue the request and return STATUS_PENDING.

> **Author's Note**
>
> *Of course, the issue for you might be precisely what constitutes "rapid completion" or a "significant period of time" to wait. There is no single correct answer to this question. The amount of time that is significant is one thing on a dedicated system used for process control, and quite another thing on a general-purpose workstation. Even then, the overall importance of the device and its requests must be taken into account. For people who simply have to have numbers, we like to tell people that if you have to wait longer than 50 microseconds, you should queue the request. If you need to wait less than 50 microseconds, call* KeStallExecutionProcessor(). *Of course, this value is completely arbitrary.*

Shutdown Notification

One unusual IRP major function code that is supported is IRP_MJ_SHUTDOWN. This Dispatch entry point can be used to request the operating system to call a

driver as the system is shutting down. Drivers export an entry point for dispatching shutdown requests the same way that they export other Dispatch
entry points, as shown in the following syntax:

```
DriverObject->MajorFunction[IRP_MJ_SHUTDOWN] = OsrShutdown;
```

Simply exporting a shutdown entry point is not sufficient to result in a driver
being called at its shutdown Dispatch routine. The driver must also call
IoRegisterShutdownNotification(), specifying one or more of its Device Objects.
Figure 14.8 shows the prototype for the IoRegisterShutdownNotification()
function. Drivers can register for shutdown processing for each Device Object
they create, or only once, depending on the driver's requirements.

NTSTATUS
IoRegisterShutdownNotification(IN PDEVICE_OBJECT *DeviceObject*);

DeviceObject: A pointer to the Device Object for which to register the
shutdown notification routine.

Figure 14.8. IoRegisterShutdownNotification() *function prototype.*

When a driver registers for shutdown notification, the I/O Manager makes an
entry in one of its internal lists. When system shutdown is requested, the I/O
Manager traverses its shutdown notification list sending IRP_MJ_SHUTDOWN IRPs
to the drivers for each registered Device Object.

Note that Dispatch shutdown routines are called in the inverse order in which
IoRegisterShutdownNotification() is called (that is, last in, first out). Drivers,
however, should not rely on this fact to ensure proper shutdown ordering
among specific devices. Shutdown notification is intended as a general notification mechanism to enable drivers to determine that system shutdown is immi-
nent. Any ordering required among drivers should be handled by the drivers
themselves. Similarly, file-structured mass storage drivers should never register
shutdown routines. Instead, these drivers should rely on the file systems and
Intermediate drivers layered above them to properly purge all pending requests.

Cancel Processing

Anytime a request is held by a driver for an extended period of time, the driver
must make provisions for that request to be cancelled. When a thread exits or

is terminated, the I/O Manager attempts to cancel any I/O requests outstanding at the time of termination for that thread.

The goal of cancel processing is for the driver to cancel the indicated IRP at its first reasonable opportunity. What makes cancel processing tricky is the need to guard against race conditions that could result in either completing the IRP multiple times (causing a system crash) or not completing the IRP at all (resulting in the ugly I/O Manager message box indicating a rundown failure). Cancellation works best in drivers designed from the beginning with the requirement to handle cancellation. Too often, it seems, driver writers complete the development of the driver and only then think about adding cancel support. This is generally not the best approach.

Windows NT uses a unique I/O request cancellation model. In this model, a driver associates a specific Cancel routine with each IRP being held in the driver. This enables the driver to specify a Cancel routine for an IRP specific to the IRP's function type or state. For example, a driver may want to use one Cancel routine for IRPs on its write queue, another for IRPs on its read queue, and a third for requests currently in progress. A driver establishes a Cancel routine in an IRP using the `IoSetCancelRoutine()` function shown in Figure 14.9.

PDRIVER_CANCEL
IoSetCancelRoutine(IN PIRP *Irp*,
      PDRIVER_CANCEL *CancelRoutine*);

Irp: The IRP for which the cancel routine is to be registered.

CancelRoutine: Pointer to a cancel routine that the I/O Manager should call if it wants to cancel the IRP.

Figure 14.9. `IoSetCancelRoutine` *function prototype.*

The `IoSetCancelRoutine()` function takes two parameters: *Irp*, which is a pointer to the IRP for which to establish the cancel routine, and *CancelRoutine*, which is a pointer to the cancel routine to be called if the I/O Manager has to cancel the IRP. If the I/O Manager has to cancel the IRP, it calls the driver's cancel routine, the prototype for which is shown in Figure 14.10.

VOID
CancelRoutine(IN PDEVICE_OBJECT *DeviceObject*,
    IN PIRP *Irp*);

DeviceObject: Pointer to a Device Object to which the I/O request was
queued.

Irp: Pointer to an I/O Request Packet to be cancelled.

When Called: To cancel an outstanding IRP

Context: Arbitrary

IRQL: DISPATCH_LEVEL

NOTE: Called with systemwide cancel spin lock held

Figure 14.10. `CancelRoutine` *entry point.*

The driver's Cancel routine is called at IRQL `DISPATCH_LEVEL` and with the
systemwide cancel spin lock held. When a driver's Cancel routine is called,
it must perform the following tasks:

- Determine whether the indicated IRP is currently being held in a cancelable state within the driver.

- If the IRP is currently held by the driver and is cancelable, the driver
  must remove the IRP from any queues on which it resides, release the systemwide cancel spin lock, set the Cancel routine in the IRP to NULL, and
  complete the IRP setting `Irp->IoStatus.Status` to `STATUS_CANCELLED` and
  `Irp->IoStatus.Information` to zero.

- If the IRP is not currently held by the driver in a cancelable state, the
  driver simply releases the systemwide cancel spin lock and returns.

The systemwide cancel spin lock is released by calling the function
`IoReleaseCancelSpinLock()`, the prototype for which appears in Figure 14.11.

VOID
IoReleaseCancelSpinLock(IN KIRQL *Irql*);

Irql: IRQL to which the system should return if the systemwide cancel
spin lock has been released.

Figure 14.11. `IoReleaseCancelSpinLock()` *function prototype.*

The *Irql* argument specifies the IRQL to which the system should return after the system-wide cancel spin lock is released. Note that when called from within a Cancel routine, the IRQL to which the system should return can be retrieved from the CancelIrql field of the IRP pointed to by the *Irp* parameter passed in to the cancel routine entry point. This is shown in Listing 14.7, later in this chapter.

At certain times, drivers have to acquire the systemwide cancel spin lock before setting the Cancel routine in the IRP. This is discussed in detail later in this section. To acquire the systemwide cancel spin lock, a driver calls the IoAcquireCancelSpinLock() function, the prototype for which is shown in Figure 14.12.

VOID
IoAcquireCancelSpinLock(OUT PKIRQL *Irql*);

Irql: Pointer to a location to which to return the IRQL at which the system was running prior to acquiring the sytemwide cancel spin lock.

Figure 14.12. IoAcquireCancelSpinLock() *function prototype.*

The I/O Manager requests cancellation of one IRP at a time. The IRP to be canceled is marked by setting the Cancel field in the fixed portion of the IRP to TRUE before the driver's Cancel routine is called. When a thread exits, the I/O Manager attempts to cancel all outstanding IRPs issued by that thread. The I/O Manager calls the Cancel routine specified in each IRP (if there is one) to effect this cancellation. The I/O Manager delays the thread's termination until all the outstanding IRPs have been completed (with STATUS_CANCELLED or any other status) or for five minutes, whichever comes first. If a thread terminates with any IRPs still outstanding, the I/O Manager displays a message box indicating the I/O rundown failure.

> ### Note
>
> *Before an IRP is completed with* STATUS_CANCELLED *or any other status, its Cancel routine must be set to* NULL. *Because the I/O is now completed and beyond the point at which cancellation is possible, it is a driver logic error to complete an IRP with a non-*NULL *Cancel routine. As an aid to driver writers, anytime an IRP is completed with a non-*NULL *Cancel routine, the Checked Build of the operating system takes a break point with an* ASSERT *failure.*

To aid driver writers in implementing simple and effective cancel strategies, both the DDK and this book suggest specific methods for implementing IRP cancellation; however, these methods are only recommendations. Any architecture that cancels IRPs reliably in a reasonably short period of time is acceptable.

System Queuing and IRP Cancellation

Drivers that use System Queuing to manage in-progress and pending IRPs must provide a mechanism to cancel IRPs that can pend for extended periods. To do this, the driver supplies a pointer to its Cancel routine in the `CancelFunction` parameter of `IoStartPacket()`. The I/O Manager calls this Cancel routine when the IRP is to be cancelled. In general, drivers that use System Queuing have to hold the systemwide cancel spin lock whenever they check or modify the cancel information in the IRP.

When the cancel routine is called to cancel an IRP pending on one of the system queues, the driver first checks to see whether the request is the current request. If it is, it releases the systemwide cancel spin lock and asks the I/O Manager to start another packet. If the request being cancelled is not the current request, the driver removes the IRP to be cancelled from the queue using the `KeRemoveEntryDeviceQueue()` function, the prototype for which appears in Figure 14.13, and releases the systemwide cancel spin lock.

BOOLEAN
KeRemoveEntryDeviceQueue(IN PKDEVICE_QUEUE *DeviceQueue*,
    IN PKDEVICE_QUEUE_ENTRY *DeviceQueueEntry*);

DeviceQueue: Pointer to the Device Queue from which to remove the entry. This is usually a pointer to the Device Queue object located in the Device Object at offset DeviceQueue.

DeviceQueueEntry: Pointer to the device queue entry to be removed. This is usually a pointer to the Tail.Overlay.DeviceQueueEntry field of an IRP to be cancelled.

Figure 14.13. `KeRemoveEntryDeviceQueue` *function prototype.*

Whether the request is current or not, the IRP is then completed by setting `IoStatus.Status` to `STATUS_CANCELLED` and `IoStatus.Information` to zero and calling `IoCompleteRequest()`. A typical Cancel routine, which follows this procedure, appears in Example 14.7.

Example 14.7. A typical Cancel routine used with System Queuing.

```
VOID
OsrCancel(IN PDEVICE_OBJECT DeviceObject, IN PIRP Irp)
{

    //
    // Is the currently in-progress request being cancelled?
    //
    if (Irp == DeviceObject->CurrentIrp) {

        //
        // Yes.  Drop the system-wide cancel spin lock and ask the
        // I/O Manager to start another packet.  We'll cancel the in-progress
        // IRP below.
        //
        IoReleaseCancelSpinLock(Irp->CancelIrql);

        IoStartNextPacket(DeviceObject, TRUE);

    } else {

        //
        // No, a queued request is being cancelled.  Take it off
        // the device queue.
        //
        KeRemoveEntryDeviceQueue(&DeviceObject->DeviceQueue,
                    &Irp->Tail.Overlay.DeviceQueueEntry);

        IoReleaseCancelSpinLock(Irp->CancelIrql);

    }

    //
    // Cancel the request
    //
    Irp->IoStatus.Status = STATUS_CANCELLED;

    Irp->IoStatus.Information = 0;

    IoCompleteRequest(Irp, IO_NO_INCREMENT);

    return;
}
```

When the driver's StartIo() routine is called to start an IRP, the driver typically wants to change or reset the Cancel routine in the IRP. This is because the IRP is no longer being held in the Device Object's Device Queue. To change the cancel routine in an IRP from within a StartIo routine, the driver does the following:

1. Acquires the systemwide cancel spin lock, using
   `IoAcquireCancelSpinLock()`.

2. Checks whether the IRP has been canceled by checking whether the
   `Cancel` field in the IRP is set to TRUE. If the IRP has been canceled, the
   driver releases the systemwide cancel spin lock (by calling
   `IoReleaseCancelSpinLock()`) and returns.

3. If the IRP has not been canceled, the driver changes the IRP's Cancel routine using `IoSetCancelRoutine()` as desired and then drops the systemwide
   cancel spin lock (using `IoReleaseCancelSpinLock()`).

Example 14.8 shows how the driver changes the Cancel routine in an IRP from
within a `StartIo()` routine.

Example 14.8. Cancel operations in a driver's `StartIo()` routine.

```
VOID
FooStartIo(IN PDEVICE_OBJECT DeviceObject, IN PIRP Irp)
{
    PDEVICE_EXTENSION devExt;
    PIO_STACK_LOCATION ioStack;
    KIRQL cancelIrql;
    NTSTATUS code;

    //
    // Was this request cancelled while it was queued?
    //
    IoAcquireCancelSpinLock(&cancelIrql);

    if (Irp->Cancel) {
        IoReleaseCancelSpinLock(cancelIrql);
        return;
    }

    //
    // Reset the Cancel routine in the IRP, making it no longer
    // cancelable.  We're going to start this request on the device.
    //
    IoSetCancelRoutine(Irp, NULL);

    IoReleaseCancelSpinLock(cancelIrql);
```

Notice that, in Example 14.8, if the request to be started is not marked as cancelled, the driver sets the IRP's Cancel routine to NULL. This makes the in-
progress request noncancellable, and frees the `DpcForIsr` from having to check
the IRP's cancel status and set the Cancel routine to NULL before completing the
request.

It is very important to realize that proper handling of cancel requests requires
that the cancel routine and `StartIo()` functions work together to appropriately

cancel pending requests. In Example 14.8, if the StartIo() routine receives an IRP that has its *Cancel* field set to TRUE, it simply drops the cancel spin lock and returns. This results in the IRP being cancelled and another IRP started, because of the way the Cancel routine shown in Example 14.7 works: When the Cancel routine in Example 14.7 is called, it checks to see whether the currently in-progress IRP is being cancelled; if it is, the Cancel routine calls IoStartNextPacket() to propagate the driver's execution and then cancels the in-progress IRP. There are, of course, numerous other ways to implement this same functionality.

Driver Queuing and IRP Cancellation

Drivers that queue requests using Driver Queuing must provide a mechanism for canceling those queued requests. In general, drivers that use Driver Queuing do not use the systemwide cancel spin lock because such drivers protect their queues with their own locking mechanisms. Thus, the only thing most drivers that use Driver Queuing have to do with the systemwide cancel spin lock is to release it immediately on entry to their cancel routines. Aside from this, the systemwide cancel spin lock can safely be ignored.

A driver that uses Driver Queuing typically sets a cancel routine into an IRP (using IoSetCancelRoutine()) before it places the IRP on one of its queues. The driver does not have to hold the systemwide cancel spin lock to do this. When its cancel routine is called, the driver typically releases the systemwide cancel spin lock immediately and then searches the appropriate queues for an IRP with Irp->Cancel set to TRUE. Note that except for using its CancelIrql field to drop the systemwide cancel spin lock, the driver ignores the pointer to the IRP passed into the Cancel routine. If the driver finds an IRP to be canceled, it removes the IRP from the queue and completes the IRP, setting IoStatus.Status to STATUS_CANCELLED and IoStatus.Information to zero. If an IRP to cancel is not found, the driver simply releases the systemwide cancel spin lock and returns. Example 14.9 shows how to implement this approach.

Example 14.9. A common implementation of a Cancel routine in a driver by using Driver Queuing.

```
VOID OsrCancelFromReadQueue(IN PDEVICE_OBJECT DeviceObject, IN PIRP Irp)
{
    PIRP irpToCancel;
    POSR_DEVICE_EXT devExt;
    KIRQL oldIrql;

    //
    // Release the system-wide cancel spin lock as soon as we can
    //
    IoReleaseCancelSpinLock(Irp->CancelIrql);
```

continues

Continued

```
        devExt = DeviceObject->DeviceExtension;

        //
        // Take out the read queue lock while running the list
        //
        KeAcquireSpinLock(&devExt->ReadQueueLock, &oldIrql);

        //
        // See whether we can find the request to cancel on the Read queue.
        // If it is found, remove it from the queue and return the pointer.
        //
        irpToCancel = OsrFindQueuedRequest(&devExt->ReadQueue);

        //
        // Drop the lock that protects the Read queue.  We're done running
        // the list.
        //
        KeReleaseSpinLock(&devExt->ReadQueueLock, oldIrql);
        //
        // If we found the request to cancel, we cancel it
        //
        if(irpToCancel) {

            //
            // We found the request to cancel
            //
            IoSetCancelRoutine(irpToCancel, NULL);

            irpToCancel->IoStatus.Status = STATUS_CANCELLED;
            irpToCancel->IoStatus.Information = 0;

            IoCompleteRequest(irpToCancel, IO_NO_INCREMENT);
        }

    }
```

The implementation of the OsrCancelFromReadQueue() function in Example 14.9 relies on a complementary implementation when a request is removed from one of the driver's queues and is started on the device. Whenever the driver removes a request from one of its queues, it checks to see whether the IRP has its Cancel field set to TRUE. If it does, the driver simply dequeues another request. If the IRP is not presently being cancelled, the driver sets the IRP's Cancel routine to NULL. The code in Example 14.10, taken from a driver's DpcForIsr, shows this approach.

Example 14.10. Handling a Cancel routine when initiating a request (Driver Queuing).

```
        //
        // See whether there's another read request to start
        //
```

```
queueEmpty = FALSE;
irp = NULL;

do {

    //
    // Acquire the lock for the read queue
    //
    KeAcquireSpinLockAtDpcLevel(&devExt->ReadQueueLock);

    //
    // Get the first entry on the queue
    //
    entry = RemoveHeadList(&devExt->ReadQueue);

    //
    // Drop the Read Queue lock...
    //
        KeReleaseSpinLockFromDpcLevel(&devExt->ReadQueueLock);
    //
    // Anything on the queue?
    //
    if (entry == &devExt->ReadQueue)  {

        //
        // NO.  Flag the queue as being empty.
        //
        queueEmpty = TRUE;

    } else {

        //
        // Yes. We have an IRP from the queue
        //
        irp =  CONTAINING_RECORD(entry, IRP, Tail.Overlay.ListEntry);

        //
        // Check to see whether it has been cancelled.
        //
        if (irp->Cancel) {

            //
            // This IRP is cancelled.
            //

            //
            // Complete the request
            irp->IoStatus.Status = STATUS_CANCELLED;
            irp->IoStatus.Information = 0;

            IoCompleteRequest(irp, IO_NO_INCREMENT);
```

continues

Continued

```
                              irp = NULL;

                   } else {

                       //
                       // Set the Cancel routine to NULL
                       //
                       IoSetCancelRoutine(irp, NULL);
                   }

             } until (queueEmpty ¦¦ irp);
```

As was true in Example 14.7, note that the approach in Example 14.10 works because the Cancel routine and cancel code in the DpcForIsr work cooperatively. Both access the driver's queue of IRPs only while holding the spin lock that protects this queue. Note that there is no reason for either routine to hold the systemwide cancel spin lock. When the cancel routine is called, it cancels the request only if it finds the request on the driver's queue. In propagating execution of the driver, when the DpcForIsr removes an entry from the driver's queue and discovers that the Cancel flag is set, the DpcForIsr immediately cancels the IRP. In both cases, the search of the queue is protected by a spin lock; therefore, there is no chance of the request being completed twice—and the request is sure to be completed. The guidelines presented in this section show just one possible way to implement cancel routines. There are many other possible (and equally valid) implementations.

Canceling In-Progress Requests

Drivers generally should avoid canceling requests in progress on a hardware device because of the complexities involved with getting the hardware to "do the right thing." The best practice is usually to avoid attempting to cancel any request that will be in progress on a device for anything less than a few seconds.

On the other hand, drivers should usually attempt to cancel any requests that can stay in progress on a device for an extended period. Fortunately, such requests are typically relatively easy to cancel. Of course, the precise method of cancellation depends on the driver and the device hardware. Recall that the absolute upper bound on the amount of time a cancelled request can pend on a device is five minutes. After five minutes, the I/O Manager displays a message box indicating its failure to successfully cancel the outstanding I/O for the existing thread.

Summary

For most drivers, initiating requests in their Dispatch routines is only the first part of the job. Drivers also have to deal with devices interrupting to indicate a change in state, such as the completion of a pending request. Chapter 15, "Interrupt Service Routines and DPCs," discusses this topic at length.

Chapter **15**

Interrupt Service Routines and DPCs

This chapter will review:

- **Interrupt Service Routines.** In this section, we discuss ISR processing. Specifically, we describe the structure of Windows NT Interrupt Service Routines and different methods for passing context information from the ISR to the DPC.

- **The DpcForIsr and CustomDpc.** Interrupt processing in Windows NT drivers is commonly deferred until a DPC can be executed. In this section, we describe the mechanics of the DpcForIsr and CustomDpc. We also discuss some typical designs used to support different types of devices.

- **ISR and DpcForIsr Design.** In this section, we discuss the ways that ISR and DpcForIsr routines are designed to work optimally together. We conclude with a discussion of ISR to DPC latency; and what can be done within the driver, within the system, and within the hardware to manage that latency.

Most devices interrupt to indicate a change in their condition to their driver. The interrupt might indicate that a previously requested I/O operation is complete, that an error has occurred, or that the device requires some other action on the part of the driver. Whatever the condition is that is being brought to the driver's attention by the device, the driver's ISR and DpcForIsr work together to service it. When a device interrupts, the driver's ISR is called. The ISR gathers information about the device by interrogating the device hardware, and passes that information along to the DpcForIsr for processing. This chapter describes how the ISR, DpcForIsr, and (optionally) CustomDpc work together to act on device requests.

Note

Remember, the HAL provides a standard interrupt architecture for use by drivers that is consistent across all processor architectures. Therefore, NT device drivers never directly access any architecture-dependent structures, such the interrupt vectors or 8259 PIC (interrupt controller chip).

Interrupt Service Routines

The connection between the interrupt vector and the device driver's Interrupt Service Routine (ISR) was established earlier during DriverEntry, as described in Chapter 13, "Driver Entry." The driver created an Interrupt Object that made the connection between the interrupt vector and the ISR by calling `IoConnectInterrupt()`. Figure 15.1 shows the prototype for the ISR entry point.

BOOLEAN
InterruptServiceRoutine(IN PKINTERRUPT *Interrupt*,
IN PVOID *ServiceContext*);

Interrupt: A pointer to the Interrupt Object that connects the ISR to the currently interrupting level and vector.

ServiceContext: A value supplied by the driver as the *ServiceContext* parameter on its call to IoConnectInterrupt. This parameter allows the driver to identify the interrupting device.

When Called: When an interrupt occurs, by any device, at the indicated vector

Context: Arbitrary

IRQL: Device IRQL—Specifically, the *SynchronizeIrql* specified by the driver on its call to IoConnectInterrupt.

Figure 15.1. *Entry point: Interrupt Service Routine.*

The ISR is called in an arbitrary thread context. The ISR runs at the DIRQL associated with its Interrupt Object, as specified by the *SynchronizeIrql* argument supplied by the driver in its call to `IoConnectInterrupt()`. The goals of a driver's ISR are as follows:

1. Determine whether the interrupt source (usually a specific device) that is described by the *ServiceContext* argument is interrupting. If it is not, the driver immediately returns from the ISR with `FALSE` as the ISR's return value.

2. Acknowledge the interrupt to the device hardware, causing the device to cease asserting its interrupt request.

3. Process the condition indicated by the interrupt appropriately, given the fact that the driver is running at DIRQL.

4. Queue a DPC to continue request processing, if complete processing of the request is either not possible or desirable within the ISR.

5. Return TRUE from the ISR to indicate that the interrupt has been recognized.

When running in the ISR for a given Interrupt Object, all interrupts on the current processor at or below the Interrupt Object's Synchronize IRQL are masked off. This means that interrupts at priorities less than or equal to the Interrupt Object's Synchronize IRQL will not be serviced on the current processor until after the ISR has completed.

Prior to entering the driver's ISR, NT acquires the interrupt spin lock associated with the Interrupt Object. This is either the spin lock within the Interrupt Object itself or the spin lock that was identified by the *SpinLock* parameter when IoConnectInterrupt() was called, as indicated by the Interrupt Object. The spin lock restricts the ISR for that Interrupt Object to running on only one processor at a time in a multiprocessor system. While the ISR is running, however, it may be interrupted at any time by a higher IRQL interrupt on the current processor. When the driver returns from the ISR, NT releases the ISR's interrupt spin lock.

> ### Note
>
> *To be absolutely clear: Only one instance of a particular ISR, associated with one Interrupt Object, will ever be running at a time because that instance of the ISR is protected by the Interrupt Object spin lock. This spin lock is automatically acquired and released by NT around the ISR, and it is not optional. The ISR runs at Synchronize IRQL, as specified by the Interrupt Object, which blocks lower-priority interrupts on the current processor (only). The ISR may be interrupted by higher-priority interrupts. Note that if two Interrupt Objects reference the same ISR, it is possible for each separate instance of the ISR to be running simultaneously on a multiprocessor system. This is the case for a system with multiple instances of the same device, for instance.*

Processing Within an ISR

In general, ISRs for NT device drivers are very short. The typical NT device driver ISR simply determines whether its device is interrupting and, if it is, acknowledges the device (perhaps disabling interrupts in the process), stores a small amount of context information away, and requests a DpcForIsr. Thus, the previously stated goals for the ISR are met while performing the least possible work within the ISR.

ISR processing is kept to a minimum both by NT convention and by the fact that you can call only a few support functions at DIRQL. Most notably, IoCompleteRequest() cannot be called from within an ISR. Therefore, any driver that completes I/O requests as a result of an interrupt must have a DPC to perform this completion.

Identifying and Acknowledging Interrupts

When a driver's ISR is called, its first task is to determine whether the device described by the *ServiceContext* parameter is interrupting. This is required because devices in Windows NT may share interrupts (see the section "Interrupt Sharing and ISRs" later in the chapter). If the indicated device is not interrupting, the ISR immediately returns the value FALSE. If the indicated device is interrupting, the ISR must return the value TRUE upon completion.

The driver acknowledges the interrupt on the device in a device-specific manner. For some devices, this simply means clearing a bit to indicate that the interrupt has been "seen" by the driver. For other devices, the interrupt may be automatically acknowledged to the device by the driver reading the device's interrupt status register. For still other types of devices, acknowledging the interrupt implies disabling interrupts for the specific interrupt source on the device. No matter how it is done, it is the driver's responsibility to acknowledge the interrupt and stop the device from actively interrupting (due to the indicated cause) before leaving the ISR.

Storing Interrupt Information for the DPC

After acknowledging the interrupt and before requesting the DpcForIsr to process the interrupt, the driver typically stores information about the interrupt's cause for the DPC to use. This can be tricky, depending on the design of the driver and its device, because multiple requests to queue a particular DPC Object may result in only a single invocation of the routine associated with that DPC Object. This was described previously in Chapter 6, "Interrupt Request Levels and DPCs." Example 15.1 shows a typical ISR.

Example 15.1. A typical ISR, storing interrupt information by accumulating bits in the Device Extension.

```
BOOLEAN AmccInterruptService(PKINTERRUPT Interrupt, PVOID ServiceContext)
{
    BOOLEAN handledInt = FALSE;
    PAMCC_DEVICE_EXT devExt = (PAMCC_DEVICE_EXT)ServiceContext;
    ULONG intRegister;
    ULONG csrRegister;
```

```
    //
    // Get the current value of the Interrupt Control and Status Register
    //
    intRegister = READ_PORT_ULONG(devExt->AmccBaseRegisterAddress+ICSR_OFF);

    //
    // Is our device interrupting?
    //
    if (intRegister & AMCC_INT_INTERRUPTED) {

        //
        // Yes, it is
        //
        handledInt = TRUE;

        //
        // Save any bits from the ICSR that are now set in our Device Extension
        //
        devExt->IntCsr |= (intRegister & AMCC_INT_ACK_BITS);

        //
        // Acknowledge the interrupt to the device
        //
        WRITE_PORT_ULONG(devExt->AmccBaseRegisterAddress+ICSR_OFF,
                intRegister);

        //
        // Request our DpcForIsr if a read or write operation is complete
        //
        if(intRegister & (AMCC_INT_READ_COMP | AMCC_INT_WRITE_COMP))  {

            IoRequestDpc(devExt->DeviceObject, 0, NULL);
        }

    }

    //
    // Return TRUE if our device was interrupting;  FALSE otherwise
    //
    return(handledInt);
}
```

Note that the *ServiceContext* parameter in Example 15.1 is a pointer to the
Device Object's device extension. This parameter was established by the driver
when it called IoConnectInterrupt(). Either a pointer to the device extension or
a pointer to the Device Object is typical as the *ServiceContext* parameter.

Requesting the Device DpcForIsr

The driver associated with the ISR shown in Example 15.1 has previously
stored a pointer to the base address of the register set of the device, as returned
by HalTranslateBusAddress() in the device extension. This enables the ISR to
locate the device's hardware. If the device associated with the device extension

is interrupting when the ISR is executed, the ISR returns TRUE. Otherwise, it returns FALSE. The example driver acknowledges the interrupt by writing the interrupt acknowledge bits in the interrupt control and status register. On the example device, this acknowledges the interrupt and resets the bits, indicating the interrupt cause. After acknowledging the interrupt on the device, the driver requests its DpcForIsr to be executed by calling the IoRequestDpc() function, the prototype for which appears in Figure 15.2.

VOID
IoRequestDpc(IN PDEVICE_OBJECT *DeviceObject*,
    IN PIRP *Irp*,
    IN PVOID *Context*);

DeviceObject: A pointer to the Device Object associated with the interrupt and DPC in a previous call to IoInitializeDpcRequest().

Irp: A pointer to the current I/O Request Packet for the interrupt and Device Object.

Context: A driver-defined context value to be passed as the *Context* parameter to the DpcForIsr.

Figure 15.2. IoRequestDpc() *function prototype.*

IoRequestDpc() is a macro that calls KeInsertQueueDpc() to attempt to queue the DPC Object embedded in the Device Object pointed to by *DeviceObject*, and thus request the execution of the driver's DpcForIsr. See Chapter 6 for a complete discussion of how DPCs are requested, queued, and executed. By convention, the *Irp* parameter to IoRequestDpc() is typically a pointer to the IRP currently in progress on the device. This is most commonly used by drivers that utilize System Queuing because such drivers have only one request active on a device at a time. In this case, the pointer to the one in-progress IRP is found in the CurrentIrp field of the Device Object. In many cases, however, setting the *Irp* parameter on IoRequestDpc() to an IRP address is either not possible or not desirable. Because the I/O Manager does not access this parameter, drivers may use both the *Irp* and *Context* parameters as driver-defined context values, which are passed (along with a pointer to the Device Object) as parameters to the DpcForIsr.

CustomDpc Routines
When a driver wants to choose among multiple DPC routines to request from within its ISR, the driver may preallocate and initialize a DPC Object to describe each of these DPC routines. These are typically called *CustomDpc*

routines, to distinguish them from the DpcForIsr that is requested by calling
IoRequestDpc(). When the driver wants to request the execution of one of these
DPC routines, the driver calls KeInsertQueueDpc() to request that the DPC
Object be inserted into the DPC queue. There is no difference in terms of how
a DPC request is handled between a driver requesting its DpcForIsr to be executed by calling IoRequestDpc(), and requesting an alternative CustomDpc
using KeInsertQueueDpc(). The I/O Manager supplies IoRequestDpc() as a convenience to driver writers to make requesting the standard DpcForIsr easy and
straightforward.

One example of the way a CustomDpc routine may be used appears in the
"intpar" driver in the DDK. Although the intpar driver typically requests its
DpcForIsr by calling IoRequestDpc(), the driver queues a CustomDpc if certain
unusual situations arise. In one particular case, the intpar driver queues
a CustomDpc (the StartBusyTimerDpc, which calls the routine
ParStartBusyTimer()) when it needs to start a timer to defer the processing
of a request until later.

Methods of Passing Context Information from ISR to DPC

In Example 15.1, the driver stores information about the cause of interrupt in
the IntCsr field of its device extension before requesting the DPC. Access to
this field is implicitly protected by the interrupt spin lock because this lock is
always held within the ISR. The driver stores the information for later use by
the DPC, so that when the DPC is invoked, it can determine what action it
needs to take.

Where, and even if, a driver stores such context information totally depends on
the device hardware and the driver's design. In Example 15.1, the ISR ORs the
bits from the device's interrupt status register into a field in the device extension. The driver in this example is careful to store the interrupt cause bits in a
manner that will preserve any previously set bits because there can be multiple
operations in progress on the device simultaneously. Thus, the code in Example
15.1 has been designed so that if two interrupts for different causes are
received before the DpcForIsr runs, the information about both interrupts is
preserved.

Accumulating interrupt cause bits is just one of many possible methods of
communicating the reason an interrupt has occurred to the DPC. In simple drivers, the reason for the interrupt is often implicit in the structure of the driver.
Consider, for example, a device that uses System Queuing and that can process
only one outstanding request at a time. The driver initiates a write on the
device in its Dispatch write entry point. The device then interrupts to indicate
that the write data has been processed. This driver's interrupt service routine
might look like Example 15.2.

Example 15.2. Example ISR for a simple device using System Queuing.

```
BOOLEAN FooIsr(IN PKINTERRUPT Interrupt, IN PVOID Context)
    {
    PDEVICE_OBJECT devObj = (PDEVICE_OBJECT)Context;
    PFOO_DEVICE_EXT devExt = devObj->DeviceExtension;
    ULONG intStatus = 0;

    //
    // Get our device's interrupt status info
    //
    intStatus = READ_PORT_ULONG(devExt->IntStatus);

    //
    // If it's not our device that's interrupting, just return
    //
    if (!(intStatus & FOO_R_INT_COMPLETE) )

        return(FALSE);

    //
    // It IS our device... Acknowledge the interrupt
    //
    WRITE_PORT_ULONG(devExt->IntStatus, FOO_W_INT_ACK);

    //
    // If no IRP outstanding, just exit
    //
    if (!devObj->CurrentIrp) {
        return(TRUE);
    }

    //
    // Request our DpcForIsr, passing back current IRP
    // and error/success status
    //
    IoRequestDpc(devObj
                 devObj->CurrentIrp,
                 (intStatus & FOO_R_INT_ERROR) );

    return(TRUE);
    }
```

Within the ISR in Example 15.2, the driver interrogates the device's interrupt status register to determine if the device is interrupting.

Because this driver has only one request outstanding on the device at a time, the driver knows that the only reason the device could be interrupting is to indicate that the one in-progress request is complete. The driver passes the DpcForIsr a pointer to the in-progress IRP via the *Irp* argument of the call to IoRequestDpc(). The driver also passes a flag to the DpcForIsr, indicating whether the device detected an error while processing the request via the

Context argument to IoRequestDpc(). Alternatively, because this driver has access to the current IRP, the ISR can set the status of the operation and the number of bytes actually transferred directly into the I/O Status Block in the IRP. The major point to note here is that when the DpcForIsr is called, the operation to be completed is the only operation in progress at the time.

A final example shows the ISR for an intelligent device that maintains a shared set of queues and structures between it and the driver. Such a device (a high-speed communications device, for example) would use Common-Buffer DMA (described in Chapter 17, "DMA Data Transfers"). This particular example device can have multiple read IRPs and multiple write IRPs in progress simultaneously.

Each individual request in progress on the device is described by a DEV_REQUEST structure in host memory, which both the driver and the device access (the device accesses these structures via DMA). The DEV_REQUEST structure is completely specified by the device architecture, and is not a standard NT structure of any type. The driver places information about the request (such as the base address and length of the transfer) in a DEV_REQUEST structure, and then puts that structure on the read or write request queue for processing by the device. The device reads the entries in the request queues (reading information about each request from the DEV_REQUEST structure), performs the indicated requests, and places the status of each completed operation in the DEV_REQUEST structure. This complicated device can have the very simple ISR demonstrated in Example 15.3.

Example 15.3. A typical ISR for an intelligent device.

```
BOOLEAN SmartDevIsr(IN PKINTERRUPT Interrupt, IN PVOID Context)
{
    PDEVICE_OBJECT devObj = (PDEVICE_OBJECT)Context;
    PFOO_DEVICE_EXT devExt = devObj->DeviceExtension;
    BOOLEAN ourInterrupt = FALSE;

    //
    // Read complete??
    //
    if ( (READ_PORT_ULONG(devExt->ReadStatus) & SMART_READ_COMPLETE) ) {

        //
        // Tell the device we've seen the interrupt
        //
        WRITE_PORT_ULONG(devExt->ReadStatus, SMART_READ_ACK);

        ourInterrupt = TRUE;

        //
        // Queue a Read Complete DPC
```

continues

Continued

```
        //
        KeInsertQueueDpc(&devExt->ReadDoneDpc, NULL, NULL);

    }

    //
    // Write compelete??
    //
    if ( (READ_PORT_ULONG(devExt->WriteStatus) & SMART_WRITE_COMPLETE) ) {

        //
        // Tell the device we've seen the interrupt
        //
        WRITE_PORT_ULONG(devExt->WriteStatus, SMART_WRITE_ACK);

        ourInterrupt = TRUE;

        //
        // Queue a Write Complete DPC
        //
        KeInsertQueueDpc(&devExt->WriteDoneDpc, NULL, NULL);

    }

    //
    // Return TRUE if it was one of ours... FALSE otherwise
    //
    return(ourInterrupt);
}
```

In Example 15.3, the ISR starts by checking the device's status to see if a read has been completed by the device. If a read has been completed, the ISR acknowledges the interrupt to the device, and queues a CustomDpc to process the read completion. The ISR then goes on to check the device's status to see whether a write has been completed; if it has, the ISR acknowledges it and queues a different CustomDpc.

Note that the driver never touches or manipulates the request queues from within the ISR. Also, note that the driver queues different DPCs to indicate read complete and write complete. There is nothing about this ISR design or device architecture that makes this strictly necessary, but it may make the DPCs easier to write, debug, and later maintain.

Finally, note that some devices have interrupt status bits that are separate from their interrupt acknowledge bits. On such devices, a driver (depending, of course, on its design) might elect to acknowledge the interrupt and return no

information to the DpcForIsr. In this case, the DpcForIsr would directly interrogate the device's interrupt status bits to determine the work that needs to be
performed.

ISR to DPC Communication Issues

The goal of ISR-to-DPC communication is for the ISR to communicate enough
information to the DPC to enable the DPC to complete whatever interrupt processing is required. The complexity involved is that there is only one DPC
Object per Device Object (unless a CustomDpc is used), and that one DPC
Object can be queued only once, to one DPC queue, at any one time.

Thus, if a given device interrupts, resulting in the driver calling IoRequestDpc(),
the DPC Object that represents the driver's DpcForIsr will be placed on the
current processor's DPC queue. If the same device interrupts again, before the
DpcForIsr has begun executing, when the ISR once again calls IoRequestDpc()
this call will be ignored because the DPC Object is already on a DPC queue.
This was discussed in detail in Chapter 6, "Interrupt Request Levels and
DPCs."

The result of this situation is that the *Irp* and *Context* parameters from the second call to IoRequestDpc(), which may have been intended to convey information to the DpcForIsr, will be lost. This issue arises only in drivers that can
have multiple requests outstanding simultaneously on one device. And, even in
such drivers, this is a problem only if the driver's design relies on passing information from the ISR to the DPC via the *Irp* and *Context* parameters.

The driver writer simply needs to be aware of the way that DPCs work, and
ensure that information is passed appropriately between the ISR and DPC. One
example of such a mechanism was shown in Example 15.1. In this example,
the ISR accumulates bits in a location in the Device Extension, which the
DpcForIsr subsequently examines. The *Irp* and *Context* parameters to
IoRequestDpc() are not used. Further, the ISR and DpcForIsr synchronize their
access to this shared status location in the Device Extension via the ISR Spin
Lock.

Interrupt Sharing and ISRs

The fact that Windows NT supports interrupt sharing affects a number of
things within a driver. NT allows sharing, regardless of interrupt mode. That
is, both LevelSensitive (that is, "level triggered") and Latched (otherwise
known as "edge triggered") interrupts may be shared. All drivers that attempt
to share a single interrupt vector must specify the same mode for the interrupt

and also must specify that they allow interrupt sharing when they call
IoConnectInterrupt(). Thus, if a driver that's not willing to share interrupts
attaches to a given interrupt vector before your driver that *wants* to share that
same vector, your call to IoConnectInterrupt() will fail.

The interrupt mode (Latched or LevelSensitive) affects the way NT calls ISRs
when an interrupt occurs. When an interrupt occurs for a vector that has been
connected by drivers as LevelSensitive, NT calls the ISRs attached to that vector until all the connected ISRs have been called or until an ISR returns TRUE,
whichever comes first. This makes sense because if more than one
LevelSensitive device is interrupting at a time, each device will continue to
interrupt until the interrupt is acknowledged.

On the other hand, if an interrupt occurs for a Latched vector, NT always calls
all the ISRs that are connected to that vector. In fact, NT will continue calling
them (going back to the beginning of the list if necessary) until *all* the connected ISRs return FALSE. All the ISRs need to be called because there is no way to
determine how many Latched interrupts have been requested.

Furthermore, the ISRs need to be called iteratively until all return FALSE, to
ensure that no interrupts are lost.

Note that the behavior described in this section is a description of how we
have observed Windows NT V4 to operate. This behavior has not been documented by Microsoft, and therefore may change in a future release or service
pack.

The DpcForIsr and CustomDpc

The goals for processing in a DpcForIsr or CustomDpc routine are as follows:

- Service all outstanding device requests. This includes calling
  IoCompleteRequest() for any newly completed IRPs.
- Propagate the execution of the driver by starting any previously queued
  I/O requests, which can now be initiated as a result of a change in the
  device's status, such as an in-progress request completing.

The DpcForIsr Entry Point

Figure 15.3 shows the prototype for the DpcForIsr entry point. Recall that
DPC routines are called at IRQL DISPATCH_LEVEL and in an arbitrary thread
context.

```
VOID
DpcForIsr(IN KDPC Dpc,
        IN PDEVICE_OBJECT DeviceObject,
        IN PIRP Irp,
        IN PVOID Context);
```

DPC: Pointer to a kernel DPC Object.

DeviceObject: A pointer to a driver-created Device Object associated with this DPC. This is the Device Object in which the DPC Object pointed to by *Dpc* is embedded.

Irp: When using system queuing, a pointer to the I/O Request Packet that is currently in progress on *DeviceObject.*

Context: A driver-defined context value, provided when IoInitializeDpcRequest() is called.

When Called: When a DPC Object is queued following a call to IoRequestDpc() for a DPC pointing to this DPC routine.

Context: Arbitrary

IRQL: DISPATCH_LEVEL

Figure 15.3. *Entry point: DpcForIsr.*

Note that in SMP systems, the same DPC routine may be executing simultaneously on more than one processor. Further, note that the DPC routine(s) that are executing can also be running in parallel with the ISR. Thus, DPC routines must be careful to appropriately serialize access to shared data. This includes queues that are updated and even hardware registers.

Note

It is absolutely correct that a single DPC routine can be executing on multiple processors at one time, contrary to the assertion in other publications that this is not the case. This is easy to see when the same DPC routine is associated with multiple Device Objects by drivers that support multiple devices. If two different devices under the driver's control interrupt on different processors, two DPC Objects will be queued and can easily be executed in parallel.

Even more interesting is the case when a single DPC Object (for example, the DPC Object describing the DpcForIsr for a single device) can be active on two processors at the same time. Consider a device that can have multiple operations in progress at one time. An interrupt occurs and

continues

Continued

the DpcForIsr is requested by calling IoRequestDpc(). *Once the DpcForIsr
starts executing, the device interrupts a second time, this time on a different processor from where the DpcForIsr is executing. The ISR once again
calls* IoRequestDpc() *to queue the DPC Object. That DPC Object can certainly be dequeued and its DPC routine started on the second processor,
prior to the DPC on the first processor existing. Thus, the same DPC
routine, with the same DPC Object, executes on two different processors
simultaneously. Thank goodness for spin locks, eh?*

The last three parameters passed into the DpcForIsr entry point are simply specific instances of the standard DPC parameters that are specified as type PVOID.
Thus, instead of *"DeferredContext, SystemArgument1,* and
SystemArgument2" (which are the last three parameters for standard DPC routines), the last three DpcForIsr parameters are *"DeviceObject, Irp, Context."*
The *Irp* and *Context* parameters (or *SystemArgument1* and *SystemArgument2*
parameters for the CustomDpc) are passed directly from the parameters of the
same name specified by the driver on its call to IoRequestDpc() (or
KeInsertQueueDpc() for the CustomDpc) that caused the DPC to be queued.

> **Note**
>
> *Remember, as mentioned previously in this chapter in the section "ISR to
> DPC Communication Issues," multiple calls made to* IoRequestDpc()
> *before the DPC begins executing result in a single invocation of the DPC
> routine. The Irp and Context parameters passed into the DPC are speci-
> fied on the first call to* IoRequestDpc(), *that is to say, the call that actually
> caused the DPC Object to be queued. The values for Irp and Context
> supplied on subsequent calls to* IoRequestDpc(), *which were made prior to
> the DPC executing, are lost.*

The differences between a DpcForIsr and CustomDpc are summarized in
Table 15.1

Table 15.1. DpcForIsr Versus CustomDpc

	DpcForIsr	CustomDpc
Parameters	PVOID *DeferredContext,* PVOID *SystemArgument1,* PVOID *SystemArgument2*	PDEVICE_OBJECT *DeviceObject,* PIRP *Irp,* PVOID *Context*
Requested via	KeInsertQueueDpc()	IoRequestDpc()
DPC Object location	Embedded in Device Object	Allocated by driver from nonpaged storage

As is clear from Table 15.1, the DpcForIsr and CustomDpc differ only slightly. Otherwise, these two routines are identical in all ways. Most drivers written for NT have only a DpcForIsr that is requested from the ISR by calling IoRequestDpc(). The less-typical driver, which needs to be able to queue DPC Objects other than the ones embedded in its Device Objects, calls KeInsertQueueDpc() directly. Because all the issues handled by the DpcForIsr and CustomDpc are identical, the remainder of this chapter will refer only to the DpcForIsr. However, all points apply equally to any CustomDpc queued from an ISR.

Processing Within the DpcForIsr

As previously mentioned, the goals for processing within the DpcForIsr are to service any device requests that were communicated to the DpcForIsr from the ISR, and also to propagate the execution of the driver. The way that the DpcForIsr meets these goals is dependent on the capabilities of the device it supports (such as whether or not the device can support multiple simultaneous operations) and the specific design chosen by the driver writer to communicate information from the ISR to the DPC.

In the following sections, we describe some of the more common DpcForIsr designs and show how these designs interact with the ISR to meet their goals.

DpcForIsr Example for Devices with One Request Outstanding

The DpcForIsr routine for devices that can have only a single request outstanding is very straightforward. Consider, for example, the DpcForIsr routine for the Foo device. This DpcForIsr (shown in Example 15.4) would run as a result of being called from the FooIsr routine shown in Example 15.2.

Example 15.4. DpcForIsr routine for the Foo device.

```
VOID FooDpc(PKDPC Dpc, PDEVICE_OBJECT DeviceObject, PIRP Irp, PVOID Context)
{
    BOOLEAN errorDuringProcessing = (BOOLEAN)Context;

    //
    // Set the I/O Status block. Note the IoStatus.Information
    // field is set with the length of the transfer in the
    // StartIo function, so we don't need to set it here unless
    // it needs to be altered.
    //
    if(errorDuringProcessing) {

        Irp->IoStatus.Status = STATUS_UNSUCCESSFUL;
        Irp->IoStatus.Information = 0;

    } else {
```

continues

Continued

```
            Irp->IoStatus.Status = STATUS_SUCCESS;

    }

    //
    // Start another request now
    //
    IoStartNextPacket(DeviceObject, TRUE);

    //
    // Complete the request
    //
    IoCompleteRequest(Irp, IO_NO_INCREMENT);

    return;
}
```

Because this DpcForIsr is called with a pointer to an IRP to complete and the
Context parameter indicates its completion status, the DPC routine itself is
very straightforward. The driver simply completes the currently outstanding
IRP and propagates the driver's execution by calling IoStartNextPacket().
Notice, however, that the DpcForIsr performs these two operations in the
opposite order than expected. This order of operation increases device utiliza-
tion and maximizes throughput. The driver attempts to start a new request on
the device as soon as possible. Calling IoStartNextPacket() results in the driver's
StartIo routine being called immediately if any IRPs are pending for the device.
With the new request in progress on the device, the driver is now free to take
whatever time might be required to complete the previous request by calling
IoCompleteRequest().

Note that there is no need to use any type of locking to guard the structures in
this example because only one request can be in progress at a time and the
queue of pending requests is managed by the I/O Manager, using System
Queuing. The I/O Manager, of course, protects the queue of pending IRPs that
it maintains in the Device Object, using an appropriate lock. Also, note that
this example assumes that the relevant StartIo function (such as FooStartIo,
shown in Example 13.8 in Chapter 14, "Dispatch Entry Points") has set the
Cancel routine to NULL before initiating the I/O operation. If this were not the
case, the DpcForIsr would need to handle it appropriately.

DpcForIsr Example for Devices with One Read and One Write
Request Outstanding

DpcForIsr processing for devices that may have only a single read and a single
write outstanding request is similarly straightforward. The DpcForIsr for such
devices checks to see the following:

1. Whether a write request is complete; and if it is, completes it.

2. Whether a write request is queued, waiting to be initiated on the device; and if it is, initiates it.

This same process is then repeated for read requests.

The "trick," if there is one, is the way the ISR communicates which operations have been completed back to the DpcForIsr. In the AmccInterruptService ISR shown in Example 15.1, this was done by accumulating status bits in the IntStatus field of the device extension. Example 15.5 shows the DpcForIsr that matches this ISR.

Example 15.5. DpcForIsr example, handling one simultaneous read and write request outstanding.

```
VOID AmccDpcForIsr(PKDPC Dpc, PDEVICE_OBJECT DeviceObject, PIRP Unused, PVOID
    Context)
{
    PAMCC_DEVICE_EXT devExt = (PAMCC_DEVICE_EXT) DeviceObject->DeviceExtension;
    PIRP irp;

    //
    // Write complete??
    //
    if( KeSynchronizeExecution(devExt->InterruptObject,
                               WriteIsDone,
                               devExt) ) {

        //
        // Yes -- Get the Write Queue lock
        //
        KeAcquireSpinLockAtDpcLevel(&devExt->WriteQueueLock);

        //
        // Get the active Write IRP to complete
        //
        irp = devExt->CurrentWriteIrp;

        //
        // Set no IRP presently in progress
        //
        devExt->CurrentWriteIrp = NULL;

        //
        // Release the Write Queue spin lock
        //
        KeReleaseSpinLockFromDpcLevel(&devExt->WriteQueueLock);

        //
        // if there is an IRP in progress, complete it
```

continues

Continued

```
        //
        if (irp) {

            //
            // Set length of data written
            //
            irp->IoStatus.Status = STATUS_SUCCESS;
            irp->IoStatus.Information = devExt->WriteTotalLength;


            //
            // Complete the request
            //
            IoCompleteRequest(irp, IO_NO_INCREMENT);
        }

        //
        //  Get the Write Queue lock again
        //
        KeAcquireSpinLockAtDpcLevel(&devExt->WriteQueueLock);

        //
        // Start the write
        //
        AmccStartNextWrite(DeviceObject);

        //
        // Release the Write Queue spin lock
        //
        KeReleaseSpinLockFromDpcLevel(&devExt->WriteQueueLock);

    }

    //
    // Read complete??
    //
    if( KeSynchronizeExecution(devExt->InterruptObject,
                               ReadIsDone,
                               devExt) ) {
        //
        // (same code as for write case, above... but processing the read queue)

    }

    return;
}
```

The function WriteIsDone(), which is called via KeSynchronizeExecution() (described later), that works with the DpcForIsr shown in Figure 15.5, appears next in Figure 15.6:

Example 15.6. `WriteIsDone()` *function.*

```
BOOLEAN WriteIsDone(IN PVOID SynchronizeContext)
{
    PAMCC_DEVICE_EXT devExt = (PAMCC_DEVICE_EXT)SynchronizeContext;

    //
    // Write complete set in the copy of the IntCsr saved in the ISR?
    //
    if(devExt->IntCsr & AMCC_INT_WRITE_COMP)  {

        //
        // Yes.  Clear it.
        //
        devExt->IntCsr &= ~AMCC_INT_WRITE_COMP;

        return(TRUE);

    }

    return(FALSE);
}
```

Note that in Example 15.5, the DpcForIsr uses `KeSynchronizeExecution()` to check whether a write operation has been completed. Figure 15.4 shows the prototype for this function.

BOOLEAN
KeSynchronizeExecution(IN PKINTERRUPT *Interrupt,*
        IN PKSYNCHRONIZE_ROUTINE *SynchronizeRoutine,*
        IN PVOID *SynchronizeContext);*

Interrupt: A pointer to an Interrupt Object, returned by a prior call to IoConnectInterrupt().

SynchronizeRoutine: A pointer to a function to call holding the Interrupt spin lock, and at the synchronize IRQL defined by *Interrupt*.

SynchronizeContext: A driver-defined context value to be passed as the *Context* parameter to the *SynchronizeRoutine*.

Figure 15.4. `KeSynchronizeExecution()` *function prototype.*

The function `KeSynchronizeExecution()` takes three parameters:

- *Interrupt*. A pointer to an Interrupt Object previously returned to the driver by calling IoConnectInterrupt().

- *SynchronizeRoutine*. A pointer to a function to be called at DIRQL and holding the interrupt spin lock used by *Interrupt*.

- *SynchronizeContext*. A parameter to be passed to *SynchronizeRoutine*. The *SynchronizeRoutine* is sometimes also called a SynchCritSection routine.

Outside of an ISR, the only way a driver can acquire an interrupt spin lock—and thus serialize its execution against an ISR—is to call `KeSynchronizeExecution()`. Unlike `KeAcquireSpinLock()`, `KeSynchronizeExecution()` does not simply acquire the indicated spin lock and return to the caller. `KeSynchronizeExecution()` asks the microkernel to acquire the interrupt spin lock associated with the indicated Interrupt Object, raise to the DIRQL of the Interrupt Object, and call the *SynchronizeRoutine*, passing *SynchronizeContext* as a parameter. The microkernel performs this call synchronously. That is, the microkernel returns from `KeSynchronizeExecution()` only after *SynchronizeRoutine* has returned. Figure 15.5 shows the prototype for the *SynchronizeRoutine* entry point.

BOOLEAN
SynchronizeRoutine(IN PVOID *SynchronizeContext*);

SynchronizeContext: A driver-defined context value, provided when KeSynchronizeExecution() was called.

When Called: As a result of a driver's call to KeSynchronizeExecution(), with a pointer (*SynchronizeRoutine*) to this function.

Context: Arbitrary

IRQL: DIRQL, specifically synchronize IRQL of the Interrupt Object provided on the call to KeSynchronizeExecution().

Figure 15.5. *Entry point: SynchronizeRoutine.*

Because the *SynchronizeRoutine* is called directly as a result of calling `KeSynchronizeExecution()`, it is called in the same context as the DpcForIsr (which is arbitrary), but it is called at DIRQL and with the ISR spin lock held. The *SynchronizeRoutine* returns a BOOLEAN value, which is returned as the return value of `KeSynchronizeExecution()`.

Returning to the Examples 15.5 and 15.6, `AmccDpcForIsr` calls `KeSynchronizeExecution()`, which in turn calls `WriteIsDone()` at DIRQL and holds the interrupt spin lock used by the indicated Interrupt Object. `WriteIsDone()` checks to see whether the write complete bit is set in the saved `IntCsr` value in the device extension. If the write complete bit is set,

WriteIsDone() clears it and returns TRUE. If the write complete bit is not set, WriteIsDone() returns FALSE. Thus, by using KeSynchronizeExecution(), the driver protects the IntCsr value in the device extension with the interrupt spin lock.

> *Note that the driver in Examples 15.5 and 15.6 could not call* KeAcquireSpinLock() *to acquire the interrupt spin lock. Further, merely acquiring an executive spinlock (via* KeAcquireSpinLock()) *will do nothing to serialize the driver with its ISR. This is because* KeAcquireSpinlock() *always raises the IRQL to DISPATCH_LEVEL. The only way to acquire the interrupt spin lock is to call* KeSynchronizeExecution().

Another thing to note in Example 15.5 is that the function holds the WriteQueueLock (a spin lock defined by the driver) whenever it is reading or updating shared data, such as the CurrentWriteIrp field in the device extension. The driver also holds the WriteQueueLock while it calls AmccStartNextWrite(), which propagates the execution of the driver (presumably checking the queue of pending write IRPs, and removing one, starting it on the device, and placing its address in CurrentWriteIrp). Holding the WriteQueueLock protects the state of the write queue and the CurrentWriteIrp field from simultaneous access by either the Dispatch routine (running on the same or a different processor) or another instance of the DpcForIsr running on a different processor.

DpcForIsr Example for Devices with Multiple Outstanding Requests

The approach taken in the DpcForIsr for a device with multiple simultaneous outstanding requests can be a bit more complex than the previously discussed cases. Example 15.7 illustrates the CustomDpc used for write completion by the SmartDevIsr shown in Example 15.3.

Example 15.7. SmartDevceWriteDoneDpc.

```
VOID SmartDevWriteDoneDpc(PKDPC Dpc,
                                        PDEVICE_OBJECT
DeviceObject,
                                        PIRP Unused1,
                                        PVOID Unused2)
{
    PSMART_DEVICE_EXT devExt = (PSMART_DEVICE_EXT)
                            DeviceObject->DeviceExtension;
    PIRP irp;
    PDEV_REQUEST request;
    BOOLEAN didOne;
```

continues

Continued

```
//
// Loop until we've no more requests to complete
//
do {

    //
    // Get the write list lock
    //
    KeAcquireSpinLockAtDpcLevel(&devExt->WriteListLock);

    //
    // Assume we'll not complete a request
    //
    didOne = FALSE;

    //
    // Get a pointer to the first entry in the write list
    //
    request = devExt->WriteListHeadVa;

    //
    // A non-zero Status field in the DEV_REQUEST structure indicates
    // the request has been completed
    //
    if(request &&
        request->Status)  {

        //
        // Remove the DEV_REQUEST structure from the write queue
        //
        devExt->WriteListHeadVa = request->Next;

        KeReleaseSpinLockFromDpcLevel(&devExt->WriteListLock);

        irp = request->Irp;

        //
        // Set the I/O Status block based on the returned
        // status of the request.  Positive value for Status
        // are the number of bytes transferred.  Negative values
        // are standard Smart Device status codes.
        //
        if(request->Status > 0)  {

            irp->IoStatus.Status = STATUS_SUCCESS;
            irp->IoStatus.Information = request->Status;

        } else  {

            irp->IoStatus.Status = STATUS_UNSUCCESSFUL;
            irp->IoStatus.Information = request->Status;
```

```
    }

    //
    // Return the DEV_REQUEST structure
    //
    SmartDevFreeBlock(request);

    //
    // Complete the request
    //
    IoCompleteRequest(irp, IO_NO_INCREMENT);

    didOne = TRUE;

  }

} while (didOne);

//
// We're outa here...
//
return;
}
```

As described prior to Example 15.3, this DPC routine operates on an intelligent device that has multiple operations in progress at a time. Each individual operation is described to the device using a shared DEV_REQUEST structure, which is a structure defined by the device's architecture. The DPC routine shown in Example 15.7 acquires the write list spin lock, and checks to see whether the entry at the head of the list of in-progress writes has been completed. If so, the DPC routine removes the entry from the list, releases the write list spin lock, returns the now unused DEV_REQUEST structure to the driver's private pool, and completes the request. Otherwise, if there are no entries remaining in the list or the entry at the head of the list is not complete, the DPC routine releases the write list spin lock and returns.

The WriteListLock protects the write list against simultaneous access from this DPC (running on another processor) or from the Dispatch routine (running on this or another processor). Note that this DPC routine does not need to do anything to propagate the driver's execution because (presumably) all incoming requests are placed directly on the device's queue. Thus, no requests are ever "pending," waiting for the device to become available. All received requests are made active on the device. Also, note that the in-progress requests are not cancelable in this example. This is due to the speed with which the device completes the requests.

What's particularly interesting about this example is that it completes requests in a loop. As long as there are requests to complete, this DPC routine keeps taking them off the list and completing them. Imagine this device being very busy in a large multiprocessor system. Let's say the DPC routine is running on Processor B on this system. If the device hardware is fast, a request could enter the driver's Dispatch write routine on Processor A, be initiated on the device, be completed on the device, and then have IoCompleteRequest() called in the DPC routine on Processor B. All this could happen while Processor B is looping in the driver's DPC routine!

Although this situation can result in very good throughput on the supported device, it can also potentially result in very long latencies for (other devices') DPCs queued after this one. This is not usually considered good driver citizenship for drivers running on general-purpose servers and workstations. All that is necessary to mitigate the impact that this design can have on another driver's latency is implementation of a "fairness counter," which limits the maximum number of iterations (and, thus, request completions) that are allowed before exiting the DPC routine. When this counter is decremented to zero, the DPC routine sets a timer that results in the DPC routine being recalled after a nominal time period has elapsed. The starting value of the fairness counter can either be hard-coded after some experimentation, or left as a tuning parameter for the running system.

ISR and DpcForIsr Design

As can be seen from the information discussed so far in this chapter, the ISR and DpcForIsr must be designed to work together. In this section, we discuss some of the issues involved when the ISR and DpcForIsr are taken together as a whole.

ISR Versus DPC

There is considerable controversy regarding how much processing should be done within the ISR itself, versus how much processing should be deferred into the DPC. Standard NT dogma, as set forth in the DDK, holds that "an ISR should return control as quickly as possible" and "must run at DIRQL for [only] the shortest possible interval" (see Chapter 8, "NT Kernel Mode Drivers Design Guide," in the *Windows NT 4.0 Device Driver Kit*). This, however, should be viewed as an implementation guideline and not as an inviolable rule.

The argument against most drivers doing extensive processing within their ISRs is sound. While the ISR is running, it blocks interrupts from all devices with lower DIRQLs on the same processor. Thus, interrupt latency will increase for lower-priority devices, the more time a driver spends in its ISR. Better aggregate device performance at the system level, and hence overall system throughput, is thus obtained when devices do not spend excessive amounts of time at DIRQL.

This is not the same, however, as a driver not being allowed to perform *any* processing within its ISR. Unfortunately, this is precisely what the Windows NT guidelines are often misinterpreted to mean.

How request processing is balanced between the ISR and DPC is a decision that must be made in light of the purpose for which the driver, device, and system are intended. For example, a lot less ISR processing is tolerable in a disk driver on a general-purpose workstation than is reasonable in a data acquisition driver for a process control system. If an entire system is dedicated to the task of running a particular device, the only limit to the amount of time that device's driver can spend in its ISR is that beyond which the remainder of the devices in the system cease to function.

In general, processing that is highly time-critical should be undertaken within the ISR. Any processing that will take a significant amount of time, or which can wait for the queued DPC to run, should be undertaken within a DPC associated with the ISR. As mentioned earlier, as a practical matter this balance is all but enforced by the fact that most utility and support routines that a driver calls are not callable above IRQL DISPATCH_LEVEL.

ISR to DPC Routine Latency

Probably the mostly frequently asked question about ISR and DpcForIsr design for NT is: How long will it take for my DPC routine to run after I call IoRequestDpc() in my ISR? Unfortunately, the only correct answer to this question is: It depends.

As discussed in Chapter 6, "Interrupt Request Levels and DPCs," a request to run a DPC routine is made by placing the DPC Object describing that routine onto a particular processor's DPC queue. This is done by calling KeInsertQueueDpc() (or, alternatively, IoRequestDpc(), which in turn calls KeInsertQueueDpc()). The length of time that elapses before a specific DPC Object is dequeued and its associated DPC routine is executed, is the sum of the following two operations:

- The length of time the system spends at IRQLs > IRQL DISPATCH_LEVEL prior to the DPC routine in question being executed

- The length of time spent within DPC routines associated with DPC Objects preceding the DPC routine in question on the DPC queue

The only time the system spends at IRQL > DISPATCH_LEVEL is time spent servicing interrupts. Only on the most interrupt-bound systems is this amount of time significant. On the other hand, the amount of time spent running the DPC routines preceding a particular DPC Object on the DPC queue is a completely unknown quantity. This depends on the design of the drivers associated with the DPC routines and the devices they are servicing.

For example, consider a driver on a multiprocessor system that requests a DPC on the same processor on which SmartDevWriteDoneDpc() (shown in Example 15.7) is running. The length of time before the driver's DPC routine runs is a function of how long SmartDevWriteDoneDpc() executes. Of course, the length of time SmartDevWriteDoneDpc() executes is a function of how busy the "SmartDev" device is. This, in turn, is a function of how many requests arrive at the device from all the other processors in the system.

Thus, the latency between requesting a DPC routine from within an ISR and when that DPC routine actually executes can vary widely. Although on most general-purpose systems, ISR-to-DPC latency is typically less than a millisecond, it can vary widely—up to several milliseconds in some cases. Just to make a point, note that the largest DPC latency that we have ever measured was 300 milliseconds! This is not characteristic, of course. It's merely the very longest time we've ever measured. (Of course, it was *our driver* that ran for 300 milliseconds within its DPC routine! This was a special-purpose device with an architecture not unlike that of the example SmartDev.)

Driver-Based Strategies for Dealing with DPC to ISR Latency

There are a number of strategies that you can use in your driver to combat this widely varying latency:

- **Move some processing from the DPC to the ISR.** As discussed earlier, the appropriateness of this strategy must be viewed within the entire scope of how a system will be used. For mass-market, general-purpose systems, doing significant amounts of processing in the ISR is typically a bad idea, and it is guaranteed to cause trouble with other drivers on the system. On the other hand, queuing a DPC for every interrupt taken by a character interrupt device may not be the best solution, either. Driver writers need to balance the time they spend at DIRQL carefully against the throughput required by their devices.

- **Use high importance DPCs.** As mentioned in Chapter 6, the manner in which DPCs are queued can be altered by changing the DPC importance. Normally, when KeInsertQueueDpc() is called, the DPC Object is placed at the end of the processor's DPC list. DPC Objects with HighImportance are queued at the head of the processor's DPC list. This can significantly decrease latency, but only if setting a DPC to HighImportance is reserved for those operations truly requiring the lowest latency levels.

- **Do as much work as possible in each DPC invocation.** If a device can have multiple requests outstanding simultaneously, doing as much work as possible each time the DPC is invoked can result in fewer total DPC invocations. This, in turn, results in lower latency—but only for the driver in question! As discussed with Example 15.7, this strategy will typically increase latency for all other drivers in the system.

Clearly, none of the listed strategies is without cost. It is the driver writer's job to choose a design that will enable devices to meet their usage requirements within their expected environments.

System-Based Strategies for Dealing with DPC-to-ISR Latency

If you can affect the configuration of the system on which your driver will be running, there are further techniques available for decreasing ISR-to-DPC latency. An obvious technique is to increase processor speed; however, this is not guaranteed to help, given that the device speed could be the limiting factor—not the speed of the processor.

Another possibility is to add more CPUs to a multiprocessor system. Because interrupts are typically distributed across processors (more or less) evenly, adding more CPUs tend to reduce the length of a given processor's DPC queue. This, in turn, results in shorter times between a driver requesting its DPC and having that DPC execute.

Hardware-Based Strategies for Dealing with DPC-to-ISR Latency

If you can affect your hardware design, there is another alternative for managing ISR-to-DPC latency that is probably the best alternative of all. This is to simply expect widely varying latency and deal with it in hardware. You can do this by measuring what you believe will be the worst-case latency level and designing your hardware so that it will not fail when that worst-case level of latency is encountered. You can do this by using deeper FIFOs, larger buffers, or some method of flow control in your hardware.

Obviously, this alternative is not without cost, either; however, it does contribute to the best system throughput possible. As Windows NT becomes more widely deployed, you can expect to see this alternative used much more frequently.

Case Study

A while ago, we had the opportunity to design a driver for a very specialized device. This device had a custom built GAsFET front end, which allowed it to sample particular kinds of data at multimegabit rates. When in use, the device generated multiple streams of data, using nearly continuous DMA back to a buffer. When one DMA operation completed, the driver needed to restart the DMA operation within microseconds to keep the data stream from failing. An entire sample was only a few seconds long; however, if *any* of the sample data were lost, none of the sample data would be usable.

This device was targeted to run on the highest possible speed system, with Windows NT as the required platform. The good news is that while the device was sampling, the entire system could be dedicated to this task. Thus, the impact that the device's driver had on the rest of the system was not of any concern.

The design we settled on was to do all device-processing at DIRQL, except for a small amount of presample initialization work. In our design, the driver locked down all required memory buffers prior to starting the sample procedure, and essentially polled the device at DIRQL to determine the end of each DMA operation.

I'll never forget a meeting we had with the client to discuss our potential design. We were discussing the use of the system during the sampling period: "We won't be using the system for anything while we're taking a sample," said the client, "so it's OK with us if the mouse doesn't move all that well while the sample is actually being taken." "That's good," I told them, "because not only won't the mouse move during the sample, the cursor won't blink either!" They were aghast.

While clearly ludicrous for use in a general-purpose system, this design met the requirements of the device in the environment for which it was intended. That's why there are few solid rules that can be applied to performance and latency issues in driver design. The only real rule is to "make the design suitable for its intended purpose."

Chapter 16

Programmed I/O Data Transfers

This chapter will review:

- **Processing Programmed I/O Data Transfers.** This section discusses the details of how Windows NT device drivers implement data transfer operations on programmed I/O devices.

- **Programmed I/O Example Driver.** To help illustrate the concepts described earlier in the chapter, this section presents a sample PIO device driver. The source code, description, and functionality is provided for each important routine in the driver.

- **Design Issues for Programmed I/O Device Drivers.** This section examines issues specific to slightly less common driver operations such as polling and synchronous I/O processing.

In this chapter, we discuss the details of how a driver implements data transfer operations for programmed I/O type (PIO) devices. Although this chapter focuses on data transfers performed in response to IRP_MJ_READ and IRP_MJ_WRITE requests, all the principles discussed may also be applied to IRP_MJ_DEVICE_CONTROL requests that are used for transferring data. The only difference, and it is minor, is the way the requestor's data buffer is located. Locating the requestor's data buffer was described in detail in Chapter 14, "Dispatch Entry Points."

Processing Programmed I/O Data Transfers

Let's review, briefly, what we've discussed up to this point in the book. The steps for processing any I/O request received at a driver's Dispatch entry point are as follows:

1. Validate the I/O request.

2. Process the IRP as far as possible.

3. Queue the IRP for further processing if immediate completion is not possible.

If a request can't be completed immediately (for example, the request can't be completed from within the driver's Dispatch or StartIo routine), the driver's ISR and DpcForIsr (or CustomDpc) will work together to complete the request.

Processing a programmed I/O data transfer is simply the process of implementing the three steps previously outlined. When an IRP is received, it is validated, as described in Chapter 13. If the request is not valid with respect to the device's general restrictions or current state, the driver fills the appropriate error status and information values into the IRP's IoStatus structure and immediately completes the request by calling IoCompleteRequest().

If the request is valid, the driver checks to see whether the device is available for the operation. The way the driver does this is dependent upon the queuing method the driver has chosen. If the driver uses System Queuing, it marks the IRP pending by calling IoMarkIrpPending(), calls IoStartPacket(), and returns STATUS_PENDING from its Dispatch routine. Example 14.3, in Chapter 14, illustrates this process (as does the example driver presented later in this chapter). Because of the IoStartPacket() call, the I/O Manager will call the driver's StartIo routine when the device is available to start processing the request.

If the driver uses Driver Queuing, the driver itself determines whether the device is available to start the particular transfer operation requested. This determination is completely device-specific. For example, many PIO devices, such as the well-known 16550 UART, can process a single read and a single write operation simultaneously. These devices cannot, however, meaningfully process more than one read or one write operation at the same time. Thus, it is up to the driver to determine whether the device is available to start the requested operation. If the device is not available (because, for example, an IRP_MJ_WRITE operation has been requested and a write is already in progress on a device that allows only a single write operation at a time), the driver will typically mark the IRP pending by calling IoMarkIrpPending(), queue the IRP, and return STATUS_PENDING from the Dispatch routine. In this case, the IRP will be started at a later time, probably from within the DpcForIsr, when the device is able to handle the request. If the device is available to start the transfer, the driver starts processing the request on the device. If the request cannot be completed in the Dispatch routine, the driver marks the IRP pending (by calling IoMarkIrpPending()) and returns STATUS_PENDING from the Dispatch routine. This entire process is shown in Figure 14.4, in Chapter 14.

Whether request processing is initiated in the StartIo routine in a driver that uses System Queuing, or in the Dispatch routine or DpcForIsr of a driver that uses Driver Queuing, the steps required to actually process the request are the same. Typically, these steps are as follows:

1. **Get the requestor's buffer address and buffer length.** Depending on the direction of the transfer, the requestor's buffer address will serve as either the source or destination of the programmed I/O data transfer. The manner in which the requestor's buffer address is determined is dependent on the buffer method chosen by the driver. The buffer length is located in the Parameters field of the IRP's current I/O Stack Location.

2. **Manipulate the device, via its control and status registers, to request and control the transfer.** Depending on the device and the operation being performed, the processing in this step may range from doing nothing to setting values into a group of device registers by using the appropriate HAL function and waiting for the device to interrupt. Further, again depending on the device, this manipulation may need to take place before the actual data transfer, after the data transfer, or may even need to take place in multiple steps.

3. **Move the data between the device and the requestor's buffer.** This entails the driver using the appropriate HAL function to copy the data in the appropriate direction between the device and the requestor's buffer. Different device architectures require the use of different HAL functions to accomplish this. Sometimes, data movement is accomplished in stages, with intervening interrupts or pauses to indicate that the device is ready to continue processing the transfer.

The following sections describe the previously outlined steps in more detail.

Getting the Requestor's Buffer Address

To perform a programmed I/O data transfer, a driver needs a kernel virtual address that corresponds to the start of the requestor's buffer. Whether this address is used as the source or destination address for the PIO data transfer is dependent on whether the request is an IRP_MJ_WRITE (which moves data to a device) or an IRP_MJ_READ (which moves data from a device). How the requestor's buffer address is determined is dependent on the buffer method that the driver specified in the Flags field of the DEVICE_OBJECT.

Getting the Buffer Address When Using Buffered I/O

If the driver utilizes Buffered I/O, the I/O Manager provides the driver with the kernel virtual address of an intermediate buffer in system space. This kernel virtual address is located in the IRP in Irp->AssociatedIrp.SystemBuffer. Because this address corresponds to a location in the system's nonpaged pool, the address is valid for use by the driver in an arbitrary thread context.

Getting the Buffer Address When Using Direct I/O

If the driver has chosen Direct I/O as its buffer method, the requestor's buffer will be described in the IRP by a Memory Descriptor List (MDL). A pointer to the MDL is stored by the I/O Manager in the IRP at Irp->MdlAddress. To map the requestor's buffer, described by the MDL, into kernel virtual address space, the driver calls the function MmGetSystemAddressForMdl(), the prototype for which is shown in Figure 16.1.

PVOID
MmGetSystemAddressForMdl(IN PMDL *Mdl*);

Mdl: A pointer to a Memory Descriptor List that describes a locked buffer.

Figure 16.1. MmGetSystemAddressForMdl() *function prototype.*

MmGetSystemAddressForMdl() takes as input a pointer to an MDL that describes a buffer, the pages of which have previously been locked into physical memory, and returns a kernel virtual address (usable in an arbitrary thread context) that corresponds to the start of the buffer. Because mapping pages into (and out of) kernel virtual address space can be expensive, MmGetSystemAddressForMdl() performs this mapping operation only if the buffer hasn't already been mapped into system space via this MDL.

MmGetSystemAddressForMdl(), which is a macro in NTDDK.H, checks a series of bits in the MDL to determine whether the buffer that the MDL describes has already been mapped into kernel virtual address space; if it has, it returns the currently mapped kernel virtual address of the buffer. If the buffer described by the MDL has not already been mapped into kernel virtual address space, the macro calls MmMapLockedPages(), which maps the pages comprising the buffer into kernel virtual address space and returns the resulting address.

> ### Note
>
> *You may notice that there is apparently no function that undoes the operation that* MmGetSystemAddressForMdl() *performs. This is deliberate, to facilitate maximum reuse of the one mapping of the buffer into kernel virtual address space. Although it is certainly possible for a driver to call* MmUnmapLockedPages() *to undo the map operation performed by* MmGetSystemAddressForMdl(), *this is at the least unnecessary, and at worst counterproductive. When an IRP with an accompanying MDL is ultimately completed, the I/O Manager and Memory Manager automatically*

perform the requisite unmap operation as part of unlocking the buffer pages from physical memory. Thus, there is almost never any need for a driver to manually unmap the pages of an MDL that have been mapped as a result of calling MmGetSystemAddressForMdl().

As previously mentioned, calling MmGetSystemAddressForMdl() to map a requestor's buffer into kernel virtual address space can be expensive in terms of the number of instructions required (although NT does attempt to take some reasonable shortcuts where possible). Even worse, the unmap operation, which takes place when the IRP is ultimately completed and the MDL is freed, can potentially require flushing processor caches on all processors (except the current one) in a multiprocessor system. Therefore, in terms of the amount of overhead incurred, it is almost always best to use Buffered I/O for devices that typically transfer fewer than one page of data per operation. This is the absolute minimum guideline, and we have gotten very good performance by using Buffered I/O on data buffers up to several pages in size.

Getting the Buffer Address When Using Neither I/O

If a driver elects to utilize the Neither I/O Buffer Method, the I/O Manager supplies the driver with requestor's virtual buffer address in the IRP's UserBuffer field. Because user virtual addresses and kernel virtual addresses below 2GB map to the same physical memory location, given the same process context, a driver can directly access a requestor's buffer using a User mode address in Kernel mode. The restriction inherent in this, of course, is that the address is valid only in the context of the calling process. As a result, Dispatch routines using Neither I/O must be called in the context of the requestor's process, as was described in Chapter 12, "Driver Structure."

If a driver that uses Neither I/O determines that it requires a kernel virtual address for the requestor's buffer that is usable in an arbitrary thread context, it must do the following:

1. Create an MDL to describe the requestor's buffer.

2. Check the pages that comprise the buffer for accessibility and lock the pages into physical memory.

3. Map the requestor's buffer described by the MDL into kernel virtual address space.

Creating an MDL to Describe the Requestor's Buffer

Although there are several methods in NT for creating MDLs, the easiest and most optimal is to call IoAllocateMdl(), the prototype for which is shown in Figure 16.2. This function returns a pointer to an allocated and initialized

MDL for use by the driver. MDLs allocated by using IoAllocateMdl() are typically taken from the I/O Manager's list of preallocated MDLs, and not allocated directly from nonpaged pool.

PMDL
IoAllocateMdl(IN PVOID *VirtualAddress,*
        IN ULONG *Length,*
        IN BOOLEAN *SecondaryBuffer,*
        IN BOOLEAN *ChargeQuota,*
        IN OUT PIRP *Irp)*;

VirtualAddress: A currently valid virtual address that points to the start of the buffer to be described by the MDL.

Length: The size, in bytes, of the buffer to be described.

SecondaryBuffer: If set to TRUE and *Irp* is non-NULL, the created MDL will be linked through the Next pointer of the MDL pointed to by *Irp->MdlAddress*.

ChargeQuota: Set to TRUE to indicate that the current thread's quota should be charged for the allocation of the MDL.

Irp: If not NULL and *SecondaryBuffer* is FALSE, a pointer to the allocated IRP is filled into the *MdlAddress* field of the indicated IRP. If not NULL and *SecondaryBuffer* is TRUE, it performs the operation described under *SecondaryBuffer*.

Figure 16.2. IoAllocateMdl() *function prototype.*

> **Tip**
>
> *When calling* IoAllocateMdl(), *if a pointer to an IRP is supplied in the* Irp *parameter, the I/O Manager will store a pointer to the allocated MDL in* Irp->MdlAddress. *This can be very handy because when the IRP is completed, the I/O Manager will automatically unmap and unlock any pages associated with this MDL, and even return the MDL appropriately.*

Checking the Pages That Comprise the Buffer for Accessibility and Locking the Pages into Physical Memory

The driver passes IoAllocateMdl() a pointer to a currently valid kernel virtual address and length of the buffer to be described by the MDL. IoAllocateMdl()

allocates and partially initializes the MDL to describe the indicated buffer. However, to complete the initialization of the MDL, the driver must next call MmProbeAndLockPages(), the prototype for which is shown in Figure 16.3.

VOID
MmProbeAndLockPages(IN OUT PMDL *MemoryDescriptorList,*
    IN KPROCESSOR_MODE *AccessMode,*
    IN LOCK_OPERATION *Operation);*

MemoryDescriptorList: A pointer to an MDL that has been partially initialized to contain the virtual address, length, and offset of a buffer.

AccessMode: Either KernelMode or UserMode, which indicates the mode in which the access check is to take place. An *AccessMode* of UserMode causes NT to check to ensure that the entire buffer resides within user address space.

Operation: Either IoReadAccess, IoWriteAccess, or IoModifyAccess. Indicates the type of access for which the function should check.

Figure 16.3. MmProbeAndLockPages() *function prototype.*

MmProbeAndLockPages() checks the pages of a buffer described by an MDL for accessibility in the mode indicated by *AccessMode*. The type of access MmProbeAndLockPages() checks is indicated by the *Operation* parameter. If the check is successful, MmProbeAndLockPages() locks (that is to say, "pins") the pages that comprise the buffer into physical memory. The pages remain locked, at least until the MDL is returned or MmUnlockPages() is called by the driver (whichever is first).

Unlike almost any other function in NT, MmProbeAndLockPages() indicates an error *by raising an exception.* Thus, any time that MmProbeAndLockPages() is called, it must be called within a try()...except() condition handler.

Tip

IoAllocateMdl() *does not, by itself, sufficiently initialize the MDL to describe a buffer in an arbitrary thread context. In fact, the page pointers within the MDL (which actually locate the buffer in physical memory— see Chapter 10, "How I/O Requests Are Described") are filled into the MDL by* MmProbeAndLockPages(). *Thus, the MDL does not contain a complete buffer description until a driver successfully returns from its call to*

MmProbeAndLockPages(). *Further, note that* MmProbeAndLockPages() *must be called in the context of the process in which the virtual address stored within the MDL is valid.*

Mapping the Requestor's Buffer Described by the MDL into Kernel Virtual Address Space

The final step in getting a kernel virtual address usable in an arbitrary thread context for a requestor's buffer is to perform the actual mapping operation. Because we have an MDL, this mapping is performed by calling MmGetSystemAddressForMdl(), as described earlier in this chapter.

Getting the Requestor's Buffer Length

The size of the buffer is located in a function-dependent field of the current IRP Stack location. For example, for IRP_MJ_WRITE operations, the length, in bytes, of the requestor's buffer appears in the current I/O Stack location in the IRP at Parameters.Write.Length. For IRP_MJ_READ operations, the length, in bytes, of the requestor's buffer is stored in the current I/O Stack location in the IRP at Parameters.Read.Length.

Keep in mind that Parameters.Write.Length and Parameters.Read.Length access the same location within the I/O Stack location. That is, the offset of these fields within the Parameters union is the same. Drivers that have common routines for processing read and write operations, including drivers that are part of Windows NT, rely on this fact. So, although few things are guaranteed not to change in later releases of the operating system, it is a fairly safe assumption to make within a driver that these two fields will refer to the same longword in the I/O Stack location. Of course, the truly paranoid among us could provide an ASSERT() statement to ensure that this remains true.

Manipulating the Device to Request and Control the Transfer

After the driver has determined the requestor's buffer address and length of the transfer, the driver must next set the device into the appropriate state for the start of the transfer. For some devices, there is nothing that the driver needs to do to ready the device for a transfer. This is the case, for example, for the standard parallel (printer) port interface. On the other hand, a driver may need to perform considerable work in this step. This is true, for example, in a serial port driver that needs to manipulate and monitor various status signals to handshake properly with a modem (that is, assert RTS and wait for the modem to assert CTS, and the like).

The only "rules" here are that the driver must perform the requisite hardware manipulation using the *translated* device address and the appropriate HAL functions. The translated device address was determined by the driver in its Driver Entry routine, as a result of calling HalTranslateBusAddress() and possibly MmMapIoSpace(). This process was described in detail in Chapter 13, "DriverEntry," in the section called "Translating Bus Addresses."

If the device registers being manipulated are in Port I/O space, the driver must use the HAL's port functions (such as READ_PORT_xxx, WRITE_PORT_xxx, READ_PORT_BUFFER_xxx, and WRITE_PORT_BUFFER_xxx, where xxx is one of UCHAR, USHORT, or ULONG) (described in Chapter 2, "Achieving Hardware Independence with the HAL"). If the device registers being accessed are in memory-mapped space, the driver must use the HAL's register functions (such as READ_REGISTER_xxx, WRITE_REGISTER_xxx, READ_REGISTER_BUFFER_xxx, and WRITE_REGISTER_BUFFER_xxx).

> ### Tip
>
> *It is very important to understand what, specifically, determines whether a driver uses the HAL register functions or the HAL port functions. The determination of which function set to use is based strictly upon the hardware implementation of the device. If the device's registers are implemented in the device hardware in Port I/O space, the driver uses the HAL port functions. This is true, regardless of whether the current processor architecture on which the driver is running has a separate Port I/O space, and irrespective of the value returned in the **AddressSpace** parameter from the driver's earlier call to HalTranslateBusAddress() (see Figure 13.14). Likewise, if the device's registers are implemented in hardware in memory space, the driver uses the HAL register functions. It is the HAL's job to access the device properly on each platform. Therefore, the choice of HAL function is determined strictly on the device's hardware, and not on any runtime consideration.*

Moving the Data Between the Device and the Requestor's Buffer

Once the driver has readied the device for the data transfer, the driver is responsible for moving the data (in the correct direction) between the requestor's data buffer and the device. On some devices, data is stored and retrieved using a register (often backed by a FIFO), which may be a byte, a word, or a longword wide. Again, the appropriate HAL function must be used to access this register.

On some devices, a driver will move data between the requestor's buffer and a buffer in "shared memory" on the device. In this architecture, the device's hardware provides a region of memory that is used for data transfers. Some devices have relatively small shared-memory areas (just a few thousand bytes, for example); other devices have many megabytes of shared memory. During initialization (typically in the driver's DriverEntry routine), the driver translates the starting address of the shared memory region by using HalTranslateBusAddress(), and maps the region into kernel virtual address space by using MmMapIoSpace(). The specific layout of this memory is, of course, device-dependent.

To access a shared memory section, the driver uses the HAL register access function. As an example, the Dispatch routine in Example 16.1 copies data from the requestor's buffer to a shared memory buffer on the device:

Example 16.1. Copying data from the requestor's buffer to a shared memory buffer on the device.

```
NTSTATUS NeitherWrite(PDEVICE_OBJECT DeviceObject, PIRP Irp)
{
    PIO_STACK_LOCATION ioStack;
    NEITHER_DEVICE_EXTENSION devExt;

    //
    // Get a pointer to the current IRP stack
    ioStack = IoGetCurrentIrpStackLocation(Irp);

    //
    // Get a pointer to our device extension
    //
    devExt = DeviceObject->DeviceExtension;

    //
    // Move the data to the device
    //
    WRITE_REGISTER_BUFFER_UCHAR(devExt->TranslatedDeviceBuffer,
                        Irp->UserBuffer,
                        ioStack->Parameters.Write.Length);

    //
    // Tell the device the data is there
    //
    WRITE_PORT_UCHAR(devExt->TranslatedWriteCtrl, NEITHER_DATA_READY);

    //
    // Complete the IRP with success
    //
    Irp->IoStatus.Status = STATUS_SUCCESS;
    Irp->IoStatus.Information =  ioStack->Parameters.Write.Length;
```

```
    IoCompleteRequest(Irp, IO_NO_INCREMENT);

    return(STATUS_SUCCESS);
}
```

Note that Example 16.1 is very simple: It assumes that the driver is always called in the context of the requesting thread and that the device is always ready to accept the transfer. Example 16.1 also does not attempt to handle the case of multiple simultaneous write requests to the device, which could lead to corrupt data. The example is simple with as low overhead as possible.

In Example 16.1, the driver has specified Neither I/O for read and write requests. Because this driver is called in the context of the calling process, the requestor's virtual address will be valid when interpreted as a kernel virtual address. The requestor's buffer address is located in the UserBuffer field of the IRP. The driver moves the data from the requestor's buffer to a shared memory buffer on the device by using the HAL function WRITE_REGISTER_BUFFER_UCHAR(). After the driver moves the data, it informs the device that the data is ready by setting the NEITHER_DATA_READY bit in one of the device's control registers.

> *Tip*
>
> *Could the driver in Example 16.1 have just called* memcpy() *(or the NT runtime library function* RtlCopyMemory()*) instead of using the HAL function* WRITE_REGISTER_BUFFER_UCHAR()*? The answer to this very common question is a resounding "NO!" Although countless drivers have been written this way, and most even appear to work most of the time, there is no guarantee that they will either continue to work or that they will work when moved to other platforms. For example, the HAL function properly flushes the internal write post buffer on Pentium processors. So, although* memcpy() ***might*** *work on a particular system, the HAL function can* ***always*** *be counted on to "do the right thing." Always use the HAL functions and avoid unforeseen difficulties!*

Also notice in Example 16.1 that the driver did not need to do anything to ready the device for the transfer. As mentioned previously, the steps that need to be taken are dependent on the specific device hardware. After the data has been moved, the driver informs the device that the data is available by setting a bit in its write control register. Because the device's hardware locates this register in Port I/O space, the driver uses the HAL function WRITE_PORT_UCHAR() to manipulate the register.

Programmed I/O Example Driver

To illustrate some of the concepts discussed so far in this chapter, let's examine parts of a complete driver example for a popular PIO device. We'll look at all the code entailed in processing transfer requests: from the Dispatch routine to the ISR, DPC, and ultimate request completion. The driver example supports the ATA (AT Attachment—popularly known as IDE) disk interface, and it is loosely based on the ATDISK driver supplied in the NT DDK. Although some IDE/ATA disks support DMA, they all support PIO. The complete code for this disk driver is available from the OSR Web site (`http://www.osr.com`). For the sake of clarity, some nonessential code (such as logic for retries and `DbgPrint()` statements) have been eliminated from the routines that appear in the book.

Before looking at the code, it might be helpful to understand a bit about how the ATA disk controller works. In PIO mode, this device is one of the simplest you can imagine. To read from the disk, the driver does the following:

1. The driver programs the controller with the sector (specified as sector, cylinder, and head) at which the read is to start and the number of sectors to be read.

2. The driver then issues a read command to the controller.

3. The controller interrupts when it has read the first sector available for the driver in its internal buffer. This buffer is a word-wide location in Port I/O space.

4. The driver then copies the data out of the controller's sector buffer to the requestor's buffer.

5. The driver interrupts again when the next sector is available.

6. The process of interrupting and copying is repeated until all sectors have been transferred.

To write to the disk, the process is almost identical:

1. The driver programs the controller with the sector (again, specifying the sector, cylinder, and head) where the write is to start and the number of sectors are to be written. The driver then gives the controller the write command.

2. When the controller indicates that it is ready (by asserting a bit in one of its registers), the driver copies one sector of data to the controller's sector buffer.

3. When the controller's sector buffer is full, it writes the data to the disk in the indicated location, and then interrupts.

4. On receiving the interrupt, the driver copies another sector of data to the controller's sector buffer.

5. This process is repeated until all the requested data has been written.

> **Note**
>
> *Attention Disk Experts! This example driver is just that; an **example**
> designed to illustrate how to write a device driver. As such, we're sure
> there are better, faster, cheaper, newer, more efficient, or more widely
> applicable methods for implementing the functionality in this driver,
> based on intimate knowledge of the ATA specification. That's not the
> point. The driver really works on the systems it was tested on. We hope
> that what it does is easy to understand, that it serves as a good illustra-
> tion of how to write drivers under Windows NT, and that it's a more
> interesting example than a parallel port. **That's** the point.*

Dispatch and StartIo Routines

Because the ATA/IDE disk controller can support only a single transfer operation at a time, we chose to implement this driver using System Queuing. Read
and write operations thus share a single Dispatch routine, as illustrated in
Example 16.2.

*Example 16.2. Read and write Dispatch entry point for the example pro-
grammed I/O driver.*

```
NTSTATUS
IdeDispatchReadWrite(IN PDEVICE_OBJECT DeviceObject,
                     IN OUT PIRP Irp)
{
    PPARTITION_DATA partitionData = (PPARTITION_DATA)DeviceObject
                                        ->DeviceExtension;
    PIDE_DEV_EXT devExt = partitionData->Partition0;
    PIO_STACK_LOCATION ioStack;
    ULONG firstSectorOfRequest;
    LONGLONG byteOffset;
    LONGLONG partitionLength;
    ULONG transferLength;

    partitionLength = partitionData->Pi.PartitionLength.QuadPart;

    //
    // Get a pointer to the current I/O stack location
    //
    ioStack = IoGetCurrentIrpStackLocation(Irp);

    //
    // Pick up some handy parameters from the current I/O Stack.
    // NOTE that although we access the parameters from the READ union,
    // we could be processing EITHER a READ or a WRITE operation. The
    // parameters are at the same locations in both I/O Stacks.
    //
```

continues

Continued

```
byteOffset = ioStack->Parameters.Read.ByteOffset.QuadPart;
transferLength = ioStack->Parameters.Read.Length;

//
// Validate the IRP
//
// Here we check to see if the parameters are valid with respect to the
// device.  Specifically:
//
//      - The transfer size must not be zero.
//      - The transfer size must not be > MAXIMUM_TRANSFER_LENGTH bytes
//      - The transfer must be entirely within one disk partition
//      - The transfer size must be an even multiple of the sector size
//
if ((transferLength == 0) ||
    (transferLength > MAXIMUM_TRANSFER_LENGTH) ||
    ((byteOffset + transferLength) > partitionLength) ||
    (transferLength % devExt->BytesPerSector)) {

    //
    // One of the parameters is not valid
    //
    Irp->IoStatus.Status = STATUS_INVALID_PARAMETER;
    Irp->IoStatus.Information = 0;

    IoCompleteRequest(Irp, IO_NO_INCREMENT);

    return(STATUS_INVALID_PARAMETER);
}

//
// The IRP is valid.  We will therefore be returning with the IRP
// pending., so mark it pending before queuing it.
//
IoMarkIrpPending(Irp);

//
// Convert the partition-relative request to one relative to the
// start of the disk, and store it back in the IRP for later use.
//
byteOffset += partitionData->Pi.StartingOffset.QuadPart;
ioStack->Parameters.Read.ByteOffset.QuadPart = byteOffset;

//
// Determine the sector at which the request starts
//
firstSectorOfRequest = (ULONG)(byteOffset >> devExt->ByteShiftToSector);

//
// Attempt to start the request.
//
```

```
// NOTE that we sort the queue of IRPs based on the starting sector
// of the request.  Because requests are processed quickly on the disk,
// we do not make them cancellable.
//
IoStartPacket(devExt->DeviceObject,
              Irp,
              &firstSectorOfRequest,
              NULL);

//
// Return with the request queued
//
return(STATUS_PENDING);
}
```

The IDE/ATA driver uses Direct I/O to describe requestor data buffers. As a result, when the I/O Manager builds an IRP to be passed to the driver, it probes the buffer for accessibility, locks the pages that comprise the requestor's buffer into physical memory, and builds an MDL describing the buffer. A pointer to the MDL is placed in Irp->MdlAddress.

On entry to the Dispatch routine, the driver validates the IRP parameters. Here, the driver checks to ensure that the requested transfer length is not zero, that it is not greater than the maximum transfer length supported by the device, and that it is an integral number of sectors (Note that disks can transfer data only a sector at a time. Thus, if an application wants to read 100 bytes from a file, the file system must read at least one sector of data from the disk and return the requested 100 bytes to the application. The sector size for IDE disks on NT is 512 bytes). The driver also checks to be sure that the transfer is completely contained within one partition on the disk. If any of the parameters in the IRP is not valid, the driver immediately completes the IRP with STATUS_INVALID_PARAMETER.

With the IRP validated, the driver marks the IRP to be pending. The driver then calculates the starting sector number of the request. Finally, the driver attempts to start the packet by calling IoStartPacket(), specifying the starting sector number as the *Key* parameter. This causes requests on the queue to be sorted by starting sector number. The driver does this as a performance optimization to keep the heads moving across the disk surface. After returning from its call to IoStartPacket(), the driver returns to the I/O Manager with STATUS_PENDING.

The careful reader might note that, because the *CancelFunction* parameter on the call to IoStartPacket() is NULL, this driver does not supply a Cancel routine for the IRPs that are queued. The writer of this driver decided that no Cancel routine was necessary because disk I/O requests complete quickly.

When the device is free, the I/O Manager will call the driver at its StartIo entry point, as illustrated in Example 16.3.

Example 16.3. StartIo entry point for the example programmed I/O driver.

```
VOID
IdeStartIo(IN PDEVICE_OBJECT DeviceObject,
          IN PIRP Irp)
{
    PIDE_DEV_EXT devExt = (PIDE_DEV_EXT)DeviceObject->DeviceExtension;
    PIO_STACK_LOCATION ioStack;

    //
    // Get a pointer to the current I/O Stack Location
    //
    ioStack = IoGetCurrentIrpStackLocation(Irp);

    //
    // Set up the major function, length, and starting sector of the transfer
    // in the device extension.  They'll be quicker to get at from the ISR
    // in the devExt than if we leave them in the IRP.
    //
    devExt->OperationType = ioStack->MajorFunction;

    devExt->RemainingTransferLength = ioStack->Parameters.Read.Length;

    devExt->FirstSectorOfRequest =
                (ULONG)(ioStack->Parameters.Read.ByteOffset.QuadPart >>
                            devExt->ByteShiftToSector);

    //
    // This driver uses Direct I/O for transfer operations.
    // Map the requestor's buffer into system address space.
    //
    ASSERT(Irp->MdlAddress);
    devExt->CurrentAddress = MmGetSystemAddressForMdl(Irp->MdlAddress);

    //
    // We start the request on this device at DIRQL so serialize
    // access to the data structures and the HW registers
    //
    (VOID)KeSynchronizeExecution(devExt->ControllerData->InterruptObject,
                            IdeStartThisRequestOnDevice,
                            devExt);

    return;
}
```

The I/O Manager calls IdeStartIo(), the driver's StartIo entry point, when the disk controller is available to process a new request. StartIo functions are always called at IRQL DISPATCH_LEVEL. This driver's StartIo function is very simple. The function starts by initializing fields in the disk's device object extension with basic information about the current transfer. This information includes the function code (which obviously determines the transfer direction), the length of the transfer, and the sector at which the transfer starts.

The StartIo function's next task in this driver is to get the kernel virtual address of the start of the requestor's data buffer. This driver (like all disk drivers on NT) utilizes Direct I/O. The driver indicated this during initialization processing, after it created its Device Object, by setting the DO_DIRECT_IO bit in the Flags field of the Device Object. Because it uses Direct I/O, the I/O Manager describes the requestor's data buffer with an MDL. Prior to passing the IRP to the driver, the I/O Manager checked the requestor's data buffer for appropriate access, and locked the requestor's data buffer pages into physical memory. To map the requestor's data buffer into kernel virtual address space, the driver calls MmGetSystemAddressForMdl(). This function returns a kernel virtual address that the driver can use to refer to the requestor's data buffer in an arbitrary thread context. Because the physical pages that comprise the requestor's buffer are locked into physical memory (that is, they are not pageable), the driver can safely refer to these pages at any IRQL without fear of a page fault.

The last thing the StartIo routine does in this driver is call IdeStartThisRequestOnDevice() via a call to the function KeSynchronizeExecution(). IdeStartThisRequstOnDevice()actually programs the controller's registers to perform the transfer. In this example driver, the controller's registers are also accessed extensively in the interrupt service routine. Therefore, the driver protects the device's registers with the Interrupt Spin Lock associated with the device's ISR to avoid any conflicts. Thus, IdeStartThisRequestOnDevice() is called with the device's Interrupt Spin Lock held, and at the device's Synchronize IRQL. A pointer to the controller's device extension is passed as the context parameter to IdeStartThisRequestOnDevice(), the syntax for which appears in Example 16.4.

Example 16.4. Starting a request in the example programmed I/O device.

```
BOOLEAN
IdeStartThisRequestOnDevice(IN OUT PVOID Context)
{
    PIDE_DEV_EXT devExt;
    PCONTROLLER_DATA controllerData;
    NTSTATUS ntStatus;
    UCHAR controllerStatus;
    UCHAR sectorCount, sectorNumber, cylinderLow, cylinderHigh,
                driveHead;

    //
    // set some locals
```

continues

Continued

```
    //
    devExt = Context;
    controllerData = devExt->ControllerData;

    //
    // get the current state of the controller
    //
    controllerStatus =
        READ_PORT_UCHAR(devExt->ControllerData->ControllerAddress +
                        STATUS_REGISTER);

    //
    // We will soon cause an interrupt that will require servicing by
    // the DPC, so set the flag to note that we require a DPC.
    //
    controllerData->InterruptRequiresDpc = TRUE;

    //
    // Determine the parameters for the controller
    //
    sectorCount = (UCHAR)(devExt->RemainingTransferLength /
                          devExt->BytesPerSector);

    sectorNumber = (UCHAR)((devExt->FirstSectorOfRequest %
                                        devExt->SectorsPerTrack) + 1);

    cylinderLow = (UCHAR)(devExt->FirstSectorOfRequest /
                              (devExt->SectorsPerTrack *
                                  devExt->TracksPerCylinder)) &
                                  0xff;

    cylinderHigh = (UCHAR)(devExt->FirstSectorOfRequest /
                              (devExt->SectorsPerTrack *
                                  devExt->TracksPerCylinder) >>
                                  8);

    driveHead = (UCHAR) (((devExt->FirstSectorOfRequest /
                              devExt->SectorsPerTrack) %
                              devExt->TracksPerCylinder) |
                                      devExt->DeviceUnit);

    //
    // Give the controller the cylinder and head of the start of the transfer.
    // Also tell it how many sectors we want to transfer.
    //
    WRITE_PORT_UCHAR(controllerData->ControllerAddress + SECTOR_COUNT_REGISTER,
                                                    sectorCount);

    WRITE_PORT_UCHAR(controllerData->ControllerAddress +
                     SECTOR_NUMBER_REGISTER,
                                                    sectorNumber);
```

```
WRITE_PORT_UCHAR(controllerData->ControllerAddress + CYLINDER_LOW_REGISTER,
                                            cylinderLow);

WRITE_PORT_UCHAR(controllerData->ControllerAddress +
                 CYLINDER_HIGH_REGISTER,
                                            cylinderHigh);

WRITE_PORT_UCHAR(controllerData->ControllerAddress + DRIVE_HEAD_REGISTER,
                                            driveHead);
//
// Actually start the request, based on the direction of the transfer.
// Note that we've already stored that length and starting VA of
// the transfer in the device extension (in the StartIo routine).
//
switch (devExt->OperationType) {

    case IRP_MJ_READ:

        //
        // Tell the controller to do a read.
        //
        // The controller will interrupt when it has a complete sector
        // of data for us to retrieve from it.
        //
        WRITE_PORT_UCHAR(controllerData->ControllerAddress +
                 COMMAND_REGISTER,
                                            devExt->ReadCommand);

        break;

    case IRP_MJ_WRITE:

        //
        // Set the write precomp
        //
        WRITE_PORT_UCHAR(
            controllerData->ControllerAddress + WRITE_PRECOMP_REGISTER,
                                            (UCHAR)(devExt->WritePrecomp));
        //
        // Give the controller the WRITE command
        //
        WRITE_PORT_UCHAR(controllerData->ControllerAddress +
                 COMMAND_REGISTER,
                                            devExt->WriteCommand);

        //
        // The way writes work is that after giving the controller the
        // WRITE command, we stuff a sector's worth of data into it. BUT,
        // before we can start stuffing, the controller has to drop its
```

continues

Continued

```
            // BUSY status, and assert DATA_REQUEST_STATUS.  That's our signal
            // to load 'er up!
            //
            (VOID)IdeWaitControllerReady(controllerData, 10, 5000);

            //
            // Get the controller status after the Wait
            //
            controllerStatus =
                READ_PORT_UCHAR(devExt->ControllerData->ControllerAddress +
                                            STATUS_REGISTER);

            //
            // As a sanity check, get it 1 more time, just in case
            //
            if (!(controllerStatus & DATA_REQUEST_STATUS)) {

                controllerStatus =
                    READ_PORT_UCHAR(devExt->ControllerData->ControllerAddress +
                                                STATUS_REGISTER);
            }

            //
            // If the controller's ready, start slamming data to it
            //
            if (controllerStatus & DATA_REQUEST_STATUS) {

                PVOID buffer;

                buffer = devExt->CurrentAddress;

                //
                // Update the address and lengths now because the
                // numbers mean "the number of bytes left to go".
                // Thus, when the interrupt occurs to signal the end
                // of this write, the bytes have "already gone".  This
                // is necessary to keep the arithmetic straight.
                //
                devExt->CurrentAddress += devExt->BytesPerInterrupt;
                devExt->RemainingTransferLength -= devExt->BytesPerInterrupt;

                //
                // Write the first buffer (which will cause an interrupt
                // when the write has been completed and it's time for us
                // to send it another sector)
                //
                WRITE_PORT_BUFFER_USHORT(
                    (PUSHORT)(controllerData->ControllerAddress +
                            DATA_REGISTER),
```

```
                    buffer,
                    devExt->BytesPerInterrupt/2);

        }

        break;

    default:

        //
        // Can't get here.
        //
        DbgBreakPoint();

        break;
    }

    return(TRUE);
}
```

IdeStartThisRequestOnDevice() actually does the somewhat messy job of programming the controller to perform the requested transfer. This function starts by calculating the starting sector of the request in the terms the controller wants to receive it (that is, the sector, cylinder, and head for the start of the transfer), as well as the number of sectors for this request. The function then programs the disk controller with this information.

Next, IdeStartThisRequestOnDevice() switches, based on the IRP major function code of the request. If the request is a read, the driver gives the controller a read command. If the request is a write, the driver gives the controller a write command and then waits for the controller to become ready for the transfer. For an IDE/ATA device, "becoming ready" entails the controller first clearing its busy bit. The driver waits for this bit to clear in the function IdeWaitControllerReady(). The second part of becoming ready requires the controller to assert its data request bit (DATA_REQUEST_STATUS, in the example). After this bit has been set, the driver then copies a sector of data to the controller's data register using the HAL function WRITE_PORT_BUFFER_USHORT(). This function takes data from the requestor's buffer (which was mapped into kernel virtual address space in the StartIo routine) and copies it to the device's data register located in Port I/O space.

Interrupt Service Routine

With either the read or the write request thus established, the driver next awaits an interrupt from the device. When the device interrupts, the driver's ISR is called, as illustrated in Example 16.5.

Example 16.5. Interrupt service routine for the example programmed I/O driver.

```
BOOLEAN
IdeISR(IN PKINTERRUPT Interrupt,
       IN OUT PVOID Context)
{
    PDEVICE_OBJECT deviceObject;
    PCONTROLLER_DATA controllerData = (PCONTROLLER_DATA)Context;
    PIDE_DEV_EXT devExt;
    PIO_STACK_LOCATION ioStack;
    UCHAR controllerStatus;

    //
    // Get the controller status.  Note that this will STOP all interrupts
    // on the controller.
    //
    controllerStatus =
          READ_PORT_UCHAR(controllerData->ControllerAddress +
                          STATUS_REGISTER);

    //
    // Check if this is an interrupt that we should service.
    //
    // We should service this interrupt if the IDE controller is not busy (i.e.
    // he's waiting for US to do something) and the driver has had a chance to
    // fully initialize (i.e. the controller data structure is set up)
    //
    if ( (controllerStatus & BUSY_STATUS) || (!controllerData->DeviceObject) ){

        return(FALSE);
    }

    //
    // Get pointer to our device object and device extension
    //
    deviceObject = controllerData->DeviceObject;

    devExt = deviceObject->DeviceExtension;

    //
    // If the controller is not indicating an error, check to see if
    // there's anything to do...
    //
    if (!(controllerStatus & ERROR_STATUS)) {

        //
        // If there's data remaining to move, do it right here.
        //
        if (devExt->RemainingTransferLength) {

            //
```

```
// if we're not ready, do 1 ping and try again
//
if (!(controllerStatus & DATA_REQUEST_STATUS)) {

    controllerStatus = READ_PORT_UCHAR(
            controllerData->ControllerAddress + STATUS_REGISTER);
}


//
// Check to be sure the device is ready
//
if (controllerStatus & DATA_REQUEST_STATUS) {

    PVOID buffer;

    //
    // Update the controller with the next chunk of data
    //

    //
    // Save the requestor's buffer address
    //
    buffer = devExt->CurrentAddress;

    //
    // adjust the address and counts in expectation
    // that this I/O will complete
    //
    devExt->RemainingTransferLength -= devExt->BytesPerInterrupt;
    devExt->CurrentAddress += devExt->BytesPerInterrupt;

    //
    // Move the data
    //
    if (devExt->OperationType == IRP_MJ_READ)  {

        //
        // Move the data from the controller to the Requestor's
        // data buffer
        //
        READ_PORT_BUFFER_USHORT(
            (PUSHORT)(controllerData->ControllerAddress +
                    DATA_REGISTER),
            buffer,
            devExt->BytesPerInterrupt/2);

    } else {

        //
        // It's a WRITE
        // Move the data from the requestor's data buffer to
        // the controller
```

continues

Continued

```
                              //
                              WRITE_PORT_BUFFER_USHORT(
                                  (PUSHORT)(controllerData->ControllerAddress +
                                          DATA_REGISTER),
                                  buffer,
                                  devExt->BytesPerInterrupt/2);

                          }


                          //
                          // If this is not the last transfer, don't
                          // request a DPC yet.
                          //
                          if ( (devExt->RemainingTransferLength) > 0) {

                              controllerData->InterruptRequiresDpc = FALSE;

                          } else {

                              controllerData->InterruptRequiresDpc = TRUE;

                          }


                  } else {

                      DbgBreakPoint();
                  }

              }

      }

      //
      // Request the DpcForIsr
      //
      if (controllerData->InterruptRequiresDpc) {

          controllerData->InterruptRequiresDpc = FALSE;

          IoRequestDpc(deviceObject,
                      deviceObject->CurrentIrp,
                      (PVOID)controllerStatus);
      }

      return(TRUE);
}
```

When the driver's ISR is entered, the driver reads the controller's status register
into a local variable. For the IDE/ATA device, reading the status register

acknowledges and clears any interrupt that may be pending. The driver then checks to see if the controller indicated by the *Context* parameter (passed into the function by the I/O Manager) is interrupting, and if the driver has been fully initialized. If either of these conditions is not the case, the driver returns from the ISR with the value FALSE.

Assuming the controller is interrupting and the driver has been fully initialized, the driver next checks to see if the controller has raised an error. If there is an error indicated, a DPC is requested. If there is no error indicated, the driver next ensures that the controller is ready for the next transfer. Assuming the controller is ready, the driver proceeds, based on whether it is processing a read or a write operation.

If a read is being processed, the driver reads a sector of data, one USHORT at a time, from the controller's data register and places it in the requestor's buffer. This operation is accomplished by calling the HAL function READ_PORT_BUFFER_USHORT().

If a write is being processed, the driver copies the next sector of data from the requestor's buffer to the controller's data register using the function WRITE_PORT_BUFFER_USHORT(). Note that the USHORT variants of these functions were chosen because the controller's data register is 16 bits (one USHORT) wide. As previously mentioned, the port HAL functions were chosen because the data register is implemented in hardware in Port I/O space.

With the next sector of data transferred, the driver checks to see if all the data to be transferred by this request is complete. If the transfer is complete, the driver requests its DpcForIsr by calling IoRequestDpc(). The driver passes the contents of the controller's status register back to the DPC as a context value.

DPC Routine

The driver's DpcForIsr routine is executed as a result of being requested from the ISR. According to the standard DPC-handling procedure, the DPC will be invoked the next time that the system attempts to transfer control to an IRQL lower than DISPATCH_LEVEL. The DpcForIsr code appears in Example 16.6:

Example 16.6. The DpcForIsr code for the example programmed I/O driver.

```
VOID
IdeDPC(IN PKDPC Dpc,
       IN PVOID DeferredContext,
       IN PVOID SystemArgument1,
       IN PVOID SystemArgument2)
{
    PDEVICE_OBJECT deviceObject;
    PIDE_DEV_EXT devExt;
```

continues

Continued

```
    PCONTROLLER_DATA controllerData;
    PIRP irp;
    PIO_STACK_LOCATION ioStack;
    NTSTATUS returnStatus;
    ULONG controllerStatus;
    NTSTATUS ntStatus;

    //
    // setup locals
    //
    deviceObject = (PDEVICE_OBJECT)DeferredContext;
    devExt = deviceObject->DeviceExtension;
    controllerData = devExt->ControllerData;

    //
    // Default to completing the IRP with success
    //
    returnStatus = STATUS_SUCCESS;

    //
    // Get the controller status.  Note that because this device only has
    // one operation in progress at a time, passing back the controller
    // status this way from the ISR presents no problem.
    //
    controllerStatus = (ULONG)SystemArgument2;

    //
    // Get a pointer to the IRP currently being processed
    //
    irp = deviceObject->CurrentIrp;

    ASSERT(irp);

    ioStack = IoGetCurrentIrpStackLocation(irp);

    //
    // If the controller is busy, wait for it to become ready...
    //
    ntStatus = IdeWaitControllerReady(controllerData, 10, 5000);

    //
    // Did the controller become ready?
    //
    if (NT_SUCCESS(ntStatus))  {

        //
        // We're not in a data request phase, right?
        //
        if (READ_PORT_UCHAR(
                controllerData->ControllerAddress + STATUS_REGISTER) &
                        DATA_REQUEST_STATUS) {
```

```
            controllerStatus |= ERROR_STATUS;

    }

} else {

    //
    // Controller stayed busy??
    //
    controllerStatus |= ERROR_STATUS;

}

//
// Was there a problem?
//
if (controllerStatus & ERROR_STATUS) {

        //
        // Do error/retry stuff here
        //

}

//
// Now, test for the success/failure of the operation.
//
if (NT_SUCCESS(returnStatus) ) {

    //
    // Success!!!
    //
    returnStatus = STATUS_SUCCESS;

    irp->IoStatus.Information = ioStack->Parameters.Read.Length;

} else {

    //
    // We tried but the request failed.  Return the error
    // status and move along...
    //
    irp->IoStatus.Information = 0;
}

//
// Time to complete the request and start another one...
//

//
// In order to properly complete a read requests we need to flush
// the I/O buffers.
```

continues

Continued

```
      //
      if (ioStack->MajorFunction == IRP_MJ_READ) {

          KeFlushIoBuffers(irp->MdlAddress, TRUE, FALSE);
      }

      //
      // Start the next packet by key... Next sector first scan to try to keep
      // the heads moving forward!  Such an optimization...
      //
      IoStartNextPacketByKey(devExt->DeviceObject,
                             FALSE,
                             devExt->FirstSectorOfRequest);

      //
      // Set the status in the IRP (Note .Information field set above)
      //
      irp->IoStatus.Status = returnStatus;

      IoCompleteRequest(irp, IO_DISK_INCREMENT);

      return;
  }
```

After the request for the DpcForIsr has been queued, on the next attempt by that processor to lower its IRQL below DISPATCH_LEVEL, NT will process that processor's DPC list. As described in Chapter 6, "Interrupt Request Levels and DPCs," processing the DPC list entails removing DPC Objects from the head of the DPC list, one at a time, and then calling the DPC routine associated with that object at IRQL DISPATCH_LEVEL. When the example driver's DPC Object is dequeued, the driver's DpcForIsr is called.

Conceptually, all that this driver needs to do in its DpcForIsr is to complete the read or write request that was in progress and attempt to start a new request to propagate the driver's execution. There is, however, just a bit more that needs to be done to ensure that the device works properly. On entry to the DpcForIsr, the driver gathers some local data. The driver then waits for the controller to become ready by calling the function IdeWaitControllerReady(). After the controller has become ready, the driver checks to see if the controller is still asserting DATA_REQUEST_STATUS. If so, this indicates data overrun or under-run during the transfer.

The driver next checks to see if the DPC or ISR has identified a controller error. If an error is identified, the driver deals with it appropriately (note that we've left this code, which isn't very interesting, out of the printed example at the location Do error/retry stuff here). If no error is detected, the driver is ready to complete the current request and start another one.

If the current request was a read request, the driver flushes the data from cache to the requestor's buffer by calling KeFlushIoBuffers(). (Note that this function is actually implemented as a NULL macro on x86 architecture processors, but it is important on various RISC processors.) The driver then calls IoStartNextPacketByKey(). This call results in the driver's StartIo routine being called to initiate the next I/O operation. Finally, the driver completes the DpcForIsr by completing the previously pending IRP by calling IoCompleteRequest(), with a priority increment of IO_DISK_INCREMENT (the standard increment value for completion of disk I/O operations). To maximize device throughput and reduce request latency (as discussed in Chapter 14), we call IoStartNextPacketByKey() before calling IoCompleteRequest() to complete the pending IRP.

DPC Versus ISR in the Example Driver

The one aspect of the example driver's design that is slightly atypical is the fact that it actually performs its I/O processing directly within the ISR. That is, the data transfer between the device and the user's buffer is almost completely implemented in the driver's ISR. In a more traditional design, each time the controller interrupts, indicating that it is ready to transfer another sector of data, the driver requests its DpcForIsr. When the DpcForIsr executes, the driver then moves the data. This is, in fact, the design used in the NT ATDISK driver upon which the example driver is based.

So, why did the designers of this driver choose to implement the data transfer in the ISR instead of in the DPC? Making the tradeoff between doing work in the DPC and doing work in the ISR was discussed in Chapter 15, "Interrupt Service Routines and DPCs." One reason for the tradeoff was that the designers, of course, knew that they were building only a sample driver, and so the decision was not a critical one. If this had been a driver for a real product, however, what would be the specific factors that resulted in making this design decision? Some of these factors are as follows:

- **The general role of disks in the system.** A disk drive usually plays an integral role in a general-purpose computer system. Thus, the thinking was that if data cannot be moved between memory and a disk rapidly, total system performance would rapidly degrade. Thus, the designers of this driver decided that the latency required by queuing a DPC for every 512 bytes transferred would adversely impact overall system performance, even at the cost of higher interrupt latency for other devices on the system.

- **The amount of work required during each interrupt.** The work done in each interrupt is limited to moving 256 words of data between an already mapped user buffer and an I/O Port. Of course, the same number of CPU cycles need to be expended to move every sector of data (ignoring the vagaries of processor caching), regardless of whether those cycles are expended in the ISR or DPC. Thus, the only issue is whether those cycles should be spent in the ISR. Although the overhead of 256 OUT instructions cannot be considered trivial, introducing this much interrupt latency on most systems was not viewed as being likely to cause a problem. In fact, no problems have been observed when the sample driver is used for general-purpose disk I/O on an NT system.

- **No parallel operation.** Because the controller does not process requests in parallel, it has at most one request in progress at a time. It is not possible, therefore, for interrupt latency caused by the driver to "add up," due to multiple simultaneous transfers.

- **The availability of other, non-CPU intensive solutions.** The designed solution places the importance of disk performance ahead of interrupt latency. By nature, the PIO-based IDE/ATA controller is a CPU-intensive method of moving data between disks and memory. If the CPU utilization or interrupt latency introduced by this driver proved unacceptable in a particular configuration, other reasonable cost solutions that do not exhibit these characteristics are available.

To summarize, we're not advocating doing all I/O processing for general-purpose devices in the ISR. As discussed in Chapter 15, most I/O processing is best done in the DPC. However, we also don't agree that it's good engineering to avoid *all* I/O processing in the ISR, as has become the conventional wisdom. The important thing is for driver designers to use good engineering judgment, consider the impact of their decisions, and carefully take into account the larger environment in which their driver will be used. If these things are done, the right decisions will typically be made—even if at times two good engineers might come to different conclusions.

Design Issues for Programmed I/O Device Drivers

The remainder of this chapter deals with specific design issues that may be encountered in drivers for programmed I/O devices. Some of these considerations include the following:

- Mapping device memory into user space

- Polling

- Synchronous driver implementations

Mapping Device Memory into User Space

One of the questions students ask us most frequently in our device driver classes is "Is there a way to map a device's shared memory into user space?" The answer to this question is always "Yes, but...". Although it is certainly possible to map a device's shared memory buffer directly into an arbitrary User mode application's address space, there are few legitimate reasons to ever do this under Windows NT.

Most of the time, people want to map device memory directly into an application's address space to more closely match the design of a system that was previously running under DOS or Windows9x. There are, in fact, many problems with implementing a similar design under Windows NT. For example, Windows NT considers it a security violation for User mode applications to have direct access to device registers in Port I/O space. As a result, on x86 architecture systems, user applications running on NT do not have the appropriate I/O Privilege Level (IOPL) to perform "IN" or "OUT" instructions.

Of course, whether an application has IOPL or not on an x86 is a moot point because NT supports multiple hardware architectures via the HAL. HAL functions such as WRITE_PORT_UCHAR() and the like are not available to User mode applications. Thus, ignoring Port I/O space access, even if a driver were to map a shared memory segment of a device into an application's address space, how would it properly move data to that device buffer? The application can't call the HAL function WRITE_REGISTER_BUFFER_UCHAR() (or whatever is appropriate). Therefore, the application would be reduced to having to understand the specific hardware on which it was running and deal with any of its complexities.

But even if a programmer were willing to accept that Port I/O space registers cannot be accessed and that the application written would be highly platform-specific, could this scheme be made to work properly? The answer to this ultimate question is "yes" for some systems, and "no" for others. For example, an application could manually flush the Pentium's internal write post buffer when moving data to the device. So, supporting the current generation of x86 systems would probably work. But there's no practical way for that same application to flush the data cache on a RISC processor. So the application could be made to work on some processors that NT supports, but not on others.

Moving data from an application directly to a device memory buffer is probably not a good idea. After all, the only difference in overhead between a driver moving the data to the device and the application doing the same is the cost of the system service invocation. This overhead is minimal, relative to the time it takes to move even a small buffer of data.

One situation that exists where it actually *might* make sense to map a device buffer directly into User mode memory is when the application can examine or operate on the data directly in the device's buffer without having to recopy it. This approach could save the overhead of the driver copying the data from the device into the user's buffer. Even this most simplified of approaches may not work on all hardware platforms, however. Thus, the cases when this is likely to be the best overall architecture are rare.

> **Note**
>
> For those rare cases in which the driver writer really wants to map device memory directly into User mode memory, the DDK has an example of one way to do this. This example is mapmem in the \ddk\src\general folder. Although this example is neither particularly well documented nor particularly well written, it does at least provide a starting point for driver writers who want to pursue this approach. Remember, however, that access to device memory without use of the HAL functions will likely result in a processor-specific implementation.

Polling

The Windows NT I/O Manager is pretty much designed around the concept of interrupt-driven device drivers. In fact, the NT V4 DDK explicitly states in section 16.3:

> An NT device driver should avoid polling its device unless it is absolutely necessary.

So, when a driver writer considers implementing a polling device driver, perhaps the question becomes: "What constitutes *absolutely necessary?*"

Few devices designed these days must be polled in the traditional sense. Here, we're talking about those old-time devices that did not support interrupts, but rather signaled a change in their status by simply setting a bit in one of their interface registers. There was no way for a driver to detect the change in the device's state, other than spinning in a loop and waiting for the appropriate bit to be set in the device's register.

There is, however, a category of high-performance devices that can go through stages where polling the device registers can be advantageous. Consider, for example, a high-speed telemetry device with a receive FIFO that can buffer only a small part of a received data block. The start of a block of data might be signaled to the device's driver through an interrupt. After the data has started to arrive, the driver could begin polling to retrieve the data from the FIFO, thus ensuring that the FIFO does not overflow. Once the complete data block has been retrieved, the driver stops polling and awaits the next interrupt from the device.

One of the difficulties of polling from NT drivers is the fact that system timers have only a resolution of about 10 milliseconds (ms), and that the actual resolution varies among processor architectures. There is no easy way to modify this timer resolution from Kernel mode. Of course, this is not a problem if a device needs to be polled fewer than 100 times per second. To do this, a driver simply calls `KeSetTimer()` or `KeSetTimeEx()` to queue a CustomDpc every 10ms or more. The prototypes for these functions are shown in Figures 16.4 and 16.5.

BOOLEAN
KeSetTimer(IN PKTIMER *Timer,*
        IN LARGE_INTEGER *DueTime,*
        IN PKDPC *Dpc*);

Timer: A pointer to timer object, located in nonpaged pool, that has been previously initialized by calling KeInitializeTimer() or KeInitializeTimerEx().

DueTime: The time at which the timer is due. If negative, this is the number of 100-nanosecond (ns) intervals from the current time at which the timer is due. If positive, this is the future absolute time when the time is due.

Dpc: An optional pointer to a DPC object, located in nonpaged pool, that has been previously initialized by calling KeInitializeDpc().

Figure 16.4. `KeSetTimer()` *function prototype.*

BOOLEAN
KeSetTimerEX(IN PKTIMER *Timer,*
        IN LARGE_INTEGER *DueTime,*
        IN LONG *Period,*
        IN PKDPC *Dpc*);

Timer: A pointer to timer object, located in nonpaged pool, that has been previously initialized by calling KeInitializeTimer() or KeInitializeTimerEx().

DueTime: The time at which the timer is to initially expire. If negative, this is the number of 100-nanosecond (ns) intervals from the current time at which the timer is to initially.

Period: The number of milliseconds for which the timer should be periodically rescheduled, after it becomes due the first time.

Dpc: An optional pointer to a DPC object, located in nonpaged pool, which has been previously initialized by calling KeInitializeDpc().

Figure 16.5. `KeSetTimerEx()` *function prototype.*

Given that Timer Objects are NT Dispatcher Objects, another way of using timers for polling is to set the timer (using one of the previously described functions) and then wait for it to be signaled using KeWaitForSingleObject(). Obviously, this wait must take place at an IRQL < DISPATCH_LEVEL. This is equivalent to the thread calling KeDelayExecutionThread(). The only other way for a kernel thread to stall for a prescribed period of time is for the thread to call KeStallExecutionProcessor(), the prototype for which is shown in Figure 16.6.

VOID
KeStallExecutionProcessor(IN ULONG *Microseconds*);

Microseconds: The number of seconds for which the processor should busy-wait, spinning within the KeStallExecutionProcessor() function, before returning to the caller.

Figure 16.6. KeStallExecutionProcessor() *function prototype.*

The KeStallExecutionProcessor() function causes the current processor to spin in a tight loop for the requested number of microseconds, before returning to the caller. Although very effective for short wait intervals, this method of delaying the execution of a driver thread is highly consumptive of CPU time. Worse yet, because the stall period is so short and the driver is busy-waiting, calling KeStallExecutionProcessor() does not result in the current thread automatically yielding control of the processor for other threads to run during the stall period.

One way that drivers can implement polling is to create a dedicated system thread. A driver may create a system thread by calling the function PsCreateSystemThread(). Figure 16.7 shows the prototype for this function.

```
NTSTATUS
PsCreateSystemThread(OUT PHANDLE ThreadHandle,
        IN ACCESS_MASK DesiredAccess,
        IN POBJECT_ATTRIBUTES ObjectAttributes,
        IN HANDLE ProcessHandle,
        OUT PCLIENT_ID ClientId,
        OUT PKSTART_ROUTINE StartRoutine,
        IN PVOID StartContext);
```

ThreadHandle: A pointer to a location to receive the returned handle for the created thread.

AccessMask: An access mask indicating the required access to the newly created thread.

ObjectAttributes: A pointer to an OBJECT_ATTRIBUTES structure describing the newly created thread.

ProcessHandle: A handle to a process in which the thread should be created. A value of NULL here causes the thread to be created within the system process.

ClientId: A pointer to a location to receive the client id of the newly created thread. This pointer is primarily useful for interprocess communication.

StartRoutine: A pointer to a function to be invoked by the newly created thread.

StartContext: A value to be passed to *StartRoutine.*

Figure 16.7. PsCreateSystemThread() *function prototype.*

In spite of what many might view as a daunting set of parameters, PsCreateSystemThread() is actually extremely easy to use from within a driver to create a worker thread. This is because many of the parameters can be defaulted or ignored. Example 16.7 demonstrates creating a thread that starts executing with the driver function ThreadFunction() with the parameter ThreadParameter.

Example 16.7. A simple way to call PsCreateSystemThread() *to create a worker thread.*

```
status = PsCreateSystemThread( &threadHandle,
                    THREAD_ALL_ACCESS,
                    NULL,
                    (HANDLE)0L,
```

continues

Continued

```
                        NULL,
                        ThreadFunction,
                        ThreadParameter);
```

To ensure reasonable performance, a driver should set the priority of any dedicated polling threads it creates to LOW_REALTIME_PRIORITY+1 or LOW_REALTIME_
PRIORITY+2. The created thread runs at IRQL PASSIVE_LEVEL. The newly created
thread can therefore poll the device at the appropriate frequency, using an
appropriate method of waiting between attempts.

> ### Note
>
> *Remember, a thread that is perennially runnable in the real-time priority
> range will result in no threads with lower priorities **ever** running. Thus,
> any time that a driver uses such a thread for polling a device, that thread
> should voluntarily relinquish control of the CPU periodically, if the per-
> formance of user applications on that CPU matters. Of course, depending
> on the overall system configuration, it is entirely possible that the perfor-
> mance of user applications on the system is of no concern during the
> polling interval. This might be the case, for example, in a process-control
> application.*

When the need arises, drivers can poll their devices from their DPC or even
from their ISR. This might be required in the case of a very high-speed device,
such as the satellite telemetry device that was previously mentioned. Note,
however, that cases where this is truly required are extremely rare. Even high-
bandwidth devices can be polled effectively at IRQL PASSIVE_LEVEL from a
driver-created system thread. The only thing gained by polling at IRQL
DISPATCH_LEVEL or above is avoidance of some operating system and ISR overhead. Before implementing a polling scheme at raised IRQL, carefully consider
the impact that this will have both on the operating system and on other
devices attempting to operate on that system. After such careful consideration,
the idea of polling in the DPC or ISR is almost universally discarded!

> ### Note
>
> *Often, the absolute best place to solve the issue of how or when to poll is
> in the hardware, not in the driver. If the hardware design for the device
> can be affected, polling could be implemented on the board, with a single
> interrupt to NT when device servicing is required. This entirely eliminates
> the need for the driver to implement polling, precisely as the DDK rec-
> ommends!*

Often seemingly small hardware changes, like increasing the size of a FIFO, can yield dramatic increases in device performance and overall system throughput. It's always preferable to design your hardware with the target operating system in mind.

Synchronous Driver Implementations

The code for the `NeitherWrite()` function, shown previously in Example 16.1, illustrates the implementation of synchronous processing for a write operation. Chapter 14, "Dispatch Entry Points," initially discussed synchronous processing. Let's now discuss it a bit further.

Although NT has an asynchronous I/O subsystem, it is typically not a problem if a driver chooses to process an I/O request synchronously. Specifically, synchronous I/O processing does not typically present a problem when:

- The application expects the request to be completed synchronously, and therefore is not adversely impacted by having to wait.

- The context in which the wait is performed is that of the application that issued the request.

If a driver processes an I/O request synchronously in the context of the requesting thread, the I/O operation will be synchronous even if the requesting thread has requested asynchronous completion. Thus, if an application expects to issue an I/O request, and then return and do useful work while the I/O request is in progress on the driver, but the driver implements the I/O operation synchronously, the result will be a synchronous I/O operation—and the application is not likely to function optimally.

Worse yet is the case when a driver processes I/O operations synchronously, but that driver is not the one initially entered by the calling application. For example, consider a disk driver that implements synchronous I/O processing. A user application issues a read request to a file system. By the time this read request winds its way down to the disk driver, the disk driver may be running in an arbitrary thread context. Therefore, if the disk driver performs its processing synchronously, it is "stealing" time from an application that is likely to be unrelated to the one issuing the file read.

If the amount of time required to synchronously complete a request is small, as it would be in the `NeitherWrite()` function shown in Example 16.1, the amount of time "stolen" from the unrelated application probably doesn't matter. The real problem occurs when the device is not free to start a transfer operation immediately. Take for example, the following slightly altered version of the `NeitherWrite()` function in Example 16.8.

Example 16.8. Even if the IRP being processed is cancelled, this driver's Cancel routine will not be called while it waits with KeWaitForSingleObject().

```
NTSTATUS NeitherWriteTwo(PDEVICE_OBJECT DeviceObject, PIRP Irp)
{
    PIO_STACK_LOCATION ioStack;
    NEITHER_DEVICE_EXTENSION devExt;

    //
    // Get a pointer to the current IRP stack
    ioStack = IoGetCurrentIrpStackLocation(Irp);

    //
    // Get a pointer to our device extension
    //
    devExt = DeviceObject->DeviceExtension;

    //
    // Before we wait, set a Cancel routine to be called
    // in case this thread wants to terminate
    //
    IoSetCancelRoutine(Irp, SynchCancel);

    //
    // Wait for the device to become available
    // before proceeding
    //
    KeWaitForSingleObject(&devExt->ReadyEvent,
                          Executive,
                          KernelMode,
                          FALSE,
                          NULL);

    //
    // No longer cancelable
    //
    IoSetCancelRoutine(Irp, NULL);

    //
    // Move the data to the device
    //
    WRITE_REGISTER_BUFFER_UCHAR(devExt->TranslatedDeviceBuffer,
                                Irp->UserBuffer,
                                ioStack->Parameters.Write.Length);

    //
    // Tell the device the data is there
    //
    WRITE_PORT_UCHAR(devExt->TranslatedWriteCtrl, NEITHER_DATA_READY);

    //
```

```
    // Complete the IRP with success
    //
    Irp->IoStatus.Status = STATUS_SUCCESS;
    Irp->IoStatus.Information =  ioStack->Parameters.Write.Length;

    IoCompleteRequest(Irp, IO_NO_INCREMENT);

    return(STATUS_SUCCESS);
}
```

Changes between this example and the original NeitherWrite() example are
shown in bold. In Example 16.8, the driver needs to wait for an event to be set
before it can process the write operation on the device. The driver sets this
event from the driver's DpcForIsr, whenever the device is available.

As stated previously, waiting for a device to be available isn't a problem as
long as the application being blocked is the application that requested the I/O
and the application is designed to expect this wait. This could be a big problem, however, if the driver waits in an arbitrary thread context. Consider what
might happen if the arbitrary thread that was blocked by the driver happened
to be the system's Modified Page Writer thread. The result could be seriously
degraded system performance (if not an outright system hang).

But there is another, more insidious problem. Note that prior to performing the
KeWaitForSingleObject() call, the driver sets a Cancel routine in the IRP by calling IoSetCancelRoutine(). However, if the thread is aborted while the wait is in
progress, the IRP's Cancel routine *will not be called*. This is true, regardless of
whether the driver waits alterable or nonalterable, or in Kernel or User mode.

Although there is no completely satisfactory way of handling this situation, one
alternative is for the driver to wait in User mode. This results in the wait being
satisfied and STATUS_USER_APC being returned to the driver in response to the
KeWaitForSingleObject() call. Although the driver's Cancel routine is still not
called, the driver could interpret the return of STATUS_USER_APC here to mean
that the pending IRP has been canceled. Obviously, this works only if there is
no other reason for the current thread to receive a User mode APC. To wait in
User mode instead of Kernel mode, the driver would specify UserMode for the
WaitMode parameter of the KeWaitForSingleObject() function call, instead of
KernelMode, as shown in the example. The only differences between waiting in
User mode and waiting in Kernel mode are that while waiting in User mode,
the delivery of User mode APCs is enabled and the driver's stack is pageable.

Example 16.9 shows the corrected code, implementing the scheme just
described.

Example 16.9. One method of handling cancel operations in drivers that perform synchronous processing.

```
NTSTATUS NeitherWriteThree(PDEVICE_OBJECT DeviceObject, PIRP Irp)
{
    PIO_STACK_LOCATION ioStack;
    NEITHER_DEVICE_EXTENSION devExt;

    //
    // Get a pointer to the current IRP stack
    ioStack = IoGetCurrentIrpStackLocation(Irp);

    //
    // Get a pointer to our device extension
    //
    devExt = DeviceObject->DeviceExtension;

    //
    // Wait for the device to become available
    // before proceeding
    //
    status = KeWaitForSingleObject(&devExt->ReadyEvent,
                        Executive,
                        UserMode,
                        FALSE,
                        NULL);

    //
    // The only reason we could wake up with a user APC being
    // delivered is if the thread is being terminated.  This means
    //   that we should cancel the current IRP.
    //
    if (status == STATUS_USER_APC)  {
        //
        // Cancel the IRP!
        //
        Irp->IoStatus.Status = STATUS_CANCELLED;
        Irp->IoStatus.Information =  0;

        IoCompleteRequest(Irp, IO_NO_INCREMENT);

        return(STATUS_CANCELLED);
    }

    //
    // Move the data to the device
    //
    WRITE_REGISTER_BUFFER_UCHAR(devExt->TranslatedDeviceBuffer,
                            Irp->UserBuffer,
                            ioStack->Parameters.Write.Length);
```

```
    //
    // Tell the device the data is there
    //
    WRITE_PORT_UCHAR(devExt->TranslatedWriteCtrl, NEITHER_DATA_READY);

    //
    // Complete the IRP with success
    //
    Irp->IoStatus.Status = STATUS_SUCCESS;
    Irp->IoStatus.Information = ioStack->Parameters.Write.Length;

    IoCompleteRequest(Irp, IO_NO_INCREMENT);

    return(STATUS_SUCCESS);
}
```

Once again, we have highlighted the differences between Example 16.9 and
Example 16.8 in bold. As previously described, the NeitherWriteThree Dispatch
routine waits for the device to be available, by waiting for a Dispatcher Object.
This wait is done in User mode. If the thread issuing the request terminates,
KeWaitForSingleObject() will return STATUS_USER_APC. The driver then interprets
this return status to mean that the pending IRP should be canceled. Note that
because the Cancel routine will never be called in this circumstance, the driver
doesn't bother setting a Cancel routine in the IRP.

Note

*Before getting too worried about the details of cancel processing in syn-
chronous drivers, it's important to keep the issue in perspective. Refer to
the discussion of cancel processing in Chapter 14. For example, if the
wait in the NeitherWriteThree Dispatch routine is going to be brief (that
is, less than a few seconds), there's probably no need to deal with request
cancellation at all.*

Chapter **17**

DMA Data Transfers

This chapter will review:

- **Processing DMA Transfer Requests.** This section briefly outlines the steps necessary for performing any DMA data transfer.

- **Adapter Objects and Map Registers.** Before getting into too much detail about how DMA data transfers are processed, we discuss the shared resources that need to be acquired by any DMA device driver. These resources are the Adapter Object and map registers.

- **DMA Device Architectures.** This section discusses the differences between packet-based and common-buffer DMA on Windows NT.

- **Packet-Based DMA Transfers.** This section discusses in detail how a driver sets up and manages packet-based DMA transfers.

- **Common-Buffer DMA Transfers.** This section discusses in detail how a driver sets up and manages common-buffer DMA transfers.

- **Packet-Based DMA Sample Driver** To help illustrate the concepts described earlier in the chapter, this section presents a sample packet-based DMA device driver. The source code, description, and functionality are provided for each important routine in the driver.

- **Design Issues.** This section examines the slightly less-common issues of data buffer alignment and System DMA support.

This chapter discusses the details of how a driver implements data transfer operations for DMA devices. As in the preceding chapter on PIO data transfers, this chapter will focus on data transfers that are performed in response to IRP_MJ_READ and IRP_MJ_WRITE requests. However, the concepts presented may also be applied to IRP_MJ_DEVICE_CONTROL requests used for transferring data via DMA.

Processing DMA Data Transfers

As is the case for any I/O request received at a driver's Dispatch entry point, the steps a driver takes to process a DMA data transfer request are as follows:

1. Validate the I/O request.

2. Process the IRP as far as possible.

3. Queue the IRP for further processing if immediate completion is not possible.

DMA data transfer requests are rarely completed immediately because the driver will typically have to wait for the DMA hardware to actually move the data. Therefore, in almost all cases, the driver will return with the IRP pending from its Dispatch routine. The obvious exception to this is when the IRP fails the driver's validation tests.

As was true for PIO data transfers, processing a DMA data transfer consists of implementing the previously stated three steps. When an IRP is received, it is validated, as described in Chapter 14, "Dispatch Entry Points." There may be special considerations for validating I/O requests to DMA devices, however, such as starting buffer alignment or buffer length. These considerations are described later in this chapter. If the request fails the driver's validation tests, the driver fills the appropriate error status and information values into the IRP's IoStatus structure and immediately completes the request by calling IoCompleteRequest().

If the request is valid, the driver checks to see whether the device is available to start the transfer. The way the driver does this is dependent upon the queuing method the driver has chosen. If the driver uses System Queuing, it marks the IRP pending by calling IoMarkIrpPending(), calls IoStartPacket(), and returns STATUS_PENDING from its Dispatch routine. This was shown in Example 14.3, in Chapter 14. As a result of the IoStartPacket() call, the I/O Manager will call the driver's StartIo routine when the device is available to start processing the request.

If the driver uses Driver Queuing, the driver itself determines if the device is available to start the particular transfer operation requested. This determination is completely device-specific. Some DMA devices, such as many devices based on the popular AMCC S5933 chip, are capable of having both a DMA read and a DMA write operation in progress at the same time. Such devices typically cannot, however, have more than one read or write operation in progress simultaneously. It is therefore up to the driver to determine whether the device is available to start the operation being requested.

If the device is not available (because, for example, an IRP_MJ_WRITE operation is being requested and a write is already in progress on a device that allows only a single write operation at a time), the driver will typically mark the IRP pending by calling IoMarkIrpPending(), queue the IRP, and return STATUS_PENDING from the Dispatch routine. In this case, the IRP will be started at a later time, probably from within the DpcForIsr, when the device is able to handle the request. If the device is available to start the transfer, the driver starts processing the request. The driver marks the IRP pending (by calling IoMarkIrpPending()) and returns STATUS_PENDING from the Dispatch routine. This entire process is shown in Example 14.4 in Chapter 14.

Throughout this chapter, our discussion of DMA focuses on Busmaster DMA operations. Unless otherwise explicitly specified, all remarks in this chapter relate only to Busmaster DMA and do not apply to System (otherwise known as "Slave-Mode") DMA. System DMA is discussed in a separate section at the end of this chapter.

Before discussing further how transfer requests are processed, you first need to understand the two resources required by a driver when performing any DMA transfer—the Adapter Object and map registers.

Adapter Objects

All DMA device drivers in Windows NT utilize one or more Adapter Objects for managing DMA transfers. The NT HAL uses Adapter Objects to synchronize access to sharable resources such as mapping registers, HAL internal intermediate buffers, system scatter/gather registers, or DMA channels (for System DMA devices). A byproduct of this is that Packet-Based DMA drivers also typically utilize the Adapter Object to serialize DMA transfers.

During initialization, DMA device drivers call HalGetAdapter() (as described in Chapter 13, "Driver Entry") to get a pointer to an Adapter Object for later use. Recall from that discussion (and Example 13.8 in that Chapter) that HalGetAdapter() takes two input parameters: a pointer to a DEVICE_DESCRIPTION data structure and a pointer to a ULONG variable, in which to return the maximum number of map registers to be used by a device at any one time. The DEVICE_DESCRIPTION data structure describes the characteristics of the DMA device, such as whether it is a Busmaster device, whether it understands 32-bit addresses, the maximum length transfer the device can support, and whether or not it supports scatter/gather. As a result of calling HalGetAdapter(), the HAL returns a pointer to an Adapter Object and also to the maximum number of map registers that the driver should use, both of which the driver stored away for later use.

In the model used by Windows NT, each DMA operation that can be in progress simultaneously requires a separate Adapter Object. Thus, drivers should allocate one Adapter Object for each DMA operation on each device that can be simultaneously in progress. For example, a driver for a device that can have a write operation and a read operation in progress simultaneously should allocate two Adapter Objects: one for use with read operations, and one for use with write operations.

Furthermore, drivers that utilize a combination of Common-Buffer DMA and Packet-Based DMA should allocate a dedicated Adapter Object for the common buffer, and separate Adapter Objects for use in the Packet-Based transfers. When calling HalGetAdapter() to get the Adapter Object for the common buffer, the driver should specify the total size of the common buffer area in the MaximumLength field of the DEVICE_DESCRIPTION data structure.

The advice to use one Adapter Object per simultaneous transfer is contrary to the conventional wisdom, and even the established practice, of many experienced NT driver writers. However, thinking the issue through shows why one Adapter Object per simultaneous transfer is the correct design. Calling HalGetAdapter() informs the HAL of future requirements for DMA resources (such as mapping registers, scatter/gather support, and the like). The HAL may use these calls to determine how many of these resources should be allocated in the system, or perhaps even reserved for use with particular Adapter Objects.

By utilizing one Adapter Object per DMA transfer, the driver accurately reflects to the HAL the level of simultaneous resource usage that the HAL can expect. This is true, even though IoAllocateAdapterChannel() (described later in this chapter) serializes Adapter Object usage because a driver's AdapterControl routine (also described later) can complete but allow the driver to continue to tie up DMA resources (by returning DeallocateObjectKeepRegisters). Further, utilizing multiple Adapter Objects allows the driver to actually initiate multiple DMA operations on a device in parallel with no delay. This is not possible, even when supported by a device, if a single Adapter Object is used.

Map Registers

In the DMA model used by NT, the memory addresses used for DMA operations are termed *logical addresses*. Logical addresses are translated to physical addresses in main host memory by map registers. Depending on the underlying processor architecture and the specific DMA operation being performed, a logical address may be identical to a physical host memory address. Alternatively, a logical address may need to be translated to a physical host memory address by software, hardware, or a combination of both. This was discussed in Chapter 8, "I/O Architectures."

Logical addresses represent the set of addresses directly accessible from a device. Map registers are used to translate such addresses to physical addresses in host memory. For example, ISA bus devices can reference addresses only below 16MB. This 16MB-address space is considered the device's logical addressing capability. Assuming that such a device has been described correctly to the HAL (via the DEVICE_DESCRIPTION data structure, passed to HalGetAdapter()), the HAL will automatically provide the driver with only appropriate logical addresses for its DMA transfers. That is, all the logical addresses provided by the HAL for such a device will always be less than 16MB. Writers of drivers for these devices, therefore, do not need to concern themselves with the location of the requestor's data buffer in physical memory.

> ### Note
>
> *The distinction between logical addresses and physical addresses is very important. DMA operations on NT are always performed to logical addresses. Drivers that perform DMA operations directly by using physical addresses (such as those returned from* MmGetPhysicalAddress()) *violate the NT DMA model. While this will work for some devices on some processor architectures (such as 32-bit Busmaster devices on the x86, where physical addresses can be used as logical addresses), it will not work for all devices on all processors. The only way to ensure cross-platform compatibility is to scrupulously observe the NT DMA model.*

Map registers are also used to implement a facility known as *system scatter/gather*. This facility (not to be confused with *System DMA*) provides devices that do not themselves support DMA transfers from multiple discontiguous physical locations in memory with the capability to transfer physically fragmented data buffers in one DMA operation. Thus, devices that do not support scatter/gather are freed from having to perform multiple DMA transfers in order to complete a request that references a physically fragmented requestor's data buffer. The HAL provides such devices with a single logical base address and length that typically allows the device to transfer the entire contents of a requestor's buffer in one operation. See Chapter 8 for a more complete discussion of how the HAL implements system scatter/gather.

The HAL is responsible for managing map registers and allocating those registers for use by drivers during DMA operations. Each map register is capable of translating, at most, one physical page (that is, PAGE_SIZE bytes) of logical to physical address space. And, like physical pages, each map register starts its addressing on a physical page boundary. Map registers may be associated with a particular Adapter Object by the HAL.

As described in Chapter 8, the way that map registers are implemented on a particular system is totally up to the HAL used on that system. Some NT

HALs, such as the standard x86 HALs, implement map registers entirely via software. Other HALs, such as some of the standard Alpha HALs, implement map registers by using a combination of hardware and software.

Irrespective of the way that map registers are implemented on a particular system, in the NT DMA model, map registers must always be allocated prior to undertaking any DMA transfer. Drivers must request that the HAL allocate enough map registers to complete the transfer, but never more than the maximum number indicated by the HAL as a result of the driver's call to HalGetAdapter() (described previously in this chapter and in Chapter 13). The transfer is then performed, using the map registers to translate from logical to physical memory addresses and to implement system scatter/gather support, if required. After the driver's use of the map registers is complete, the driver must return the map registers it used for the transfer to the HAL for reuse.

> *Tip*
>
> *Map registers are a limited resource that the HAL allocates to drivers as they are needed. Except for drivers that implement Common-Buffer DMA architectures, driver writers should not retain map registers for extended periods of time. This can lead to poor throughput on other devices in the system, and ultimately may even result in total system failure.*

It is extremely important to understand that logical addresses and map registers, like Adapter Objects and the system scatter/gather facility, are conceptual abstractions exported by the HAL. That is, these things are part of the Windows NT conceptual model of DMA processing. There may or may not be any real, hardware, map registers in a given system. However, this is largely irrelevant to the driver writer. As discussed in Chapter 2, "Achieving Hardware Independence with the HAL," the HAL provides driver writers with a single, unchanging, model of processor resources and facilities. Driver writers design and develop their drivers according to this model. The HAL is responsible for converting, as efficiently as possible, between its abstract model and the actual processor resources that happen to be present on a particular system.

Also, as discussed in Chapter 2, performing this conversion efficiently means that the HAL tries not to introduce unnecessary overhead in the process. This is particularly true on systems such as the x86, where the functionality provided by some of the HAL's abstractions is not required. For example, because 32-bit DMA devices can address all of main memory on most x86 systems, the logical addresses used by these devices are in fact physical addresses. If such devices support scatter/gather, the HAL does not actually allocate any map registers during DMA operations by these devices. This is because x86 processors typically do not implement map registers in hardware, and 32-bit Busmaster

DMA devices that support scatter/gather have no need for any additional software-provided support from the HAL. For such devices, the HAL simply provides the driver with the base address and length of each fragment of the requestor's data buffer (via the `IoMapTransfer()` function, discussed later), and gets out of the way while the driver performs the transfer.

On the other hand, typical x86 systems do not provide any hardware facility for implementing features such as system scatter/gather. Therefore, how do typical x86 HALs implement this facility? On standard x86 systems, when a driver for a device that does not support scatter/gather sets up a Packet-Based DMA transfer (using the standard NT DMA procedures), the HAL provides a physically contiguous intermediate buffer for use during the transfer. Thus, for a write operation, the HAL copies the contents of the requestor's physically fragmented data buffer to a physically contiguous intermediate buffer that the HAL allocates and manages internally. The HAL then provides the driver with the logical base address and length of the physically contiguous buffer for use as the base address for the DMA transfer.

The bottom line is that, except in extraordinary circumstances, drivers should follow the NT DMA model. Let the HAL do its job. By programming to the architecture implemented by the HAL, driver writers have the best level of cross-platform compatibility.

DMA Device Architectures

As described previously in Chapter 8, "I/O Architectures," DMA operations in Windows NT fall into one of two categories: Packet-Based DMA and Common-Buffer DMA. Devices, and hence drivers, may utilize one or both of these DMA architectures. The following sections describe the basic characteristics of Packet-Based DMA and Common-Buffer DMA, explain Common-Buffer and Packet-Based DMA transfers, and provide a practical Packet-Based DMA driver example.

Packet-Based DMA

Packet-Based DMA is by far the most common type of DMA used in standard Kernel mode device drivers. In Packet-Based DMA, drivers utilize Direct I/O to describe the requestor's data buffers. The driver provides the logical address and length of each physical fragment of the requestor's data buffer, and the transfer direction, to the device. If a device supports scatter/gather, the driver supplies the device with multiple base address and length pairs per transfer to describe a physically fragmented data buffer. The number of base address and length pairs (and, hence, the number of data buffer fragments) that can be provided to a device at one time is device-dependent. Well-designed scatter/gather devices will typically allow a driver to specify enough fragments to completely describe even an unusually fragmented requestor's buffer, thus allowing the buffer to be transferred in a single DMA operation.

Devices that do not support scatter/gather can process only a single logical base address and length per DMA operation. Therefore, such devices would need to perform multiple DMA operations to transfer a fragmented data buffer. Setting up and managing these multiple DMA transfers can result in significant overhead. To avoid this overhead for non-scatter/gather devices, the NT DMA model provides a facility called *system scatter/gather*. This facility provides the driver with a single logical base address and length, which is then used by the device to transfer the entire requestor's buffer in one DMA operation. One common DMA engine used in PCI devices is the AMCC S5933 (a sample driver for this appears later in this chapter).

Common-Buffer DMA

Common-Buffer DMA operations utilize the same data buffer repeatedly for DMA transfers between the host and the device. The most frequently encountered Common-Buffer architecture is one in which the device and the driver share a buffer in host memory containing device-specific data structures. This is often referred to as "continuous" DMA. An example of this type of device is the "SmartDev" device, described in Chapter 15, "Interrupt Service Routines and DPCs." During the initialization of such a device, a driver typically provides to its device the logical address of a buffer in host memory that the driver has previously allocated and initialized. The driver and device then manipulate the device-defined data structures within this buffer, as required to initiate and complete data transfers. The device will typically access the data structures in host memory, via DMA, without further programming by the driver. Thus, the driver is not necessarily aware of when the device is performing its DMA operations. The device will typically interrupt to indicate a change in status. This interrupt will usually cause the driver to interrogate the data structures in shared memory to determine the action taken by the device. In this approach, the data to be transferred may be copied by the driver between the data structures in shared memory and the requestor's data buffer. More commonly, however, the device-defined data structures in shared memory contain the logical addresses of the physical fragments of the data buffers to be used for the transfer.

Common-Buffer DMA of this kind is most frequently used by high-speed intelligent devices, such as network interface cards or high-end disk devices. The Common-Buffer DMA architecture is well suited for use with these devices because a single device can often have many requests in each direction in progress simultaneously. Using a set of shared data structures in host memory to manage such transfers is often more convenient and efficient than having the driver repeatedly program registers on the device. Because support for this architecture requires firmware in the device, whether or not a driver uses this type of Common-Buffer DMA is inherent in the design of the device.

Another less-frequently utilized form of Common-Buffer DMA is actually a cross between the DMA and PIO architectures. In this approach, the driver allocates a common buffer in host memory that serves as an intermediate buffer for all DMA transfer operations. The driver may provide the logical base address of this buffer to the device during driver initialization. To process a transfer request, the driver moves (under program control) the data to be transferred between the requestor's data buffer and the common buffer in host memory. To start the transfer, the driver programs the device with the length of the transfer and the transfer direction. For example, in devices of this design, when processing a write operation the driver will copy the contents of the requestor's data buffer to the prereserved buffer in host memory. The driver then starts the request on the device by providing the byte count to the device and transferring direction of the DMA operation. The device generates an interrupt when it has finished transferring the data from the common buffer via DMA. In a variant of this scheme, a driver allocates two intermediate common buffers for use by the device: one for read operations and the other for write operations. The decision of whether to implement this type of Common-Buffer DMA is a decision that is made by the driver writer. It is most often used for devices that do not support scatter/gather, and when DMA transfers on the device are expected to be few. However, Windows NT's Packet-Based DMA architecture, and its inherent support for agglomerating physical buffer fragments for devices that do not support scatter/gather, typically makes the use of this design unnecessary.

Comparing Packet-Based DMA with Common-Buffer DMA

The following table summarizes the differences between the Packet-Based and Common-Buffer DMA architectures.

	Packet-Based DMA	Common-Buffer DMA (with requestor data recopy)	Common-Buffer (with transfer directly from requestor's data buffer pages)
DMA operation	Driver programming device	Data structures in common buffer	Data structures in common

continues

	Packet-Based DMA	Common-Buffer DMA (with re-questor data recopy)	Common-Buffer (with transfer directly from requestor's data buffer pages)
	registers	shared between device and driver	buffer shared between device and driver
Requestor's data DMA'd	Original requestor's buffer pages	Common buffer area	Original requestor's buffer pages
Map registers allocated	For each transfer via Io Allocate Adapter Channel()	During initialization via HalAllocate CommonBuffer()	Both during initialization via HalAllocate CommonBuffer() and for each transfer via Io AllocateAdapter Channel()
Map registers returned	After each transfer via IoFreeMap Registers()	On driver unload via HalFreeCommon Buffer()	Registers allocated per transfer freed via IoFreeMap Registers(); Registers allocated for common buffer freed via HalFreeCommon Buffer()

Packet-Based DMA Transfers

When a driver determines that the device that it supports is free to perform a DMA transfer, it initiates the request on the device. The steps required to process the request are typically as follows:

1. **Prepare for the transfer.** This step includes flushing processor cache back to memory, determining the number of map registers to be used for the current transfer, and requesting the HAL (via the I/O Manager) to allocate an Adapter Object and whatever shared resources that might be

required to perform the transfer. When the Adapter Object is free and the HAL has the necessary resources for the transfer available, the driver's AdapterControl routine is called to perform the next step.

2. **Program the device with request information.** In this step, the driver gets the logical base address and length of one or more fragments of the requestor's data buffer, and passes them on to the device. A driver for a device that supports scatter/gather will retrieve and provide the device with multiple base address and length pairs. With the user buffer logical address determined, the driver programs the device to start the transfer.

3. **Complete the transfer.** Once the transfer is complete, the driver flushes any data from system internal DMA caches; and returns any shared resources, such as map registers, that may still be in use.

4. **Propagate the execution of the driver.** The driver next checks to see if the entire request is completed as a result of the transfer just completed. This might not be the case, for example, if a request had to be divided into multiple transfers due to restrictions on the availability of mapping registers. If the request is complete, the driver calls `IoCompleteRequest()` and attempts to initiate a new request, if one is pending. If the request is not complete, the driver initiates a new transfer for the next portion of the request.

The following sections describe the preceding steps in more detail.

Preparing for the Transfer

After a particular IRP to process has been selected, and it has been determined that the device is available to perform a request, a driver undertakes a few steps in preparation for a Packet-Based DMA data transfer. This preparation involves ensuring that the driver, the device, and the HAL are all in the proper state for the DMA transfer to be requested. If a driver uses System Queuing for management of its IRPs, this preparation phase will typically take place in the StartIo routine. In a driver that uses Driver Queuing, the preparation will be done after the driver has determined that a request can be started on a given device.

The first thing a driver does to prepare the system for the transfer is to ensure that the contents of the requestor's data buffer is sufficiently coherent with the host's processor cache to allow the transfer. This is done by calling the function `KeFlushIoBuffers()`, the prototype for which is shown in Figure 17.1:

VOID
KeFlushIoBuffers(IN PMDL *Mdl*,
    IN BOOLEAN *ReadOperation*,
    IN BOOLEAN *DmaOperation*);

Mdl: A pointer to an MDL that describes the buffer to be flushed.

ReadOperation: A boolean value, indicating the direction of the transfer planned for the buffer. TRUE indicates the transfer will be a read operation (out of memory and to the device).

DmaOperation: If set to TRUE, indicates that the buffer is planned for transfer via DMA.

Figure 17.1. `KeFlushIoBuffers()` *function prototype.*

On some RISC processors, DMA operations are not coherent with respect to the contents of processor cache. That is, DMA write operations (from memory to the device) are performed on main memory without consideration of the contents of the processor's cache. Likewise, DMA read operations (from the device into memory) update main memory but do not necessarily automatically update or invalidate the contents of the processor cache for the requestor's buffer. The result of this lack of coherency is that the processor cache and main memory can hold different values, and the DMA operation appears to "not work right."

To avoid this problem, drivers call `KeFlushIoBuffers()` prior to performing any DMA operations. This function takes a pointer to the MDL that describes the requestor's buffer, as well as a pair of BOOLEAN values that indicates whether the request is a DMA request and the direction of the transfer. `KeFlushIoBuffers()` uses this information and flushes the requestor's data buffer from processor cache to host main memory, if this is required to correctly perform the DMA operation. Note that x86 architecture systems are cache-coherent with respect to DMA operations. Therefore, `KeFlushIoBuffers()` is defined in NTDDK.H for x86 systems as a null macro.

After calling `KeFlushIoBuffers()`, the driver next determines the number of map registers it will request from the HAL for this transfer. In the NT DMA model, a driver requests and returns map registers for every DMA transfer. The HAL determines whether the map registers are actually required, and provides them only if necessary. The number of map registers that the driver requests will typically be the number required to completely map the requestor's data buffer. One map register is required for each physical memory page that contains data to be transferred. The driver may determine the number of physical memory pages spanned by the requestor's buffer by using the macro ADDRESS_AND_SIZE_TO_SPAN_PAGES. Figure 17.2 illustrates this macro.

ULONG
ADDRESS_AND_SIZE_TO_SPAN_PAGES(IN PVOID *Va*,
   IN ULONG *Size*);

Va: An address, not necessarily in the current operating mode, indicating the start of a buffer

Size: Length, in bytes, of the buffer

Figure 17.2. `ADDRESS_AND_SIZE_TO_SPAN_PAGES` *macro.*

Using the virtual address and size of the requestor's data buffer, the `ADDRESS_AND_SIZE_TO_SPAN_PAGES` macro determines the number of physical pages that the data buffer references.

The virtual address of the requestor's buffer (in the requestor's mode), which is passed to the macro as the *Va* parameter, can be retrieved from the MDL by using the function `MmGetMdlVirtualAddress()`, which is shown in Figure 17.3.

VOID
MmGetMdlVirtualAddress(IN PMDL *Mdl*);

Mdl: A pointer to an initialized MDL.

Figure 17.3. `MmGetMdlVirtualAddress()` *function prototype.*

Remember that the MDL is an opaque data structure. It is never a good idea to directly access the fields within the MDL. Always use the functions supplied by the Memory Manager. In most cases, these functions are actually macros that expand to reference the appropriate MDL fields. This is the case, for example, with `MmGetMdlVirtualAddress()`.

Note

Don't confuse the functions `MmGetMdlVirtualAddress()` *(used here) and* `MmGetSystemAddressForMdl()` *(described in Chapter 16, "Programmed I/O Data Transfers")! These are two very different Memory Manager functions with similar-sounding names. Both take as input a pointer to an MDL and return a* PVOID. `MmGetMdlVirtualAddress()` *returns the requestor's virtual address of the start of the data buffer described by an MDL, simply by returning the contents of one of the MDL's internal fields.* `MmGetSystemAddressForMdl()`, *on the other hand, performs a memory-management operation that maps the requestor's data buffer described by an MDL into kernel virtual address space.*

Referring to Figure 17.3, you'll note that even a data buffer that is less than one page long can span memory in two physical pages. This is because the data can start at the end of one page and continue into the start of another, as shown in Figure 17.4.

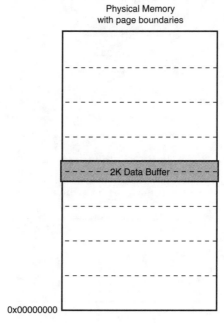

Figure 17.4. *A 2K-user data buffer spanning two physical memory pages.*

A driver is not always allowed to request the number of map registers required to map the entire requestor's buffer, however. Recall that when the driver called HalGetAdapter() during initialization, the HAL returned the maximum number of map registers that the driver could use at one time. The driver is therefore constrained to request no more than this number of map registers for a given transfer. Thus, if a requestor's buffer requires more map registers than the HAL will allow the driver to request, the driver must request only the maximum number allowed by the HAL. This will result in the driver having to process the request as multiple DMA transfers, each one using no more than the maximum number of map registers allowed by the HAL.

The code segment in Example 17.1 that follows shows the process of determining the number of map registers that will be requested by the driver:

Example 17.1. Determining the number of map registers that will be used by the driver for a particular transfer.

```
//
// How many map registers are need to entirely map the requestor's
// buffer?
//
requestorsVa = MmGetMdlVirtualAddress(Irp->MdlAddress);

mapRegsNeeded =
    ADDRESS_AND_SIZE_TO_SPAN_PAGES(requestorsVa,
                                   ioStack->Parameters.Write.Length);

//
// Determine the number of map registers we'll request from the HAL
// for this transfer.  Use the number required to map the entire
// requestor's buffer unless that exceeds the maximum number the
// HAL told us we could ask for when we called HalGetAdapter()
//
if (mapRegsNeeded > devExt->MapRegsGot) {

    devExt->MapRegsThisDma = devExt->MapRegsGot;

} else {

    devExt->MapRegsThisDma = mapRegsNeeded;
}
```

The driver in the example code determines the requestor's virtual buffer address, given the MDL address in the IRP being processed by calling `MmGetMdlVirtualAddress()`. The resulting value is passed—along with the length of the requestor's buffer, as determined from the `Parameters.Write.Length` field in the IRP's current I/O Stack Location—to the `ADDRESS_AND_SIZE_TO_SPAN_PAGES` macro. This macro returns the number of pages, and hence the number of map registers, required to completely map the requestor's data buffer. The driver determines the number of map registers it will request from the HAL by using this value. However, the driver limits the number of map registers it will request to the maximum number of map registers that the HAL indicated the driver may request as a return value from `HalGetAdapter()`. Example 13.8 in Chapter 13 shows where this maximum value is returned. The driver stores the number of map registers that will be used for the current DMA operation in its device extension for later use.

Once the driver has flushed the requestor's data buffer from processor cache and determines the number of map registers to be requested for the current transfer, the driver is ready to request the HAL to allocate the resources required for the transfer. The driver does this by calling `IoAllocateAdapterChannel()`. The prototype is shown in Figure 17.5.

NTSTATUS
IoAllocateAdapterChannel(IN PADAPTER_OBJECT *AdapterObject,*
        IN PDEVICE_OBJECT *DeviceObject,*
        IN ULONG *NumberOfMapRegisters,*
        IN PDRIVER_CONTROL *ExecutionRoutine,*
        IN PVOID *Context*);

AdapterObject: A pointer to the Adapter Object for the transfer

DeviceObject: A pointer to the Device Object representing the device for the transfer.

NumberOfMapRegisters: The number of map registers the driver is requesting the HAL to reserve for this transfer.

ExecutionRoutine: A pointer to the driver's AdapterControl routine.

Context: A driver-defined context argument to be passed to the driver's AdapterControl routine.

Figure 17.5. *IoAllocateAdapterChannel() function prototype.*

IoAllocateAdapterChannel() takes as input a pointer to the Adapter Object and Device Object, as well as the number of map registers being requested for the transfer. This function also takes a pointer to the driver's AdapterControl routine and a context value to be passed to that routine. The only "trick" to calling IoAllocateAdapterChannel() is that it must be called at IRQL DISPATCH_LEVEL. This is not usually a problem because drivers often call this function from either their StartIo or DpcForIsr routines, which are already running at IRQL DISPATCH_LEVEL. If a driver is running at an IRQL lower than DISPATCH_LEVEL, it need only call KeRaiseIrql() to raise its IRQL to DISPATCH_LEVEL, call IoAllocateAdapterChannel(), and then call KeLowerIrql() to return the IRQL to the previous level.

When the adapter pointed to by *AdapterObject* and the number of map registers indicated by *NumberOfMapRegisters* are available, the HAL calls the driver's AdapterControl routine pointed to by *ExecutionRoutine*, passing *Context* as a parameter. Figure 17.6 shows the prototype for the driver's AdapterControl routine. It is within the driver's AdapterControl routine that the driver can program the device to actually perform the transfer.

IO_ALLOCATION_ACTION
AdapterControl(IN PDEVICE_OBJECT *DeviceObject*,
    IN PIRP *Irp*,
    IN PVOID *MapRegisterBase*,
    IN PVOID *Context*);

DeviceObject: A pointer to the Device Object representing the device for the transfer.

Irp: If the driver uses System Queuing, this is a pointer to the IRP currently in progress on *DeviceObject*. Otherwise, this parameter is unused.

MapRegisterBase: A handle returned by the HAL, indicating the start of a range of map registers reserved for the transfer.

Context: A driver-defined context argument passed from the driver's call to IoAllocateAdapterChannel().

When Called: When requested DMA resources are available, as a result of a driver's call to IoAllocateAdapterObject().

Context: Arbitrary

IRQL: DISPATCH_LEVEL

Figure 17.6. *AdapterControl routine entry point.*

Programming the Device

The HAL calls the driver's AdapterControl routine when all of the resources required to perform the transfer are available. The AdapterControl routine is always called at IRQL DISPATCH_LEVEL and in an arbitrary thread context. The HAL passes four parameters in to the AdapterControl routine, as follows:

- *DeviceObject*. A pointer to the Device Object on which the transfer is to be requested.

- *Irp*. The contents of DeviceObject->CurrentIrp, which is a pointer to the current IRP to be processed *if the driver uses System Queuing*. If the driver does not use System Queuing, this parameter is meaningless and should be ignored.

- *MapRegisterBase*. A handle that the HAL uses to identify the block of map registers that have been reserved for use by this transfer operation. The driver will provide this handle as input to IoMapTransfer(), described later.

- *Context*. The *Context* parameter, passed by the driver in its call to IoAllocateAdapterChannel(). For drivers that use Driver Queuing, this parameter is often a pointer to the IRP to be processed.

It is the goal of the driver's AdapterControl routine to program the device and initiate the DMA transfer. To do this, the driver will get the logical base address and length of the fragments that comprise the requestor's data buffer. Recall that if the device supports scatter/gather, multiple logical base address and length pair will likely be required to describe the requestor's buffer. Also, recall that if the device does not support scatter/gather, NT's system scatter/gather facility (as provided by the HAL) will agglomerate the physically fragmented requestor's buffer and provide a single logical base address and length that the driver will use for the transfer.

However, there is a slight complication involved. The driver may not use more map registers for the transfer than were reserved by the HAL. The number of map registers reserved by the HAL was either the number of map registers required to completely map the requestor's buffer, or the maximum number of map registers that the driver is allowed by the HAL to request at one time, whichever is smaller. The number of map registers to request the HAL to reserve was determined by the driver prior to calling IoAllocateAdapterChannel(), and passed as a parameter to the function call.

This complication means that within the AdapterControl routine, the driver may not be able to initiate a single DMA request that will handle all of the requestor's data buffer. This is true, irrespective of whether or not the device supports scatter/gather. When the requestor's data buffer is larger than can be mapped with the maximum number of map registers that the driver is allowed to request, the request will need to be split into multiple transfers.

To get the logical base address and length of the requestor's data buffer fragments, the driver calls the function IoMapTransfer(). The prototype is shown in Figure 17.7.

PHYSICAL_ADDRESS
IoMapTransfer(IN PADAPTER_OBJECT *AdapterObject,*
    IN PMDL *Mdl,*
    IN PVOID *MapRegisterBase,*
    IN PVOID *CurrentVa,*
    IN OUT PULONG *Length*
    IN BOOLEAN *WriteToDevice*);

AdapterObject: A pointer to the Adapter Object for the transfer.

Mdl: A pointer to the MDL that represents the requestor's buffer for the transfer.

MapRegisterBase: The HAL-supplied handle of the same name, passed in to the driver at its AdapterControl routine.

CurrentVa: A pointer, in the requestor's address space, to the starting location in *Mdl* for this transfer.

Length: Length, in bytes, of the transfer.

WriteToDevice: BOOLEAN indicating the direction of the transfer. TRUE indicates a transfer to the device (out of memory).

Figure 17.7. `IoMapTransfer()` *function prototype.*

`IoMapTransfer()` is a rather inconvenient and even confusing function to call. Parameters to this function include a pointer to the Adapter Object to be used for the transfer (*AdapterObject*); a pointer to the MDL that describes the requestor's data buffer to be used for the transfer (*Mdl*); and the MapRegisterBase value, as passed into the AdapterControl routine. Note that drivers of Busmaster devices traditionally pass NULL as the pointer to the Adapter Object when calling this function. However, either NULL or a pointer to the Adapter Object may actually be passed. `IoMapTransfer()` also takes a BOOLEAN (*WriteToDevice*) that indicates the direction of the transfer (set to TRUE if the operation is a DMA write operation—going to the device). These parameters are all easy enough to manage.

`IoMapTransfer()` takes two additional parameters, described in the following short list:

- *CurrentVa.* This is a pointer to the next location in the requestor's data buffer to be transferred, in the requestor's virtual address space. This pointer is used by `IoMapTransfer()` as an index into the current data buffer. The initial value for this parameter is obtained by the driver calling `MmGetMdlVirtualAddress()` with a pointer to the MDL describing the requestor's data buffer. After each call to IoMapTransfer(), this pointer must be incremented by the length of the requestor's data buffer fragment returned from the call.

- *Length*. This is a pointer to a ULONG variable. On input to IoMapTransfer(), the content of this variable is the remaining length of the requestor's data buffer. That is, it contains the number of bytes of the requestor's data buffer that have not yet been described by logical base address and length pairs returned by IoMapTransfer(). On output from IoMapTransfer(), the content of this variable contains the size, in bytes, of the current fragment of the requestor's buffer.

The return value from a call to IoMapTransfer() is the logical base address of the fragment of the requestor's buffer that starts at *CurrentVa*. As previously mentioned, the length of that fragment is returned as the contents of the *Length* parameter.

Drivers that do not implement scatter/gather will make a single call to IoMapTransfer(), as shown in Example 17.2 that follows.

Example 17.2. Calling IoMapTransfer() *in a driver for a non-scatter/gather device.*

```
totalLength = ioStack->Parameters.Write.Length;
length = totalLength;
baseVirtualAddress = MmGetMdlVirtualAddress(irp->MdlAddress);

logicalBaseAddress = IoMapTransfer(NULL,
                        irp->MdlAddress,
                        MapRegisterBase,
                        baseVirtualAddress,
                        &length,
                        TRUE);      // WriteToDevice
```

On return from the call to IoMapTransfer() in Example 17.2, logicalBaseAddress contains the logical base address to be used for the DMA transfer, and length contains the length of the fragment starting at logicalBaseAddress. Note that the total length of the request is saved in totalLength. The only time that the returned length of the requestor's buffer fragment will not be equal to the total length of the requestor's buffer (that is, length != totalLength) is if the number of map registers reserved for the operation is insufficient to map the entire requestor's buffer. If this is the case, the driver will need to initiate another DMA transfer to complete the request when this transfer is complete.

Although it is true that one map register is capable of mapping only one physical page at one time, typical NT HALs provide drivers with the obvious optimization: When IoMapTransfer() *is called, if map registers span adjacent logical pages, the HAL will return the logical base address of the first map register as the base of the fragment, and the total length of the spanned area as the fragment length. Therefore, for example, if a 10K-transfer is mapped by three adjacent map registers,* IoMapTransfer() *on most HALs will return the logical base address of the first map register and a length of 10K (as opposed to returning three separate fragments). Of course, different HALs can do different things, so there is no guarantee that this optimization will be provided.*

Recall from the earlier discussion that typical x86 HALs implement NT's system scatter/gather facility (used by devices that do not themselves support scatter/gather) by copying data between the physically fragmented requestor's buffer to a physically contiguous, HAL-controlled intermediate buffer. It is during the call to IoMapTransfer() that the HALs typically do this copy for write operations.

The process of calling IoMapTransfer() is slightly more complicated for drivers of devices that implement scatter/gather. Example 17.3 shows a complete AdapterControl function for a scatter/gather driver:

Example 17.3. Calling IoMapTransfer() *in a driver for a device that supports scatter/gather.*

```
FooAdapterControlWrite(PDEVICE_OBJECT DevObj, PIRP Irp,
                  PVOID MapRegisterBase, PVOID Context)
{
    PVOID baseVa;
    ULONG length, mapRegsLeft;
    PHYSICAL_ADDRESS laToGiveDevice;
    PIO_STACK_LOCATION ioStack;
    FOO_DEVICE_EXTENSION devExt;

    devExt = DevObj->DeviceExtension;

    ioStack=IoGetCurrentIrpStackLocation(Irp);

    //
    // Save the map register base for use in the DpcForIsr.
    // We'll need this to call both IoFlushAdapterBuffers() and
    // IoFreeMapRegisters()
    //
    devExt->MapRegBase = MapRegisterBase;
```

continues

Continued

```
//
// Get the length of the current request.  At this point,
// devExt->LengthSoFar contains either zero (if this is the
// first part of this request) or the length already transferred
// (if we've had to split a request into multiple transfers due
// to the length of the requestor's data buffer exceeding
// the maximum number of map registers available).
//
length = ioStack->Parameters.Write.Length -
                              devExt->LengthSoFar;


//
// Remember where this request started.  We'll need this in the
// DpcForIsr to call IoFlushAdapterBuffers().
//
devExt->StartingOffset = devExt->LengthSoFar;


//
// Pointer to start of the transfer, in requestor's virtual
// address space.
//
baseVa = MmGetMdlVirtualAddress(Irp->MdlAddress);


//
// Number of map registers requested when IoAllocateAdapterChannel()
// was called
//
mapRegsLeft = devExt->MapRegsThisDma;


//
// As long as there are still fragments to map, and we have
// map registers, map them, and put them into scatter/gather list
//
While(length && mapRegsLeft--) {

    laToGiveDevice = IoMapTransfer(NULL,
                                   Irp->MdlAddress,
                                   MapRegisterBase,
                                   baseVa+devExt->LengthSoFar,
                                   &length,
                                   TRUE);


    //
    // Store the logical address/length pair for our device.
    // Note that the precise mechanism used to do this is
    // a function of our device, not NT.
    //
    FooSetFragToWrite(laToGiveDevice, length);

    devExt->LengthSoFar += length;
```

```
        length = ioStack->Parameters.Write.Length -
                        devExt->LengthSoFar
    }

    //
    // Program the device to start the DMA write.
    // Again, the manner we use to accomplish this is
    // a function of our device, not NT.
    //
    FooStartTheDmaWrite(devExt);

    return(DeallocateObjectKeepRegisters);
}
```

The code in Example 17.3 iteratively calls IoMapTransfer(), receiving back from each call the logical base address and length of a fragment of the requestor's data buffer. Each time after returning from IoMapTransfer(), the driver immediately calls its own internal function FooSetFragToWrite(), which passes the logical base address and length pair to the device. When all the fragments that comprise the buffer have been retrieved, or when the number of available map registers has been reached, the driver calls its own internal function FooStartTheDmaWrite() to initiate the DMA request on the device.

As was the case for the non-scatter/gather device driver, the only time that this driver will leave its AdapterControl routine without having set up a DMA operation for the entire requestor's buffer is if the requestor's buffer required more map registers than the HAL allowed the driver to reserve at one time.

With its device programmed to initiate the DMA transfer, the driver returns from its AdapterControl routine. However, on return from its AdapterControl routine, the driver must tell the HAL what to do with the Adapter Object and map registers that it reserved prior to AdapterControl being called. To do this, the driver must return one of the following three return values from its AdapterControl routine:

- **KeepObject.** This status value indicates that the driver does not want the HAL to return either the allocated Adapter Object or the allocated map registers. This value is typically returned by drivers of System (that is, Slave-mode) DMA devices. Drivers returning this status will need to manually return both the Adapter Object and the map registers used during the transfer.

- **DeallocateObject.** This status indicates that the HAL should return both the allocated Adapter Object and the allocated map registers. This value might be used by a Busmaster DMA driver that determines, for some unusual reason, that a transfer will not be started from its AdapterControl routine.

- **DeallocateObjectKeepRegisters.** This status instructs the HAL that the Adapter Object is free, but the mapping registers that have been allocated for the driver are still in use. This is the status that most Busmaster DMA device drivers return from their AdapterControl routines. Drivers that return this status will need to manually return the map registers after the transfer has completed.

With the DMA operation requested on the device, the driver waits for the device to indicate that it has completed the transfer.

Completing the Transfer

Once the device has completed the DMA transfer, it will typically interrupt. When the driver's interrupt service routine is called, it will usually request a DpcForIsr. The driver completes the transfer within the DpcForIsr routine.

Completing the transfer involves flushing caches and returning resources that were reserved for the transfer.

Flushing Caches

To flush any data that may remain in the DMA controller on some systems, drivers call the function IoFlushAdapterBuffers(), the prototype for which appears in Figure 17.8.

BOOLEAN
IoFlushAdapterBuffers(IN PADAPTER_OBJECT *AdapterObject,*
        IN PMDL *Mdl,*
        IN PVOID *MapRegisterBase,*
        IN PVOID *CurrentVa,*
        IN OUT PULONG *Length*
        IN BOOLEAN *WriteToDevice*);

AdapterObject: A pointer to the Adapter Object for the transfer.

Mdl: A pointer to the MDL that represents the requestor's buffer for the transfer.

MapRegisterBase: The HAL-supplied handle of the same name, passed in to the driver at its AdapterControl routine.

CurrentVa: Pointer, in the requestor's address space, to the starting location in *Mdl* for this transfer.

Length: Length, in bytes, of the transfer.

WriteToDevice: BOOLEAN indicating the direction of the transfer. TRUE indicates a transfer to the device (out of memory).

Figure 17.8. IoFlushAdapterBuffers() *function prototype.*

The `IoFlushAdapterBuffers()` function must be called by all DMA drivers to complete a DMA transfer. Note that the following are all input parameters to this function: a pointer to the MDL describing the data buffer, the map register base used during the transfer, the starting virtual address of the transfer in the requestor's virtual address space, and the length of the transfer. These values must therefore be stored away by the driver in the AdapterControl routine, so that they are available for this function call.

> **Note**
>
> *Recall from the earlier discussion that typical x86 HALs implement NT's system scatter/gather facility (used by devices that do not themselves support scatter/gather) by copying data between the physically fragmented requestor's buffer and a physically contiguous, HAL-controlled intermediate buffer. HALs typically do this copy for read operations during the call to* `IoFlushAdapterBuffers()`.

Returning Resources Used During the Transfer

After calling `IoFlushAdapterBuffers()`, drivers must return any resources that were reserved for use during the transfer operation, but not freed on return from the AdapterControl routine. For Busmaster DMA devices, this means returning the map registers that were retained when the AdapterControl routine returned the status `DeallocateObjectKeepRegisters`. To return the retained map registers, drivers call `IoFreeMapRegisters()`, the prototype for which is shown in Figure 17.9

VOID
IoFreeMapRegisters(IN PADAPTER_OBJECT *AdapterObject*,
    IN PVOID *MapRegisterBase*,
    IN ULONG *NumberOfMapRegisters*);

AdapterObject: A pointer to the Adapter Object for the transfer.

MapRegisterBase: The HAL-supplied handle of the same name, passed in to the driver at its AdapterControl routine.

NumberOfMapRegisters: The number of map registers allocated for the (now complete) transfer, as specified when the driver called IoAllocateAdapterChannel().

Figure 17.9. `IoFreeMapRegisters()` *function prototype.*

As shown in the prototype, `IoFreeMapRegsiters()` takes as input a pointer to the Adapter Object used for the transfer, as well as the map register base and the number of map registers used for the transfer. Note that as a result of freeing the map registers, drivers that had called `IoAllocateAdapterChannel()` but were awaiting map registers before their AdapterControl routine could be called, may have their wait satisfied.

> ### Note
>
> *Drivers must correctly track the number of map registers they are using and the associated map register base. Typical HALs do not track the map registers that devices have outstanding, once the Adapter Object associated with that transfer has been returned. Thus, failure to call* `IoFreeMapRegister()`, *or calling* `IoFreeMapRegisters()` *with incorrect values for MapRegisterBase and NumberOfMapRegisters, can result in undesirable system behavior.*

With the adapter buffers flushed and the map registers returned, it is time for the driver to complete the current request, if possible, and propagate its execution by finding the next operation to perform.

Propagating Driver Execution

With a DMA transfer operation completed, the driver must next determine whether the entire current request is complete. In most cases, it will be; however, in the case in which the transfer was limited by the number of map registers available to the driver, the driver will have to set up and perform another DMA transfer for the remaining part of the requestor's buffer. If the entire current request is complete, the driver completes the IRP describing the request, and attempts to start another request on the now free device. Example 17.4 illustrates these steps.

Example 17.4. DMA completion processing.

```
//
// Did this completed transfer also complete the entire current
// request?
//
if( (ioStack->Parameters.Write.Length - devExt->LengthSoFar) > 0) {

    //
    // Nope.  More left to do.  Re-allocate the Adapter Object and
    // necessary map registers and continue.  First, determine how many
    // map registers we'll request for this transfer.
    //
    baseVa = MmGetMdlVirtualAddress(irp->MdlAddress) + devExt->LengthSoFar;

    length = ioStack->Parameters.Write.Length - devExt->LengthSoFar;

    mapRegsNeeded = ADDRESS_AND_SIZE_TO_SPAN_PAGES(baseVa, length);

    //
```

```
                // Limit the number of map registers being requested to the maximum
                // the HAL said we could ask for.
                //
                if (mapRegsNeeded > devExt->MapRegsGot) {

                    devExt->MapRegsThisDma = devExt->MapRegsGot;

                } else {

                    devExt->MapRegsThisDma = mapRegsNeeded;

                }

                IoAllocateAdapterChannel(devExt->Adapter,
                                DevObj,
                                devExt->MapRegsThisDma,
                                FooAdapterControlWrite,
                                NULL);
            } else {

                //
                // The current IRP is done.  Complete it and attempt to start another
                //
                Irp->IoStatus.Status = STATUS_SUCCESS;

                Irp->IoStatus.Information = ioStack->parameters.write.length;

                IoCompleteRequest(Irp, IO_NO_INCREMENT);

                devExt->LengthSoFar = 0;

                IoStartNextPacket(DevObj, FALSE);
            }
```

As Example 17.4 demonstrates, if the current transfer completed the pending request, the driver completes the IRP describing the pending request, and attempts to start a new request. If the driver uses System Queuing, as in the preceding example, the driver calls IoStartNextPacket() to inform the I/O Manager that the device represented by DevObj is available to start another request. If using Driver Queuing, the driver checks its own internal queues to determine whether there is another request to be started.

On the other hand, if the entire requestor's buffer has not yet been processed, the driver sets up to process the remaining piece of the user's buffer. This entails determining the number of map registers to be requested. The number requested is either the number required to map the remainder of the requestor's buffer or the maximum number the driver is allowed by the HAL to use, whichever is smaller. And, again, IoAllocateAdapterChannel() is called to reserve the resources required for the transfer.

Note

If you find it too cumbersome to track how much of the requestor's buffer has been transferred, and to check whether it will require additional transfers to complete a request, here's an idea. If practical for your device and applications, you can limit the maximum size transfer that your driver will accept to the maximum size that can be described using the number of map registers that HAL will allow your driver to reserve. Simply take the maximum number of map registers value returned by the HAL from HalGetAdapter(), subtract one, and multiply by PAGE_SIZE. *Then reject any requests that are larger than the resulting value in your Dispatch routine with* STATUS_INVALID_PARAMETER. *This results in your driver always being able to process a DMA request in one transfer.*

Although this may sound a bit extreme (and, we admit, it is a bit of a "hack"), it's not as bad as it first sounds. Further, taking this approach can eliminate coding and testing a lot of cumbersome code.

The reason this approach isn't quite as bad as it may at first seem is that the number of mapping registers that the standard HALs allow drivers to reserve is not typically determined dynamically based on system load. Thus, the value returned is not likely to change for a given platform. In most cases, you will find that this approach results in a maximum transfer length of at least 64KB.

Further, drivers for 32-bit Busmaster DMA devices that support scatter/gather can use this strategy particularly effectively. This strategy is effective because these drivers are rarely limited in the number of map registers they are allowed to allocate by the HAL. In fact, on typical x86 processors, drivers for these devices do not, in fact, utilize any map registers at all.

Of course, this "trick" works only if you have control of the applications that will be using your driver. If applications are written to try larger buffer sizes, but back off to smaller ones, this approach can be useful. Of course, if you must support existing applications that don't back off, this won't work for you. Although we don't recommend this approach be used for most typical drivers, there are special cases where it might be worthwhile.

Common-Buffer DMA Transfers

The steps required to process Common-Buffer DMA transfers are far more device-specific than those required for Packet-Based DMA transfers. In general, the following steps will be required to process Common-Buffer DMA transfers:

1. **Allocate the common buffer.** During initialization, the driver will usually allocate a common buffer. This buffer will comprise the shared ("common") memory area accessed by both the device and the driver.

2. **Perform the transfer using the common buffer.** This may be as simple as copying data from the requestor's buffer to the common buffer, or as complex as setting up a Packet-Based DMA transfer with the scatter/gather list stored in a device-specific data structure in the common buffer. In either case, the driver uses device-specific means to complete the transfer.

3. **Propagate the driver's execution.** The device will typically interrupt when there is work for the driver to do. The driver will typically interrogate the device-specific structures in shared memory, and determine if in-progress requests may be completed and if pending requests may be started.

The following sections describe the preceding steps in more detail.

Allocating the Common Buffer

The first step to setting up a driver to support Common-Buffer DMA is, not surprisingly, allocating the buffer. The common buffer should usually be allocated as early as possible in the driver, preferably during driver initialization processing. This gives the driver the best chance to get the contiguous memory required for the buffer.

Drivers that perform Common-Buffer DMA operations should get an Adapter Object from the HAL, exclusively for use with the common buffer. To do this, drivers should specify the total size of the common buffer area in the MaximumLength field of the DEVICE_DESCRIPTION data structure. Drivers should also indicate that their devices support scatter/gather by setting the ScatterGather field of the DEVICE_DESCRIPTION data structure to TRUE.

A common buffer for DMA operations is allocated by using the function HalAllocateCommonBuffer(). This function and the process of allocating the common buffer were described in Chapter 13, "Driver Entry," in the section "Common Buffers for DMA Devices." Refer to that section to review the important details on how common buffers are allocated.

To briefly review the information discussed in Chapter 13, HalAllocateCommonBuffer() takes as input a pointer to an Adapter Object, the length of the buffer to allocate, and a BOOLEAN value indicating whether the memory should be cached or noncached. Drivers should typically allocate noncached memory for a common buffer. The function returns both the kernel virtual address and the logical address of the common buffer for use in DMA operations. HalAllocateCommonBuffer() is a very clever function that refers to the Adapter Object passed as input and allocates memory that is appropriate for the device. That is, when a driver for an ISA bus device calls `HalAllocateCommonBuffer()`, the logical address of the memory returned will always be less than 16MB.

> **Note**
>
> *We said it in Chapter 13, but it's worth repeating here: Drivers that require buffers for DMA operations must allocate them by using* `HalAllocateCommonBuffer()` *(or a manual alternative to this function). A very common driver error is to allocate memory for DMA transfers by calling* `MmAllocateContiguousMemory()` *and then getting the physical address by calling* `MmGetPhysicalAddress()`. *This is obviously incorrect because in the NT model, DMA operations are performed to logical addresses, not physical addresses. And while this will work on current x86 platforms (where physical addresses can be used directly as logical addresses), this will not work on other systems.*

Performing the Transfer

Common-Buffer Busmaster DMA processing is very different, depending on the type of device being supported. For simple Common-Buffer devices, in which the driver copies the data between the requestor's data buffer and the common buffer, performing a transfer is much like performing a PIO request to a shared memory block. The driver manipulates structures within the common buffer to control transfers.

Unlike shared memory in PIO devices, however, drivers for Common-Buffer devices may copy data between the requestor's data buffer and the common buffer by using `RtlCopyMemory()`, which is the NT runtime library equivalent of `memcpy()`. This is because the common buffer actually resides in host memory, not on a device (as with PIO shared memory). As is the case for PIO device drivers, Common-Buffer drivers typically use whatever method is convenient (Direct I/O, Buffered I/O, or Neither I/O) to describe I/O requests.

> **Note**
>
> *If the common buffer was allocated cached, which is normally not a good idea, drivers will need to flush data back from processor cache to the common buffer at appropriate times by using* `KeFlushIoBuffers()`. *In order to call* `KeFlushIoBuffers()`, *a driver must build an MDL (using* `IoAllocateMdl()` *and* `MmBuildMdlForNonPagedPool()`, *which are described later) to describe the common buffer. Note that there is no equivalent for* `IoFlushAdapterBuffers()`, *which is used (or needed) for Common-Buffer DMA.*

Some Common-Buffer DMA devices utilize a shared set of data structures in memory that contain one or more scatter/gather lists for DMA operations. Figure 17.10 shows an example of such a set of data structures.

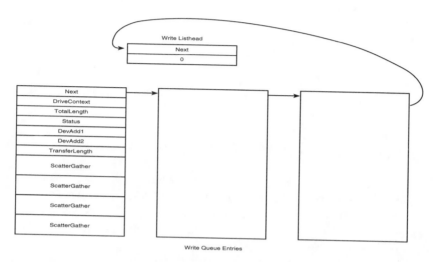

Figure 17.10. *Example of Common-Buffer DMA data structures.*

These drivers are identical to Packet-Based DMA drivers, except that the device is controlled via shared data structures in host memory, instead of via I/O Ports or memory-based registers. Thus, drivers for these devices utilize Direct I/O and Driver Queuing to manage incoming requests.

On receiving a request in its Dispatch routine, the driver determines if the device is available to initiate a new operation; if it is, the driver determines the number of map registers to request from the HAL. Just as for Packet-Based DMA, drivers for these devices are subject to the HAL-imposed limit on the number of map registers that can be used. The driver next marks the IRP pending (calling IoMarkIrpPending()), and calls HalGetAdapter() to allocate the Adapter Object and any necessary map registers. The driver then returns STATUS_PENDING from its Dispatch routine to the I/O Manager.

In the AdapterControl routine, the driver iteratively calls IoMapTransfer() to build the scatter/gather list to give the device. The driver then fills in the appropriate shared structures in the common buffer to appropriately program the device and initiate the transfer.

Propagating Driver Execution

Common-Buffer DMA devices typically indicate a change of status via an interrupt. When an interrupt is received, the driver will typically query the shared memory data structures to determine what actions to take. Taking the data structures shown in Figure 17.10 as an example once again, on receiving an interrupt, the driver requests a DpcForIsr. In the DpcForIsr, the driver traverses the write request queue, checking the status field in each entry, to determine if it is complete. If the request is complete, the driver will remove the request from the list and call IoCompleteRequest() on the IRP associated with the request.

When one or more operations are completed, the driver determines whether others may be started. Again, this operation is completely device- and driver-specific.

Packet-Based DMA Driver Example

To illustrate some of the concepts discussed so far in this chapter, let's examine parts of a complete driver example for a popular DMA device. Just as we did in Chapter 16 on PIO, we'll look at all the code entailed in processing a transfer request, starting with the Dispatch routine and completing in the DpcForIsr. This driver example supports the AMCC S5933 DMA controller, as used in the DK1 evaluation board for that device (the PCI Matchmaker Controller Developer's Kit, available from AMCC distributors). Of course, the complete code for this driver is available from OSR's Web site (http://www.osr.com). For the sake of clarity, some nonessential code (such as logic for error handling and some DbgPrint() statements) have been eliminated from the routines as they appear in this book.

The DK1 is a simple evaluation board that allows the basic facilities of the S5933 DMA controller chip to be exercised. The device does not support scatter/gather, but is capable of performing both DMA reads and DMA writes in parallel. That is, a single transfer of each type may be in progress on the device at one time. Because the device allows multiple I/O operations to be in progress simultaneously, the driver uses Driver Queuing to manage its queue of IRPs.

To program the device, it is provided with the 32-bit base address of the requestor's buffer, the length of the transfer in bytes, and the transfer direction. The maximum transfer length for the device is limited to 64M-1 bytes (0x3FFFFFF). The device interrupts on transfer completion. The reason for this interrupt is contained in the device's interrupt status register.

> ### Note
>
> *One eccentricity of this device is that it requires the start of the requestor's buffers to be aligned on an even longword boundary. That is, the low two bits of the logical address of the requestor's buffer are*

ignored by the device. This driver manages this restriction "automatically" using NT's system scatter/gather facility. Therefore, the driver doesn't worry about it. See the section on alignment and length issues later in this chapter for a more complete discussion of the issues involved.

Dispatch Routine

Processing starts, of course, in the Dispatch routine, where the driver is called by the I/O Manager with an IRP to be processed. The code for this driver's Dispatch write routine appears in Example 17.5. The code for the Dispatch read routine is identical, with the exception of the specific operation being performed.

Example 17.5. Dispatch write routine for the example DMA driver.

```
NTSTATUS OsrWrite(PDEVICE_OBJECT DeviceObject, PIRP Irp)
{
    POSR_DEVICE_EXT devExt = DeviceObject->DeviceExtension;
    KIRQL oldIrql;
    NTSTATUS code = STATUS_SUCCESS;
    BOOLEAN listWasEmpty;
    PIO_STACK_LOCATION ioStack;
    ULONG temp;

    //
    // Validate the IRP we've received
    //
    ioStack = IoGetCurrentIrpStackLocation(Irp);

    //
    // If the length of the requested transfer is either zero or too long,
    // we immediately compelte the IRP with an error status.
    //
    if (ioStack->Parameters.Write.Length == 0 ||
        ioStack->Parameters.Write.Length > OSR_PCI_MAX_TXFER)  {

        Irp->IoStatus.Status = STATUS_INVALID_USER_BUFFER;
        Irp->IoStatus.Information = 0;

        IoCompleteRequest(Irp, IO_NO_INCREMENT);

        return(STATUS_INVALID_USER_BUFFER);

    }

    // Take out the Write list lock, since we'll insert this IRP
    // onto the write queue
    //
    KeAcquireSpinLock(&devExt->WriteQueueLock, &oldIrql);
```

continues

Continued

```
//
// Since we'll probably be queuing this request, set a routine
// to be called by the I/O Manager in case he needs to cancel
// this IRP.
//
IoSetCancelRoutine(Irp, OsrCancelFromWriteQueue);


//
// Before we queue this request, has it been cancelled??
//
// What we're doing here is closing that tiny window between the time
// the Dispatch routine is called and when we acquired the queue spin
// lock.  Once the queue spin lock is held, and the IRP is queued, the
// cancellation routine will deal with any requests to cancel the IRP.
//
if (Irp->Cancel)  {
    //
    // Can't complete a request with a valid cancel routine!
    //
    IoSetCancelRoutine(Irp, OsrCancelFromWriteQueue);

    KeReleaseSpinLock(&devExt->WriteQueueLock, oldIrql);

    Irp->IoStatus.Status = STATUS_CANCELLED;
    Irp->IoStatus.Information = 0;

    IoCompleteRequest(Irp, IO_NO_INCREMENT);

    return(STATUS_CANCELLED);
}


//
// If we get this far, we will return with this request pending
//
IoMarkIrpPending(Irp);


//
// Do we need to start this request on the device?
//
// If there is no IRP currently in progress, we'll start the
// one we've just received.
//
if (devExt->CurrentWriteIrp == NULL)  {

    //
    // No write presently active.  Start this request...
    // (Note that we're still holding the queue lock here)
    //
    OsrStartWriteIrp(DeviceObject,Irp);

} else {
```

```
        //
        // Put this request on the end of the write queue
        //
        InsertTailList(&devExt->WriteQueue, &Irp->Tail.Overlay.ListEntry);

    }

    //
    // We're done playing with the write queue now
    //
    KeReleaseSpinLock(&devExt->WriteQueueLock, oldIrql);

    return(STATUS_PENDING);
}
```

The routine starts by validating the received write request. Validation for this device is straightforward:

1. The driver checks to see if the requested transfer length is zero or if it exceeds the maximum supported by the device.

2. If either of these conditions is true, the driver immediately completes the request with STATUS_INVALID_USER_BUFFER and returns to the I/O Manager with that same status.

If the request is valid, the driver acquires the write queue spin lock. The driver uses this lock to protect the queue of write requests to the device. While holding the lock, the driver sets the Cancel routine in the IRP and then checks to see if the IRP has been cancelled. If it has, the lock is immediately dropped, the Cancel routine is reset, and the request is completed with STATUS_CANCELLED. The driver returns STATUS_CANCELLED to the I/O Manager.

The driver performs the check for the request being cancelled while holding the write queue lock because, in this driver, the queue lock appropriate to the request is also used to guard cancel processing. This check for IRP cancellation guards against the possibility that the IRP was cancelled prior to the driver acquiring the write queue spin lock. If the IRP is subsequently cancelled prior to being initiated on the device, the driver's Cancel routine finds the IRP on the write queue (after acquiring the write queue lock, of course), and cancels it.

If the incoming IRP has not been cancelled, the driver marks the IRP pending by calling IoMarkIrpPending(). If a write request is not already in progress on the device, the driver calls OsrStartWriteIrp() to start the request. If a write request is already busy on the device, the driver inserts the received IRP at the end of the write queue. In either case, the driver returns STATUS_PENDING from its Dispatch routine.

Preparing for the Transfer

Given that the device is available to start a write transfer and that the IRP to be started is at the head of the write queue, the `OsrStartWriteIrp()` function is called. The code for this function appears in Example 17.6.

Example 17.6. Starting the write request for the example DMA driver.

```
VOID
OsrStartWriteIrp(PDEVICE_OBJECT DeviceObject, PIRP Irp)
{
    POSR_DEVICE_EXT devExt = DeviceObject->DeviceExtension;
    PIO_STACK_LOCATION ioStack;
    ULONG mapRegsNeeded;

    ioStack = IoGetCurrentIrpStackLocation(Irp);

    //
    // In progress IRPs cannot be cancelled
    //
    IoSetCancelRoutine(Irp, NULL);

    //
    // There is no in-progress request.  Start this request on the
    // device.
    //
    devExt->CurrentWriteIrp = Irp;

    devExt->WriteTotalLength = ioStack->Parameters.Write.Length;

    devExt->WriteSoFar = 0;

    devExt->WriteStartingOffset = 0;

    //
    // Start the watchdog timer on this IRP
    //
    (ULONG)Irp->Tail.Overlay.DriverContext[0] = OSR_WATCHDOG_INTERVAL;

    //
    // Since we're about to initiate a DMA operation, ensure the user's data
    // buffer is flushed from the cache back into memory, on processors that
    // are non-DMA cache coherent.
    //
    KeFlushIoBuffers(Irp->MdlAddress, FALSE, TRUE);

    //
    // Determine the number of map registers we'll need for this transfer
    //
    mapRegsNeeded =
        ADDRESS_AND_SIZE_TO_SPAN_PAGES(MmGetMdlVirtualAddress(Irp->MdlAddress),
                                       ioStack->Parameters.Write.Length);
```

```
    //
    // If the number of map registers required for this transfer exceeds the
    // maximum we're allowed to use (as reported to us from HalGetAdapter() ),
    // we'll need to limit ourselves to the maximum we're allowed.
    //
    devExt->MapRegsThisWrite = ((mapRegsNeeded > devExt->WriteMapRegsGot) ?
                              devExt->WriteMapRegsGot : mapRegsNeeded);

    //
    // Ready to GO! Allocate the appropriate Adapter Object and map registers.
    //
    IoAllocateAdapterChannel(devExt->WriteAdapter,
                      DeviceObject,
                      devExt->MapRegsThisWrite,
                      OsrAdapterControlWrite,
                      Irp);
}
```

The OsrStartWriteIrp() function starts by setting the Cancel routine for the newly in-progress IRP to NULL. This results in the IRP not being cancellable while it is in progress on the device. The driver next saves a pointer to the IRP in the CurrentWriteIrp field of the device extension. The driver then starts the "watchdog timer" value into one of the driver's context fields in the IRP. Each second, the driver's watchdog timer code will run and decrement this count in the in-progress IRP. In the rare case that the count reaches zero, the device is assumed to have stopped functioning. The driver therefore does a soft reset on the device, and the currently in-progress request is cancelled by the driver.

The driver continues by calling KeFlushIoBuffers() to flush the contents of the requestor's data buffer from processor cache to main memory on systems where this is required. The driver then determines the number of map registers required to completely map the requestor's buffer, and determines the number of map registers that it will request from the HAL. This is the number of map registers required to map the user's buffer, up to the limit imposed by the HAL.

The driver then asks the HAL to reserve its Adapter Object and map registers for the transfer by calling IoAllocateAdapterChannel(). The HAL calls the driver's AdapterControl routine (in this instance, OsrAdapterControlWrite()) when the resources for the transfer are available. As a convenience, the driver passes a pointer to the IRP to be processed to its AdapterControl routine in the Context parameter of the IoAllocateAdapterChannel() function. This is necessary because the Irp parameter that the HAL passes into the AdapterControl routine is not valid (because the example driver uses Driver Queuing).

On return from its call to IoAllocateAdapterChannel(), the driver returns from the OsrStartWriteIrp() function. This results in returning to the Dispatch routine, which called it (OsrDispatchWrite()), and a return the I/O Manager with the status STATUS_PENDING.

Programming the Device

When the Adapter Object and map registers are available for this transfer, the HAL calls the driver at the AdapterControl routine specified on the call to `IoAllocateAdapterChannel()`. This function is called at IRQL DISPATCH_LEVEL in an arbitrary thread context. The code for the AdapterControl routine `OsrAdapterControlWrite()` appears in Example 17.7.

Example 17.7. AdapterControl routine for the sample DMA driver.

```
IO_ALLOCATION_ACTION
OsrAdapterControlWrite(IN PDEVICE_OBJECT DeviceObject, IN PIRP NotUsed,
                            IN PVOID MapRegisterBase, IN PVOID Context)

{
    PIRP irp = (PIRP) Context;
    PIO_STACK_LOCATION ioStack;
    POSR_DEVICE_EXT devExt;
    PUCHAR baseVa;

    devExt = DeviceObject->DeviceExtension;

    ioStack = IoGetCurrentIrpStackLocation(irp);

    devExt->WriteLength = ioStack->Parameters.Write.Length -
                        devExt->WriteSoFar;

    //
    // Get set-up for the transfer
    //
    devExt->WriteMapRegBase = MapRegisterBase;

    baseVa = MmGetMdlVirtualAddress(irp->MdlAddress);

    devExt->WriteStartingOffset =  devExt->WriteSoFar;

    //
    // Get the base address and length of the segment to write.
    //
    devExt->WritePaToDevice = IoMapTransfer(NULL,
                            irp->MdlAddress,
                            MapRegisterBase,
                            baseVa+(devExt->WriteSoFar),
                            &devExt->WriteLength,
                            TRUE);       // WriteToDevice

    //
    // Update the length transfered so far
    //
    devExt->WriteSoFar += devExt->WriteLength;

    //
    // Put the request on the device
```

```
//
(VOID)KeSynchronizeExecution(devExt->InterruptObject,
                             OsrStartWriteOnDevice,
                             DeviceObject);

    return(DeallocateObjectKeepRegisters);
}
```

OsrAdapterControlWrite() is also a rather straightforward function. On entry, the driver adjusts the length of the request to reflect any previous transfers that have been performed on this buffer. This will be the case only when you have re-entered this routine to continue processing a requestor buffer that could not be completely mapped by NT's system scatter/gather facility. The driver then performs some simple bookkeeping—storing away the map register base and starting offset for this transfer for later use in the DpcForIsr.

The driver then calls IoMapTransfer(), passing in the traditional NULL as the pointer to the Adapter Object, a pointer to the IRP describing the requestor's buffer, the map register base, the base virtual address (in the requestor's address space) of the start of the transfer, the remaining length of the transfer, and a value of TRUE—indicating that the current operation is a write operation. IoMapTransfer() returns the logical address to be passed to the device, as well as the length to be written. Both these parameters are stored in the device extension by the driver. The driver then stores the number of bytes that this request will have successfully written so far.

At this point, the driver is ready to program the device to perform the DMA write operation. The starting logical address and length of the transfer have been stored in the device extension. The driver next requests the kernel to call the driver's routine that actually programs the device while holding the ISR spin lock (in order to interlock this check against the driver's ISR). The driver does this by calling KeSynchronizeExecution(), which was described fully in Chapter 15, "Interrupt Service Routines and DPCs" (see Figure 15.4 for the function prototype).

KeSynchronizeExecution() raises to the synchronize IRQL of the device's ISR, acquires the ISR spin lock, and directly calls the driver function OsrStartWriteOnDevice(). OsrStartWriteOnDevice() programs the AMCC device hardware for the write operation, using the appropriate HAL functions (WRITE_PORT_ULONG and READ_PORT_ULONG). When OsrStartWriteOnDevice() returns, KeSynchronizeExecution() returns to the caller in OsrAdapterControlWrite(). At this point, the device has been programmed to perform the indicated transfer. The device will interrupt when the transfer is complete. The driver returns from its AdapterControl routine with the status DeallocateObjectKeepRegisters, which indicates that the HAL may free the Adapter Object, but that the driver retains the map registers for the duration of the transfer. These map registers will be explicitly returned by the driver in the DpcForIsr.

Because OsrStartWriteOnDevice() is totally device-specific, and rather ugly and boring, this code has been omitted. We pick up the flow of control in the Interrupt Service Routine.

Interrupt Service Routine

When the transfer is complete, the device generates an interrupt. This results in the driver's ISR being called. The code for the ISR appears in Example 17.8.

Example 17.8. Interrupt Service Routine for the example DMA driver.

```
BOOLEAN
OsrHandleInterrupt(PKINTERRUPT Interrupt, PVOID ServiceContext)
{
    BOOLEAN ourDeviceInterrupting = FALSE;
    POSR_DEVICE_EXT devExt = (POSR_DEVICE_EXT)ServiceContext;
    ULONG intRegister;
    ULONG csrRegister;

    //
    // Get the current interrupt CSR from our device
    //
    intRegister = READ_PORT_ULONG(devExt->AmccBaseRegisterAddress+ICSR_OFF);

    //
    // Is our device presently interrupting?
    //
    if (intRegister & AMCC_INT_INTERRUPTED) {

        //
        // Yes, it is!
        //
        ourDeviceInterrupting = TRUE;

        //
        // Store away some context so when we get to our DpcForIsr we'll know
        // what caused the interrupt.  Specifically, we accumulate bits in the
        // "IntCsr" field of our device extenstion indicating what interrupts
        // we've seen from the device.  Note that since we support simultaneous
        // read and write DMA operations, we could get both a read complete
        // interrupt and a write complete interrupt before the DpcForIsr has
        // had a chance to execute.  Thus, we must carefully ACCUMULATE the
        // bits.
        //
        // N.B.  We guard these bits with the Interrupt Spin Lock, which is
        // automatically acquired by NT before entering the ISR.  The bits
        // cannot be set or cleared unless holding that lock.
        //
        devExt->IntCsr |= (intRegister & AMCC_INT_ACK_BITS);
```

```
//
// Acknowledge the interrupt on the device
//
WRITE_PORT_ULONG(devExt->AmccBaseRegisterAddress+ICSR_OFF,
                            intRegister);

//
// IF the interrupt was as a result of a READ or WRITE operation
// completing (either with success or error) request our DpcForIsr.
//
if(intRegister & (AMCC_INT_READ_COMP | AMCC_INT_WRITE_COMP))  {

    IoRequestDpc(devExt->DeviceObject, 0, NULL);

}

}

return(ourDeviceInterrupting);
}
```

The ISR is entered at the device's synchronize IRQL, as specified on the driver's call to IoConnectInterrupt(), and in an arbitrary thread context. When entered, the system is holding the ISR spin lock associated with this ISR's Interrupt Object.

As in any ISR, this routine first checks to see if the device described by the *ServiceContext* parameter passed into the ISR is interrupting. If it is not, the ISR returns FALSE.

If the driver's device is interrupting, the driver carefully accumulates bits indicating the reason for the interrupt in a storage location in its device extension. These bits indicate, for example, whether a DMA read operation is complete or a DMA write operation is complete.

The driver next acknowledges the interrupt on the device, and requests its DpcForIsr by calling IoRequestDpc(). Note that the driver does not attempt to pass any context back from its ISR to its DpcForIsr via the *Context* parameter to IoRequestDpc() because multiple DMA operations can be in progress at one time. Thus, any attempt to pass context back via IoRequestDpc() would be futile, because multiple requests to invoke the DpcForIsr, prior to the DpcForIsr running, will result in one DpcForIsr invocation. This was discussed previously in Chapter 15, in the section "DpcForIsr and CustomDpc."

The ISR returns TRUE to indicate that its device was interrupting when the ISR was called. As a result of calling IoRequestDpc(), the next routine entered is the driver's DpcForIsr.

Completing the Transfer and Propagating Driver Execution

When the processor next attempts to return to an IRQL below DISPATCH_LEVEL, the DPC Object for the example driver will be dequeued, and the driver's DpcForIsr will be called. The code for this DpcForIsr appears in Example 17.9.

Example 17.9. DpcForIsr for the sample DMA driver.

```
VOID
OsrDpcForIsr(PKDPC Dpc, PDEVICE_OBJECT DeviceObject, PIRP Unused, PVOID
              Context)
{
    POSR_DEVICE_EXT devExt = (POSR_DEVICE_EXT) DeviceObject->DeviceExtension;
    PLIST_ENTRY entry;
    PIRP irp;
    PVOID baseVa;
    ULONG mapRegsNeeded;

    //
    // Write complete??
    //
    if( KeSynchronizeExecution(devExt->InterruptObject,
                              WriteIsDone,
                              devExt) ) {
        //
        // Get the write queue lock
        //
        KeAcquireSpinLockAtDpcLevel(&devExt->WriteQueueLock);

        //
        // Get the address of the in-progress request
        //
        irp = devExt->CurrentWriteIrp;

        //
        // See if there's an entry on the Write queue that needs to be
        // completed or continued.
        //
        if (irp) {

            //
            // There is an IRP currently in progress.
            //
            baseVa = (PUCHAR)MmGetMdlVirtualAddress(irp->MdlAddress)+
                            devExt->WriteStartingOffset;

            IoFlushAdapterBuffers(devExt->WriteAdapter,
                            irp->MdlAddress,
                            devExt->WriteMapRegBase,
                            baseVa,
                            devExt->WriteSoFar-
                            devExt->WriteStartingOffset,
```

```
                          TRUE);      // writeToDevice == TRUE

    //
    // Tell the HAL the map registers we were using are free
    //
    IoFreeMapRegisters(devExt->WriteAdapter,
                       devExt->WriteMapRegBase,
                       devExt->MapRegsThisWrite);

    //
    // See if there's more of the user's buffer left for us to DMA.
    // Be sure the request was not cancelled whilst in progress.
    //
    if( (devExt->WriteTotalLength - devExt->WriteSoFar) &&
        (!irp->Cancel) )  {

        //
        // The user buffer has NOT been completely DMA'ed.
        // How many map regs can we use this time?
        //
        mapRegsNeeded =
            ADDRESS_AND_SIZE_TO_SPAN_PAGES(
                MmGetMdlVirtualAddress(irp->MdlAddress)+
                    devExt->WriteSoFar,
                    devExt->WriteTotalLength-devExt->WriteSoFar);

        devExt->MapRegsThisWrite =
                ((mapRegsNeeded > devExt->WriteMapRegsGot) ?
                            devExt->WriteMapRegsGot :
                            mapRegsNeeded);

        IoAllocateAdapterChannel(devExt->WriteAdapter,
                                 DeviceObject,
                                 devExt->MapRegsThisWrite,
                                 OsrAdapterControlWrite,
                                 irp);
    } else  {

        //
        // We're going to complete this request
        //

        //
        // Information field contains number of bytes written
        //
        irp->IoStatus.Information = devExt->WriteTotalLength;

        // and all requests are completed with success...
        //
        irp->IoStatus.Status = STATUS_SUCCESS;
```

continues

Continued

```
//
//
// ...unless the in-progress I/O operation is cancelled.
//
if(irp->Cancel == TRUE)  {

    irp->IoStatus.Status = STATUS_CANCELLED;
    irp->IoStatus.Information = 0;

}

//
// Complete the request now
//
IoCompleteRequest(irp, IO_NO_INCREMENT);

//
// N.B.  We're STILL HOLDING the write queue lock.
//

//
// No write in progress right now
//
devExt->CurrentWriteIrp = NULL;

//
// Keep removing entries until we start one.
//
while ( !devExt->CurrentWriteIrp &&
        !IsListEmpty(&devExt->WriteQueue) ) {

    entry = RemoveHeadList(&devExt->WriteQueue);

    irp =  CONTAINING_RECORD(entry,
                 IRP,
                 Tail.Overlay.ListEntry);

    //
    // If this IRP is cancelled, cancel it now, without
    // initiating it on the device
    //
    if (irp->Cancel) {

        irp->IoStatus.Status = STATUS_CANCELLED;
        irp->IoStatus.Information = 0;

        //
        // Complete the request now
        //
        IoCompleteRequest(irp, IO_NO_INCREMENT);
```

```
                         } else {

                               //
                               // Make this IRP the current write IRP, and
                               // start the request on the device.  This routine
                               // sets devExt->CurrentWriteIrp
                               //
                               OsrStartWriteIrp(DeviceObject, irp);
                         }

                  }    // while (!devExt->CurrentWriteIrp &&
                       //          !IsListEmpty(devExt->WriteQueue) )
            }
      }

      //
      // Drop the lock
      //
      KeReleaseSpinLockFromDpcLevel(&devExt->WriteQueueLock);

   }

   //
   // Read Complete??
   //
   if( KeSynchronizeExecution(devExt->InterruptObject,
                              ReadIsDone,
                              devExt) )  {

         //
         // Code eliminated from listing...
         //

   }

   //
   // We're outa here...
   //
   return;
}
```

For the sake of brevity, we have included only the DpcForIsr code related to write completion here. Suffice it to say that the code for read completion is identical, except that it refers to the appropriate data structures.

On entry to the DpcForIsr, the driver checks to see if it needs to process a write completion. The driver checks this by calling the function KeSynchronizeExecution(), which in turn calls the driver's WriteIsDone() routine at synchronize IRQL, while holding the ISR spin lock. As described in Chapter 15, this operation is required because in this driver, the accumulated status bits in the device extension are protected by the ISR spin lock.

If a write is not complete, the DpcForIsr continues on to check whether a read is complete.

If a write is complete, the driver acquires the write queue spin lock and checks to see whether a write request is in progress. If no write request is in progress, the driver falls out of the if statement and proceeds to check to see whether a read request is complete. If there is a write request in progress, the driver completes the DMA transfer by flushing any remaining data from the adapter buffers by calling IoFlushAdapterBuffers(). The driver then returns the map registers that were reserved, calling IoFreeMapRegisters(). Note that both the map register base and the number of map registers reserved were stored away previously by the driver for use in this call.

Next, the driver checks to see whether part of the requestor's buffer remains to be transferred. That is, the driver checks to see whether there were too few map registers available on the last transfer to completely map the requestor's buffer. If the entire request has not yet been completed, and if the outstanding request has not been cancelled, the driver determines the number of map registers to request, and once again calls IoAllocateAdapterChannel() to continue with the request. This call results in OsrAdapterControlWrite() being called, which will set up for another piece of the user buffer to be transferred. The driver releases the write queue lock and proceeds to check to see whether a read has been completed.

If the current write transfer completed the entire request (or if the current request had the cancel flag set while it was in progress), the driver sets the result status in the IRP's IoStatusBlock fields. If the current IRP has had its cancel flag set, the driver sets the completion status to STATUS_CANCELLED and the IRP's IoStatus.Information field to zero. The driver then calls IoCompleteRequest() to complete the IRP.

Finally, with the previous operation complete, the driver propagates its execution by checking to see if there are any requests remaining on the write queue. If there are, the driver removes the request and checks to see if it has been cancelled. Note that this cancel check determines if the request has been cancelled in the time that the DpcForIsr has been holding the write queue spin lock. If the request had been cancelled prior to the DpcForIsr acquiring the write queue spin lock, the request would have been removed from the write queue and cancelled by the driver's cancel routine. If the new request has its cancel flag set, the driver completes the request with STATUS_CANCELLED and attempts to dequeue another IRP from the write queue. If the newly dequeued request does not have its cancel flag set, the driver calls OsrStartWriteIrp() (the code for which appears Example 17.6) to begin the processing of this next request.

Design Issues for DMA Device Drivers

The remainder of this chapter deals with specific issues that may be encountered in drivers for DMA devices. The following issues are discussed:

- Alignment restrictions

- System DMA

Alignment Restrictions

As discussed several times previously, the first step that a driver performs to process any transfer request is to validate the parameters passed in the IRP. This validation normally includes checking things such as the length of the transfer to ensure that they meet the device's requirements. DMA devices, however, sometimes have additional hardware restrictions concerning data buffers that drivers will need to check before they can consider a particular request valid. These restrictions typically apply to the alignment, length, or fragmentation of the requestor's data buffer.

It is not uncommon for DMA devices to require that requestor data buffers begin on particular memory boundaries. For example, the AMCC S5933 DMA controller used as our Packet-Based DMA driver example requires all fragments of the requestor's data buffer to be aligned, starting on an even longword boundary. In Windows NT, a driver has only two options for enforcing such requirements:

- **Pass the requirement on to the user.** That is, inform users of the device that all data buffers used for data transfers must be properly aligned, and/or must be of an appropriate length. The alignment requirement can be enforced by the driver appropriately setting the `AlignmentRequirement` field in the Device Object. Because buffer alignment in virtual address space is the same as buffer alignment in physical address space, users can actually control whether this requirement is met. Thus, the physical (but not logical) alignment of the requestor's data buffer can be ascertained by examining the `Irp->UserBuffer` field in the IRP.

- **Rebuffer the request if a received requestor's data buffer does not meet the alignment requirements.** If a request cannot be refused due to faulty alignment, the driver has no choice but to provide an appropriately aligned intermediate buffer for use in the transfer. The driver is then responsible for copying the data between the intermediate buffer and the actual requestor's data buffer.

Compounding the problem of validating requests for buffer alignment is the fact that the driver can't be sure that an alignment requirement will not be met until it receives the logical address for the transfer back from IoMapTransfer(). Consider, for example, the case of a device that does not support scatter/gather and a HAL that performs intermediate buffering for the purpose of buffer fragment agglomeration. This is the case for the AMCC example driver and the standard x86 HAL. In this case, checking the base address of the data buffer prior to the intermediate buffering operation will be pointless. In fact, when the HAL rebuffers requests, it will typically use an internal buffer that is aligned on a page boundary.

The solution most often offered by hardware colleagues, that of moving the first few bytes of the data via PIO to achieve the required alignment, is rarely possible. In most hardware designs, DMA input is directly wired to device output. There is rarely a "way around" the DMA mechanism that allows a random few bytes to be moved prior to a DMA transfer.

> **Note**
>
> *Although alignment restrictions are not unique to NT, several UNIX variants rebuffer requests on nicely aligned boundaries. Therefore, even software-savvy hardware designers often make the mistake of thinking that alignment requirements are not onerous to driver writers.*

There is no ideal solution to the problem of alignment constraints on NT. The best solution, of course, is to intervene early in the hardware design process to ensure that such restrictions aren't introduced. If this is not possible, remember that rebuffering requests to make them aligned really isn't that bad.

System DMA

As described in Chapter 8, "I/O Architectures," System DMA utilizes the hardware system-supplied controller to perform DMA operations. System DMA is a legacy of the original PC design and few devices that are developed today use system DMA. The notable exceptions are sound cards and floppy disk drivers, both of which are typically System DMA devices.

System DMA transfers are performed by using DMA channels. On NT, multiple devices may share one DMA channel. Access to a device's DMA channel is coordinated by using the Adapter Object, along with its access to map registers. Because System DMA devices can have only one request in progress at a time, drivers for these devices typically use System Queuing of IRPs.

Packet-Based System DMA

The procedures for a driver to support Packet-Based System DMA are almost identical to Packet-Based Busmaster DMA. Because they perform Packet-Based

DMA operations, drivers for Packet-Based System DMA devices typically have their requests described by using Direct I/O. System DMA devices do not support scatter/gather. Thus, drivers for these devices will call IoMapTransfer() one time within their AdapterControl routine.

When a Packet-Based System DMA device calls IoMapTransfer(), the HAL programs the system DMA controller for the transfer. After IoMapTransfer() has been called, the driver programs the device with the transfer information and requests it to start the transfer. The device subsequently interacts with the system DMA controller to actually move the data between the device and the requestor's data buffer.

AdapterControl routines for System DMA devices return the status KeepObject to indicate to the HAL that they need to retain their Adapter Object and the associated DMA Channel and map registers. As a result of this, in the DpcForIsr the driver will need to return the Adapter Object to the HAL by calling IoFreeAdapterChannel(). This function also automatically returns any map registers that were reserved. The prototype for this function appears in Figure 17.11:

VOID
IoFreeAdapterChannel(IN PADAPTER_OBJECT *AdapterObject*);

AdapterObject: A pointer to the Adapter Object for the transfer

---

Figure 17.11. IoFreeAdapterChannel() *function prototype.*

After the Adapter Object has been freed, the driver completes the outstanding request. The driver completes its processing in the DpcForIsr by propagating its execution, typically by calling IoStartNextPacket().

Common-Buffer System DMA
Common-Buffer System DMA is a bit more complicated to implement. This type of DMA is used by drivers that utilize "auto-initialize" System DMA mode.

A Common-Buffer System DMA driver works much like a cross between a Packet-Based and Common-Buffer Busmaster driver. During initialization, the driver gets a pointer to its adapter by calling HalGetAdapter(). Drivers for System DMA devices should get one Adapter Object per supported simultaneous transfer. For most devices, this will mean that the driver gets only a single Adapter Object. Due to the coordination required with the system DMA controller, drivers for Common-Buffer System DMA devices must not call HalGetAdapter() to allocate a separate Adapter Object for use with the common buffer (unlike Common-Buffer Busmaster DMA drivers).

During driver initialization, the driver allocates the common buffer by calling
`HalAllocateCommonBuffer()`. Using the logical address returned by
`HalAllocateCommonBuffer()`, the driver next builds an MDL to describe the common buffer. This MDL is required in order to call `IoMapTransfer()`, later during
processing of a particular I/O request. The MDL is built by calling
`IoAllocateMdl()` (the prototype for which appears in Figure 16.2 in Chapter
16), and the unlikely sounding function `MmBuildMdlForNonPagedPool()`. This
function, the prototype for which is shown in Figure 17.12, builds an MDL
for any nonpageable system memory, including nonpaged pool and common
buffers for DMA.

VOID
MmBuildMdlForNonPagedPool(IN PMDL *Mdl*);

Mdl: A pointer to a partially initialized MDL.

Figure 17.12. `MmBuildMdlForNonPagedPool()` *function prototype.*

When a request is received, the driver will typically validate the request, mark
it pending by calling `IoMarkIrpPending()`, and call `IoStartPacket()`. When the
device is available, the I/O Manager will call the driver's StartIo routine.
Within this routine, if the request is a write to the device, the driver moves the
data from the requestor's data buffer to the common buffer. The driver then
calls `IoAllocateAdapterChannel()` to request the HAL to allocate the Adapter
Object, System DMA channel, and any map registers that may be required to
perform the transfer.

Once in its AdapterControl routine, the driver calls `IoMapTransfer()` once, providing the MDL built earlier to describe the common buffer area. This results
in the HAL programming the appropriate system DMA controller for the
transfer. The driver then programs the device appropriately, using the returned
logical address and length of the data to be transferred. The driver then returns
`KeepObject` from its AdapterControl routine.

Note

*It may seem like there's a natural optimization to the process just dis-
cussed: Perhaps you could call* `IoMapTransfer()` *only once, during initialization, instead of calling it every time from the AdapterControl routine.
However, this optimization is not possible. This is because*
`IoMapTransfer()` *does much more than just return the contents of the
MDL. For System –DMA,* `IoMapTransfer()` *actually programs the System
DMA controller for the transfer.*

When the transfer is completed, the device will interrupt and the driver will request a DpcForIsr. Within the DpcForIsr, the driver must flush the adapter buffers to ensure that the transfer is complete. This is accomplished by calling `IoFlushAdapterBuffers()`. The driver must then return the Adapter Object, DMA channel, and map registers that were allocated for the transfer by calling `IoFreeAdapterChannel()`. The driver then completes the I/O request and propagates its execution, most likely by calling `IoStartNextPacket()`.

Chapter **18**

Building and Debugging Drivers

This chapter will review:

- **Setting Up the Driver Development Environment.** Installing and configuring the software needed to develop, test, and debug drivers can be difficult for driver developers who are new to the Windows NT environment. This section describes in detail all the steps needed to set up a fully functional driver development environment.

- **Building Drivers.** This section describes the utilities, control files, and procedures used for compiling and linking drivers.

- **Driver Debugging.** With your driver built and your environment established, how do you actually debug your driver? This section answers all of your questions about debugging.

- **Debugging and Testing Hints and Tips.** Debugging kernel drivers is a slow process. This section provides several tips learned through long experience that will help you along the way.

- **Behind the Blue Screen.** When Windows NT crashes, it displays the ominous "blue screen of death." This section provides an introduction to the blue screen, and helps you interpret its meaning.

- **Crash Dumps.** Many driver writers are not aware that Windows NT contains support for post-mortem debugging. This brief section describes how to enable this feature and how to debug the resulting dump files.

This chapter discusses how you set up a driver development environment, including what you need to build drivers for Windows NT, as well as the steps that are necessary to set up the debugger. The chapter concludes with some hints and tips for driver testing and debugging.

Setting Up the Driver Development Environment

Setting up the environment needed to support Windows NT driver development entails setting up two systems: a Development System and a Test System. We describe this process in several steps, which are as follows:

1. Getting the necessary software. You'll need an appropriate compiler and the other Microsoft components that supply the header files, libraries, test environment, and the utilities necessary for driver development.

2. Setting up the systems. This step entails installing two systems, with appropriate versions of the operating system and other software you accumulated in Step 1.

3. Setting up debugging. In this step, you'll enable kernel-debugging support on the Test System, and configure the kernel debugger on the Development System.

The following sections describe these steps in detail.

Getting the Necessary Software

To build drivers under Windows NT, you'll need a compiler. For all practical purposes, this means that you must use Microsoft Visual C++ (MSVC). For Windows NT V4, you'll need at least MSVC V4.1 or later. Although it is possible to use other vendors' C compilers, the Windows NT Device Driver Kit (DDK) and debugger software assume that you're using MSVC. This means the necessary header files have been optimized for use with MSVC. Thus, unless you have a specific and compelling reason to do otherwise, we strongly recommend that you stick with MSVC.

The compiler itself is not enough, however. The next thing you'll need is a subscription to the Microsoft Developer's Network (MSDN), available directly from Microsoft (see http://www.microsoft.com/MSDN). Because MSDN subscriptions come in several different flavors, you'll need at least a subscription to the Professional Edition. When you subscribe, you'll need to *specifically request* the DDK (Device Driver Kit) CDs. While you're at it, if you're writing code for other than the United States market or you would find the international versions of Windows NT useful, you can also specifically request the international CDs. There is no extra cost associated with requesting either the DDK or the international CDs as part of the MSDN Professional Edition subscription. However, these components *do* have to be specifically requested or you will not get them as part of your subscription.

The MSDN CDs contain lots of Microsoft software, not just the software necessary for writing drivers. Distributions of Windows 9x, Windows NT, and many development kits are provided. In addition to the Windows NT operating system software itself, there are three things that MSDN provides that pertain to writing drivers: The Microsoft Developer Network Library CDs, the Platform Software Development Kit (SDK), and the DDK.

The DDK contains the documentation and header files that are needed to write NT drivers. The documentation is provided in online format, accessed via InfoViewer. This makes it easily searchable, and it's even moderately easy to print hard copies of the documentation for casual perusing.

What is most impressive and useful about the DDK is that it comes complete with source code examples of more than 50 real Windows NT drivers. The provided samples span (almost) the entire range of the NT driver-writing realm: from SCSI Miniport drivers to standard Kernel mode drivers and almost everything in between. Only file system examples are absent (and those are available as part of the separately licensed Windows NT Installable File Systems Kit). Here is what's particularly useful about the provided samples: When the name of one of the sample drivers is the same as a "real" driver that is provided as part of the regular Windows NT distribution kit, the sample driver is usually the actual source code for that driver on the NT Kit. This allows you to see and understand how many things work in the NT I/O subsystem. This benefit also allows you to build and modify one of the provided sample drivers from source, substitute it for the existing NT driver, and watch how it works.

The SDK contains all the header files and tools normally required to build User mode applications for Windows NT. For driver building, you need to install only the SDK tools. The most important tool to install is WinDbg, the debugger from the SDK that supports Kernel mode debugging.

Finally, there are the MSDN Library CDs. These CDs contains a wealth of wide-ranging information about software development on all the supported Microsoft platforms. The Library CDs include the Knowledge Base (KB). The Knowledge Base is a collection of articles written to address specific issues (often as the result of a problem or bug report). Some KB articles describe otherwise undocumented features or system behavior. Others describe known problems and workarounds. The KB is searchable by keyword. It is worth your time to wander through the KB periodically and check what new things pop up.

Setting Up the Systems

To develop drivers on Windows NT using the Microsoft-supplied tools, you will need two systems that are capable of running Windows NT. One of these systems will be your Development System, which is the system on which you will edit and build your driver. This will also be the system on which you run the debugger. The goal is to keep this system stable and not subject it to the random crashes that running a new driver tends to cause. For maximum productivity, your Development System should be configured with a reasonable CPU and as much memory as possible. While CPU speed is nice to have, there really is no substitute for lots of memory. A 120MHz Pentium and 64MB of memory is really the minimum for good performance on your Development System. Doubling the memory and CPU speed is not at all unreasonable.

The second system will be your Test System. Your Test System will be the system on which you will be running your driver under test. The Test System can be much more conservatively configured than your Development System. Whatever Pentium CPU is available and 32MB of memory will typically serve as a reasonable Test System. As described in detail later, you will use your Development System to control your Test System, via the kernel debugger.

Note

Numega Technologies, Inc. has a product for Windows NT called SoftICE. This product allows driver development and debugging by using a single system. Even if you use SoftICE, we recommend that you use two systems for driver development. This prevents the potential problems of losing files if your driver crashes and, by a stroke of bad luck, wipes out your file system. While not likely, this is certainly possible.

Setting Up the Test System

There are two versions of the Windows NT operating system that are provided with MSDN and used during driver development. These two versions are known as the *Free Build* (also sometimes called the *Retail Build*) and the *Checked Build* (also known as the *Debug Build*).

The Free Build is the normal, ordinary Windows NT binary distribution kit. It doesn't say anything unusual on the MSDN distribution CD. This version is intended for regular distribution, and is built by Microsoft using compiler optimizations and without much cross-checking or debug-specific code. In contrast, the Checked Build is a version of NT that Microsoft specifically designed for use by device driver writers. It is clearly labeled "Checked Build" on the MSDN distribution CD. When the Checked Build is compiled by Microsoft, it is compiled with many fewer optimizations (making the code easier to trace). It also has the symbol DBG defined at compile time. Defining this symbol in the operating system source code causes lots of conditional debugging code to be included in the build. This debugging code checks many function parameters for "reasonableness," and in general attempts to identify and trap various run-time errors.

The Checked Build is only intended for use on a Test System. While it could be used on a regular Development System, the inclusion of all the debugging code and lack of compiler optimizations makes it run slower than the Free Build. This is especially true because when you install the Checked Build, you get the checked version of *everything*. You get a checked NT operating system, a checked HAL, plus the checked versions of every single driver and Kernel mode DLL in the system.

You can install the Checked Build on your Test System by using the Checked Build distribution kit included in MSDN. This build of the operating system is installed in the same way as any other version of Windows NT. However, as mentioned previously, this installs checked versions of every component in the system, which can result in a rather slow system.

One alternative to installing the complete Checked Build on your Test System is to install the Free Build, and then replace the individual Free Build components of interest to use with their Checked Build counterparts. Thus, for example, if you are writing a standard Kernel mode driver, you would install the Free Build of NT on the Test System. You would then replace the Free version of the operating system (ntoskrnl.exe or ntkrnlmp.exe, depending on whether the system is single processor or multiprocessor) and HAL (hal.dll) with the same files from the Checked Build.

The only difficulty with this alternative approach is that finding and replacing these files may not be quite as simple as it sounds. First, you *absolutely must* replace the HAL and NTOS images together. You can't have, for example, the Checked version of the HAL and the Free version of NTOS. They either both have to be Checked or they both have to be Free, or the system will not boot. These files all live in the \SystemRoot\System32 directory. To replace the Free versions with the Checked versions, copy the files you want to replace from the \i386 or \alpha directory of the Windows NT Checked Build distribution disk supplied with MSDN to the \SystemRoot\System32 directory of your Test System.

There are still a couple of "tricks" left to discuss, however. One is that you might need to determine which HAL your Test System is using. The file in \SystemRoot\System32 is *always* called HAL.DLL. However, the original HAL file that was copied to create this file might be named something else. This will be true, for example, when your Test System is a multiprocessor system. To find out which HAL is installed on your Test System, check the contents of the file \SystemRoot\Repair\setup.log. This file will contain a line such as the following:

```
\WINNT\system32\hal.dll = "halmps.dll","1a01c"
```

This shows that the HAL being used on the current system is actually halmps.dll. If you have trouble even finding setup.log in the \SystemRoot\Repair\ directory, it's because it's a *hidden file*. Just attrib it -h and you should have no problem!

The remaining trick is that the image of the HAL on the Checked distribution kit might be compressed. This is a good trick to know in general because the files that are distributed compressed on the Windows NT kit disk can change over time. You can identify a compressed file by a file type that ends with an underscore. Thus, if the HALMPS image is not compressed on the Checked distribution kit, you'll be able to find it in the \i386\ directory and it will be named halmps.dll. On the other hand, if the file *is* compressed, it will be in the \i386\ directory and will be named halmps.dl_.

To expand a compressed file, use Microsoft's Expand utility. The easiest way to do this is to copy the desired file to its ultimate location by copying halmps.dl_ from the \i386\ directory on the Checked Build CD to \SystemRoot\system32\HALMPD.DL_. Then, simply use the expand command from the command shell, as follows:

```
expand -r halmps.dl_
```

The preceding command expands the file and automatically names the resulting expanded file halmps.dll.

A second alternative to installing the complete Checked Build on your Test System is to install the Free Build, and then copy the Checked Build components of interest to your Test System—placing them in their usual directories, but with unique names. Thus, instead of copying the appropriate files from the checked distribution kit to the \SystemRoot\System32 directory and naming them ntoskrnl.exe and hal.dll, you copy these same files (the checked kernel and HAL images) and name them, for example, ntoscheck.exe and halcheck.dll. You may then create a boot option, specifying these checked system components by editing the file boot.ini and specifying the /KERNEL= and /HAL= switches. The process of editing boot.ini is discussed later.

Note

When you're developing a driver, make sure you test it on both the Free and Checked versions of NT! The timings on these systems are very different, due to the extra parameter checking in the Checked Build of the operating system. You should use the Checked version of NT exclusively during the early stages of driver development. Once the majority of your driver code is running, switch to testing and debugging on the Free Build of the system. Prior to release, run a complete set of tests on both the Checked and the Free Builds of Windows NT.

Setting Up the Development System

To properly set up your Development System, install the Free Build of Windows NT with whatever service packs or hot fixes that are required to make it most current. You also must install MSVC, the DDK, and the SDK on the Development System. To maximize the ease of installation and later use, install these software components by using the account from which you'll be doing your driver development. In addition, it usually works best to install the SDK first, followed by MSVC, and then the DDK. Note that you do not need to install these components on your Test System—they are installed only on your Development System.

Connecting the Development and Test Systems

In the standard Windows NT driver development environment, the Test System is controlled by the debugger running on the Development System. The two systems are connected via a serial null-modem cable, attached to a serial port on each system. Choose a free serial port on each system and connect the two systems via a serial null-modem cable. Remember which serial port you use on each system, because later you'll have to tell the software which port to use.

> **Note**
>
> *Some people have trouble determining what specific type of serial null-modem cable to use to connect the Development System and the Test System. In fact, the cheapest possible serial cable wired in a null-modem configuration will typically work best. This configuration wires pin 2 on one end of the cable to pin 3 on the other, pin 3 on one end of the cable to pin 2 on the other, and connects the ground pins together. We have had particularly good luck ordering serial LapLink™ cables as debugger cables. Not only do they work, but also they typically have both 9-pin and 25-pin connectors at each end.*

Setting Up Debugging

To set up the Windows NT dual-system debugging environment used for driver debugging, you need to do two things:

1. Enable kernel debugging on your Test System, which will allow you to control the Test System from the debugger on the Development System.

2. Set up and start the debugger on your Development System. This process entails setting all the right options in the debugger to enable it to communicate with the kernel debugger running on the Test System.

The next two sections specifically discuss these procedures.

Enabling Kernel Debugging on the Test System

Kernel-debugging support is included in all Windows NT systems, regardless of whether the system is Free or Checked. Ordinarily, kernel debugging is not enabled on a system. To enable it on your Test System, you need to instruct Windows NT to turn on debugging support at boot time. On x86 architecture systems, you do this by editing the file boot.ini in the root directory of the boot volume.

> **Note**
>
> *To enable kernel debugging on Alpha systems, instead of editing boot.ini,*
> *you modify the* OSLOADOPTIONS *environment variable from the ARC*
> *console firmware. You use the same switches (such as* /DEBUGPORT=x
> /BAUDRATE=y*), described later in this chapter for x86 systems.*

boot.ini is the control file that directs the Windows NT boot process. Figure 18.1 illustrates what the contents of boot.ini look like when Windows NT v4 is initially installed on a system.

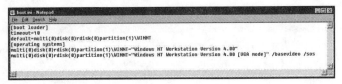

Figure 18.1. boot.ini *before editing to enable debugging.*

Each line in the [operating systems] section of the file points to the SystemRoot (that is, the base directory into which Windows NT was installed on the system) of a Windows NT system that can be potentially started. During NT system startup, the ntldr program reads boot.ini and displays this list of systems. The user selects the operating system that they want to start from this list. If no selection is made, a default choice is taken after a timeout period.

Debugging support is enabled in an NT system by adding switches to a particular operating system line in boot.ini. These switches tell NT which system files to load, whether or not kernel debugging support should be enabled when the system is started, and (if kernel debugging support is enabled) how to communicate with the remote debugger. Some of the most common switches used to control kernel-debugging options are as follows:

- **/DEBUG.** Enables kernel-debugging support and indicates that during system bootup the system should attempt to connect with the remote kernel debugger.

- **/DEBUGPORT=x**. Specifies that serial port *x* should be dedicated to use with the kernel debugger. Implies /DEBUG.

- **/BAUDRATE=y**. Indicates the speed at which serial port *x* should be set. Obviously, this speed must be the same as that used by the kernel debugger on the Development System.

- **/KERNEL=filename**. Indicates that for this boot option the kernel image named filename should be loaded from the \SystemRoot\System32\ directory.

- **/HAL=filename**. Indicates that for this boot option, the HAL image named filename should be loaded from the \SystemRoot\System32\ directory.

The best way to enable kernel debugging for a system is to add an additional choice to the list of systems to start. If kernel-debugging support is desired, the system with kernel-debugging support can be selected from the list shown at boot time. If kernel-debugging support is not required, a system without kernel-debugging support enabled can be started.

To add an additional choice to boot.ini, simply copy the line in the [operating systems] section that describes the operating system image that you want to boot. Put this copy on a line by itself in boot.ini and append the appropriate debugger control switches listed previously. Figure 18.2 shows a version of boot.ini that has been updated to include a third operating system option to be started, which has debugging enabled.

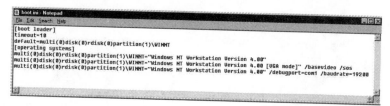

Figure 18.2. boot.ini *after it has been edited to add a boot choice with kernel debugging enabled.*

Note in Figure 18.2 that COM1 has been chosen as the serial port on the Test System that will be connected via the null-modem cable to the Development System. The speed chosen for this port is 19200 bps.

Note

When setting up our Test and Development Systems, we always initially choose a very low baud rate. This makes it easier to establish the initial connection between the two systems. Later, when you have veri-

continues

Continued

> *fied connectivity between the two systems, you can raise the baud rate
> (on both) to the highest working speed (typically 115200). Using a
> higher speed makes debugging a lot more pleasant.*

The next time that NT is started on the Test System with the boot.ini that
appears in Figure 18.2, there will be three choices of which system to start displayed. The third choice will indicate that the debugger is enabled. To enable
kernel debugging on the Test System, reboot the system and select the choice
with debugging enabled.

There is one trick that you have to be aware of when you edit boot.ini. This is
the fact that, by default, boot.ini is a read only, system, hidden file. Therefore,
before you can edit boot.ini successfully, you will need to change its attributes
(by using Explorer or another appropriate utility) to remove at least the read
only attribute. The other attributes do not have to be changed. Further, after
editing boot.ini, there is no need to restore the read only attribute.

Setting Up and Running the Debugger on the Development System

Enabling kernel debugging on your Test System merely allows that system to
be controlled by another system running an appropriate kernel debugger. The
next step in the process of getting a driver development environment established entails setting up and running the kernel debugger on your Development
System.

The standard remote debugger that is supplied as part of the Windows NT
SDK is WinDbg (pronounced "wind bag" by all those who know and love it).
This debugger includes kernel-debugging support, which will let you control
your Test System from your Development System. To set WinDbg up with
kernel-debugging support, start WinDbg (by selecting \Start\Platform
SDK...\Tools...\WinDbg), and select Options from the View Menu Item. In the
WinDebug Options dialog box, select the Kernel Debugger tab, as shown in
Figure 18.3.

To enable kernel debugging, click the Enable Kernel Debugging check box in
the Flags section of the WinDebug Options dialog box. In the Communications
section of this same dialog box, set the appropriate options regarding your
communications setup. Set the Baud Rate option to the baud rate for the null-
modem connection to the kernel debugger. This must match the baud rate that
you previously set in boot.ini on the Test System. Using the Port option, select
the port on your Development System that will be connected via the null-
modem cable to the Test System. The Cache Size parameter indicates the initial

size of WinDbg's cache, which is used to hold values. The default is usually sufficient. Finally, set the Platform option to correctly indicate the processor architecture (x86 or Alpha) of the Test System. When satisfied with your selections, click on the Symbols tab of the WinDebug Options dialog box to proceed to setting up the symbol search path. Figure 18.4 shows the Symbols tab of the Options dialog box.

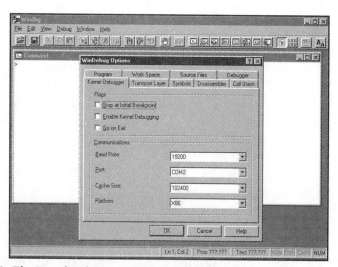

Figure 18.3. The Kernel Debugger tab of the WinDebug Options dialog box.

Figure 18.4. The Symbols tab of the WinDebug Options dialog box.

Note

Note that WinDbg can be used to debug drivers on an Alpha system from an x86 architecture system, or vice versa; by selecting the

continues

Continued

appropriate processor architecture as WinDbg's Platform value. This cross-platform setup can be useful in a pinch. However, it's not ideal as a normal environment because the MSVC compilers are not cross-compilers. To produce an Alpha architecture executable, you run the Alpha version of the MSVC compiler on an Alpha system. This means your Development System will have to be an Alpha system, as well as your Test System.

From the Symbols tab, enter the path that WinDbg should search for debugging symbols in the text box labeled "Path used to search for the debugging symbols." You should dedicate a directory on your Development System to hold debugging symbols, such as C:\DEBUG. This will be referred to as your *dedicated debugging directory*. When you first set up WinDbg, your dedicated debugging directory should be empty. The contents of this directory are discussed later. The remaining options, such as Load Time and Symbol Suffix, in the Symbols tab of the WinDebug Options dialog box may be ignored.

When you are satisfied with your choices, click OK. Then start WinDbg by selecting the Go option from the Debug menu (or hit F5). WinDbg should display a message similar to that shown in Figure 18.5.

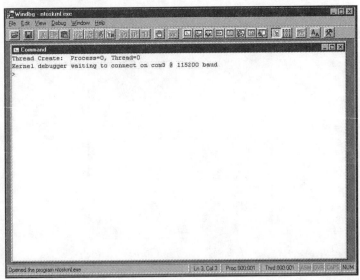

Figure 18.5. *WinDbg, ready and waiting to establish a kernel debugger connection.*

> **Note**
>
> *There are many other tabs that have other selections you could make in the WinDebug Options dialog box. Our best advice is to stay away from options other than those mentioned specifically in this chapter. Most of the other options are not applicable to Kernel mode debugging but can still cause nasty side effects when using the kernel debugger. For example, while it is indeed possible (and may even seem reasonable) to alter the settings in the Transport Layer tab, do not change any of the settings shown. LOCAL must remain the selected transport, although you're not doing kernel debugging on the same machine. Changing these settings will cause WinDbg to not function properly.*

The message in WinDbg's command window indicates that it is waiting to establish a kernel debugger connection on a particular port at a specific speed. Check this information to be sure it's correct. If your Test System is already running, is connected to your Development System via the null-modem cable, and has been booted with debugging enabled; you can try to get WinDbg and your Test System to "sync up." You can either select the Debug menu item, and then choose Break; or type Control-C in WinDbg's command window. If you have a good connection between WinDbg and your Test System, and if the parameters in both boot.ini on your Test System and in WinDbg are correct, WinDbg should respond to the control-break by issuing a message similar to that shown in Figure 18.6.

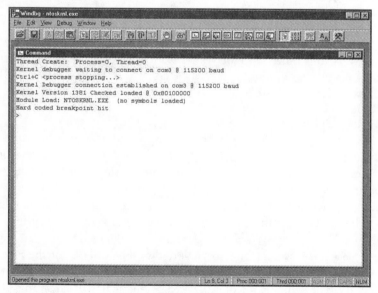

Figure 18.6. *WinDbg, stopped by typing Control-C, with a connection established to a Test System with kernel debugging enabled.*

Note that the last message displayed in the WinDbg command window is Hard coded breakpoint hit. This is WinDbg's quaint way of telling you that your Test System is now stopped. At this point, you may enter other debugging commands (discussed later) via the Debug menu, or by typing directly into the command window. Enter the KS command to show the contents of the kernel stack. You should see a display similar to that in Figure 18.7.

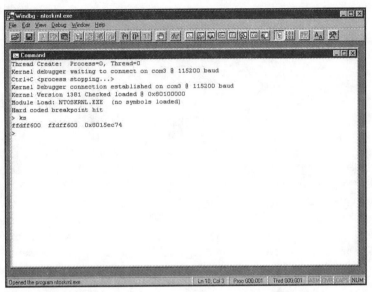

Figure 18.7. *A WinDbg kernel stack trace, without symbols set up.*

Note that at this point, the information displayed is not very helpful! We'll fix that shortly. At this time, continue your Test System by pressing F5, selecting the Debug menu's Go option (or type the g command—followed by a carriage return, of course) in the command window.

Setting Up Debugging Symbols

To enable you to get traces with symbolic names, and also to allow you to manipulate variables and other symbols in your driver code under development, WinDbg needs access to symbol table information. The operating system components, such as the kernel, the HAL, and the operating system-supplied drivers, have the symbol table information removed from their executable images. The symbols for these operating system components are typically located on the operating system distribution disk, under the \Support\Debug\i386\Symbols directory. Note that the symbols for the Free (Retail) components appear on the standard (Free, Retail) distribution kit in this directory. The symbols for the Checked components appear in this directory on the Checked (debug) distribution kit. You must use the symbols for the build (that is, Checked or Free) that match the components you have installed on your test machine. Thus, if you installed the Checked versions of the NTOSKRNL.EXE and HAL.DLL, as recommended previously, you need to provide the Checked versions of the symbols (from the Checked distribution kit) to the debugger.

All symbol files supplied with Windows NT have the file type .DBG. To make it a bit easier to find particular files (and because components that differ by only file type can't be in the same directory), Microsoft separates the symbol files under the \Support\Debug\i386\Symbols directory by file type. Under this directory, there are subdirectories named Acm, Com, Cpl, Dll, Drv, Exe, Scr, and Sys. Thus, the symbols for NTOSKRNL.SYS for the x86 architecture would be located in the file \Support\Debug\i386\Symbols\Sys\NTOSKRNL.DBG. The symbols for HAL.DLL would be located in \Support\Debug\i386\Symbols\Dll\HAL.DBG.

Now that you can find the appropriate symbols, copy the symbols for any components of interest from the appropriate distribution kit to your dedicated debug directory on your Development System. This directory is the one that you entered the path to in the Symbols tab of the WinDebug Options dialog box, discussed earlier. Typically, you should always copy the symbols for the kernel (NTOSKRNL) and the HAL (remember to copy the correct version of the HAL symbols and rename it HAL.DBG in the debug directory!).

Note

Updates to Windows NT that are issued by Microsoft between versions are called service packs. *The executable images of the kernel, HAL, and the drivers can change in each service pack release. Thus, the symbols for these components change. Check your MSDN disks for the most recent service pack and the symbols that correspond to that service pack. Service packs (and other vital fixes, called hot fixes) and symbol files are usually available online from Microsoft. Check out*
ftp://ftp.microsoft.com/bussys/winnt/winnt-public/fixes/.

Once your symbols have been correctly set up, if you tell WinDbg to stop executing the Test System (by selecting Debug and then Break, or by typing Control-C in the command window), you should be able to get a symbolic stack dump, as shown in Figure 18.8.

Note that in Figure 18.8, you now see the name of the function at which the system is stopped. The system was stopped in the function RtlpBreakWithStatusInstruction, in the module NT, which was called from the function KeUpdateSystemTime, which was called from the function KiIdleLoop. If you did not see a symbolic stack dump, try issuing the .RELOAD command.

(That's a period, immediately followed by the word RELOAD.) This command causes WinDbg to attempt to scan for and reload any symbol-table files.

At this point, you should have a kernel driver development and debugging environment completely set up. You have communications established and tested between your Development System and your Test System. Now, it's time to move on to actually building and debugging your driver.

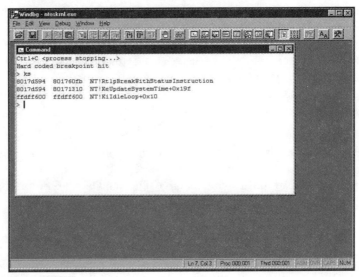

Figure 18.8. *A WinDbg kernel stack trace, showing symbolic debugging information.*

Building Drivers

The standard driver development environment at present is not integrated into MSVC's Developer Studio. Thus, drivers are built from the command line. From the Windows NT DDK program group, select either the Checked Build Environment or Free Build Environment icon, depending on which type of driver you want to build. This will result in the display of a command window. If you select Checked Build Environment, for example, any drivers built in the displayed command window will be checked. That is, they will have the symbol DBG set equal to one, will be built with symbols in their executable images, and will be built with fewer compiler optimizations (to facilitate debugging).

*possible to simply use the default Developer Studio environment to build drivers under NT. It is, however, possible to use Developer Studio to build drivers if the right build procedures are established. An explanation of how to do this, and a working build command procedure for use with Developer Studio, is available on the OSR Web site (*http://www.osr.com*).*

Note

Note that the version of NT may be either Free or Checked; in addition, you may build either a Free or Checked version of your driver. You can run either the Free or Checked version of your driver on either the Free or Checked version of the operating system.

Driver development is controlled by the BUILD utility. This utility, located in the \ddk\bin directory, provides a DDK-specific front end to the driver building process. BUILD (and NMAKE, which it directly controls) reads inputs from files named sources, dirs, and makefile. BUILD creates files named build.log, build.err, and build.wrn as outputs. If all goes well, the ultimate result of executing the BUILD utility is the creation of an executable version of your driver. This file will have a .sys file type.

The BUILD utility supports a wide variety of command options. To obtain a list of these options, which are self-explanatory, use the command BUILD -?.

BUILD must be run in a command window, with the default directory set to the directory that BUILD is to start processing. That directory must contain either a DIRS file, or a SOURCES file and a makefile file.

The DIRS file contains a list of directories for BUILD to process. These directories must all be subdirectories of the current directory. Figure 18.9 shows a sample DIRS file from the \ddk\src\comm directory of the NTv4 DDK.

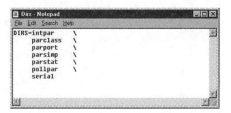

Figure 18.9. *A sample* DIRS *file.*

This file directs BUILD to look in the specified directories (named intpar, parclass, and so forth in Figure 18.9) under the current directory. In each of these directories, BUILD will either find another DIRS file, or a SOURCES file and a makefile file, instructing it how to proceed.

Continuing with the example, in the intpar directory of the DDK (to be specific, that's the directory \ddk\src\comm\intpar), there is a SOURCES file that tells the
BUILD utility how to build the source files contained in that directory. Figure
18.10 shows the SOURCES file.

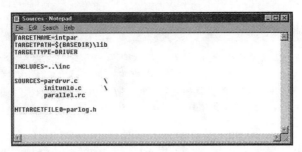

Figure 18.10. *A sample* SOURCES *file.*

The SOURCES file contains macros that instruct the BUILD utility about what to
build, where to get inputs, and where to put outputs. Microsoft supplies some
documentation for BUILD in the DDK Programmer's Guide. Although many of
the BUILD macros are self-explanatory, some of the more common BUILD
directives are listed in Table 18.1 for easy reference.

Table 18.1. Brief list of BUILD utility directives.

Command	Use
C_DEFINES=	Used to provide #define switches to the compiler. For example, C_DEFINES=/DFT_BUILD defines the symbol FT_BUILD.
INCLUDES=	Set equal to the path indicating directories to search for INCLUDE files.
MSC_WARNING_LEVEL=	Allows warning switches to be set. For example, MSC_WARNING_LEVEL=/W4 enables warnings at level 4.
NTTARGETFILE0=	Creates the indicated file as part of pass zero of the build, by executing the commands in makefile.inc in the current directory.
SOURCES=	Set to the list of source files in the current directory to be compiled. Filenames can be separated with spaces or tabs.
TARGETNAME=	Specifies the name for the executable file being built.
TARGETPATH=	Indicates where the executable image should be placed. Note that $(BASEDIR) refers to the base direc- tory where the DDK was installed (typically \ddk).
TARGETTYPE=	Indicates type of image being created. Typically one of DRIVER or DYNLINK.

The file named `makefile` is a standard file that must appear unchanged in every directory with a `SOURCES` file, the contents of which are illustrated in Figure 18.11.

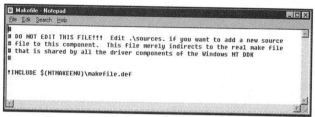

Figure 18.11. *The standard* `makefile`.

Notice that the purpose of a `makefile` is simply to include `makefile.def` from the `\ddk\inc` directory as part of the build process.

Note

> `\ddk\inc\makefile.def` *can be very interesting reading! Once you have mastered the basics of building drivers in the NT environment, take the time to read the contents of* `makefile.def`—*it has a lot of interesting information about the default driver build environment.*

To compile and link a driver, set your default directory in the appropriate DDK environment command prompt window to the directory at which you want to start the build. Then, all you need to do is type `BUILD`, followed by a carriage return. If the compiler, SDK, and DDK have all been installed correctly, the result will be similar to that shown in Figure 18.12.

Figure 18.12. *Output from BUILD.*

When BUILD is run, it potentially creates several output files. BUILD always creates the file build.log in the current directory. This file lists the detailed output from the compiler and linker. If BUILD encounters any warnings during the build process, it places the warning messages in the file build.wrn. If BUILD encounters any errors during the build process, it places the error messages in the file build.err. If there are no warnings and no errors, neither of these files is created.

The executable driver image is placed in the location indicated in the SOURCES file. This is typically based in the \ddk\lib directory. BUILD automatically distributes executables based on target process architecture, and the Free or Checked status of the driver being built. BUILD uses a hierarchy of subdirectories, based on processor architecture and Free or Checked status. Thus, the executable image for a driver will be placed in *targetpath**arch**status*, where *targetpath* is the directory specified in the TARGETPATH= macro in the SOURCES file; *arch* is either i386 for x86 architecture systems or Alpha for Alpha systems; and *status* is free if building a Free build of the driver, and Checked if a Checked version of the driver is being built.

This may sound confusing, but an example or two should clear things up. Assume that TARGETPATH= in the SOURCES file specifies $(BASEDIR)\lib, as do most of the examples in the DDK, and that the DDK was installed into a directory named \ddk. Then, if a Free x86 architecture driver is built, the executable will be placed in the \ddk\lib\i386\free directory. If a Checked x86 architecture driver is built, the executable will wind up in the directory \ddk\lib\i386\checked. If a Free Build of the driver is created for an Alpha architecture system, the driver executable will be located in \ddk\lib\alpha\free. If a Checked version of an Alpha driver is created, it will be located in \ddk\lib\alpha\checked. The default file type for a Windows NT driver is .sys.

> ### Note
>
> *While at first this distribution of output files may seem cumbersome, it actually comes in handy if you're building executables for multiple architectures. Because BUILD will automatically distribute the executables, you can direct the output of your build process to a single server volume. This volume can then contain Alpha and x86 architecture executables, with no conflict in directories used.*

Driver Debugging

Once your driver is built, if you want to debug it you'll need to copy the executable image to two places:

- **The Test System.** Place your driver in the expected location so it can be started. By default, executable driver images are located in the `\NT\System32\Drivers` directory.

- **The Dedicated Debugging Directory.** Copy your driver executable image to the dedicated debugging (symbol) directory on your Development System that you identified when you set up the WinDbg. By default, driver images include debugging symbols (this is true for both the free and the checked builds of drivers). Thus, putting a copy of your executable driver image into your dedicated debugging directory will allow WinDbg to access symbol information while your driver is running on your Test System.

Assuming that your driver has been copied to the two locations mentioned previously, installed, and started, you may begin debugging your driver.

> **Note**
>
> *Here, we assume that you've installed your driver by making the necessary entries in the Registry. This process is described in detail in Chapter 20, "Installing and Starting Drivers."*

WinDbg is a full-featured multi-window debugger. It supports source-level debugging in either C or assembler language. You may set breakpoints of all types (static, conditional, and the like) by using your driver's source code; examine and change local variables; single-step program execution (stepping either into or over called functions); and view and even walk back up the call stack. Figure 18.13 shows an example of a WinDbg driver-debugging session in progress.

> **Note**
>
> *Does it all sound too good to be true? Full multi-window source-level debugging available to driver writers? Well, it is true. The NT driver debugging environment is far superior to any other we've used. But, there is a catch: While WinDbg is very useful, it is also absolutely famous among the NT development community for being flaky. Sometimes it ignores breakpoints. Sometimes it just hangs. Sometimes it gets its symbol table confused. If you encounter any these problems or others (and if you use WinDbg, you will), just exit and restart WinDbg. Microsoft is slowly working on the problems and has said that they are dedicated to making WinDbg the best debugger available anywhere. Reaching this goal will likely take some time.*

How do you actually use WinDbg? For the most part, you use it precisely like any other debugger. You'll just have to experiment. However, to get you started on the right foot, the outlined procedure for setting a breakpoint in the source code of your Kernel mode driver follows. This procedure assumes that your Test and Development Systems have been set up correctly, as described earlier, that your driver executable file has been copied to your dedicated debugging directory, and that your driver executable file has been copied to and is running on the Test System. To set a breakpoint in a currently loaded driver, do the following:

1. From WinDbg's File menu, select Open Source File.

2. In the Open Source File dialog box, select one of your driver's source files in the location in which it was built.

3. Page through the newly opened source file (using the Page Up and Page Down keys, or the up and down arrow keys) until you find a source code line at which you would like to set a breakpoint. Place the mouse on this source code line and click the left mouse button.

4. Stop the Test System by selecting WinDbg's Debug menu and then choosing Break. The message Hard coded breakpoint hit will be displayed in WinDbg's command window.

5. To set a breakpoint at the location currently indicated by the cursor in the source file window, click on the Insert/Remove BreakPoint icon on the toolbar. This icon looks like an open hand, signaling STOP. The selected line in the source code window should be highlighted in red. The red highlighting means that the breakpoint has been set succesfully.

6. If, at this point, after a long pause, the selected line in the source code window is highlighted in purple instead of red, the breakpoint has been requested but not instantiated. This is typically due to WinDbg not being able to find the symbol table for the driver. The most frequent causes of this problem are that the driver executable was not being copied to the dedicated debugging directory, or that the dedicated debugging directory was not properly set up in WinDbg's View\Options...\Symbols dialog box, as described earlier in this chapter.

7. If the breakpoint was set successfully, execution of the Test System can be resumed by selecting Go from WinDbg's Debug menu. When the driver next attempts to execute the line of code where the breakpoint appears, the Test System will stop and the message Breakpoint #0 hit will be displayed in WinDbg's command window.

Kernel Debugger Extensions

In addition to the standard retinue of debugging commands, WinDbg also provides an extensible command interface. You can write your own extensions, starting from the samples provided in the ddk's \src\krnldbg\kdexts directory.

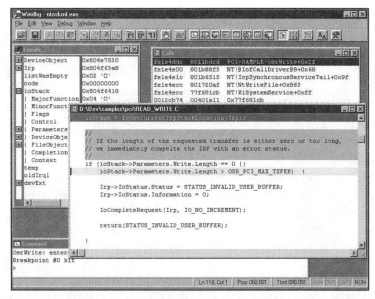

Figure 18.13. *A WinDbg driver debugging session.*

Windows NT also supplies a set of kernel debugger extensions that can be useful when debugging drivers. Before these extensions can be used, the DLL containing the appropriate version of the extensions must be copied from the \support\debug\i386 or \support\debug\alpha directory on the distribution kit (depending on the system on which WinDbg is running) to the \ddk\bin directory on the Development System. The filename of the x86 kernel debugger extension library is kdextx86.dll; the filename of the Alpha kernel debugger library is kdextalp.dll. Note that the Checked and Free versions of the extension libraries are not the same. The extension library must match the kernel and HAL being debugged. Thus, a checked version of the extensions library must be copied from the Checked distribution kit if the Checked version of the kernel and HAL is running on Test System.

The kernel debugger extensions provide many powerful debugging commands. All kernel debugger extension commands start with the exclamation point (!) character. For a complete list of kernel debugger extension commands, enter !? in the WinDbg command window.

Debugging and Testing Hints and Tips

This section contains a mostly random collection of hints and tips regarding driver debugging.

Displaying Output in WinDbg

Drivers can display output that appears in WinDbg's command window by using the DbgPrint () macro. This macro is the Kernel mode equivalent of C's standard printf () function. Since DbgPrint () is active in both Free and Checked versions of the driver, it is often enclosed in #if DBG and #endif conditionals. This results in the DbgPrint () statements appearing only in Checked versions of the driver.

Where to Build Your Project

Until you are familiar with the location of the various files, it's usually easiest to build your drivers in the Microsoft-supplied DDK source tree. Simply add one or more of your own directories under the \ddk\src\ directory, and build your project there. Once you become familiar with other environment variables that may need to be changed, feel free to use an arbitrary directory for your drivers.

Installing Multiple System Images on Your Test System

Using the various options in boot.ini, you can install multiple system images on your test system. This can allow you to have a Free, a Checked, and possibly several different versions (such as a released version of NTv4 and a beta test release of NTv5) installed on the same Test System. You can choose the image you want to start at boot time.

Turning Up the Serial Port Speed

Once you verify that you have a kernel debugger connection properly established between your Development System and your Test System, crank the speed up on the serial port as high as you can. 115200 works on most systems. Don't forget to change the speed in boot.ini on the Test System and in WinDbg!

SysRq Stops the Test System

Is your Test System caught up in a tight loop? Is it ignoring requests from WinDbg to stop? Just hit the SysRq key on the keyboard of the Test System. The system will stop immediately in the debugger, showing the familiar Hard coded breakpoint hit message.

Asserting Assumptions

A well-known Microsoft technique for writing solid code is the use of the ASSERT() macro. This function allows you to check, at runtime, that your assumptions are true. For example, suppose that a pointer is passed into one of your functions as a parameter. Further, suppose that one of the rules for using this function is that this pointer can never be NULL. Instead of just "trusting" that your function was called correctly, you could ASSERT() that the pointer was not equal to NULL, as follows:

```
VOID GetAOne(PULONG MyValue)
{
     ASSERT(MyValue != NULL);
     *MyValue = 1;
}
```

In the preceding example, the first statement uses the ASSERT() macro to ensure that the value of the parameter *MyValue* is not equal to NULL. If this assertion is correct, execution continues. If the statement within the parentheses evaluates to FALSE, however, the system displays a message in WinDbg's command window that indicates that an assertion failed. This message includes the source filename and line number of the assertion, and optionally allows you to take a breakpoint.

This facility is terrific, but see the next hint.

ASSERT() Works Only in the Checked Build

The ASSERT() macro does nothing if you build your driver Free, or if you run your Checked driver on a Free build of Windows NT. For ASSERT() to work, your driver must be built Checked, and your Checked driver must be running on a Checked Build of Windows NT. If you find this constraining, there's always the next hint...

Define Your Own ASSERT() Macro

Do you like the idea of the ASSERT() macro but prefer it did something different (such as something in the Free Build of the operating system)? Define your own macro for ASSERT() and override the system-provided one. Personal preference plays a big role here, but one option might be the following:

```
#define ASSERT(_c) \
    if(!(_c))  \
        DbgPrint("Assert Failed in file %s, line %d.\n", \
            __FILE__,__LINE__)
```

Test on MP Systems

Assuming that your driver is supported on multiprocessor configurations of NT (as it probably should be), be sure to test your driver on multiprocessor systems prior to its release. There is *absolutely no way* you can be sure your driver is MP safe without actually testing it on an MP system. To speed up your testing, use a system with as many processors as possible. Quad-processor systems are more than twice as good at finding multiprocessor errors as dual-processor systems are.

Use the Tools Supplied in the DDK

There are a number of extremely useful tools in the DDK's \bin directory. Most useful of these to writers of standard Kernel mode drivers are the POOLMON and KERNPROF utilities.

POOLMON provides a dynamically updating display of both paged and non-paged pool usage by pool tag. The utility must be run on a system with pool-tracking enabled, such as the Checked Build. For more information on POOLMON, run it, and then type an h to display a help screen.

KERNPROF is a utility that can be used to profile the amount of time spent in various kernel routines. This utility will allow you to pinpoint hot spots in your driver. For more information on KERNPROF, enter the command KERNPROF -?.

Unfortunately, the POOLMON and KERNPROF utilities are neither comprehensively documented nor supported by Microsoft.

Check Your Driver with Performance Monitor

The standard Windows NT Performance Monitor utility can be very useful in debugging device drivers. Using this utility, you can monitor system internal behavior. Things such as the number of interrupts processed and DPCs queued per second by the system can be clues to how your driver is working.

Enable Pool Checking

Windows NT has a terrific set of pool-validation features built into it. Unfortunately, some of the most helpful features for driver writers appear in the Checked Build, but are not enabled by default.

Pool tail checking places guard words after each allocated pool block. The system checks these guard words to ensure that the caller has not written past the end of the allocated segment.

Pool free checking sets freed pool segments to a defined value. Using this value, the system can check to see whether a pool segment is written to after it has been freed.

To enable either of these features, you have to manually set the appropriate NT GlobalFlags (Enable Pool Tail Checking, Enable Pool Free Checking) in the Registry, either manually or by using the GFLAGS utility from the Windows

NT Resource Kit (supplied as part of MSDN). Make the Registry change and reboot. Again, note that these features only appear to be active in the Checked Build.

According to Microsoft Knowledge Base article Q147314:

```
FLG_POOL_ENABLE_TAIL_CHECK      0x00000100
FLG_POOL_ENABLE_FREE_CHECK      0x00000200
```

We recommend that everyone start testing their code with these values ON by default. If the system finds an error, it takes a breakpoint after displaying a cryptic error message.

> ### Note
> *Be careful! You can't be "clever" and decide to turn this checking on from your driver by setting these values on a running system. They need to be enabled when the system starts, or the appropriate signature is not initially written into pool, and everything looks like an error.*

Test on Both the Free and Checked Builds

The road is littered with the bodies of developers whose last words were: "It worked in the Checked Build." Be sure you test the Free Build of your driver on both the Free and Checked Builds of Windows NT prior to shipping.

Stay Up-to-Date

Regularly check the Microsoft Web site for information on driver development issues. At the time this book went to press, the locations on Microsoft's Web site with the best information for driver writers were
http://www.microsoft.com/hwdev and
http://support.microsoft.com/support/ddk_hardware/NTDDK/.

Turn to the World for Help

Although the signal-to-noise ratio can sometimes get a bit too high, the best source for online peer assistance is the Usenet newsgroup comp.os.ms-windows.programmer.nt.kernel-mode. Lots of knowledgeable people answer questions in this forum, including this book's authors and many of the Microsoft support people. Remember, Usenet assistance is "unfiltered"...take any advice proffered from whence it comes.

Behind the Blue Screen

When a Windows NT system, either Free or Checked, encounters what it considers to be an unacceptably fatal condition, it stops and displays a blue screen with white letters. This is called "the blue screen of death," or "BSOD," by driver writers—who typically get to see this screen much more frequently than they would hope. Figure 18.14 shows a sample BSOD.

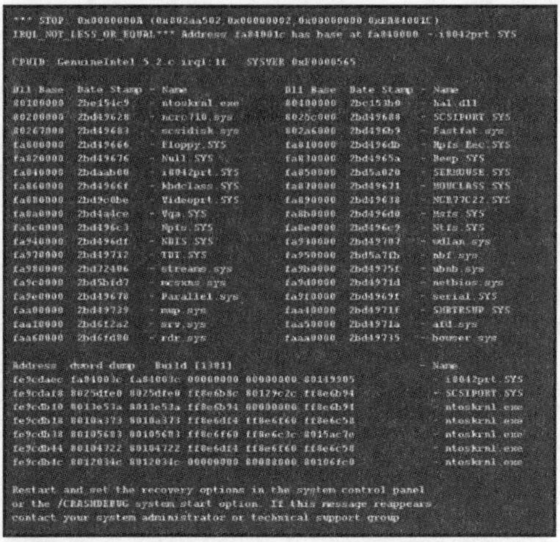

Figure 18.14. *Windows NT's infamous blue screen of death.*

There is a lot of mythology about "debugging" system problems from the blue screen. Unfortunately, often there is not enough information displayed on the blue screen to allow even a highly experienced driver writer to identify the underlying reason that the system crashed.

This section provides a brief introduction to the blue screen, and provides some basic guidelines to help you understand it and deal with it. Much more information is available on MSDN and at the Microsoft support Web site (http://support.microsoft.com).

Blue Screen Format

The blue screen itself is divided into five sections. The first section, located at the top of the screen, provides the reason for the system failure. In Figure 18.13, this section reads:

```
*** Stop: 0x0000000A (0x802aa502, 0x00000002, 0x00000000, 0xFA84001c)
IRQL_NOT_LESS_OR_EQUAL***  Address fa84001c has base at fa840000 -
i8042prt.sys
```

This section is the most important part of the blue screen display. The first line contains the system bug check code and parameters. The complete list of Windows NT bug check codes appears in the DDK-provided file \ddk\inc\ bugcodes.h. The second line provides an interpretation of the error code, and a guess as to the driver or component that might be the cause of the crash.

In the preceding example, the system bug check code is 0x0000000A, which translates to the error IRQL_NOT_LESS_OR_EQUAL, as shown on the second line. The values in parentheses on the first line are parameters to the bug check. The meaning of these parameters varies by bug check code, and even by the location at which the bug check is encountered.

The second section of the blue screen identifies the system on which the crash occurred. In Figure 18.13, the data in the second section reads:

```
CPUID: GenuineIntel 5.2.c  irql: 1f  SYSVER:0xF00000565
```

This line indicates the type of processor on which the crash occurred. The irql represents the IRQL at the time the blue screen is displayed, which on x86 architecture systems is always 1f. Note that this is *not* the IRQL at which the system was running when the problem occurred. The SYSVER variable indicates the type of system and the Windows NT baselevel number. In the example, the baselevel number in hex is 565, which translates to the decimal value 1381, which is the baselevel for Windows NT V4.0.

The third section of the blue screen contains a list of the drivers and Kernel mode DLLs that were loaded in the system when it crashed. The base address, date stamp, and name of each of these modules are listed. The date stamp is taken from the header that was created when the driver or DLL was linked, and can be used to verify the version of the driver that was running. It can be matched with the date displayed by the SDK's dumpbin utility.

The fourth section of the blue screen comprises a dump of the kernel stack, taken at the time the system crashed. The stack address appears in the first column, and the contents of the stack appear in the subsequent columns. In the rightmost column, the name of the driver corresponding to the stack information is displayed.

The stack dump can be useful in identifying what drivers were running and were on the call stack when the system crashed. Typically, the module that caused the crash is located in the first or second stack entry.

The final section of the blue screen contains the information message telling you to contact your system administrator or technical support group.

Reporting or Interpreting Blue Screens

Suppose you're trying to identify the reason the system crashed. To do this, you'll need a record of the information on the blue screen. But you don't have to copy down all the hex values that are displayed. You need to record only the "important stuff."

Anytime the system crashes and you want to identify the cause yourself or you want to work with Microsoft support to identify the cause, be sure to write down all the information from the first section of the blue screen. Without the information displayed in the first two lines of the blue screen, there is nothing anybody can do to identify the reason for the crash.

In addition to this, at a bare minimum, you'll want to copy down the names of the drivers or modules on the kernel stack (shown in the rightmost column of section four of the blue screen). It is rarely helpful to copy down any more of the information from this section.

With this information in hand, either you or a support person might be able to at least get a clue as to the cause of the problem.

Crash Dumps

Windows NT systems can optionally be set up to save the contents of memory to a debugging or "crash dump" file when a crash occurs. This option can be enabled on the Recovery section of the Startup/Shutdown tab of the System Control Panel Applet, as shown in Figure 18.15.

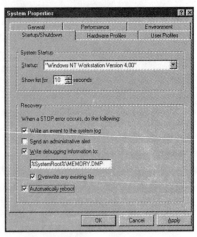

Figure 18.15. *Enabling crash dumps.*

Once a crash dump has been saved, it may be debugged by using WinDbg. Many of the standard techniques used for debugging on a running system can be used to debug a crash dump.

The crash dump file can be opened from WinDbg's File menu. WinDbg can then be used to examine the crashed system in an attempt to determine the cause of the crash.

Chapter 19

Creating a Finished Driver

This chapter will review:

- **Driver Error Logging.** One part of creating a finished driver is having the driver write useful, human-readable messages to the system event log. This section shows you how.

- **Defining Driver Version Resources.** This section describes how to create version resources that will allow both driver writers and users to easily identify which version of a driver is in use.

This chapter discusses some of the smaller, optional items that can help make your driver seem to be truly "finished." Specifically, you'll learn about error logging and driver version resources.

Driver Error Logging

There are many reasons for drivers to log information to persistent storage for later review. For example, it's often useful to have your driver log information about software or hardware problems that are encountered. This can be particularly useful for diagnosing problems at customer sites, when a driver-debugging environment is not available. Drivers may also just want to log information about their normal operation, which might include logging dynamically determined parameters, major state transitions, or other operational information.

Windows NT provides a centralized facility for logging events of significance. This facility, known as the Event Logging Facility, is extensively documented in the Platform SDK. There are actually three event logs—one each for system events, security events, and application events. All of these logs are located by default in the directory %SystemRoot%\System32\config. The content of these logs is stored in binary, and is interpreted and viewed by applications, including the Event Viewer system application.

The I/O Manager provides an interface that drivers can use to write information to the system event log. This interface includes a well-defined structure for event log entries from drivers. This structure is the IO_ERROR_LOG_PACKET. The information provided by the driver in this packet includes:

- An error message code, corresponding to a predefined textual error message. This may be either a generic message that has been defined by the I/O Manager for use by drivers, or an error message of the driver's devising that has been compiled by the Message Compiler and linked with the driver.

- A set of I/O Manager-defined parameters. These parameters are filled into the IO_ERROR_LOG_PACKET by the driver.

- Optional Unicode text strings to be inserted in the textual error message.

- An optional block of binary "dump data."

Note

The standard logging mechanism in Windows NT is known as the Event Logging Facility. The I/O Manager interface to this facility, however, uses the term error log rather than event log. The error log that the I/O Manager mentions and the Windows NT event log are the same thing.

Defining Error Messages

Error messages are logged and stored in the event log file by error message code. The message code is interpreted by the Event Viewer application when a user reviews the contents of the event log. This scheme makes the internationalization of event log messages easy.

The I/O Manager provides a standard set of error messages, which are defined in the file \ddk\inc\ntiologc.h. The messages provided allow a driver to easily log errors such as common configuration errors, parity errors, timeouts, and the like. To use these messages, a driver needs only to include ntiologc.h at compile time.

The problem with the I/O Manager's standard error definitions is that they are generic, sometimes to the point of being confusing. If you are going to go through the effort to add error logging to the driver, do you really want to log a message such as "Driver detects an internal error in its data structures?" If the point of error logging is to make your driver more supportable, you probably don't want to generate event log messages that themselves are the cause of support calls. Therefore, most complex drivers tend to define their own custom error messages for the event log.

Custom error messages for the event log are defined by using the Microsoft
Windows Message Compiler, which is a standard part of the SDK. This compiler (MC.EXE) compiles an error message-definition file into a binary resource-
definition (.RC) file. This file may then be either directly compiled by the
Resource Compiler, or included in the driver's existing resource-definition file
for compilation by the Resource Compiler.

The Message Compiler reads an error message-definition (.MC) file and creates
two standard output files. These output files have the same name as the input
.MC file, but are different file types. There does not appear to be any way to
change the filenames that the Message Compiler generates. For example, if the
file Message.MC is successfully compiled by the Message Compiler, the following
two files will be generated:

- Message.H. A header file for inclusion in your driver source code that
  defines the error message codes. ntiologc.h and ntstatus.h are examples
  of the .h file that the Message Compiler generates.

- Message.RC. The resource-definition file that defines the messages. This file
  is to be further compiled by the Resource Compiler.

In addition to these two files, the Message Compiler generates a set of .BIN
files named MSG0000x.BIN, where x is the language number. English-language
error messages are created in the file MSG00001.BIN. The contents of these files
are the binary message texts to be included in your driver's executable image
file.

The DDK contains a number of sample error message-definition (.MC) files and
even a sample that is dedicated specifically to error logging
(\ddk\src\general\errorlog). Example 19.1 provides another example.

Example 19.1. Sample error message-definition file.

```
;//
;//Module Name:
;//
;//    NOTHING_MSG.MC
;//
;//Abstract:
;//
;//    Message definitions
;//
;//Revision History:
;//
;
;#ifndef _NOTHINGLOG_
```

continues

Continued

```
;#define _NOTHINGLOG_
;
;//
;//  Status values are 32 bit values layed out as follows:
;//
;//   3 3 2 2 2 2 2 2 2 2 2 2 1 1 1 1 1 1 1 1 1 1
;//   1 0 9 8 7 6 5 4 3 2 1 0 9 8 7 6 5 4 3 2 1 0 9 8 7 6 5 4 3 2 1 0
;//  +---+-+-----------------------+-------------------------------+
;//  |Sev|C|       Facility        |             Code              |
;//  +---+-+-----------------------+-------------------------------+
;//
;//  where
;//
;//      Sev - is the severity code
;//
;//          00 - Success
;//          01 - Informational
;//          10 - Warning
;//          11 - Error
;//
;//      C - is the Customer code flag
;//
;//      Facility - is the facility code
;//
;//      Code - is the facility's status code
;//
;
MessageIdTypedef=NTSTATUS

SeverityNames=(Success=0x0:STATUS_SEVERITY_SUCCESS
               Informational=0x1:STATUS_SEVERITY_INFORMATIONAL
               Warning=0x2:STATUS_SEVERITY_WARNING
               Error=0x3:STATUS_SEVERITY_ERROR
               )

FacilityNames=(System=0x0
               RpcRuntime=0x2:FACILITY_RPC_RUNTIME
               RpcStubs=0x3:FACILITY_RPC_STUBS
               Io=0x4:FACILITY_IO_ERROR_CODE
               NOTHING=0x7:FACILITY_NOTHING_ERROR_CODE
               )

MessageId=0x0001 Facility=NOTHING Severity=Error SymbolicName=NOTHING_MESSAGE_1
Language=English
This is sample message number 1
.


MessageId=0x0002 Facility=NOTHING Severity=ErrorSymbolicName=NOTHING_SAMPLE
Language=English
This is another sample message.
.
```

```
MessageId=0x0003 Facility=NOTHING Severity=Informational SymbolicName=NOTHING-
MSG-VALUE
Language=English
%1 logs the following message: %2
.


;#endif    // _NOTHINGLOG_
```

The format of the .MC file shown in Example 19.1 is fairly self-explanatory. Documentation of the .MC file format is provided as part of the Platform SDK. In Example 19.1, lines preceded by semicolons (;) are treated as comments by the Message Compiler. The Message Compiler removes the semicolons and copies the remaining contents of the line to the output .H file. Severity and facility names are defined by using the SeverityNames and FacilityNames for use in the later message file definitions. Note that the "facility" code needs to be a unique value among the messages generated by your driver. The standard system error messages (such as STATUS_INVALID_PARAMETER) use facility code zero. The I/O Manager's standard error-logging messages, defined in ntiologc.h, use facility code four. Therefore, drivers typically use facility codes greater than four for private error messages. Example 19.1 uses a facility code value of seven.

Note

Don't worry about having to choose a value for a facility code that's unique among all drivers. Just choose one that is not used by the standard NT components. As previously stated, using any value greater than four will work. As a matter of convention, most driver writers use either five or seven.

The message-definition section of the .MC file contains the error message ID, symbolic name, error severity, and text to be displayed by the Event Viewer when a message with the indicated Message ID is logged. The text may be provided in multiple languages. Text strings may be optionally inserted into these messages, using the escape sequence %n, where "n" is the number of the text string to insert. The I/O Manager always provides text string number one, which is defined as being the name of the device logging the message (if the *IoObject* specified when the error packet is allocated is a pointer to a Device Object, as described later in this section). Therefore, text strings, which are provided by the driver to be inserted into the error message, start with %2. A few other escape sequences are available for use in message definitions. Refer to the SDK for the complete list. The text of each error message is terminated by a period . as the first character on the line.

Note

Even though there is a severity STATUS_SEVERITY_SUCCESS, *and it is possible to define messages with this severity, this is not an acceptable severity level in the Windows NT event-logging model. In fact, the Event Viewer application will display any messages logged with* STATUS_SEVERITY_ SUCCESS *with an Error severity.*

Allocating the Error Log Packet

When a driver wants to write a message to the error log, it allocates an error log packet large enough to hold the standard I/O Manager error log information packet, plus any additional data (such as text-insertion strings or even binary data) that it wants to record. This packet is allocated by using the function IoAllocateErrorLogEntry(), the prototype for which is shown in Figure 19.1.

PVOID
IoAllocateErrorLogEntry(IN PVOID *IoObject*,
        IN UCHAR *EntrySize*);

IoObject: A pointer to either the driver's Driver Object or Device Object associated with this error. If an error is associated with a particular device, the driver should provide a Device Object pointer for this parameter.

EntrySize: The total size in bytes of the error log packet to be allocated, including any arguments or data provided by the driver. This must not exceed ERROR_LOG_MAXIMUM_SIZE bytes.

Figure 19.1. IoAllocateErrorLogEntry() *function prototype.*

The *IoObject* argument to IoAllocateErrorLogEntry() dictates the translation of the %1 parameter in the error message string. If the *IoObject* parameter is set to a pointer to a Device Object, the name of the device replaces %1 in the error-message definitions. If the *IoObject* is a pointer to a Driver Object, the %1 parameter is replaced by the I/O Manager with a NULL.

The driver-accessible fields of the IO_ERROR_LOG_PACKET structure are zeroed by the I/O Manager before the packet is returned to the driver. The packet contains the following fields that are filled in by drivers:

- MajorFunctionCode. This field indicates the IRP major function code associated with the request that was in progress when the error was detected.

- `RetryCount`. This field contains the number of attempts the driver has made prior to logging this error.

- `DumpDataSize`. This field indicates the length of any binary data that the driver will log. This value is the size over and above the size of the `IO_ERROR_LOG_PACKET` structure itself and the size of any text strings to be inserted into the log message.

- `NumberOfStrings`. This field indicates the number of driver-supplied text strings to be inserted into the log message.

- `TextOffset`. This field indicates the offset in bytes from the start of the `IO_ERROR_LOG_PACKET` to the start of the first null-terminated Unicode character string to be inserted into the log message.

- `EventCategory`. According to the documentation, this is an optional "event category" from a driver's custom-defined message file. We hate to say it, but we don't understand what that means and we don't know what this field is supposed to be for. We've never seen it used, and we've never seen a system component log a message that uses it. We do know that a driver can set this to any USHORT value it wants, and that value will be displayed (in decimal) in the Category column in the Event Viewer.

- `ErrorCode`. This field indicates the code for the event log message to be displayed. This is the symbolic name from either a system-defined or driver-defined message file.

- `UniqueErrorValue`. This field is a driver-defined value that uniquely identifies the location or cause of the error. Drivers most often use this value as a further qualifier to the `ErrorCode`. For example, there may be a number of places where a driver logs an `IO_ERR_CONFIGURATION_ERROR` ErrorCode value. Each location that logs this error will utilize a unique `UniqueErrorValue` that allows the driver's developers to identify the specific cause of the error.

- `FinalStatus`. This field indicates the ultimate NTSTATUS in which the operation in error resulted.

- `SequenceNumber`. This field indicates a monotonically increasing IRP sequence number kept by the driver.

- `IoControlCode`. If the `MajorFunction` field indicates an error on an `IRP_MJ_DEVICE_CONTROL` or `IRP_MJ_INTERNAL_DEVICE_CONTROL` operation, this field contains the I/O Control Code.

- `DeviceOffset`. This value is the offset into the device where the error occurred. Obviously, this field is more relevant to disk and tape drivers than it would be for, say, a serial port driver.

- `DumpData`. This field indicates the start of a driver-defined area of `DumpDataSize` bytes that contains binary data that the driver wants to log along with the standard I/O Manager error log packet.

As is evident from the preceding descriptions, the fields in the I/O Manager's error log packet structure are fairly rigidly defined. Driver writers don't need to be constrained by the documented meanings of the fields in the `IO_ERROR_LOG_PACKET`, however. For example, drivers of devices that don't have a "device offset" can use the `DeviceOffset` field of the `IO_ERROR_LOG_PACKET` for anything the driver wants. Similarly, although the I/O Manager's error-logging guidelines require it, most drivers do not implement IRP sequence numbers for the `SequenceNumber` field. A common use of this field is to hold a value that is incremented for each packet written to the event log.

Writing Packets to the Event Log

Once an `IO_ERROR_LOG_PACKET` has been allocated and filled in, the driver calls the I/O Manager function `IoWriteErrorLogEntry()`, the prototype for which appears in Figure 19.2.

PVOID
IoWriteErrorLogEntry(IN PVOID *ElEntry*);

ElEntry: A pointer to a filled-in error log packet that has been previously allocated by calling IoAllocateErrorLogEntry().

Figure 19.2. `IoWriteErrorLogEntry()` *function prototype.*

The `IoWriteErrorLogEntry()` function passes the error log packet to the I/O Manager, who in turn passes it to the systemwide event-logging facility. The `IO_ERROR_LOG_PACKET` is automatically returned by the I/O Manager; the driver does not deallocate or return this packet. Example 19.2 shows how to use the `IoAllocateErrorLogEntry()` and `IoWriteErrorLogEntry()` functions, including inserting a text string.

Example 19.2. Allocating, filling in, and writing an error log entry.

```
//
// Log a message to the error log
//
logMsg = L"Error processing WRITE request.";

len = (UCHAR)wcslen(logMsg)*sizeof(WCHAR) + sizeof(WCHAR);
```

```
//
// Allocate the packet with enough space for the insertion string.
//
errorLogEntry = (PIO_ERROR_LOG_PACKET)
                IoAllocateErrorLogEntry(devObj,
                    (UCHAR)(sizeof(IO_ERROR_LOG_PACKET)+len) );

//
// Initialize the packet
//
errorLogEntry->ErrorCode = (ULONG) NOTHING_MSG_VALUE;
errorLogEntry->NumberOfStrings = 1;
errorLogEntry->StringOffset = FIELD_OFFSET(IO_ERROR_LOG_PACKET,
                                                DumpData);

//
// The rest of the fields are "optional" - That is, the message will be
// written even if they are not supplied.
//
errorLogEntry->MajorFunction = ioStack->MajorFunction;
errorLogEntry->UniqueErrorValue = WriteErrorBaseValue+12;
errorLogEntry->FinalStatus = STATUS_INVALID_DEVICE_REQUEST;
errorLogEntry->SequenceNumber = ErrorLogSequenceNumber++;

//
// Copy the insertion string to the packet
//
RtlCopyMemory(&errorLogEntry->DumpData[0], logMsg, len);

//
// Write the packet to the event log
//
IoWriteErrorLogEntry(errorLogEntry);
```

The code in Example 19.2 shows how the error log packet is allocated, filled in, and written by the driver. Note that some of the I/O Manager-defined fields are filled in. Other fields, such as the SequenceNumber field, are filled in but with a slightly different interpretation than the ordinary one used by the I/O Manager. Other fields are not referenced at all.

Note

We must admit that our favorite way to use the event log is to define a single error message at each severity level with the content "%1: %2". This lets us write any string we want—preprocessed by sprintf(), if required—to the event log. Granted, this makes internationalization difficult. But it makes adding concise, specific error messages very easy. This is especially true during debugging.

Invoking the Message Compiler with BUILD

You've decided to include error logging in your driver. How do you actually get the Message Compiler to process your .MC file as part of the build process?

Unfortunately, the BUILD utility does not automatically know how to process .MC files. Therefore, the driver writer will need to create a makefile.inc file, including the rules defining how to build the message file. BUILD is then directed to read this file by using the macro NTTARGETFILE0 in the SOURCES file for the driver. Figure 19.3 shows a sample SOURCES file that uses NTTARGETFILE0 to cause BUILD to read and process makefile.inc, located in the same directory. Figure 19.4 shows the associated makefile.inc file that directs the compilation of the message-definition file.

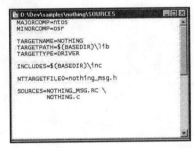

Figure 19.3. *SOURCES* file illustrating the use of NTTARGETFILE0 *to compile a message-definition file.*

Figure 19.4. makefile.inc *with rules for compiling a message-definition file.*

Note in Figure 19.4 that the Message Compiler is invoked with the -c switch. This causes the "customer code flag" bit to be set in the generated messages. While not absolutely necessary, it is correct to set this bit for messages that are not defined by Microsoft.

Registering Your Driver As an Event Logging Source

Drivers that define their own error messages must register themselves as an event logging source. This enables Event Viewer and other applications to interpret log entries written by the driver.

All that is required to register your driver as an event logging source is to create a key in the Registry under the key
HKEY_LOCAL_MACHINE\SYSTEM\CurrentControlSet\Services\EventLog\System. The key you create must be equal to the name of your driver. The values placed under this key must be as follows:

- **EventMessageFile**. Set this value equal to the REG_EXPAND_SZ string that is the path to your driver's executable image file. This value may contain paths to multiple files that define event log messages—each separated by a semicolon. Thus, for example, if a driver writes both standard NT I/O Manager messages and its own event log messages, this value must be set equal to the path to the driver's image file and also equal to the path to the I/O Manager's message file, which is
%SystemRoot\System32\IoLogMsg.DLL.

- **TypesSupported**. Set this value to a REG_DWORD equal to the facility number (typically 0x07) that your driver implements.

These Registry changes are normally made as part of the driver's installation procedure.

Defining Driver Version Resources

Although not a crucial design element, the capability to quickly and easily determine the version of a driver can save a lot of time and frustration. One thing that makes such identification easy is adding a version resource (technically, a VERSIONINFO resource) to your driver. This resource can be viewed from the Windows NT Explorer (right-click on the file, select Properties, and choose the Version tab).

The VERSIONINFO resource is defined in the driver's resource-definition (.RC) file. Complete documentation on creating VERSIONINFO resources appears in the Platform SDK documentation. This section provides a brief overview of this topic as it relates specifically to NT drivers.

Defining .RC Files from the Microsoft-Supplied Templates

If you look through the DDK example drivers (which, as we said earlier, are mostly sources for "real" NT drivers from the distribution kit), you'll find many resource-definition (.RC) files that resemble the one shown in Example 19.3, which is taken from the DDK's parport driver.

Example 19.3. A Microsoft standard resource-definition file from the DDK.

```
#include <windows.h>

#include <ntverp.h>

#define     VER_FILETYPE                    VFT_DRV
#define     VER_FILESUBTYPE                 VFT2_DRV_SYSTEM
#define     VER_FILEDESCRIPTION_STR         "Parallel Port Driver"
#define     VER_INTERNALNAME_STR            "parport.sys"
#define     VER_ORIGINALFILENAME_STR        "parport.sys"

#include "common.ver"

#include "parlog.rc"
```

Notice in Example 19.3 that the file begins by including NTVERP.H (from the \ddk\inc directory), lists a set of definitions, and then goes on to include COMMON.VER (also from the \ddk\inc directory). The last line in the example includes PARLOG.RC, which is the .RC file created by the Message Compiler for error logging.

NTVERP.H is Microsoft's systemwide, standard version-definition file that includes definitions relevant to Windows NT for the build number, version, company name, product name, and legal trademark. COMMON.VER is a template that actually defines the version resource. Note that the version-specific definitions in all these files (such as VFT_DRV, VFT2_DRV_SYSTEM, and the like) are defined in the SDK include file, WINVER.H.

Driver writers can define version resources for their drivers by building standard resource files using the Microsoft-supplied templates. In this case, unless you override the supplied values, you will get Microsoft's information. You can override these values in your .RC file, as shown in Example 19.4, which is the .RC file for OSR's "nothing" example driver.

Example 19.4. A resource-definition file to override standard Microsoft resources.

```
//
// Resources
//
#include <windows.h>
#include <ntverp.h>

#ifdef VER_COMPANYNAME_STR
#undef VER_COMPANYNAME_STR
#endif

#ifdef VER_PRODUCTNAME_STR
#undef VER_PRODUCTNAME_STR
```

```
#endif

#ifdef VER_PRODUCTVERSION_STR
#undef VER_PRODUCTVERSION_STR
#endif

#ifdef VER_PRODUCTVERSION
#undef VER_PRODUCTVERSION
#endif

#define VER_COMPANYNAME_STR        "OSR Open Systems Resources, Inc."
#define VER_FILEDESCRIPTION_STR    "The OSR Nothing Driver"
#define VER_FILEVERSION_STR        "3.0a"
#define VER_INTERNALNAME_STR       "nothing"
#define VER_LEGALCOPYRIGHT_STR  " ©1998 OSR Open Systems Resources, Inc."
#define VER_ORIGINALFILENAME_STR   "nothing.sys"

#define VER_PRODUCTNAME_STR        "Developing Windows NT Device Drivers"
#define VER_PRODUCTVERSION_STR     "Windows NT V4"

#define VER_FILEVERSION            4,00,01,001
#define VER_PRODUCTVERSION         4,00,01,001
#define VER_FILETYPE               VFT_DRV          // Type is Driver
#define VER_FILESUBTYPE            VFT2_DRV_SYSTEM

#include <common.ver>

#include "nothing_msg.rc"
```

Example 19.4 redefines all the resources that you'll need to override to avoid defaulting any parameters (not counting the FILEFLAGS and FILEFLAGS mask. See the SDK.) to Microsoft-specific values.

Creating Your Own Resource-Definition File

By the time you override all the Microsoft-specific values, we think the result is complicated and ugly enough that you might just as well create your own version resource-definition file. It's easy enough to do. Example 19.5 shows a sample version resource-definition file.

Example 19.5 A custom resource-definition file.

```
//
// Resources
//
#include <winver.h>

#ifdef RC_INVOKED

#if DBG
```

continues

Continued

```
#define VER_DBG VS_FF_DEBUG
#else
#define VER_DBG
#endif

VS_VERSION_INFO VERSIONINFO
FILEVERSION    3,00,01,00
PRODUCTVERSION 3,00,01,00
FILEFLAGSMASK  VS_FFI_FILEFLAGSMASK
FILEFLAGS      VER_DBG
FILEOS         VOS_NT
FILETYPE       VFT_DRV
FILESUBTYPE    VFT2_DRV_SYSTEM
BEGIN
    BLOCK "StringFileInfo"
    BEGIN
        BLOCK "040904B0"
        BEGIN
            VALUE "CompanyName",      "OSR Open Systems Resources, Inc."
            VALUE "FileDescription",  "The Nothing Driver"
            VALUE "FileVersion",      "V3.0a"
            VALUE "InternalName",     "Nothing"
            VALUE "LegalCopyright","  ©1998 OSR Open Systems Resources, Inc."
            VALUE "OriginalFilename", "Nothing.Sys"
            VALUE "ProductName",      "Developing Windows NT Device Drivers"
            VALUE "ProductVersion",   "NT V4.0"
            VALUE "For Support Call", "OSR at (603) 595-6500"
        END

    END

    BLOCK "VarFileInfo"
    BEGIN
        VALUE "Translation", 0x0409, 0x04B0
    END
END

#endif

#include "nothing_msg.rc"
```

Example 19.5 shows a custom resource-definition file for the "nothing" driver. This file is only slightly longer than Example 19.4, which uses the Microsoft templates. This file has the advantage of omitting Microsoft-specific information (like the copyright notice) that you might overlook when overwriting the file, and which might consequently incur the wrath of your company's lawyers. Defining your own version resource also has the added advantage of allowing you to define your own driver- or company-specific values. In Example 19.5, note the addition of a "For Support Call" value.

Chapter **20**

Installing and Starting Drivers

This chapter will review:

- **How Drivers Are Started.** Device drivers in Windows NT are all started dynamically. This section describes how drivers are started and how the startup order of device driver may be specified.

- **Driver- and Device-Specific Parameters.** Most drivers need to store some sort of driver- or device-specific parameters during their installation procedure. This section makes some suggestions as to where those parameters may be stored.

- **Driver Installation.** This section describes the different methods for installing device drivers on a Windows NT system.

As mentioned several times previously in the book, Windows NT drivers are dynamically started, typically during the process of bootstrapping the system. Precisely when a driver is started or whether it is automatically started at all, is dependent on information stored in the Registry about the driver. This chapter covers installation procedures for Windows NT device drivers, and the Registry entries needed to control how and when a driver is started.

As in the rest of the book, we limit our discussion in this chapter to standard Kernel mode device drivers. Although we mention in passing some issues related to the installation and startup of mini-port drivers (such as video, SCSI, or NDIS drivers) and User mode drivers (such as multimedia drivers); we do not pretend to thoroughly or completely address the issues related to the installation of drivers for these types of devices. The NT DDK includes both clear explanations and examples of how to install these devices.

How Drivers Are Started

Kernel mode drivers are started according to information in the Windows NT Registry. Each driver in Windows NT must have its own key in the Registry, named with the driver's name, under the HKEY_LOCAL_MACHINE\SYSTEM\CurrentControlSet\Services key. Values stored under the driver's key tell the system when and if a driver is to be started. Figure 20.1 shows the Registry key (displayed by the regedt32 utility) for the standard Windows NT "Beep" driver.

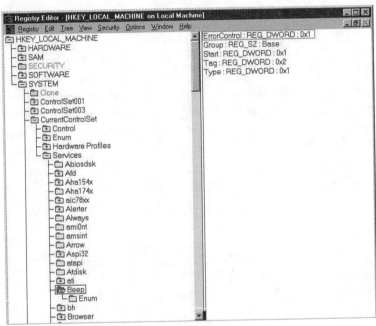

Figure 20.1. *Services key for the Beep driver.*

As you can see in Figure 20.1, the Beep driver has a key named HKLM\SYSTEM\CurrentControlSet\Services\Beep. Under this key (in the right pane in Figure 20.1), are value entries named ErrorControl, Group, Start, Tag, and Type. These value entries provide the information the system needs to be able to start the Beep driver at the appropriate time. Briefly, the value entries relevant to driver startup that may appear under a driver's Services key are as follows:

- **Type.** This value indicates the type of component (driver, file system, or application, for example) that this entry represents.

- **Start.** This value tells the system whether it should attempt to start this driver during system startup and, if so, during what phase of system startup it should attempt it.

- **Group.** This value allows the driver writer to specify a specific startup order for their driver order within a given system startup phase.

- **Tag.** This value allows the driver writer to establish a specific order within a particular startup group.

- **ErrorControl.** This value indicates what action the system should take if it attempts to start a driver but fails.

- **DependOnGroup/DependOnService.** This value identifies a prerequisite group or specific driver on which the driver depends.

- **ImagePath.** This value contains the path to the driver image file.

- **DisplayName.** This is the text name of the driver to be displayed.

In addition to drivers, Windows NT services also have entries with these values under the Services key in the Registry. Services are User mode applications (similar to daemons on UNIX) that run automatically, in the background, at system startup.

Driver Service Entries

Each of the value entries relevant to driver startup is described in detail in the sections that follow. In these sections, for those value entries with DWORD values, the hex value, as well as the Service Control Manager symbolic values, are shown. Coverage of how the Service Control Manager CreateService() function can be used to build a custom installation procedure is provided later in this chapter.

> ### Note
>
> *Case is not significant in Registry keys or, typically, Registry values. Thus, although the case of various value entries or values is set by convention (such as \HKEY_LOCAL_MACHINE\SYSTEM being uppercase); be assured that whether a key, value entry, or value related to driver installation and startup is specified in upper-, lower-, or mixed case is of no significance to the system.*

Type

The Type value entry is set to a REG_DWORD that indicates the general service type that this Registry entry represents. Table 20.1 shows the values for Type that are relevant to drivers.

Table 20.1. Type value entries.

Hex Value	Service Control Manager Definition	Meaning
0x01	SERVICE_KERNEL_DRIVER	Entry is a Kernel mode driver
0x02	SERVICE_FILE_SYSTEM_DRIVER	Entry is a file system driver
0x04	SERVICE_ADAPTER	Entry is a network adapter or component
0x08	SERVICE_RECOGNIZER_DRIVER	Entry is a file system recognizer

There are other valid values for Type, for use by Win32 services. Unless a driver is a file system or file system recognizer, it should use type SERVICE_KERNEL_DRIVER.

Start

The Start value entry (a REG_DWORD) indicates if and when a driver is to be started. If the driver is to be started automatically during system startup, Start also indicates the phase of system startup during which the driver should be started. Table 20.2 lists the value entries for Start.

Table 20.2. Start value entries.

Hex Value	Service Control Manager Definition	Startup Type Shown by Device Control Panel Applet	Meaning
0x00	SERVICE_BOOT_START	Boot	Driver is started at the first opportunity during the bootstrap process by ntldr
0x01	SERVICE_SYSTEM_START	System	Driver is started with the "core" set of system drivers
0x02	SERVICE_AUTO_START	Automatic	Driver is started by the Service Control Manager during system and application startup
0x03	SERVICE_DEMAND_START	Manual	Driver is started on request
0x04	SERVICE_DISABLED	Disabled	Driver cannot be started, even if explicitly requested

Drivers that start at boot start time (Start value of 0x00) are loaded from the boot media by the ntldr utility by using a special boot file system, and are started during operating system initialization. The only drivers that should start at boot start time are those that are required for the operating system to boot. Because the operating system is still in the process of initializing during boot start, drivers that start at this time will encounter certain limitations. Such limitations include the fact that drive letters are not yet assigned, much of the Registry has not yet been loaded, and the event-logging service has not been started. Examples of standard NT drivers that start at boot start time are the SCSI adapter driver and class driver that control the boot disk.

Drivers that start at system start time (*Start* value of 0x01) start with the core set of NT drivers. Unless you have a specific reason to start your driver earlier or later, this is probably the start time to use for your driver. System start time begins while the startup "blue screen" is still being displayed and continues approximately until you see the logon prompt displayed. Most standard NT drivers start at system start time, including drivers for the keyboard, floppy disk, CD-ROM, video display, and sound system.

Auto-start time (Start value of 0x02) takes place immediately following system start. This is the last opportunity for drivers to be automatically started during the system boot process. Auto-start time is typically used by network components and services, as well as by low-priority Kernel mode drivers. NT ordinarily starts the parallel and serial port drivers, as well as the network adapter driver, during this phase of startup. It is worth noting that users might be able to log into the Windows NT system before all the drivers that are scheduled to start at Auto-start time have started. This means that drivers started at Auto-start time may not be immediately available as soon as a user gains access to the system.

A driver with its Start entry set to SERVICE_DEMAND_START will be started only on request. This can be by request of a user, for example, by using the appropriate Control Panel applet, or programmatically via the service control manager interface. Drivers that are set to demand start may also be started automatically during system startup, if they are indicated as a prerequisite, via the DependOnGroup or DependOnService value entries, for a driver that starts in the Auto-start group. See the description of DependOnGroup/DependOnService later in this chapter for a complete explanation of this phenomenon.

> **Tip**
>
> *When debugging or testing a driver, it's usually most convenient to start it manually, if this is possible. Thus, the Start entry would be set to* SERVICE_DEMAND_START. *Starting the driver manually avoids the problem of having the driver crash the system during startup, thus preventing the driver writer from easily replacing the driver!*

It is important to understand that the value of Start determines driver start time at the coarsest possible level. Therefore, all drivers with Start set to SERVICE_BOOT_START will be started before any drivers with Start values of SERVICE_SYSTEM_START. Likewise, all drivers with Start values indicating

SERVICE_SYSTEM_START will be started before any drivers set to
SERVICE_AUTO_START will be started.

Group

The Group value entry indicates the load order group to which the driver
belongs. The load order group determines when the driver starts, *within its
indicated start time*. The load order group is specified as a REG_SZ value, taken
from a list of values in HKEY_LOCAL_MACHINE\SYSTEM\CurrentControlSet\Control\
ServiceGroupOrder\List. This value entry is a REG_MULTI_SZ that contains an
order listed of load order groups. ...\ServiceGroupOrder\List by default contains the following groups:

1. System Bus Extender

2. SCSI miniport

3. port

4. Primary disk

5. SCSI class

6. SCSI CDROM class

7. filter

8. boot file system

9. Base

10. Pointer Port

11. Keyboard Port

12. Pointer Class

13. Keyboard Class

14. Video Init

15. Video

16. Video Save

17. file system

18. Event log

19. Streams Drivers

20. PNP_TDI

21. NDIS

22. TDI

23. NetBIOSGroup

24. SpoolerGroup

25. NetDDEGroup

26. Parallel arbitrator

27. extended base

28. RemoteValidation

29. PCI Configuration

This list indicates that within a given start time, a driver that sets its Group value entry to System Bus Extender will be started before a driver with the Group value entry SCSI miniport. Similarly, drivers with the Group value entry SCSI miniport will be started before drivers with a Group value entry port, and so on. Drivers that have a Group value that does not appear in ...\ServiceGroupOrder\List are started after the drivers that list a valid Group value. Drivers that provide no Group value entry are started last within their start time.

> **Note**
>
> *The Windows NT DDK documentation claims in at least one place that the Group value entry is used only for drivers that start at boot start and system start times. This is not correct. The Group value is also used to order the startup of drivers started at auto-start time.*

Tag

The value for Tag sets the order in which a driver starts *within its startup group* if the driver starts within boot start or system start time. The system ignores Tag values for drivers that start at auto-start time. Possible values for Tag are specified for each group in the Registry under the key HKEY_LOCAL_MACHINE\CurrentControlSet\Control\GroupOrderList. Under this key is a set of value entries, the name of which corresponds to the names of the various startup groups. Each value entry comprises a tag vector.

Figure 20.2 shows the ...\Control\GroupOrderList key opened in the regedt32 application. In the right pane are the value entries that are stored under this key. Notice that not every group that appears in the ...\ServiceGroupOrder\List value entry has a value under ...\Control\GroupOrderList. This is because only those groups that need to control the startup order of drivers within the group require value entries under the ...\Control\GroupOrderList key.

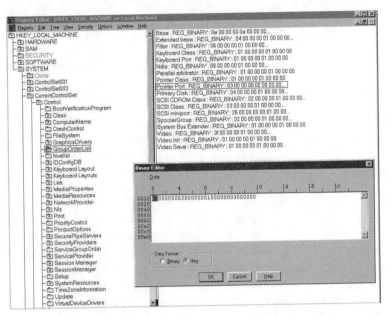

Figure 20.2. GroupOrderList *key in the Registry.*

The format of the tag vector is rather arcane. The tag vector is in REG_BINARY format. The first byte of the tag vector indicates the number of longword tags that appear. The subsequent longwords comprise an ordered list of tag values.

The tag vector for the Pointer Port group is shown opened in regedt32's binary editor in Figure 20.2. Note that this tag vector has 0x03 tags indicated. The tags, in the order that they appear in the tag vector, are 0x00000002, 0x00000001, and 0x00000003. Note that the tag vector is rounded out to an integral number of longwords. The Pointer Port tag vector indicates that there are three tags. Among the drivers within the group Pointer Port, the driver with its Tag value entry set to 0x02 will be started first, the driver with a Tag of 0x01 starts next, and the driver with Tag 0x03 starts third.

Figure 20.3 shows the Registry entry for the serial mouse (Sermouse) driver.

Figure 20.3 shows that the Sermouse driver is *Type* : SERVICE_KERNEL_DRIVER (0x01); starts at system start time (Start is set to SERVICE_SYSTEM_START which is 0x01); and during system start time, starts within the startup group Pointer Port (Group is set equal to Pointer Port). Within the startup group Pointer Port, Sermouse will be the first driver started. This is because the Sermouse driver has a *Tag* value entry of 0x02, and 0x02 is the first value in Pointer Port tag vector (stored under the value entry ...\Control\GroupOrderList\Pointer Port).

Figure 20.3. *Sermouse driver Registry entry.*

ErrorControl

The value entry `ErrorControl` determines what action the system takes if a driver fails to successfully start at boot, system, or auto-start time. The reason for the failure could be due to errors in its Registry service key or the driver returning a status other than `STATUS_SUCCESS` from its driver entry routine. `ErrorControl` is ignored for drivers that start at auto-start time. Table 20.3 shows the possible values for `ErrorControl` and their meanings.

Table 20.3. `ErrorControl` *value entries.*

Hex Value	Service Control Manager Definition	Meaning
0x00	SERVICE_ERROR_IGNORE	Load errors are ignored.
0x01	SERVICE_ERROR_NORMAL	Load errors are logged to the system event log; system continues booting.
0x02	SERVICE_ERROR_SEVERE	Load errors are logged to the system event log; if Last Known Good configuration is being booted, load continues; otherwise, the system is restarted by using Last Known Good configuration.
0x03	SERVICE_ERROR_CRITICAL	Load errors are logged to the system event log; if the Last Known Good configuration is being booted, the boot is aborted; otherwise, the system is restarted by using Last Known Good configuration.

Whenever the CurrentControlSet in the Registry is modified, the Registry makes a backup copy of the previous control set that was used to successfully start the system. This backup control set is known as the *Last Known Good* control set.

If a driver specifies an ErrorControl value of SERVICE_ERROR_SEVERE, if the driver fails to start, the boot process checks to see whether it is already starting by using the last known good control set. If the driver is not already started by using the *Last Known Good* control set, the system is rebooted by using the *Last Known Good* control set. Once the system is started by using the *Last Known Good* control set, the system startup process continues.

The only difference between an ErrorControl value of SERVICE_ERROR_CRITICAL and SERVICE_ERROR_SEVERE is that if a driver specifying SERVICE_ERROR_CRITICAL fails to start, and the *Last Known Good* control set is already being used, the system boot process is halted by a system crash.

> **Note**
>
> *Obviously, it's important to use the* ErrorControl *values* SERVICE_ERROR_SEVERE *and* SERVICE_ERROR_CRITICAL *carefully. Failure to do so can result in an unbootable system! Further, our experience has been that although* SERVICE_ERROR_SEVERE *and* SERVICE_ERROR_CRITICAL *do indeed result in the system being rebooted, they do not always result in the system being rebooted with the Last Known Good control set. Thus, if you have a driver that specifies one of these* ErrorControl *values, and the driver encounters an error, you may have to manually reboot the system and then manually elect to start the system by using the Last Known Good control set.*

DependOnGroup/DependOnService

The DependOnGroup and DependOnService value entries cause more confusion than any other entries about how Windows NT drivers are started. Documentation to the contrary, these two value entries appear to apply only during auto-start time. Further, their actual actions can be quite surprising.

DependOnGroup is a REG_MULTI_SZ that contains one or more startup groups on which the driver is dependent. At auto-start time, when a driver with a DependOnGroup is started, the Service Control Manager will attempt to start all the drivers in the prerequisite groups that have not already been started and are not explicitly marked as SERVICE_DISABLED. Thus, even drivers in a prerequisite group that are marked as SERVICE_DEMAND_START will be started. Such drivers are still started at the time specified by their *Group* value, however. If any of the drivers in the prerequisite group start, the driver with the dependency will be started.

An example might make this a little clearer. Assume that you have the following drivers to start:

```
Nothing.sys    Type: REG_DWORD: SERVICE_KERNEL_DRIVER
               Start: REG_DWORD: SERVICE_AUTO_START
               Group: REG_SZ: Primary disk
               DependOnGroup: REG_MULTI_SZ: MyGroup

Fred.sys       Type: REG_DWORD: SERVICE_KERNEL_DRIVER
               Start: REG_DWORD: SERVICE_DEMAND_START
               Group: REG_SZ: MyGroup
```

In this example, when the Service Control Manager encounters Nothing.sys with its prerequisite group MyGroup, it will attempt to start all the drivers not already started and not set to SERVICE_DISABLED, including Fred.sys. If any of the drivers in MyGroup started successfully, either because they started successfully during their normal start opportunity or because they were started as a result of a dependency for Nothing.sys, Nothing.sys will be started. Note that the prerequisite drivers can have been started at boot start time, system start time, or auto-start time.

This gets complicated, however. Suppose the group Primary disk appears in the ...\Control\ServiceGroupOrder\List before MyGroup, and there are no other drivers in MyGroup other than Fred.sys. In this case, the dependency will fail (and Nothing.sys will not be started) because Fred.sys will not actually be started until it is MyGroup's turn, according to the ...\Control\ServiceGroupOrder\List.

DependOnService works the same way that DependOnGroup works, except it works on a specific driver (or service) name, instead of on an entire group of drivers. Thus, if DriverA is listed in a DependOnService value entry for DriverB, when DriverA is successfully started, DriverB will also start successfully.

> **Note**
>
> *We admit it: We've given up trying to figure out all the nuances of how DependOnGroup and DependOnService really work. What's clear is that these value entries do not appear to us to work either the way they are documented, or the way many people seem to think they work. It's our practice to avoid these two value entries and order our drivers using the Group value entry. If one of our drivers is dependent on another, we simply have the dependent driver check in its Driver Entry routine to see whether the prerequisite driver has created its Device Object. If it hasn't, we know the prerequisite driver did not load successfully.*

ImagePath

The ImagePath value entry specifies the location of the driver image on disk. This value entry lets you locate your driver executable file in a location other than `%SystemRoot%\System32\Drivers`, which is the default. Precisely how this entry is specified is a function of the start time of the driver.

For drivers that start at boot start time, the value for ImagePath must either start with a leading slash and be an absolute ARC path name, or not start with a leading slash and indicate a path relative to `%SystemRoot%`. This is because the Object Manager's directory structure has not been set up when the driver is loaded. For example, for a boot start driver, specifying the value `Win32\MyDrivers\Nothing.Sys` locates the indicated driver in `%SystemRoot%\Win32\MyDrivers` directory.

For drivers that start at system start time, the `ImagePath` value cannot use traditional drive letters because these will not necessarily be created yet. Thus, instead of specifying `C:\MyDirectory\Nothing.Sys`, you must specify `\Device\HardDisk0\Partition1\MyDirectory\Nothing.Sys` (assuming that `C:` corresponds to `\HardDisk0\Partition0`, of course). The path must point to a local (non-network) volume. The relative syntax supported for drivers started at boot time, where a path without a leading slash indicates a path relative to `%SystemRoot%`, also appears to work.

For drivers that start at either auto-start or demand start, the `ImagePath` is only constrained to be on a local partition. Driver images cannot be opened and loaded across the network.

DisplayName

The DisplayName value entry contains a Unicode text string that identifies the driver. If a DisplayName value is not supplied, the driver's filename is used.

Driver- and Device-Specific Parameters

Drivers typically store driver- and device-specific information under a `\Parameters` subkey of their service entry. Figure 20.3 shows the Sermouse's service entry, including a `\Parameters` subkey. Device- or driver-specific information might include tuning parameters, licensing information, or configuration information.

As mentioned in Chapter 13, "Driver Entry," information stored under the `\Parameters` subkey is entirely device- or driver-specific. The system does not retrieve or attempt to interpret any of the information stored under this key. The structure of the data stored under the Parameter's key is entirely up to the driver. There is no specific NT convention that applies.

The installation procedure for drivers that do not support dynamic configuration, such as those for ISA bus devices, typically store static configuration information under the \Parameters subkey. This information, including the port address, shared memory address, or IRQ for the device, is retrieved by the driver during the Driver Entry routine.

In addition to the \Parameters subkey of the driver's service entry, drivers often store information in the Registry under the Software key. The convention is that information should be stored under what's called a *description* subkey. The entire key has the following form:

\HKEY_LOCAL_MACHINE\SOFTWARE\CompanyName\ProductName\ProductVersion.

Again, the information stored in these keys is entirely up to the driver.

Driver Installation

Installing device drivers on Windows NT is extremely simple. The entire process consists of only two steps:

1. **Copy the necessary files to the system.** These files include the driver executable image (.sys) file, as well as any other files (such as files containing microcode or configuration information) that are required by the driver.

2. **Create the necessary Registry entries, as described in the previous section.** These entries indicate when the driver is to be started, and also store any driver- or device-specific information (such as IRQ or device I/O addresses) that the driver may need during its initialization processing.

Depending on the type of driver being installed and when it is installed, there are three options for how the two installation steps are implemented:

- For Keyboard and Mouse drivers (as well as display and SCSI adapter drivers) that need to be installed during the NT system installation process, Text Setup installation is used. This process requires the creation of a simple TXTSETUP.OEM file that describes the files to be copied and the Registry entries to be made.

- For Keyboard, Mouse, PC Card, Port and Tape drivers (as well as SCSI Adapter, display, modem, Telephony, and Multimedia drivers) installed after Windows NT has been installed, GUI setup is used. This process is directed from a particular Control Panel applet (CPA), and requires the creation of an OEMSETUP.INF file to describe the files to be copied and the Registry entries to be made.

- For all other standard Kernel mode device drivers, a custom installation procedure is used. This requires the driver writer to create a custom installation program to copy the files and make the necessary Registry entries. Alternatively, a third-party installation product such as InstallShield can be used.

As should be evident from the preceding list, most standard Kernel mode drivers will be installed using a custom installation procedure. Fear not, however, because the actual installation process is very simple.

Text Setup

Drivers that are installed during the Windows NT system installation procedure are installed using a process called *text setup*. These drivers include keyboard and mouse drivers, as well as display and SCSI adapter drivers. Custom HALs are also installed by using this method.

Text setup requires the creation of an installation script called TXTSETUP.OEM. The format of this file is well-defined by the DDK documentation, and several examples exist in the \ddk\src\setup directory. This file directs the setup program to copy the files and create the Registry entries necessary to install the driver.

The TXTSETUP.OEM file contains a series of sections. Each section in the file is prefixed by the name of the section in square brackets. For example, the first section is the Disks section. This section is identified in TXTSETUP.OEM by [Disks] appearing on a line by itself.

Within the TXTSETUP.OEM file itself, lines that start with a hash mark ("#") or a semicolon (";") indicate comment lines. Text scripts are enclosed in double quotation marks.

The sections in TXTSETUP.OEM include:

- [Disks]

- [Defaults]

- [Component]

- [Files.*component.id*]

- [Config.*component.id*]

[Disks] Section of TXTSETUP.OEM

The [Disks] section of the TXTSETUP.OEM file identifies the disks that make up the distribution kit for the component to be installed. Each disk is identified by one script line. The format of script lines in the disk section is:

```
disk = description, tagfile, directory
```

where:

- *disk* is the name used later in the script to identify the particular disk in the installation kit.

- *description* is a text string with the human-readable description of the disk; used to prompt the user for the right disk to insert.

- *tagfile* is a path, without the device name, that points to a file on the distribution disk. Setup looks for this file during installation to determine whether the correct disk has been inserted by the user.

- *directory* is the base directory on the disk from which the file will be copied during installation.

The following example shows how the [Disks] section of the TXTSETUP.OEM file might appear.

```
[Disks]

Disk1= "Rocket Blaster Mouse Driver Disk 1", \rbmouse.1, \
```

In the preceding example, the user will be prompted to "Rocket Blaster Mouse Driver Disk 1" when files from that disk are to be copied. When a disk is inserted, setup will check to see whether it finds the file rbmouse.1 in the root directory of the disk to verify that the proper disk has been inserted by the user. Files will be copied from the root directory of the volume.

[Defaults] Section of TXTSETUP.OEM

The [Defaults] section of the TXTSETUP.OEM file provides the default selection for the hardware "components" listed in [component] sections. The format for script lines in this section is as follows:

```
component = id
```

where:

- *component* is the hardware component name. This must be one of computer, display, keyboard, mouse, CD-ROM, or SCSI.

- *id* is the string that identifies the option ID for the component.

The following example shows how the [Defaults] section of the TXTSETUP.OEM file might appear.

```
[Defaults]

mouse = RBMFAST
```

In the preceding example, the default option for the hardware mouse component is the RBMFAST option. The following section covers hardware component options in greater detail.

[Component] Section of TXTSETUP.OEM

The [Component] section of the TXTSETUP.OEM file identifies the hardware-component options that the user can select to be installed. The name of this section is the hardware component name, which is one of computer, display, keyboard, mouse, CD-ROM, or SCSI. Each line represents one option. The default option is indicated by the [Defaults] section, previously in the script. If no default for a component is present, the first line in the component section is used. The format for script lines in this section is:

```
id = description, key-name
```

where:

- *id* is the string that identifies the option id for the component. This is the same *id* string that can appear in the [Defaults] section.

- *description* is the human-readable text string that identifies this component to the user. The user will be asked to choose which option to install among the various component options listed.

- *key-name* is the name of the services key to create in the Registry for this component.

The following example shows how the [Defaults] section of the TXTSETUP.OEM file might appear.

```
[mouse]

RBMFAST = "Rocket Blaster FAST mouse", RBMOUSE
RBMCORRECT = "Rocket Blaster working mouse", RBMOUSE
RBMGEN = "Generic rocket blaster mouse driver", RBMOUSE
```

In the preceding example, there are three choices for the mouse component. Each choice is represented by a separate line in the [mouse] component section of the file. The user will be prompted to choose among the listed description strings from a menu. Regardless of which option is chosen, the services key in the Registry will be named RBOUSE.

[Files.*component.id*] Section of TXTSETUP.OEM

The [Files.*component.id*] section of the TXTSETUP.OEM file identifies the files that are to be copied for the particular option of a particular component. Each line in the script file identifies the type of file to be copied, its disk in the installation kit, and the name of the file to be copied. The name of the section uses the word "Files" followed by a period, followed by a hardware component name, and then followed by an id that matches a component option id in the component section of the script. The format of script lines in this section is as follows:

```
component = disk, filename
```

where:

- *component* is the hardware component name.

- *disk* is the identifier, defined in the [Disks] section of the script file, that indicates the disk from which the file is to be copied.

- *filename* is a file specification that, when appended to the directory specification of the matching [Disks] script line, forms the full path and file name of the file to be copied.

The following example shows how the [Files.*component.id*] section of the TXTSETUP.OEM file might appear.

```
[Files.mouse.RBMFAST]
driver = Disk1, fast\rbmouse.sys

[Files.mouse.RBMCORRECT]
driver = Disk1, right\rbmouse.sys
```

In the preceding example, there are two sections shown. The first is processed when the user selects the RBMFAST option from the component section. In this section, the mouse driver is copied from Disk1 (which matches the Disk1 specification in the [Disks] section at the top of this script file) from the \fast\ directory. The file copied is RBMOUSE.SYS.

[Config.*component.id*] Section of TXTSETUP.OEM

The [Config.*component.id*] section of the TXTSETUP.OEM file identifies any additional Registry entries that need to be made during installation, beyond those that are minimally required to start the driver. The format of the script lines in this section is as follows:

```
value = subkeyname, valuename, valuetype, valuetoset
```

where:

- *value* is a keyword.

- *subkeyname* is the name of the subkey to be used for the indicated value under the \HKEY_LOCAL_MACHINE\CurrentControlSet\Services*key-name* key in the Registry (where *key-name* is defined in the *component* section of the script). If the key does not exist, it is created. To place a value directly under the driver's services key, specify a null string in this *subkeyname* field.

- *valuename* is the name of the value entry to create.

- *valuetype* is the Registry-defined value entry type, such as REG_DWORD, REG_SZ, REG_EXPAND_SZ, or REG_BINARY.

- *valuetoset* is the actual value to be set in the indicated location.

The following example shows how the [Component.*component.id*] section of the
TXTSETUP.OEM file might appear:

```
[Config.mouse.RBMFAST]
value = Parameters, GoFast, REG_DWORD, 01

[Config.mouse.RBMCORRECT]
value = Parameters, GoFast, REG_DWORD, 00
```

In the preceding example, two sections are shown. The section processed
depends on the user's selection during installation. If the RBMFAST component
option was selected, the value entry named GoFast is created with the value of
0x01 in the Registry under \HKLM\CCS\Services\RBMOUSE\Parameters key.

GUI Setup

Drivers for standard devices that are installed after Windows NT has been fully
set up, or those that are installed during system installation but can be tailored
later, use GUI setup procedures. The devices that are supported by GUI setup
are the keyboard, mouse, PC card, and port and tape devices (as well as the
SCSI adapter, display, modem, telephony, and multimedia devices). This procedure is directed by an .INF file, which has a format that is shared between
Windows NT and Windows 95.

The .INF file format is well documented in the DDK, and we will not repeat
that documentation here. There are also numerous examples in the
\ddk\src\setup directory of the DDK that can be used as a guide.

One caution about .INF file format is worth mentioning: Although it is indeed
true that Windows 95 and Windows NT share a common .INF file format, not
all sections are supported by both platforms. Thus, it is common to have a
shared .INF file that has different sections used for Windows NT GUI setup
and Windows 95 GUI setup.

Custom Setup

Most device drivers for Windows NT (at least most of the device drivers developed outside of Microsoft!) are installed by using a custom setup procedure.
This is because most drivers are installed after the system is installed, and do
not fit in the category of those devices supported by GUI setup.

Because device-driver installation is so simple on Windows NT, creation of a
Win32 program to properly install the drivers is a straightforward task. A
Win32 installation program can be as elegant or as simple as required. All that
is required is to copy the needed files so that they are properly accessible at
start time, and to make the required Registry entries. More complex installation programs query the user for configuration parameters, and store these
parameters under the driver's \Parameters subkey.

Creating the required Registry entries for a driver is made even easier by using the Win32 Service Control Manager API function `CreateService()`. This function, which is fully documented in the SDK, creates the necessary Service entry for the driver and adds the required value entries. An example of installing and starting a driver using the Service Control Manager API even appears in the DDK in the `\ddk\src\general\instdrv` directory. Figure 20.4 shows the prototype for the `CreateService()` function.

```
SC_HANDLE
CreateService(SC_HANDLE hSCManager,
        LPCTSTR lpServiceName,
        LPCTSTR lpDisplayName,
        DWORD dwDesiredAccess,
        DWORD dwServiceType,
        DWORD dwStartType,
        DWORD dwErrorControl,
        LPCTSTR lpBinaryPathName,
        LPCTSTR lpLoadOrderGroup,
        LPDWORD lpdwTagId,
        LPCTSTR lpDependencies,
        LPCTSTR lpServiceStartName,
        LPCTSTR lpPassword);
```

hSCManager: A handle to the Service Control Manager, previously opened using the OpenSCManager() function.

lpServiceName: A pointer to a NULL-terminated string that contains the name of the service key to be created in the \HKLM\CCS\System\Services directory.

LpDisplayName: A pointer that contains a NULL-terminated string for the DisplayName value entry in the Registry entry for this driver.

dwDesiredAccess: The access desired to the service, once it has been created. Typically, SERVICE_ALL_ACCESS. See the SDK for details.

dwServiceType: The value for the value entry Type for this driver.

dwStartType: The value for the Start value for this driver.

dwErrorControl: The value to the ErrorControl value entry for this driver.

lpBinaryPathName: A pointer to a NULL-terminated string that contains the value for the LoadImage value entry for this driver.

---

lpLoadOrderGroup: A pointer to a NULL-terminated string that contains the value for the Group value entry for this driver. If no group value is required, specify NULL.

lpdwTagId: A pointer to a DWORD containing the value for the Tag value entry. If no tag is required, specify NULL.

lpDependencies: A pointer to a string to a list of group or service dependencies. Each entry in the list must be terminated with a single NULL character, and the entire list must be terminated with two NULL characters. By default, any listed entries are placed in the DependOnService value entry for the driver. Entries that start with the identifier SC_GROUP_IDENTIFIER are placed in the DependOnGroup value entry for the driver. If this driver has no dependencies, specify NULL.

lpServiceStartName: A pointer to a NULL-terminated string that specifies the ObjectName value entry. For Kernel mode drivers, this value should be NULL.

lpPassword: A pointer to a NULL-terminated string that provides a password. For Kernel mode drivers, this value should be NULL.

Figure 20.4. `CreateService()` *Win32 function prototype.*

Of course, the requisite Registry entries can also be created by using the RTL or Registry Win32 functions. One advantage to using the Service Control Manager API, however, is that services that are created by using `CreateService()` can be immediately started without rebooting the system by using the `StartService()` function.

Installation with InstallShield

Custom setup routines may also be crafted by using InstallShield, a product made by InstallShield Software Corporation. Most developers working on PC platforms have probably encountered InstallShield at one time or another because it is the most common program used for application installation and removal. InstallShield provides an attractive and easily customized splash screen, as well as application installation and removal.

Part III

Alternate NT Driver Architectures

Please note that it is not possible to learn how to write File System drivers, Video Miniport drivers, SCSI Miniport drivers, or NDIS Miniport drivers using the information presented in the four chapters in this part of the book. The goal of this part is to simply provide a brief introduction to these alternative NT drivers, and to relate the structure of these drivers to the standard Kernel mode device drivers discussed previously in this book.

Chapter 21

File System Drivers

This chapter will review:

- **File System Driver Characteristics.** This section describes the characteristics that make File System drivers unique among Windows NT Kernel mode drivers.

- **Learning More About Developing File System Drivers.** This section provides information on where and how to find out more about developing FSDs.

This chapter briefly compares and contrasts File System drivers with the standard Kernel mode device drivers that were discussed extensively in Part II. At the end of the chapter, you'll find a few pointers on where you can learn more about developing File System drivers.

Please note that it is not possible to learn how to write a File System driver using the information presented in this chapter. The goal of this chapter is to simply provide a brief introduction to File System drivers, and to relate the structure of these drivers to the standard Kernel mode device drivers discussed previously in this book.

File System Driver Characteristics

File System drivers (FSDs) are Windows NT standard Kernel mode drivers. When most people first think of "File System drivers," they typically think of FSDs that implement physical media file systems, such as NTFS or FAT. Although NT FSDs can implement physical media file systems, they are also used to implement many more things. FSDs in Windows NT may implement network file systems and logical namespace file systems, as well.

The most common example of a network file system is a redirector, such as the Windows NT "RDR" file system. A redirector is responsible for mapping drive letters to remote volumes, accessible over the network. The remote volume is shared via a paired server.

Network file systems may also implement interprocess communications facilities. Examples of these include Windows NT's Named Pipe File System (NPFS) and Mail Slot File System (MSFS). The FSD provides a generic I/O interface (`CreateFile()`, `ReadFile()` and `WriteFile()` from Win32) to interprocess communications.

There are a wide variety of FSDs that fall into the category of logical namespace File System drivers. A simple example would be an FSD that exports a content-addressable data store as a hierarchy of directories and files. One example of this type of FSD that we've seen was based on storage for publications: A volume represented a publication, a top-level directory on the volume represented a chapter in the publication, and the subdirectories within the chapters each represented separate parts of the chapter.

Other examples of logical namespace file systems are hierarchical storage subsystems. Again, there are many different things that fall into this category. However, the most common variation manages the storage of data, both online and "near line" (near line being in a juke box system, for example). All the data files in the system appear to the user to be available online at all times. Access to the near line data is transparent to the user, except for the delay in its initial access. The more sophisticated types of hierarchical storage subsystems dynamically balance what data is stored where, thus allowing fast access to frequently used data, but providing vast amounts of storage space for infrequently accessed information.

One obvious characteristic that sets an FSD apart from a device driver is that the lower-edge interface of an FSD is another driver typically accessed via `IoCallDriver()`, instead of a device accessed via the HAL. Apart from this, however, there are specific differences that allow FSDs to fulfill their special roles in Windows NT systems. Some of these characteristics include:

- FSDs are guaranteed to be called in the context of the requesting thread.

- FSDs are tightly integrated with the NT Memory Manager and Cache Manager subsystems.

- FSDs are closely intertwined with the NT I/O and Object Managers.

Figure 21.1 shows the file system's place in the stack of Windows NT drivers. The following sections discuss each of the FSD characteristics in more detail.

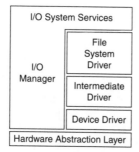

Figure 21.1. *File System drivers are at the top of the Windows NT driver stack.*

FSDs Are Called in the Context of the Requesting Thread

As discussed in Chapter 11, "The Layered Driver Model," and shown in Figure 21.1, FSDs are always logically located at the top of a Windows NT stack of drivers. A File System driver is thus always guaranteed to be initially called with a request, in the context of the thread making the request. This guarantee makes it possible for FSDs to use Neither I/O for describing requests and to implement Fast I/O entry points.

Implementing Neither I/O allows an FSD to manipulate data by using the requestor's virtual address. This avoids the overhead of locking buffers in memory and creating alternate mappings (as would be required with Direct I/O), or copying data to intermediate buffers (as would be required with Buffered I/O). When a request cannot be conveniently processed immediately in the context of the requesting thread by an FSD, the FSD builds an MDL to describe the requestor's buffer. This MDL is, of course, usable in an arbitrary thread context. An FSD may utilize "worker threads" to process such requests.

Because file systems are called in the context of the calling thread, they also typically implement Fast I/O. Fast I/O, described in Chapter 11, is a procedure-based interface between the I/O Manager and drivers. The Fast I/O entry point is shown in Figure 21.2. The Fast I/O interface makes it possible for FSDs to process certain operations, including some read and write operations, without the use of IRPs.

In Fast I/O, request parameters are passed from the I/O Manager to the FSD as function parameters. As an example of a Fast I/O entry point, Figure 21.3 shows the parameters passed by the I/O Manager to an FSD's `FastIoRead()` entry point. Because the FSD is called in the context of the requesting thread, the parameters that are passed in are all that the FSD requires to process the request.

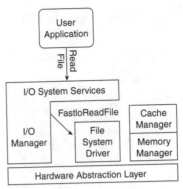

Figure 21.2. *Fast I/O processing for a Read operation.*

```
BOOLEAN
FastIoRead(IN PFILE_OBJECT FileObject,
          IN PLARGE_INTEGER FileOffset,
          IN ULONG Length,
          IN BOOLEAN Wait,
          IN ULONG LockKey,
          OUT PVOID Buffer,
          OUR PIO_STATUS_BLOCK IoStatus,
          IN PDEVICE_OBJECT DeviceObject);
```

Figure 21.3. FastIoRead() *FSD entry point.*

Note that the FastIoRead() routine is of type BOOLEAN. This allows the FSD to inform the I/O Manager about whether it was able to process the request. If the FSD was able to completely process the request in its Fast I/O routine, the FSD returns TRUE as the status of its Fast I/O routine. This results in the I/O Manager completing the request back to the requestor, with the I/O status returned in the I/O Status Block. If the FSD could not completely process the request, it returns FALSE from its Fast I/O routine. In this case, the I/O Manager builds an IRP (typically using Neither I/O, as described previously) that describes the I/O request and calls the FSD at the appropriate Dispatch entry point.

> **Note**
>
> *Remember: Only File System drivers can implement Fast I/O entry points for read and write operations. The I/O Manager will not call the read or write Fast I/O entry points of intermediate or device drivers, even if such a driver is at the top of its driver stack.*

FSDs Are Tightly Integrated with the VM Subsystem

Probably the single greatest differentiating factor between File System drivers and other drivers is that FSDs tightly integrate with the Windows NT Memory Manager and Cache Manager subsystems. Figure 21.4 shows an example of this integration.

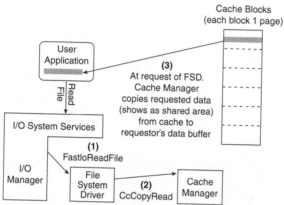

Figure 21.4. *FSD and Cache Manager integration.*

In Figure 21.4, the FSD is called at one of its Fast I/O entry points to process a read request from a User mode application (Step (**1**)). In response to this call, assuming that the file was not opened non-cached, the FSD calls the Cache Manager (via its CcCopyRead() function) to copy the requested data from the system cache to the requestor's data buffer (Step (**2**)). All of the requested data exists in the cache, so the Cache Manager copies the data from the system cache to the user's data buffer (Step (**3**)).

If all of the requested data does not presently reside in cache, the FSD can (optionally) wait while the Cache Manager reads the data from disk. When the Cache Manager has to go to disk for data, it performs read-ahead on the requested file. Therefore, disk reads are always at least one page in length, and are frequently longer.

The Cache Manager does not simply issue a read for the data from disk, however. The Cache Manager page faults the disk data into memory. The data itself is thus loaded from the disk file by the Memory Manager. The Memory Manager builds a paging I/O request for the data from disk, and sends it to the file system, as shown in Step (**3**) in Figure 21.5. This results in the data being read from the disk, into the system cache (Step (**4**)). The user's read is eventually completed using this data.

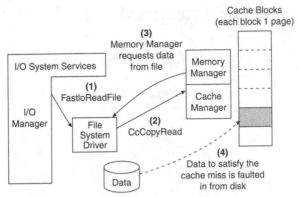

Figure 21.5. *The Cache Manager goes to disk for data.*

The data is read from disk and placed in an appropriate cache block. On completion of the in-page (disk read) operation, the Cache Manager copies the data from the newly filled cache block to the requestor's data buffer.

> **Note**
>
> *Please be aware that this explanation leaves out many of the complex details of the file system, Cache Manager, and Memory Manager's interaction. Our goal is only to provide enough information for you to reach an understanding of how file systems differ from device drivers. Actually implementing a file system requires a bit more information than we can include in these few pages!*

FSDs Are Closely Intertwined with the I/O and Object Managers

The final difference between File Systems drivers and device drivers is in the level of integration between FSDs and the I/O and Object Managers. File systems in Windows NT are each responsible for implementing part of the system's namespace.

When a request to open a file named `c:\mydir\fred.txt` for read access is received by the I/O Manager, the I/O Manager calls the Object Manager to help resolve the name that was passed in. The Object Manager traverses its namespace, finding the Device Object that corresponds to `c:`. Decoding the remainder of the name, however, is the province of the I/O Manager and the File System driver. The decoding process is as follows:

1. The Object Manager calls the parse method associated with the identified Device Object. This parse method is provided by the I/O Manager.

2. The I/O Manager locates the FSD that has the volume mounted.

3. The I/O Manager then builds an IRP with an IRP_MJ_CREATE major function code and passes this IRP to the FSD.

4. The FSD is then responsible for parsing the remaining parts of the path and filename in a file system-dependent manner.

5. When the name has been parsed, the FSD builds a data structure in memory called a File Control Block (FCB), which describes the file.

Although the format of the FCB is generally file system-dependent, part of the FCB's structure is known to various NT subsystems such as the I/O Manager.

The capability to parse and resolve names in I/O requests is one of a file system's most powerful capabilities. It is this capability that makes file systems useful for more than just the support of on-disk structures.

Learning More About Developing File System Drivers

Unfortunately, File System driver development is not supported by Microsoft at the present time. Microsoft has released an installable file systems development kit, available separately from MSDN, which enables file system development. This kit provides the necessary header file with prototypes of the required functions, plus a sample code for a couple of example file systems. More information on the kit is available on the Web at
http://www.microsoft.com/hwdev/ntifskit/default.htm.

The only resource for learning, in detail, how to develop FSDs is OSR's Windows NT File Systems Development seminar. This seminar is taught in public and private settings all over the world. In the interest of full disclosure, this seminar is taught by one of the authors. Check out http://www.osr.com for more information, including a seminar outline and the current schedule.

Rajeev Nagar has authored a very good book, titled *Windows NT File Systems Internals: A Developer's Guide* (O'Reilly, ISBN: 1-56592-249-2). The book is a great resource that is clearly written and describes many heretofore undocumented details about file-system development. Take care, however, because the book is more correct for NT V3.51 than it is for later versions of NT.

Chapter 22

Video Miniport Drivers

We are grateful to our resident graphics expert, OSR Consulting Associate Pete Nishimoto, for contributing this chapter.

This chapter will review:

- **Video Port/Miniport Drivers.** This section briefly describes the design and architecture of Video Miniport drivers.

- **Display Drivers.** Video Miniport drivers provide only part of the support needed for graphics devices on NT. This section describes Device Display Interface (DDI) drivers.

- **DMA and Video Display Drivers.** This section highlights some issues regarding DMA support in Video display drivers.

- **Learning More About Developing Video Display Drivers.** This section provides information on where you can learn more about developing Video Display drivers.

This chapter briefly discusses the structure of Video Display drivers, and compares and contrasts their structure to that of standard Kernel mode device drivers. The chapter ends with a section that provides information on where you can learn more about developing Video Display drivers.

Please note that it is not possible to learn how to write Video Display drivers by using only the information presented in this chapter. The goal of this chapter is to simply provide a brief introduction to Video Display drivers, and to relate the structure of these drivers to the standard Kernel mode device drivers discussed previously in this book.

A Video Display driver actually consists of two separate drivers: a Device Display Interface (DDI) driver and a Video Miniport driver. The DDI is a Kernel mode DLL that is responsible for all rendering activities. That is, the DDI receives graphics requests from the Win32 subsystem and then interfaces with the video display hardware to produce the correct graphical representation. The Video Miniport driver is a Kernel mode driver that is responsible for the nonrendering tasks required by a DDI for a particular graphics adapter (for instance, tasks such as graphics-adapter initialization, mapping of adapter registers, or allocation of resources). The Video Miniport driver and DDI driver are a matched pair and, together, are considered to be a Video Display driver.

Video Port/Miniport Drivers

Video Miniport drivers have some of the same characteristics of other Minidrivers in Windows NT. That is, the Video Miniport drivers are "wrapped" by a higher-level driver (the Video Port driver), and the Miniport driver (if written correctly) is compatible across Windows NT platform architectures. The Video Miniport driver for Windows NT, however, is not compatible with the Video Miniport drivers for Windows 9x platforms.

Video Port Drivers

The Video Port driver (videoprt.sys) is implemented as a standard NT Kernel mode driver. There exists an export library (videoprt.lib) to which the Video Miniport driver links. When the Video Port driver is loaded, Windows NT will invoke its DriverEntry routine, which will perform the normal device driver initialization (routine registration, object creation, and so forth). Once loaded, the Video Port driver then queries the Registry for the available video services, and, when found, the Video Miniport driver for that service will then be loaded.

The purpose of the Video Port driver is to

- Isolate Video Miniport drivers from the operating system

- Perform as much common processing as possible

The Video Port driver exports a standard interface for use by all Video Miniport drivers. The Video Port driver then employs NT mechanisms to implement the interface. Video Miniport drivers normally call only those functions exported by the Video Port driver; however, because the Video Miniport is linked within the environment of standard Window NT Kernel mode drivers, the Video Miniport driver may make Windows NT executive function calls directly.

A major goal for the Video Port/Miniport architecture is to keep the Video Miniport drivers from having to deal with most typical NT device driver processing. To achieve this, the Video Port driver handles interfacing to the remainder of the NT operating system (such as the I/O Manager), and presents a restricted and controlled view of the NT environment. This frees the Video Miniport drivers to concentrate on the display hardware-specific aspects of their adapter.

Video Miniport Drivers

Because the Video Miniport drivers are wrapped by the Video Port driver, their format and interface are much simpler than that of standard Kernel mode device drivers. As a result, Video Miniport drivers are typically shorter and simpler than an equivalent standard Kernel mode driver. Additionally, the standard structure of a Windows NT Kernel mode driver does not apply to Video Miniport drivers. This section briefly discusses the Video Miniport driver structure, including the actions performed by the driver at some of its major entry points, including initialization, request initiation, and interrupt service.

> ### Note
>
> *The Video Port/Video Miniport interface is a call-return interface, and therefore all access to a graphics adapter is serialized. Additionally, there is a per-adapter resource lock that the Video Port driver must obtain before any request is submitted to the Video Miniport driver, thus imposing a single-threaded access paradigm for all Video Miniport requests and thus, single-threaded access to the graphics adapter itself.*

Initialization

Like all drivers in Windows NT, the Video Miniport driver starts with a DriverEntry routine that is called when the driver is loaded; however, this is where the similarities between the Video Miniport drivers and normal Kernel mode drivers end. Initialization consists of a number of sequential calls between the Video Miniport and the Video Port driver, culminating in an ultimate return from the Video Miniport's DriverEntry routine.

Within its DriverEntry, the Video Miniport driver allocates and initializes the VIDEO_HW_INITIALIZATION_DATA structure. This data structure contains

- Pointers to the Video Miniport functional entry points

- Size of the device extension data area that is to be allocated for use for device-specific data

- Some basic information about the devices that will be supported

After the VIDEO_HW_INITIALIZATION_DATA structure has been initialized, the Video Miniport driver calls the Video Port driver's VideoPortInitialize() routine, passing a pointer to the allocated VIDEO_HW_INITIALIZATION_DATA structure and a pointer to the Video Miniport's Driver Object (one of the parameters supplied with the DriverEntry call). Within the VideoPortInitialize() function, the

Video Port driver performs much of the normal Kernel mode device driver DriverEntry processing, including initializing the Driver Object dispatch table and creating Device Objects for the graphics adapter.

During `VideoPortInitilaize()`, the Video Port driver allocates the Device Extension data area. The Video Port driver then calls back into the Video Miniport driver at the `HwVidFindAdapter()` entry point, as defined in the `VIDEO_HW_INITIALIZATION_DATA` structure. Within its `HwVidFindAdapter()` routine, the Video Miniport driver locates and configures the graphics adapter that it will control. The Video Port driver exports a number of functions to facilitate the Video Miniport driver with this process. One such function is `VideoPortGetAccessRanges()`. This routine retrieves bus-configuration information and will attempt to claim these resources in the Registry. Another function is `VideoPortGetDeviceBase()`, which combines the NT functions `HalTranslateBusAddress()` and `MmMapIoSpace()`. There are other helper routines that are just wrappers for the HAL routines, such as `VideoPortGetBusData()`, (`HalGetBusDataByOffset()`), and `VideoPortReadRegisterUlong()` (`READ_REGISTER_ULONG()`).

> **Note**
>
> *The* Again *parameter to* `HwVidFindAdapter()` *is used to indicate whether the Video Miniport driver wants to be called again at its* `HwVidFindAdapter()` *routine to process the next adapter. However, Windows NT 4.0 SP3 officially supports only a single graphics adapter and does not support multiheaded configurations. Setting* Again *to* TRUE, *so that* `HwVidFindAdapter()` *is called multiple times, does not deleteriously affect the operation of Windows NT, and does indeed result in the Video Miniport's* `HwVidFindAdapter()` *routine being called again. However, this alone is not at all sufficient to enable multihead support. There is much more to providing multihead support than just setting* Again *to* TRUE.

Upon return from `HwVidFindAdapter()`, the Video Port driver completes many of the standard NT device-driver tasks: reserving resources for the Video Miniport driver, obtaining interrupt vectors and connects to that interrupt, initializing timers, and creating symbolic links.

Request Initiation

Video Miniport drivers do not use IRPs. Instead, the Video Port driver will repackage the IRPs it receives into Video Request Packets (VRPs). And when it creates the Device Object for the Video Miniport, the Video Port indicates that requests should be described by using Buffered I/O. The fields of the originally received IRP are copied to the VRP, with the added restriction that the input and output buffers have been set up for Buffered I/O.

When the Video Port driver receives a request to be processed, it calls the Video Miniport driver at its HwVidStartIO() routine (as specified in the VIDEO_HW_INITIALIZATION_DATA structure). The parameters passed to this routine are the adapter's Device Extension and a pointer to the VRP. The IoControlCode field of the VRP identifies the function to be performed. The InputBuffer and OutputBuffer fields identify the data buffers for the request. The StatusBlock field is used to communicate the completion information for this request back to the Port driver.

There is a minimum set of IoControlCodes that must be supported for every Video Miniport. These include:

- IOCTL_VIDEO_QUERY_NUM_AVAIL_MODES

- IOCTL_VIDEO_QUERY_AVAIL_MODES

- IOCTL_VIDEO_SET_CURRENT_MODE

- IOCTL_VIDEO_MAP_MEMORY

- IOCTL_VIDEO_RESET_DEVICE

Interrupt Service

When the graphics adapter interrupts, the Video Port driver calls the Video Miniport driver's HwVidInterrupt() routine with a pointer to the adapter's device extension. In this case, the Video Miniport driver's responsibilities are exactly those of a normal Kernel mode driver.

The HwVidInterrupt() function must determine whether this interrupt is being generated by the graphics adapter. If not, HwVidInterrupt() must return FALSE. If this is an interrupt that is generated by the graphics adapter, HwVidInterrupt() must dismiss the interrupt, do any necessary processing to complete the operation, and then return TRUE back to the Video Port driver. There are restrictions on the Video Port driver routines that may be called from HwVidInterrupt(), but most of the functions normally employed during an ISR (notably VideoPortReadXxxx() and VideoPortWriteXxxx()) may be called.

Display Drivers

The architecture for the Kernel mode graphics-rendering subsystem for Windows NT is notably different from the other Kernel mode subsystems. It consists of a device-independent device driver, known as the Kernel mode Graphics Device Interface (GDI). The GDI receives User mode graphics requests, and determines how these are to be rendered upon the display device. GDI will then make graphics requests to the resident device-dependent, graphics-rendering driver (DDI).

Like the Video Port driver, the GDI is a wrapper for the DDI. However, it is not a standard wrapper architecture in the Port/Miniport sense, as is the case with the Video Miniport driver. For example, the initial entry point for the DDI is not called DriverEntry, there is no type of StartIO routine, and the DDI does not handle anything like IRPs.

GDI is implemented as a Kernel mode driver (win32k.sys). It maintains an export library (win32k.lib), against which the DDI links. GDI is loaded after the Video Port and Video Miniport drivers have been loaded. The GDI then loads the DDI (known through its association with the Video Miniport that had been loaded), once the User mode graphics DLLs have also been loaded. The purpose of the GDI is threefold:

- Isolate the DDI from the operating system.
- Isolate the DDI from the Win32 API.
- Perform as much graphics adapter-independent processing as possible.

To isolate the DDI from the operating system, the GDI exports a well-defined interface for use by all DDIs. The GDI then employs the NT mechanisms to implement the interface. The DDI can call only those functions exported by the GDI driver, via the win32k.lib library. Linking to any other library other than win32k.lib (and libcnptr.lib) will result in a DDI that GDI will refuse to load.

With regard to isolating the DDI from the Win32 API, the interface that is exported by the DDI does not exactly match the Win32 graphics API. In fact, there is usually a one-to-many mapping of Win32 graphics routine requests to the actual requests that are serviced by the DDI. The GDI will decompose each Win32 graphics request into simpler graphics requests and present these requests to the DDI. This architecture allows the reduction in the number of graphics primitives that a DDI must implement, and therefore reduces the complexity of the supporting graphics software and adapter.

A major goal for the GDI architecture is to keep the DDI from having to deal with any of the processing, either NT driver or graphical processing, which would be independent graphics adapter architecture. To achieve the NT driver-processing independence, the GDI handles the entire interface with the Windows NT operating system, and presents a restricted and controlled view of the NT environment to the DDI. Consequently, the DDI has no access to any NT kernel executive functions, except for those exported by the GDI. To achieve the graphical-processing independence, the GDI handles all the Win32 graphics state management, which is not dependent upon graphics display characteristics (such as Win32 primitive composition, display resolution, color bits per pixel, graphics memory, and so forth). The GDI also determines, in a consistent manner, the graphical primitives that are to be rendered. This frees the DDI to concentrate on only the rendering aspects of the specific graphics adapter for a known set of graphic-rendering primitives.

> ### Note
>
> *DDIs cannot call any non GDI-supplied functions. This is an important distinction between the GDI wrapper architecture and that used by other wrapped Miniport drivers, such as Video Miniport drivers and SCSI Miniport drivers. The Video Miniport driver can call Windows NT Kernel mode functions. As mentioned, the GDI will refuse to load the DDI if it tries to call any function other than those supplied by the GDI.*

Device Display Interface (DDI) Drivers

DDIs are typically straightforward in implementation, but may contain a large amount of rendering code. Furthermore, the standard structure of a Windows NT Kernel mode driver does not apply to DDIs. This section briefly discusses DDI structure, as well as the actions performed by the driver at some of its major entry points, including initialization, drawing requests, and serialization. Coverage of other graphics interfaces is also included.

Initialization

The DDI has a unique initialization entry point and initialization handshake with the GDI. When the GDI determines which DDI to load (based on the Video Miniport loaded), the DDI is entered at the DrvEnableDriver() entry point. Within DrvEnableDriver(), the DDI builds a table of index/function entry point pairs, as specified in the DRVENABLEDATA structure. This table describes to the GDI which rendering and graphics-related functions are supported by the DDI.

GDI then invokes the DrvEnablePDEV() function (contained within the DRVENABLEDATA structure). This function allocates and initializes the DDI's Physical DEVice data structure (PDEV), which is the DDI's context block. The GDI then requests that the DDI initialize itself into a specific mode (that is, resolution, refresh rate, color bits per pixel, and so forth). The DDI returns to the GDI an updated DEVINFO structure that details the specific graphics capabilities at this mode setting. If the requested mode is supported by the DDI, upon return to the GDI, all initial GDI-related resources are allocated and initialized.

After the graphics state of the DDI has been generated, the GDI then invokes the DrvEnableSurface() function (contained within the DRVENABLEDATA structure). This will create a drawing surface upon which the GDI can request the DDI to render. At this point, the DDI is sufficiently initialized to accept all rendering requests from the GDI for all surfaces, including the main display surface—the screen/desktop.

Drawing Requests

When a Win32 drawing/rendering request is received by the GDI, it is potentially broken down into more than one DDI-rendering request. The GDI has
the capability of performing all graphics operations, regardless of the diversity
and complexity of the graphics-request parameters by using a software render-
er. Software rendering is likely to be slower, however, than the adapter-specific,
hardware-assisted rendering that the DDI can perform.

As the GDI receives Win32 drawing/rendering requests, it processes these
requests via calls to one or more of the DDI routines specified in the
DRVENABLEDATA structure vector table. Most request parameters consist of a target surface, the primitive (such as line, rectangle, and so on), a list of clipping
rectangles (source and/or destination), and raster operation. The actual parameter list is specific to the graphics function and may contain more GDI graphics objects. The DDI graphics function must then traverse the clip list for each
clip rectangle and perform the rendering operation, returning either TRUE (if
successful) or FALSE. If FALSE is returned, an error is logged. More importantly,
this means that the graphics request did not complete, and therefore the display will be missing the graphical update—the desktop display may be "corrupted."

There may be cases in which the requested operation may be too difficult for
the DDI to perform. This may be due to the complexities of the rendering
operation in conjunction with the specified raster operand, or may be due to
the fact that the underlying graphics adapter cannot perform the operation,
based on the request parameters. Instead of returning FALSE and not performing
any graphics update (and, therefore, "corrupting" the display), the DDI will
call back into the GDI and have the GDI's Graphics Rendering Engine (GRE)
perform the graphics request to a temporary surface. After the GDI has done
the rendering, the DDI will then copy the contents of the temporary surface to
the target surface and complete the operation by returning TRUE. This technique
is known as *punting* the request. With this technique, all graphics operations
can be realized by the DDI, there will not be any lost graphics, and thus, there
will be no corrupted displays. This also decreases the burden upon the DDI to
support all possible variations of the GDI's graphics requests, either in the
graphics adapter itself or in DDI software emulation.

Serialization

An interesting aspect of DDI drivers is that the DDI can optionally specify
whether or not GDI's access to the DDI is single-threaded. By default, GDI
allows for multiple threads to access different surfaces simultaneously.
However, this multithreaded access is constrained by GDI, allowing only
single-threaded access to each surface. But this means that multiple threads can
be accessing different surfaces simultaneously. DDI can further augment this

constraint by specifying that all accesses to *all* surfaces are single-threaded, effectively making GDI's overall access to DDI single-threaded.

This single-threaded mode may be desired for some graphics adapters that process graphic requests at a rate different from that of the host CPU. Specifically, it is assumed that upon return from the graphics request, the DDI has completed the entire rendering activity; and the contents of the display (or surface) is complete and available for the next request. This has obvious ramifications if the graphics adapter is still updating an area of the display while another GDI thread is accessing that same display area.

Other Graphics Interfaces

As stated previously, the GDI/DDI interface maintains the Win32 graphics API functionality. However, with the emergence of 3D graphics technology, the question was whether to expand the Win32 graphics API or use/create new APIs. The current environment for 3D graphics requests is in the form of DirectDraw or OpenGL requests. Both of these sets of requests are not part of the Win32 graphics API architecture, but are separate entities that require separate major functional modules to be implemented.

GDI will perform full software emulation for DirectDraw if it is not supported by a particular DDI. The DDI can indicate to GDI that it natively supports DirectDraw by supplying the DrvEnableDirectDraw() entry point in the DRVENABLEDATA structure vector table.

An OpenGL implementation is not required for a DDI, as opposed to DirectDraw, and so there is no software emulation of OpenGL in the GDI. DDI can indicate that it supports OpenGL by trapping and returning success values for the OpenGL escape query parameters OPENGL_GETINFO and OPENGL_CMD for the GDI draw escape QUERYESCSUPPORT. (The GDI draw escape handling is done in the DDI routine DrvDrawEscape()).

DMA and Video Display Drivers

As application graphics requirements increase and graphics adapter technology evolves, the call/return architecture for each graphics requests proves to be a performance bottleneck. To get around this problem, graphics adapter architectures have moved toward using DMA for data exchange, buffering graphics commands in shared memory, and dispensing them directly to the graphics adapter. These graphics commands can take various forms: the translation of GDI requests into graphics adapter-specific commands, the buffering of DirectDraw/OpenGL requests, or the buffering of intermediate rendering primitives specific to the graphics adapter.

However, in Windows NT v4 SP3, the video display architecture (DDI and the Video Miniport) does not include direct support for DMA. Because the DDI and the Video Miniport drivers are both wrappers, by rule, they should not call routines outside of their wrapped interfaces. In addition, DDI is prohibited from linking/calling any function outside of GDI (win32k.sys) because Windows NT will refuse to load any DDI that has linked against other libraries.

Although DDI has this hard restriction, the Video Miniport driver does not have the same restrictions. So, although the Video Port driver does not currently (as of Windows NT v4 SP3) contain direct support for DMA functionality (such as memory functions, event functions, and so forth), the Video Miniport driver may use the various NT executive routines to perform the necessary ancillary activities to enable DMA. In addition, the DDI can communicate with the Video Miniport via IOCTLs (EngDeviceIoControl() as exported from the GDI). Given these basic tools, DMA functionality can be supported in a graphics device driver subsystem.

Learning More About Developing Video Display Drivers

Because both the Video Miniport and Device Dependent Interface (DDI) drivers are wrappers, the implementation of both drivers is fairly straightforward; it depends upon the complexity of the graphics adapter, the applicability of the graphics adapter functionality to the functionality required by GDI, and the level of I/O activity for the graphics adapter (DMA, for example). The DDK does a reasonably good job of documenting how to write DDIs and Video Miniport drivers, and includes the source code for four graphics devices.

Chapter 23

SCSI Miniport Drivers

This chapter will review:

- **SCSI Miniport Driver Characteristics.** SCSI Miniport drivers are a special category of driver, which utilize the SCSI Port driver as a wrapper. This section discusses the general attributes of SCSI Miniport drivers.

- **SCSI Miniport Driver Structure.** This section discusses the structure of the SCSI Miniport driver, which is atypical of standard Windows NT Kernel mode drivers. Coverage of initialization, request initiation, interrupt service, and serialization is also included.

- **Learning More About Developing SCSI Miniport Drivers.** This section points you to the relevant part of the DDK that describes SCSI Miniport drivers.

This chapter briefly discusses the structure of SCSI Miniport drivers, and compares and contrasts their structure with that that of standard Kernel mode device drivers. The chapter ends with a section on where you can learn more about developing SCSI Miniport drivers.

Please note that it is not possible to learn how to write a SCSI Miniport driver using the information presented in this chapter alone. The goal of this chapter is to simply provide a brief introduction to SCSI Miniport drivers, and relate the structure of these drivers to the standard Kernel mode device drivers discussed previously in this book.

SCSI Miniport Driver Characteristics

As described in Chapter 11, "The Layered Driver Model," SCSI Miniport drivers are a particular type of device driver. SCSI Miniport drivers exist within the wrapper environment created by the SCSI Port Driver. Figure 23.1 shows the relationship of SCSI Miniport drivers to other NT Kernel mode components.

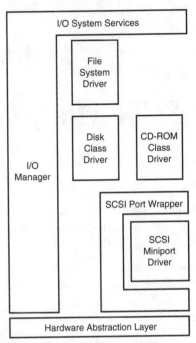

Figure 23.1. *SCSI Miniport driver in a stack of NT drivers.*

SCSI Miniport drivers, like other mini-drivers, share a common format between Windows NT and Windows 9x platforms, which means that the same SCSI Miniport driver will work on both platforms. The SCSI Miniport driver's format and interface are controlled by the SCSI Port driver.

The SCSI Port driver is implemented as a Kernel mode DLL to which the SCSI Miniport driver links. The SCSI Port driver is loaded when the first SCSI Miniport driver is loaded on the system. Since it is a DLL, the SCSI Port driver does not have its own DriverEntry entry point, or create device objects for its own use. The purpose of the SCSI Port driver is to perform the following tasks:

- **Isolate SCSI Miniport drivers from the operating system.** The SCSI Port driver exports a standard interface for use by SCSI Miniport drivers. The Port driver then uses operating system specific features to implement this interface. SCSI Miniport drivers may call only those functions explicitly provided by the SCSI Port driver. SCSI Miniport drivers that call other functions will, obviously, not be compatible across operating system platforms.

- **Perform as much common processing as possible.** One of the major goals of the SCSI Port driver is to keep the SCSI Miniport drivers from having to deal with most of the common processing that's required for handling

SCSI requests. To achieve this, the SCSI Port driver works in consort with the various class drivers. This allows SCSI Miniport drivers to deal only with the hardware-specific aspects of their adapters.

- **Provide a custom-tailored interface, specific to SCSI devices.** The interface the Port driver provides to the SCSI Miniport driver is SCSI-specific. Both functions and data structures are specifically designed with the goal facilitating the support of SCSI adapters.

Because SCSI Miniport drivers are wrapped by the SCSI Port driver, their format and interface are much simpler than those of standard Kernel mode device drivers. As a result, SCSI Miniport drivers are typically shorter and simpler than an equivalent standard Kernel mode driver.

Another characteristic of SCSI Miniport drivers is that their execution is always serialized. Therefore, SCSI Miniport drivers do not have to be concerned about acquiring spin locks for shared data. This serialization (presumably) occurs in the SCSI Port driver, where a lock is acquired before the SCSI Miniport driver is entered.

> *Note*
>
> *As previously mentioned, SCSI Miniport drivers are typically restricted to calling only functions supplied by the SCSI Port driver (and defined in* miniport.h, *which is the standard include file for SCSI Miniport drivers). SCSI Miniport drivers that do not comply with this restriction can be built, but they might not be certified by Microsoft, and will not be compatible across operating system platforms.*

SCSI Miniport Driver Structure

Because the SCSI Miniport driver's interfaces are dictated by the SCSI Port wrapper, the standard structure of a Windows NT Kernel mode driver does not apply to SCSI Miniport drivers. The topics within this section briefly discuss the structure of a SCSI Miniport driver, including the actions performed by the driver at some of its major entry points, such as:

- Initialization, performed at the DriverEntry() and HwScsiFindAdapter() entry points.

- Request initiation, performed at the HwScsiStartIo() entry point.

- Interrupt service, performed at the HwScsiInterrupt() entry point

Initialization

Like all drivers in Windows NT, SCSI Miniport drivers start with a
DriverEntry routine that is called when the driver is loaded. This is where the
obvious similarities with standard Kernel mode drivers end, however. Within
DriverEntry, the SCSI Miniport driver builds and initializes an
HW_INITIALIZATION_DATA data structure. This data structure includes pointers to
the SCSI Miniport driver's entry points, the size of the Device Extension
required by the SCSI Miniport driver for each device supported, and rudimen-
tary information about the type of SCSI adapter supported. A pointer to the
HW_INITIALIZATION_DATA data structure, and a pointer to the SCSI Miniport's
Driver Object (which was provided, as it is to all Kernel mode drivers, as a
parameter to driver entry) is passed to the SCSI Port driver when the SCSI
Miniport driver calls ScsiPortInitialize().

The SCSI Port and SCSI Miniport drivers work together to implement what is
really a single standard Kernel mode device driver. When ScsiPortInitialize()
is called by the SCSI Miniport driver, the SCSI Port driver performs the operating system-specific part of DriverEntry processing. On Windows NT, this
means that the SCSI Port driver fills in the Driver Object with pointers to its
Dispatch entry points and creates a Device Object for each SCSI Adapter supported.

Before leaving DriverEntry, and from within the ScsiPortInitialize() function,
the SCSI Port driver calls the SCSI Miniport driver back at its
HwScsiFindAdapter() entry point. In this routine, the SCSI Miniport driver
locates and configures each SCSI adapter that it will control. The SCSI Port
driver passes a pointer to a Device Extension of the size requested by the SCSI
Miniport driver to the SCSI Miniport driver's HwScsiFindAdapter() entry point.
The SCSI Miniport driver may use this Device Extension for storage of device-
specific data.

> **Note**
>
> *The SCSI Miniport Device Extension is not identical to the NT Device
> Extension pointed to by the SCSI Port Device Object.*

The SCSI Port driver provides the SCSI Miniport driver with a set of functions
it can call to facilitate its work in the HwScsiFindAdapter() function. Sometimes
these functions are simply re-exported versions of standard NT functions;
other times the Port driver's functions combine the functionality of multiple
standard NT functions. For example, the ScsiPortGetDeviceBase() function
combines the standard functions HalTranslateBusAddress() and MmMapIoSpace().
On the other hand, the function ScsiPortReadPortUchar() is simply a thinly
disguised version of the similarly named HAL routine.

On return from its call to the Miniport's HwScsiFindAdapter() function, the SCSI Port driver performs all the functions that one would expect from a typical Kernel mode device driver, including reserving resources for the SCSI Miniport driver, getting a pointer to an Adapter Object (if the SCSI adapter is a DMA device), and connecting to interrupts. The SCSI Port driver iteratively calls HwScsiFindAdapter() until the SCSI Miniport driver indicates that there are no more adapters for it to find.

Request Initiation

SCSI Miniport drivers do not use IRPs. Instead, SCSI requests are described to the SCSI Miniport driver using a SCSI Request Block (SRB). Figure 23.2 illustrates the SRB format.

SrbStatus	Function	Length	
Lun	TargetId	PathId	ScsiStatus
SenseInfoBuffer Length	CdbLength	QueueAction	QueueTag
SrbFlags			
DataTransferLength			
TimeoutValue			
DataBuffer			
SenseIoBuffer			
NextSrb			
OriginalRequest			
SrbExtension			
QueueSortKey			
UCHAR Cdb[16]			

Figure 23.2. *The SCSI Request Block (SRB).*

Except for a few specific fields, SCSI Miniport drivers treat the SRB as a read-only structure. Private data may be stored by the Miniport driver in the SRB Extension (Srb->SrbExtension), the size of which is communicated to the SCSI Port driver via the HW_INITIALIZATION_DATA structure.

The SRB typically contains all the information necessary for the SCSI Miniport driver to issue the SCSI request. Note that even the SCSI Command Descriptor Block (CDB) has been pre-built for the SCSI Miniport driver.

To process a typical SCSI request, the SCSI Miniport driver is called at its HwScsiStartIo() routine by the Port driver. The parameters passed into this routine are a pointer to the SCSI Miniport driver's Device Extension (which identifies the adapter for the request) and a pointer to an SRB (which describes the request to be processed). The SRB's Function file indicates the type of function to be performed.

By far the most common type of function is SRB_FUNCTION_EXECUTE_SCSI, which requests the SCSI Miniport driver to execute a SCSI command. To process this function, the SCSI Miniport driver typically need only provide the CDB from the SRB to the appropriate adapter under its control.

Interrupt Service

When the adapter interrupts, the SCSI Port driver calls the SCSI Miniport driver's HwScsiInterrupt() routine with a pointer to the adapter's Device Extension.

SCSI Miniport drivers do not have DpcForIsr routines like standard Kernel mode drivers. Instead, when the SCSI Miniport driver's HwScsiInterrupt() routine is called, the SCSI Miniport driver checks to see if the adapter denoted by the Device Extension is currently interrupting. If the adapter is not interrupting, the SCSI Miniport driver returns FALSE from its HwScsiInterrupt() function.

If the current adapter is interrupting, the SCSI Miniport driver determines that cause of the interrupt and may then signal the SCSI Port driver to deal with it. For example, if a request is initiated on the SCSI adapter, and the adapter interrupts to indicate that the request is complete, the SCSI Miniport driver will call ScsiPortNotification() with a pointer to the SRB to complete. The SCSI Port driver then will typically call ScsiPortNotification() a second time, requesting the SCSI Port driver to start another request. The SCSI Port driver then schedules a DPC where the request represented by the SRB is completed back to the I/O Manager and a new request is initiated.

Learning More About Developing SCSI Miniport Drivers

The typical SCSI Miniport driver is very simple to write. The DDK does a reasonably good job of documenting how to write SCSI Miniport drivers. The DDK also presently includes source code for five real SCSI Miniport drivers, including the SCSI Miniport driver that implements the ATAPI (IDE) disk driver. These files can be found in the DDK in the \ddk\src\storage\miniport directory.

Chapter 24

NDIS Miniport Drivers

This chapter will review:

- **The NDIS Family of Standards.** This section provides an overview of the origins and evolution of the Network Driver Interface Specification.

- **The Windows NT Networking Architecture.** This section provides the big picture of how NDIS drivers and the NDIS library fit into the overall scheme of network operations.

- **NDIS Driver Types and the NDIS Library.** This section summarizes the three types of NDIS drivers and the role that the NDIS Library plays in supporting NDIS drivers.

- **NDIS (LAN) Miniport Drivers.** This section discusses the structure and actions performed in a typical NDIS (LAN) Miniport driver. Coverage of initialization, transmit processing, interrupt and DPC processing, transmit completion, message reception, and serialization is used to compare and contrast NDIS drivers with other Kernel mode drivers.

- **Learning More About Developing NDIS Drivers.** This section covers the level of support provided in the DDK for developing NDIS drivers.

This chapter briefly discusses the NT networking environment in general and NDIS drivers in particular. The structure of NDIS (LAN) Miniport drivers is then compared and contrasted to that of standard Kernel mode device drivers. The chapter ends with a section on where you can learn more about developing NDIS drivers.

Please note that to fully explain the various types of NDIS drivers would require an entire book! The goal of this chapter is to simply provide a brief introduction to the various kinds of NDIS Miniport drivers, and to relate the structure of these drivers to the standard Kernel mode device drivers discussed previously in this book.

The NDIS Family of Standards

The Network Driver Interface Specification (NDIS) was originally conceived as an interface to separate a LAN card's driver logic from its protocol implementation. If you remember correctly, the original specification was restricted to x86 Assembly language for systems running LAN Manager.

From these humble beginnings, NDIS has become a whole family of networking standards. Today, this family encompasses two different types of local area network (LAN) card driver standards, a wide area networking (WAN) driver standard, and a standard for intermediate drivers that exist somewhere between protocols and net cards. In the next release of NDIS (which is scheduled for release with Windows NTV5), connection-oriented media support will be introduced (via so-called CO-NDIS).

More than any other driver standard on NT, NDIS has evolved to keep pace with changing technologies and feedback from developers. PC networking has undergone a number of fundamental changes since the days when NDIS was born, when a single LAN card running NetBEUI at 10Mbps was considered a "big deal." Today, people regularly run multiple 100Mbps LAN cards in machines, and often use much higher speeds (such as 622Mbps) via ATM and other technologies. The need for the throughput to support such network speeds was never dreamt of when NDIS was originally created.

Dial-up networking support was originally a "roll-your-own" affair for network driver writers. When dial-up networking because ubiquitous, NDIS introduced a WAN networking standard, integrated with Microsoft's Remote Access Server (RAS) and Telephony API (TAPI).

Finally, the initial NDIS specification for Windows NT (NDIS V3.0) made it exquisitely painful to implement certain typical functions. Based on developer feedback and first-person experience, a revised NDIS specification was introduced that supported a new type of driver to overcome these difficulties.

All these changes have not been without cost, however. As a result of both gradual evolution and significant innovation, the NDIS standard has grown to encompass the wide variety of driver types and interfaces it now includes.

The Windows NT Networking Architecture

Figure 24.1 shows the networking "big picture." User-written NDIS drivers appear in gray blocks. Microsoft-supplied components appear in white blocks.

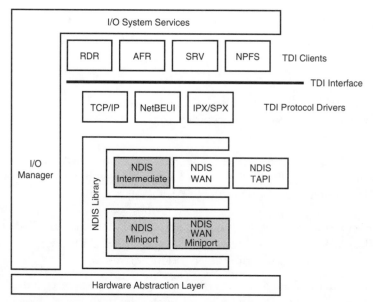

Figure 24.1. *The Networking "Big Picture."*

At the top of the stack of drivers shown in Figure 24.1 are four sample TDI Clients. The examples are RDR (the Microsoft networking redirector), AFD (the Kernel mode side of the Winsock interface), SRV (the Microsoft networking file server), and NPFS (the Named Pipe File System). All these drivers, except for SRV (which is a standard Kernel mode driver) are Windows NT File System drivers. These TDI clients interface to the protocol implementations installed on the system via the Transport Driver Interface (TDI).

Networking protocols, or "TDI drivers" as they are called, are in fact relatively standard Windows NT intermediate layer drivers. They implement a standard upper edge, as defined by the TDI specification. This upper edge interface is based mostly on receiving and processing IRP_MJ_DEVICE_CONTROL IRPs containing TDI-specified control code values. On their lower edge, TDI drivers interface to the NDIS Library (or NDIS "Wrapper" as it is often called).

The NDIS Library is implemented as a Kernel mode DLL, similar to the SCSI Port driver. The NDIS Library implements the interface among components that reference it: TDI drivers, NDIS Intermediate drivers, the NDIS WAN support driver, and NDIS LAN and WAN Miniport drivers. The interface implemented by the NDIS Library is a "call and return" interface. Drivers call functions located in the NDIS Library. The NDIS Library in turn may call functions in other drivers to perform operations. IRPs are not utilized in the NDIS specification.

NDIS Driver Types and the NDIS Library

The three most common types of NDIS drivers are as follows:

- **NDIS (LAN) Miniport drivers.** These drivers support LAN Network Interface Cards (NICs) and conform to the NDIS V3.1 or NDIS V4.0 standard.

- **NDIS WAN Miniport drivers.** These drivers support WAN interfaces, including ISDN, Frame Relay, and Switched 56 with NT Remote Access Services (RAS). Support for the PPP framing, authentication, compression, and other options are provided to these drivers via the NDISWAN driver (which is itself implemented as an NDIS Intermediate driver). NDIS WAN Miniport drivers may also act as a TAPI Service Provider (TSPI) in conjunction with the NDISTAPI driver.

- **NDIS Intermediate drivers.** NDIS Intermediate drivers receive data from protocols, just like NDIS LAN and WAN Miniport drivers. However, the bottom edge of an NDIS Intermediate driver is another driver, not the NDIS Library interface to a LAN or WAN NIC. NDIS Intermediate drivers are very powerful, and can serve multiple purposes, including filtering NDIS NIC drivers, implementing specialized protocols, or other such functions.

Since NDIS drivers existing within the environment are created by the NDIS Library, the structure and interfaces used by these drivers are defined by the NDIS Library. This allows NDIS Miniport drivers to be binary compatible across operating system platforms. Thus, the same executable image of an NDIS Miniport driver will work on Windows NT and Windows 9x operating systems.

The purposes of the NDIS Library are as follows:

- **Isolate NDIS Miniport and Intermediate drivers from the operating system.** The NDIS Library exports a set of standard interfaces used by all NDIS drivers, as well as drivers (such as TDI drivers) that interface to NDIS. The NDIS Library uses operating system-specific features to implement this interface. NDIS drivers may call only those functions explicitly provided by the NDIS Library. NDIS drivers that call other functions will, obviously, not be compatible across operating-system platforms.

- **Perform as much common processing as possible.** One of the major goals of the NDIS Library is to keep common processing code out of NDIS drivers. This means that most NDIS drivers, and Miniport drivers in particular, need to implement only the smallest amount code necessary to deal with the hardware-specific aspects of their NICs.

- **Provide a custom-tailored interface, specific to networking.** The interface the NDIS Library provides to NDIS drivers is designed for networking. Network data has many unique attributes, including the fact that it often arrives unsolicited. Another interesting attribute of networking data is that as a network message travels down protocol layers, headers (and less often, trailers) can be added to the original message at each layer. The NDIS specification makes it possible to prepend and append such structures without having to recopy the original date message. This capability to build network messages without recopying the data is absolutely vital to achieving high levels of network performance. The NDIS Library and interface standard is designed specifically to make it convenient for drivers to handle networking data and to deal with issues specific to networking support.

Thus, the NDIS Library creates an entire custom environment for NDIS drivers that is both specifically tailored to networking and portable across operating systems. The NDIS Library offloads from drivers the burden of dealing with many routine chores and provides network-specific facilities that are not normally available to standard Kernel mode drivers.

NDIS LAN Miniport Drivers

As mentioned previously, a proper discussion of NDIS drivers would require its own book. To help illustrate how NDIS drivers are implemented on Windows NT, this section discusses NDIS (LAN) Miniport drivers and actions performed at the entry points, including:

- Initialization, performed in the `DriverEntry()` and `MiniportInitialize()` entry points.

- Transmit processing, performed in the `MiniportSend()` or `MiniportSendPackets()` entry point.

- Interrupt and DPC processing, performed in the `MiniportIsr()` and `MiniportHandleInterrupt()` routines.

- Transmit Completion and Message Reception, performed in the `MiniportHandleInterrupt()` entry point.

Through this discussion, the NDIS LAN Miniport driver architecture is compared and contrasted with that of standard Kernel mode drivers discussed in most of the book.

> ### Note
>
> *NDIS LAN Miniport drivers have the same basic structure as other NDIS Miniport drivers; however, each type of NDIS driver has a number of unique attributes. To keep things clear, the description in the following sections is restricted to NDIS LAN Miniport drivers.*

Initialization

Since NDIS Miniport drivers are indeed standard Kernel mode device drivers, initialization processing takes place in the driver's DriverEntry routine. This routine is far different from that found in a standard Kernel mode driver, however.

The first thing an NDIS Miniport driver does in its DriverEntry routine is call NdisMInitializeWrapper(), passing as parameters the parameters it received from the I/O Manager at DriverEntry. Calling this function ensures that the NDIS Library is loaded, and provides the Library with a pointer to the NDIS Miniport's Driver Object. NdisMInitializeWrapper() exports its entry points in the Device Object, so when an IRP is received, the I/O Manager calls the NDIS Library.

The NDIS Miniport driver next builds an NDIS_MINIPORT_CHARATERISTICS data structure. This structure contains pointers to the NDIS Miniport's entry points. The NDIS Miniport driver passes a pointer to this data structure to the NDIS Library by calling NdisMRegisterMiniport().

From within NdisMRegsiterMiniport(), the NDIS Library calls the NDIS Miniport driver's MiniportInitialize() function once for every adapter configured for the driver during installation. Within its MiniportInitialize() function, the NDIS Miniport driver reads information from the Registry by using NdisReadConfiguration(), which is merely a private function that calls RtlQueryRegistryValues(). Also provided by the NDIS Library for use by the NDIS Miniport driver are calls such as NdisReadPciSlotInformation() and NdisReadEisaSlotInformation(). These functions are the NDIS variants of the standard HAL functions HalGetBusData(). Another NDIS Library provided function is NdisMRegisterIoPortRange(). This function combines the functions of HalTranslateBusAddress(), MmMapIoSpace(), and IoReportResourceUsage().

For each adapter supporting interrupts, the NDIS Miniport driver calls NdisMRegisterInterrupt(). NdisMRegisterInterrupt() in turn translates the interrupt, calls IoConnectInterrupt(), and registers the DpcForIsr on behalf of the NDIS Miniport driver. The interrupt is connected to a function in the NDIS Library, not directly to the NDIS Miniport's interrupt service routine.

On return from the `NdisMRegisterMiniport()` function, the NDIS Miniport driver's initialization is complete. It returns from DriverEntry with `NDIS_STATUS_SUCCESS`, which is of course a private version of NT's ordinary `STATUS_SUCCESS` status.

Transmit Processing

When a TDI client, such as a protocol driver, has a message to transmit, it calls the NDIS Library with that message. The NDIS Library in turn calls the appropriate NDIS Miniport driver's `MiniportSend()` or `MiniportSendPackets()` routine.

NDISv4 supports the option of sending multiple packets with one call to the NDIS Miniport driver. These packets are described by an array of pointers, each of which is a pointer to an NDIS packet to be sent. This is done via the `MiniportSendPackets()` routine.

NDIS Miniport drivers that do not support the option of sending multiple packets at one time are called by the NDIS Library at their `MiniportSend()` routine with a pointer to an NDIS Packet describing the message to be sent.

A transmitted or received message is described by an `NDIS_PACKET`. The structure of an `NDIS_PACKET` is opaque to NDIS drivers. The NDIS Library provides the functions necessary to retrieve information about and manipulate the packet and the message it describes. Each `NDIS_PACKET` comprises one or more `NDIS_BUFFERS`, which are also opaque. Each `NDIS_BUFFER` describes a virtually contiguous part of a message located in kernel virtual memory.

`NDIS_BUFFERS` in Windows NT are in fact MDLs. However, unlike MDLs used by standard Kernel mode drivers, MDLs used by NT networking are chained through their `Mdl->Next` pointers. This allows TDI drivers to build messages made up of virtually discontiguous buffers. Each buffer can hold a separate part of the message. Figure 24.2 illustrates the relationship of the `NDIS_PACKET` and `NDIS_BUFFER` data structures, and the fragments of the message that each `NDIS_BUFFER` represents.

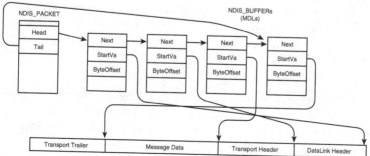

Figure 24.2. `NDIS_PACKET`s *point to* `NDIS_BUFFER`s *which point to message fragments.*

When called at its `MiniportSend()` entry point with a packet to transmit, the NDIS Miniport driver makes the request active on its adapter. The NDIS Miniport driver may call a wide variety of support routines in the NDIS Library to facilitate this process.

Interrupt and DPC Processing

When an adapter interrupts, Windows NT calls the NDIS Library's interrupt service routine. What happens next depends on how the NDIS Miniport is configured. If the NDIS Miniport driver has registered a `MiniportIsr()` routine, the NDIS Library calls that routine. If the `MiniportIsr()` returns TRUE, a DpcForIsr is requested.

The NDIS specification encourages Miniport drivers to not register a `MiniportIsr()` routine. In this case, when the NDIS Library receives the interrupt, it automatically requests a DpcForIsr.

The DpcForIsr routine is part of the NDIS Library. When this function is entered, the NDIS Library acquires a lock and calls the NDIS Miniport driver's `MiniportHandleInterrupt()` routine, which is in effect the NDIS Miniport's DpcForIsr. It is interesting to note that the NDIS Library serializes NDIS Miniport DPC routine execution. Thus, unlike in standard Kernel mode drivers, NDIS DPC routines cannot be re-entered multiple times or active on multiple processors simultaneously.

Transmit Completion

When the NDIS Miniport driver's `MiniportHandleInterrupt()` routine is called to indicate that a previously transmitted operation is complete, the NDIS Miniport driver calls `NdisMSendComplete()`, with a pointer to the NDIS_PACKET that has been completed and the ultimate status of the transmit operation.

After completing a transmit operation, NDIS Miniport drivers typically do not notify the NDIS Library that it may initiate a new transmit operation (the exception to this would be a driver that has disabled further transmit operations due to lack of resources). Rather, the NDIS architecture assumes that multiple transmit packets can be in progress in the driver simultaneously. Therefore, the driver continues to be called at its `MiniportSend()` routine to transmit packets even while other packets are in progress.

Message Reception

Of course, the NIC may interrupt because it has received a message. Network drivers are unusual in that they must deal with a significant volume of unsolicited input compared to other drivers. Depending on the adapter hardware and the version of NDIS being supported, NDIS Miniport drivers will typically preallocate and supply the adapter with data buffers for message reception.

In the `MiniportHandleInterrupt()` routine that runs as a result of an interrupt, the driver sees that a new message has been received. How the NDIS Miniport driver passes this message to the NDIS Library, and subsequently to TDI drivers, depends on the version of NDIS being supported and the features the driver supports.

In most cases, however, a message is received and buffered internally by the NDIS Miniport driver. To inform the NDIS Library that a message has been received, the NDIS Miniport driver calls a function such as `NdisMEthIndicateReceive()` (the actual name of the function depends on the LAN protocol being used—this example assumes Ethernet).

From within `NdisMEthIndicateReceive()`, the NDIS Library informs the various protocols that a message has been received by an adapter driver. Each protocol driver that wants a copy of the message then calls the NDIS Library with a pointer to an `NDIS_PACKET`. In response to this request, the NDIS Library calls back the NDIS Miniport driver at its `MiniportTransferData()` routine. In this routine, the NDIS Miniport driver copies the received message from its internally allocated data buffer to the `NDIS_PACKET` provided by the TDI protocol driver.

> ### Note
>
> *The preceding example is one among many ways that NDIS drivers handle incoming packets. There are others, some of which are more efficient than the method described.*

Serialization

The execution of NDIS Miniport drivers is typically "automatically" serialized by the NDIS Library. The NDIS Library holds a spin lock to ensure this serialization while it is executing within an NDIS Miniport driver. This frees NDIS Miniport drivers from having to worry about most synchronization issues.

Learning More About Developing NDIS Drivers

NDIS LAN Miniport drivers are well documented in the Windows NT DDK. The source code for several example NDIS (LAN) Miniport drivers is provided. NDIS WAN Miniport drivers and NDIS Intermediate drivers are also documented in the Windows NT DDK, but not nearly as thoroughly as are NDIS LAN Miniport drivers. A sample NDIS WAN Miniport driver appears on the DDK, and a sample NDIS Intermediate driver is available from Microsoft. These files can be found in the `\ddk\src\network` directory.

Part **IV**

Appendixes

Appendix A

Windows NT Status Codes/ Win32 Error Codes

This appendix contains a list of Windows NT status codes (STATUS_xxxx) and the corresponding values returned by Win32. Note that NT status values are shown in the table in hex (as they are traditionally displayed), but Win32 error values are shown in the table in decimal (their traditional format).

Table A.1 is sorted in alphabetical order by NT status code name. Table A.2 is sorted by Win32 error code name. Note that because there are fewer Win32 error codes than there are NT status codes, multiple NT status codes map to the same Win32 error code.

Table A.1. Windows NT Status codes and corresponding Win32 error codes.

NT Status	NT Status Value	Win32 Error Code	Win32 Error Value
STATUS_ABIOS_INVALID_COMMAND	0xC0000113	ERROR_MR_MID_NOT_FOUND	317
STATUS_ABIOS_INVALID_LID	0xC0000114	ERROR_MR_MID_NOT_FOUND	317
STATUS_ABIOS_INVALID_SELECTOR	0xC0000116	ERROR_MR_MID_NOT_FOUND	317
STATUS_ABIOS_LID_ALREADY_OWNED	0xC0000111	ERROR_MR_MID_NOT_FOUND	317
STATUS_ABIOS_LID_NOT_EXIST	0xC0000110	ERROR_MR_MID_NOT_FOUND	317
STATUS_ABIOS_NOT_LID_OWNER	0xC0000112	ERROR_MR_MID_NOT_FOUND	317
STATUS_ABIOS_NOT_PRESENT	0xC000010F	ERROR_MR_MID_NOT_FOUND	317
STATUS_ABIOS_SELECTOR_NOT_AVAILABLE	0xC0000115	ERROR_MR_MID_NOT_FOUND	317
STATUS_ACCESS_DENIED	0xC0000022	ERROR_ACCESS_DENIED	5
STATUS_ACCESS_VIOLATION	0xC0000005	ERROR_NOACCESS	998
STATUS_ACCOUNT_DISABLED	0xC0000072	ERROR_ACCOUNT_DISABLED	1331
STATUS_ACCOUNT_EXPIRED	0xC0000193	ERROR_ACCOUNT_EXPIRED	1793
STATUS_ACCOUNT_LOCKED_OUT	0xC0000234	ERROR_ACCOUNT_LOCKED_OUT	1909
STATUS_ACCOUNT_RESTRICTION	0xC000006E	ERROR_ACCOUNT_RESTRICTION	1327
STATUS_ADAPTER_HARDWARE_ERROR	0xC00000C2	ERROR_ADAP_HDW_ERR	57
STATUS_ADDRESS_ALREADY_ASSOCIATED	0xC0000238	ERROR_ADDRESS_ALREADY_ASSOCIATED	1227
STATUS_ADDRESS_ALREADY_EXISTS	0xC000020A	ERROR_DUP_NAME	52
STATUS_ADDRESS_CLOSED	0xC000020B	ERROR_NETNAME_DELETED	64
STATUS_ADDRESS_NOT_ASSOCIATED	0xC0000239	ERROR_ADDRESS_NOT_ASSOCIATED	1228
STATUS_AGENTS_EXHAUSTED	0xC0000085	ERROR_NO_MORE_ITEMS	259
STATUS_ALIAS_EXISTS	0xC0000154	ERROR_ALIAS_EXISTS	1379
STATUS_ALLOCATE_BUCKET	0xC000022F	ERROR_MR_MID_NOT_FOUND	317
STATUS_ALLOTTED_SPACE_EXCEEDED	0xC0000099	ERROR_ALLOTTED_SPACE_EXCEEDED	1344
STATUS_ALREADY_COMMITTED	0xC0000021	ERROR_ACCESS_DENIED	5
STATUS_APP_INIT_FAILURE	0xC0000145	ERROR_MR_MID_NOT_FOUND	317
STATUS_ARRAY_BOUNDS_EXCEEDED	0xC000008C	STATUS_ARRAY_BOUNDS_EXCEEDED	3221225612
STATUS_AUDIT_FAILED	0xC0000244	ERROR_MR_MID_NOT_FOUND	317
STATUS_BACKUP_CONTROLLER	0xC0000187	ERROR_MR_MID_NOT_FOUND	317
STATUS_BAD_COMPRESSION_BUFFER	0xC0000242	ERROR_MR_MID_NOT_FOUND	317
STATUS_BAD_DESCRIPTOR_FORMAT	0xC00000E7	ERROR_BAD_DESCRIPTOR_FORMAT	1361

STATUS	Code	ERROR	Number
STATUS_BAD_DEVICE_TYPE	0xC00000CB	ERROR_BAD_DEV_TYPE	66
STATUS_BAD_DLL_ENTRYPOINT	0xC0000251	ERROR_MR_MID_NOT_FOUND	317
STATUS_BAD_FUNCTION_TABLE	0xC00000FF	ERROR_MR_MID_NOT_FOUND	317
STATUS_BAD_IMPERSONATION_LEVEL	0xC00000A5	ERROR_BAD_IMPERSONATION_LEVEL	1346
STATUS_BAD_INHERITANCE_ACL	0xC000007D	ERROR_BAD_INHERITANCE_ACL	1340
STATUS_BAD_INITIAL_PC	0xC000000A	ERROR_BAD_EXE_FORMAT	193
STATUS_BAD_INITIAL_STACK	0xC0000009	ERROR_STACK_OVERFLOW	1001
STATUS_BAD_LOGON_SESSION_STATE	0xC0000104	ERROR_BAD_LOGON_SESSION_STATE	1365
STATUS_BAD_MASTER_BOOT_RECORD	0xC00000A9	ERROR_MR_MID_NOT_FOUND	317
STATUS_BAD_NETWORK_NAME	0xC00000CC	ERROR_BAD_NET_NAME	67
STATUS_BAD_NETWORK_PATH	0xC00000BE	ERROR_BAD_NETPATH	53
STATUS_BAD_REMOTE_ADAPTER	0xC00000C5	ERROR_BAD_REM_ADAP	60
STATUS_BAD_SERVICE_ENTRYPOINT	0xC0000252	ERROR_MR_MID_NOT_FOUND	317
STATUS_BAD_STACK	0xC0000028	ERROR_MR_MID_NOT_FOUND	317
STATUS_BAD_TOKEN_TYPE	0xC00000A8	ERROR_BAD_TOKEN_TYPE	1349
STATUS_BAD_VALIDATION_CLASS	0xC00000A7	ERROR_BAD_VALIDATION_CLASS	1348
STATUS_BAD_WORKING_SET_LIMIT	0xC000004C	ERROR_INVALID_PARAMETER	87
STATUS_BIOS_FAILED_TO_CONNECT_INTERRUPT	0xC000016E	ERROR_MR_MID_NOT_FOUND	317
STATUS_BUFFER_TOO_SMALL	0xC0000023	ERROR_INSUFFICIENT_BUFFER	122
STATUS_CANCELLED	0xC0000120	ERROR_OPERATION_ABORTED	995
STATUS_CANNOT_DELETE	0xC0000121	ERROR_ACCESS_DENIED	5
STATUS_CANNOT_IMPERSONATE	0xC000010D	ERROR_CANNOT_IMPERSONATE	1368
STATUS_CANNOT_LOAD_REGISTRY_FILE	0xC0000218	ERROR_MR_MID_NOT_FOUND	317
STATUS_CANT_ACCESS_DOMAIN_INFO	0xC00000DA	ERROR_CANT_ACCESS_DOMAIN_INFO	1351
STATUS_CANT_DISABLE_MANDATORY	0xC000005D	ERROR_CANT_DISABLE_MANDATORY	1310
STATUS_CANT_OPEN_ANONYMOUS	0xC00000A6	ERROR_CANT_OPEN_ANONYMOUS	1347
STATUS_CANT_TERMINATE_SELF	0xC00000DB	ERROR_MR_MID_NOT_FOUND	317
STATUS_CANT_WAIT	0xC00000D8	ERROR_MR_MID_NOT_FOUND	317
STATUS_CHILD_MUST_BE_VOLATILE	0xC0000181	ERROR_CHILD_MUST_BE_VOLATILE	1021
STATUS_CLIENT_SERVER_PARAMETERS_INVALID	0xC0000223	ERROR_MR_MID_NOT_FOUND	317
STATUS_COMMITMENT_LIMIT	0xC000012D	ERROR_COMMITMENT_LIMIT	1455
STATUS_CONFLICTING_ADDRESSES	0xC0000018	ERROR_INVALID_ADDRESS	487

continues

Table A.1. Continued

NT Status	NT Status Value	Win32 Error Code	Win32 Error Value
STATUS_CONNECTION_ABORTED	0xC0000241	ERROR_CONNECTION_ABORTED	1236
STATUS_CONNECTION_ACTIVE	0xC000023B	ERROR_CONNECTION_ACTIVE	1230
STATUS_CONNECTION_COUNT_LIMIT	0xC0000246	ERROR_CONNECTION_COUNT_LIMIT	1238
STATUS_CONNECTION_DISCONNECTED	0xC000020C	ERROR_NETNAME_DELETED	64
STATUS_CONNECTION_IN_USE	0xC0000108	ERROR_DEVICE_IN_USE	2404
STATUS_CONNECTION_INVALID	0xC000023A	ERROR_CONNECTION_INVALID	1229
STATUS_CONNECTION_REFUSED	0xC0000236	ERROR_CONNECTION_REFUSED	1225
STATUS_CONNECTION_RESET	0xC000020D	ERROR_NETNAME_DELETED	64
STATUS_CONTROL_C_EXIT	0xC000013A	ERROR_MR_MID_NOT_FOUND	317
STATUS_CONVERT_TO_LARGE	0xC000022C	ERROR_MR_MID_NOT_FOUND	317
STATUS_COULD_NOT_INTERPRET	0xC00000B9	ERROR_MR_MID_NOT_FOUND	317
STATUS_CRC_ERROR	0xC000003F	ERROR_CRC	23
STATUS_CTL_FILE_NOT_SUPPORTED	0xC0000057	ERROR_NOT_SUPPORTED	50
STATUS_DATA_ERROR	0xC000003E	ERROR_CRC	23
STATUS_DATA_LATE_ERROR	0xC000003D	ERROR_IO_DEVICE	1117
STATUS_DATA_NOT_ACCEPTED	0xC000021B	ERROR_MR_MID_NOT_FOUND	317
STATUS_DATA_OVERRUN	0xC000003C	ERROR_IO_DEVICE	1117
STATUS_DEBUG_ATTACH_FAILED	0xC0000219	ERROR_MR_MID_NOT_FOUND	317
STATUS_DELETE_PENDING	0xC0000056	ERROR_ACCESS_DENIED	5
STATUS_DEVICE_ALREADY_ATTACHED	0xC0000038	ERROR_MR_MID_NOT_FOUND	317
STATUS_DEVICE_CONFIGURATION_ERROR	0xC0000182	ERROR_INVALID_PARAMETER	87
STATUS_DEVICE_DATA_ERROR	0xC000009C	ERROR_CRC	23
STATUS_DEVICE_DOES_NOT_EXIST	0xC00000C0	ERROR_DEV_NOT_EXIST	55
STATUS_DEVICE_NOT_CONNECTED	0xC000009D	ERROR_NOT_READY	21
STATUS_DEVICE_NOT_PARTITIONED	0xC0000174	ERROR_DEVICE_NOT_PARTITIONED	1107
STATUS_DEVICE_NOT_READY	0xC00000A3	ERROR_NOT_READY	21
STATUS_DEVICE_POWER_FAILURE	0xC000009E	ERROR_NOT_READY	21
STATUS_DEVICE_PROTOCOL_ERROR	0xC0000186	ERROR_IO_DEVICE	1117
STATUS_DFS_EXIT_PATH_FOUND	0xC000009B	ERROR_PATH_NOT_FOUND	3
STATUS_DFS_UNAVAILABLE	0xC000026D	ERROR_MR_MID_NOT_FOUND	317

STATUS Code	Hex	ERROR Code	Number
STATUS_DIRECTORY_NOT_EMPTY	0xC0000101	ERROR_DIR_NOT_EMPTY	145
STATUS_DISK_CORRUPT_ERROR	0xC0000032	ERROR_DISK_CORRUPT	1393
STATUS_DISK_FULL	0xC000007F	ERROR_DISK_FULL	112
STATUS_DISK_OPERATION_FAILED	0xC000016A	ERROR_DISK_OPERATION_FAILED	1127
STATUS_DISK_RECALIBRATE_FAILED	0xC0000169	ERROR_DISK_RECALIBRATE_FAILED	1126
STATUS_DISK_RESET_FAILED	0xC000016B	ERROR_DISK_RESET_FAILED	1128
STATUS_DLL_INIT_FAILED	0xC0000142	ERROR_DLL_INIT_FAILED	1114
STATUS_DLL_INIT_FAILED_LOGOFF	0xC000026B	ERROR_MR_MID_NOT_FOUND	317
STATUS_DLL_NOT_FOUND	0xC0000135	ERROR_MOD_NOT_FOUND	126
STATUS_DOMAIN_CONTROLLER_NOT_FOUND	0xC0000233	ERROR_DOMAIN_CONTROLLER_NOT_FOUND	1908
STATUS_DOMAIN_CTRLR_CONFIG_ERROR	0xC000015E	ERROR_MR_MID_NOT_FOUND	317
STATUS_DOMAIN_EXISTS	0xC00000E0	ERROR_DOMAIN_EXISTS	1356
STATUS_DOMAIN_LIMIT_EXCEEDED	0xC00000E1	ERROR_DOMAIN_LIMIT_EXCEEDED	1357
STATUS_DOMAIN_TRUST_INCONSISTENT	0xC000019B	ERROR_DOMAIN_TRUST_INCONSISTENT	1810
STATUS_DRIVER_CANCEL_TIMEOUT	0xC000021E	ERROR_MR_MID_NOT_FOUND	317
STATUS_DRIVER_ENTRYPOINT_NOT_FOUND	0xC0000263	ERROR_PROC_NOT_FOUND	127
STATUS_DRIVER_INTERNAL_ERROR	0xC0000183	ERROR_IO_DEVICE	1117
STATUS_DRIVER_ORDINAL_NOT_FOUND	0xC0000262	ERROR_INVALID_ORDINAL	182
STATUS_DRIVER_UNABLE_TO_LOAD	0xC000026C	ERROR_MR_MID_NOT_FOUND	317
STATUS_DUPLICATE_NAME	0xC00000BD	ERROR_DUP_NAME	52
STATUS_DUPLICATE_OBJECTID	0xC000022A	STATUS_DUPLICATE_OBJECTID	3221226026
STATUS_EA_CORRUPT_ERROR	0xC0000053	ERROR_FILE_CORRUPT	1392
STATUS_EA_TOO_LARGE	0xC0000050	ERROR_EA_LIST_INCONSISTENT	255
STATUS_EAS_NOT_SUPPORTED	0xC000004F	ERROR_MR_MID_NOT_FOUND	317
STATUS_END_OF_FILE	0xC0000011	ERROR_HANDLE_EOF	38
STATUS_ENTRYPOINT_NOT_FOUND	0xC0000139	ERROR_PROC_NOT_FOUND	127
STATUS_EOM_OVERFLOW	0xC0000177	ERROR_EOM_OVERFLOW	1129
STATUS_EVALUATION_EXPIRATION	0xC0000268	ERROR_MR_MID_NOT_FOUND	317
STATUS_EVENTLOG_CANT_START	0xC000018F	ERROR_EVENTLOG_CANT_START	1501
STATUS_EVENTLOG_FILE_CHANGED	0xC0000197	ERROR_EVENTLOG_FILE_CHANGED	1503
STATUS_EVENTLOG_FILE_CORRUPT	0xC000018E	ERROR_EVENTLOG_FILE_CORRUPT	1500
STATUS_FAIL_CHECK	0xC0000229	ERROR_MR_MID_NOT_FOUND	317

continues

Table A.1. Continued

NT Status	NT Status Value	Win32 Error Code	Win32 Error Value
STATUS_FILE_CLOSED	0xC0000128	ERROR_INVALID_HANDLE	6
STATUS_FILE_CORRUPT_ERROR	0xC0000102	ERROR_FILE_CORRUPT	1392
STATUS_FILE_DELETED	0xC0000123	ERROR_ACCESS_DENIED	5
STATUS_FILE_FORCED_CLOSED	0xC00000B6	ERROR_HANDLE_EOF	38
STATUS_FILE_INVALID	0xC0000098	ERROR_FILE_INVALID	1006
STATUS_FILE_IS_A_DIRECTORY	0xC00000BA	ERROR_ACCESS_DENIED	5
STATUS_FILE_IS_OFFLINE	0xC0000267	ERROR_MR_MID_NOT_FOUND	317
STATUS_FILE_LOCK_CONFLICT	0xC0000054	ERROR_LOCK_VIOLATION	33
STATUS_FILE_RENAMED	0xC00000D5	ERROR_MR_MID_NOT_FOUND	317
STATUS_FILES_OPEN	0xC0000107	ERROR_MR_MID_NOT_FOUND	317
STATUS_FLOAT_DENORMAL_OPERAND	0xC000008D	STATUS_FLOAT_DENORMAL_OPERAND	3221225613
STATUS_FLOAT_DIVIDE_BY_ZERO	0xC000008E	STATUS_FLOAT_DIVIDE_BY_ZERO	3221225614
STATUS_FLOAT_INEXACT_RESULT	0xC000008F	STATUS_FLOAT_INEXACT_RESULT	3221225615
STATUS_FLOAT_INVALID_OPERATION	0xC0000090	STATUS_FLOAT_INVALID_OPERATION	3221225616
STATUS_FLOAT_OVERFLOW	0xC0000091	STATUS_FLOAT_OVERFLOW	3221225617
STATUS_FLOAT_STACK_CHECK	0xC0000092	STATUS_FLOAT_STACK_CHECK	3221225618
STATUS_FLOAT_UNDERFLOW	0xC0000093	STATUS_FLOAT_UNDERFLOW	3221225619
STATUS_FLOPPY_BAD_REGISTERS	0xC0000168	ERROR_FLOPPY_BAD_REGISTERS	1125
STATUS_FLOPPY_ID_MARK_NOT_FOUND	0xC0000165	ERROR_FLOPPY_ID_MARK_NOT_FOUND	1122
STATUS_FLOPPY_UNKNOWN_ERROR	0xC0000167	ERROR_FLOPPY_UNKNOWN_ERROR	1124
STATUS_FLOPPY_VOLUME	0xC0000164	ERROR_MR_MID_NOT_FOUND	317
STATUS_FLOPPY_WRONG_CYLINDER	0xC0000166	ERROR_FLOPPY_WRONG_CYLINDER	1123
STATUS_FOUND_OUT_OF_SCOPE	0xC000022E	ERROR_MR_MID_NOT_FOUND	317
STATUS_FREE_VM_NOT_AT_BASE	0xC000009F	ERROR_INVALID_ADDRESS	487
STATUS_FS_DRIVER_REQUIRED	0xC000019C	ERROR_MR_MID_NOT_FOUND	317
STATUS_FT_MISSING_MEMBER	0xC000015F	ERROR_IO_DEVICE	1117
STATUS_FT_ORPHANING	0xC000016D	ERROR_IO_DEVICE	1117
STATUS_FULLSCREEN_MODE	0xC0000159	ERROR_FULLSCREEN_MODE	1007
STATUS_GENERIC_NOT_MAPPED	0xC00000E6	ERROR_GENERIC_NOT_MAPPED	1360
STATUS_GRACEFUL_DISCONNECT	0xC0000237	ERROR_GRACEFUL_DISCONNECT	1226

Status Code	Hex	Win32 Error	Number
STATUS_GROUP_EXISTS	0xC0000065	ERROR_GROUP_EXISTS	1318
STATUS_GUIDS_EXHAUSTED	0xC0000083	ERROR_NO_MORE_ITEMS	259
STATUS_HANDLE_NOT_CLOSABLE	0xC0000235	ERROR_INVALID_HANDLE	6
STATUS_HOST_UNREACHABLE	0xC000023D	ERROR_HOST_UNREACHABLE	1232
STATUS_ILL_FORMED_PASSWORD	0xC000006B	ERROR_ILL_FORMED_PASSWORD	1324
STATUS_ILL_FORMED_SERVICE_ENTRY	0xC0000160	ERROR_MR_MID_NOT_FOUND	317
STATUS_ILLEGAL_CHARACTER	0xC0000161	ERROR_MR_MID_NOT_FOUND	317
STATUS_ILLEGAL_DLL_RELOCATION	0xC0000269	ERROR_MR_MID_NOT_FOUND	317
STATUS_ILLEGAL_FLOAT_CONTEXT	0xC000014A	ERROR_MR_MID_NOT_FOUND	317
STATUS_ILLEGAL_FUNCTION	0xC00000AF	ERROR_INVALID_FUNCTION	1
STATUS_ILLEGAL_INSTRUCTION	0xC000001D	STATUS_ILLEGAL_INSTRUCTION	3221225501
STATUS_IMAGE_ALREADY_LOADED	0xC000010E	ERROR_SERVICE_ALREADY_RUNNING	1056
STATUS_IMAGE_CHECKSUM_MISMATCH	0xC0000221	ERROR_BAD_EXE_FORMAT	193
STATUS_IMAGE_MP_UP_MISMATCH	0xC0000249	ERROR_BAD_EXE_FORMAT	193
STATUS_IN_PAGE_ERROR	0xC0000006	ERROR_SWAPERROR	999
STATUS_INCOMPATIBLE_FILE_MAP	0xC000004D	ERROR_INVALID_PARAMETER	87
STATUS_INFO_LENGTH_MISMATCH	0xC0000004	ERROR_BAD_LENGTH	24
STATUS_INSTANCE_NOT_AVAILABLE	0xC00000AB	ERROR_PIPE_BUSY	231
STATUS_INSTRUCTION_MISALIGNMENT	0xC00000AA	ERROR_MR_MID_NOT_FOUND	317
STATUS_INSUFF_SERVER_RESOURCES	0xC0000205	ERROR_NOT_ENOUGH_SERVER_MEMORY	1130
STATUS_INSUFFICIENT_LOGON_INFO	0xC0000250	ERROR_MR_MID_NOT_FOUND	317
STATUS_INSUFFICIENT_RESOURCES	0xC000009A	ERROR_NO_SYSTEM_RESOURCES	1450
STATUS_INTEGER_DIVIDE_BY_ZERO	0xC0000094	STATUS_INTEGER_DIVIDE_BY_ZERO	3221225620
STATUS_INTEGER_OVERFLOW	0xC0000095	ERROR_ARITHMETIC_OVERFLOW	534
STATUS_INTERNAL_DB_CORRUPTION	0xC00000E4	ERROR_INTERNAL_DB_CORRUPTION	1358
STATUS_INTERNAL_DB_ERROR	0xC0000158	ERROR_INTERNAL_DB_ERROR	1383
STATUS_INTERNAL_ERROR	0xC00000E5	ERROR_INTERNAL_ERROR	1359
STATUS_INVALID_ACCOUNT_NAME	0xC0000062	ERROR_INVALID_ACCOUNT_NAME	1315
STATUS_INVALID_ACL	0xC0000077	ERROR_INVALID_ACL	1336
STATUS_INVALID_ADDRESS	0xC0000141	ERROR_UNEXP_NET_ERR	59
STATUS_INVALID_ADDRESS_COMPONENT	0xC0000207	ERROR_INVALID_NETNAME	1214
STATUS_INVALID_ADDRESS_WILDCARD	0xC0000208	ERROR_INVALID_NETNAME	1214

continues

Table A.1. Continued

NT Status	NT Status Value	Win32 Error Code	Win32 Error Value
STATUS_INVALID_BLOCK_LENGTH	0xC0000173	ERROR_INVALID_BLOCK_LENGTH	1106
STATUS_INVALID_BUFFER_SIZE	0xC0000206	ERROR_INVALID_USER_BUFFER	1784
STATUS_INVALID_CID	0xC000000B	ERROR_INVALID_PARAMETER	87
STATUS_INVALID_COMPUTER_NAME	0xC0000122	ERROR_INVALID_COMPUTERNAME	1210
STATUS_INVALID_CONNECTION	0xC0000140	ERROR_UNEXP_NET_ERR	59
STATUS_INVALID_DEVICE_REQUEST	0xC0000010	ERROR_INVALID_FUNCTION	1
STATUS_INVALID_DEVICE_STATE	0xC0000184	ERROR_BAD_COMMAND	22
STATUS_INVALID_DISPOSITION	0xC0000026	STATUS_INVALID_DISPOSITION	3221225510
STATUS_INVALID_DOMAIN_ROLE	0xC00000DE	ERROR_INVALID_DOMAIN_ROLE	1354
STATUS_INVALID_DOMAIN_STATE	0xC00000DD	ERROR_INVALID_DOMAIN_STATE	1353
STATUS_INVALID_FILE_FOR_SECTION	0xC0000020	ERROR_BAD_EXE_FORMAT	193
STATUS_INVALID_GROUP_ATTRIBUTES	0xC00000A4	ERROR_INVALID_GROUP_ATTRIBUTES	1345
STATUS_INVALID_HANDLE	0xC0000008	ERROR_INVALID_HANDLE	6
STATUS_INVALID_HW_PROFILE	0xC0000260	ERROR_MR_MID_NOT_FOUND	317
STATUS_INVALID_ID_AUTHORITY	0xC0000084	ERROR_INVALID_ID_AUTHORITY	1343
STATUS_INVALID_IMAGE_FORMAT	0xC000007B	ERROR_BAD_EXE_FORMAT	193
STATUS_INVALID_IMAGE_LE_FORMAT	0xC000012E	ERROR_BAD_EXE_FORMAT	193
STATUS_INVALID_IMAGE_NE_FORMAT	0xC000011B	ERROR_BAD_EXE_FORMAT	193
STATUS_INVALID_IMAGE_NOT_MZ	0xC000012F	ERROR_BAD_EXE_FORMAT	193
STATUS_INVALID_IMAGE_PROTECT	0xC0000130	ERROR_BAD_EXE_FORMAT	193
STATUS_INVALID_IMAGE_WIN_16	0xC0000131	ERROR_BAD_EXE_FORMAT	193
STATUS_INVALID_INFO_CLASS	0xC0000003	ERROR_INVALID_PARAMETER	87
STATUS_INVALID_LDT_DESCRIPTOR	0xC000011A	ERROR_MR_MID_NOT_FOUND	317
STATUS_INVALID_LDT_OFFSET	0xC0000119	ERROR_MR_MID_NOT_FOUND	317
STATUS_INVALID_LDT_SIZE	0xC0000118	ERROR_MR_MID_NOT_FOUND	317
STATUS_INVALID_LEVEL	0xC0000148	ERROR_INVALID_LEVEL	124
STATUS_INVALID_LOCK_SEQUENCE	0xC000001E	ERROR_ACCESS_DENIED	5
STATUS_INVALID_LOGON_HOURS	0xC000006F	ERROR_INVALID_LOGON_HOURS	1328
STATUS_INVALID_LOGON_TYPE	0xC000010B	ERROR_INVALID_LOGON_TYPE	1367
STATUS_INVALID_MEMBER	0xC000017B	ERROR_INVALID_MEMBER	1388

STATUS_INVALID_NETWORK_RESPONSE	0xC00000C3	ERROR_BAD_NET_RESP	58
STATUS_INVALID_OPLOCK_PROTOCOL	0xC00000E3	ERROR_MR_MID_NOT_FOUND	317
STATUS_INVALID_OWNER	0xC000005A	ERROR_INVALID_OWNER	1307
STATUS_INVALID_PAGE_PROTECTION	0xC0000045	ERROR_INVALID_PARAMETER	87
STATUS_INVALID_PARAMETER	0xC000000D	ERROR_INVALID_PARAMETER	87
STATUS_INVALID_PARAMETER_1	0xC00000EF	ERROR_INVALID_PARAMETER	87
STATUS_INVALID_PARAMETER_10	0xC00000F8	ERROR_INVALID_PARAMETER	87
STATUS_INVALID_PARAMETER_11	0xC00000F9	ERROR_INVALID_PARAMETER	87
STATUS_INVALID_PARAMETER_12	0xC00000FA	ERROR_INVALID_PARAMETER	87
STATUS_INVALID_PARAMETER_2	0xC00000F0	ERROR_INVALID_PARAMETER	87
STATUS_INVALID_PARAMETER_3	0xC00000F1	ERROR_INVALID_PARAMETER	87
STATUS_INVALID_PARAMETER_4	0xC00000F2	ERROR_INVALID_PARAMETER	87
STATUS_INVALID_PARAMETER_5	0xC00000F3	ERROR_INVALID_PARAMETER	87
STATUS_INVALID_PARAMETER_6	0xC00000F4	ERROR_INVALID_PARAMETER	87
STATUS_INVALID_PARAMETER_7	0xC00000F5	ERROR_INVALID_PARAMETER	87
STATUS_INVALID_PARAMETER_8	0xC00000F6	ERROR_INVALID_PARAMETER	87
STATUS_INVALID_PARAMETER_9	0xC00000F7	ERROR_INVALID_PARAMETER	87
STATUS_INVALID_PARAMETER_MIX	0xC0000030	ERROR_INVALID_PARAMETER	87
STATUS_INVALID_PIPE_STATE	0xC00000AD	ERROR_BAD_PIPE	230
STATUS_INVALID_PLUGPLAY_DEVICE_PATH	0xC0000261	ERROR_MR_MID_NOT_FOUND	317
STATUS_INVALID_PORT_ATTRIBUTES	0xC000002E	ERROR_MR_MID_NOT_FOUND	317
STATUS_INVALID_PORT_HANDLE	0xC0000042	ERROR_INVALID_HANDLE	6
STATUS_INVALID_PRIMARY_GROUP	0xC000005B	ERROR_INVALID_PRIMARY_GROUP	1308
STATUS_INVALID_QUOTA_LOWER	0xC0000031	ERROR_MR_MID_NOT_FOUND	317
STATUS_INVALID_READ_MODE	0xC00000B4	ERROR_BAD_PIPE	230
STATUS_INVALID_SECURITY_DESCR	0xC0000079	ERROR_INVALID_SECURITY_DESCR	1338
STATUS_INVALID_SERVER_STATE	0xC00000DC	ERROR_INVALID_SERVER_STATE	1352
STATUS_INVALID_SID	0xC0000078	ERROR_INVALID_SID	1337
STATUS_INVALID_SUB_AUTHORITY	0xC0000076	ERROR_INVALID_SUB_AUTHORITY	1335
STATUS_INVALID_SYSTEM_SERVICE	0xC000001C	ERROR_INVALID_FUNCTION	1
STATUS_INVALID_UNWIND_TARGET	0xC0000029	ERROR_MR_MID_NOT_FOUND	317
STATUS_INVALID_USER_BUFFER	0xC00000E8	ERROR_INVALID_USER_BUFFER	1784

continues

Table A.1. Continued

NT Status	NT Status Value	Win32 Error Code	Win32 Error Value
STATUS_INVALID_VARIANT	0xC0000232	ERROR_MR_MID_NOT_FOUND	317
STATUS_INVALID_VIEW_SIZE	0xC000001F	ERROR_ACCESS_DENIED	5
STATUS_INVALID_VOLUME_LABEL	0xC0000086	ERROR_LABEL_TOO_LONG	154
STATUS_INVALID_WORKSTATION	0xC0000070	ERROR_INVALID_WORKSTATION	1329
STATUS_IO_DEVICE_ERROR	0xC0000185	ERROR_IO_DEVICE	1117
STATUS_IO_PRIVILEGE_FAILED	0xC0000137	ERROR_MR_MID_NOT_FOUND	317
STATUS_IO_TIMEOUT	0xC00000B5	ERROR_SEM_TIMEOUT	121
STATUS_IP_ADDRESS_CONFLICT1	0xC0000254	ERROR_MR_MID_NOT_FOUND	317
STATUS_IP_ADDRESS_CONFLICT2	0xC0000255	ERROR_MR_MID_NOT_FOUND	317
STATUS_KEY_DELETED	0xC000017C	ERROR_KEY_DELETED	1018
STATUS_KEY_HAS_CHILDREN	0xC0000180	ERROR_KEY_HAS_CHILDREN	1020
STATUS_LAST_ADMIN	0xC0000069	ERROR_LAST_ADMIN	1322
STATUS_LICENSE_QUOTA_EXCEEDED	0xC0000259	ERROR_LICENSE_QUOTA_EXCEEDED	1395
STATUS_LICENSE_VIOLATION	0xC000026A	ERROR_MR_MID_NOT_FOUND	317
STATUS_LINK_FAILED	0xC000013E	ERROR_UNEXP_NET_ERR	59
STATUS_LINK_TIMEOUT	0xC000013F	ERROR_UNEXP_NET_ERR	59
STATUS_LM_CROSS_ENCRYPTION_REQUIRED	0xC000017F	ERROR_LM_CROSS_ENCRYPTION_REQUIRED	1390
STATUS_LOCAL_DISCONNECT	0xC000013B	ERROR_NETNAME_DELETED	64
STATUS_LOCK_NOT_GRANTED	0xC0000055	ERROR_LOCK_VIOLATION	33
STATUS_LOG_FILE_FULL	0xC0000188	ERROR_LOG_FILE_FULL	1502
STATUS_LOGIN_TIME_RESTRICTION	0xC0000247	ERROR_LOGIN_TIME_RESTRICTION	1239
STATUS_LOGIN_WKSTA_RESTRICTION	0xC0000248	ERROR_LOGIN_WKSTA_RESTRICTION	1240
STATUS_LOGON_FAILURE	0xC000006D	ERROR_LOGON_FAILURE	1326
STATUS_LOGON_NOT_GRANTED	0xC0000155	ERROR_LOGON_NOT_GRANTED	1380
STATUS_LOGON_SERVER_CONFLICT	0xC0000132	ERROR_MR_MID_NOT_FOUND	317
STATUS_LOGON_SESSION_COLLISION	0xC0000105	ERROR_LOGON_SESSION_COLLISION	1366
STATUS_LOGON_SESSION_EXISTS	0xC00000EE	ERROR_LOGON_SESSION_EXISTS	1363
STATUS_LOGON_TYPE_NOT_GRANTED	0xC000015B	ERROR_LOGON_TYPE_NOT_GRANTED	1385
STATUS_LOST_WRITEBEHIND_DATA	0xC0000222	ERROR_MR_MID_NOT_FOUND	317
STATUS_LPC_REPLY_LOST	0xC0000253	ERROR_INTERNAL_ERROR	1359

STATUS_LUIDS_EXHAUSTED	0xC0000075	ERROR_LUIDS_EXHAUSTED	1334
STATUS_MAPPED_ALIGNMENT	0xC0000220	ERROR_MAPPED_ALIGNMENT	1132
STATUS_MAPPED_FILE_SIZE_ZERO	0xC000011E	ERROR_FILE_INVALID	1006
STATUS_MARSHALL_OVERFLOW	0xC0000231	ERROR_MR_MID_NOT_FOUND	317
STATUS_MEDIA_WRITE_PROTECTED	0xC00000A2	ERROR_WRITE_PROTECT	19
STATUS_MEMBER_IN_ALIAS	0xC0000153	ERROR_MEMBER_IN_ALIAS	1378
STATUS_MEMBER_IN_GROUP	0xC0000067	ERROR_MEMBER_IN_GROUP	1320
STATUS_MEMBER_NOT_IN_ALIAS	0xC0000152	ERROR_MEMBER_NOT_IN_ALIAS	1377
STATUS_MEMBER_NOT_IN_GROUP	0xC0000068	ERROR_MEMBER_NOT_IN_GROUP	1321
STATUS_MEMBERS_PRIMARY_GROUP	0xC0000127	ERROR_MEMBERS_PRIMARY_GROUP	1374
STATUS_MEMORY_NOT_ALLOCATED	0xC00000A0	ERROR_INVALID_ADDRESS	487
STATUS_MESSAGE_NOT_FOUND	0xC0000109	ERROR_MR_MID_NOT_FOUND	317
STATUS_MISSING_SYSTEMFILE	0xC0000143	ERROR_MR_MID_NOT_FOUND	317
STATUS_MORE_PROCESSING_REQUIRED	0xC0000016	ERROR_MORE_DATA	234
STATUS_MUTANT_LIMIT_EXCEEDED	0xC0000191	ERROR_MR_MID_NOT_FOUND	317
STATUS_MUTANT_NOT_OWNED	0xC0000046	ERROR_NOT_OWNER	288
STATUS_NAME_TOO_LONG	0xC0000106	ERROR_FILENAME_EXCED_RANGE	206
STATUS_NET_WRITE_FAULT	0xC00000D2	ERROR_NET_WRITE_FAULT	88
STATUS_NETLOGON_NOT_STARTED	0xC0000192	ERROR_NETLOGON_NOT_STARTED	1792
STATUS_NETWORK_ACCESS_DENIED	0xC00000CA	ERROR_NETWORK_ACCESS_DENIED	65
STATUS_NETWORK_BUSY	0xC00000BF	ERROR_NETWORK_BUSY	54
STATUS_NETWORK_CREDENTIAL_CONFLICT	0xC0000195	ERROR_SESSION_CREDENTIAL_CONFLICT	1219
STATUS_NETWORK_NAME_DELETED	0xC00000C9	ERROR_NETNAME_DELETED	64
STATUS_NETWORK_UNREACHABLE	0xC000023C	ERROR_NETWORK_UNREACHABLE	1231
STATUS_NO_BROWSER_SERVERS_FOUND	0xC000021C	ERROR_NO_BROWSER_SERVERS_FOUND	6118
STATUS_NO_CALLBACK_ACTIVE	0xC0000258	ERROR_MR_MID_NOT_FOUND	317
STATUS_NO_EAS_ON_FILE	0xC0000052	ERROR_FILE_CORRUPT	1392
STATUS_NO_EVENT_PAIR	0xC000014E	ERROR_MR_MID_NOT_FOUND	317
STATUS_NO_GUID_TRANSLATION	0xC000010C	ERROR_MR_MID_NOT_FOUND	317
STATUS_NO_IMPERSONATION_TOKEN	0xC000005C	ERROR_NO_IMPERSONATION_TOKEN	1309
STATUS_NO_LDT	0xC0000117	ERROR_MR_MID_NOT_FOUND	317
STATUS_NO_LOG_SPACE	0xC000017D	ERROR_NO_LOG_SPACE	1019

continues

Table A.1. Continued

NT Status	NT Status Value	Win32 Error Code	Win32 Error Value
STATUS_NO_LOGON_SERVERS	0xC000005E	ERROR_NO_LOGON_SERVERS	1311
STATUS_NO_MEDIA	0xC0000178	ERROR_NO_MEDIA_IN_DRIVE	1112
STATUS_NO_MEDIA_IN_DEVICE	0xC0000013	ERROR_NOT_READY	21
STATUS_NO_MEMORY	0xC0000017	ERROR_NOT_ENOUGH_MEMORY	8
STATUS_NO_PAGEFILE	0xC0000147	ERROR_MR_MID_NOT_FOUND	317
STATUS_NO_SECURITY_ON_OBJECT	0xC00000D7	ERROR_NO_SECURITY_ON_OBJECT	1350
STATUS_NO_SPOOL_SPACE	0xC00000C7	ERROR_NO_SPOOL_SPACE	62
STATUS_NO_SUCH_ALIAS	0xC0000151	ERROR_NO_SUCH_ALIAS	1376
STATUS_NO_SUCH_DEVICE	0xC000000E	ERROR_FILE_NOT_FOUND	2
STATUS_NO_SUCH_DOMAIN	0xC00000DF	ERROR_NO_SUCH_DOMAIN	1355
STATUS_NO_SUCH_FILE	0xC000000F	ERROR_FILE_NOT_FOUND	2
STATUS_NO_SUCH_GROUP	0xC0000066	ERROR_NO_SUCH_GROUP	1319
STATUS_NO_SUCH_LOGON_SESSION	0xC000005F	ERROR_NO_SUCH_LOGON_SESSION	1312
STATUS_NO_SUCH_MEMBER	0xC000017A	ERROR_NO_SUCH_MEMBER	1387
STATUS_NO_SUCH_PACKAGE	0xC00000FE	ERROR_NO_SUCH_PACKAGE	1364
STATUS_NO_SUCH_PRIVILEGE	0xC0000060	ERROR_NO_SUCH_PRIVILEGE	1313
STATUS_NO_SUCH_USER	0xC0000064	ERROR_NO_SUCH_USER	1317
STATUS_NO_TOKEN	0xC000007C	ERROR_NO_TOKEN	1008
STATUS_NO_TRUST_LSA_SECRET	0xC000018A	ERROR_NO_TRUST_LSA_SECRET	1786
STATUS_NO_TRUST_SAM_ACCOUNT	0xC000018B	ERROR_NO_TRUST_SAM_ACCOUNT	1787
STATUS_NO_USER_SESSION_KEY	0xC0000202	ERROR_NO_USER_SESSION_KEY	1394
STATUS_NOLOGON_INTERDOMAIN_TRUST_ACCOUNT	0xC0000198	ERROR_NOLOGON_INTERDOMAIN_TRUST_ACCOUNT	1807
STATUS_NOLOGON_SERVER_TRUST_ACCOUNT	0xC000019A	ERROR_NOLOGON_SERVER_TRUST_ACCOUNT	1809
STATUS_NOLOGON_WORKSTATION_TRUST_ACCOUNT	0xC0000199	ERROR_NOLOGON_WORKSTATION_TRUST_ACCOUNT	1808
STATUS_NONCONTINUABLE_EXCEPTION	0xC0000025	STATUS_NONCONTINUABLE_EXCEPTION	3221225509
STATUS_NONE_MAPPED	0xC0000073	ERROR_NONE_MAPPED	1332
STATUS_NONEXISTENT_EA_ENTRY	0xC0000051	ERROR_FILE_CORRUPT	1392
STATUS_NONEXISTENT_SECTOR	0xC0000015	ERROR_SECTOR_NOT_FOUND	27
STATUS_NOT_A_DIRECTORY	0xC0000103	ERROR_DIRECTORY	267
STATUS_NOT_CLIENT_SESSION	0xC0000217	ERROR_NOT_SUPPORTED	50

STATUS	Hex	ERROR	Decimal
STATUS_NOT_COMMITTED	0xC000002D	ERROR_INVALID_ADDRESS	487
STATUS_NOT_FOUND	0xC0000225	ERROR_MR_MID_NOT_FOUND	317
STATUS_NOT_IMPLEMENTED	0xC0000002	ERROR_INVALID_FUNCTION	1
STATUS_NOT_LOCKED	0xC000002A	ERROR_NOT_LOCKED	158
STATUS_NOT_LOGON_PROCESS	0xC00000ED	ERROR_NOT_LOGON_PROCESS	1362
STATUS_NOT_MAPPED_DATA	0xC0000088	ERROR_INVALID_ADDRESS	487
STATUS_NOT_MAPPED_VIEW	0xC0000019	ERROR_INVALID_ADDRESS	487
STATUS_NOT_REGISTRY_FILE	0xC000015C	ERROR_NOT_REGISTRY_FILE	1017
STATUS_NOT_SAME_DEVICE	0xC00000D4	ERROR_NOT_SAME_DEVICE	17
STATUS_NOT_SERVER_SESSION	0xC0000216	ERROR_NOT_SUPPORTED	50
STATUS_NOT_SUPPORTED	0xC00000BB	ERROR_NOT_SUPPORTED	50
STATUS_NOT_TINY_STREAM	0xC0000226	ERROR_MR_MID_NOT_FOUND	317
STATUS_NT_CROSS_ENCRYPTION_REQUIRED	0xC000015D	ERROR_NT_CROSS_ENCRYPTION_REQUIRED	1386
STATUS_OBJECT_NAME_COLLISION	0xC0000035	ERROR_ALREADY_EXISTS	183
STATUS_OBJECT_NAME_INVALID	0xC0000033	ERROR_INVALID_NAME	123
STATUS_OBJECT_NAME_NOT_FOUND	0xC0000034	ERROR_FILE_NOT_FOUND	2
STATUS_OBJECT_PATH_INVALID	0xC0000039	ERROR_BAD_PATHNAME	161
STATUS_OBJECT_PATH_NOT_FOUND	0xC000003A	ERROR_PATH_NOT_FOUND	3
STATUS_OBJECT_PATH_SYNTAX_BAD	0xC000003B	ERROR_BAD_PATHNAME	161
STATUS_OBJECT_TYPE_MISMATCH	0xC0000024	ERROR_INVALID_HANDLE	6
STATUS_OBJECTID_EXISTS	0xC000022B	STATUS_OBJECTID_EXISTS	3221226027
STATUS_OPEN_FAILED	0xC0000136	ERROR_MR_MID_NOT_FOUND	317
STATUS_OPLOCK_NOT_GRANTED	0xC00000E2	ERROR_MR_MID_NOT_FOUND	317
STATUS_ORDINAL_NOT_FOUND	0xC0000138	ERROR_INVALID_ORDINAL	182
STATUS_PAGEFILE_CREATE_FAILED	0xC0000146	ERROR_MR_MID_NOT_FOUND	317
STATUS_PAGEFILE_QUOTA	0xC0000007	ERROR_PAGEFILE_QUOTA	1454
STATUS_PAGEFILE_QUOTA_EXCEEDED	0xC000012C	ERROR_MR_MID_NOT_FOUND	317
STATUS_PARITY_ERROR	0xC000002B	STATUS_PARITY_ERROR	3221225515
STATUS_PARTITION_FAILURE	0xC0000172	ERROR_PARTITION_FAILURE	1105
STATUS_PASSWORD_EXPIRED	0xC0000071	ERROR_PASSWORD_EXPIRED	1330
STATUS_PASSWORD_MUST_CHANGE	0xC0000224	ERROR_PASSWORD_MUST_CHANGE	1907
STATUS_PASSWORD_RESTRICTION	0xC000006C	ERROR_PASSWORD_RESTRICTION	1325

continues

Table A.1. Continued

NT Status	NT Status Value	Win32 Error Code	Win32 Error Value
STATUS_PATH_NOT_COVERED	0xC0000257	ERROR_HOST_UNREACHABLE	1232
STATUS_PIPE_BROKEN	0xC000014B	ERROR_BROKEN_PIPE	109
STATUS_PIPE_BUSY	0xC00000AE	ERROR_PIPE_BUSY	231
STATUS_PIPE_CLOSING	0xC00000B1	ERROR_NO_DATA	232
STATUS_PIPE_CONNECTED	0xC00000B2	ERROR_PIPE_CONNECTED	535
STATUS_PIPE_DISCONNECTED	0xC00000B0	ERROR_PIPE_NOT_CONNECTED	233
STATUS_PIPE_EMPTY	0xC00000D9	ERROR_NO_DATA	232
STATUS_PIPE_LISTENING	0xC00000B3	ERROR_PIPE_LISTENING	536
STATUS_PIPE_NOT_AVAILABLE	0xC00000AC	ERROR_PIPE_BUSY	231
STATUS_PLUGPLAY_NO_DEVICE	0xC000025E	ERROR_SERVICE_DISABLED	1058
STATUS_PORT_ALREADY_SET	0xC0000048	ERROR_INVALID_PARAMETER	87
STATUS_PORT_CONNECTION_REFUSED	0xC0000041	ERROR_ACCESS_DENIED	5
STATUS_PORT_DISCONNECTED	0xC0000037	ERROR_INVALID_HANDLE	6
STATUS_PORT_MESSAGE_TOO_LONG	0xC000002F	ERROR_MR_MID_NOT_FOUND	317
STATUS_PORT_UNREACHABLE	0xC000023F	ERROR_PORT_UNREACHABLE	1234
STATUS_POSSIBLE_DEADLOCK	0xC0000194	ERROR_POSSIBLE_DEADLOCK	1131
STATUS_PRINT_CANCELLED	0xC00000C8	ERROR_PRINT_CANCELLED	63
STATUS_PRINT_QUEUE_FULL	0xC00000C6	ERROR_PRINTQ_FULL	61
STATUS_PRIVILEGE_NOT_HELD	0xC0000061	ERROR_PRIVILEGE_NOT_HELD	1314
STATUS_PRIVILEGED_INSTRUCTION	0xC0000096	STATUS_PRIVILEGED_INSTRUCTION	3221225622
STATUS_PROCEDURE_NOT_FOUND	0xC000007A	ERROR_PROC_NOT_FOUND	127
STATUS_PROCESS_IS_TERMINATING	0xC000010A	ERROR_ACCESS_DENIED	5
STATUS_PROFILING_AT_LIMIT	0xC00000D3	ERROR_MR_MID_NOT_FOUND	317
STATUS_PROFILING_NOT_STARTED	0xC00000B7	ERROR_MR_MID_NOT_FOUND	317
STATUS_PROFILING_NOT_STOPPED	0xC00000B8	ERROR_MR_MID_NOT_FOUND	317
STATUS_PROPSET_NOT_FOUND	0xC0000230	ERROR_MR_MID_NOT_FOUND	317
STATUS_PROTOCOL_UNREACHABLE	0xC000023E	ERROR_PROTOCOL_UNREACHABLE	1233
STATUS_PWD_HISTORY_CONFLICT	0xC000025C	ERROR_MR_MID_NOT_FOUND	317
STATUS_PWD_TOO_RECENT	0xC000025B	ERROR_MR_MID_NOT_FOUND	317
STATUS_PWD_TOO_SHORT	0xC000025A	ERROR_MR_MID_NOT_FOUND	317

STATUS code	Hex	Win32 error	Number
STATUS_QUOTA_EXCEEDED	0xC0000044	ERROR_NOT_ENOUGH_QUOTA	1816
STATUS_QUOTA_LIST_INCONSISTENT	0xC0000266	ERROR_MR_MID_NOT_FOUND	317
STATUS_RANGE_NOT_LOCKED	0xC000007E	ERROR_NOT_LOCKED	158
STATUS_RECOVERY_FAILURE	0xC0000227	ERROR_MR_MID_NOT_FOUND	317
STATUS_REDIRECTOR_NOT_STARTED	0xC00000FB	ERROR_PATH_NOT_FOUND	3
STATUS_REDIRECTOR_PAUSED	0xC00000D1	ERROR_REDIR_PAUSED	72
STATUS_REDIRECTOR_STARTED	0xC00000FC	ERROR_MR_MID_NOT_FOUND	317
STATUS_REGISTRY_CORRUPT	0xC000014C	ERROR_BADDB	1009
STATUS_REGISTRY_IO_FAILED	0xC000014D	ERROR_REGISTRY_IO_FAILED	1016
STATUS_REGISTRY_QUOTA_LIMIT	0xC0000256	ERROR_MR_MID_NOT_FOUND	317
STATUS_REMOTE_DISCONNECT	0xC000013C	ERROR_NETNAME_DELETED	64
STATUS_REMOTE_NOT_LISTENING	0xC00000BC	ERROR_REM_NOT_LIST	51
STATUS_REMOTE_RESOURCES	0xC000013D	ERROR_REM_NOT_LIST	51
STATUS_REMOTE_SESSION_LIMIT	0xC0000196	ERROR_REMOTE_SESSION_LIMIT_EXCEEDED	1220
STATUS_REPLY_MESSAGE_MISMATCH	0xC000021F	ERROR_MR_MID_NOT_FOUND	317
STATUS_REQUEST_ABORTED	0xC0000240	ERROR_REQUEST_ABORTED	1235
STATUS_REQUEST_NOT_ACCEPTED	0xC00000D0	ERROR_REQ_NOT_ACCEP	71
STATUS_RESOURCE_DATA_NOT_FOUND	0xC0000089	ERROR_RESOURCE_DATA_NOT_FOUND	1812
STATUS_RESOURCE_LANG_NOT_FOUND	0xC0000204	ERROR_RESOURCE_LANG_NOT_FOUND	1815
STATUS_RESOURCE_NAME_NOT_FOUND	0xC000008B	ERROR_RESOURCE_NAME_NOT_FOUND	1814
STATUS_RESOURCE_NOT_OWNED	0xC0000264	ERROR_NOT_OWNER	288
STATUS_RESOURCE_TYPE_NOT_FOUND	0xC000008A	ERROR_RESOURCE_TYPE_NOT_FOUND	1813
STATUS_RETRY	0xC000022D	ERROR_MR_MID_NOT_FOUND	317
STATUS_REVISION_MISMATCH	0xC0000059	ERROR_REVISION_MISMATCH	1306
STATUS_RXACT_COMMIT_FAILURE	0xC000011D	ERROR_RXACT_COMMIT_FAILURE	1370
STATUS_RXACT_INVALID_STATE	0xC000011C	ERROR_RXACT_INVALID_STATE	1369
STATUS_SECRET_TOO_LONG	0xC0000157	ERROR_SECRET_TOO_LONG	1382
STATUS_SECTION_NOT_EXTENDED	0xC0000087	ERROR_OUTOFMEMORY	14
STATUS_SECTION_NOT_IMAGE	0xC0000049	ERROR_INVALID_PARAMETER	87
STATUS_SECTION_PROTECTION	0xC000004E	ERROR_INVALID_PARAMETER	87
STATUS_SECTION_TOO_BIG	0xC0000040	ERROR_NOT_ENOUGH_MEMORY	8
STATUS_SEMAPHORE_LIMIT_EXCEEDED	0xC0000047	ERROR_TOO_MANY_POSTS	298

continues

Table A.1. Continued

NT Status	NT Status Value	Win32 Error Code	Win32 Error Value
STATUS_SERIAL_NO_DEVICE_INITED	0xC0000150	ERROR_SERIAL_NO_DEVICE	1118
STATUS_SERVER_DISABLED	0xC0000080	ERROR_SERVER_DISABLED	1341
STATUS_SERVER_NOT_DISABLED	0xC0000081	ERROR_SERVER_NOT_DISABLED	1342
STATUS_SHARED_IRQ_BUSY	0xC000016C	ERROR_IRQ_BUSY	1119
STATUS_SHARING_PAUSED	0xC00000CF	ERROR_SHARING_PAUSED	70
STATUS_SHARING_VIOLATION	0xC0000043	ERROR_SHARING_VIOLATION	32
STATUS_SPECIAL_ACCOUNT	0xC0000124	ERROR_SPECIAL_ACCOUNT	1371
STATUS_SPECIAL_GROUP	0xC0000125	ERROR_SPECIAL_GROUP	1372
STATUS_SPECIAL_USER	0xC0000126	ERROR_SPECIAL_USER	1373
STATUS_STACK_OVERFLOW	0xC00000FD	ERROR_STACK_OVERFLOW	1001
STATUS_STACK_OVERFLOW_READ	0xC0000228	ERROR_MR_MID_NOT_FOUND	317
STATUS_SUSPEND_COUNT_EXCEEDED	0xC000004A	ERROR_SIGNAL_REFUSED	156
STATUS_SYNCHRONIZATION_REQUIRED	0xC0000134	ERROR_MR_MID_NOT_FOUND	317
STATUS_SYSTEM_PROCESS_TERMINATED	0xC000021A	ERROR_MR_MID_NOT_FOUND	317
STATUS_THREAD_IS_TERMINATING	0xC000004B	ERROR_ACCESS_DENIED	5
STATUS_THREAD_NOT_IN_PROCESS	0xC000012A	ERROR_MR_MID_NOT_FOUND	317
STATUS_TIME_DIFFERENCE_AT_DC	0xC0000133	ERROR_MR_MID_NOT_FOUND	317
STATUS_TIMER_NOT_CANCELED	0xC000000C	ERROR_MR_MID_NOT_FOUND	317
STATUS_TIMER_RESOLUTION_NOT_SET	0xC0000245	ERROR_MR_MID_NOT_FOUND	317
STATUS_TOKEN_ALREADY_IN_USE	0xC000012B	ERROR_TOKEN_ALREADY_IN_USE	1375
STATUS_TOO_LATE	0xC0000189	ERROR_WRITE_PROTECT	19
STATUS_TOO_MANY_ADDRESSES	0xC0000209	ERROR_TOO_MANY_NAMES	68
STATUS_TOO_MANY_COMMANDS	0xC00000C1	ERROR_TOO_MANY_CMDS	56
STATUS_TOO_MANY_CONTEXT_IDS	0xC000015A	ERROR_TOO_MANY_CONTEXT_IDS	1384
STATUS_TOO_MANY_GUIDS_REQUESTED	0xC0000082	ERROR_TOO_MANY_NAMES	68
STATUS_TOO_MANY_LINKS	0xC0000265	ERROR_TOO_MANY_LINKS	1142
STATUS_TOO_MANY_LUIDS_REQUESTED	0xC0000074	ERROR_TOO_MANY_LUIDS_REQUESTED	1333
STATUS_TOO_MANY_NAMES	0xC00000CD	ERROR_TOO_MANY_NAMES	68
STATUS_TOO_MANY_NODES	0xC000020E	ERROR_TOO_MANY_NAMES	68
STATUS_TOO_MANY_OPENED_FILES	0xC000011F	ERROR_TOO_MANY_OPEN_FILES	4

STATUS	Hex	ERROR	Value
STATUS_TOO_MANY_PAGING_FILES	0xC0000097	ERROR_NOT_ENOUGH_MEMORY	8
STATUS_TOO_MANY_SECRETS	0xC0000156	ERROR_TOO_MANY_SECRETS	1381
STATUS_TOO_MANY_SESSIONS	0xC00000CE	ERROR_TOO_MANY_SESS	69
STATUS_TOO_MANY_SIDS	0xC000017E	ERROR_TOO_MANY_SIDS	1389
STATUS_TOO_MANY_THREADS	0xC0000129	ERROR_MR_MID_NOT_FOUND	317
STATUS_TRANSACTION_ABORTED	0xC000020F	ERROR_UNEXP_NET_ERR	59
STATUS_TRANSACTION_INVALID_ID	0xC0000214	ERROR_UNEXP_NET_ERR	59
STATUS_TRANSACTION_INVALID_TYPE	0xC0000215	ERROR_UNEXP_NET_ERR	59
STATUS_TRANSACTION_NO_MATCH	0xC0000212	ERROR_UNEXP_NET_ERR	59
STATUS_TRANSACTION_NO_RELEASE	0xC0000211	ERROR_UNEXP_NET_ERR	59
STATUS_TRANSACTION_RESPONDED	0xC0000213	ERROR_UNEXP_NET_ERR	59
STATUS_TRANSACTION_TIMED_OUT	0xC0000210	ERROR_UNEXP_NET_ERR	59
STATUS_TRUST_FAILURE	0xC0000190	ERROR_TRUST_FAILURE	1790
STATUS_TRUSTED_DOMAIN_FAILURE	0xC000018C	ERROR_TRUSTED_DOMAIN_FAILURE	1788
STATUS_TRUSTED_RELATIONSHIP_FAILURE	0xC000018D	ERROR_TRUSTED_RELATIONSHIP_FAILURE	1789
STATUS_UNABLE_TO_DECOMMIT_VM	0xC000002C	ERROR_INVALID_ADDRESS	487
STATUS_UNABLE_TO_DELETE_SECTION	0xC000001B	ERROR_INVALID_PARAMETER	87
STATUS_UNABLE_TO_FREE_VM	0xC000001A	ERROR_INVALID_PARAMETER	87
STATUS_UNABLE_TO_LOCK_MEDIA	0xC0000175	ERROR_UNABLE_TO_LOCK_MEDIA	1108
STATUS_UNABLE_TO_UNLOAD_MEDIA	0xC0000176	ERROR_UNABLE_TO_UNLOAD_MEDIA	1109
STATUS_UNDEFINED_CHARACTER	0xC0000163	ERROR_MR_MID_NOT_FOUND	317
STATUS_UNEXPECTED_IO_ERROR	0xC00000E9	ERROR_MR_MID_NOT_FOUND	317
STATUS_UNEXPECTED_MM_CREATE_ERR	0xC00000EA	ERROR_MR_MID_NOT_FOUND	317
STATUS_UNEXPECTED_MM_EXTEND_ERR	0xC00000EC	ERROR_MR_MID_NOT_FOUND	317
STATUS_UNEXPECTED_MM_MAP_ERROR	0xC00000EB	ERROR_MR_MID_NOT_FOUND	317
STATUS_UNEXPECTED_NETWORK_ERROR	0xC00000C4	ERROR_UNEXP_NET_ERR	59
STATUS_UNHANDLED_EXCEPTION	0xC0000144	ERROR_MR_MID_NOT_FOUND	317
STATUS_UNKNOWN_REVISION	0xC0000058	ERROR_UNKNOWN_REVISION	1305
STATUS_UNMAPPABLE_CHARACTER	0xC0000162	ERROR_NO_UNICODE_TRANSLATION	1113
STATUS_UNRECOGNIZED_MEDIA	0xC0000014	ERROR_UNRECOGNIZED_MEDIA	1785
STATUS_UNRECOGNIZED_VOLUME	0xC000014F	ERROR_UNRECOGNIZED_VOLUME	1005
STATUS_UNSUCCESSFUL	0xC0000001	ERROR_GEN_FAILURE	31

continues

Table A.1. Continued

NT Status	NT Status Value	Win32 Error Code	Win32 Error Value
STATUS_UNSUPPORTED_COMPRESSION	0xC000025F	ERROR_MR_MID_NOT_FOUND	317
STATUS_UNWIND	0xC0000027	ERROR_MR_MID_NOT_FOUND	317
STATUS_USER_EXISTS	0xC0000063	ERROR_USER_EXISTS	1316
STATUS_USER_MAPPED_FILE	0xC0000243	ERROR_USER_MAPPED_FILE	1224
STATUS_USER_SESSION_DELETED	0xC0000203	ERROR_UNEXP_NET_ERR	59
STATUS_VARIABLE_NOT_FOUND	0xC0000100	ERROR_ENVVAR_NOT_FOUND	203
STATUS_VDM_HARD_ERROR	0xC000021D	ERROR_MR_MID_NOT_FOUND	317
STATUS_VIRTUAL_CIRCUIT_CLOSED	0xC00000D6	ERROR_VC_DISCONNECTED	240
STATUS_VOLUME_DISMOUNTED	0xC000026E	ERROR_MR_MID_NOT_FOUND	317
STATUS_WORKING_SET_QUOTA	0xC00000A1	ERROR_WORKING_SET_QUOTA	1453
STATUS_WRONG_PASSWORD	0xC000006A	ERROR_INVALID_PASSWORD	86
STATUS_WRONG_PASSWORD_CORE	0xC0000149	ERROR_INVALID_PASSWORD	86
STATUS_WRONG_VOLUME	0xC0000012	ERROR_WRONG_DISK	34
STATUS_WX86_FLOAT_STACK_CHECK	0xC0000270	ERROR_MR_MID_NOT_FOUND	317
STATUS_WX86_INTERNAL_ERROR	0xC000026F	ERROR_MR_MID_NOT_FOUND	317

Table A.2 maps Win32 error return codes to their NT status equivalents.

Table A.2. Win32 error codes and corresponding Windows NT Status codes.

Win32 Error Code	Win32 Error Value	NT Status	NT Status Value
ERROR_ACCESS_DENIED	5	STATUS_ACCESS_DENIED	0xC0000022
ERROR_ACCESS_DENIED	5	STATUS_ALREADY_COMMITTED	0xC0000021
ERROR_ACCESS_DENIED	5	STATUS_CANNOT_DELETE	0xC0000121
ERROR_ACCESS_DENIED	5	STATUS_DELETE_PENDING	0xC0000056
ERROR_ACCESS_DENIED	5	STATUS_FILE_DELETED	0xC0000123
ERROR_ACCESS_DENIED	5	STATUS_FILE_IS_A_DIRECTORY	0xC00000BA
ERROR_ACCESS_DENIED	5	STATUS_INVALID_LOCK_SEQUENCE	0xC000001E
ERROR_ACCESS_DENIED	5	STATUS_INVALID_VIEW_SIZE	0xC000001F
ERROR_ACCESS_DENIED	5	STATUS_PORT_CONNECTION_REFUSED	0xC0000041
ERROR_ACCESS_DENIED	5	STATUS_PROCESS_IS_TERMINATING	0xC000010A
ERROR_ACCESS_DENIED	5	STATUS_THREAD_IS_TERMINATING	0xC000004B
ERROR_ACCOUNT_DISABLED	1331	STATUS_ACCOUNT_DISABLED	0xC0000072
ERROR_ACCOUNT_EXPIRED	1793	STATUS_ACCOUNT_EXPIRED	0xC0000193
ERROR_ACCOUNT_LOCKED_OUT	1909	STATUS_ACCOUNT_LOCKED_OUT	0xC0000234
ERROR_ACCOUNT_RESTRICTION	1327	STATUS_ACCOUNT_RESTRICTION	0xC000006E
ERROR_ADAP_HDW_ERR	57	STATUS_ADAPTER_HARDWARE_ERROR	0xC00000C2
ERROR_ADDRESS_ALREADY_ASSOCIATED	1227	STATUS_ADDRESS_ALREADY_ASSOCIATED	0xC0000238
ERROR_ADDRESS_NOT_ASSOCIATED	1228	STATUS_ADDRESS_NOT_ASSOCIATED	0xC0000239
ERROR_ALIAS_EXISTS	1379	STATUS_ALIAS_EXISTS	0xC0000154
ERROR_ALLOTTED_SPACE_EXCEEDED	1344	STATUS_ALLOTTED_SPACE_EXCEEDED	0xC0000099
ERROR_ALREADY_EXISTS	183	STATUS_OBJECT_NAME_COLLISION	0xC0000035
ERROR_ARITHMETIC_OVERFLOW	534	STATUS_INTEGER_OVERFLOW	0xC0000095
ERROR_BAD_COMMAND	22	STATUS_INVALID_DEVICE_STATE	0xC0000184
ERROR_BAD_DESCRIPTOR_FORMAT	1361	STATUS_BAD_DESCRIPTOR_FORMAT	0xC00000E7
ERROR_BAD_DEV_TYPE	66	STATUS_BAD_DEVICE_TYPE	0xC00000CB
ERROR_BAD_EXE_FORMAT	193	STATUS_BAD_INITIAL_PC	0xC000000A

continues

Table A.1. Continued

NT Status	NT Status Value	Win32 Error Code	Win32 Error Value
ERROR_BAD_EXE_FORMAT	193	STATUS_IMAGE_CHECKSUM_MISMATCH	0xC0000221
ERROR_BAD_EXE_FORMAT	193	STATUS_IMAGE_MP_UP_MISMATCH	0xC0000249
ERROR_BAD_EXE_FORMAT	193	STATUS_INVALID_FILE_FOR_SECTION	0xC0000020
ERROR_BAD_EXE_FORMAT	193	STATUS_INVALID_IMAGE_FORMAT	0xC000007B
ERROR_BAD_EXE_FORMAT	193	STATUS_INVALID_IMAGE_LE_FORMAT	0xC000012E
ERROR_BAD_EXE_FORMAT	193	STATUS_INVALID_IMAGE_NE_FORMAT	0xC000011B
ERROR_BAD_EXE_FORMAT	193	STATUS_INVALID_IMAGE_NOT_MZ	0xC000012F
ERROR_BAD_EXE_FORMAT	193	STATUS_INVALID_IMAGE_PROTECT	0xC0000130
ERROR_BAD_EXE_FORMAT	193	STATUS_INVALID_IMAGE_WIN_16	0xC0000131
ERROR_BAD_IMPERSONATION_LEVEL	1346	STATUS_BAD_IMPERSONATION_LEVEL	0xC00000A5
ERROR_BAD_INHERITANCE_ACL	1340	STATUS_BAD_INHERITANCE_ACL	0xC000007D
ERROR_BAD_LENGTH	24	STATUS_INFO_LENGTH_MISMATCH	0xC0000004
ERROR_BAD_LOGON_SESSION_STATE	1365	STATUS_BAD_LOGON_SESSION_STATE	0xC0000104
ERROR_BAD_NET_NAME	67	STATUS_BAD_NETWORK_NAME	0xC00000CC
ERROR_BAD_NET_RESP	58	STATUS_INVALID_NETWORK_RESPONSE	0xC00000C3
ERROR_BAD_NETPATH	53	STATUS_BAD_NETWORK_PATH	0xC00000BE
ERROR_BAD_PATHNAME	161	STATUS_OBJECT_PATH_INVALID	0xC0000039
ERROR_BAD_PATHNAME	161	STATUS_OBJECT_PATH_SYNTAX_BAD	0xC000003B
ERROR_BAD_PIPE	230	STATUS_INVALID_PIPE_STATE	0xC00000AD
ERROR_BAD_PIPE	230	STATUS_INVALID_READ_MODE	0xC00000B4
ERROR_BAD_REM_ADAP	60	STATUS_BAD_REMOTE_ADAPTER	0xC00000C5
ERROR_BAD_TOKEN_TYPE	1349	STATUS_BAD_TOKEN_TYPE	0xC00000A8
ERROR_BAD_VALIDATION_CLASS	1348	STATUS_BAD_VALIDATION_CLASS	0xC00000A7
ERROR_BADDB	1009	STATUS_REGISTRY_CORRUPT	0xC000014C
ERROR_BROKEN_PIPE	109	STATUS_PIPE_BROKEN	0xC000014B
ERROR_CANNOT_IMPERSONATE	1368	STATUS_CANNOT_IMPERSONATE	0xC000010D
ERROR_CANT_ACCESS_DOMAIN_INFO	1351	STATUS_CANT_ACCESS_DOMAIN_INFO	0xC00000DA
ERROR_CANT_DISABLE_MANDATORY	1310	STATUS_CANT_DISABLE_MANDATORY	0xC000005D
ERROR_CANT_OPEN_ANONYMOUS	1347	STATUS_CANT_OPEN_ANONYMOUS	0xC00000A6
ERROR_CHILD_MUST_BE_VOLATILE	1021	STATUS_CHILD_MUST_BE_VOLATILE	0xC0000181

Win32 Error Code	Number	NT Status Code	Status Value
ERROR_COMMITMENT_LIMIT	1455	STATUS_COMMITMENT_LIMIT	0xC000012D
ERROR_CONNECTION_ABORTED	1236	STATUS_CONNECTION_ABORTED	0xC0000241
ERROR_CONNECTION_ACTIVE	1230	STATUS_CONNECTION_ACTIVE	0xC000023B
ERROR_CONNECTION_COUNT_LIMIT	1238	STATUS_CONNECTION_COUNT_LIMIT	0xC0000246
ERROR_CONNECTION_INVALID	1229	STATUS_CONNECTION_INVALID	0xC000023A
ERROR_CONNECTION_REFUSED	1225	STATUS_CONNECTION_REFUSED	0xC0000236
ERROR_CRC	23	STATUS_CRC_ERROR	0xC000003F
ERROR_CRC	23	STATUS_DATA_ERROR	0xC000003E
ERROR_CRC	23	STATUS_DEVICE_DATA_ERROR	0xC000009C
ERROR_DEV_NOT_EXIST	55	STATUS_DEVICE_DOES_NOT_EXIST	0xC00000C0
ERROR_DEVICE_IN_USE	2404	STATUS_CONNECTION_IN_USE	0xC0000108
ERROR_DEVICE_NOT_PARTITIONED	1107	STATUS_DEVICE_NOT_PARTITIONED	0xC0000174
ERROR_DIR_NOT_EMPTY	145	STATUS_DIRECTORY_NOT_EMPTY	0xC0000101
ERROR_DIRECTORY	267	STATUS_NOT_A_DIRECTORY	0xC0000103
ERROR_DISK_CORRUPT	1393	STATUS_DISK_CORRUPT_ERROR	0xC0000032
ERROR_DISK_FULL	112	STATUS_DISK_FULL	0xC000007F
ERROR_DISK_OPERATION_FAILED	1127	STATUS_DISK_OPERATION_FAILED	0xC000016A
ERROR_DISK_RECALIBRATE_FAILED	1126	STATUS_DISK_RECALIBRATE_FAILED	0xC0000169
ERROR_DISK_RESET_FAILED	1128	STATUS_DISK_RESET_FAILED	0xC000016B
ERROR_DLL_INIT_FAILED	1114	STATUS_DLL_INIT_FAILED	0xC0000142
ERROR_DOMAIN_CONTROLLER_NOT_FOUND	1908	STATUS_DOMAIN_CONTROLLER_NOT_FOUND	0xC0000233
ERROR_DOMAIN_EXISTS	1356	STATUS_DOMAIN_EXISTS	0xC00000E0
ERROR_DOMAIN_LIMIT_EXCEEDED	1357	STATUS_DOMAIN_LIMIT_EXCEEDED	0xC00000E1
ERROR_DOMAIN_TRUST_INCONSISTENT	1810	STATUS_DOMAIN_TRUST_INCONSISTENT	0xC000019B
ERROR_DUP_NAME	52	STATUS_ADDRESS_ALREADY_EXISTS	0xC000020A
ERROR_DUP_NAME	52	STATUS_DUPLICATE_NAME	0xC00000BD
ERROR_EA_LIST_INCONSISTENT	255	STATUS_EA_TOO_LARGE	0xC0000050
ERROR_ENVVAR_NOT_FOUND	203	STATUS_VARIABLE_NOT_FOUND	0xC0000100
ERROR_EOM_OVERFLOW	1129	STATUS_EOM_OVERFLOW	0xC0000177
ERROR_EVENTLOG_CANT_START	1501	STATUS_EVENTLOG_CANT_START	0xC000018F
ERROR_EVENTLOG_FILE_CHANGED	1503	STATUS_EVENTLOG_FILE_CHANGED	0xC0000197
ERROR_EVENTLOG_FILE_CORRUPT	1500	STATUS_EVENTLOG_FILE_CORRUPT	0xC000018E

continues

Table A.1. Continued

NT Status	NT Status Value	Win32 Error Code	Win32 Error Value
ERROR_FILE_CORRUPT	1392	STATUS_EA_CORRUPT_ERROR	0xC0000053
ERROR_FILE_CORRUPT	1392	STATUS_FILE_CORRUPT_ERROR	0xC0000102
ERROR_FILE_CORRUPT	1392	STATUS_NO_EAS_ON_FILE	0xC0000052
ERROR_FILE_CORRUPT	1392	STATUS_NONEXISTENT_EA_ENTRY	0xC0000051
ERROR_FILE_INVALID	1006	STATUS_FILE_INVALID	0xC0000098
ERROR_FILE_INVALID	1006	STATUS_MAPPED_FILE_SIZE_ZERO	0xC000011E
ERROR_FILE_NOT_FOUND	2	STATUS_NO_SUCH_DEVICE	0xC000000E
ERROR_FILE_NOT_FOUND	2	STATUS_NO_SUCH_FILE	0xC000000F
ERROR_FILE_NOT_FOUND	2	STATUS_OBJECT_NAME_NOT_FOUND	0xC0000034
ERROR_FILENAME_EXCED_RANGE	206	STATUS_NAME_TOO_LONG	0xC0000106
ERROR_FLOPPY_BAD_REGISTERS	1125	STATUS_FLOPPY_BAD_REGISTERS	0xC0000168
ERROR_FLOPPY_ID_MARK_NOT_FOUND	1122	STATUS_FLOPPY_ID_MARK_NOT_FOUND	0xC0000165
ERROR_FLOPPY_UNKNOWN_ERROR	1124	STATUS_FLOPPY_UNKNOWN_ERROR	0xC0000167
ERROR_FLOPPY_WRONG_CYLINDER	1123	STATUS_FLOPPY_WRONG_CYLINDER	0xC0000166
ERROR_FULLSCREEN_MODE	1007	STATUS_FULLSCREEN_MODE	0xC0000159
ERROR_GEN_FAILURE	31	STATUS_UNSUCCESSFUL	0xC0000001
ERROR_GENERIC_NOT_MAPPED	1360	STATUS_GENERIC_NOT_MAPPED	0xC00000E6
ERROR_GRACEFUL_DISCONNECT	1226	STATUS_GRACEFUL_DISCONNECT	0xC0000237
ERROR_GROUP_EXISTS	1318	STATUS_GROUP_EXISTS	0xC0000065
ERROR_HANDLE_EOF	38	STATUS_END_OF_FILE	0xC0000011
ERROR_HANDLE_EOF	38	STATUS_FILE_FORCED_CLOSED	0xC00000B6
ERROR_HOST_UNREACHABLE	1232	STATUS_HOST_UNREACHABLE	0xC000023D
ERROR_HOST_UNREACHABLE	1232	STATUS_PATH_NOT_COVERED	0xC0000257
ERROR_ILL_FORMED_PASSWORD	1324	STATUS_ILL_FORMED_PASSWORD	0xC000006B
ERROR_INSUFFICIENT_BUFFER	122	STATUS_BUFFER_TOO_SMALL	0xC0000023
ERROR_INTERNAL_DB_CORRUPTION	1358	STATUS_INTERNAL_DB_CORRUPTION	0xC00000E4
ERROR_INTERNAL_DB_ERROR	1383	STATUS_INTERNAL_DB_ERROR	0xC0000158
ERROR_INTERNAL_ERROR	1359	STATUS_INTERNAL_ERROR	0xC00000E5
ERROR_INTERNAL_ERROR	1359	STATUS_LPC_REPLY_LOST	0xC0000253
ERROR_INVALID_ACCOUNT_NAME	1315	STATUS_INVALID_ACCOUNT_NAME	0xC0000062

Win32 Error	Decimal	NT Status	Hex
ERROR_INVALID_ACL	1336	STATUS_INVALID_ACL	0xC0000077
ERROR_INVALID_ADDRESS	487	STATUS_CONFLICTING_ADDRESSES	0xC0000018
ERROR_INVALID_ADDRESS	487	STATUS_FREE_VM_NOT_AT_BASE	0xC000009F
ERROR_INVALID_ADDRESS	487	STATUS_MEMORY_NOT_ALLOCATED	0xC00000A0
ERROR_INVALID_ADDRESS	487	STATUS_NOT_COMMITTED	0xC000002D
ERROR_INVALID_ADDRESS	487	STATUS_NOT_MAPPED_DATA	0xC0000088
ERROR_INVALID_ADDRESS	487	STATUS_NOT_MAPPED_VIEW	0xC0000019
ERROR_INVALID_ADDRESS	487	STATUS_UNABLE_TO_DECOMMIT_VM	0xC000002C
ERROR_INVALID_BLOCK_LENGTH	1106	STATUS_INVALID_BLOCK_LENGTH	0xC0000173
ERROR_INVALID_COMPUTERNAME	1210	STATUS_INVALID_COMPUTER_NAME	0xC0000122
ERROR_INVALID_DOMAIN_ROLE	1354	STATUS_INVALID_DOMAIN_ROLE	0xC00000DE
ERROR_INVALID_DOMAIN_STATE	1353	STATUS_INVALID_DOMAIN_STATE	0xC00000DD
ERROR_INVALID_FUNCTION	1	STATUS_ILLEGAL_FUNCTION	0xC00000AF
ERROR_INVALID_FUNCTION	1	STATUS_INVALID_DEVICE_REQUEST	0xC0000010
ERROR_INVALID_FUNCTION	1	STATUS_INVALID_SYSTEM_SERVICE	0xC000001C
ERROR_INVALID_FUNCTION	1	STATUS_NOT_IMPLEMENTED	0xC0000002
ERROR_INVALID_GROUP_ATTRIBUTES	1345	STATUS_INVALID_GROUP_ATTRIBUTES	0xC00000A4
ERROR_INVALID_HANDLE	6	STATUS_FILE_CLOSED	0xC0000128
ERROR_INVALID_HANDLE	6	STATUS_HANDLE_NOT_CLOSABLE	0xC0000235
ERROR_INVALID_HANDLE	6	STATUS_INVALID_HANDLE	0xC0000008
ERROR_INVALID_HANDLE	6	STATUS_INVALID_PORT_HANDLE	0xC0000042
ERROR_INVALID_HANDLE	6	STATUS_OBJECT_TYPE_MISMATCH	0xC0000024
ERROR_INVALID_HANDLE	6	STATUS_PORT_DISCONNECTED	0xC0000037
ERROR_INVALID_ID_AUTHORITY	1343	STATUS_INVALID_ID_AUTHORITY	0xC0000084
ERROR_INVALID_LEVEL	124	STATUS_INVALID_LEVEL	0xC0000148
ERROR_INVALID_LOGON_HOURS	1328	STATUS_INVALID_LOGON_HOURS	0xC000006F
ERROR_INVALID_LOGON_TYPE	1367	STATUS_INVALID_LOGON_TYPE	0xC000010B
ERROR_INVALID_MEMBER	1388	STATUS_INVALID_MEMBER	0xC000017B
ERROR_INVALID_NAME	123	STATUS_OBJECT_NAME_INVALID	0xC0000033
ERROR_INVALID_NETNAME	1214	STATUS_INVALID_ADDRESS_COMPONENT	0xC0000207
ERROR_INVALID_NETNAME	1214	STATUS_INVALID_ADDRESS_WILDCARD	0xC0000208
ERROR_INVALID_ORDINAL	182	STATUS_DRIVER_ORDINAL_NOT_FOUND	0xC0000262

continues

Table A.2. Continued

NT Status	NT Status Value	Win32 Error Code	Win32 Error Value
ERROR_INVALID_ORDINAL	182	STATUS_ORDINAL_NOT_FOUND	0xC0000138
ERROR_INVALID_OWNER	1307	STATUS_INVALID_OWNER	0xC000005A
ERROR_INVALID_PARAMETER	87	STATUS_BAD_WORKING_SET_LIMIT	0xC000004C
ERROR_INVALID_PARAMETER	87	STATUS_DEVICE_CONFIGURATION_ERROR	0xC0000182
ERROR_INVALID_PARAMETER	87	STATUS_INCOMPATIBLE_FILE_MAP	0xC000004D
ERROR_INVALID_PARAMETER	87	STATUS_INVALID_CID	0xC000000B
ERROR_INVALID_PARAMETER	87	STATUS_INVALID_INFO_CLASS	0xC0000003
ERROR_INVALID_PARAMETER	87	STATUS_INVALID_PAGE_PROTECTION	0xC0000045
ERROR_INVALID_PARAMETER	87	STATUS_INVALID_PARAMETER	0xC000000D
ERROR_INVALID_PARAMETER	87	STATUS_INVALID_PARAMETER_1	0xC00000EF
ERROR_INVALID_PARAMETER	87	STATUS_INVALID_PARAMETER_10	0xC00000F8
ERROR_INVALID_PARAMETER	87	STATUS_INVALID_PARAMETER_11	0xC00000F9
ERROR_INVALID_PARAMETER	87	STATUS_INVALID_PARAMETER_12	0xC00000FA
ERROR_INVALID_PARAMETER	87	STATUS_INVALID_PARAMETER_2	0xC00000F0
ERROR_INVALID_PARAMETER	87	STATUS_INVALID_PARAMETER_3	0xC00000F1
ERROR_INVALID_PARAMETER	87	STATUS_INVALID_PARAMETER_4	0xC00000F2
ERROR_INVALID_PARAMETER	87	STATUS_INVALID_PARAMETER_5	0xC00000F3
ERROR_INVALID_PARAMETER	87	STATUS_INVALID_PARAMETER_6	0xC00000F4
ERROR_INVALID_PARAMETER	87	STATUS_INVALID_PARAMETER_7	0xC00000F5
ERROR_INVALID_PARAMETER	87	STATUS_INVALID_PARAMETER_8	0xC00000F6
ERROR_INVALID_PARAMETER	87	STATUS_INVALID_PARAMETER_9	0xC00000F7
ERROR_INVALID_PARAMETER	87	STATUS_INVALID_PARAMETER_MIX	0xC0000030
ERROR_INVALID_PARAMETER	87	STATUS_PORT_ALREADY_SET	0xC0000048
ERROR_INVALID_PARAMETER	87	STATUS_SECTION_NOT_IMAGE	0xC0000049
ERROR_INVALID_PARAMETER	87	STATUS_SECTION_PROTECTION	0xC000004E
ERROR_INVALID_PARAMETER	87	STATUS_UNABLE_TO_DELETE_SECTION	0xC000001B
ERROR_INVALID_PARAMETER	87	STATUS_UNABLE_TO_FREE_VM	0xC000001A
ERROR_INVALID_PASSWORD	86	STATUS_WRONG_PASSWORD	0xC000006A
ERROR_INVALID_PASSWORD	86	STATUS_WRONG_PASSWORD_CORE	0xC0000149
ERROR_INVALID_PRIMARY_GROUP	1308	STATUS_INVALID_PRIMARY_GROUP	0xC000005B

Win32 Error Code	Decimal	NT Status Code	Hex
ERROR_INVALID_SECURITY_DESCR	1338	STATUS_INVALID_SECURITY_DESCR	0xC0000079
ERROR_INVALID_SERVER_STATE	1352	STATUS_INVALID_SERVER_STATE	0xC00000DC
ERROR_INVALID_SID	1337	STATUS_INVALID_SID	0xC0000078
ERROR_INVALID_SUB_AUTHORITY	1335	STATUS_INVALID_SUB_AUTHORITY	0xC0000076
ERROR_INVALID_USER_BUFFER	1784	STATUS_INVALID_BUFFER_SIZE	0xC0000206
ERROR_INVALID_USER_BUFFER	1784	STATUS_INVALID_USER_BUFFER	0xC00000E8
ERROR_INVALID_WORKSTATION	1329	STATUS_INVALID_WORKSTATION	0xC0000070
ERROR_IO_DEVICE	1117	STATUS_DATA_LATE_ERROR	0xC000003D
ERROR_IO_DEVICE	1117	STATUS_DATA_OVERRUN	0xC000003C
ERROR_IO_DEVICE	1117	STATUS_DEVICE_PROTOCOL_ERROR	0xC0000186
ERROR_IO_DEVICE	1117	STATUS_DRIVER_INTERNAL_ERROR	0xC0000183
ERROR_IO_DEVICE	1117	STATUS_FT_MISSING_MEMBER	0xC000015F
ERROR_IO_DEVICE	1117	STATUS_FT_ORPHANING	0xC000016D
ERROR_IRQ_BUSY	1119	STATUS_IO_DEVICE_ERROR	0xC0000185
ERROR_KEY_DELETED	1018	STATUS_SHARED_IRQ_BUSY	0xC000016C
ERROR_KEY_HAS_CHILDREN	1020	STATUS_KEY_DELETED	0xC000017C
ERROR_LABEL_TOO_LONG	154	STATUS_KEY_HAS_CHILDREN	0xC0000180
ERROR_LAST_ADMIN	1322	STATUS_INVALID_VOLUME_LABEL	0xC0000086
ERROR_LICENSE_QUOTA_EXCEEDED	1395	STATUS_LAST_ADMIN	0xC0000069
ERROR_LM_CROSS_ENCRYPTION_REQUIRED	1390	STATUS_LICENSE_QUOTA_EXCEEDED	0xC0000259
ERROR_LOCK_VIOLATION	33	STATUS_LM_CROSS_ENCRYPTION_REQUIRED	0xC000017F
ERROR_LOCK_VIOLATION	33	STATUS_FILE_LOCK_CONFLICT	0xC0000054
ERROR_LOG_FILE_FULL	1502	STATUS_LOCK_NOT_GRANTED	0xC0000055
ERROR_LOGIN_TIME_RESTRICTION	1239	STATUS_LOG_FILE_FULL	0xC0000188
ERROR_LOGIN_WKSTA_RESTRICTION	1240	STATUS_LOGIN_TIME_RESTRICTION	0xC0000247
ERROR_LOGON_FAILURE	1326	STATUS_LOGIN_WKSTA_RESTRICTION	0xC0000248
ERROR_LOGON_NOT_GRANTED	1380	STATUS_LOGON_FAILURE	0xC000006D
ERROR_LOGON_SESSION_COLLISION	1366	STATUS_LOGON_NOT_GRANTED	0xC0000155
ERROR_LOGON_SESSION_EXISTS	1363	STATUS_LOGON_SESSION_COLLISION	0xC0000105
ERROR_LOGON_TYPE_NOT_GRANTED	1385	STATUS_LOGON_SESSION_EXISTS	0xC00000EE
ERROR_LUIDS_EXHAUSTED	1334	STATUS_LOGON_TYPE_NOT_GRANTED	0xC000015B
		STATUS_LUIDS_EXHAUSTED	0xC0000075

continues

Table A.2. Continued

NT Status	NT Status Value	Win32 Error Code	Win32 Error Value
ERROR_MAPPED_ALIGNMENT	1132	STATUS_MAPPED_ALIGNMENT	0xC0000220
ERROR_MEMBER_IN_ALIAS	1378	STATUS_MEMBER_IN_ALIAS	0xC0000153
ERROR_MEMBER_IN_GROUP	1320	STATUS_MEMBER_IN_GROUP	0xC0000067
ERROR_MEMBER_NOT_IN_ALIAS	1377	STATUS_MEMBER_NOT_IN_ALIAS	0xC0000152
ERROR_MEMBER_NOT_IN_GROUP	1321	STATUS_MEMBER_NOT_IN_GROUP	0xC0000068
ERROR_MEMBERS_PRIMARY_GROUP	1374	STATUS_MEMBERS_PRIMARY_GROUP	0xC0000127
ERROR_MOD_NOT_FOUND	126	STATUS_DLL_NOT_FOUND	0xC0000135
ERROR_MORE_DATA	234	STATUS_MORE_PROCESSING_REQUIRED	0xC0000016
ERROR_MR_MID_NOT_FOUND	317	STATUS_ABIOS_INVALID_COMMAND	0xC0000113
ERROR_MR_MID_NOT_FOUND	317	STATUS_ABIOS_INVALID_LID	0xC0000114
ERROR_MR_MID_NOT_FOUND	317	STATUS_ABIOS_INVALID_SELECTOR	0xC0000116
ERROR_MR_MID_NOT_FOUND	317	STATUS_ABIOS_LID_ALREADY_OWNED	0xC0000111
ERROR_MR_MID_NOT_FOUND	317	STATUS_ABIOS_LID_NOT_EXIST	0xC0000110
ERROR_MR_MID_NOT_FOUND	317	STATUS_ABIOS_NOT_LID_OWNER	0xC0000112
ERROR_MR_MID_NOT_FOUND	317	STATUS_ABIOS_NOT_PRESENT	0xC000010F
ERROR_MR_MID_NOT_FOUND	317	STATUS_ABIOS_SELECTOR_NOT_AVAILABLE	0xC0000115
ERROR_MR_MID_NOT_FOUND	317	STATUS_ALLOCATE_BUCKET	0xC000022F
ERROR_MR_MID_NOT_FOUND	317	STATUS_APP_INIT_FAILURE	0xC0000145
ERROR_MR_MID_NOT_FOUND	317	STATUS_AUDIT_FAILED	0xC0000244
ERROR_MR_MID_NOT_FOUND	317	STATUS_BACKUP_CONTROLLER	0xC0000187
ERROR_MR_MID_NOT_FOUND	317	STATUS_BAD_COMPRESSION_BUFFER	0xC0000242
ERROR_MR_MID_NOT_FOUND	317	STATUS_BAD_DLL_ENTRYPOINT	0xC0000251
ERROR_MR_MID_NOT_FOUND	317	STATUS_BAD_FUNCTION_TABLE	0xC00000FF
ERROR_MR_MID_NOT_FOUND	317	STATUS_BAD_MASTER_BOOT_RECORD	0xC00000A9
ERROR_MR_MID_NOT_FOUND	317	STATUS_BAD_SERVICE_ENTRYPOINT	0xC0000252
ERROR_MR_MID_NOT_FOUND	317	STATUS_BAD_STACK	0xC0000028
ERROR_MR_MID_NOT_FOUND	317	STATUS_BIOS_FAILED_TO_CONNECT_INTERRUPT	0xC000016E
ERROR_MR_MID_NOT_FOUND	317	STATUS_CANNOT_LOAD_REGISTRY_FILE	0xC0000218
ERROR_MR_MID_NOT_FOUND	317	STATUS_CANT_TERMINATE_SELF	0xC00000DB
ERROR_MR_MID_NOT_FOUND	317	STATUS_CANT_WAIT	0xC00000D8

Status Code	Hex		Win32 Error
STATUS_CLIENT_SERVER_PARAMETERS_INVALID	0xC0000223	317	ERROR_MR_MID_NOT_FOUND
STATUS_CONTROL_C_EXIT	0xC000013A	317	ERROR_MR_MID_NOT_FOUND
STATUS_CONVERT_TO_LARGE	0xC000022C	317	ERROR_MR_MID_NOT_FOUND
STATUS_COULD_NOT_INTERPRET	0xC00000B9	317	ERROR_MR_MID_NOT_FOUND
STATUS_DATA_NOT_ACCEPTED	0xC000021B	317	ERROR_MR_MID_NOT_FOUND
STATUS_DEBUG_ATTACH_FAILED	0xC0000219	317	ERROR_MR_MID_NOT_FOUND
STATUS_DEVICE_ALREADY_ATTACHED	0xC0000038	317	ERROR_MR_MID_NOT_FOUND
STATUS_DFS_UNAVAILABLE	0xC000026D	317	ERROR_MR_MID_NOT_FOUND
STATUS_DLL_INIT_FAILED_LOGOFF	0xC000026B	317	ERROR_MR_MID_NOT_FOUND
STATUS_DOMAIN_CTRLR_CONFIG_ERROR	0xC000015E	317	ERROR_MR_MID_NOT_FOUND
STATUS_DRIVER_CANCEL_TIMEOUT	0xC000021E	317	ERROR_MR_MID_NOT_FOUND
STATUS_DRIVER_UNABLE_TO_LOAD	0xC000026C	317	ERROR_MR_MID_NOT_FOUND
STATUS_EAS_NOT_SUPPORTED	0xC000004F	317	ERROR_MR_MID_NOT_FOUND
STATUS_EVALUATION_EXPIRATION	0xC0000268	317	ERROR_MR_MID_NOT_FOUND
STATUS_FAIL_CHECK	0xC0000229	317	ERROR_MR_MID_NOT_FOUND
STATUS_FILE_IS_OFFLINE	0xC0000267	317	ERROR_MR_MID_NOT_FOUND
STATUS_FILE_RENAMED	0xC00000D5	317	ERROR_MR_MID_NOT_FOUND
STATUS_FILES_OPEN	0xC0000107	317	ERROR_MR_MID_NOT_FOUND
STATUS_FLOPPY_VOLUME	0xC0000164	317	ERROR_MR_MID_NOT_FOUND
STATUS_FOUND_OUT_OF_SCOPE	0xC000022E	317	ERROR_MR_MID_NOT_FOUND
STATUS_FS_DRIVER_REQUIRED	0xC000019C	317	ERROR_MR_MID_NOT_FOUND
STATUS_ILL_FORMED_SERVICE_ENTRY	0xC0000160	317	ERROR_MR_MID_NOT_FOUND
STATUS_ILLEGAL_CHARACTER	0xC0000161	317	ERROR_MR_MID_NOT_FOUND
STATUS_ILLEGAL_DLL_RELOCATION	0xC0000269	317	ERROR_MR_MID_NOT_FOUND
STATUS_ILLEGAL_FLOAT_CONTEXT	0xC000014A	317	ERROR_MR_MID_NOT_FOUND
STATUS_INSTRUCTION_MISALIGNMENT	0xC00000AA	317	ERROR_MR_MID_NOT_FOUND
STATUS_INSUFFICIENT_LOGON_INFO	0xC0000250	317	ERROR_MR_MID_NOT_FOUND
STATUS_INVALID_HW_PROFILE	0xC0000260	317	ERROR_MR_MID_NOT_FOUND
STATUS_INVALID_LDT_DESCRIPTOR	0xC000011A	317	ERROR_MR_MID_NOT_FOUND
STATUS_INVALID_LDT_OFFSET	0xC0000119	317	ERROR_MR_MID_NOT_FOUND
STATUS_INVALID_LDT_SIZE	0xC0000118	317	ERROR_MR_MID_NOT_FOUND
STATUS_INVALID_OPLOCK_PROTOCOL	0xC00000E3	317	ERROR_MR_MID_NOT_FOUND

continues

Table A.2. Continued

NT Status	NT Status Value	Win32 Error Code	Win32 Error Value
ERROR_MR_MID_NOT_FOUND	317	STATUS_INVALID_PLUGPLAY_DEVICE_PATH	0xC0000261
ERROR_MR_MID_NOT_FOUND	317	STATUS_INVALID_PORT_ATTRIBUTES	0xC000002E
ERROR_MR_MID_NOT_FOUND	317	STATUS_INVALID_QUOTA_LOWER	0xC0000031
ERROR_MR_MID_NOT_FOUND	317	STATUS_INVALID_UNWIND_TARGET	0xC0000029
ERROR_MR_MID_NOT_FOUND	317	STATUS_INVALID_VARIANT	0xC0000232
ERROR_MR_MID_NOT_FOUND	317	STATUS_IO_PRIVILEGE_FAILED	0xC0000137
ERROR_MR_MID_NOT_FOUND	317	STATUS_IP_ADDRESS_CONFLICT1	0xC0000254
ERROR_MR_MID_NOT_FOUND	317	STATUS_IP_ADDRESS_CONFLICT2	0xC0000255
ERROR_MR_MID_NOT_FOUND	317	STATUS_LICENSE_VIOLATION	0xC000026A
ERROR_MR_MID_NOT_FOUND	317	STATUS_LOGON_SERVER_CONFLICT	0xC0000132
ERROR_MR_MID_NOT_FOUND	317	STATUS_LOST_WRITEBEHIND_DATA	0xC0000222
ERROR_MR_MID_NOT_FOUND	317	STATUS_MARSHALL_OVERFLOW	0xC0000231
ERROR_MR_MID_NOT_FOUND	317	STATUS_MESSAGE_NOT_FOUND	0xC0000109
ERROR_MR_MID_NOT_FOUND	317	STATUS_MISSING_SYSTEMFILE	0xC0000143
ERROR_MR_MID_NOT_FOUND	317	STATUS_MUTANT_LIMIT_EXCEEDED	0xC0000191
ERROR_MR_MID_NOT_FOUND	317	STATUS_NO_CALLBACK_ACTIVE	0xC0000258
ERROR_MR_MID_NOT_FOUND	317	STATUS_NO_EVENT_PAIR	0xC000014E
ERROR_MR_MID_NOT_FOUND	317	STATUS_NO_GUID_TRANSLATION	0xC000010C
ERROR_MR_MID_NOT_FOUND	317	STATUS_NO_LDT	0xC0000117
ERROR_MR_MID_NOT_FOUND	317	STATUS_NO_PAGEFILE	0xC0000147
ERROR_MR_MID_NOT_FOUND	317	STATUS_NOT_FOUND	0xC0000225
ERROR_MR_MID_NOT_FOUND	317	STATUS_NOT_TINY_STREAM	0xC0000226
ERROR_MR_MID_NOT_FOUND	317	STATUS_OPEN_FAILED	0xC0000136
ERROR_MR_MID_NOT_FOUND	317	STATUS_OPLOCK_NOT_GRANTED	0xC00000E2
ERROR_MR_MID_NOT_FOUND	317	STATUS_PAGEFILE_CREATE_FAILED	0xC0000146
ERROR_MR_MID_NOT_FOUND	317	STATUS_PAGEFILE_QUOTA_EXCEEDED	0xC000012C
ERROR_MR_MID_NOT_FOUND	317	STATUS_PORT_MESSAGE_TOO_LONG	0xC000002F
ERROR_MR_MID_NOT_FOUND	317	STATUS_PROFILING_AT_LIMIT	0xC00000D3
ERROR_MR_MID_NOT_FOUND	317	STATUS_PROFILING_NOT_STARTED	0xC00000B7
ERROR_MR_MID_NOT_FOUND	317	STATUS_PROFILING_NOT_STOPPED	0xC00000B8

ERROR_MR_MID_NOT_FOUND	317	STATUS_PROPSET_NOT_FOUND	0xC0000230
ERROR_MR_MID_NOT_FOUND	317	STATUS_PWD_HISTORY_CONFLICT	0xC000025C
ERROR_MR_MID_NOT_FOUND	317	STATUS_PWD_TOO_RECENT	0xC000025B
ERROR_MR_MID_NOT_FOUND	317	STATUS_PWD_TOO_SHORT	0xC000025A
ERROR_MR_MID_NOT_FOUND	317	STATUS_QUOTA_LIST_INCONSISTENT	0xC0000266
ERROR_MR_MID_NOT_FOUND	317	STATUS_RECOVERY_FAILURE	0xC0000227
ERROR_MR_MID_NOT_FOUND	317	STATUS_REDIRECTOR_STARTED	0xC00000FC
ERROR_MR_MID_NOT_FOUND	317	STATUS_REGISTRY_QUOTA_LIMIT	0xC0000256
ERROR_MR_MID_NOT_FOUND	317	STATUS_REPLY_MESSAGE_MISMATCH	0xC000021F
ERROR_MR_MID_NOT_FOUND	317	STATUS_RETRY	0xC000022D
ERROR_MR_MID_NOT_FOUND	317	STATUS_STACK_OVERFLOW_READ	0xC0000228
ERROR_MR_MID_NOT_FOUND	317	STATUS_SYNCHRONIZATION_REQUIRED	0xC0000134
ERROR_MR_MID_NOT_FOUND	317	STATUS_SYSTEM_PROCESS_TERMINATED	0xC000021A
ERROR_MR_MID_NOT_FOUND	317	STATUS_THREAD_NOT_IN_PROCESS	0xC000012A
ERROR_MR_MID_NOT_FOUND	317	STATUS_TIME_DIFFERENCE_AT_DC	0xC0000133
ERROR_MR_MID_NOT_FOUND	317	STATUS_TIMER_NOT_CANCELED	0xC000000C
ERROR_MR_MID_NOT_FOUND	317	STATUS_TIMER_RESOLUTION_NOT_SET	0xC0000245
ERROR_MR_MID_NOT_FOUND	317	STATUS_TOO_MANY_THREADS	0xC0000129
ERROR_MR_MID_NOT_FOUND	317	STATUS_UNDEFINED_CHARACTER	0xC0000163
ERROR_MR_MID_NOT_FOUND	317	STATUS_UNEXPECTED_IO_ERROR	0xC00000E9
ERROR_MR_MID_NOT_FOUND	317	STATUS_UNEXPECTED_MM_CREATE_ERR	0xC00000EA
ERROR_MR_MID_NOT_FOUND	317	STATUS_UNEXPECTED_MM_EXTEND_ERR	0xC00000EC
ERROR_MR_MID_NOT_FOUND	317	STATUS_UNEXPECTED_MM_MAP_ERROR	0xC00000EB
ERROR_MR_MID_NOT_FOUND	317	STATUS_UNHANDLED_EXCEPTION	0xC0000144
ERROR_MR_MID_NOT_FOUND	317	STATUS_UNSUPPORTED_COMPRESSION	0xC000025F
ERROR_MR_MID_NOT_FOUND	317	STATUS_UNWIND	0xC0000027
ERROR_MR_MID_NOT_FOUND	317	STATUS_VDM_HARD_ERROR	0xC000021D
ERROR_MR_MID_NOT_FOUND	317	STATUS_VOLUME_DISMOUNTED	0xC000026E
ERROR_MR_MID_NOT_FOUND	317	STATUS_WX86_FLOAT_STACK_CHECK	0xC0000270
ERROR_MR_MID_NOT_FOUND	317	STATUS_WX86_INTERNAL_ERROR	0xC000026F
ERROR_NET_WRITE_FAULT	88	STATUS_NET_WRITE_FAULT	0xC00000D2
ERROR_NETLOGON_NOT_STARTED	1792	STATUS_NETLOGON_NOT_STARTED	0xC0000192

continues

Table A.2. Continued

NT Status	NT Status Value	Win32 Error Code	Win32 Error Value
ERROR_NETNAME_DELETED	64	STATUS_ADDRESS_CLOSED	0xC000020B
ERROR_NETNAME_DELETED	64	STATUS_CONNECTION_DISCONNECTED	0xC000020C
ERROR_NETNAME_DELETED	64	STATUS_CONNECTION_RESET	0xC000020D
ERROR_NETNAME_DELETED	64	STATUS_LOCAL_DISCONNECT	0xC000013B
ERROR_NETNAME_DELETED	64	STATUS_NETWORK_NAME_DELETED	0xC00000C9
ERROR_NETNAME_DELETED	64	STATUS_REMOTE_DISCONNECT	0xC000013C
ERROR_NETWORK_ACCESS_DENIED	65	STATUS_NETWORK_ACCESS_DENIED	0xC00000CA
ERROR_NETWORK_BUSY	54	STATUS_NETWORK_BUSY	0xC00000BF
ERROR_NETWORK_UNREACHABLE	1231	STATUS_NETWORK_UNREACHABLE	0xC000023C
ERROR_NO_BROWSER_SERVERS_FOUND	6118	STATUS_NO_BROWSER_SERVERS_FOUND	0xC000021C
ERROR_NO_DATA	232	STATUS_PIPE_CLOSING	0xC00000B1
ERROR_NO_DATA	232	STATUS_PIPE_EMPTY	0xC00000D9
ERROR_NO_IMPERSONATION_TOKEN	1309	STATUS_NO_IMPERSONATION_TOKEN	0xC000005C
ERROR_NO_LOG_SPACE	1019	STATUS_NO_LOG_SPACE	0xC000017D
ERROR_NO_LOGON_SERVERS	1311	STATUS_NO_LOGON_SERVERS	0xC000005E
ERROR_NO_MEDIA_IN_DRIVE	1112	STATUS_NO_MEDIA	0xC0000178
ERROR_NO_MORE_ITEMS	259	STATUS_AGENTS_EXHAUSTED	0xC0000085
ERROR_NO_MORE_ITEMS	259	STATUS_GUIDS_EXHAUSTED	0xC0000083
ERROR_NO_SECURITY_ON_OBJECT	1350	STATUS_NO_SECURITY_ON_OBJECT	0xC00000D7
ERROR_NO_SPOOL_SPACE	62	STATUS_NO_SPOOL_SPACE	0xC00000C7
ERROR_NO_SUCH_ALIAS	1376	STATUS_NO_SUCH_ALIAS	0xC0000151
ERROR_NO_SUCH_DOMAIN	1355	STATUS_NO_SUCH_DOMAIN	0xC00000DF
ERROR_NO_SUCH_GROUP	1319	STATUS_NO_SUCH_GROUP	0xC0000066
ERROR_NO_SUCH_LOGON_SESSION	1312	STATUS_NO_SUCH_LOGON_SESSION	0xC000005F
ERROR_NO_SUCH_MEMBER	1387	STATUS_NO_SUCH_MEMBER	0xC000017A
ERROR_NO_SUCH_PACKAGE	1364	STATUS_NO_SUCH_PACKAGE	0xC00000FE
ERROR_NO_SUCH_PRIVILEGE	1313	STATUS_NO_SUCH_PRIVILEGE	0xC0000060
ERROR_NO_SUCH_USER	1317	STATUS_NO_SUCH_USER	0xC0000064
ERROR_NO_SYSTEM_RESOURCES	1450	STATUS_INSUFFICIENT_RESOURCES	0xC000009A
ERROR_NO_TOKEN	1008	STATUS_NO_TOKEN	0xC000007C

ERROR_NO_TRUST_LSA_SECRET	1786	STATUS_NO_TRUST_LSA_SECRET	0xC000018A
ERROR_NO_TRUST_SAM_ACCOUNT	1787	STATUS_NO_TRUST_SAM_ACCOUNT	0xC000018B
ERROR_NO_UNICODE_TRANSLATION	1113	STATUS_UNMAPPABLE_CHARACTER	0xC0000162
ERROR_NO_USER_SESSION_KEY	1394	STATUS_NO_USER_SESSION_KEY	0xC0000202
ERROR_NOACCESS	998	STATUS_ACCESS_VIOLATION	0xC0000005
ERROR_NOLOGON_INTERDOMAIN_TRUST_ACCOUNT	1807	STATUS_NOLOGON_INTERDOMAIN_TRUST_ACCOUNT	0xC0000198
ERROR_NOLOGON_SERVER_TRUST_ACCOUNT	1809	STATUS_NOLOGON_SERVER_TRUST_ACCOUNT	0xC000019A
ERROR_NOLOGON_WORKSTATION_TRUST_ACCOUNT	1808	STATUS_NOLOGON_WORKSTATION_TRUST_ACCOUNT	0xC0000199
ERROR_NONE_MAPPED	1332	STATUS_NONE_MAPPED	0xC0000073
ERROR_NOT_ENOUGH_MEMORY	8	STATUS_NO_MEMORY	0xC0000017
ERROR_NOT_ENOUGH_MEMORY	8	STATUS_SECTION_TOO_BIG	0xC0000040
ERROR_NOT_ENOUGH_MEMORY	8	STATUS_TOO_MANY_PAGING_FILES	0xC0000097
ERROR_NOT_ENOUGH_QUOTA	1816	STATUS_QUOTA_EXCEEDED	0xC0000044
ERROR_NOT_ENOUGH_SERVER_MEMORY	1130	STATUS_INSUFF_SERVER_RESOURCES	0xC0000205
ERROR_NOT_LOCKED	158	STATUS_NOT_LOCKED	0xC000002A
ERROR_NOT_LOCKED	158	STATUS_RANGE_NOT_LOCKED	0xC000007E
ERROR_NOT_LOGON_PROCESS	1362	STATUS_NOT_LOGON_PROCESS	0xC00000ED
ERROR_NOT_OWNER	288	STATUS_MUTANT_NOT_OWNED	0xC0000046
ERROR_NOT_OWNER	288	STATUS_RESOURCE_NOT_OWNED	0xC0000264
ERROR_NOT_READY	21	STATUS_DEVICE_NOT_CONNECTED	0xC000009D
ERROR_NOT_READY	21	STATUS_DEVICE_NOT_READY	0xC00000A3
ERROR_NOT_READY	21	STATUS_DEVICE_POWER_FAILURE	0xC000009E
ERROR_NOT_READY	21	STATUS_NO_MEDIA_IN_DEVICE	0xC0000013
ERROR_NOT_REGISTRY_FILE	1017	STATUS_NOT_REGISTRY_FILE	0xC000015C
ERROR_NOT_SAME_DEVICE	17	STATUS_NOT_SAME_DEVICE	0xC00000D4
ERROR_NOT_SUPPORTED	50	STATUS_CTL_FILE_NOT_SUPPORTED	0xC0000057
ERROR_NOT_SUPPORTED	50	STATUS_NOT_CLIENT_SESSION	0xC0000217
ERROR_NOT_SUPPORTED	50	STATUS_NOT_SERVER_SESSION	0xC0000216
ERROR_NOT_SUPPORTED	50	STATUS_NOT_SUPPORTED	0xC00000BB
ERROR_NT_CROSS_ENCRYPTION_REQUIRED	1386	STATUS_NT_CROSS_ENCRYPTION_REQUIRED	0xC000015D
ERROR_OPERATION_ABORTED	995	STATUS_CANCELLED	0xC0000120
ERROR_OUTOFMEMORY	14	STATUS_SECTION_NOT_EXTENDED	0xC0000087

continues

Table A.2. Continued

NT Status	NT Status Value	Win32 Error Code	Win32 Error Value
ERROR_PAGEFILE_QUOTA	1454	STATUS_PAGEFILE_QUOTA	0xC0000007
ERROR_PARTITION_FAILURE	1105	STATUS_PARTITION_FAILURE	0xC0000172
ERROR_PASSWORD_EXPIRED	1330	STATUS_PASSWORD_EXPIRED	0xC0000071
ERROR_PASSWORD_MUST_CHANGE	1907	STATUS_PASSWORD_MUST_CHANGE	0xC0000224
ERROR_PASSWORD_RESTRICTION	1325	STATUS_PASSWORD_RESTRICTION	0xC000006C
ERROR_PATH_NOT_FOUND	3	STATUS_DFS_EXIT_PATH_FOUND	0xC000009B
ERROR_PATH_NOT_FOUND	3	STATUS_OBJECT_PATH_NOT_FOUND	0xC000003A
ERROR_PATH_NOT_FOUND	3	STATUS_REDIRECTOR_NOT_STARTED	0xC00000FB
ERROR_PIPE_BUSY	231	STATUS_INSTANCE_NOT_AVAILABLE	0xC00000AB
ERROR_PIPE_BUSY	231	STATUS_PIPE_BUSY	0xC00000AE
ERROR_PIPE_BUSY	231	STATUS_PIPE_NOT_AVAILABLE	0xC00000AC
ERROR_PIPE_CONNECTED	535	STATUS_PIPE_CONNECTED	0xC00000B2
ERROR_PIPE_LISTENING	536	STATUS_PIPE_LISTENING	0xC00000B3
ERROR_PIPE_NOT_CONNECTED	233	STATUS_PIPE_DISCONNECTED	0xC00000B0
ERROR_PORT_UNREACHABLE	1234	STATUS_PORT_UNREACHABLE	0xC000023F
ERROR_POSSIBLE_DEADLOCK	1131	STATUS_POSSIBLE_DEADLOCK	0xC0000194
ERROR_PRINT_CANCELLED	63	STATUS_PRINT_CANCELLED	0xC00000C8
ERROR_PRINTQ_FULL	61	STATUS_PRINT_QUEUE_FULL	0xC00000C6
ERROR_PRIVILEGE_NOT_HELD	1314	STATUS_PRIVILEGE_NOT_HELD	0xC0000061
ERROR_PROC_NOT_FOUND	127	STATUS_DRIVER_ENTRYPOINT_NOT_FOUND	0xC0000263
ERROR_PROC_NOT_FOUND	127	STATUS_ENTRYPOINT_NOT_FOUND	0xC0000139
ERROR_PROC_NOT_FOUND	127	STATUS_PROCEDURE_NOT_FOUND	0xC000007A
ERROR_PROTOCOL_UNREACHABLE	1233	STATUS_PROTOCOL_UNREACHABLE	0xC000023E
ERROR_REDIR_PAUSED	72	STATUS_REDIRECTOR_PAUSED	0xC00000D1
ERROR_REGISTRY_IO_FAILED	1016	STATUS_REGISTRY_IO_FAILED	0xC000014D
ERROR_REM_NOT_LIST	51	STATUS_REMOTE_NOT_LISTENING	0xC00000BC
ERROR_REM_NOT_LIST	51	STATUS_REMOTE_RESOURCES	0xC000013D
ERROR_REMOTE_SESSION_LIMIT_EXCEEDED	1220	STATUS_REMOTE_SESSION_LIMIT	0xC0000196
ERROR_REQ_NOT_ACCEP	71	STATUS_REQUEST_NOT_ACCEPTED	0xC00000D0
ERROR_REQUEST_ABORTED	1235	STATUS_REQUEST_ABORTED	0xC0000240

ERROR		STATUS	
ERROR_RESOURCE_DATA_NOT_FOUND	1812	STATUS_RESOURCE_DATA_NOT_FOUND	0xC0000089
ERROR_RESOURCE_LANG_NOT_FOUND	1815	STATUS_RESOURCE_LANG_NOT_FOUND	0xC0000204
ERROR_RESOURCE_NAME_NOT_FOUND	1814	STATUS_RESOURCE_NAME_NOT_FOUND	0xC000008B
ERROR_RESOURCE_TYPE_NOT_FOUND	1813	STATUS_RESOURCE_TYPE_NOT_FOUND	0xC000008A
ERROR_REVISION_MISMATCH	1306	STATUS_REVISION_MISMATCH	0xC0000059
ERROR_RXACT_COMMIT_FAILURE	1370	STATUS_RXACT_COMMIT_FAILURE	0xC000011D
ERROR_RXACT_INVALID_STATE	1369	STATUS_RXACT_INVALID_STATE	0xC000011C
ERROR_SECRET_TOO_LONG	1382	STATUS_SECRET_TOO_LONG	0xC0000157
ERROR_SECTOR_NOT_FOUND	27	STATUS_NONEXISTENT_SECTOR	0xC0000015
ERROR_SEM_TIMEOUT	121	STATUS_IO_TIMEOUT	0xC00000B5
ERROR_SERIAL_NO_DEVICE	1118	STATUS_SERIAL_NO_DEVICE_INITED	0xC0000150
ERROR_SERVER_DISABLED	1341	STATUS_SERVER_DISABLED	0xC0000080
ERROR_SERVER_NOT_DISABLED	1342	STATUS_SERVER_NOT_DISABLED	0xC0000081
ERROR_SERVICE_ALREADY_RUNNING	1056	STATUS_IMAGE_ALREADY_LOADED	0xC000010E
ERROR_SERVICE_DISABLED	1058	STATUS_PLUGPLAY_NO_DEVICE	0xC000025E
ERROR_SESSION_CREDENTIAL_CONFLICT	1219	STATUS_NETWORK_CREDENTIAL_CONFLICT	0xC0000195
ERROR_SHARING_PAUSED	70	STATUS_SHARING_PAUSED	0xC00000CF
ERROR_SHARING_VIOLATION	32	STATUS_SHARING_VIOLATION	0xC0000043
ERROR_SIGNAL_REFUSED	156	STATUS_SUSPEND_COUNT_EXCEEDED	0xC000004A
ERROR_SPECIAL_ACCOUNT	1371	STATUS_SPECIAL_ACCOUNT	0xC0000124
ERROR_SPECIAL_GROUP	1372	STATUS_SPECIAL_GROUP	0xC0000125
ERROR_SPECIAL_USER	1373	STATUS_SPECIAL_USER	0xC0000126
ERROR_STACK_OVERFLOW	1001	STATUS_BAD_INITIAL_STACK	0xC0000009
ERROR_STACK_OVERFLOW	1001	STATUS_STACK_OVERFLOW	0xC00000FD
ERROR_SWAPERROR	999	STATUS_IN_PAGE_ERROR	0xC0000006
ERROR_TOKEN_ALREADY_IN_USE	1375	STATUS_TOKEN_ALREADY_IN_USE	0xC000012B
ERROR_TOO_MANY_CMDS	56	STATUS_TOO_MANY_COMMANDS	0xC00000C1
ERROR_TOO_MANY_CONTEXT_IDS	1384	STATUS_TOO_MANY_CONTEXT_IDS	0xC000015A
ERROR_TOO_MANY_LINKS	1142	STATUS_TOO_MANY_LINKS	0xC0000265
ERROR_TOO_MANY_LUIDS_REQUESTED	1333	STATUS_TOO_MANY_LUIDS_REQUESTED	0xC0000074
ERROR_TOO_MANY_NAMES	68	STATUS_TOO_MANY_ADDRESSES	0xC0000209
ERROR_TOO_MANY_NAMES	68	STATUS_TOO_MANY_GUIDS_REQUESTED	0xC0000082

continues

Table A.2. Continued

NT Status	NT Status Value	Win32 Error Code	Win32 Error Value
ERROR_TOO_MANY_NAMES	68	STATUS_TOO_MANY_NAMES	0xC00000CD
ERROR_TOO_MANY_NAMES	68	STATUS_TOO_MANY_NODES	0xC000020E
ERROR_TOO_MANY_OPEN_FILES	4	STATUS_TOO_MANY_OPENED_FILES	0xC000011F
ERROR_TOO_MANY_POSTS	298	STATUS_SEMAPHORE_LIMIT_EXCEEDED	0xC0000047
ERROR_TOO_MANY_SECRETS	1381	STATUS_TOO_MANY_SECRETS	0xC0000156
ERROR_TOO_MANY_SESS	69	STATUS_TOO_MANY_SESSIONS	0xC00000CE
ERROR_TOO_MANY_SIDS	1389	STATUS_TOO_MANY_SIDS	0xC000017E
ERROR_TRUST_FAILURE	1790	STATUS_TRUST_FAILURE	0xC0000190
ERROR_TRUSTED_DOMAIN_FAILURE	1788	STATUS_TRUSTED_DOMAIN_FAILURE	0xC000018C
ERROR_TRUSTED_RELATIONSHIP_FAILURE	1789	STATUS_TRUSTED_RELATIONSHIP_FAILURE	0xC000018D
ERROR_UNABLE_TO_LOCK_MEDIA	1108	STATUS_UNABLE_TO_LOCK_MEDIA	0xC0000175
ERROR_UNABLE_TO_UNLOAD_MEDIA	1109	STATUS_UNABLE_TO_UNLOAD_MEDIA	0xC0000176
ERROR_UNEXP_NET_ERR	59	STATUS_INVALID_ADDRESS	0xC0000141
ERROR_UNEXP_NET_ERR	59	STATUS_INVALID_CONNECTION	0xC0000140
ERROR_UNEXP_NET_ERR	59	STATUS_LINK_FAILED	0xC000013E
ERROR_UNEXP_NET_ERR	59	STATUS_LINK_TIMEOUT	0xC000013F
ERROR_UNEXP_NET_ERR	59	STATUS_TRANSACTION_ABORTED	0xC000020F
ERROR_UNEXP_NET_ERR	59	STATUS_TRANSACTION_INVALID_ID	0xC0000214
ERROR_UNEXP_NET_ERR	59	STATUS_TRANSACTION_INVALID_TYPE	0xC0000215
ERROR_UNEXP_NET_ERR	59	STATUS_TRANSACTION_NO_MATCH	0xC0000212
ERROR_UNEXP_NET_ERR	59	STATUS_TRANSACTION_NO_RELEASE	0xC0000211
ERROR_UNEXP_NET_ERR	59	STATUS_TRANSACTION_RESPONDED	0xC0000213
ERROR_UNEXP_NET_ERR	59	STATUS_TRANSACTION_TIMED_OUT	0xC0000210
ERROR_UNEXP_NET_ERR	59	STATUS_UNEXPECTED_NETWORK_ERROR	0xC00000C4
ERROR_UNEXP_NET_ERR	59	STATUS_USER_SESSION_DELETED	0xC0000203
ERROR_UNKNOWN_REVISION	1305	STATUS_UNKNOWN_REVISION	0xC0000058
ERROR_UNRECOGNIZED_MEDIA	1785	STATUS_UNRECOGNIZED_MEDIA	0xC0000014
ERROR_UNRECOGNIZED_VOLUME	1005	STATUS_UNRECOGNIZED_VOLUME	0xC000014F
ERROR_USER_EXISTS	1316	STATUS_USER_EXISTS	0xC0000063
ERROR_USER_MAPPED_FILE	1224	STATUS_USER_MAPPED_FILE	0xC0000243

ERROR_VC_DISCONNECTED	240	STATUS_VIRTUAL_CIRCUIT_CLOSED	0xC00000D6
ERROR_WORKING_SET_QUOTA	1453	STATUS_WORKING_SET_QUOTA	0xC00000A1
ERROR_WRITE_PROTECT	19	STATUS_MEDIA_WRITE_PROTECTED	0xC00000A2
ERROR_WRITE_PROTECT	19	STATUS_TOO_LATE	0xC0000189
ERROR_WRONG_DISK	34	STATUS_WRONG_VOLUME	0xC0000012
STATUS_ARRAY_BOUNDS_EXCEEDED	3221225612	STATUS_ARRAY_BOUNDS_EXCEEDED	0xC000008C
STATUS_DUPLICATE_OBJECTID	3221226026	STATUS_DUPLICATE_OBJECTID	0xC000022A
STATUS_FLOAT_DENORMAL_OPERAND	3221225613	STATUS_FLOAT_DENORMAL_OPERAND	0xC000008D
STATUS_FLOAT_DIVIDE_BY_ZERO	3221225614	STATUS_FLOAT_DIVIDE_BY_ZERO	0xC000008E
STATUS_FLOAT_INEXACT_RESULT	3221225615	STATUS_FLOAT_INEXACT_RESULT	0xC000008F
STATUS_FLOAT_INVALID_OPERATION	3221225616	STATUS_FLOAT_INVALID_OPERATION	0xC0000090
STATUS_FLOAT_OVERFLOW	3221225617	STATUS_FLOAT_OVERFLOW	0xC0000091
STATUS_FLOAT_STACK_CHECK	3221225618	STATUS_FLOAT_STACK_CHECK	0xC0000092
STATUS_FLOAT_UNDERFLOW	3221225619	STATUS_FLOAT_UNDERFLOW	0xC0000093
STATUS_ILLEGAL_INSTRUCTION	3221225501	STATUS_ILLEGAL_INSTRUCTION	0xC000001D
STATUS_INTEGER_DIVIDE_BY_ZERO	3221225620	STATUS_INTEGER_DIVIDE_BY_ZERO	0xC0000094
STATUS_INVALID_DISPOSITION	3221225510	STATUS_INVALID_DISPOSITION	0xC0000026
STATUS_NONCONTINUABLE_EXCEPTION	3221225509	STATUS_NONCONTINUABLE_EXCEPTION	0xC0000025
STATUS_OBJECTID_EXISTS	3221226027	STATUS_OBJECTID_EXISTS	0xC000022B
STATUS_PARITY_ERROR	3221225515	STATUS_PARITY_ERROR	0xC000002B
STATUS_PRIVILEGED_INSTRUCTION	3221225622	STATUS_PRIVILEGED_INSTRUCTION	0xC0000096

Appendix B

Sources of Information for Driver Writers

Hopefully, this book will serve as a solid starting point for your journey into writing NT Kernel mode device drivers. No one source can have absolutely every piece of information, however. This appendix assembles some additional sources to which you can turn for more help.

Windows NT systems internals in general, and device driver development in particular, are fields that lots of people claim to "know about," but relatively few people actually practice in. Thus, when utilizing any of the resources listed in this appendix, please carefully consider the source of the information that you're getting. Even though an article appears in a reputable publication, it doesn't necessarily mean that the article has been carefully technically reviewed. Consider the credentials of the author. We're sorry to say it, but we've seen articles about Windows NT systems internals in typically trustworthy publications that were so wrong that they were laughable. So, caveat driver writer!

This Book's Web Pages

We've dedicated a set of Web pages to the support of this book. On those pages, you'll find source code for the two complete sample drivers that appear in Chapters 16 and 17 (one PIO and other DMA), book errata, and lots of other assorted information. Check out http://www.osr.com/book.

Periodicals and Journals

The NT Insider

The cover says it all: "The only publication dedicated entirely to Windows NT system software development." This bi-monthly journal is published by OSR Open Systems Resources, Inc. (the consulting firm in which the authors are partners). Each issue runs about 20 pages, all of which is about NT drivers, file systems, and other NT systems internals issues. It may be hard to believe, but one-year *free subscriptions* are available on OSR's Web site at http://www.osr.com. Even if we didn't write for this publication, we'd still say it's the best deal going.

Windows NT Magazine

Even though this publication is aimed more at systems administrators than driver writers, there always seems to be one or two articles per issue that we find interesting. Because driver writers need to be aware of a wide variety of systems issues, this publication is certainly worth reading. There's also a regular column on NT internals that can at times be a good read, although it's usually rather superficial. See http://www.winntmag.com for subscription information.

Dr. Dobb's Journal

A long-time publication aimed at "Software tools for the professional programmer," DDJ (as it's called) has published several driver-related articles in the past year or so. A recent issue described Windows NT device driver toolkits, for example. Because this publication covers the entire realm of programming, NT systems software is merely a sidelight. See http://www.ddj.com for more information.

Microsoft's Knowledge Base

The Microsoft Knowledge Base, or KB as it's more commonly known, is the collection of known bugs, issues, and workarounds for Microsoft software. A subset of the KB comes with MSDN. The KB can be searched online from the Web site http://support.microsoft.com/support. The online version is a gold mine of information, and can even be searched for new articles on a particular topic "within the past 30 days." If you're having problems with NT, this is an important place to check.

Newsgroups, Mailing Lists, and FAQs

Here the caveats to inquiring driver writers certainly apply; only much, much stronger.

comp.os.ms-windows.programmer.nt.kernel-mode

This is the only solid newsgroup for Kernel mode driver writers. The Microsoft support folks hang out here and will occasionally answer questions purely in the interest of being nice guys. Many other experienced driver writers and consultants regularly participate, including the authors. The signal-to-noise ratio of this group has gotten much higher in the past year; if you read it frequently, you will get sick of seeing the same questions posted over and over and over (my favorite being "Can I write drivers using a C-Compiler other than MSVC++?"). Hey, what can we say, it's Usenet, right? Despite its flaws, this group remains a very important resource.

microsoft.public.win32.programmer.kernel

This is an official Microsoft newsgroup that generally has a lot of Win32 questions that somehow the author thinks are related to Kernel mode. Some consultants and driver writers answer questions here. Not much in this newsgroup is aimed squarely at NT driver writing.

NTDEV Mailing List

To subscribe, send email to Majordomo@atria.com with "SUBSCRIBE NTDEV" in the body of the message. An interesting and ever-changing exchange of issues. Worth watching.

NTFSD Mailing List

To subscribe, send email to Majordomo@atria.com, with "SUBSCRIBE NTFSD" in the body of the message. This mailing list is the only place in the known universe where NT file systems' development issues are regularly discussed, except for *The NT Insider*. Interesting to watch for driver writers, just to gain some insight into nondevice-related systems internals issues.

DDK-L Mailing List

Moderated by Daniel Norton of Windows 3.x VxD fame, this mailing list actually costs money ($15/year after a free 30-day trial period) to subscribe to. We guess the idea of the subscription price is to raise a barrier to the casual participation of dilettantes. See http://www.albany.net/~danorton/ddk/ddk-l/.

The Windows NT Kernel-Mode Driver FAQ

This list of "Frequently Asked Questions" lives at
http://www.cmkrnl.com/faq.html. Though it hasn't been updated in almost two
years and is now hopelessly out of date, this FAQ will still be useful to neo-
phyte driver writers. Jamie Hanrahan of Kernel Mode Systems, one of the few
good guys in this field who actually knows what he's talking about, put this
FAQ together.

Seminars

OSR Open Systems Resources, Inc.
(http://www.osr.com)

This is the company where the authors are consulting partners, and it is the
largest provider of NT Kernel mode training, by far. OSR teaches both lecture
and lab seminars throughout the world on writing Windows NT device drivers,
file systems, and video drivers. Both public and custom on-site seminar presen-
tations are available.

David Solomon Expert Seminars
(http://www.solsem.com)

Another company that does NT training.

Appendix **C**

Changes in NT V5.0

As this book is being written, Widows NT V5.0 is being developed. In fact, this book was completed after the Beta 1 release of Windows NT V5.0, but before the Beta 2 release. Thus, the precise details of what will be in Windows NT V5.0 is anybody's guess. Until it has been released by Microsoft, nobody knows what will be in the final version.

We'd like to give you some clue, however, about what is likely to change—in our opinion—in Windows NT V5.0. While nothing is cast in concrete, some things are very clear. For example, it is clear that the main principles underlying driver development on Windows NT will remain the same from NT V4.0 to NT V5.0. It is also clear that there are a number of specific things that will change.

This Appendix attempts to address the few issues that are clear at this book's press time. As we get more information, we'll be posting it on the OSR Web site (http://www.osr.com) for readers of this book. In addition, we expect to have a working copy of the major example drivers presented in Chapters 16 and 17 updated and commented for NT V5.0 as soon as we have enough information to do this. Check in with us often!

Note

Although we have done our best to get the most recent and accurate information possible on NT V5.0, almost all of the information in this chapter is still speculative. Until NT V5.0 ships, we won't know precisely how things will really work. Thus, before using the information in this chapter for a major project, be sure to check the OSR Web site, the Microsoft Web sites, and MSDN for any updated information on NT V5.0.

NT V4.0 Device Drivers on NT V5.0.0

In general, as far as we know, standard Kernel mode drivers written and compiled on NT V4.0 will run unchanged on NT V5.0 systems. This means that the type of device drivers described in this book should work on NT V5.0 systems without any change.

Of course, NT V4.0 drivers will not be able to participate in plug and play or power-management activities on NT V5.0. For many devices and systems, this won't be important. However, for other devices or for certain users this can be a significant disadvantage. Suppose, for example, that a user has a laptop running NT V5.0 that they want to suspend. If one of the drivers on that laptop doesn't support power management, the user will at least be warned that suspending the laptop is risky (precisely how this will work isn't yet clear). If the user chooses to force a suspension, the NT V4.0 driver may not properly reinitialize its device when the system is resumed.

Driver Entry Changes

In NT V4, DriverEntry() was the function that handled everything necessary to initialize drivers and devices. In DriverEntry(), we export our entry points via the Driver Object. We also typically identify our device and create a Device Object for each device found. This ordinarily means scanning the bus to find the device(s), and calling IoCreateDevice(). Next, in an NT V4.0 driver, we reserve the hardware resources to be used by the device. For PCI devices, this typically means calling HalAssignSlotResources() and IoAssignResources() to get a CM_RESOURCE_LIST of the hardware resources that each of the devices will use. These resources include ports, shared memory areas, IRQs, DMA Channels, and whatever other hardware resources our device(s) require. We also connect to interrupts from our device within the Driver Entry routine, and, in general, do whatever is necessary to become ready to process requests on our device.

In NT V5.0, the functions previously performed in DriverEntry() are separated out into three parts:

- **Things to do with initializing the driver itself.** These things, like exporting entry points, are still performed in the Driver Entry routine.

- **Things to do with discovering the devices our driver needs to support.** This step, including creating a Device Object, is now performed in the driver's AddDevice() entry point. This is a new entry point in NT V5.0.

- **Things to do with device resources and device initialization.** Things to do with the device hardware itself actually wait until we're called with an IRP_MJ_PNP IRP with an IRP_MN_START_DEVICE minor function. In this function, we do stuff like connect to interrupts.

Driver Entry in NT V5.0

Just like in NT V4.0, a driver's DriverEntry() entry point is called in NT V5.0 at IRQL PASSIVE_LEVEL, in the context of the system process when our driver is first loaded.

DriverEntry() in NT V5.0 is typically restricted to doing things related to initializing the driver as a whole. This includes exporting entry points via the Driver Object. Two new important entry points that NT V5.0 drivers will need to export are as follows:

- An AddDevice() entry point, a pointer to which is placed in DriverObject->DriverExtension->AddDevice.

- The Dispatch entry point for processing IRP_MJ_PNP IRPs (a pointer to which must be placed in DriverObject->MajorFunction[IRP_MJ_PNP]).

Although not normally required, before exiting DriverEntry(), you'll have to save the Registry path information if you'll need it later. You should really need this only if you call one of those functions that requires it as a parameter (such as IoRegisterDriverReinitialization(), HalAssignSlotResources(), or IoAssignResources()); or you need to do some Registry lookups in your AddDevice() routine (described in the next section). Of course, good NT V5.0 drivers won't typically call any of these routines (with the possible exception of IoRegisterDriverReinitialization()). If you do need to save the Registry path, be sure to actually save the Registry path data itself, not just a pointer to the Registry path. The I/O Manager apparently deallocates the Registry path immediately on return from its call to DriverEntry().

Although it doesn't say so in the preliminary NT V5.0 documentation, it is possible to still create Device Objects during DriverEntry(). However, this is no longer typically done. In fact, the only Device Object you might want to create in DriverEntry() in an NT V5.0 driver would be an object for an overall driver control type device. Perhaps this would be some sort of operation, administration, or management device. If you *do* create any Device Objects in DriverEntry(), the DO_DEVICE_INITIALIZING bit is still cleared as before NT V5.0.

That's really all there is to the "all new and improved" version of DriverEntry(). What has traditionally been the longest function in many NT standard Kernel mode drivers is now rather short indeed! Processing continues when the driver's AddDevice() entry point is called.

The AddDevice Entry Point

At some point after your driver has returned from the Driver Entry routine, any time a device that is your driver's responsibility is added to the system, the I/O Manager calls your driver's AddDevice() entry point, the prototype for which is shown in Figure C.1.

NTSTATUS
AddDevice (IN PDRIVER_OBJECT *DriverObject,*
   IN PDEVICE_OBJECT *PhysicalDeviceObject*);

DriverObject: A pointer to the Driver Object. This is, of course, the same Driver Object pointer provided in DriverEntry.

PhysicalDeviceObject: A pointer to the physical device object (PDO) that represents this device.

Figure C.1. AddDevice() *entry point.*

The *DriverObject* parameter passed into this routine is the same pointer passed into your DriverEntry() entry point. The *PhysicalDeviceObject* parameter is a pointer to the Physical Device Object (PDO) that represents your device. This Device Object was created by the bus driver when it scanned the bus to see what devices were physically connected to the bus. The PDO is used as the point of communication between the bus driver, Plug and Play Manager, and your driver to inform you of PnP events (such as somebody disconnecting your device). Figure C.2 illustrates the connection between the FDO and the PDO.

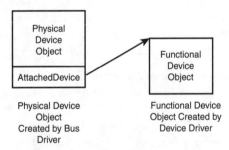

Figure C.2. *Functional Device Object attached to Physical Device Object.*

When you're called at your AddDevice() entry point, there are two major activities for your driver to undertake:

1. Create one or more Device Objects (and optionally, Device Extensions) to represent your device. This is done in the traditional way by calling

`IoCallDriver()`. Don't forget that because you're calling `IoCreateDevice()` outside of your `DriverEntry()` entry point, you need to manually clear the `DO_DEVICE_INITIALIZING` bit in `DeviceObject->Flags`. This is an important detail—unless this bit is cleared, other Device Objects cannot be attached to yours. If you forget to clear this bit, the I/O Manager will remind you with a little message in the Checked Build. If required, also create a symbolic link to point to your Device Object using `IoCreateSymbolicLink()`, just like in NT V4.0, as described in Chapter 13, "Driver Entry."

2. Attach the newly created Device Object (or, indeed, Device Objects) to the physical device that the bus driver has created to describe your device. This attachment is done by calling `IoAttachDeviceToDeviceStack()`, passing in the pointer to your newly created Device Object and the Physical Device Object passed into your `AddDevice()` entry point. `IoAttachDeviceToDeviceStack()` returns a pointer to the actual Device Object to which you attached. Be sure to save this away because you're going to need it later.

Before leaving your `AddDevice()` entry point, you should perform any per-device initialization that can be performed *without touching your hardware*. This might include checking the Registry (if you saved the path away earlier!) for device-specific information or anything else you can dream up.

Note

To emphasize the point, we'll say it again: No references to your hardware *are permitted from within the* `AddDevice()` *routine. Your driver still has not been given any hardware resources. Your driver has been informed only that a device owned by your driver has been found. That comes in the next step.*

Also, because you now have a Device Object, it is entirely possible for users to issue I/O requests to that Device Object. Because you're not allowed to touch your hardware yet, it would be a serious mistake to just go ahead and try to process any requests that you receive. Proper NT V5.0 etiquette requires that you keep track of the fact that this device has been created but not yet started (that is, you've received an `AddDevice()` call for this device, but not an `IRP_MN_START_DEVICE` request—more about that later) and queue any IRPs that you receive for later processing on your device. The preliminary NT V5.0 documentation suggests keeping a flag in the Device Extension for this purpose. This sure seems like a good idea to us!

Leave `AddDevice()` with `STATUS_SUCCESS` if you were successful in your work in this routine. Returning an error status results in the load sequence for your driver being aborted.

Processing Plug and Play IRPs

When one of the previously added devices is to be started, the Plug and Play Manager will call your driver with an IRP containing an IRP_MJ_PNP major function code and an IRP_MN_START_DEVICE minor function code. IRP_MJ_PNP is used to identify IRPs that are queued to your driver as a result of plug-and-play events. There are seven minor function codes that uniquely identify the type of plug-and-play request to the driver (see Table C.1). In NT V5.0, device drivers sit atop a driver stack that may include an underlying bus driver. This leads to two issues in a driver handling PnP requests:

- All IRP_MJ_PNP IRPs must be passed by your device driver to the underlying bus driver. This is vital for correct system operation.

- Some PnP IRPs must be processed (successfully) by the underlying bus driver before they can be processed by your device driver. On the other hand, some PnP IRPs need to be processed (successfully) by your driver before being passed on to the underlying bus driver.

It is your driver's task to determine who processes each particular PNP IRP first (you or the underlying bus driver, depending on the IRP minor function code), and then (typically) to pass the IRP to the underlying driver in the normal way by calling IoCallDriver(). The Device Object used as the target for the IoCallDriverCall() is the PDEVICE_OBJECT returned when the driver called IoAttachDeviceToDeviceStack() in its AddDevice() entry point. Fortunately, it's pretty easy to figure out from the documentation who is supposed to handle which IRP_MN functions when. Table C.1 resolves the dilemma of which drivers handle a given IRP_MN function and when.

Table C.1. Driver processing of IRP_MN functions.

IRP_MN_ Function Code	Who Processes It First?
IRP_MN_START_DEVICE	Bus driver
IRP_MN_STOP_DEVICE	Device driver
IRP_MN_QUERY_STOP_DEVICE	Device driver
IRP_MN_CANCEL_STOP_DEVICE	Bus driver
IRP_MN_QUERY_REMOVE_DEVICE	Device driver
IRP_MN_REMOVE_DEVICE	Device driver
IRP_MN_CANCEL_REMOVE_DEVICE	Bus driver
IRP_MN_QUERY_CAPABILITIES	Bus driver

When we say the device driver processes a request "first," we mean that upon receipt, the device driver examines the request. If the request can be accommodated, the device driver does what is necessary to carry out the request. When the device driver has completed processing the request successfully, it sends the request to the underlying bus driver. If the request cannot be accommodated, the device driver completes the request in the ordinary way with an appropriate error status. In this case, the IRP does not need to be passed to the underlying bus driver.

Passing an IRP on to another driver given a pointer to the target driver's Device Object is done the same way in NT V5.0 as it was done in NT V4.0. The only difference is that in NT V5.0, we now have a handy macro to use to make things a bit easier. To pass a request to an underlying driver, you simply copy the current I/O Stack location to the next I/O Stack location, register a completion routine if you want one, and pass the IRP to the next driver using IoCallDriver().

When the device driver processes the IRP_MJ_PNP IRP first, a completion routine is not normally required. This is because the underlying driver will send your driver another PnP IRP, telling you to cancel the operation if it finds the PnP operation that you approved unacceptable. Example C.1 provides code that demonstrates passing on the IRP in this case:

Example C.1. Passing an IRP to the underlying driver—with no Completion routine supplied.

```
//
// Invoke the handy stack copy macro, new to NT V5.
//
IoCopyCurrentIrpStackLocationToNext(Irp);

//
// Send the request to the bus driver and return
//
return(IoCallDriver(DeviceExtension->PdoPointer, Irp));
```

When the bus driver processes the request first, things are a bit more tricky. To indicate that your device can be started, you receive an IRP_MN_START_DEVICE IRP that needs to be processed by the bus driver first. When the device driver receives the request, it passes the request to the bus driver. During this transaction, the device driver does not do any of the request-processing itself.

Again, just as in NT V4.0, when a driver passes a request to an underlying driver, it is later notified about the request completion by setting a Completion routine in the IRP, prior to passing the IRP to the underlying driver. Passing requests from driver to driver was discussed in detail in Chapter 11, "The Layered Driver Model." None of the concepts will change in NT V5.0. The I/O Manager will call the completion routine when the underlying driver(s) have completed the request. Only when the completion routine has been called may the IRP actually be processed by the device driver. Unfortunately, recall that completion routines may be called at IRQL >= DISPATCH_LEVEL. This makes completion processing more complex than you might like.

Although there are many ways to actually code up the solution to this problem, we agree with the preliminary DDK that the best solution is to wait for an
event in the device driver's Dispatch Routine. When the Completion routine is
called, it signals the event, thus awakening the Dispatch Routine code, in
which the IRP is processed to completion. The Completion routine reclaims
"ownership" of the IRP by returning STATUS_MORE_PROCESSING_REQUIRED to the
I/O Manager. Example C.2 shows the code for the Dispatch Routine to do this.

*Example C.2. Passing on an IRP to the underlying driver, supplying a comple-
tion routine.*

```
//
// Copy the current IRP Stack Location to the next one, using
// the new macro supplied with NT V5 strictly for this purpose
//
IoCopyCurrentIrpStackLocationToNext(Irp);


//
// Set a completion routine for this IRP.  Have it called regardless
// of the IRP's completion status.  The context passed into the
// completion routine is a pointer to the event to signal.
//
IoSetCompletionRoutine(Irp,
                OsrPnpCompRoutine,
                &pnpEvent,
                TRUE,
                TRUE,
                TRUE);

//
// Initialize an event which will be signaled from the
// completion routine.
//
KeInitializeEvent(&pnpEvent,
                NotificationEvent,
                FALSE);

status = IoCallDriver(devExt->NextDriverObject, Irp);

//
// Wait on the event to be signaled by the completion routine.
// The completion routine will "reclaim" the IRP so we may
// continue to process it below.
//
KeWaitForSingleObject(&pnpEvent,
                Executive,
                KernelMode,
                FALSE,
                NULL);

//
```

```
// After the completion routine wakes us, get the ultimate
// status of the operation from the IRP.
//
status = Irp->IoStatus.Status;

if (NT_SUCCESS (status)) {

    //
    // Since the bus driver was happy, we can FINALLY try to
    // process the IRP.
    //

    status = OsrProcessPnPIrp(Irp);

}

//
// Since the completion routine ALWAYS reclaims the IRP by
// returning STATUS_MORE_PROCESSING_REQUIRED, we need to
// actually complete the IRP here.
//
Irp->IoStatus.Status = status;

Irp->IoStatus.Information = 0;

IoCompleteRequest (Irp, IO_NO_INCREMENT);
```

As previously described, this code not only passes the IRP to the underlying driver, it also creates an event and waits for that event to be signaled. The event is set to be signaled from the driver's Completion routine, shown in Example C.3.

Example C.3. Sample Completion routine.

```
NTSTATUS
OsrPnpCompRoutine(IN PDEVICE_OBJECT DeviceObject,
                  IN PIRP Irp,
                  IN PVOID Context)
{
    PKEVENT event = (PKEVENT)Context;

    //
    // IF this request pended, make sure we mark it as
    // having done so in the current IRP stack location
    //
    if (Irp->PendingReturned) {

        IoMarkIrpPending( Irp );

    }

    //
```

continues

Continued

```
// Set the event on which the Dispatch Routine is waiting
//
KeSetEvent(event, 0, FALSE);

//
// Re-claim IRP to that the Dispatch Routine can continue
// to process it.
//
// N.B. Dispatch Routine must recall IoCompleteRequest
//
return STATUS_MORE_PROCESSING_REQUIRED;
}
```

Admittedly, Example C.3 provides a pretty simple Completion routine, but it does handle all the basics. One step worth noting is the need to call `IoMarkIrpPending()` in the Completion routine if `Irp->PendingReturned` is set. The reasons behind this are complex, and haven't changed between NT V5.0 and NT V4.0. Unfortunately, these reasons are well beyond the scope of this appendix. Suffice it to say that this really is required.

As recommended in the preliminary DDK documentation, the approach shown in Examples C.2 and C.3 is probably the best method for handling IRPs that need to be processed by the bus driver first. Because it is possible that your Completion routine could be called at elevated IRQL, we wait in the Dispatch routine instead of trying to process the request in the actual Completion routine. When the Completion routine is called, the IRP is reclaimed by the device driver (by returning `STATUS_MORE_PROCESSING_REQUIRED`). The Completion routine then wakes the Dispatch Routine by setting the event. Any necessary processing is then performed by the device driver in the context of the Dispatch routine. The device driver then completes the IRP, calling `IoCompleteRequest()`, with an appropriate status.

Processing `IRP_MN_START_DEVICE` Requests

Given the general process for handling `IRP_MJ_PNP` requests, you should become familiar with the way you specifically process `IRP_MN_START_DEVICE` requests.

As stated previously, when the Plug and Play Manager wants you to start your device, it sends you an `IRP_MJ_PNP` IRP with an `IRP_MN_START_DEVICE` minor function. The device to be started is, obviously, the one represented by the Device Object pointer received in the Dispatch PNP routine.

Recall that IRP_MN_PNP IRPs must be processed by the bus driver before being processed by the device driver. Thus, on receiving one of these IRPs, the device driver simply passes it on down to the bus driver, and waits for its Completion routine to be called. Assume that you'll use the design shown in Examples C.2 and C.3, where you wait in the Dispatch Routine for an event to be signaled by the Completion Routine. In this case, you wake back up in the Dispatch routine, and proceed to process the IRP_MN_START_DEVICE request.

How do we process this request? Recall that up to this point, we still have neither identified nor reserved the hardware resources required by our device. Providing us a list of these resources is the main purpose of the IRP_MN_START_DEVICE IRP.

Contained in the current I/O Stack location of the IRP_MN_START_DEVICE IRP are two parameters of specific interest: Parameters.StartDevice.AllocatedResources (which is a pointer to a CM_RESOURCE_LIST that describes the device's resources), and Parameters.StartDevice.AllocatedResourcesTranslated (which is a pointer to a CM_RESOURCE_LIST that contains the translated values for the device's resources). These parameters are the resources that the PnP Manager, the I/O Manager, and the HAL have agreed on and allocated for your device's use. In NT V4.0 for a PCI device (for example), the untranslated resources are those that would have been returned by HalAssignSlotResources(). The Translated version of these resources are equivalent to the output from HalTranslateBusAddress() and HalGetInterruptVector().

Given the CM_RESOURCE_LIST, the driver may access, initialize, and program its device just as in NT V4.0. And, just like in NT V4.0, if a resource is in memory space the driver will need to call MmMapIoSpace() to assign kernel virtual addresses to it. And, of course, the driver will need to connect to interrupt by calling IoConnectInterrupt() just as it did in NT V4.

DMA Implementation Changes

The overall architectural abstraction and model used for DMA support in Windows NT V5.0 is only slightly changed from that in NT V4. In NT V5.0, a number of concepts specifically related to Adapter Objects are clarified and further defined.

For example, instead of calling HalGetAdapter() to identify the characteristics of a device to the HAL and get a pointer to an Adapter Object, in NT V5.0, drivers call IoGetDmaAdapter(), the prototype for which is shown in Figure C.3.

PDMA_ADAPTER

IoGetDmaAdapter (IN PDEVICE_OBJECT *PhysicalDeviceObject,*
    IN PDEVICE_DESCRIPTION *DeviceDescription,*
    IN PULONG *NumberOfMapRegisters*);

PhysicalDeviceObject: A pointer to the physical device object (PDO) that represents this device.

DeviceDescription: A pointer to the DEVICE_DESCRIPTION data structure (no change from NT V4.0).

NumberOfMapRegisters: A pointer to a ULONG, into which is returned the maximum number of map registers that a driver may use at one time (no change from NT V4.0).

Figure C.3. `IoGetDmaAdapter()` *function prototype.*

Note that this function takes one parameter that `HalGetAdapter()` didn't. This is a pointer to the Physical Device Object associated with the device. In addition, instead of a pointer to an Adapter Object, this function returns a pointer to a `DMA_ADAPTER`. This new structure starts with a version and size field, and contains a pointer to a `DMA_OPERATIONS` structure, in addition to HAL and bus driver specific data. The `DMA_OPERATIONS` structure comprises pointers to bus-specific functions that perform common DMA support activities.

The `DMA_OPERATIONS` structure is, in fact, key to the NT V5.0 implementation of the NT DMA model. This was necessary due to bus driver support being moved from only in the HAL to being in standard Kernel mode drivers. In versions of NT prior to NT V5.0, when a driver called a bus-specific function such as `IoMapTransfer()` or `IoFreeMapRegisters()`, the I/O Manager called the HAL, which in turned called the support routine for the appropriate bus on which the operation was to take place.

In NT V5.0, it appears that bus drivers are moved from being exclusively in the HAL to also being within Kernel mode drivers. This eases support for different types of buses, extends NT's processor hardware abstraction architecture, and facilitates PNP, power management, and other types of bus support. Thus, in NT V5.0, a driver acquires a pointer to its `DMA_ADPATER` structure.

In early versions of NT V5.0 that we've seen, macros have been defined in `ntddk.h` that redefine NT V4.0 calls which take an `ADAPTER_OBJECT` as an argument, to take a `DMA_ADAPTER` in its place and perform the NT V5.0 function of calling the appropriate function from within the `DMA_OPERATIONS` vector of the

DMA_ADAPTER structure. This allows drivers that call the NT V4.0 functions to be recompiled and work correctly with the NT V5.0 DMA_ADAPTER structure.

According to the existing DDK documentation, a new set of support functions will also be defined. The parameters to these functions, and the ways these functions are used, remains unchanged from NT V4.0, with the exception that instead of a PADAPTER_OBJECT (returned by HalGetAdapter()), these functions take a PDMA_ADAPTER (returned by IoGetDmaAdapter()). Table C.2 lists the NT V4.0 DMA functions and their NT V5.0 equivalents.

Table C.2. NT V4.0/NT V5.0 DMA functions.

NT V4.0 DMA Function	NT V5.0 DMA Function
HalAllocateCommonBuffer()	AllocateCommonBuffer()
HalFreeCommonBuffer()	FreeCommonBuffer()
IoAllocateAdapterChannel()	AllocateAdapterChannel()
IoFlushAdapterBuffers()	FlushAdapterBuffers()
IoFreeAdapterChannel()	FreeAdapterChannel()
IoFreeMapRegisters()	FreeMapRegisters()
IoMapTransfer()	MapTransfer()
HalGetDmaAlignmentRequirement()	GetDmaAlignment()

It is not clear at the time of this writing what the final implementation of the new DMA interface will be in NT V5.0. All we can advise on this point is to visit the OSR Web site for the latest information.

> **Note**
>
> *One small yet significant change in the functions mentioned previously is in* MapTransfer(). *When calling this function, drivers for Busmaster devices* must *supply a pointer to their* DMA_ADAPTER. *This is in contrast with the convention established prior to NT V5.0, in which Busmaster device drivers passed* NULL *to* IoMapTransfer() *as a pointer to their* ADAPTER_OBJECT.

Power Management

Power management one of the biggest changes between NT V4 and NT V5.0. It is also one of the changes about which the least information was available when this chapter was written. Thus, in this section we present only a brief overview of power management. Check the OSR Web site for updated information!

Support for power management in a device driver requires supporting three new IRP minor function codes of the IRP_MJ_POWER function, as follows:

- IRP_MN_QUERY_POWER
- IRP_MN_SET_POWER
- IRP_MN_WAIT_WAKE

Support for a fourth minor function code, IRP_MN_POWER_SEQUENCE, is optional.

When a driver receives a power management IRP, it has a choice of ways to process it:

1. If the driver cannot perform the indicated operation (that is, the driver cannot enter a power-down state when it receives an IRP_MN_QUERY_POWER request), it immediately completes the IRP with an error code.

2. If the driver can perform the indicated operation, it calls PoCallDriver() to pass the request on to other drivers. When the request reaches the bus driver, it will ultimately be completed with success.

In either case, the driver attempts to dequeue another power request by calling PoStartNextPowerIrp().

IRP_MN_QUERY_POWER

The IRP_MN_QUERY_POWER request is sent to a driver when the Power Manager needs to determine whether the device can enter a sleeping power state. If the device can, it calls PoCallDriver() to pass the request along. At this point, the driver also stops processing any new requests it receives (queuing them for later processing).

If the driver is not in a state where it can enter a sleep state, it immediately completes the IRP with an error status.

IRP_MN_SET_POWER

Processing the IRP_MN_SET_POWER request is a bit more complicated than processing IRP_MN_QUERY_POWER. This is because the driver may receive set power requests that indicate a change in either the device's or the system's power state. In addition, the driver may receive a set power request when its device is already in the requested state.

On receiving a set power request, the device driver checks to see whether the device is already in the requested state. If it is, it simply completes the IRP with success. Device power states are represented by the values D0, D1, D2, and

D3. D0 represents fully powered-on device state. D3 represents fully powered-off state. States D1 and D2 represent intermediate states between fully powered-on and fully powered-off.

If the device is not in the requested state when a set power request is received, the way the driver proceeds depends on the request:

- If the request is to enter power-down state, the device driver calls PoSetPowerState() to indicate that it is leaving fully powered state to enter power-down state. It then powers the device down, and completes the IRP with success.

- If the request is to enter the power-on state, the device driver powers up the device, and when it has reached power-on state, it calls PoSetPowerState(). It then completes the IRP with success.

IRP_MN_WAIT_WAKE

This minor function code is sent by a device driver to indicate that one or more of its devices can wake the system, causing the system to return to a fully powered state. Unfortunately, we have no further information on this function at this time.

Index

B

T

U

V

X-Z